BLACK CONFEDERATES AND AFRO-YANKEES IN CIVIL WAR VIRGINIA

Ervin L. Jordan, Jr.

D1173023

University Press of Virginia

Charlottesville and London

The University Press of Virginia
Copyright © 1995 by the Rector and Visitors
of the University of Virginia
First published 1995

Library of Congress Cataloging-in-Publication Data
Jordan, Ervin L.
    Black Confederates and Afro-Yankees in Civil War Virginia / Ervin
L. Jordan, Jr.
        p.   cm.—(A Nation divided : new studies in Civil War
history)
    Includes bibliographical references and index.
    ISBN 0-8139-1544-9.—ISBN 0-8139-1545-7 (pbk.)
    1. Virginia—History—Civil War, 1861–1865—Afro-Americans.
2. United States—History—Civil War, 1861–1865—Afro-Americans.
3. Afro-Americans—Virginia—History—19th century.   I. Title.
II. Series: Nation divided.
E585.A35J67   1995
973.7'4755—dc20   94-16923
                                                   CIP

Printed in the United States of America

For My Parents
Ervin Leon Jordan, Sr.
& Carrie Edwards Jordan
Norfolk, Virginia
and
My Parents-in-Law
Estelle (Frye) & John Bracey
Madison County, Virginia

Write the things thou hast seen,
and the things which are,
and the things which shall be hereafter.
Revelations 1:19

Previous books by the author

19th Virginia Infantry (with Herbert Thomas)

Charlottesville and the University of Virginia in the Civil War

Contents

Appendixes

Illustrations

Tables

Preface

Some time ago I had the pleasure of meeting the renowned American scholar Vincent Harding and told him of my plans for this book. He encouragingly inscribed a copy of his book: "For Brother Ervin—Keep the story well, Share the story widely!" His message sums up the responsibility of anyone attempting to narrate any aspect of African-American history.[1]

The record of the Civil War is woefully incomplete without consideration of the many roles that African-Americans played. This narrative seeks to show African-Americans as human beings who took an active part in Confederate Virginia. It is concerned with the toil of slavery and the effects of everyday backbreaking, mind-numbing slave labor. It explores the black community's culture and its resilience in the face of a constant effort to obscure and minimize the contributions of its members and their significance as human beings.

Humankind has always fought over something, be it land, water, wealth, power, religion, or honor. The Confederacy fought for a way of life which included the right to continue to hold blacks in bondage and reap economic and political benefits. W. E. B. Du Bois characterized Southerners as possessing an abundance of fearlessness but lacking the moral courage to fight on behalf of justice and liberty.[2]

The experiences of Afro-Virginians—slave and free, homefront and battlefield, Confederate and Union—epitomized the war's major issues. I have organized the book in topical chapters to look first, in Part One, "Uncertain Trumpet," at the scope of Afro-Virginian domestic life and labor and the attitudes that both slaves and free blacks encountered within and outside of the legal system. These first seven chapters also demonstrate a growing concern about black resistance and what roles blacks might play in the war. Part Two, "Give Us a Flag," examines wartime civilian and military roles defined by and for Afro-Virginians: as free blacks and slaves within a disintegrating society, as body servants taken to war, as soldiers and spies choosing to serve on both sides.

Who were Afro-Virginians? How did they survive during the Confederacy? These and similar questions must be answered, but there are inherent difficulties in researching the black Civil War experience. The preponderance of surviving documents are white accounts of black life and culture. Much of what Afro-Virginians did and said comes to us only through the views of white Virginians. Written records about black slaves are abundant—and worth citing—but primary sources generated by free blacks and black soldiers are rare. I have particularly tried to highlight such sources, for it is imperative that they be sought out, recognized, and properly housed and cataloged in manuscript repositories.[3]

A word about nomenclature. *Afro-Virginians* denotes slaves and free blacks born in Virginia, blacks freed or enslaved there, those transported to or from the state, and those who resided there. *Afro-Confederates* were pro-Southern blacks who privately or publicly supported and allied themselves with the Confederacy; *Afro-Yankees* were Southern blacks who supported the Union. Whenever possible I use individual names (most slaves had but one).[4]

The first arrival of African slaves occurred in 1619 in Virginia; the freeing of their descendants, in 1865. Present in America for nearly four hundred years, African-Americans have experienced freedom for only one-third of that time. While there were always some free blacks, the overall African-American existence has been one of bondage. The United States has never officially apologized to African-Americans for slavery; history has compelled us to become realists with long memories. African-American history is not for the squeamish.

This study attempts to preserve the record and tell the stories of Afro-Virginians as participants in, not objects of, history. I have been influenced by the writings of such pioneers as George Washington Williams, Joseph T. Wilson, Carter G. Woodson, Luther Porter Jackson, and James H. Brewer, author of the only previous book-length study of black Virginians during the war. The writing of *Black Confederates and Afro-Yankees in Civil War Virginia* has been a disturbing, enlightening, and mystical experience.

Acknowledgments

I BENEFITED FROM the advice and assistance of several persons and institutions in Virginia (unless otherwise noted). Members of my family were particularly supportive. My wife, Lorraine Frye Jordan, provided moral support and uncomplainingly accompanied me on various research trips. My parents, Ervin, Sr., and Carrie Jordan, believed in me even when I did not believe in myself; my brother, Robert E. Jordan, and sister, Patricia Anne Jordan, constantly reassured me that I would complete this project. Randall and Sylvia Yancey of Gaithersburg, Maryland, were sympathetic and hospitable.

At the University of Virginia persons who deserve special mention include: Donna Barbour, Interlibrary Loan Office, Alderman Library; Edmund Berkeley, Jr., Director, Michael Plunkett, Curator, Manuscripts Division, and William Runge, Rare Book Division, Special Collections Department; Robert E. Campbell, Senior Program Analyst, Academic Computing Center; Marie Carter, Executive Secretary, Alderman Library; Joan E. Klein, Historical Collections, Claude Moore Health Sciences Library. Christina W. Sharretts, Electronic Services Librarian, Science and Engineering Library, expertly repaired my computer.

The staff of the University Press of Virginia were pleasant, patient, and professional, especially Nancy Essig. Also deserving of special mention is Harold E. Howard of Lynchburg. This book was originally scheduled as a volume for his Virginia Battles and Leaders Series, but he generously allowed it to be submitted to another publisher.

Mrs. James Howard Brewer of Durham, North Carolina, was a gracious hostess and deserves thanks for granting access to her late husband's papers and patiently answering hundreds of questions. She extended to me the honor of sitting at the very desk where Professor Brewer wrote *The Confederate Negro*.

Virginia residents and Civil War scholars offered advice and expertise including: Chris Calkins, Park Historian, Petersburg National Battlefield; Robert K. Krick, Chief Historian, Fredericksburg and Spotsylvania National Military Park; Louis H. Manarin, State Archivist, Virginia State Library and Archives, Richmond; James I. Robertson, Jr., Alumni Distinguished Professor in History, Virginia Polytechnic Institute and State University, Blacksburg; Philip J. Schwarz, Chairman, Department of History and Geography,

Virginia Commonwealth University, Richmond; Thomas R. Towers, Gooch-land; Sheldon Vanauken, Lynchburg; John H. Walker, Scottsville; Lee A. Wallace, Falls Church.

Out-of-state specialists were no less supportive: Edward Agran, Department of Humanities, Centre College, Danville, Kentucky; Joseph T. Glatthaar, University of Houston; Richard Pindell, State University of New York at Binghamton; Robert J. Trout, Myerstown, Pennsylvania; Ronald L. Waddell, Lebanon, Pennsylvania; Howard C. Westwood, Washington, D.C. Scholars who bravely read all or portions of the manuscript and provided much-appreciated suggestions and criticism include Deborah White, Rutgers University; Delores P. Aldridge, Emory University; Lucious Edwards, Jr., University Archivist, Virginia State University; Paul D. Escott, Department of History, Wake Forest University; and Matthew Holden, Jr., Henry L. and Grace M. Doherty Professor, Woodrow Wilson Department of Government and Foreign Affairs, University of Virginia.

Fellow archivists supportive beyond the call of duty were Ronald L. Becker, Special Collections and Archives, Rutgers University Libraries, New Brunswick, New Jersey; Barbara Benson, Historical Society of Delaware, Wilmington; Barney Bloom, Vermont Historical Society, Montpelier; Tommy L. Bogger, Norfolk State University Archives, Norfolk; Barbara J. Brown, Washington and Lee University, Lexington; Dean Burgess, Portsmouth Public Library, Portsmouth, Virginia; Yvonne Carignan, Lloyd House, Alexandria Library, Alexandria; Thomas E. Camden, University of Georgia, Athens; Margaret Cook, Swem Library, College of William and Mary, Williamsburg; Rebecca A. Ebert, The Handley Library, Winchester; Ralph L. Elder, University of Texas at Austin; Melinda B. Frierson, Albemarle County Historical Society, Charlottesville; Gregg Kimball, Valentine Museum, Richmond; Tony Jenkins, Duke University, Durham, North Carolina; Thomas Knoles, American Antiquarian Society, Worcester, Masachusetts; Jesse R. Lankford, Jr., North Carolina Department of Cultural Resources, Raleigh; Linda Leazer, E. Lee Shepard, and the late Waverly Winfree, Virginia Historical Society, Richmond; Minnie Lee McGehee, Fluvanna County Historical Society, Palmyra; Michael P. Musick, National Archives, Washington, D.C.; Carolyn S. Parson and Minor Weisiger, Virginia State Library and Archives, Richmond; Diana Franzusoff Peterson, Haverford College, Haverford, Pennsylvania; Edmund Raus, Manassas National Battlefield Park, Manassas, Virginia; Laura Katz Smith, Jack Straw, and Glen McMullen, Special Collections Department, Virginia Polytechnic Institute and State University, Blacksburg; Richard A. Shrader, University of North Carolina at Chapel Hill; and Guy R. Swanson, Museum of the Confederacy, Richmond. They courteously granted access and permission to copy and quote from their materials.

A month's paid leave of absence and travel funding was provided by the Library Faculty Research Committee of the University of Virginia Library during the summer of 1990. Also, research was greatly facilitated by 1990 fellowship support from the Virginia Foundation for the Humanities and Public Policy (under the auspices of the National Endowment for the Humanities). Its director, Robert Vaughan, and staff were affable and encouraging.

I owe a special debt of thanks to a group of new colleagues, all esteemed scholars, for suggestions and intellectual encouragement during my tenure at the Virginia Foundation: Professor Dina Copelman, George Mason University, Fairfax, for advice on the use and placement of statistical tables; Susan Ford, independent scholar, on self-promotion and negotiation of book contracts; Reverend Max R. Harris, independent scholar, for prodding me to define Afro-Confederates; Professor Larry Sabato, University of Virginia, for advice on the pitfalls of book publishing; and Sarah Shaver Hughes, Shippensburg University, Pennsylvania, for lively discussions on chapter titles.

BLACK CONFEDERATES AND AFRO-YANKEES IN CIVIL WAR VIRGINIA

PROLOGUE
Sphinxes Wearing Masks: Afro-Virginians and the Coming of Secession, 1855–61

I don't think the people of the slave States will ever consider the subject of slavery in its true light till some other argument is resorted to than moral suasion.
—*John Brown, October 1859*

The shining black mask they wear does not show a ripple of change—sphinxes.
—*Mary Boykin Chesnut*

THE RECORD of America's greatest internal crisis, the Civil War, is incomplete without considering the history of African-Americans. This narrative depicts African-Americans as human beings who were an integral component of Confederate Virginia, a democratic commonwealth based on slavery. While such knowledge is finite (complete details of the past are forever veiled), this book is representative of their perspective. African-Americans shaped the birth and fleeting existence of the Southern Confederacy.

The first casualty of the Civil War was a free black Virginian named Heyward Shepherd, a train depot baggagemaster at Harpers Ferry, Jefferson County. He died on 16 October 1859 when John Brown led sixteen whites and five blacks into the town in an attempt to capture its Federal arsenal and inspire slaves to rebellion. Having spent three years in the planning, Brown believed his "army" could expropriate enough weapons to arm slaves and establish mountain bases for a black revolutionary republic as a place of refuge and a rallying point for slave insurgencies. However, Jefferson County's Afro-Virginians comprised barely 30 percent of the population.[1]

Among Brown's men were five blacks: John Anthony Copeland, Shields Green, Lewis Sheridan Leary, Dangerfield Newby, and Osborne Perry Anderson; only Newby, born a slave in 1815 in Fauquier County, was a Virginian. Green, too, had been a slave; Anderson, Copeland, and his uncle Leary were free blacks. Newby's wife Harriet, a slave, may have known of the plot, for she unintentionally wrote incriminating letters to her husband.[2]

The "army of liberation" achieved part of its objectives on the night of

1

16 October, but the first Virginia civilian killed, Heyward Shepherd, a free black, was shot in the back when he tried to warn the town. Although Brown's men took forty hostages, wrathful townspeople drove the attackers to an armory engine house. Besieged, the raiders were able to hold them at bay until the arrival of Colonel Robert E. Lee, Lieutenant James Ewell Brown Stuart, and ninety marines.

The marines stormed the building, and when the shooting and bayoneting ceased, ten of the raiders, including two of Brown's sons and Leary and Newby, were dead, several were captive, and five (Anderson among them) escaped. Copeland and Green were hanged. Four townspeople, two local slaves, and one marine also died. Brown himself died on the gallows at Charles Town in December, his body dangling from the noose for nearly forty minutes. A *New York Tribune* reporter contributed to his immortality by concocting a believable myth that Brown kissed a black child en route to his execution; the myth became "fact" after publication as a poem.[3]

Heyward Shepherd was buried in Winchester with full military honors. The United Daughters of the Confederacy and the Sons of Confederate Veterans erected a monument honoring him as a "faithful Negro" in 1931. On 2 December 1859, the day of Brown's execution, a group of Scottsville blacks led by a slave named Ben hanged him in effigy as an "old murderer, horse thief and traitor" and proclaimed their willingness to use his pikes to defend their masters against abolitionists. But four years later Union prisoner of war Colonel Daniel Ullmann was surprised to hear Warrenton slaves singing "John Brown's Body" and asked why they were permitted to sing it. Their owner replied that he was unable to prevent them: it was their favorite.[4]

The lone black survivor among the raiders, Osborne Anderson, published his account in 1861. According to him, fourteen slaves and one free black joined Brown, saying they had long prayed and dreamed of their liberation. "Cowardly Virginians and slaveholders" meekly surrendered to the blacks. The "poor white trash" who normally did their "dirty work" cringingly remained behind their doors safe at home, though several participated in the subsequent harassment and the "cowardly judicial murdering" of innocent blacks. Anderson escaped to Canada, and although he implied that his flight was a solo effort, it is reasonable to assume that Brown's supporters and the Underground Railroad network assisted him. He fought in the war kindled by Brown and died in 1871 in Washington.[5]

Why did Brown fail? Local whites outnumbered blacks roughly three to one and possessed superior communications, reinforcements, and weapons. Brown underestimated Virginian slaveholders: they had spent their lives dreading black insurrection, so when it arrived instead of fleeing they mobilized and appealed to the government for Federal troops. Brown's scheme was too pretentious: he made no plans for providing the raiders with food, executed little or no prior reconnaissance, and unrealistically assumed that it would be enough merely to place hundreds of pikes and rifles into the hands of slaves, most of whom had never used firearms and were not inclined to leave their plantations to follow white strangers. The raid was more of a publicity gambit than anything else, and Frederick Douglass knew it; he wisely declined to join Brown. Reverend Willis Augustus Hodges, a freeborn black Virginian living in New York, was acquainted with Brown and knew of his plans. But he, too, like Douglass, advised that the time for black men to take up arms against the slavocracy had not yet arrived.[6]

The Harpers Ferry raid provoked partisan songs and poetry. One Massachusetts "Dirge" stated:

> Today, beside Potomac's wave,
> Beneath Virginia's sky,
> They slay the man who loved the slave,
> And dared for him to die.[7]

But a pro-Southern reactionary song entitled "Old John Brown: A Song for Every Southern Man," warned:

> Now all you Southern darkies, a word to you I'll say;
> Always mind your masters, and never run away,
> And don't mind these Northern agents, they tell to you a lie,
> They get you at the North, and starve you 'till you die.[8]

A poem predicted Brown would cause more trouble dead than alive:

> And Old Brown,
> Old Osawatomie Brown,
> May trouble you more than ever, when you've nailed his coffin down![9]

Racial backlash and white hysteria were swift and relentless. Whites who publicly spoke anything less than contempt of Brown and his followers were visited by vigilante committees. A man named Haines who uttered "abolitionist sentiments" at Harrisonburg was the victim of a mock hanging. "He had the rope around his neck and was about to be swung up," said one eyewitness, "and would have been if it had not been for Judge Kenney who told [the vigilantes] the evidence was not sufficiently strong to hang him." David Rumgarner was spared by Page County vigilantes after claiming to be "as good a democrat as any body" and a foe of abolitionism.[10]

An unsigned broadside urged nonslaveholders and slaves to eradicate slavery by killing slave owners. This *Plan for the Abolition of Slavery* advised the creation of "Vigilance Committees and Leagues of Freedom" in every neighborhood to make war on slaveholders and their nonhuman property, particularly slave-hunting dogs. Slaves were to be told "the state of Slavery is a state of war," and as for their owners: "We especially advised the flogging of individual Slaveholders. This is a case where the medical principle, the like cures like, will certainly succeed. Give the Slaveholders, then, a taste of their own whips. Spare their lives, but not their backs. The arrogance they have acquired by the use of the lash upon others, will be soon applied to themselves." With plots such as this in circulation, white Virginians had ample grounds to distrust and be concerned about Afro-Virginians.[11]

Antebellum Virginia was part of a Southern oligarchy in which economic pursuits directly established social strata. The common people comprised two groups. Yeomen were mostly farmers descended from German, Dutch, and English stock. The second category consisted of poor whites. Rural paupers who lived in mountainous areas and other regions of inadequate soils, they fiercely protected what little was theirs, especially small plots of land.

Poor whites, having no sympathy for runaway slaves, became slave catchers, and this line of work rewarded them with hard cash and a sense of racial solidarity with the upper classes. Moncure Daniel Conway characterized them as "serfs of the soil . . . employed in doing nothing" except producing "innumerable brats and squalid children"; they were no more than white slaves. Their only value, said Conway, was as overseers and bumpkin voters duped into putting rich, smooth-talking slaveholders into office who then ignored them until the next election.[12]

By definition and custom a slave was a black human being held in hereditary servitude whose body, labor, liberty, and property were under the legal control of a white person from cradle to grave. Any black or mulatto was considered prima facie a slave, and the burden of proof of being free rested on them, not on those who would enslave them. Slaves could not vote, learn how to read and write, possess firearms, or acquire property. It was illegal for them to own dogs, boats, books, or paper in any form, possess cash, ride on trains, or attend any type of assemblage without a white person present.

They could be sold, borrowed, traded, raffled, mortgaged, or transported to another place at any time; they could be distributed to heirs or wagered in card games. Slaves were subject to the will and whims of their owners or, in their absence, any white person capable to giving commands. The slightest indication of disobedience by a slave of any command, moral or immoral, precipitated some form of threat or punishment. Slave owners were answerable only to their consciences and pocketbooks.

Slavery was one of the state's economic backbones. Slave traders recommended Virginia slaves to potential buyers as the best available black merchandise. From 1830 to 1860, 280,000 Virginia slaves were marketed to the Deep South; during the first half century of the nineteenth century, nearly 600 black convicts were sold by the state. One resident somberly noted that Virginia had become the place where "negroes were raised and sold; a nursery of slavery." Cities and towns like Alexandria and Richmond were slave marts for the South. Richmond slave trader Hector Davis in January 1860 told his clients that slaves were "selling very high at this time." He enclosed a listing of current values:

Best Young Men 19 to 24:	$1550 to $1650
Fair Young Men:	$1350 to $1500
Best Black Girls 16 to 20:	$1400 to $1525
Fair Girls:	$1250 to $1350

"Good Boys & Girls" ages twelve to sixteen were fetching higher prices than before, but "Good young women with one & two children" under the age of ten were not selling as well. "You cannot go wrong in . . . good grown negroes," he concluded. According to *De Bow's Review* the average price paid in 1860 for a Virginia slave was $1,500.[13]

Louis Hughes, a Virginia slave, saw female slaves being sold for $500 to $700, housemaids for $1,000 to $1,200, and blacksmiths for $1,600 to $1,800. In 1864 five-year-old Booker T. Washington was valued at $400. Eight Buckingham County slaves sold at an estate sale in February 1861 netted $5,655, about $700 each. An auctioneer rejected as too low bids of $850 and $890 for a middle-aged black woman and her three girls (an infant of three months, a two-year-old, and a three-year-old). Slaves were sometimes sold by weight. A female slave recalled the sale of one of her playmates in Prince Edward County. This boy, Little Joe, son of the plantation cook, was dressed in his Sunday best and placed on a pair of scales. This slaveling was sold at an agreed-upon rate per pound, and his master used the proceeds to buy some hogs. His mother was whipped for grieving over her child. Richmond slave dealers regularly advertised and sold slave children by height.[14]

Slaveholders encouraged slave breeding. They traded and forced fertile young black girls and boys to mate and replenish their stock; slave males were purchased for stud service. "Will you be so good as [to] look out for me a breeding negro woman under twenty years of age?" wrote G. B. Wallace of Strawberry Hill to a fellow planter. "Also a young active negro man." Expatriate Virginians James and Emily Jackson in Kentucky wrote to Alfred and Nancy Dearing in Rappahannock County to inquire about the prices of "men and Boys and girls of different ages" on behalf of their son, a resident of Kentucky who wanted to purchase Old Dominion slaves because they represented quality and fertility at an affordable price. Elige Davison told an interviewer seventy years afterward that his master had compelled him to have fifteen wives and sire several children with each. Davison estimated he had fathered more than a hundred sons and daughters.[15]

Louis Hughes, sold at age twelve for $380 at the Richmond Exchange, remembered the awful moment when he first met his new owner, a wealthy Mississippi cotton planter who purchased sixty slaves. "When I was placed upon the block, a Mr. [Edward] McGee came up and felt of me and asked me what I could do. 'You look like a right smart nigger,' said he. 'Virginia always produces good darkies.'" Peter Randolph recalled the sale of a slave family. The husband and father, Emanuel, was auctioned first, followed by the oldest child, Lucy (age seventeen), then Harry (age fifteen) and Mary. As the mother, Jenny, screamed for her children, the slave trader warned her to stop her "hollering" else he would give her something to holler about. Having thus lost her husband and children and deadened with grief, Jenny was the last of the family sold.[16]

Nonslaveholders often were horrified the first time they saw slaves sold. John S. Wise, taken to a sale by his uncle, noted that "bucks" (unmarried black males ages eighteen to twenty-five) were offered first. Potential buyers examined their eyes, hearing, and teeth, "ran their hands over the muscles of their backs and arms," and felt their legs. Next were young unmarried women, and some of the questions asked of them were "indecent and shocking." Members of the crowd exclaimed with delight over the value of slaves: "Niggers is high." But when one slave family was offered, only the mother was sold; no one bid on her husband and two children. Her new owner told her to cheer up and promised she would find a new husband and have more children. A lawyer, unable to bear the unfolding tragedy, stepped forward with an offer for the entire hapless family but was refused.[17]

British tourists in Richmond were critical. Eyre Crowe, an artist accompanying William Thackeray's American tour, was appalled by the "stifling atmosphere of human traffic." William Chambers told of a bleak conversation he had with a Madison County slave woman at an auction house shortly before her sale. The mother of seven children, she told him that her owner was selling her in order to purchase more land. But as the year 1860 drew to a close, slave dealers were gloomy: "The financial crisis still rages and is not likely to abate for some months. We have no hope for any political change which will give peace and confidence in commercial matters. . . . Very few sales have been made this month."[18]

Geographically speaking, Virginia's 61,352 square miles (including what later became West Virginia) constituted eastern and western regions divided by the Blue Ridge Mountains, the easternmost range of the Appalachian Mountains that sweeps from Harpers Ferry into Georgia. The state's rivers bore the names of long-vanished Indian tribes and an English king: Potomac, Rappahannock, Appomattox, Kanawha, Monongahela, and the mighty James. The climate dispensed perennial rains vital to farming, infrequent snowfalls of short duration, and long growing seasons; mineral resources were abundant and diverse in the form of coal, copper, gold, lead, and salt. Agriculture was the focal sector of the state's economy and provided not only food for its inhabitants but raw materials for industries and agricultural products for export. The fertile soil burst forth with wheat, rye, corn, oats, barley, peas, beans, tobacco, cotton, and potatoes; grasslands nurtured beef cattle, milch cows, hogs, mules, oxen, and sheep. Health spas at hot springs, numerous caverns and grottoes, and the spectacular beauty of mountains and forests attracted legions of enthralled tourists.[19]

From east to west were four regions: the tidewater, piedmont, valley, and Trans-Allegheny. Tidewater, located on the coastal plain of the Chesapeake Bay (an inlet of the Atlantic Ocean fed by estuaries of the Potomac, James, York, and Rappahannock rivers) was where most of the state's earliest large-scale cotton and tobacco plantations were founded and where the first European immigrants had settled; here, too, resided most of Virginia's free blacks and slaves. Although farming and fishing (corn and oysters) remained the major industries, this had become a commercial and manufacturing sector; Petersburg, Richmond, and Norfolk (with its shipyards and a secure harbor at Hampton Roads, located between the mouth of the James River and the entrance to Chesapeake Bay) were worthy of the designation of "city." The names of Gloucester, James City, Northampton, and York counties were among those which betokened the state's British colonial heritage. To the southeast the Great Dismal Swamp, a 700-square-mile freshwater marsh, provided runaway slaves a place of refuge among its cypress trees.[20]

Virginia's population, in order of size, consisted of whites, slaves and free blacks. Between 1800 and 1860 the number of whites had increased by 50 percent, slaves by 70 percent, and freed blacks by 34 percent (table 0.1). Eighty-nine percent of Afro-Virginians were chattel slaves, and their numbers had increased every decade since 1800 except for a 20,770 decrease in 1840 after a decade of particularly great relocation by planters to the Deep South and Midwest. Between 1800 and 1830 free black and slave inhabitants

TABLE 0.1. POPULATION CHANGES IN ANTEBELLUM VIRGINIA

Decade	Free blacks	Slaves	Whites
1800–1810	+10,446	+46,720	+37,234
1810–1820	+6,313	+32,623	+51,821
1820–1830	+10,465	+44,609	+90,965
1830–1840	+2,494	−20,770	+46,668
1840–1850	+4,491	+23,541	+153,832
1850–1860	+3,709	+18,337	+152,611

Source: U.S. census returns, Virginia, 1800–1860.

TABLE 0.2. FREE PERSONS AND SLAVE INHABITANTS OF VIRGINIA, 1800–1860

Year	Whites	Free blacks	Slaves
1800	514,280	20,124	345,796
1810	551,514	30,570	392,516
1820	603,335	36,883	425,148
1830	694,300	47,348	469,757
1840	740,968	49,842	448,987
1850	894,800	54,333	472,528
1860	1,047,299	58,042	490,865

Source: U.S. Department of Commerce, Bureau of the Census, *Negro Population in the United States, 1790–1915* (1918; reprint, New York, 1968), 44, 55, tables 6, 13; U.S. Department of Interior, *Statistics of the United States . . .* (Washington, D.C.: GPO, 1866), 50; Joseph C. G. Kennedy, Superintendent of the Census, *Agriculture of the United States in 1860* (Washington, D.C.: GPO, 1864), 243–45; Kennedy, *Population of the United States in 1860; Compiled from the Original Returns of the Eighth Census, under the Direction of the Secretary of the Interior* (Washington, D.C.: GPO, 1864), 518. The Commerce Department placed the 1860 white Virginia populace at 1,047,299 whereas the other sources list it as 1,047,411, a difference of 112 persons in the form of Indians counted as whites for the higher estimate (ibid., 518).

experienced their greatest antebellum population gains in Virginia (table 0.2). The 1840s and 1850s saw slower growth; in the decade ending in 1850 blacks had increased in the state by 30,000 but constituted only 37 percent of the Old Dominion's residents.

The 1860 census indicates that Virginia's 1,596,146 inhabitants averaged twenty-six persons per square mile; blacks (35 percent of the population) were outnumbered two to one by whites (65 percent of the population).[21] A typical 1860 state county possessed 10,817 residents: 7,076 whites, 3,338 slaves, and 403 free blacks. And yet, census returns also show an evolution of the Old Dominion into a biracial commonwealth. Of its 148 counties, 41 percent were either predominantly or nearly half black (table 0.3). Mostly located in the tidewater or piedmont regions but including Clarke County to the northwest and Pittsylvania County to the central south, there were forty-four counties where Afro-Virginians, at 51 to 74 percent, were the majority, especially in Nottoway (74 percent), Amelia (73 percent), and Cumberland and Charles City (70 percent); Greensville, King William, Powhatan, and Sussex counties each had a black majority of 69 percent. (A complete racial synopsis of each county is in Appendix A.)

The preponderance of Afro-Virginians in a given county did not by any means require whites to share political power by granting voting rights to blacks or even to tolerate them as social equals. Afro-Virginians were kept down by narrow ordinances, taxation, and other proven techniques of racial control. They lacked not only education but a well-versed, focused leadership capable of gaining white acceptance as spokesmen for their communities and the means to communicate with each other regularly on a statewide basis. Hypothetically, each of Virginia's thirteen members of the United States House of Representatives represented 122,780 Virginians. Even though its 550,000 black residents were barred from the political process and free blacks were assessed at a higher tax rate than whites, the presence of Afro-Virginians enabled the state to reap political benefits by giving it four congressmen more than it would have had without the three-fifths clause in the United States Constitution.[22]

Free blacks were widespread in rural and urban areas of Virginia though in none were they the majority. Accomack (3,418), Dinwiddie (3,746), and Henrico (3,599) counties held significant portions of them, but only one black person lived in each of six counties that later became part of West Virginia (Boone, Buchanan, Calhoun, Doddridge, Hancock, and Logan). Alone among Virginia's shires was the southwestern county of McDowell: no slaves or free blacks resided there.

Free blacks preferred urban environments and were twice as likely to live in a town or city than slaves, who were primarily agricultural workers. In 1860, 83 percent of free Afro-Virginian city dwellers lived in Alexandria, Farmville, Fredericksburg, Lynchburg, Norfolk, Petersburg, Portsmouth, Richmond and Manchester, and Winchester, while only 8 percent of urban slaves lived in these localities (table 0.4). Towns and cities offered free blacks greater opportunities for employment, exposure to literature, professional services, and the company of other blacks. Attacks against free blacks in the more rural, isolated counties usually arose in the aftermath of slave plots; in cosmopolitan areas whites seemed more assured about their ability to control blacks. Eighteen percent of the Old Dominion's slaves were in urban locales, mainly Richmond (34 percent) and Petersburg (16 percent).[23]

TABLE 0.3. VIRGINIA COUNTIES WITH POPULATIONS AT LEAST 40 PERCENT BLACK, 1860

County	Population	Black	White
Accomack	18,586	7,925 (43%)	10,661 (57%)
Albemarle	26,625	14,522 (54%)	12,103 (46%)
Amelia	10,741	7,844 (73%)	2,897 (37%)
Amherst	13,742	6,575 (48%)	7,167 (52%)
Appomattox	8,889	4,771 (53%)	4,118 (47%)
Bedford	25,068	10,680 (42%)	14,388 (58%)
Brunswick	14,809	9,817 (66%)	4,992 (34%)
Buckingham	15,212	9,171 (60%)	6,041 (40%)
Campbell	26,197	12,609 (48%)	13,588 (52%)
Caroline	18,464	11,516 (63%)	6,948 (37%)
Charles City	5,609	3,803 (67%)	1,806 (33%)
Charlotte	14,471	9,490 (65%)	4,981 (35%)
Chesterfield	19,016	8,997 (47%)	10,019 (53%)
Clarke	7,146	3,439 (48%)	3,707 (52%)
Culpeper	12,063	7,104 (58%)	4,959 (42%)
Cumberland	9,961	7,015 (70%)	2,946 (30%)
Dinwiddie	30,198	16,520 (54%)	13,678 (46%)
Elizabeth City	5,798	2,618 (45%)	3,180 (55%)
Essex	10,469	7,173 (68.5%)	3,296 (31.5%)
Fauquier	21,706	11,276 (51%)	10,430 (49%)
Fluvanna	10,353	5,260 (51%)	5,095 (49%)
Gloucester	10,956	6,439 (58%)	4,517 (42%)
Goochland	10,656	6,842 (64%)	3,184 (36%)
Greensville	6,347	4,400 (69%)	1,974 (31%)
Halifax	26,520	15,460 (58%)	11,060 (42%)
Hanover	17,222	9,740 (56%)	7,482 (44%)
Henry	12,105	5,332 (44%)	6,773 (56%)
Isle of Wight	9,977	4,940 (49%)	5,037 (51%)
James City	5,798	3,631 (62%)	2,167 (38%)
King George	6,571	4,061 (61%)	2,510 (39%)
King and Queen	10,328	6,527 (63%)	3,801 (37%)
King William	8,530	5,941 (69%)	2,589 (31%)
Lancaster	5,151	3,170 (61%)	1,981 (39%)
Louisa	16,701	10,518 (63%)	6,183 (37%)
Lunenburg	11,983	7,562 (63%)	4,421 (37%)
Madison	8,854	4,494 (50%)	4,360 (49%)
Mathews	7,091	3,226 (45%)	3,865 (55%)
Mecklenburg	20,096	13,318 (66%)	6,778 (34%)
Middlesex	4,364	2,501 (57%)	1,863 (43%)

TABLE 0.3. CONTINUED

County	Population	Black	White
Nansemond	13,693	7,961 (58%)	5,732 (42%)
Nelson	13,015	6,366 (48%)	6,649 (52%)
New Kent	5,883	3,738 (63%)	2,145 (37%)
Northampton	7,832	4,834 (61%)	2,998 (39%)
Northumberland	7,531	3,661 (48%)	3,870 (52%)
Nottoway	8,836	6,566 (74%)	2,270 (26%)
Orange	10,851	6,298 (58%)	4,553 (42%)
Pittsylvania	32,104	14,999 (46%)	17,105 (54%)
Powhatan	8,392	5,812 (69%)	2,580 (31%)
Prince Edward	11,844	7,807 (65%)	4,037 (35%)
Prince George	8,411	5,512 (65%)	2,899 (35%)
Princess Anne	7,714	3,381 (43%)	4,333 (57%)
Rappahannock	8,850	3,832 (43%)	5,018 (57%)
Richmond	6,856	3,286 (47%)	3,570 (52%)
Southampton	12,915	7,202 (55%)	5,713 (45%)
Spotsylvania	16,076	8,360 (52%)	7,716 (48%)
Stafford	8,555	3,633 (42%)	4,922 (58%)
Surry	6,133	3,799 (61%)	2,334 (38%)
Sussex	10,175	7,057 (69%)	3,118 (30%)
Warwick	1,740	1,078 (61%)	662 (39%)
Westmoreland	8,282	4,895 (59%)	3,387 (41%)
York	4,949	2,607 (52%)	2,342 (48%)

Source: Joseph C. G. Kennedy, *Population of the United States in 1860* . . . (Washington, D.C.: GPO, 1864), 501–13, 516–18.

Twenty-five percent of the state's 201,523 families (52,128 slaveholding families) owned its 490,865 slaves. Individually, a typical slave owner (33 percent of the population) possessed at least 2 slaves; 609 owned 40 to 50 slaves, 503 owned 50 to 70 slaves, and, according to the eighth Federal census, one white Virginian owned more than 300. This individual was a Mr. Morson of Goochland who maintained 800 slaves, but apparently this same census missed Samuel Hairston of Henry County who in 1860 owned 1,600 slaves and Philip St. George Cocke, owner of 660 slaves with a combined value of $580,650. Another member of Henry County's Hairston clan, Marshal, held 171 slaves, including a 112-year-old female. One fourth of all white Virginians were slaveholders, and the state auditor estimated the net worth of the slaves in the state at more than $313 million dollars.[24]

Counties with exceptional numbers of slaveholders were east of the Appalachians: Henrico (2,339); Dinwiddie (1,826); and Campbell (1,705). Web-

TABLE O.4. DISTRIBUTION OF AFRO-VIRGINIANS IN TEN VIRGINIA
MUNICIPALITIES, 1860

Free blacks		Slaves	
Petersburg	3,244	Richmond	11,699
Richmond	2,576	Petersburg	5,680
Alexandria	1,415	Winchester	4,392
Norfolk	1,046	Norfolk	3,284
Winchester	680	Lynchburg	2,694
Portsmouth	543	Woodstock	2,113
Fredericksburg	422	Alexandria	1,386
Lynchburg	357	Fredericksburg	1,291
Farmville	241	Portsmouth	934
Manchester	222	Staunton	900
Total	10,746	Total	34,373

Source: Joseph C. G. Kennedy, *Population of the United States in 1860* . . . (Washington, D.C.: GPO, 1864), 518–20. Returns for a few cities and towns such as Charlottesville are missing.

ster County had but one slaveholder, Calhoun and Clay, three each, and McDowell, none. The general population of black Virginians had declined by 532 free blacks and 8,567 slaves by 1861. The overall number of Afro-Virginian women and men was approximately equal (271,000 and 277,000, respectively); 49 percent of the slaves and 52 percent of the free blacks were female (table 0.5).[25]

In a case similar to the 1857 Dred Scott decision, a group of Virginia slaves played a minor role in the impending crisis. The Lemmon Slave Case began when Jonathan and Juliet Lemmon, residents of Bath County, decided in 1852 to move to Texas and take with them eight slaves whom Mrs. Lemmon had inherited from her father. The Lemmons made their plans and departed on 18 October 1852, reaching Richmond twelve days later; from there they proceed to Norfolk where they intended to book passage on a ship bound for New Orleans. A change in plans necessitated their traveling from Norfolk to New York City on the steamer *City of Richmond*, which arrived at four o'clock on the afternoon of 5 November.

Aware that the city was in a free state and was a hotbed of abolitionism that raised the likelihood of rescue efforts, Jonathan Lemmon made plans to transfer their slaves at night to the steamer *Memphis*, scheduled to depart for New Orleans the next morning. But his plans went awry, and the slaves were confined at a boardinghouse on Carlisle Street. A free black named Louis Napoleon discovered the slaves and shortly thereafter boldly petitioned the

TABLE 0.5. RACE AND GENDER IN VIRGINIA, 1860

Gender/Race/Status	Total	Percentage
Whites	1,047,411	65.5%
Blacks	548,907	34.3
Males, both races	806,101	50.5
Females, both races	790,217	49.5
White males	528,897	33.1
White females	518,514	32.4
Black males	277,204	17.3
Black females	271,703	17.0
Slaves, male	249,483	50.9
Slaves, female	241,382	49.1
Free black males	27,721	47.8
Free black females	30,321	52.2

Source: Joseph C. G. Kennedy, *Population of the United States in 1860* . . . (Washington, D.C.: GPO 1864), 505, 509, 513, 518. According to this source, Virginia's 1860 population was 1,596,318; Indians are omitted from this table, resulting in a core of figure of 1,596,206.

Supreme Court of New York for a writ of habeas corpus on their behalf, despite the fact that he could not even sign his name to his intrepid petition.[26]

The petition was granted, a constable located the slaves and their owners, and the contending parties were brought before Justice Elijah Paine. The Afro-Virginians were Emeline, age twenty-three; Lewis, brother of Emeline, sixteen; Edward, brother of Emeline, thirteen; Amanda, daughter of Emeline, two; Lewis and Edward, twin sons of Nancy, seven; Nancy, twenty; and Ann, daughter of Nancy, five. Newspaper accounts described them as strong, healthy, and well-cared for. These two slave families of four persons each nervously awaited the verdict; the courtroom was packed with African-American spectators. Before the arrival of Justice Paine, Juliet Lemmon approached Nancy and Emeline and unsuccessfully attempted to persuade the two women to return, all sins forgiven, and pleaded for them "not to rob her of their labor."[27]

Through his attorney Jonathan Lemmon argued that his wife was the legal owner of the slaves and had been for several years. He cited the right of the transit of property and asserted that the eight slaves were legally recognized as property in Virginia, by the Supreme Court, and in Texas. Lemmon denied Napoleon's accusations that he was a slave trader and that his slaves were confined and restrained against their will. The Virginian claimed that since the slaves "had never touched, landed, or come into the harbor or State of New York except for the mere purpose of passage and transit," they should be permitted to remain in his custody and the Lemmons allowed to proceed on their journey.

Justice Paine announced his decision in the case of *Jonathan Lemmon v. Louis Napoleon* on 13 November 1852. Citing the antislavery statues of New York, he ordered the slaves freed. The black spectators "appeared to be intoxicated with joy" as the newly freed slaves were taken in two carriages to safe houses. Paine's decision was commended by Northern newspapers, but a group of New York merchants raised funds to compensate the Lemmons, who in the meantime appealed to the state supreme court to overturn Paine's ruling. Virginia governor Joseph Johnson and an outraged General Assembly pledged to assist the Lemmons. Johnson told legislators that the couple planned to free the slaves if they won their appeal because they had been adequately compensated, but he worried that if the decision went against them, the value of slave property in general would be seriously affected. Meanwhile, the ex-slaves were sent to the safety of Canada out of the reach of American authorities. The Lemmons received $5,200 as indemnity from city merchants and returned to Virginia.[28]

The New York Court of Appeals later ruled in favor of the eight slaves in March 1860 (future president Chester A. Arthur served as one of their attorneys). Newspaper editorials defended the right of slaves to sue for freedom in that "errors committed in behalf of the slave are nobler that errors committed on behalf of the slaveholder." Southerners castigated the ruling as a dangerous interference of property rights. Only the coming of civil war prevented the case from being heard and decided by the country's highest tribunal.[29]

Black involuntary servitude by 1860 had all but vanished in most of the states above the Mason-Dixon Line but flourished below it. The North, antislavery but antiblack, at first would fight for the preservation of the American Union and only later affixed the abolishment of involuntary servitude to its cause. The South, proslavery and antiblack, sought independence with black slavery as its cornerstone and white freedom and liberty as its aspiration. African-Americans were increasingly blamed by white contemporaries as the cause of the national estrangement.

Conveniently forgotten was the realization that if a choice were offered, black Americans would not have selected the kind of existence they had known and endured in the United States, an existence of victimization and desperate injustice. Secession became an euphemism for slavery, and when the war was over, only two ideologies were forever eradicated from political, economic, and moral contention in the United States: slavery and secession. Both were defended by Southerners as a duty and a legitimate part of government.

In Atlanta, Georgia, Harrison Berry, a forty-year-old slave shoemaker and the property of S. W. Price of Covington, published a pamphlet which urged African-American slaves to be submissive to their white owners. Taught to read and write, Berry became perhaps the sole Southern slave to address the nation directly and one of few blacks to state complete support of slavery in a published tract. His twenty-five-cent pamphlet, *Slavery and Abolitionism, as Viewed by a Georgia Slave*, appeared shortly after Lincoln's election and before South Carolina's secession. He had little if anything positive to say about Northerners or abolitionists and accused both of promising to help slaves escape but ignoring them afterwards; he warned potential runaways that "subordination of the poor colored man North, is greater than that of the slave South." Berry carried his arguments further by saying that he would rather have his wife be a slave with a master bound by law and self-interest to protect her than to be with her and their children as free persons without any means of support.[30]

Afro-Virginians in Fredericksburg were rewarded with a huge banquet at the courthouse in their honor in 1861 after exhibiting conspicuous heroism and devotion toward protecting their masters' property by successfully battling fires. They were waited on by whites, and the Christianburg Amateur Band serenaded them as they feasted; afterwards the blacks retired to the Masonic Hall for speeches of praise and dancing to the music of "the fiddle, triangle and banjo."[31]

The *Alexandria Gazette and Virginia Advertiser*, observing a group of well-dressed slaves at the city's West End district on "hiring day," declared they were happily "eating, drinking, fiddling and dancing" while anxious contractors and farmers haggled and competed for their services as cooks, dining room servants, field hands, house servants, and mechanics. This "was not at all strange," said the *Gazette*, "for, being incapable of ambitious aspirations . . . a negro enjoys a mundane heaven, if he has plenty to eat and drink, and is not worked hard."[32]

But the Union came to an end with the election of Abraham Lincoln as president of the United States in November 1860. He received less than two thousand votes in Virginia, and a conference called by the General Assembly to resolve the crisis met at Washington in February but accomplished nothing. South Carolina had already seceded from the Union and had been joined by five other slave states in establishing a provisional Confederate government. According to Elizabeth Keckley, an ex-Virginia slave,

Southerners held secret meetings at Jefferson Davis's Washington residence in 1860 even before Lincoln's nomination to devise their secession strategy.[33]

A commentator for the Richmond *Examiner* put the crisis in perspective when he claimed that the enemies of slavery were foes of the state: "Virginia is the particular object of abolition envy, hatred and arrogance. As the doomed and damned of Tophet hate the blessed in Paradise, so do the mean, hungry, avaricious, lying, cheating, hypocritical, cunning, cowardly Yankees hate the high-toned Southerner, but above all, the Virginian." Lincoln's call for 75,000 volunteers to suppress the insurrection was met by defiance from the Old Dominion. Confederate propagandists cautioned Virginia, the nation's most populous slave state, of dire consequences, including the freeing of its slaves.[34]

Culpeper County residents held a public meeting in favor of secession during December 1860 which was appropriately prefaced by a large sale of slaves; a visiting Mississippi congressman declared himself surprised but delighted by their secession sentiments. Pittsylvania County residents demanded respect for the Southern way of life: "While many of us do not believed that the election of a sectional president even with odious and dangerous sentiment would of itself be sufficient cause for extreme measures, yet all feel that is it an alarming indication of . . . schemes of treason, plundered outrage to the South . . . and . . . fanaticism." Rockingham County residents sang:

> Shoulder to shoulder, son and sire!
> All, call all! to the feast of fire!
> Mother and maiden, and child and slave,
> A common triumph or a single grave.[35]

Not everyone was as electrified about imminent bloodshed, and the naysayers warned that the commonwealth should expect to become the dominant theater for military campaigns as God's retribution for its slavery sins. A Warrenton newspaper said: "Virginia! Mother of Harlots—Plunderer of Cradles—she who has grown fat by selling her own children in the slave shambles: Virginia! Butcher—Pirate—Kidnapper—Slavocrat—the murderer of John Brown and his gallant band—at last, will meet her just doom." On April 18, 1861, the day after Virginia's secession, a melancholy William Johnson Pegram warned a friend: "Virginia has seceded, and we are now out of the old government in the new. But we are going to have a terrible war." Little did the applauding newest Confederates realize the magnitude of grief and suffering awaiting their state. Not only would it lose most of its western counties, but nearly all of its western counties would come to reject and despise Confederate rule to the extent that many became openly Unionist in sentiment and practically lawless from 1863 to 1865. But for the moment, white and black Virginians plunged into the martial spirit convinced they had nothing to fear from each other or the Yankees.[36]

Although the majority of Virginians were proud to call themselves rebels, there were those whose first sights of Confederate soldiers left unfavorable impressions; a visitor to Richmond in the fall of 1861 sneeringly called it a "City of loafers and dirty Soldiers." Neither were some slave patricians as committed to a society of white male social and political equality as they had publicly indicated. A Salt Sulphur Springs slaveowner named Harnson advocated a slavocracy of hereditary aristocratic Southern slave lords as the best form of Confederate government. He predicted a new regime based on a royal ruling class of white masters over black and poor white slaves and the establishment of "a limited or absolute Monarchy."[37]

Afro-Virginians were at the mercy of white capriciousness and the General Assembly. A new state constitution drafted by a convention in December 1861 stated the basis, foundation, and duty of government to be the furnishing of "common benefit, protection and security of the people." Afro-Virginians were badly destitute of these, as well as of equal rights and justice, but the promise of the Declaration of Rights that "no man or set of men are entitled to exclusively or separate . . . privileges from the community" amounted to empty words wherever the status of the two races was compared.

There were other impediments. The third article of the proposed constitution dashed any limited expectations by the state's free blacks by declaring that only white males could qualify as voters. The fact that voting was by voice, not written ballots, deterred any attempt at free black voter registration. Freedom of the press, speech, and worship was reaffirmed, but blacks could expect the continuation of the oppression and discrimination they had always weathered. To make certain that future, less conservative legislators dare not alter the racial status quo, this document required manumitted slaves to forfeit their freedom if they stayed in the Old Dominion more than one year. The General Assembly was given the authority to ban slave emancipation and, "for the relief of the Commonwealth," to deport free black residents. Blacks did not have any recognized rights but were liable for obligations such as taxes.[38]

As the Old Dominion withdrew from the Union, other white Virginians were holding their own discussions in the northwestern part of the state.

Map of Virginia counties showing percentage of slave inhabitants, 1860. (*Courtesy of the Virginia State Library and Archives*)

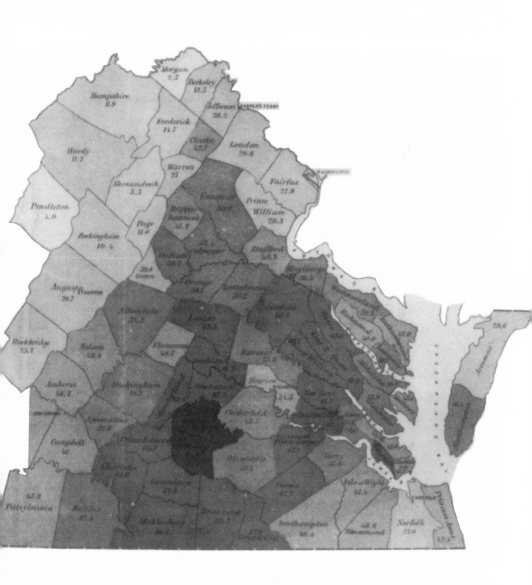

After a preliminary gathering held late in April, a convention of delegates met at Wheeling in May to denounce secession and reaffirm their support of the Union. For several years these western counties had felt they were being shortchanged of their fair share of wealth and political power. They operated their farms operated with few or no slaves, and because slaves under the age of twelve could not be taxed but livestock could, western Virginians bitterly complained that their property was overtaxed in comparison to that of easterners.

Slave owners could be reimbursed if their human chattels were executed by the state for crimes, and the coffers of the commonwealth paid for the return of black runaways, so that the westerners were paying taxes for benefits they did not use. They also had legitimate complaints about the dearth of educational funding. A Wheeling convention which met during the summer of 1861 declared the formation of a new state, Kanawha, with forty-eight counties and set up a shadow bureaucracy which offered itself as the "true" government of Virginia. Both of these "governments" operated out of Wheeling with Francis H. Pierpont serving as governor until the new state could be organized. The Kanawha secessionists petitioned the Federal Congress for admission to the Union as a new state.[39]

But what of Afro-Virginians? Pierpont, a long-term Unionist later known as the "Father of West Virginia," believed that slaves were entitled to emancipation and equitable treatment under the law. The General Assembly of the Restored State of Virginia at Alexandria promised that when the rebellion was suppressed, the government would be returned to loyal authorities who were nonslaveholders and the slaves would be freed. He asked Lincoln for Federal troops to suppress counterrevolutionaries. The proposed Kanawha constitution, while ordaining gradual emancipation after 4 July 1863 for slaves within certain age limits, prohibited ex-slaves or free blacks from permanent residency in the new state.

The presidential proclamation of admission was issued on 20 April 1863, and the state of West Virginia officially joined the Union on 20 June, the only group of Unionists to secede successfully from the Confederacy. The West Virginia government was put into place with Arthur Boreman elected as its first governor. Pierpont was recognized as the legal governor of "Loyal Virginia" and held civil authority over Federally occupied areas of the rebel commonwealth in cities like Alexandria (which became his capital), Norfolk, and Portsmouth and the counties of Accomack, Berkeley, Elizabeth City, Fairfax, Loudoun, Norfolk, Northampton, Prince William, and York.

Slavery, however, continued; the loyal state represented by Pierpont's government was exempted from the provisions of the Emancipation Proclamation until it ratified the Thirteenth Amendment in February 1865. B. F. Caldwell complained to Governor Pierpont about slaves obtaining passes from Union officers to leave the state; he had lost six in this manner and wanted the governor not only to recover his chattels but to take steps to prevent officers from "robbing" owners of their human property in the future. An army officer writing from Taylor County warned that the local press "is doing much mischief here. The secesh . . . seem to take courage and renew their old favorite hobby (the Nigger) with renewed zeal." He quoted one of his soldiers as saying that if the proclamation went into effect, he would quit the army.[40]

Of the Confederacy's 3,653,000 blacks, 548,907, or one in six, resided in Virginia. The South perceived of blacks as invaluable assets and instruments for waging and winning the war. On 26 April 1861 C. M. Hubbard of James City County advised Governor John Letcher to employ Afro-Virginian males between the ages of eighteen and fifty for military labor. The Richmond secession convention passed an ordinance in July 1861 allowing local governments to draft all able-bodied free black males to work on fortifications and similar tasks for up to sixty days at a time without their consent; their white commandants were to furnish them "compensation, rations, quarters and medical attendance." Afro-Virginian men were subject to charges of treason, desertion, and disobedience of orders and to any resulting penalties if they failed to meet at the designated rendezvous points.[41]

Most Afro-Virginians were not easily deceived by Confederate propaganda which wanted them to believe that Union soldiers were coming South not to free them but to kill blacks and use their bodies as fertilizer or to sell them to Haiti and Cuba. "Masters have tried to make us believe that the Yankees only wished to sell us to Cuba, to get money to carry on the war," a group of runaway slaves told a visiting Northern clergyman during September 1861. Here and there a few absentee masters sent word to their slaves that the Yankees would not harm them and that they were free to go with them if they preferred. Several astute slaves went into business for themselves, selling fruit, cider, fresh meat, food pies, and cakes to hungry Union soldiers and sailors. Some of these self-emancipated slaves procured boats ("bumboats"), loaded them with delicacies, and rowed out to Union vessels where eager customers paid seventy-five cents for cakes that in peacetime sold for fifteen cents.[42]

Afro-Virginians wore inscrutable masks, watermelon smiles, and feigned indifference. Eliza Wilson of Rockbridge County was guaranteed sanctuary by her worried brother in New York who feared an Afro-Virginian uprising: "Neither your state governments nor the federal government can prevent raids of free negroes . . . bands of whom are already formed & thoroughly drilled for the purpose of distributing themselves through the seceded states & inciting insurrections. We cannot contemplate this without horror, & yet we cant prevent it: & should you remain I regard your destruction as inevitable." He urged his sister to relocate to New York as soon as she could pack.[43]

However, most slaveholders trusted their slaves to protect their families and property. Robert Winn Snead, an Amherst County soldier, commended the care of his family to Aunt Peggy in a long, solemn farewell letter on the eve of his departure. "I can only commit to you my servants the safe keeping of My dear wife and children, how far you will discharge your duties time will tell," he wrote in July 1861. "You will take care of them, try and conduct yourselves to as not get in any trouble or difficulty while I am gone." He enclosed a photograph of himself and asked Peggy to remember him in her prayers.[44]

Other owners took no chances. Three months before Virginia's secession John Ewell decided to move his nine slaves from Prince William County to Texas. He purchased a farm and hired out his slaves, but the reluctant Afro-Virginian exiles were unhappy and missed their families. Ewell dismissed their concerns as whining that would "wear off with time & they are not competent judges of what is best for them."[45]

Armed with slaves, bountiful farms, railroads, shipyards, factories, and arrogance, Virginia appeared a calm lake on a still summer's morn with tranquil waters concealing undertows of uncertainty. The slave masters of the Old Dominion expressed vociferous confidence that the peculiar institution would be a boon for the Confederacy and reassured each other that "Cuffee" and his fellow slaves could best be employed to repel any invasion directly in their age-old roles of field hands and industrial laborers. After the passage of the secession ordinance, a patriotic Nelson County planter named one of his newborn slaves "Jeff Davis." The citizens of Richmond celebrated by playfully hoisting a grinning, ragged-looking black man upon the shoulders of Jean Antoine Houdon's statue of George Washington in the State Capitol. This would have more accurately symbolized of the plight of Afro-Virginians had the statue been placed on the black man's back.[46]

Southern blacks lived hard lives yet displayed fortitude and a sense of dignity. In the pages that follow, Afro-Virginians are depicted in a range of activities and behaviors: assimilators, builders, farmers, husbands and wives, negotiators, parents, pragmatists, teachers, and warriors. Blacks and whites were neighbors yet strangers to each other. Both faced a paradoxical Confederate States of America with pretensions of democracy. Southern whites rallied on the basis of race for independence, justice, and freedom yet were antagonistic to Afro-Southerners' basic civic rights and aspirations for self-determination. Slavery and racism were grim idiosyncrasies of the Confederate republic, an oxymoronic nation which systematically repressed blacks while insisting on their allegiance.[47]

PART ONE
UNCERTAIN TRUMPET

1 HERITAGE OF SERVITUDE
Slave Life and Labor on the Plantation

We were worked hard. They kept us busy.
—*William I. Johnson, Jr., Virginia ex-slave*

Sometimes I feel discouraged,
And think my work's in vain.
—*African-American spiritual*

THE EVERYDAY LIFE of slaves in wartime Virginia at first seemed unchanged. They labored on, hopeful yet alert, while their masters anxiously watched for any changes in their demeanor. Clothing continued to be provided though the cost increased as the war progressed. Slaveholders' expenses included not only purchases and repair of slave clothing; some planters felt obliged to issue spending money to slaves in order to prevent trouble.[1]

Cotton and hemp "Negro-cloth" produced in the mills of New England and a heavy, rough cotton cloth known as osnaburg were available for slaves in two sizes: small and large. Virginia slave males wore gray woolen coats and pants, colored cotton neckcloths, and coarse woolen socks. Slave women wore woolen dresses and white aprons and tied handkerchiefs around their heads. Both sexes wore their white folks' hand-me-downs, jeans, calico outfits, and remnants of discarded Confederate and Yankee uniforms. The only time slaves looked their best was on Sundays or at auctions; one Northern tourist described the clothing worn by Afro-Virginians as resembling prison uniforms. Owners were advised to purchase woolen cloth by the yard, leather by the pound, and shoes by the dozen from Richmond to minimize costs. Prices ranged from eight cents to a dollar a yard.[2]

Shoes were another story. Ex-slaves complained they never had any or at least none that fitted properly. Those who received them usually got one pair a year if they were lucky, but shoddy material made most "Negro shoes" last barely a few months. Richard Toler claimed his master never provided shoes for his slaves. They worked barefoot in the snow all winter, and their feet became frostbitten. "We just greased them with tallow when they cracked open" and kept on working, recalled another slave, Peter Randolph.[3]

Elizabeth Keckley's first garment was a short dress and white apron.

Booker T. Washington's was a "tow shirt"; and if his owner did not issue him a new one, Washington went naked. This type of shirt, made of "refuse flax," was stiff and coarse and irritated the skin during a breaking-in period of six weeks; it felt like "a thousand needle points prickling the flesh." To his dying day the sight of a new shirt reminded Washington of his former agonies. Washington's master issued shoes with wooden soles and raw leather uppers but only after the onset of extreme winter cold.[4]

Slaves were seen laboring in the fields practically nude. There was a decline in the availability of wool; most of the state's wool was produced in its western counties, and when they seceded as West Virginia there was little left to clothe whites, much less slaves. "I do not know how we will clothe the negroes," a worried Isaetta Hubard wrote to her mother in May 1862, "unless we get the wool." Her husband eventually procured "half-worn Yankee overcoats, cheap" from prisoners of war hospitalized in Richmond.[5]

Francis T. Glasgow, superintendent of Catawba Furnace in Botetourt County, complained in March 1863 that his slave laborers had been unable to work for weeks "for want of clothing and shoes." A King and Queen County slave owner tried to maintain a close rein on the costs of clothing her slaves during 1864–65 by personally doling out cloth, wool, and cow's hair for them make their own garments. Gloucester County owners were hard pressed to provide meat for their slaves after Yankee raiders passed through, and Colin Clarke, grousing over the high cost of wool and cotton, asked his son about obtaining for his slaves the clothing of soldiers who had died in Richmond hospitals.[6]

Ownership of slaves meant attending to their needs of food and housing just as for livestock, but unlike animals religious instruction was necessary for their souls' moral development. Slaves were not to be worked beyond their physical capacities and were to be furnished with the proper tools to carry out their tasks. Masters who strayed from these guidelines risked ostracism. Nevertheless, there were state laws that expressly placed responsibility for adequate treatment of slaves on their owners.[7]

The hard times of war made it increasingly difficult for owners to clothe their slaves properly, and the phrase "tatterdemalion Negroes" was accurate as most slaves were barefoot and dressed in rags. Barefoot Confederate soldiers customarily appropriated shoes from blacks. Wooden shoes (sabots) were cheaper than leather, and penny-pinching planters issued them to cut costs, but slaves universally refused to wear them. At other times only leather or wooden soles were available, and blacks had to make do with next to nothing. Some preferred nothing.

Whites were accustomed to the "Negro look": old straw hats, hand-me-down dresses, faded cotton shirts, tattered pants, handkerchiefs, brogans, and coarse sacks for children with three holes cut for their heads and arms. They were quick to suspect as a thief any black dressed in ostentatious finery; one newspaper declared, "It is surprising that their means of obtaining such finery are not more frequently inquired into." Afro-Virginian women disregarded society's restrictions on their wardrobes and were represented as being extremely well-dressed as they promenaded down the streets of wartime Richmond adorned in pink muslin dresses and velvet cloaks. Shabby-clothed runaways who reached Union lines later appeared with umbrellas, suits, white cotton gloves, walking sticks, top hats, or bonnets. Whites considered such displays to reflect pretensions of social equality.[8]

Afro-Virginians had their own language and jargon. They were quoted as speaking in minstrel dialects ("dis" for *this*, "chillums" for *children*, "I'se" for *I am* or *I have*, "nusin" for *nothing*, "hab" for *have*, and yet African words found their way into the everyday language of their oppressors, words like *banana* (West African in origin), *banjo* (*mbanza*, a African stringed instrument having a fretted neck), *goober* (*nguba*, used for peanuts), *okra* (in West African parlance *nkruma*), *gumbo* (*gombo*, a Bantu word describing a thick, rich soup containing okra), and *yams* (*njam* in the Gullah dialect), i.e., orange-colored sweet potatoes.[9]

Tote, a word commonly used by slaves, meant "to carry or to bear." When Abraham Lincoln visited Petersburg on 8 April 1865, a ragged Afro-Virginian boy was invited aboard the president's train and questioned by him and members of his party, including Elizabeth Keckley, born a slave in the Old Dominion and now the confidante of Mrs. Lincoln. Keckley noted that when the boy used the word *tote* and was asked to define it, he enthusiastically explained, "Why, massa, to tote um on your back." An intrigued Lincoln asked one of his traveling companions, Senator Charles Sumner, about the word's origins. Sumner, in a condescending tone, remarked that it had African and Latin roots; he did not consider it an elegant or even a good word but admitted its widespread colloquial usage among black Southerners gave it validity.[10]

Much of the food that slaves had was edibles that whites ordinarily did not eat such as chicken necks, gizzards, and feet (used for soups) and chitlins (the small intestines of hogs, described by a white writer as "rubbery and tasteless"). *Kush,* a mixture of cornbread cooked with gravy and ham, ashcake, and hoecake were enjoyed by the slaves. They were allowed to grow their own vegetables and trapped and consumed as many opossums, raccoons, squirrels, rabbits, and fish as they could catch to supplement their rationed diet. Rarely was meat given to them other than leftovers of ubiquitous hogs and chickens. Molasses, salt pork, okra, bacon, peas, collard greens, turnips, and black-eyed peas were among the foods issued to slaves along with daily or weekly rations of salt, corn, and cornmeal. With only two meals a day (reduced to one a day on some farms during the war), slaves suffered from scurvy, cholera, tuberculosis, smallpox, and pellagra, a deficiency of proteins and niacin caused by protracted diets of a limited number of food types, mainly cornmeal, grits, molasses, and pork.[11]

From April to October meals were served in the fields at eight in the morning and one in the afternoon (breakfast and supper) with three-quarters of an hour to an hour and a half allowed for eating. Some field hands and children ate from troughs. Slaves composed songs about their preference for ham and cabbage:

> Hannah, boil em' down,
> De cabbage just pulled out de ground,
> Boil 'em in de pot
> And make him smoking hot.[12]

Was slave food plentiful and nutritious? Pork, corn, fish, and potatoes provided carbohydrates, proteins, and vitamins if sufficient quantities were served. In their narratives slaves remembered always being hungry; even if they had been well fed as claimed by proslavery writers, the methods of food preparation and preservation left much to be desired. Food was boiled in communal pots, and slaves had to gulp it down while standing, using their bare hands.[13]

Slaves devised their own amusements when not at work, though most slept or rested in their spare time. Others performed personal chores: mending clothing, visiting sick and elderly relatives, and comparable family activities. They tended vegetable gardens, fished and hunted, gambled and held cockfights, or plotted escapes. Each season had its own entertainments and expectations; Sundays, Christmas, New Year's, and election days were opportunities to celebrate with drinking, dancing, music, sports, barbecues, and preaching.[14]

Marbles, pitching horseshoes, storytelling, and footraces were among their amusements. Head butting was a popular way of demonstrating prowess, though whites typically initiated these contests and wagered on the outcomes. Two husky male slaves would seize each other by the shoulders and violently bang their heads together until one gave up or was knocked unconscious. Albert Woods and Colin Hodgins were slaves renowned for their head-butting stamina. Hodgins, who bore numerous scars of his victories on his head, arms, and back, would not permit any white to punish him by whipping.[15]

Music and dancing were favored pastimes, and Richmond blacks held several dances by invitation only throughout the war years. Union and Confederate soldiers both commented on the slaves' affinity for dancing and singing and noted that at those moments they seemed happiest. Frederick Douglass asserted that the slaves sang not because they were happy or to forget their troubles but because they were sad about their bondage and wanted to be free.[16]

Spirituals were religious songs that expressed the depths of the slaves' emotions, burdens, trepidations, and hopes. The music thinly disguised their true feelings, and the interplay between lead singers and choruses gave vent to hand-clapping, foot-stomping, low-moaning laments or shouts of hope and dogged resolve to be free in this world and the next. Out of these songs and feelings came the blues, ragtime, and jazz.[17]

Afro-Virginians sang:

I don't feel weary and noways tired,
　　O glory hallelujah
Just let me in the kingdom while the world
　　Is all on fire,
　　O glory hallelujah.

Songs contained double, even triple, surreptitious messages such as "The Hypocrite and the Concubine," a condemnation of whites and slavery:

Hypocrite and concubine,
Living among the swine,
They ran to God with lips
And tongue,
And leave all heart behind.

Caroline County slaves, in one of their favorite hymns, sang of freedom:

Bending knees a-aching
Body racked with pain,
I wished I was a child of God,
I'd get home by and by.[18]

Many slaves began their autobiographies by stating the year, sometimes the complete date and place, of their birth, but one of the things most slaves did not do was celebrate birthdays. Slaves such as Lorenzo Ivy, who knew he was about fifteen years in 1866 because the war had ended the

TABLE I.I. AGES OF NELSON COUNTY SLAVES, 1861

Name	Birth date	Age
Archie	September 1841	29
George	February 1837	24
Clara Ann	July 1859	2
Anenah	1 December 1848	13
James	20 October 1855	6
Eliza Ann	October 1853	18
Primus	1 December 1853	8
Ben	December 1850	11
Drury	4 June 1859	2
George	30 March 1860	1

Source: "Register of My Negroes in Nelson," 1856–62, Robert Thurston Hubard Papers, 8708, box 10, UVA.

previous year, calculated their ages from famous local, state, and national events: Nat Turner's rebellion, John Brown's raid, the Civil War, Lee's surrender, severe weather, and similar events. Slaveholders were supposed to know the ages of their slaves because they became taxable at age twelve.[19]

Frederick County owner George L. Severs meticulously listed his female slaves and their children. His notations before 1846 show only years of birth, but during the war the precise day and month were included. The slave register of Nelson County slave owner Robert Thurston Hubard shows similar record keeping (table 1.1). The Hubard register and hundreds like it that have survived are invaluable to Afro-Virginian genealogical research.[20]

Elderly slaves (those aged fifty and older) were respected and venerated within the Afro-Virginian community as survivors and fountains of wisdom. There were eighty-two black Virginians over the age of 100 in 1860 (twenty-seven males, fifty-five females), but unless a slave was enfeebled, he or she was put to work. On the Louisa County plantation of Thomas Watson, "Old Lucy" had charge of slave infants and children too young for the fields and was paid $3.25 a day. As the oldest slave on the plantation, "Old Cupid" for many years had had no labor required of him and considered himself worthy of the Watson family's respect and support. Lucy and Cupid received regular stipends to spend as they pleased for shoes and other luxuries. During Watson's absences he left instructions for his overseer to continue presenting small sums of cash to this retired slave couple. The age which slaves were allowed to "retire" varied according to owner preference.[21]

Many Virginian slaveholders considered aged slaves to be unproductive burdens. When this point was reached, it became "cheaper to buy poison than medicine." Dinah Browne, an Afro-Virginian slave who escaped from Petersburg, flatly accused whites of murdering old slaves. She recalled seeing overseers giving doses of a black juice to slaves too aged and sick to work; this juice "sent them to sleep, and that for ever." Elderly slaves were auctioned in Petersburg for $15 to $30 each; in Lynchburg, nine days before Christmas 1862, a seventy-year-old black woman was sold for $10 and a black man between the age of seventy-five and one hundred went under the hammer for $300.[22]

Plantations were a combination of labor camps, racial indoctrination barracks, and Christianization bureaus. Days and nights of intimidation, toil, and punishment harshly enforced the will of planters. The typical field hand, male or female, was a dark-skinned, broad-nosed, thick-lipped, and kinky black-haired individual in his or her twenties. They toiled until darkness and then were required to work by torch or moonlight, especially during the height of the cornhusking and harvest seasons of October and November when they might be in the fields from dawn until one o'clock the following morning. "Mark me," Charles City County planter Richard Eppes warned his slaves, "laziness, playing possum, insolence to overseer or neglect of your work or anything of that kind, no one who has committed them need apply to me for any favor as I am determined every tub shall stand on its own bottom."[23]

Austin Steward, who slaved in Prince William County, recalled workdays as beginning at sunrise; when summoned by the blowing of a horn or conch shell, slaves had thirty minutes to get to the fields where, to use a Virginia expression, they immediately were hard at work "betimes in the morning." Steward recalled breakfast (usually bread) as being served at nine for half an hour, then it was back to work until noon for another communal meal; afterwards the labors resumed, for the overseer was "always on hand to attend all delinquents . . . [who] never failed to feel the blows of his heavy whip." Slaves retaliated against their forced labor by malingering and sabotage. One overseer's manual advised: "It is almost universal with negroes to lie, feign ignorance or prevaricate when called upon to give evidence against others. This sort of combination must be broken up, and when detected in such practices, the offender must be punished according to the degree of the offense." To eliminate some of the drudgery, white supervisors tried to turn work into play; cornshucking competitions were held to determine bragging rights for the fastest shucker on the plantation, and corn liquor was freely available to speed up the pace. Hog-killing time became a festive occasion though it was bloody, smelly work producing sweetbreads, chitlins, hams, and bacon.[24]

Slavery was a system of control and deceit. It held unpleasant memories for those who suffered under it, but Southern whites looked back on it as a congenial, simpler time. "There slavery wore its kindliest aspect," a Charlotte County resident wrote of her home and its slaves. Plantations were domiciles of "affectionate relationships between the servers and the served." Sundays for whites were days of rest, of churchgoing and visits with friends, but down in the slave quarters the Sabbath was a day of inspection, with slaves forming long lines near the Big House, dressed in their best clothes, mentally steeling themselves for another week in the fields under the merciless Virginia sun.[25]

Elaborate rules and regulations were issued periodically from owners to their slaves for the governance of behavior. Slaveholders considered these to be legal contracts between themselves and their slaves. The edicts prohibited stealing, lying, reporting late to work, striking masters or overseers, adultery, fighting and quarreling, drunkenness, slovenly dress, malingering, running away, sabotage, and ownership of boats or dogs. Penalties varied from head shaving, confinement, and whippings to reduction of weekly allowances or denial of special privileges. One slaveholder devised a unique punishment for quarreling: "The parties shall be stripped naked placed in a closed room each with a cowhide whip and made to whip each other until they are commanded to stop." As a reward for appropriate behavior, slaves were granted passes to visit spouses, their own garden plots and the right to raise chickens, extra rations of pork, meal, and wood, Christmas and Easter holidays, cash payments for overtime, or half days on Saturdays.[26]

Approximately forty slave tobacco workers employed at Frederick's Hall plantation were handsomely paid for their overwork (overtime) in cash. These payments ranged from $4 to $50 per worker in December 1863; exactly one year later payments of $80 to $100 were routine, due to galloping inflation.[27]

Slaves were categorized as four types of laborers: "full hands" (a full-grown able-bodied male) "three-quarters hands" (young adults), "half hands" (nursing mothers and children age twelve or older), "quarter hands" (children below the age of six, elderly slaves, and those recovering from minor illnesses or accidents). On several farms specialized tasks were assigned to each slave, sometimes more than one. A male slave at any given moment could be a gravedigger, hog feeder, carriage driver, or slave driver; women were field hands, water toters, house servants, cooks, and seamstresses. Slaves as young as three were allocated a share of labor. Four-year-old Elizabeth Keckley was placed in charge of her mistress's infant, rocking its cradle, shooing away flies, and not letting it cry. She rocked too hard, the child was flung upon the floor, and her mistress ordered Keckley whipped. "This was the first time I was punished in this cruel way," Keckley laconically remarked in her autobiography, "but not the last."[28]

Tobacco, a labor-intensive crop, required several closely monitored activities: seeding, hilling, transplanting, pruning, topping, worming, cutting, drying, sorting, and packing. The worming process demanded the removal of large green worms whose voracious appetites could obliterate an entire crop. They had to be killed, crushed by bare hands one by one. Six-year-old Nancy Williams suffered an outlandish penalty for her lackadaisical attitude toward this chore; though warned by another slave girl to pick every one in sight and kill each one, Nancy merely dropped the worms to the ground and moved on down the rows. Her owner rushed over and stuffed a handful in her mouth: "Lordy knows how many of them things I done swallered, but I sho' picked 'em off careful arter dat." Simon Stokes's overseer required him to suffer three lashes for every worm missed or else eat them. Stokes always choose the worms; chewing them was but a temporary discomfort, "but dem lashes done last a pow'full long time."[29]

The historic image of the overseer is one of cruelty and unscrupulousness, and slave narratives seldom have anything positive to say about them. Union soldier Francis Colburn Adams was part of a Federal force which overran one Virginia plantation in 1862. He described its overseer as "a little, lean, leathery man, with a sallow complexion ... no complexion at all, a sharp, angular visage, and a small dull eye. He wore a shabby grey coat, that reached almost to his heels, a soft hat slouched over his eyes, and seemed to be shirtless. He was a strange and quaint item ... this sovereign of the lash." His employer had fled and left him in charge of only children, women, and old men who ignored his orders and laughed at his efforts to punish them. When he tried to use the whip, Union soldiers threatened to put him in irons and confine him in their guardhouse. This shattered his sanity, causing him to stare into space for hours, muttering to himself.[30]

The hiring of overseers varied by master and locale, but usually written contracts were drawn up and signed by both parties. An agreement between Sarah B. Saunders of Buckingham County and N. L. Gregory for 15 November 1862 to 15 November 1863 required Gregory "to be sober, constant & industrious, to stay regularly with his hands, to attend to his stock, and ... take good care of them." The phrase "to be sober" was repeated later in the document with good reason: drunken overseers not only were unable to manage slaves but presented a bad impression of whites as a whole to ever-watchful blacks. Saunders promised Gregory a house, a garden, five barrels of corn, eight slaves, and four workhorses for his personal use and one-ninth of the crops.[31]

Overseers between the ages of twenty-five and forty, in good health, honest, of sound judgment, and "fond of home and fond of his calling" were preferred. Individuals heavily in debt were rejected because "an overseer in debt, has his mind too much troubled with his own anxieties and affairs." They were to be treated well but not as equals. "Do not interfere between your negroes & overseer," one planter cautioned his sons, "and give your orders to *your negroes* in person, but *give your directions to your overseer and tell him what is to be done.* This prevents confusion." Extravagant wages were impractical because of the uncertainties of prices and crops. But for managing plantations of twenty-five to thirty slaves, overseers could expect salaries of $200 to $300 annually.[32]

Although the daily responsibility for any given plantation rested with overseers, planters were wont to set goals, devise timetables, and offer unsolicited advice for the management of their properties. One planter's "Standing Rules for the Government of Slaves" (see Appendix B) was prefaced by six cardinal rules:

> *Rule 1st* No negro should be permitted to go off the Plantation on his or her own business without a written Pass
> *2nd* No negro should be presented to sell any thing without a written Permit
> *3d* Fighting should be strictly forbidden
> *4th* It should [be] made the duty of every negro to take up or give information to the Overseer of every negro who may come among them & cannot give a strict account of himself, they should be especially prohibited from entertaining watermen
> *5th* Quarrelling, or vexations & insulting language, from one to another & especially from a younger to an older negro, should be strictly forbidden
> *6th* Every working hand under the authority of the Overseer upon the plantation should appear with a clean shirt & decent clothes every [Sunday?] morning.

Overseers were assisted by a corps of black slave drivers (headmen or foremen). More than a few of these suboverseers zealously punished fellow slaves, for they could be disciplined and reduced in rank if they or their charges failed to obey regulations. Drivers summoned slaves to work and acted as the eyes and ears of the overseer. In return, they obtained extra food and clothing and the right to raise hogs for profit.[33]

Wartime urgencies made overseers indispensable to their employers, and their value to the South was reflected in Confederate law. The Conscription Act of 16 April 1862 exempted overseers or masters of plantations with twenty or more slaves. Critics blasted it as blatant favoritism to slave owners, but it was one technique for maintaining control of blacks. From 1863 on, affidavits were required to prove eligibility for this exemption, and only those persons employed as professional overseers before the 1862 act were exempted. Though the number of required slaves was reduced to fifteen by an amendment of February 1864, the payment of a $500 fee by planters (and their promise to sell agricultural products to the government at its prices) and two witnesses became necessary in order to secure an overseer's exemption. The amendment subjected white males between the ages of sixteen and fifty to military service but allowed exemptions in areas where slave labor could not be safely employed without the presence of able-bodied white men.[34]

Averse to losing their seasoned surrogates, planters sought exemption on their behalf as early as May 1861. Charles C. Wellford, a wealthy Confederate sympathizer near Fredericksburg, appealed for the exemption of the county's overseers from military duty else "large bodies of negroes" would overwhelm white civilians. John J. Werth successfully entreated Confederate secretary of war Judah P. Benjamin for the discharge of John Houston and William M. Wade so they could return to overseeing duties at the Carbon Hill Mines, Virginia's chief supplier of natural coke (a substitute for anthracite coal) for the treasury, war, and quartermaster departments, the post office, and Richmond's hospitals. Houston and Wade, wrote Werth in desperation, were essential for the supervision of the mine's one hundred slave workers for they were the last of its "intelligent and experienced white men" who could control them.[35]

An alarmed eighty-three-year-old Fluvanna County planter, John Hartwell Cocke, petitioned President Jefferson Davis in 1863 for an exemption for overseer Albert Wood, pleading his poor health and need of Wood's experience in handling slaves on his 300-acre estate. The planter informed Davis that Wood's expertise had enabled his farm to produce 900 bushels of wheat, 100 pounds of corn, and 40,000 pounds of hay for the Confederate government and insisted that Wood was indispensable.[36]

The relationship between plantation owners and overseers could be adversarial. Robert Ritchie complained in October 1861 that his family's overseer was taking advantage of an elderly uncle and not obeying his orders; Ritchie feared his uncle had developed "too great [a] delicacy in making suggestions" for the management of the family estate. In September 1863 Edmund Ruffin bemoaned that "there seems to be no chance or prospect" of hiring competent overseers. His son Julian was able to hire a man in April 1864 who was exempted from military service because he had only one hand, but this disabled overseer had little if any experience in farming or dealing with slaves. The disgusted Ruffin branded the entire overseer class as a pestilence to planters.[37]

Meddling slave owners and sullen slaves posed dilemmas for overseers. William Wakefield, an overseer who claimed to be a Unionist but not an abolitionist, voiced his opposition to "Negro equality" and criticized two Northern white women domiciled with his family for violating Southern social etiquette by visiting blacks at their cabins and greeting them with a kiss. This conduct, he fumed, hampered his ability to keep the slaves at their work and gave them false ideas of their caste. A Henrico County slave named Richard was convicted in April 1863 and hanged for the attempted murder of an overseer. Another slave, the father of Nancy Williams, was known for his temper and one day rebelled after an overseer tried to make him perform some unidentified task. When the overseer cursed and threatened him, Williams's father pulled a knife and tried to cut the white man's throat but was prevented by the intervention of fellow slaves. The owner's response was unconventional: he fired the white overseer and put Williams's father in charge of the plantation. Under his leadership production and profits soared, and he received a cash share of the proceeds.[38]

The war took a toll on owner-overseer relationships. One overseer named Nash evidently was appreciated by his employer, William Gordon of Nelson County, until 1862 when the two men had a falling-out. "On farm matters," wrote Gordon in his diary, "my business has been going dreadfully" because Nash "the worst overseer & meanest man I ever knew left me on the 15th Nov. [1862] but not till he had nearly ruined me. We made nothing for market last year." Slave shoes and cloth, coffee, sugar, corn, nails, and flour were "out of the question as I have nothing left to sell."[39]

Another element of slavery involved slave traders and agents. Slave apologist Beverly Munford inaccurately held that the general opprobrium of slave traders was proof that the Old Dominion was not in the business of breeding slaves; many state residents angrily denied breeding charges as lies by Northerners. The distinction between selling slaves and breeding and raising them for market was heeded by professional slave auctioneers and brokers. Pulliam & Company of Richmond, mindful of such community sensitivities, advertised itself as "Auctioneers for Sale of Negroes—*Have no connection with the Negro Trade.*" One Confederate periodical declared slave breeding as merely a concomitant of the Southern climate's stimulating effects.[40]

Dickinson and Hill, Richmond's foremost slave auctioneers, had sales of $2 million, and other city dealers sold another $2 million worth of human stock just before the war. Slave advertisements were scanned avidly by slave owners and would-be masters:

Hector Davis
Auctioneer and Commission Merchant for
The Sale of Negroes,
Franklin Street, Richmond, Va.,
Sells Negroes both publicly and privately,
and pledges his best efforts to obtain the
Highest Market Prices.
He has a safe and commodious Jail, where
he will board all Negroes intended for his
sales at 30 cents per day.[41]

Alexandria was the state's main slave-trading center. Franklin and Armfield's slave pens remained in business until the Union seizure of the town in May 1861. This establishment shipped up to one hundred slaves at a time to New Orleans chained in pairs and in the custody of armed guards. Alexandria was also home for Kephart and Company; after the town's capture this firm's building was converted into a jail for Confederate prisoners of war. In the fall of 1862 a Union soldier stationed at Alexandria wrote his wife: "Today I find myself at the *Slave pens* where for years human beings have been sold at auction by the slave dealer. This is the great headquarters of the slave trade for the whole state of Virginia. The pens are now used to confine rebel prisoners." The office of Price, Birch & Company, "Dealers In Slaves," housed slaves in cells with earthen floors, no windows, and iron manacles and bars on the doors. It was later used to house troublesome Union soldiers.[42]

Dealers purchased slaves and had them shaved, washed, dressed, and fattened up to look sleek and healthy for prospective buyers. Afro-Virginians were shipped south by boat or packed in railroad cars like cattle. Mulattoes were prized: the whiter the slave, the greater his or her market value. Full- and mixed-blood Afro-Virginian women "were much sought after" as dependable breeders. Persons engaged in the wholesale business of selling or hiring of slaves on commission paid state and county licensing fees.[43]

The firm of Dickinson, Hill and Company received inquiries from Lieutenant John Garrett of Gloucester Point in the fall of 1861 about "what a valuable young negro man very likely would bring put in market now. I have one I wish *to sell* if I can do so without making a great sacrifice." Another owner simply shipped three slaves named "London, Kitty, and Jim" to the company with orders to keep them in custody pending higher prices. So profitable was slavery early in the war that Dr. J. H. Burnett of North Carolina could confidently write to E. H. Stokes, a Richmond dealer: "A friend of yours informed me that you were now selling negroes. I have a boy about 16 years old . . . a cotton hand & another about 25 black [field] hand. What can you get for them?" Stokes replied that the sixteen-year-old could be worth $1,900 and the twenty-five-year-old $1,000 or more on the current market. By March 1862 Richmond was crowded with slaves; slave bricklayers and plasterers were selling at $11,000 apiece, and $950 to $1,000 was offered for slave girls.[44]

In December 1862, 120 slaves were sold in Lynchburg; one went for almost $3,000. Fourteen days earlier a sixteen-year-old boy had sold for $2,150; a twenty-year-old gardener and carpenter, $1,850; a family consisting of a twenty-five-year-old man, his twenty-year-old wife, and their three children ages ten, eight and six were sold for $4,000. It is an irony that Abraham Lincoln's first inauguration and his Emancipation Proclamation contributed to an economic boost for Virginia slave prices. "If old Abe will issue another proclamation, he will up prices of negroes so high that a poor man will not be able to own one," the Lynchburg *Daily Republican* observed facetiously. As Union general Hugh Judson Kilpatrick passed near Fredericksburg, he heard a bell tolling, and when he asked why, he was told a slave auction was about to commence. Kilpatrick entered the town and saw five male slaves on the block as an auctioneer started the proceedings by saying, "Who bids?" The general thereupon stepped forth and said in a loud voice, "I bid." The five slaves were handed over, and Kilpatrick took them to freedom.[45]

The highest prices for Confederate slaves were found in the Old Dominion. Prices escalated from $1,000 in 1861, to $1,300 in 1862, $1,500 in 1863, $3,000 in 1864, and $5,000 by early 1865. Texas experienced prices well below Virginia's ($664 in 1863 and $691 in 1864); however, Georgia (where prices averaged at $1,500 in late 1862) also experienced steady rises in prices. Cotton prices, inflation, credit strains, the risk for dealers in transferring large groups of slaves from one state to another in the middle of a war, all interfered with the business.[46]

Regardless of the war many Virginia slave dealers could genuinely proclaim, "Slavery is our business, and business is good." Silas and R. H. Omohundro of Richmond saw increasing profits even though their merchandise's availability became uncertain. During 1863–64 this firm's quarterly sales were more than $13,000; in July 1864 the sale of just four slaves netted $18,550.[47]

Rockingham County dealers John B. Smith and James E. Carson were so bullish on slavery that their newspaper advertisements bragged of their having $100,000 in cash reserved exclusively for purchasing able-bodied young slaves on the spot from owners. The year 1863 saw more increasing prices: thirteen slaves from the estates of John Randolph and N. Tobert were sold for $21,365 ($1,700 each), and eleven slaves went for $13,915 when auctioned by Staunton dealers Bruce & Peck. During the latter sale a twenty-five-year-old male sold for $1,500, a fourteen-year-old girl the same, and a sixty-year-old man, $1,615. A month after the Emancipation Proclamation, the Richmond firm of Lee and James sold a group of slave men and boys at prices varying from $2,100 to $2,500 and women and girls from $1,200 to $2,500; one mulatto girl went for $3,000 in cash.

The proclamation did not immediately jeopardize slave sales. Wythe County merchant and ironworks owner David Graham purchased a "sound and healthy" Richmond slave named Green for $1,995 on 20 January 1863; forty-two-year-old Mary, purchased by Martha Thornton of Farmville for $1,500 on 16 January, was warranted to be of sound body and mind; Mrs. B. L. Blankenship of Nottoway County purchased from R. H. Dickinson & Brother, Richmond, "a small healthy negro girl—ten or twelve years old . . . a Dark Mulatto" for cash on 16 January.[48]

Estate appraisals and inventories supported the optimism of slaveholding Virginians. The 1,200-acre Pea Hill plantation in Brunswick County was worth $47,000 in January 1863 and possessed nearly fifty slaves ages two months to seventy-four years and tobacco, fodder, oats, wheat, corn, and similar crops. The crops were valued at $16,784.25, but the slaves were worth $29,750, 63 percent of Pea Hill's wealth (a 10 percent decrease from 1860 when the plantation's then forty-three slaves were worth approximately $33,350). Table 1.2 shows this plantation's inventory with slaves' names, ages, occupational skills and assessed values.[49]

When a court decree divided twenty-six slaves worth $5,500 into seven lots for distribution to the heirs of Mrs. Frances Hamilton, slave mothers and their children were greedily claimed. Esther, age thirty-four, "not healthy," and her two children (three-month-old Jarretta and three-year-old Mack) were appraised at $1,750; two separate fatherless, husbandless families consisting of Lindy, age twenty-six, and her two children (nine-month-old William Henry and four-year-old Millow), and thirty-one-year-old Lucy and her two children (two-year-old Newton and four-year-old Jim) were worth $3,500 each.[50]

One Albemarle County resident paid $2,360 apiece for five slaves in January 1864; fifteen slaves were purchased at Amelia Court House in December at $2,500 each. By March 1865 a Richmond resident was complaining that male slaves were going for $10,000 each and expressed concern that such prices would ruin the state. The demand for slaves never lessened, though fewer Virginians were able to afford them. Second-, third-, and fourth-rate slaves (diseased, defective, aged, unruly) were eagerly sought

TABLE I.2. PEA HILL PLANTATION SLAVE INVENTORY, BRUNSWICK COUNTY,
I JANUARY 1863

Slave	Age	Occupation	Value
Claiborne	74	Foreman	$100
Willis	54		$300
Pleasant	33		$1,500
Joshua	36		$1,200
Stephen	32		$1,500
Allen	36		$1,200
Horrace	29		$1,500
Rebecca	40		$800
Minty	32		$1,000
Julia	24		$1,000
Patsy	20		$1,200
Sarah	14		$1,100
Parthenia	14		$1,200
Nazareth	15		$1,000
Augustus	17		$1,500
Wyche	14		$1,200
Susan	15	Field hand	$800
Sally	75	Spinner	
Gada	63	Spinner	
Cherry	62	Blind	
Betsy	62	Cook	
Nancy	40	Weaver	$800
Serena	30	Seamstress	$900
Rhoda	20	Spinner	$1,000
Caty	59	Cook	
Ellen	13		$800
Virginious	8		$600
Joe	5		$500
Peter	13		$800
Williamson	12		$600
Nalley	10		$600
Harriet	9		$600
Manaa(?)	6		$400
Meritt	4		$400
Toby	9		$600
Saphrenia	9		$400
Robin	5		$500
Lucunia(?)	3		$350
Cornelia	5		$300
Myra	2		$200

TABLE I.2. CONTINUED

Slave	Age	Occupation	Value
Epperson	2		$250
John	2		$250
Lidia	1		$150
Junious	1		$150
Levan	1		$150
Claiborn	1		$150
Vina	3 months		$100
Gaton	3 months		$100
Govan	2 months		$100

Source: "Inventory of Negroes upon Pea Hill Plantation Taken from 1st January 1863," Cocke Family Papers, 640, UVA.

after as bargains. At one Richmond auction an "ugly" nineteen-year-old girl sold for $1,350, and $450 was the final price for a ailing fifty-five-year-old man.[51]

Probably the most useless slaves to slaveholders were elderly black females unable to bear children or perform hard manual labor. Among a parcel of slaves shipped to the heirs of one deceased owner was Betsy, "a nearly blind and valueless" sixty-two-year-old woman. The other slaves, appraised at $38,000, were parceled out, but no one would take Betsy because she was no longer worth the expense of keeping her in bondage. In desperation the legatees paid the sum of $500 "for the keeping for life the said slave" to one of the reluctant heirs. But a male slave of the same age, Tom, valued at $700, was accepted without complaint.[52]

Some female slaves demonstrated managerial skills and established relationships of mutual respect with their owners. Lucy Skipwith and Fluvanna County planter John Hartwell Cocke forged a remarkable association. She dutifully corresponded with him from Hopewell, his plantation in Greene County, Alabama, throughout the war after some of his slaves were transferred there from Virginia. It was Cocke's plan to implement self-sufficient plantations managed solely by slaves, and he hoped eventually to send them to Liberia. Lucy (who had a daughter, Maria, by a white overseer) strove to be worthy of the trust Cocke placed in her.

Skipwith was the de facto mistress of the Hopewell plantation since Cocke was unable to visit it. She sent neatly written monthly reports describing the condition of the property, tasks accomplished, and the status of the crops. She also provided local gossip, health reports of neighboring whites, pleas for redress from his overseers, and requests for additional authority over the other slaves. Lucy's official duties included serving as "instructor to the young negroes" and foreman of the adults. In the first of her wartime letters she wrote: "We have preaching regularly at the Chapel. I send you a piece that Mr. [Brown?] has had published . . . about the plantation. . . . he made a little mistake in the number of people but that makes little difference." On 5 August 1861 she plaintively wrote: "I often think of you and fear sometimes that we shall never meet again. . . . I hope we shall meet in heaven where parting shall be no more."[53]

Two crises intervened in the smooth patterns of her life. Smith Powell, the overseer of Cocke's New Hope plantation, sought to hire out her daughter Maria in May 1862. Lucy successfully appealed to Cocke as a distressed parent: "I am willing to part with Maria for the sake of mother as she is old and has no child of her own to help her but . . . it will be hard for me to give [her] up." Two years later another crisis appeared when Richard D. Powell, formerly Cocke's overseer, obtained his own plantation and asked to purchase Maria. Lucy refused: "Mr. Powell asked my consent to buy Maria from you & I having to much respect for him hated to tell him my mind upon the subject but told him that he could propose the thing to you & see what you say about it." In a carefully worded letter filled with parental pleading, moral persuasion, implied threats of the possible disruption of the plantation, and just the right touch of self-righteous indignation, Lucy pleaded her case: "I do not wish Maria sold to him for she is a child after my own heart & I hate to part from her. . . . It goes hard with me to think of parting with her. I would like for him [to be] accommodated but it seems that nothing will do for him but Maria if he must have her I would rather he hired to him [her] & myself other than be parted from her. My other poor child came very near being ruined while away from me. There is nothing like a mother's watchful eye over a child." Her daring gambit worked; Cocke wisely avoided trouble with his trusted black female steward by vetoing Maria's sale.[54]

Lucy wrote to her ex-master in December 1865 after he had arranged for Federal protection of his property and again offered to send her to Liberia. She was pleased to hear from him but tactfully turned down the one-way trip. Instead, she wanted to return to Virginia and as their spokesman informed him that none of the former Hopewell slaves wished to leave the United States. Lucy had become a teacher, her parents lived nearby, and she hoped to build a proper schoolhouse. In her final "Dear Master" letter she concluded: "We are all here but I cannot tell how it will be another year. I will now bring my letter to a close hoping soon to hear from you again. I am as ever your Servant Lucy Skipwith."[55]

The hiring and buying, selling and trading of slaves was a profitable business in Confederate Virginia; runaways, Union incursions, and wartime vicissitudes did not seriously impair slavery's economic vitality until the end of 1863. By then, inflation and war made slaves increasingly unaffordable for many Virginians, and more of them took to hiring slaves rather than buying them. Prices skyrocketed, advertisements for sales decreased, notices of servants for hire increased, and in an effort to cut expenses a number of families no longer used slaves in any capacity.

Hiring out was the practice by which slaveholders rented their slaves ("hirelings") to whites who could not or did not wish to purchase them but needed their labor for a short or long term. Slaveholders earned extra cash, slaves perhaps got a taste of homesickness or gained their freedom by saving their earnings to purchase themselves and their families, and nonslaveholders experienced the benefits of slave labor without the responsibilities of full-time ownership. The hiring-out season usually began in December (near Christmas) or late January after harvest and planting seasons ended. A few slaves were allowed to hire themselves out and sent portions of their earnings to their owners.

The Rockingham County firm of S. M. & R. Brown offered "No. 1" slave men as farmhands for hire by the month in 1861. The quartermaster office in Fredericksburg placed an ad for a male cook to serve an officers' mess, and the Virginia and Tennessee Railroad office in Lynchburg needed 500 slaves for work in its shops as laborers, train hands, carpenters, and blacksmiths. A Staunton owner offered a young woman who "is a First-Rate washer and ironer, and good House Servant. She has good capacity, and could learn to do any kind of work. A situation in the county preferred." Experienced slave women cooks, washers, and ironers were advertised in Lexington, and J. W. Harper of Danville sought to employ 50 slaves between the ages of four and twelve but did not specify for what purpose. R. W. Richardson of Wakefield in Hanover County advertised the availability of his 40 slaves but with certain restrictions: "They will be hired as farm hands and house servants—in no instance to labor on works of internal improvement, or in occupations considered hazardous." Those who hired them were required to post bond.[56]

Contracts for slave hires were simple documents wherein employers promised to pay a specific sum in installments for the use of slaves whose names and physical descriptions were carefully recorded. One such contract signed by the first lady of the Confederacy, Varina Davis, in 1865 stated: "On the 1st January next we bind ourselves, our heirs to pay Thomas Bindford, his heirs or assigns four hundred dollars for the hire of a negro woman Fannie payable quarterly, for the present year. Said negro woman to be returned at Christmas next well clothed and blanket." By 1864 "negro blankets" were impossible to obtain.[57]

Hirelings were to be treated humanely and not to be carried out of the state or hired out to third parties, and they were to be returned at an agreed-upon time, usually 1 January or Christmas. Hats, two pairs of shoes, and blankets were to be supplied to the slave at the hirer's expense. Hire notices were uncompromising about clothing the slaves: "All who hire for the year . . . will confer a favor by returning servants properly clothed," or "The hirers to furnish servants with usual clothing, summer and winter." If these admonishments were ignored, owners protested. "When Carter came to me at Xmas, he told me you had not given him his clothes, nor his winter shoes," wrote one annoyed owner during January 1865. "This is a hardship on the negro as he can't do services. I hope you will attend to this without delay, if you please."[58]

A Richmond *Sentinel* article quipped that due to the high costs of hiring black female cooks, white women would have the opportunity of becoming reacquainted with "that unknown locality, the kitchen" and learn again that skill of which the majority were "utterly ignorant": the art of cooking. Nevertheless, the dependency on hired slaves caused agonizing separations of Afro-Virginian families. Female hirelings "without encumbrances" (childless women or mothers separated from their children) were prized even though they cost more to hire. "Negroes hire at a very high price even here," an Albemarle County woman lamented in 1863. She reminded her correspondent of the availability of one of her slaves for the hiring season: "I wanted to consult you about Hannah, if you want her why have you not mentioned it. She can be hired for a high price. I think I will sell Kathy. [But] Hannah has given satisfaction." Eleven slaves of Henry C. Page of Nelson County were employed at the Mount Torry Furnace in Augusta County as woodcutters to the great benefit of his finances.[59]

Charles Tibbs, hired out to a Covington farm, was forced to leave behind his sick wife. After her death an anguished Tibbs poured out his grief to their owner: "I seat myself to rite you a few lines and I hope that they may find you and Mistress well. I was very sorry to come away [hired out] and leave my wife sick I would have liked to have stayed until she got well but I learned a few days ago that she was dead. . . . Dear Master I trust she has gone to a better plase than in this veil of sin and sorrow. Mr. Ward says he can spare the time for me to come if you will pay my way back." Tibbs requested permission to return in order to make arrangements for the care of his young son and an elderly slave woman (an in-law?), Aunt Betsy.[60]

John J. Fry hired out four female slaves to William Cabell of Nelson

County in 1863 for $440, but when Cabell expressed a wish to add their children to his bond so that they might remain with their mothers, Fry callously replied: "What are they there for? I never give a bond for children." A slave woman named Gracey and her two children, the property of R. H. Crabb, were sent to work at the Glenwood Furnace in Rockbridge County but at least avoided being separated.[61]

William Mitchell of Pittsylvania County leased Philada and her two children to Samuel Blair for one year for $640. Just three days after their 28 December 1864 return, Philada and children were rented out again, this time to John H. Reynolds, for $790. Reynolds had been the lowest bidder at an hiring-out market where twelve other Mitchell slaves (including one named Henry hired out for a mere $6) were leased for the year. Mitchell grossed nearly $6,000 in slave rentals while Philada and the others earned the usual clothing and "humane treatment." Some slaves avoided hiring out by making themselves invaluable to their owners: slaves belonging to Richard O. Morris were so successful at raising and selling chickens that he became their partner and biggest customer and paid fair prices for their fowls and eggs. Some earned $20 a month through this arrangement and were able to remain at home with their families.[62]

The Confederate government rarely, if ever, purchased slaves outright (however, the commonwealth of Virginia owned at least sixty slaves between the ages of fifteen and seventy), although its officials did discuss the possibility of buying and then emancipating them after the war as reward for loyal service. It hired slaves from contractors and private citizens until it eventually conscripted slaves outright. General John Bankhead Magruder successfully appealed for authorization to hire 600 Afro-Virginian slaves at $100 each in 1861–62 for his engineering and quartermaster departments. Magruder said these slaves were more economical to lease than to purchase and promised their absence would not interfere with local agricultural operations.[63]

Intolerable as forced military labor may have been, it was particularly odious to free blacks. Isaac, slave of James M. Taylor of Henrico County, was hired out to the Richmond headquarters of the Engineering Department in April 1863 as a laborer for the public defenses. Thousands of slaves were likewise rented to the military, but in this case Isaac was a substitute for an Henrico County free black named J. H. Pearman. Isaac toiled for $25 a month through June 1864 as a laborer and hostler while Taylor pocketed his wages. Slavery not only set Afro-Virginians against each other but free blacks against slaves.[64]

Civilians earned tremendous profits hiring out or for providing services to hired government slaves. E. W. Massey boarded black workers at Bacon's

Quarter Branch near Richmond; over a seven-month period of July 1863 to January 1864 he boarded 723 blacks, charging the government $5 to $8 a head for 17 to 60 boarders a week. Massey earned maximal profits when he housed 67 hirelings and conscripted laborers at $8 each, resulting in $536 in reimbursements after he submitted a meticulous voucher bearing the names of each free black and slave boarder. An appreciable percentage of the Afro-Virginians mentioned in Massey's vouchers were free blacks.[65]

Some hired slaves escaped. Davy, held in custody by Richmond and Danville Railroad field agent T. J. Sampson, had attempted to escape from Danville in 1862 by posing as a faithful slave en route to visit his master in the Valley. His ploy soon came to grief: "LOST NEGRO MAN FOUND. Davy, a tall, black, negro man, with short whiskers and moustache, and clothed in homespun about half worn, was delivered to me for safekeeping by Conductor W. Taylor last Saturday week. Davy says he belongs to Joe Wright of Pittsylvania County, about 30 miles from Danville, and was on his way to wait on his young master, who is a Lieutenant in Gen. Wise's Brigade. The owner will please come forward, prove property, owe charges, and take his servant." Before his owner (a Mr. Cardozo?) could reclaim Davy, he had to pay Sampson $51 for outlays in recovering the runaway: $5.50 in train fares, $26.50 for newspaper notices, and $19.00 in jail fees.[66]

Hirelings necessitated other risks. A $400 reward was offered in January 1863 by Wilkins W. Hunt of Farish House, Charlottesville, for the apprehension of the murderers of James F. Hunt of the 4th Texas Regiment. Hunt left Charlottesville for Fredericksburg on 11 December 1862 in charge of a coffle of four hired slaves. His body was found four days later in Caroline County. The slaves, Henry and Tom of Albemarle County and John and Jacob of Augusta County, vanished but were believed to have killed Hunt before fleeing to Union lines.[67]

The families and neighbors of Confederate soldiers expected their absent menfolks to offer advice and long-distance supervision of slaves. A. J. Rike of the 3d Virginia Infantry, formerly an overseer for Mrs. Majette, was asked by her to handle the details concerning the hiring out of her slave, Henry, in February 1865. Rike ruefully reminded her of his inability to maintain a juggling act between military and slave overseer duties: "I am in the Army and a man in service cannot attend to business."[68] The stability of the Old Dominion's wartime slavery came to depend on the collective action and needs of Afro-Virginians, not whites.

2 THE COLOR OF SWEAT
Slave Life and Labor beyond the Plantation

The whole machinery of slavery was so constructed as to cause labor to be looked upon as a badge of degradation, of inferiority.
—*Booker T. Washington*

Although slaves were the prime working element necessary for Confederate agriculture, their use as urban workers also became indispensable. Industrial slavery was vital to Virginia's military and governmental infrastructure, and free blacks, too, were hired in greater numbers than the previous decade to sustain the economy of war. Due to white labor shortages, more free Afro-Virginians were able to earn higher, more regular salaries and slightly improved standards of living.[1]

Hired slaves were available at half the annual wages paid to white factory workers and could be pushed to greater levels of productivity. Certain industries, tobacco for one, preferred hired slaves over whites. One scholar has determined that slaves and free blacks in the South could be found in over 270 skilled occupations including apothecaries, bricklayers, caulkers, glaziers, soapmakers, typesetters, and nail makers. As time passed, more Afro-Virginians were sucked into the Confederate war effort in occupations formerly held by white males in mining, saltworks, ironworks, military fortifications, ordnance, shipyards, and similar industries. At Mayo's Tobacco Factory in Richmond black workers earned the best wages of their lives, but their toil was hard and tiresome. In their tobacco works songs they sang of their longings:

> I hope my mother will be there,
>> In that beautiful world on high,
> That used to join me in prayer,
>> In that beautiful world on high.

Danville tobacco workers sang of "Bright sparkles in de church-yard, Give light unto de tomb, Bright summer, springs over, sweet flowers in der bloom."[2]

49

Black convicts were also hired out as extra labor. Afro-Virginians sentenced to be sold or transported beyond the limits of the Confederacy were instead hired out by the state to ironworks where they manufactured munitions and cannon or to saltworks following a law enacted by the General Assembly on 6 December 1861; two years later Afro-Virginian convicts were hired out to coal mines and their wages returned to the public treasury as surplus. By February 1864 any male slave condemned to life imprisonment for a crime could be sold to any employer who posted a $1,000 bond; female slave convicts and their children were available without these conditions. Numerous Southern industrialists were able to purchase outright additional slave workers for their factories thanks to this law, and Governor Letcher defended these practices by pointing out that after the war surplus slave industrial workers could be sold at a profit back to civilians.[3]

Confederate Virginia increased its demands for slave hirelings. Twenty were sought by Glenwood Furnace in Rockingham County during August 1861; the superintendent of niter operations at Salem advertised for fifty blacks in 1862. Black workers were motivated by bonuses, overtime pay, and extra rations such as whiskey, but furloughs were the most effective tool in managing them. During 1863–64, 150 black miners at the Dover and Tuckahoe Pits cost the company $40,500 annually; free blacks were paid $3 a day, fair wages for whites or blacks considering the times. The custom of employing more blacks resulted in the government's issuing a scale of wages, rations, and clothing allowances for them on a daily, monthly, or yearly basis; civilian employers were to pay blacks at the rate of $2.50 a day, $30 a month, or $550 a year; the state government pledged salaries of $1.50, $50, and $300, respectively.[4]

Industrial labor was dangerous, and improper ventilation, food, health care, and harsh working conditions made factory work hazardous. On 6 August 1864 five blacks were killed when the G. O. Bradley Machine Works in Manchester was devastated by a huge explosion. Two wagons driven by black teamsters had just pulled up to the gateway with shells retrieved from the battlefields around Richmond and Petersburg; during unloading one of the blacks accidentally dropped a shell into a pile of live ammunition. The resultant blast, accompanied by a deafening roar and a blinding flash like lightning, rattled windows across the river in Richmond. The dead were slaves: Davy, Charles Porter, Robert Moody, and two identified as "Teamster No. 15 and Teamster No. 51."[5]

Another dangerous occupation was that of strikebreaker. When Hollywood Cemetery's Irish gravediggers struck in the summer of 1864 for higher wages, they were fired. Blacks were hired to replace them and worked until noon when the unemployed whites attacked and drove them from the cemetery. The authorities, unwilling to pay the Irishmen more than the usual $7 per day, replaced these blacks with another group: black convicts from the nearby penitentiary who went about their work without any interruption guarded by Confederate troops.[6]

Afro-Virginian industrial workers were present in a wide range of logistical industries, especially ironmaking. The most famous of these, the Tredegar Iron Works, located near the James River and Kanawha Canal in Richmond, was founded in 1836; its proprietor, Joseph Reid Anderson, owned sixty slaves between the ages of one and forty-five in 1860. Situated near sources of high-quality iron ore and coal mines by way of the canal, this facility has been described as the Confederacy's single most important factory. It was capable of casting field artillery in large quantities as well as railroad equipment, torpedoes (underwater mines), and submarines (at a cost of $6,500 each). Tredegar produced the iron plate used for both wings and the dome of the United States Capitol and later cast armor plate for the CSS *Virginia*. In all, 1,600 cannon and 90 percent of the South's shot and cannonballs were cast at this establishment.

Tredegar employed more than 1,200 slaves and free blacks in Richmond and associated plants and furnaces in Alleghany, Botetourt, Chesterfield, Goochland, Henrico, and Rockbridge counties. Afro-Virginians worked in every occupation from common laborers to engineers. Black hands shaped plate iron, nails, cannon, boilers, and locomotives, and between 1862 and 1865 Tredegar purchased 33 skilled slave workers at an annual cost of nearly $70,000. Slaves were paid $1.25 per day in 1861, but this increased to a daily wage of $4 by 1864; the company kept some of its expenses low by paying certain slave hirelings in cash but requiring them to purchase their own food and lodging.

Eventually Tredegar found it cheaper to house, feed, clothe, and provide medical care for its workers on site since blacks made up more than half of the force by 1864 and were becoming harder to acquire. The supervisor of the company's Glenwood Furnace in Rockbridge County requested permission in 1863 to hire 100 Afro-Virginians solely for the purpose of cultivating 300 acres to grow wheat to feed the black workers. Slaves represented other benefits to Tredegar: their labor was economical and less prone to strikes, and they could be paid in iron bars or even rails which their owners happily sold for cash or exchanged for other finished goods.[7]

Tredegar could not get enough black workers. Francis T. Glasgow, superintendent in charge of seven furnaces, reported on 29 May 1863 that his integrated force of 576 slaves, black and white convicts, and white laborers were employed at company pig iron furnaces in Botetourt County (Catawba, Cloverdale, Grace, and Rebecca) and Rockbridge (Glenwood); of these workers 59 percent (343) were slaves, 32 percent (187) were white, and the remaining 9 percent (53) were convict laborers. In 1862 Tredegar owners purchased the Dover Coal Mine and hired 150 blacks for the Tuckahoe Mines in Henrico County as teamsters, firemen, engineers, puddlers, and axmen at yearly salaries of $300 each. The company sought 1,000 slaves for its Alleghany, Goochland, Henrico, Richmond, and Rockbridge operations in January 1864 and hired another 113 free black convicts. The company's problems with runaways and convicts were transformed by Governor Letcher into a statewide dilemma in December 1863: "Several of the convict negroes hired to J. R. Anderson & Co. have absconded within the last year, and are supposed to have made their escape into the enemy's lines, as they have not since been heard of. In time of war these convicts, hired at furnaces near the lines of the contending parties, are hard to restrain and keep in proper subjection, and are therefore much more likely to effect their escape.... Thus a necessity is shown for a change of our policy in regard of them.... I renew my recommendation ... to make sale of them ... [their] number is increasing so rapidly that it will soon become a difficult question to manage." Blacks joined their white coworkers as members of the 6th Tredegar Battalion, Local Defense Troops, and saved the ironworks from looting by mobs when Richmond was evacuated in April 1865.[8]

David Graham and Son Iron Works operated in Wythe County at Graham's Forge, and for this and adjunct enterprises the Grahams relied on and hired slaves. Their agent, John W. Robinson, scoured the region for skilled blacks and, if all else failed, hired unskilled ones. These slaves were rehired the following year including a slave named Waller hired from John Cork for the period of 1 March to 25 December 1862. Waller was to be supplied with the necessary "summer and winter clothing," and the Grahams were to pay the county and state taxes for him. Cork was to receive payment of $110 on Christmas Day for Waller's work. Robinson's hire of ten slaves from William B. Crumb in 1862 cost Graham and Son only $995, a relatively modest expenditure in light of the booming profits the firm earned from their biggest customer, the Confederate government.[9]

At Rockbridge County's Buffalo Forge pig and forged iron were produced. This plant was a thriving enterprise which employed Afro-Virginians throughout its existence. Ledgers, journals, diaries, letter books, and "Negro Books" recorded wages, overtime pay, medical care, hires, contracts, and individual accounts for slaves and free blacks. Some slaves accumulated savings that they could withdraw to purchase necessities for their families; and their overtime work not only resulted in direct payments of cash, but in several cases they chose to receive wages as compensatory leave so that they could visit their families.

The experience and skills of Buffalo Forge's black employees caused several to be rehired for two- or three-year periods. One register of these men indicates their ages (twenty-one to forty-eight years), height, skin color, health status, and assignments. Most were blacksmiths, wagoners, or wood-choppers. Wages for the twenty-seven hirelings cost Buffalo Forge $12,000 annually. Afro-Virginians were hired at three times the average white Confederate soldier's pay at Buffalo Forge with some earning annual wages of $350 to $600, more than any private and most Confederate army officers, yet another paradox of a paradoxical war. Several of this forge's slaves continued their employment as free laborers after the war.[10]

Blacks were employed by railroads, saltworks, and canal companies. Governor Letcher urged that free black labor be employed exclusively for rail repairs because they could secure satisfying wages, which would reduce their motive for deserting to the Union. Letcher reminded the General Assembly that many Afro-Virginian free blacks were skilled mechanics and by employing them slaves could be left on the farms. He believed the services of free blacks and slaves could aid the commonwealth's industries and agricultural operations simultaneously. Blacks were invaluable logistical components supporting the Confederate military.

It was indeed hazardous to be a black railroad laborer. Bezaliel G. Brown of the 7th Virginia Infantry wrote his brother in December 1861 that an elderly slave named Reubin was forced to work at the same killing pace as younger slaves during the construction of a railroad line: "They have commenced on the railroad. They are working negroes on [it], all convicts. Cousin [Thomas] Maupin's old Reubin is with them—he jumps around like a boy—if he does not they will *knock him down with anything they get hold of.*" The Richmond *Sentinel* of 8 July 1863 reported the death of a free black fireman, James Trent, killed in the explosion of a train called "Jeff Davis" on the Richmond and Petersburg Railroad.[11]

The Old Dominion was the South's chief producer of salt with operations at Saltville, located in Washington County. Salt not only preserved meat for long periods of time but was necessary to provide minerals for livestock, especially cattle and horses. Its production involved drilling into a bed of fossilized salt and then pumping in water to form brine. This brine was pumped to the surface, poured into kettles, and boiled to form salt crystals. During the process the heavy concentration of the salt in the surrounding air made workers appear to be laboring in the middle of a snowstorm, covered with hoarfrost.

Every hundred gallons of brine produced twenty-two gallons of pure salt. Slaves were hired by saltworks, and such was the need for the product that they were worked around the clock in shifts. Accidents involving scalding and diseases such as smallpox and malaria were common, but there was a medicinal benefit in that saline vapors were considered a cure for throat and lung diseases. A niter and mining bureau was established in 1863 because niter was needed to make gunpowder after shortages caused by the Union naval blockade. Black employees worked in damp, smelly caves preparing and refining the niter; in November 1864 Colonel Isaac M. St. John, head of the bureau, reported that 1,016 Afro-Virginians were employed but another 508 were needed for the 1865 season.[12]

One essential private corporation was the James River and Kanawha Canal Company, founded in 1785. The canal, five feet deep and thirty feet wide, was a thoroughfare for soldiers and carrier of bulk supplies required by Confederate armies. Its white workers joined the army in such numbers that black boatmen, masons, and dredge-boat hands were increasingly relied on to maintain the canal and its equipment, and the company president praised their efficiency and patriotism.

Overseers and free blacks were exhorted "to the most vigorous and energetic efforts to put and keep the canal open in the best possible condition" after a Union raid at Covington near Clifton Forge, site of a company furnace, made it "impossible to employ white labor." The board of directors informed stockholders that it expected subsidies from the General Assembly to enable the hiring of slaves and seventy-five free blacks between the ages of fifteen and fifty from Campbell, Amherst, Bedford, Rockbridge, and Botetourt counties. General Philip H. Sheridan destroyed over eighty-nine miles of the canal in March 1865, along with thirty-four locks, thirty bridges, nine boats, and all of the workshops, tools, provisions, and timber supplies at Scottsville and Columbia. Although several black employees joined Sheridan, other Afro-Virginians were rushed from Richmond to begin repairs.[13]

Newspapers, too, increasingly employed slaves. The Richmond *Examiner*'s expenditures between 1 March 1862 to 21 January 1865 included payments to hired slaves and supplemental expenses such as boarding. They were paid at rates of $2 to $8 per week in 1862; one slave, Jake, cost the *Examiner* $5 a week in boarding fees during October 1863. As inflation escalated, these expenses consumed substantial chunks of the *Examiner*'s profits.[14]

Afro-Virginians were vital for hospital work. In December 1861 the medical director of the Army of Northern Virginia, Thomas H. Williams, ordered military general hospitals to hire or draft slaves and free blacks if not enough white men were available. Confederate surgeons pleaded for permission to hire blacks as nurses, attendants, and cooks for their facilities and eventually paid them an average of $30 a month. The Charlottesville General Hospital, established in July 1861, hired free blacks and conscripted

Albemarle County slaves as cooks, laundresses, nurses, and scavengers. At any given month in 1862 it was employing 60 slaves and free blacks. By 1863, 445 blacks were employed by Richmond's Chimborazo Hospital, and 280 worked for the Richmond's Winder General Hospital with another 122 at Danville, 139 at Farmville, and 100 at Charlottesville. These were among Virginia's most important military medical centers.[15]

The Staunton military hospital advertised in the *Vindicator* for eight female slave laundresses "healthy and unencumbered" (meaning no small children) at $25 a month and comfortable furnished quarters. The surgeon in charge of Chimborazo Hospital No. 1 wanted ten black men for his staff, and in a Lynchburg newspaper medical director J. A. Forbes promised good wages and equitable treatment for the first fifty to seventy-five Afro-Virginian males and females hired by his hospital. The Eastern State Lunatic Asylum in Williamsburg employed hired slaves, but most fled by 1862 because they had not been paid the previous eighteen months.[16]

Confederate military physicians were not alone in providing medical care for black hospital employees. The governor reported black patients in the Medical College of Virginia's public ward at a cost of $5 per week in 1861, the same rate as white soldiers. The chief surgeon of the Engineer Bureau's hospital also served as a civilian physician contracted to care for sick and injured black laborers. Each patient was carefully examined, black nurses were assigned to their wards, and no expense was spared to make their quarters clean and neat.[17]

Not all military doctors were as considerate of black patients. Dr. C. D. Rice, surgeon in charge at Richmond's Howard Grove Hospital in 1862, had little sympathy with owners of hired-out slaves who, fearing infection, had removed them from this smallpox hospital without permission and in violation of their contracts with the government. (There were several smallpox outbreaks during 1862–64 at Staunton, Danville, Lexington, Portsmouth, and similar areas of urban concentration.) When Rice and other physicians complained, the secretary of war sided with them and ordered that slave owners and slaves must take their chances, warning that force would be used to keep the blacks at their posts. Eventually black hospital workers became the nucleus of the Confederate States Colored Troops; 83 percent of the male slaves at Richmond's Jackson Hospital volunteered in February 1865 to fight Yankees. As members of the Jackson Battalion, they proved themselves in combat the ensuing month when they served for a week in the Petersburg trenches.[18]

At Graham's Forge in Wythe County, Afro-Virginian slave ironworkers resided at their work sites with their families; the owners believed this arrangement would keep the men content and less likely to run away. Health benefits, including smallpox vaccinations, were extended to their families, and Dr. R. W. Saunders was hired as their physician. Between 3 August 1862 and 30 April 1865 Sanders made seventy-four house calls at a cost to David Graham and Son of $278, or about $3.80 per visit. On 8 September 1862 Sanders charged $3 for treating a black child at the forge; almost a year later he treated three cases of gonorrhea for $25. He helped a slave woman named Clara deliver her baby on 16 June 1864 for $10, extracted a tooth on 27 December for $3.50, made an emergency night visit to a sick child on 1 January 1865, and charged $3 for lancing the breast of a black woman on 2 February. He made numerous night visits during which he provided treatments such as bleeding, lancing jaws, fixing broken legs, and prescribing blue pills at fifty cents a box.[19]

The majority of noncombatant slave laborers were sent away from their families, and malingering and escapes were frequent. The manager of the Etna Furnace (a producer of pig iron) groused in 1862 about two slave employees, Par, a woodchopper, and Griffen. Par always feigned illness except when visits to his wife were imminent, and Griffen pretended illness so frequently that he ultimately was returned to his owner. Rewards of $250 apiece were offered for three slaves who fled from the Buena Vista Furnace in Rockbridge County during 1863: Sandy, age twenty-five, Jerry, age twenty-one and Bryant, age twenty-three; the furnace's owners believed they were heading for Union forces in the Valley. Of the five slaves who escaped from the Lucy Selina Furnace in Alleghany County, three were recent purchases from North Carolina and two, Hubbard (of Dinwiddie County) and Winston, were native Virginians; a $125 reward was offered for the capture of any of the escapees. After a series of Union raids, residents of Lynchburg and the counties of Buchanan and Craig were so afraid of black strangers that several Afro-Virginians with legitimate work passes were jailed.[20]

Union forays precipitated headaches for furnace and slave owners. In June 1864 a Yankee cavalry raid led by General David ("Black Dave") Hunter through the Valley provided slaves with a welcome opportunity to abscond. "I regret to inform you that your boy Beverly went off with the enemy upon that raid through this county on 12 June," a chagrined David Brady wrote to James Stewart from Buffalo Forge. "I lost three of my own & they captured Mr. Rex my manager, whom they took off with them. . . . I was fortunate in escaping myself. . . . They destroy[ed] Samuel Jordan's furnace . . . burn[ed] his furnace, mill, corn cob . . . saw mill . . . & carpenter shop." As other raids took place, black defections escalated. William, "a bushy hair, smiling countenance, and polite mannered" mulatto, deserted the James River and Kanawha Canal Company in September 1864, and a $500 reward was posted in December for Sam, a runaway from Richmond's Chimborazo Hospital.

By the spring of 1865 hired slaves and free blacks, aware that the South had lost, deserted Virginia's industries in record numbers.[21]

The North underestimated Confederate initiative in the utilization of blacks as military laborers. The *New York Daily Tribune* forecast a short war: "It is just absurd to talk of a three years' war for the Union. An Army and a General competent to beat the Rebels will be competent to *pin* them so that they must fight or throw down their arms. A protracted war can not be maintained in the South . . . amid such peasantry as the Slaves."[22] But the young Confederacy rapidly mobilized slaves for its struggle; food, weapons, and other essentials were produced, gathered, packaged, and shipped by blacks via transportation networks maintained by gangs of supervised slaves. In every branch of the Confederate military—quartermaster, commissary, naval, ordnance, hospital, and agricultural—the toil of Afro-Virginians fueled its military and civilian industries.

Slaves were employed at South Carolina and Alabama fortifications as early as January 1861 although Florida was the first Southern state actually to enact provisions for the impressment of slaves. The Confederate Congress ordered registration and enrolling of free blacks for miliary labor on 1 July 1861; during the summer of 1862 the Old Dominion's General Assembly authorized the impressment of 10,000 Afro-Virginian slaves between the ages of eighteen and forty-five for up to sixty days' service at $16 a month. In spite of the urgency, unauthorized impressments by Confederate officers were punishable as misdemeanors with fines fixed at twice the slaves' value.[23]

A Confederate soldier stationed at Gloucester Point during May 1861 marveled at the sight of one white engineering officer supervising sixty blacks and commented that "they had already accomplished a good deal" and could easily throw up breastworks faster than any number of white men. At Yorktown an engineering officer employed nineteen New Kent County slaves for an average of eleven days each at thirty-three to fifty cents per day from October to December 1861. When an Alabama officer complained to his superiors about his white troops having to unload ships at Yorktown, slaves were rounded up from neighboring plantations for the job.[24]

During a July 1861 meeting of the Richmond city council, it was announced that 120 free Afro-Virginian males had volunteered to serve the Confederacy, but previously a "Virginia Fugitive" declared that the South eagerly accepted and employed free black labor because it permitted the rebel military to keep close tabs on those African-Americans most likely to provoke slave rebellions. "To correct a great evil in this city" the council enforced fines against anyone who hired themselves out or hired slaves without their owners' consent, allowed slaves to go about unsupervised, or employed free blacks who lacked official papers of their free status and registration as required by state law. In some locales free blacks were jailed at the end of each working day to prevent conspiracies.[25]

The war required great sacrifices, especially by the slaveholding class. In 1861 complaints from former president John Tyler (owner of thirty-nine slaves and a member of the Confederate Congress) on behalf of constituents in Charles City and New Kent counties failed to prevent the military's requisition of more than half of these counties' slaves. General Magruder, charged with the responsibility of defending Williamsburg, complained to Richmond during September 1861 about wealthy planters in Lancaster and Surry counties who ignored proclamations to surrender their slaves for fortification work. Secretary of War Benjamin, sensitive to the rights of property, decreed that ownership rights and the state's agricultural needs outranked the military's. Magruder responded by ordering his troops to bring in every black they could find, but this drastic temporary measure only energized civilian protests.[26]

For Thomas Garland and Jason Douglass of Albemarle County and other owners who tried to comply with military requisitions, it was just as frustrating to bring their quota of slaves to the nearest town for transport to fortifications only to be told upon arrival that transportation was not available or to have their quota of slaves arbitrarily increased. Garland (his slave was employed building boats and burying Confederate dead at the Richmond fortifications) and Douglass objected to furnishing more of their slaves as military laborers, complained they had provided their fair share of slaves, and appealed to their elected state representatives for relief. Any delays could put owners in violation of legal requirements and subject them to no end of trouble with both Confederate and state authorities. The General Assembly, worried about the excessive use of the state's slaves for the war, passed resolutions calling for their release from this assignment.[27]

The Confederate military sought "the most intelligent and faithful negroes" as substitutes for white enlisted men who were returned to regiments at the front. The Confederate Congress passed legislation in 1862 for the impressment of slaves as musicians and cooks for the army and gradually authorized the use of all black Southern males as necessary. Richmond's provost marshal stressed the need of 300 blacks to serve two months for the construction of military roads. One meal per day and $20 a month was to be their compensation. The General Assembly's answer to chronic shortages of white laborers and lagging by slave owners was the initiation of slave conscription in an "Act for the Public Defense" passed on 3 October 1862 which empowered the governor to call out a percentage of slaves from each locality by means of requisitions to county court clerks. The clerks were to summon the county justices, who in turn ordered sheriffs to collect the required number of slaves and convey them to the military. In theory this system called out, located, and shipped slaves to the military within three days, but if any county was unable to meet its quota, the governor could take no more than 5 percent of its slave population at his discretion.[28]

Blacks between the ages of eighteen and forty-five were sought, and this act stipulated that owners were to be paid $16 a month for their labor. It also provided a loophole: if an owner supplied more than thirty but less than forty slaves, he had the right to place them under the supervision of his own overseer for sixty days, with the overseer's salary to be paid by the government. Jefferson Davis wasted little time after the law's passage. On 10 October he informed Governor Letcher that the Engineer Bureau needed 4,500 Afro-Virginians immediately; bureau chief Jeremy Francis Gilmer ordered county agents to deliver their slaves to Richmond. Letcher promised that state counties would meet their quotas promptly and cheerfully.[29]

Before a male slave joined the ranks of military laborers, he underwent a process of selection, appraisal, description, separation, and transportation. He had no voice in the matter; his owner chose the unlucky few in response to a summons by a select committee of the county's freeholders. As the sheriff or military agent gathered slaves, the freeholder committee appraised, assigned, and recorded their value and prepared written physical descriptions of each slave; they were then forwarded to the nearest railroad station for shipment to their work site or else walked for most if not all of the entire distance.

Slaves were appraised at about $1,000 to $8,000 per individual. A group of thirteen slaves from three north and south central counties had a combined value of $50,000; two of these men, Harrison and Gil Bass, were worth $6,000 apiece in 1864 and went to labor at the Richmond and Danville fortifications. Andrew was described for the record as "entirely sound"; Spencer and Tarleton belonged to the J. B. McClellan estate; Ben, Carter, and Willis represented a $9,400 risk for C. C. Cocke of Fluvanna County; Samuel Pannill Wilson's Gil Bass, Charles, and Peter were appraised at $12,500 by Pittsylvania County's enrollment officer; George Clements of the same county stood to lose $26,500 if his slaves Henry, Reuben, and Wiley died or escaped. These slaves were only a few of the thousands employed. After completing their contracted duty, conscripted slaves were given passes and sent home, but not a word of thanks or praise accompanied them on their solitary journey homeward. They could expect to be returned to the fortifications at any time.[30]

Confederate attorney general Thomas Bragg declared slaves were property but also ruled that they were "rational human beings." In November 1862, 4,150 slaves were requisitioned, and in December 1864 another 1,162 were required. The 1863 requisition tried to make up for the significant deficit of October 1862, but few counties reached their quotas. Pittsylvania's 1863 target of 307 slaves included 170 not received during the 1862 call-up; Brunswick's quota of 222 included 125 missing from the previous request, and Halifax's 242 included 57 missing from the 1862 summons. Of twenty-nine counties only Louisa, Orange, and Rockbridge were given reduced quotas due to losses caused by Union incursions.[31]

The 13 March 1863 amendment to the "Act for the Public Defense" permitted the governor to exempt counties near or within enemy lines or where large numbers of slaves had escaped. It also increased the age range to eighteen to fifty-five, increased monthly wages to $20, and ordered that only one slave belonging to a soldier or a widow could be requisitioned. A maximum of 10,000 slaves was set, and those seized from owners who had disobeyed summonses to bring them forth were to labor for three months instead of two. Virginian slave owners viewed this provision as a hardship. "On the 7th Nov 1862, seven of my Nelson men & boys went to Richmond to work on the fortification," resignedly wrote Robert Thurston Hubard. "For their services I am to be paid $16 per month the negroes will probably be absent 60 days." Two months later the government requisitioned seven more from his Nelson County farm and five from his Buckingham County plantation. A later amendment made a few minor changes in the law; slaves removed from an area by owners because of the enemy's presence (and not just to evade requisitions) were exempted from confiscation.[32]

Rockbridge County slave owners began the war in cheerful compliance with slave requisitions and voluntarily furnished eighty-nine slaves during September 1863. A newspaper article highlighting the services of Rockbridge blacks at the York River Railroad described their camps as orderly and comfortable, with tents sturdy enough to house fireplaces and each camp having the services of experienced cooks. Each slave received a pound of bacon and eighteen ounces of flour daily. Hospital facilities were accessible, and when asked if there was anything they lacked, these Afro-Virginians requested more "hog meat," beans, hominy, and dried apples.[33]

Hiring out slaves cost the state on average $30 apiece per month, and it is small wonder the Confederacy preferred to impress them at about half this rate. As additional slaves were requisitioned, more counties (Amelia, Chesterfield, Dinwiddie, Goochland, Hanover, King and Queen, King William, Powhatan, Spotsylvania, Southampton, and Sussex) were exempted due to heavy losses in runaways. Approximately 340 slaves were called up from Craig, Giles, Grayson, Floyd, Russell, Smyth, Tazewell, Washington, and Wythe counties for work at Saltville to maintain production levels. Its superintendent was promised an extra twenty-five slaves by one citizen in exchange for payment in salt.[34]

During the fall of 1863 new orders from Richmond allowed generals to confiscate as many local slaves as they needed but also cautioned them to cooperate with state authorities to avoid complications, especially if it meant interfering with slaves at plantations that provided grain and other provisions to the army. If a slave was delivered in pursuance of requisitions, his owner earned $20 monthly; if one was seized from those trying to dodge this responsibility, only $15 a month was paid. Owners protested that each slave removed from farm operations would hurt food production, not to mention the financial reverses suffered whenever they absconded. Governor Letcher accused several counties of not furnishing their share of slaves, and to make up for this lack of compliance he conscripted black convicts from the state penitentiary.[35]

To allay owner concerns, the Confederate Congress passed an act in December 1863 guaranteeing reimbursement for impressed slaves lost for one reason or another while in the public service. This act also served as a remedy for an opinion rendered by the attorney general the previous month that the government was not liable for the value of any impressed slaves used on a temporary basis. Slave claims boards comprising two members, one appointed by the president and the other by the governor of the slave's home state, met to determine the value of each slave accepted for military employment. A subsequent attorney general's opinion held that these boards lacked jurisdiction over claims for slaves killed or who escaped while in the process of being transported to their posts.[36]

Occasionally, Virginia resorted to drastic methods involving press-gangs and massive, unannounced sweeps to obtain blacks for military labor. On 5 October 1864, Confederate soldiers seized and led off every able-bodied black Richmond male they could catch. From shops, streets, and alleys, even from carts and on horseback, blacks were hustled off to fortifications and factories, but somehow word leaked out and many took refuge with their owners or stayed home. The *Richmond Daily Examiner* ignored the anguish this incident caused among black families, remarking that "the great bulk will be made to do the country a service for the next few days, which patriotic citizens should not begrudge for the sake of the common cause."[37]

The Engineer Bureau of the Confederate War Department received these and other similarly seized blacks. The department also requested an appropriation of $3,108,000 just to cover claims for slaves lost in the service or who died shortly after their discharge from "laboring on the public de-fenses." Estimates for deaths or escapes of Afro-Virginian totaled $500,000; between 1861 and 1864 the government made payments of $708,000 for 354 of these Afro-Virginian slaves. Alfred Landon Rives, head of the bureau, cate-gorized such losses as serious and indicated they were not uncommon. He estimated another 1,554 escapees might generate additional claims with 22 percent of these as Virginia's share of the losses. These appropriations were approved, but two months later Rives's successor, Major General Gilmer, pleaded for yet $1.5 million to cover claims for irretrievable slaves.[38]

In February 1864 the Confederate Congress enacted "An Act to increase the efficiency of the Army by the employment of free negroes and slaves in certain capacities." This measure called for more slaves and ordered up to 20,000 "male free negroes and other persons of color, not including those who are free under the treaty of Paris of eighteen hundred and three, or under the treaty with Spain of eighteen hundred and nineteen, resident in the Confederate States" to make themselves available for duty as teamsters and other laboring ranks. Although the act recognized the rights and exemp-tions of certain free blacks, it nonetheless required they be impressed if enough slaves could not be procured. Since there were more slaves than free blacks in the Confederacy, the measure indicates the South's predicament: prior to this time slaves were deemed sufficient to meet its labor demands.[39]

By joint resolution the General Assembly directed Governor William Smith to warn that such measures would incite free blacks to desert to the Union at a time when the state needed them. In partial response to these and equivalent protests, the Confederate Congress increased the pay of con-scripted free blacks in the army to $18 a month. Under the Conscription Act of 1864, 1,464 were enrolled by the Conscription Bureau before the war's end; these conscripts were employed as shoemakers, wheelwrights, tanners, built and repaired roads, and worked as cooks, waiters, and teamsters.[40]

Pleas from the General Assembly for relief from slave impressments were ignored by the War Department. When asked to grant the emergency release of slaves to prevent interference with farming activities, Secretary of War James A. Seddon expressed sympathy for the seriousness of the situa-tion but rejected leniency. Another competing employer of Afro-Virginians was the Union army, and General Ulysses S. Grant wanted every able-bodied black male as a soldier or military laborer. He sent out expeditions to bring in all the Afro-Virginians they could find.[41]

Between September and November 1864 General Robert E. Lee and Engineer Bureau head Jeremy Gilmer planned to organize black conscripts into Confederate Negro Labor Battalions as companies, regiments, and bat-talions supervised by overseers. To instill a sense of patriotism and esprit de corps, free blacks were enrolled into labor battalions within their home counties. One hundred blacks would comprise a gang under a manager assisted by three white overseers. Eight gangs (800 black men and 32 whites) formed a battalion or section commanded by a superintendent and assigned an assistant purveyor, a clerk, and a physician; three battalions (2,400 blacks and 96 whites) made up a "force" under the single command of a director assisted by two clerks. The chief engineers of each Confederate army were to be the officers at the top of these hierarchies. The blacks were forwarded to their camps under heavy guard and once there were enrolled into the service at regular conscript camps by field grade officers with muster rolls, regular inspections, individual service records on file, and other trappings of military order and discipline with the exception of being armed.

It went without saying that this organization would prove useful if a decision was made to enroll blacks as soldiers. Lee suggested a system of rewards for individual good conduct with extra wages paid directly to worthy blacks because "most of the negroes are accustomed to something of this sort on the plantations." He also advised "promotions" to the position of foreman for a few deserving token blacks; each gang could promote up to four black foremen.[42]

The Bureau of Conscription called up 5,000 more slaves on 21 September 1864 for the army and ordered that they be forwarded to Richmond's Camp Lee; nine days later free blacks between the ages of eighteen and fifty were sought. Generally, one out of every five male slaves was drafted in this manner. Black enrollment had top priority and was to proceed with "extraordinary diligence and vigor." In their haste to meet quotas two counties impressed female slaves between the ages of eighteen and forty-five, but Confederate officials soon acknowledged this as a mistake and returned the women to their owners.[43]

In his November message to Congress, Jefferson Davis admitted that slaves were human beings (before the war he was of the opinion that blacks were intelligent and rational) but suggested that his government purchase them for military work and emancipate them afterwards as a reward for loyal service with permission to reside in any state they claimed as home. This proposal implied government acceptance of a free blacks as a class in the postwar Confederacy. His secretary of war sent a message to Virginia explaining and justifying the conscription of another several thousand slaves as the legitimate power and duty of government to seize private property for the public good.[44]

After a December 1864 request for 2,250 slaves fell far short of its goal, Lee asked for an additional 5,010 (the final tally was 5,140) Afro-Virginians, and Davis appealed directly to Governor Smith to do whatever he could to provide them. More counties were refusing to comply, but the Engineer Bureau tried another tactic to secure the slaves it needed. County sheriffs were advised that for each slave or free black delivered, the government would pay $5 plus expenses. Neither this nor Smith's executive order ("It is of great importance that the quota should be immediately furnished") accomplished the task. Forty-four counties were asked provide 107 slaves, but a mere 26 were forwarded. Sixteen counties were unable to fill their quotas; only Grayson County met its goal. This dismal response can be explained only by indifference, obstinacy, and owner fears that their human chattels might escape, die, or return in poor health. Albemarle County was among the shirkers. One of the largest counties in the state, it possessed 14,000 slaves; during 1861–64 it was asked to furnish 940 slaves but consistently failed to meet its quotas.[45]

Counties and owners either refused altogether or willfully delayed sending their slaves; black males became extremely skilled in making themselves scarce whenever conscription officers scheduled visits to their localities. Slave owners remained suspicious about the treatment of their slaves away from home. James H. Evans, a resident of Prince Edward County, petitioned the government for three years for reimbursement of his loss in the form of a deceased slave named Elijah. Apparently a healthy and experienced farmhand, Elijah was conscripted on 29 October 1862 and sent to the Richmond fortifications. Two months later, on 11 December, he was dead of an unspecified disease contracted while in the service. Evans was still seeking compensation in early 1865.[46]

Thomas S. Bocock, speaker of the Confederate House of Representatives, became embroiled in a personal controversy during December 1864 over the impressment of nine of his slaves. Two were seized and sent to the Petersburg fortifications; he sent the others to work on a bridge near his estate under the supervision of his overseer to avoid surrendering them to enrolling officers. Meanwhile, one of his Petersburg slaves escaped and apparently made his way back to Bocock, who also sought the prompt release of Collin, another of his slaves under arrest for an escape attempt. Using his influence and buttressed by claims of having "furnished more Negroes for Government Service than any man [in Appomattox County] owning the same number of slaves," Bocock pressured county enrolling officer Lieutenant W. T. Fentress to "most cordially recommend the release of his boy Collin" on 29 December and to grant permission for the Petersburg runaway to remain with Bocock.[47]

Governor Smith considered hesitancy about forwarding slaves to the military as treasonous. When a Lynchburg court clerk replied that the city was unable to comply with the governor's December 1864 requisition order on the grounds that no more than one hundred slaves were available, Smith exploded in a caustic letter that labeled the clerk a liar and white Lynchburgers and others like them unpatriotic and selfish for refusing to loan their slaves: "I have to express my deep regret at the manifest reluctance of the Counties, cities, and towns in filling these requisitions called for the public defense. At a time when the slave Institution itself is in peril, and our inability to hold Richmond would make our interest in slave property worthless, a call made at the instance of General Lee to enable him to hold this city is too frequently responded to with such coldness and reluctance as to fill the hearts of those deeply anxious for our Liberty and Independence with anguish if not despondency."[48]

Two weeks later Lee protested that of the 5,000 slaves requisitioned, only 502 (10 percent) had arrived at Petersburg, and he warned that his troops were stretched thin working at trench repairs, cutting wood, gathering supplies, and fighting the Yankees at the same time. Smith decided the time had come for Virginia to play its free back card and asked the General Assembly for authorization to establish volunteer organizations of slave and free Afro-Virginians for the state's defense, holding out hope that their use might demoralize the enemy. Furthermore, he wanted the laws changed to permit blacks to be armed as part of their new military duties and sought crackdowns on the exemptions to requisitions by instituting a flat 10 percent conscription of each county's slaves. Stiff fines of $10 per day were imposed on owners for each slave illegally withheld; sheriffs could be fined up to $2,000, and they and county clerks who refused to perform these duties satisfactorily were liable to be found guilty of malfeasance and removed from office.

The only slaves not subject to this final draft were those belonging to persons who owned but one slave; to soften some of the act's harshness, owners were promised $60 a month and the right to have their slaves supervised by their own overseers with the slaves' rations, medical care, and expenses paid for by the government. Governor Smith's final requisitioning demands of slaves were sent to the counties with the warning that the new laws would be strictly executed. The upshot of this eleventh-hour request for 1,942 slaves was that by March 1865 1,614 were received, a success rate of 83 percent (table 2.1). Forty-nine counties responded, and of these fourteen met or exceeded their quotas. Their slaves were distributed among the Army of Northern Virginia, the Richmond and Danville Railroad, the Piedmont Railroad, the Engineer Bureau, and the quartermaster and commissary departments.[49]

TABLE 2.I. FINAL REQUISITION OF VIRGINIA SLAVES, FEBRUARY–MARCH 1865

County	Quota	Slaves	Percentage
Albemarle	95	75	78%
Alleghany	5	1	20
Amelia	50	48	96
Amherst	40	39	97
Appomattox	25	22	88
Bath	5	2	40
Bedford	70	45	64
Botetourt	20	18	90
Brunswick	73	46	63
Buckingham	66	59	89
Campbell	68	69	101
Caroline	30	30	100
Carroll	2	2	100
Charlotte	80	80	100
Chesterfield	30	23	76
Cumberland	50	48	96
Dinwiddie	30	17	56
Essex	20	14	70
Floyd	3	1	25
Fluvanna	40	39	97
Franklin	50	49	98
Giles	4	4	100
Goochland	48	46	95
Grayson	4	4	100
Greene	10	13	130
Halifax	110	103	93
Hanover	50	37	74
Henrico	45	19	42
Henry	40	40	100
King William	15	14	93
Louisa	65	55	84
Lunenburg	60	54	90
Lynchburg (city)	12	9	75
Madison	17	5	29
Mecklenburg	103	95	92
Monroe	7	6	85
Montgomery	13	13	100
Nelson	35	31	88
Nottoway	50	50	100
Orange	30	15	50
Pittsylvania	104	104	100

TABLE 2.1. CONTINUED

County	Quota	Slaves	Percentage
Powhatan	30	30	100
Prince Edward	55	49	89
Pulaski	10	9	90
Richmond (city)	60	21	35
Roanoke	15	14	93
Rockbridge	20	23	+115
Russell	5	3	60
Shenandoah	2	2	100
Washington	17	6	35
Wythe	14	12	85
Total	1,942	1,614	83%

Source: William F. Fry, Report of Negro Slaves Impressed in the State of Virginia under Circular No. 69, Conscript Office, 1864 to 1st March 1865, M-331, War Department Collection of Confederate Records, 109: Generals, Staff Officers, Compiled Military Records, NA.

From the middle of 1864 until January 1865, 1,540 free black male Virginians were enrolled at Camp Lee outside Richmond. Some were as young as seventeen, others were in their sixties. All except one were Virginia-born. Among their ranks were shoemakers, farmers, coopers, wheelwrights, machinists, bookkeepers, horse grooms, dockworkers, carpenters, barbers, and bricklayers. Thirty-two-year-old Irving Baily was a Surry County distiller; Kiah Berry of Richmond had been a train fireman; Dock Harris of Pittsylvania County, a twenty-three-year-old army waiter. Most were draftees, but some were volunteers.

Those with appropriate skills were allocated to railroads as brakemen, firemen, and engine cleaners; to hospitals as attendants; to the trenches as military engineers; to the Nitre Bureau, the Ordnance Department, naval depots, or the staffs of generals. Some were excused or exempted from duty due to ill health, and a few deserted or were officially listed as captured by the enemy or for one reason or another were unassigned or unaccounted for by enrolling officers. Some were sent to other states for duty.[50]

Nearly 180,000 Afro-Virginians toiled as logistical support for Confederate Virginia. As reward for their services, the General Assembly enacted legislation during the 1920s awarding annual pensions of $25 to those who had been body servants or military laborers. Black laborers were vital manpower sources for the Confederate army and the state's military forces. The fortifications they built stopped Yankee bullets and dampened the explosions of shells; the factories where they lifted, heaved, and pushed shaped the instruments of war to kept the Southern armies equipped; the labors of industrial-military slaves fueled local economies. Without them, the South would have gone down to defeat much sooner.

3 MANY THOUSANDS GONE
Runaways and Contrabands

Virginia Slave Owner: "Come here, you black rascal!"
Virginia Slave: "Can't come back nohow, massa; Dis chile's CONTRABAND!"
—*from a Union patriotic envelope*

BEFORE THE war a group of freed slaves tried to establish themselves on property purchased for them in Mercer County, but they were driven out by whites who warned that the blacks would be killed if they ever attempted to return because Mercer was a "white man's county." The *Charlottesville Advocate* claimed that freedom was "not the normal condition of the negro race" and argued that it was harmful to black mental health. It cited census statistics that seemingly indicated a higher frequency of lunacy among Northern free blacks than Southern slaves: Louisiana, one in 2,477; South Carolina, one in 3,000; Massachusetts, one in 43; Maine, one in 14.[1]

An estimated 30,000 to 60,000 slaves out of a population of four million deserted slavery via the Underground Railroad between 1830 and 1860, but it is also true that the Railroad's effectiveness has been exaggerated: most slaves, until the end of the war, sojourned in bondage for life. William Still, himself an escaped slave, served as an agent or "conductor" for the Railroad and later described several Virginia escapes during the 1850s by slaves on foot or horseback, by steamship or aboveground rail, or in carriages. Daniel M. Norton and his brother escaped to New York where Daniel became a physician. He returned to Virginia in 1864 and headed a political machine in York County for forty years. Richard Slaughter, another ex-slave, agreed on the Railroad's successes in the state and told of slaves smuggled in the hulls or topsails of vessels bound for the North.[2]

Fugitives from Virginia crossed the Ohio River, or in the southeast found sanctuary in the Great Dismal Swamp in colonies of slaves from the tidewater area; the Eastern Shore was one "road" for the passage of slaves to liberty. A favorite and heavily used route for runaways from the Confederate capital during the war was the Mechanicsville Turnpike, crossing the Pamunkey and Mattaponi rivers to the Rappahannock River and Bowler's Wharf near Tappahannock; from there they continued on to King George or Westmoreland counties and then either crossed the Potomac River into

Maryland or took a boat upriver to Washington.[3] The Railroad's Virginia network enabled a few black families to maintain contact by mail with those still in slavery. When his daughter Rosette fell in love and fled with her slave-husband John Henry Hill, Rosette's father, free black Petersburg caterer John McCray, sent the young couple money. Rosette's husband, John, hid out in Richmond, Norfolk, and Philadelphia for nine months before it was safe for him to continue to Canada, and she then followed him to Canada; the couple returned to Virginia after the war. Jane Marie Chester, born a slave in 1806, fled to Pennsylvania where her son Thomas was born in 1834. Years afterwards he returned to his mother's native state as a reporter for a Philadelphia newspaper to chronicle the final months of the Civil War.[4]

At the very beginning of the war slaves were convinced it would be the long-prayed-for millennium of freedom. They had always foreseen the coming of the great turning point that would end their bondage and were acquainted with the course of national events despite slave owners' efforts to adulterate the details. Two slave women, Annetta M. Lane of Norfolk and Harriet R. Taylor of Hampton, founded the United Order of Tents as a black benevolence society in Norfolk. In fact, it was a front for an Underground Railroad station. It became the first black female lodge to be chartered in the state after the war.[5]

John Quincy Adams of Frederick County took advantage of the passage of the contending armies to escape. One of fifteen children (including two sets of twins), Adams was sold to Winchester, but his parents urged him to prepare for freedom and predicted blacks would not be slaves much longer. Adams equally hungered for education and freedom; to him schooling and knowledge were "man's greatest privilege," but the South had always opposed any education for blacks. On 27 June 1862 Adams and a large part of his family (his father, mother, four brothers, and two sisters) escaped and ultimately reached Harrisburg, Pennsylvania. There they prospered, and Adams became a hotel bell tender and dining room waiter. He did not see his twin brother Aaron again until three years after the war.[6]

One unidentified Virginia slave became the focus of an intense skirmish when he attempted an escape on the spur of the moment while driving a Confederate wagon between hostile lines. The rebel pickets saw him going but could not stop him. Surprised as he was by the success of his escape, the black man was even more amazed when a Union quartermaster paid him several hundred dollars for the mules and the wagon.[7]

Some slaves, if they felt they were being overworked, would temporarily abscond and returned only in exchange for amnesty. Norfolk County planter George T. Wallace, his crops rotting in the fields, desperately sent word through an intermediary to nine runaway slaves: "If you can, induce [them] to return. . . . You can safely promise *all* of them . . . that I will not whip them. . . . I need labor *now* very much & if these negroes intend to return I wish them to do so this week. Do what you can to get them back." Wallace and other slaveholders had to negotiate with such slaves as if they were wage laborers.[8]

Many slaves were motivated to escape after a taste of the lash. Robert, a hired-out slave, fled after an overseer "struck him four or five Licks" in August 1861. Covesville resident Cornelia Boaz advised her brother not to whip his slaves unless he wanted them to run away: "I believe it will not do to correct servants much now. Dr. Boaz [her husband] whipped Phillis about two or nearly three months ago for some offence and she left and has not been seen or heard of since." Joshua, "alias Ditcher," fled to parts unknown in 1861; three years later someone saw him working in Petersburg as a tanner and shoemaker. His owner still wanted him back and placed a newspaper advertisement providing a detailed description: "He is about 33 years old dark complected 5 feet 10 or 11 inches high, has red, muddy casted eyes, slooped about the neck, and a small scar on his right cheek." Fluvanna County slave James Henry Woodson fled from a brutal master and became a guide for Philip Sheridan's cavalry during its 1864–65 Virginia raids. His son, born in 1875 in Buckingham County, became the "Father of Black History," Carter G. Woodson.[9]

In June 1862 slave owner H. B. White successfully completed a grueling trip from Richmond through Union pickets to his Hanover County home. A rude shock spoiled his arrival, for "seven of my negroes [were] missing of course they are in Yankee Land, they were Henry Jefferson, Jackson, little Henry, Milly, Martha, Eliza and Betsy (Azruiss' child). Milly left Antony behind I suppose she and Azruiss had a Swap, they took nothing with them but what they had on." Although most of his slaves remained on the farm, a dismayed White could not help but wonder "how *long* they will remain, can't say should be not surprised any morning to find that most of the balance had gone."[10]

Prominent Confederate slaveholders, too, were vexed by runaways. Thirty-year-old William Andrew Jackson, a coachman for Jefferson Davis, ran away in May 1862 and was described as an "extremely intelligent" because he knew how to read and write. Jackson, previously employed as a Richmond court messenger and a hack driver, characterized the Confederate president as "disheartened and querulous"; by November, Jackson arrived in Great Britain with a letter of introduction from one of Davis's archfoes, abolitionist William Lloyd Garrison. When Jim Turner, body servant of former governor Henry A. Wise, escaped during the Union offensive against Norfolk in 1862, Wise wrathfully declared that runaways should be shot on sight. Years later, Turner reappeared—at Wise's funeral.[11]

Several runaway slaves, despite and against the odds, continued to press their rations of luck after their initial escape. Cornelius, another slave of Jefferson Davis's, fled with enough food for a week but soon was recaptured. By means of one of the oldest subterfuges, asking for water, he again escaped after knocking his jailer down with the empty water cup. A West Point, Virginia, slave named Claiborne found employment as a Union scout; during a reconnaissance he barely evaded recapture by a Confederate regiment. Other slaves escaped by way of aboveground railroads on the pretense of carrying out errands for their owners. As a result, blacks were no longer issued tickets or allowed to board trains unless whites had procured their tickets. These and other methods were ineffective; fifty slaves absconded from Isle of Wight County, and thirty "Yankee contrabands" crossed from south of the James River to Old Point Comfort; sixteen more, ages three to fifty-six, fled from a single plantation in Stafford County during September 1862. The increased pace of slave escapes from the state demoralized slave owners.[12]

Slaveholders professed astonishment that slaves would run away and blamed Northern distortions and abolitionist exaggerations. Newspaper advertisements frequently were suffixed with "absconded without visible cause" or "without provocation or complaint." The number of Afro-Virginians fleeing the state increased. Of 490,865 slaves in 1860, 117 ran away; but as of 1863, 37,706 slaves out of a population of 346,848 were able to abscond successfully in spite of slave patrols, Confederate troops, and state militia.[13]

Chapter 105 of the 1860 state code detailed the legal procedures required for the processing of captured runaways. Following arrest the slave was to be taken before a county justice who would certify him or her as a runaway. Any person apprehending a fugitive was entitled to a reward of $5 if the slave had been arrested within fifty miles of his owner's home county or $10 for those seized beyond fifty miles. Additional rewards ranged from 15 to 25 percent of the fugitive's value. Runaways belonging to unidentified owners could be jailed for no more than a month before the jailer had to place a notice describing both the captive and his apparel in Richmond newspapers. If unclaimed four months after the advertisement, the slave was to be sold at a public auction. Officials who failed to abide by these legal provisions could be fined of up to $100.[14]

These policies applied to Union officers, who also risked monetary penalties for helping slaves to escape. Among the first ordinances passed by the

Virginia State Convention in May 1861 were those directed against Yankee officers who incited, counseled, or abetted slave revolts and escapes; these offenses were deemed felonies and were punishable by fines up to $10,000 and imprisonment in the state penitentiary for twenty years. The House of Delegates' Committee on Military Affairs even studied the possibility of removing all slaves from counties invaded by or in proximity to the Union army.[15]

The General Assembly passed a law on 3 October 1862 requiring those found guilty to pay double the value of the slave plus 6 percent interest. Another law established penalties for Union officers who employed runaway slaves; fines of $50 per day for each slave were ordered for this offense. Under Virginia law the only time a slave could testify against whites was in cases where runaways had been seized or harbored under the authority of Union military officers.[16]

State agencies were directed to report any expenditures resulting from the capture and jailing of runaways. The Central Lunatic Asylum reported costs of $90.61 for the year ending 30 September 1863. The legislature anticipated a Confederate victory and the need for diplomatic negotiations to secure the return of runaways who reached Union territory; another measure enacted in March 1863 required commissioners of revenue in every town and county to forward the names, sex, ages, and numbers of their black fugitives and the names of their owners to the state auditor of public accounts.

Commissioners' reports were sent to the auditor of public accounts in Richmond; some enumerated 1863 runways, whereas others such as the Greensville County report included slaves who escaped during 1861–62. During 1861–63 approximately 5,127 slaves fled successfully. Eleven percent of these runaways escaped during the first two years of the war. Orange County suffered 621 escapes; Charles City County's runaways included 42 black children between the ages of two and six who followed the retreat of General George B. McClellan's army during August 1862. The governor reported the escape of 38,000 Virginia slaves in 1863.[17]

The Confederate Constitution (Article IV, section 2) enumerated provisions for the return of escaped slaves. An 1861 opinion by Attorney General Bragg ruled that the government should pay all expenses incurred in the recapture of slaves employed on government projects whether they were hired or impressed labor. Runaways belonging to members of allied Indian tribes were dealt with under an enactment of 17 February 1862. Fugitive slaves owned by "friendly" Indians were to be delivered to a superintendent of Indian affairs for return to the chief of the appropriate tribe; free blacks were specifically exempted from this proviso if they could prove their free status.[18]

Large sums were offered for runaways. Rewards were based on gender, skills, skin color, and temperament. S. E. Edmonds of News Ferry, Halifax County, promised $3,000 for his five runaway slaves in October 1864; later that same year $2,000 was offered for Burnett, a runaway who escaped from Richmond with his mother, an Amelia County slave. Matilda, a thirty-five-year-old light-complexioned slave woman, was worth $250 to anyone sharp-eyed enough to catch her; a Lynchburg advertisement of July 1863 warned she was heading for Fauquier County because she had lived there previously. The reward for twenty-one-year-old George, a "copper color, nose talking, cock-eyed" literate slave from Pittsylvania County that same year was $50. A Culpeper County slave who escaped was asked by Union officers about the latest news from his county. He replied tongue in cheek that there was a man in Culpeper who had lost a good and valuable servant and prophesied he would probably lose more.[19]

With so many escapes taking place, owners found it expedient to become more knowledgeable about the physical marks and idiosyncracies of their slaves. William, the property of Captain W. T. Peterson of Petersburg, escaped from Richmond's American Hotel in September 1864 to join his wife in Amelia County; he was described simply as a twenty-year-old "bushy head." William House absconded from Madison County in a stolen "good suit of Confederate gray." Sarah, a Hardy County slave, was characterized as "very black . . . with short upper lip, long white teeth" and likely to speak in "rather a *Yankeelike style*" when addressed.[20]

Physical peculiarities were especially emphasized. Malachi, who fled during April 1863, was a forty-eight-year-old male purchased from Greenville, North Carolina, who had possessed an usually coarse, loud voice and because of poor eyesight always wore green eyeglasses. A Petersburg newspaper notice characterized eighteen-year-old Louisa as having "eye teeth grown above the others" which could be seen only when she laughed, "stout" with waved hair, and suspected of posing as a free black while employed at one of the city's hospitals. One of the highest rewards for an individual slave, $2,000, was promised in 1864 for the return of Burnett (or Beenard), a "good looking and well spoken" twenty-nine-year-old despite bad front teeth. He escaped in a wagon and was presumed to be on his way to Richmond County. When a thirteen-year-old named Colin escaped during March 1865, his owner's advertisement made mention of a small scar under his left jaw caused by scrofula (tuberculosis).[21]

Teeth and complexion were frequently noted to distinguish one slave from another. "All three had good teeth," advised Henry E. Graves in a Petersburg newspaper after the escape of Aaron, James, and Paschal. Booker, a Bedford County fugitive slave, possessed a complexion resembling "brown gingerbread." Jordan, a male slave in Buffalo Springs, Amherst County, was described as of "copper color, 25 years old, stout built . . . had on his breast three small blisters about the size of a pea." Another slave with "decayed teeth," eighteen-year-old Mary Randolph, escaped on 2 August 1861, taking several dresses with her. Two months later her brother, fifteen-year-old Frederick, though described by their owner as "not very intelligent," also fled. A reward of $50 apiece was promised if they were recaptured in Clarke County or $60 if caught in Frederick County.[22]

Apparently, runaway black slaves were far more valuable and worth the trouble of recapture than white Confederate deserters or civilian apprentices. Advertisements for fugitive white apprentices were similar to those for runaway blacks but differed in at least one crucial aspect: the amount of the rewards promised. If these whites were apprehended, they were worth as little as twenty-five cents. John H. Moore promised a five-cent reward for a nine-year-old white boy, John B. Kibler, in 1863, but among the most worthless sums on record were one-cent rewards pledged for the return of apprentices Samuel H. Swisher and John E. M. Guy in September 1861 and January 1863.[23]

Even rarer were "runaway slave notices" deliberately devised to take advantage of the public's interest in the monetary gains to be had through slave catching. These false advertisements were actually eye-catching announcements of services offered by white entrepreneurs. Archibald Davis, a carriage and house painter and paperhanger, introduced his services to Rockbridge County residents by prefacing his advertisement with the heading "$500 Reward" wherein he trumpeted his willingness to accept "country produce" instead of cash as payment for his work.[24]

At the end of 1864 Virginia's hopes for peace and a Confederate victory were diminishing. More slaves were fleeing, and some even established their own underground networks to smuggle themselves across enemy lines or initiated contacts with Union soldiers in personal bids for freedom. George, a slave of Dr. George Leftwitch, was arrested by two Richmond constables in March 1864 for aiding slaves to escape and carrying them to Union-held territories. Edmonia, sent on an errand to the camp of the 12th Ohio Regiment, returned to her owner's home after a considerable delay. Soon afterwards sixty of the soldiers arrived saying they only wanted potatoes, but they also tried to take the family's horses. Apparently Edmonia had reached an understanding with these troops because she departed with them but not before they took all of the plantation's supply of flour. Upon the advice and assistance of the Yankees, she opened trunks of the family's possessions and "took all she could carry." Slavery was becoming a fragile reality, and Afro-Virginians were contributing to its deterioration.[25]

Collectively and individually Afro-Virginians gauged the progress of the conflict and chose to cast their lot with the winning side. The family of Richmond barber Robert Francis reached the safety of Union-held Bermuda Hundred with their bedding and 920 pounds of tobacco. Sixty weary yet happy runaways arrived in Alexandria from Sussex County; nearly all were from the same plantation. Mary Pope and her husband Joe Dardin fled from Southampton County to Norfolk. Mary's owner had sold Joe in Richmond in 1861 because he constantly visited her with or without official permission. When the war began Mary feared she and her three children would be sold away; she and six other slaves stole some chickens, meat, and cornmeal and fled. Four Botetourt County white men guarding three imprisoned slaves named Haws, Moses, and Peter were tricked when the trio received permission "to attend to the calls of Nature." They escaped, and two of them, Moses and Peter, reached a Yankee patrol and were seen two months later in Craig County. Haws required medical attention after being tortured by angry Confederates.[26]

Boats and rivers were a habitual mode of quick escape for runaways. After overhearing plans by local whites to arm and send them into battle against Yankees, six slaves escaped from Mathews County in July 1861 to Stingaree Lighthouse where they were rescued by Union sailors. Stafford Cook of York County lost his slaves after telling a neighbor of his plan to sell them south; a slave overhead the conversation and warned Cook's slaves, and they fled to Union-held Yorktown. A Lancaster County farmer complained to the commander of the Potomac Flotilla after seven of his own slaves and seven others hired out to him escaped by boarding a ship on the Rappahannock River from which they were eventually forwarded to the safety of Fort Monroe. One of these slaves, Charles, was blind, but his comrades took him with them at great risk to the entire party. Five slaves who fled down the Nansemond River to Fort Monroe in late 1861 reported in detail on the construction, layout, and garrisons of Confederate batteries and the location of infantry and cavalry camps along the river and in Isle of Wight County, Smithfield, Chuckatuck, and Suffolk. These runaways complained that farmers were starving slaves to feed soldiers.[27]

The General Assembly enacted laws in March 1861 and February 1864 to curtail escapes by boat. The first measure was directed at tidewater slaves; unattended boats were subject to removal and destruction upon a petition of any three white freeholders, and the value of the craft was to be paid to its owner. The other law ordered any person who transported a slave by boat without the permission of his owner to be punished with fines, imprisonment, paying the value of the slave, and repayment of double the expenses the owner incurred if he failed to recapture his property.[28]

But slaves continued to desert plantations by boat. In June 1862 six slaves belonging to James R. Saunders of Norfolk County but hired out to George T. Wallace stole a vessel and fled after a Portsmouth runaway persuaded them to make their bid for freedom; of Wallace's fifty-one slaves only eight remained, and three were so sick that he feared his crop would be lost. A Gloucester County resident named Bryan who previously had lost eighty-seven slaves was powerless to prevent nineteen more from making good their escape by boat during August 1862, including "Jack, Old Becky . . . & that wretch and villain Oliver." Nine conscripted slave laborers from Nelson and Cumberland counties abandoned the Chaffin's Farm headquarters of General (and former governor) Henry Wise in October 1862.[29]

Hill Carter of Charles City County attributed his losses to the proximity of Union vessels. On 14 July 1863 he noted, "10 of the best negro men ran off to the gunboats this morning"; two days later "5 more . . . ran off to the Yankee Gunboats . . . nearly all the men have gone off, *no women* . . . this makes in all 33 negroes have gone off." By June 1864 seventy-two of Carter's slaves had escaped.[30]

Across the James River, Edmund Ruffin, Jr. (son of the secessionist), chronicled the war's effect on his Beechwood plantation in Prince George County. The presence of Union soldiers induced many of his slaves to escape during May 1862, including his carriage driver, a houseboy, a carpenter, and slaves he had hired to raise a corn crop. He then hired eight slave boys and women from his father's Evelynton plantation because of the escape of six other slaves, but within a week forty-one of his slaves escaped. Ruffin took his remaining fifty-nine slaves, mostly women and children, to Petersburg and sold half of them for $11,000 in June 1862. Later that summer the Yankees visited Beechwood, stole all of the movable property, and carried off more slaves. The estate, within Grant's lines during the Petersburg siege, was used by Union quartermasters as a grazing ground for army cattle. Ruffin was finally able to return to Beechwood in April 1865, only to find it occupied by black squatters.[31]

Naval forays galvanized slaves to escape, and plantations located near rivers were vulnerable to amphibious assault. During January 1864 an expedition set out by ship from Norfolk and Newport News up the James River toward Brandon and landed at the plantation of a Dr. Ritchie. The doctor, a contractor for the Confederacy, and his overseers were arrested; 5,000 bushels of corn and 24,000 pounds of pork were destroyed. Approximately 137 slaves were freed during this thirty-hour raid, and most returned with the troops to Norfolk. While many slaves were content to flee alone or in groups, others frequently returned to the area on their own or with Union troops to pillage, rescue family members, and establish bases for raiding parties. An example of slave retribution occurred at Gwynn's Island near the mouth of the Piankatank River in Mathews County. Five hundred black men who landed at Cobb's Creek in March 1864 under the ostensible control of white Union officers brutally and thoroughly plundered the neighborhood; at each house and farm they took everything of value. These raids challenged and broke the power of county slave owners; a fifty-four-year-old ex-slave named Bill became the "master of the land."[32]

There were runaways who returned to their former plantations not for retaliation but to rescue their families and retrieve personal belongings. Sigismunda Stribling Kimball of Shenandoah County, whose husband was serving in the Confederate army, had few difficulties at the beginning of the war in managing her black laborers alone. After Union raids in March 1862, Kimball described the Valley as being so desolate that "even the chickens forgot to crow." A Union officer warned her that the military "had plenty of ladies prisoners and they are the worst traitors in the world."[33]

A month after the issuance of the Emancipation Proclamation, a group of soldiers led by two black men, Clifton and William, arrived at the Kimball farm where Clifton's wife Emily and children were held as slaves. Upon their arrival Clifton and William hurriedly led the soldiers to the slave quarters while the officer in charge rode up to the front porch to bid the white women good morning. He pompously announced that he had come "to take that man's (pointing to William) brother's wife (Fairinda) away." Exasperated, Kimball demanded his name, and he brusquely answered, "Captain William Clagget, I was born near Richmond and am what you would call poor White Trash." Four horses were hitched to a wagon, and Fairinda, her child, chests, and barrels of flour were packed in. Clagget told the slave woman that if she wanted meat, flour, or anything on the farm, it was hers for asking. Fairinda, anxious to be away, responded that she did not want anything but herself. The next morning a squad of Union soldiers returned with the runaways so they could pack up the clothes they had left behind in their haste to be away.[34]

Despite a day of heavy rains a runaway named Abner returned to the Kimball farm with soldiers to retrieve his wife Lucy and family on the afternoon of 7 March 1863 and for good measure took flour, bedclothing, and miscellaneous supplies. The lieutenant in charge, a man named McVicar, was not entirely unsympathetic and, unlike Clagget, took pains to explain that he had written orders. Unfortunately he had "left them in town," but he excused his own forgetfulness since this was the first time he ever participated in this sort of assignment. "I have come for this gentlemen's family,"

McVicar announced, and even though he admitted that the entire proceeding was "an disagreeable business," orders were orders. After all, "this is the way to break down the rebellion[:] take the labor away, the South could secede, let her face the consequences."[35]

Several runaway slaves were able to escape beyond the state's boundaries but when caught provided little if any information as to the identity of their owners. Forty-eight-year-old George Stuart, arrested in Ohio, denied being a runaway and refused to acknowledge an owner. An April 1861 advertisement described him as wearing a black cashmere coat, black pants, a white cotton shirt, and shabby shoes. Lunsford, captured in Bedford County, identified his owner as one Welfinbarger of Grainger County in east Tennessee. When Peter, a runaway who hid out in Richmond, was captured in November 1864, he had been on the run for four years and was disguised as a washerwoman and laundress employed by a free black woman.[36]

Slaves fled whenever opportunities seemed favorable. In 1864 a column of slaves being marched under guard from a Confederate hospital in Richmond suddenly scattered. Their guards caught most of them, but one named Royall continued to run until he reached the docks. There he jumped into the James River and drowned. Henrietta, slave of George W. Gary of Richmond, carefully laid her plans to finance her escape by stealing and selling select items belonging to her owners. While the family was away for tea, she took $5,000 worth of watches, jewelry, dresses, shoes, cash, and bonds, put on the best of the dresses, and tried to pass herself off as a free black. Twenty-four hours later she was discovered hiding at the home of Margaret, another slave; both women received thirty-nine lashes. Jim Woods in an 1864 letter complained about a slave named Henry who deserted while on an errand to Staunton. Woods feared "the morale effect on the balance of my Negroes will be very [serious]." He was hoping that Henry might have been impressed as labor for military fortifications and sent another slave, William, to look for him. Ten days later Henry, whose absence had been an escape attempt, was in a Harrisonburg jail, and Woods decided to sell him in the hope that he would be "taken South where he will have but little chance to get to the Yankees."[37]

In the fall of 1862 Richmond newspapers reported the Confederate military's recapture of ninety-eight blacks consisting of forty-six slaves and fifty-two "Northern free negroes," body servants of Yankee officers. The slaves were housed in Libby Prison where their owners might reclaim them, but no one knew what to do with the free blacks. Slave runaways had a 90 percent chance of recapture, and most managed to flee no more than twenty to fifty miles from their owners. The Confederate government established three depots in the state where such slaves were confined until their owners reclaimed them, at Richmond, Petersburg, and Dublin Station. It was not a coincidence that these depots were near army camps; soldiers not only provided ample security but were not above seeking out black fugitives to earn extra cash. At the depots captured slaves were put to work as laborers, cooks, teamsters, and body servants; their names and those of their owners were printed in Richmond newspapers.[38]

Runaways were capable of traveling throughout most of the Confederacy's most important and heavily fortified state. Seventy-five men and women and boys and girls were held at Richmond's Castle Thunder and Libby prisons during the summer of 1863; their owners were mostly Virginians, but a number of these fugitives had fled from Maryland, Tennessee, and Washington, D. C. Among them were a family of five blacks named Green, the property of a Williamsburg slaveholder.[39]

Of a group of thirteen slaves listed in an 1864 newspaper advertisement, only two (James Bush and Revel Garrison) claimed their current owners' surnames as their own. These Afro-Virginian males fled across distances ranging from a mere 20 miles (George and William, from Chesterfield); 50 miles (Phillip, from Essex); 105 miles (Charles, from Portsmouth); 170 miles (George, from Alleghany); up to more than 220 miles (James Bush, from Montgomery, and Jim, from North Carolina). With the exception of Elijah, these black males journeyed, on average, in excess of a hundred miles, the equivalent of the distance between America's two wartime capitals.[40]

Union incursions contributed to the fugitive slave population. When Yankees raiders struck at the Augusta County farm of Nancy Emerson during July 1864, they took with them all of her horses and slave men and boys and told the slave women they would be taken next time. A week later they kept their promise, and one of Emerson's youngest slaves revealed the hiding place of family valuables. To preclude additional losses of items and slaves (and thwart their collaboration with the enemy), Emerson sent the last of her slaves off "to seek their fortunes"; one of them, Eva, supposedly deathly ill with pneumonia, underwent a instantaneous recovery after a gulping down a cup of coffee and hurried to join the others. John, a twelve-year-old, had been hired out by Emerson to a local farmer who secreted him in the woods day and night to keep the Yankees from finding him.[41]

Between 1,300 and 1,500 slaves were carried away from or otherwise fled Essex County in June 1864, practically depopulating the county of its labor force. During the Wilson-Kautz raid near Petersburg, cavalrymen under the command of General James Harrison Wilson captured all the African-American males they could find on the farms and plantations of Dinwiddie, Nottoway, and Lunenburg counties. Their mission, to destroy Lee's southern and western railroad supply lines into Petersburg, proceeded well until Confederate troops confronted them in force at Stony Creek Station near the Petersburg and Weldon Railroad as the Federals tried to return to Grant's lines. After a sharp fight approximately 700 slaves were recaptured, perhaps the largest group ever regained by the Confederacy at one time during the war. Among them were old and young, robust and infirm, blacks and mulattoes. Some were well dressed, others were in rags; the youngest was a few days old, the eldest, age sixty. They were marched down Richmond's Bank Street to the office of the provost marshal, gawked at by crowds. As the slaves tramped to the city under heavy guard, one woman gave birth in a military ambulance; mother and infant later convalesced in a guardhouse.

And so it was that on 4 July 1864 (the eighty-eighth anniversary of the Declaration of Independence) 624 slaves were listed by name in two newspaper columns for their owners to reclaim them. (On this same day in neighboring Hanover County sixteen slaves commemorated their own independence day by successfully deserting the Wickham family plantation.) They were from Nottoway, Brunswick, Powhatan, Prince Edward, Sussex, Mecklenburg, Dinwiddie, Lunenburg, Culpeper, Charlotte, and Greensville counties. Perhaps with none too gentle prodding and the threat of whippings, they were encouraged to provide the names and residences of their masters, most of whom would need only to secure one or two slaves. William H. Trotter received the largest number of errant slaves, thirty-five; a Dr. Taylor of Mecklenburg and Edward Wyatt both had twenty-seven slaves awaiting repatriation; George Field reclaimed twenty-five; George Parham of Sussex, thirty slaves.[42]

Several runaways were luckless enough to be caught in Union army uniforms. Black soldiers (and their officers) were considered to be participating in slave insurrections, a crime punishable by death. One Confederate War Department proclamation in November 1862 warned: "Slaves in flagrant rebellion are subject to death by the laws of every slave-holding State; and did circumstances admit without too great delays and military inconveniences, might be handed over to the civil tribunals for condemnation. They cannot be recognized in any way as soldiers subject to the rules of war and to trial by military courts . . . summary execution must therefore be inflicted on those taken."[43]

George C. Council, Henry Worthington, William Harrison, and Henry Kirk were captured after the 16 July 1863 engagement at James Island, South Carolina, as members of the 54th Massachusetts (Colored) Infantry, an all-black Union regiment commanded by white officers. They were indicted and tried by the Charleston Police Court, Charleston Military District, in

September on charges of being runaways engaged in insurrection and treason against South Carolina. Council and Worthington were described in the
indictment as "negro slaves owned in Virginia"; Harrison and Kirk as Missouri slaves. A Charleston court decided the case was not within its bailiwick
and ordered the blacks returned to jail. Harrison and Worthington later died
in a Florence, South Carolina, prison camp in 1865.[44]

An unidentified black Union soldier, taken to Richmond in May 1864
and treated as a curiosity, was recognized as having been a slave of the firm
of Rawlings and Brothers of Norfolk. He claimed to have been in the Union
army for eight months and told how Northern whites deliberately kept
black soldiers so ignorant that they could only mark the passage of time "by
counting the number of suns over them." He asked to be returned to his
Norfolk owners, but because that city was under Union occupation it seems
clear that he hoped to avoid being executed. Confederate officers threatened
to kill him if he did not demonstrate the drills he had learned while in Lincoln's army. The situation was enough to make any man nervous, but "he
went through it with alacrity and no little skill," conceded one account, "ani-
mation being imparted to his evolutions by the threat that he was to die if
he did not perform well."[45]

Gilbert Adams, yet another slave runaway, had his release secured from
Libby Prison by his master, French Tilghman. One day as Tilghman passed
by the prison, he recognized the voice of Adams calling to him, "Marse
French! Marse French! For God's sake get me out of here!" He did so—and
sold Adams south to Georgia as punishment.[46]

The runaway slave problem and a sense of imminent defeat caused a
decline in runaway notices in many of the state's newspapers, and rewards
offered in the twilight of the Confederacy were substantially depreciated. In
early 1865 $100 was promised for the return of a forty-year-old Henrico
County runaway named Robert if he was captured before reaching his family in Goochland. David, the hired slave of a physician, fled on horseback
from the camp of the 9th Virginia Cavalry near Stony Creek Station; the
notice of his escape promised $100 for the return of the pony, saddle, and
bridle but only $50 for his capture.[47]

Runaways who reached Union lines became "contrabands." Those who used
the label or were officially designated contraband included slaves who
sought protection by the Union army and were employed by it as cooks,
teamsters, and body servants; fugitive slaves forwarded to contraband
camps; runaways who preferred the designation as opposed to "fugitive" or
"runaway"; and finally, black families under the provisional care and protec-

tion of the Federal army while their husbands, sons, fathers, and brothers served as soldiers or military laborers.

To be addressed as a contraband was a means to claim nominal citizenship, but escaped slaves disliked the term. Union soldiers claimed "darkey" was habitually applied by the contrabands to each other, though whenever they were addressed as such the blacks protested, "What d'ye call us that for?" One Northern journal, the *Liberator*, advised whites to use "colored refugees" because "the word 'Contrabands' is not a proper term to be applied to human beings. In fact, no one word expresses their condition. They are not exactly slaves, and, to the disgrace of our Government, they are not exactly freedmen. Let them be called Colored Refugees, until we can obtain for them a recognized freedom and citizenship."[48]

At Fort Monroe in September 1861, Union major general John E. Wool complained to Secretary of War Simon Cameron about the number of runaways flocking to the Union's most important Virginia stronghold: "I would be much gratified if you would tell me what I am to do with the negro slaves that are almost daily arriving at this post from the interior. Am I to find food and shelter for the women and children, who can do nothing for themselves? Thus far we have been able to employ in various ways most of the adults. . . . I hope you will give me instructions on this very important subject. Humanity requires that they should be taken care of."[49]

The first contrabands were three Virginia slave field hands who appeared at the fort on 23 May 1861: Shepard Mallory, Frank Baker, and James Townshend. They informed Union officials that they were about to be shipped to North Carolina to labor on Confederate fortifications. Their owner, Confederate colonel Charles K. Mallory, 115th Virginia Militia, demanded their return under the provisions of the Fugitive Slave Act of 1850 and appealed to Major General Benjamin F. Butler through his emissary, Major M. B. Carey. Carey and Butler met under a flag of truce at Mill Creek Bridge near Hampton to discuss the situation; Butler initially denied the request in order to confer with his superiors. By the end of May, Butler formally refused to return the three slaves, pointing out that since Virginia had seceded, it could no longer claim the protection and privileges of Federal law: "I am under no constitutional obligations to a foreign country, which Virginia now claims to be." He proclaimed as "contrabands of war" any slave who reached Union lines or had been previously employed as military labor for the Confederacy.

Later, Butler would deny that he had used "contrabands" as meaning anything other than coal, ships, buildings, and inanimate property and claimed that as a lawyer he was never very proud of his decision to apply the term to human beings until a member of his staff reminded him that "contrabands of war" was the maxim which freed the slaves. Mallory, Baker, and Townshend, now free men, were hired as brickmasons. Other escapees were put to work in the same capacities they had held under slavery—cooks, servants, and teamsters—but now received wages. When the black grapevine telegraphed these developments, slaves struck out for Federal camps and liberty. Eight more arrived on May 26; 59 more between the ages of three months and eighty-five years reached the fort the following day, and by 30 July 1861 900 Afro-Virginian refugees were living at Fort Monroe, which blacks nicknamed "Freedom's Fortress" because of its sanctuary for escaped slaves. They spread the news:

> Wake up snakes, pelicans, and Sesh'ners!
> Don't yer hear 'um coming'—
>> Comin' on de run?
> Wake up, I tell yer! Get up, Jefferson!
>> Bobolishion's coming'—
>> Bob-o-lish-i-on.[50]

Contrabands wanted the same treatment as other free men and women: decent work and fair, regular wages; no floggings as punishment and fair treatment by employers; that their families not be separated; education for their children; freedom of movement; voting rights; and equal treatment under the law and access to public facilities. Agencies such as the American Missionary Association hurried volunteers south to preach the gospel and try to improve the social and economic condition of the ex-slaves. By January 1864 the association, whose major goal was the creation of schools for freedpeople in the South, had spent $17,000 on behalf of ex-slaves, and more than a hundred of its teachers, missionaries, and assistants were providing elementary and religious instruction at Arlington Heights, Craney Island, Hampton, Newport News, Norfolk, Portsmouth, Sewell's Point, and Yorktown.

A school was organized by the American Tract Society at the Freedmen's Village, Greene Heights, Arlington, on 7 December 1863 with Henry E. Simmons, formerly a member of the 11th Rhode Island Volunteers, as its principal. As a whole, Afro-Virginian refugees were industrious, sober, honest, and "intensely human." They were capable of improvement, commented one Northern missionary, and would "become a great people." An escaped slave echoed those expectations: "Our masters have always told us that we could not live without them, but [we] will show them that liberty makes men; that we can, and will be something."[51]

Fort Monroe became the first of the war's racial uplift laboratories.

There, contraband employees were placed in two categories: Class 1 comprised males over the age of eighteen paid $10 a month, one ration a day, and clothing; Class 2 were boys aged twelve to eighteen or sickly or infirm males paid $5 a month, one daily ration, and the necessary amount of clothing. Superintendent of Contrabands Captain Charles B. Wilder, in testimony before the American Freedmen's Inquiry Commission, stated that 10,000 blacks fled to Fort Monroe, chiefly from the areas between Richmond and North Carolina; one woman traveled 200 miles alone disguised as a man. By August 1863, 26,110 were under Union protection in tidewater (8 percent were literate), but a year later they were suffering mortality rates of 25 percent. Joyous celebrations occurred as black families were reunited; one Norfolk slave woman found a daughter who had been sold from her as a child. The now eighteen-year-old woman was marked by whipping scars from head to toe.[52]

At contraband camps near Washington, blacks were badly treated, poorly fed, and inadequately housed in ever-present filth and squalor. They could not get gainful employment because prejudiced Northerners refused to hire them. The sight of black refugees invoked the pity of some Virginia slave owners. "Runaway negroes from the county around continue to come in every day," a Fredericksburg woman observed in June 1862. "It is a curious and pitiful sight to see the footsore and weary looking cornfield hands with their packets on their backs and handkerchiefs tied over their heads—men, women, little children and babies coming in gangs of ten and twenty at a time. They all look anxious and unhappy. Many of them are sent to the North. . . . Many are shipped direct for [Haiti] from here."[53]

Union officials had little choice but to establish quarters for blacks near urban areas of occupied Virginia; Confederates retaliated by destroying towns and villages to thwart their use as sites for contraband camps. Hampton was burned on 7 August 1861 for this reason. William Martin of the 11th Pennsylvania Cavalry told his sister in December 1862 that the town's burning and the destruction of the mansion of former president John Tyler were intended to deny their use as housing for contrabands and schools for black children. Martin was of the opinion that the slaves should have "stayed At home" in the first place and derided them as "Miserable Looking Devels." Another soldier contended that contrabands were "a lazy pack of fellows and won't hurt themselves with work."[54]

In September 1862 General Wool's successor, Major General John A. Dix, advised Secretary of War Edwin M. Stanton that contrabands were gathering in such enormous numbers at Fort Monroe that they had become "a very great source of embarrassment to the troops in this garrison and in the camps hereabout and to the white population of . . . this neighborhood."

The general applied for and received permission to ship 2,000 black refugees to Newport News under the supervision of Captain Wilder (appointed six months previously as superintendent of contrabands) pending their eventual transfer north. However, Northern governors almost to a man vetoed black immigration to their states, and Dix decided to move the unfortunate refugees to Craney Island and turn the problem over to Brigadier General Michael Corcoran. Two months later, upon hearing reports that the blacks were being mistreated and denied food and shelter, Dix sternly reminded Corcoran of his (and the Union army's) responsibility: "These people are in our care and we are bound by every principle of humanity to treat them with kindness and protect them from exposure and injury in their persons and property."[55]

Field-workers of the American Freedmen's Inquiry Commission, overwhelmed with Afro-Virginians fleeing from slavery, were hard pressed to clothe, feed, shelter, and employ them. As of 8 May 1863 there were 90 contrabands employed at the Fairfax Seminary Hospital; 624 rations were provided for 950 blacks, of whom nearly a hundred were hospital patients. As one Alexandria official compiled his monthly report, another 150 contrabands unexpectedly arrived at his tent.[56]

The counties of Accomack, Elizabeth City, Norfolk, Northampton, Princess Anne, and York and the cities of Alexandria, Norfolk, Portsmouth, and Suffolk were under Union occupation by January 1863. At Alexandria 1,230 black refugees (475 men, 276 women, and 439 children) resided in twenty-five houses. Each building was twelve feet square and provided shelter for up to twelve persons; all able-bodied males were gainfully employed except those necessary to care for the children and the elderly. There was not enough clothing and blankets for the women and children. As of 1863, 3,000 were in residence; a year later, 4,000 more arrived.

Contraband barracks were constructed, but blacks also took the initiative to build and whitewash their own shanties. Those employed by the government were paid $20 a month; others hired themselves out privately and planted gardens to supplement their rations. Black Alexandrians were particularly desirous of education and were known for taking out spelling books and studying during work breaks. A school instituted by convalescent Federal soldiers taught a hundred young black students. But black passengers were forced to ride in the cattle cars of the Orange and Alexandria Railroad until the War Department ordered that no distinction of race or color would be tolerated in public transportation; ridership was to henceforth be on a first-come, first-seated basis.[57]

A freedpeople's village consisting of neat houses surrounded by farms cultivated by the ex-slaves was founded in 1863 at Robert E. Lee's confiscated Arlington estate. It possessed a church, a 159-bed hospital, several workshops (blacksmiths, wheelwrights, carpenters, tailors, and shoemakers), a school with 135 pupils, and a home for elderly blacks built by members of this community. As aspiring entrepreneurs the blacks amazed whites by proving to be astute negotiators when making contracts. A lifetime of servitude and dealing with the harshest employers in the world—slave owners—taught them invaluable lessons of survival. They produced $6,000 worth of hay and $2,300 of corn fodder, and the profits they earned, $60,000 by the end of 1863, were deposited in their own savings bank.

Newspapers characterized this village's main street as clean and prosperous-looking throughout its quarter-mile length. Its residents received training as house servants or seamstresses, with sewing machines being provided for their practicum. Under this system every advantage was provided for them, and after they successfully completed their training, the former slaves were provided with employment. The village survived as a black community until 1900.[58]

Three prosperous free black women residents of Winchester contributed food to the Union hospital there in 1862: Marcia Weaver, owner of two houses; Evelina Orrick, a sixty-year-old, six-foot-tall mother of twenty-six children (five by white men); and Mary Strange. Yet conditions for contrabands at the Fort Norfolk camp were not inspiring; 962 ex-slaves lived there, but all able-bodied men were sent elsewhere for government service, and 633 women, children, the sick, and the old were left behind. Of these, half suffered from measles and whooping cough, and deaths easily exceeded births. Wretchedly clothed, they were housed in a warehouse previously used to store guano which was usually filled with smoke because it had no chimneys. This lifestyle was little better than slavery, yet "we are willing," said one freedwoman, "to endure and suffer this and more for the prospect of freedom."[59]

The crowded conditions of some of the camps and at cities under Union occupation caused social tensions among the blacks. They took abandoned and vacant houses for housing, and sometimes disputes broke out over scarce shelters. Throughout these tenements one could see and hear fighting and squabbles among the occupants. Three Winchester black women were seen dragging a fourth from a house one summer morning; they beat her unmercifully and stripped her of her clothing to the stares of passersby and the delight of leering Union soldiers.[60]

Federal governmental policies toward contrabands ranged from indifference to hostility to sincere concern. Private organizations such as the

United States Commission for the Relief of the National Freedman sought and obtained permission to furnish supplies, schoolbooks, and subsistence. Among the relief agencies active in Virginia on behalf of the freedpeople were: the American Colonization Society; the American Freedmen's Inquiry Commission; the American Missionary Association; the American Tract Society; the Bureau for the Relief of Freedmen and Refugees (established by Congress in March 1865 and commonly known as the Freedmen's Bureau); the Education Commission for Freedmen (later the New England Freedmen's Aid Society); the National Freedmen's Relief Association (New York City); and the Office for Freedmen (Brooklyn, New York).

Elizabeth Keckley, the former Virginia slave who by hard work and resourcefulness became one of Washington's best-known seamstresses, yearned to help her people. Her only child was killed in action in 1861, and in her grief she pledged herself to the alleviation of some of the burdens that newly arrived contrabands encountered in the unfriendly society of freedom. Keckley noted that the Federal capital regularly held events for the benefit of its sick and wounded white soldiers and suggested to the city's black churches that a benevolent society be instituted by and for African-Americans.

The Contraband Relief Association was founded in August 1862 with Keckley as president, and this extraordinary woman personally conducted fund-raising campaigns in Boston and New York. Contributions were received from the Sheffield Anti-Slavery Society of England, and Frederick Douglass, the nation's greatest orator and spokesman for black Americans, donated $200 and lectured on behalf of the association. Keckley unflaggingly toiled to put an end to the abuse and neglect of blacks: "For one kind word spoken, two harsh ones were uttered . . . the road was rugged and full of thorns . . . the mute appeals for help too often were answered by cold neglect. . . . Bright dreams were too rudely dispelled." Her agency became the Freedmen's and Soldiers' Relief Association of Washington when blacks were permitted to join the Union army after the promulgation of the Emancipation Proclamation.[61]

Contrabands experienced the vicissitudes of life as they sought to live as free men and women. In lessons and tracts for their edification bearing appropriate titles such as *Advice to Freedmen* (1863) and *Friendly Counsels for Freedmen* (1864), Northern missionaries urged them to become good Christians and providers for their families, truthful, punctual, sober, and respectful to one another. In 1864 Robert Dale Owen, author of a foresighted volume entitled *The Wrong of Slavery, the Right of Emancipation, and the Future of the African Race in the United States*, proclaimed Southern blacks just as worthy of assistance as white Unionists because both were opponents of secession and needed the protection of the Federal government. A freedmen's bureau would be necessary, Owen predicted, not because slaves were black but because they were human beings who had been deprived of their rights for generations. They were qualified for the same treatment as other free citizens and not to be subjected to compulsory labor, blind contracts, or discriminatory wages. Any supervision over them should be advisory, with no restrictions on their decisions or movements.[62]

Several slaves managed to find happier lives in the North. After Martha Mortimer and her family made their way to New York, she wrote to a friend: "We are very much pleased with the *North*, as well as we expected, & there is but one thing that mars, or one thing that is needed to make us happy now, as other things are working pretty well, that is, *education*, you know what is needed to take us along. Oh! how it makes my blood boil! when I think that *we five Children*, out of eleven, of the same flesh & blood, had to picked out, and placed in darkness. No wonder God has cursed *Virginia*, but there is an old saying, 'no use crying over spilled milk.'" Mortimer's father was also her owner. Her neighbors often asked about slavery and in particular wanted to know if there were many more white slaves in the South.[63]

Northern free blacks extended assistance to their less fortunate Afro-Virginian brethren. A Plymouth, Massachusetts, free black named Norbert visited a contraband camp, adopted a ten-year-old Virginia orphan boy, Austin Smith of Northumberland County, and promised to "care & rear [him] as one of his own family." Back in Virginia, the American Missionary Association established the Ferry Point Orphanage, between Portsmouth and Norfolk, under the supervision of Miss R. G. C. Patten, "a whole-souled friend" of ex-slaves. Among the children in her care were a six-month-old child and its four brothers and sisters whose mother had been accidentally shot by a Union sentry.[64]

The quarrels of black teamsters in army camps became public entertainment for bored soldiers; there were several instances of African-American teamsters lashing each other with their long whips over some petty misunderstanding to the laughter of white spectators. A thousand contrabands in late April 1865 were put to work by Union quartermasters cleaning up Richmond's docks and forced to perform the extremely dangerous task of removing captured Confederate ordnance, a chore better suited to and more appropriate for rebel prisoners of war.

To some Afro-Virginians, their treatment at the hands of the Yankees was not unlike what they had known under the Confederacy, and in some cases it was worse. Alfred Dickinson fled from his owner in 1863 to join the

Union army but received such rough treatment that he deserted a year later while employed as a laborer on the Dutch Gap Canal. Captured by Confederates in Nelson County, Dickinson wore a hand-me-down blue uniform but when asked about his experiences replied that the behavior of both sides very left much to be desired.[65]

4 BODY AND SOUL
Health, Education, and Religion

Once you learn to read you will forever be free.
—*Frederick Douglass*

A new thing under the sun! A Sabbath-school among Virginia freedmen!
—*Reverend Lewis C. Lockwood, 16 September 1861*

As THE war continued slave owners exchanged information on how to keep medical costs down and slaves healthy. One desperate slave owner beseeched a Buckingham County doctor to treat her slave woman in 1862: "The negro woman Spicy is no Better She says She gets weaker every Day and her cough is no Better and complains of [pains?] in her breast. She throws up Every other Day She says the Stuff She throws up is very Bitter. I still continue giving her those drops you sent. . . . She spits some little blood . . . come as soon as you can. . . . Please to send Spicy something to Take I have told you how She complains, She sweats very much of Nights and rests very little."[1]

One planter advised his sons to develop expertise as self-trained general practitioners to provide inexpensive care for their slaves: "Keep a good supply of medicine and study some few works on the practice of medicine. By doing so and by attentively studying the symptoms of ordinary cases of sicknesses you will be able to relieve most of your negroes & thus avoid the expense of sending for a Doctor when unnecessary. . . . Observe with care, think calmly, and if then you find it best to send for a Doctor do so but avoid all silly alarms & precipitations."[2]

Slaveholders fretted over the health of slaves conscripted as military laborers. This concern often placed them on the horns of a dilemma: they wanted to be loyal Confederate citizens but were loath to do so if their slaves were repeatedly placed at risk after being seized by Confederate officers.

Rockbridge County's 2,087 slaves, valued at $735,863 in 1862, were called out to military labor, but this did not preclude slaveholders from seeking exemptions. Henry, a slave of Hetty J. Walker, was certified unfit because he suffered from pneumonia of the left lung and "several hemorrhages." Walker worried that Henry's life would be endangered by exposure to military camps. Amherst County planter Lancelot Minor grumbled in his 1863 diary that the repeated use of his slave by the military during the previous three months was an example of the government's unjustified infringement on the rights of slaveholders: "John has been in 'the service' as they call it . . . since 17 of Sept. greatly to my pecuniary inconvenience . . . is again called away to Richmond from which I scarcely expect him to be returned alive because of small Pox & other diseases. Howbeit it [is] all right except that the Gov. annoyed me greatly in the first instance or the last."[3]

The grumbling of Minor and other Virginia slave masters was not without foundation. Jacob, "a remarkably fine and athletic" twenty-four-year-old slave of "excellent character" belonging to Mary Clark of Washington County, was impressed along with other country slaves by Governor Letcher and sent to work on the Richmond fortifications in February 1863. There he labored for fifty-one days until his discharge on 12 April for return home by rail on the Virginia and Tennessee Railroad. He became violently ill with pneumonia during the trip from exposure suffered while laboring for the military; three Washington County slaves helped him off the train near Emory and Henry College and made their way on foot with him to the home of his mistress's neighbor, William Edmondson.

Anxious to return to his mistress but too ill to continue on foot, Jacob borrowed a horse and, accompanied by two other slaves, proceeded to the Clark residence. A physician, Dr. William Barr of Abingdon, was summoned on the thirteenth at four in the morning, and after a brief examination pronounced the case hopeless but began treating him at Clark's insistence. Jacob's sisters and Clark took turns ministering the sick man with Barr in constant attendance for the next five days, but Jacob died on the morning of 18 April despite all efforts. Clark later petitioned the Confederate Congress for compensation for property "lost to her in the service and defence of the Confederacy" and placed Jacob's value at $3,000.[4]

Slaves owned by W. H. Glenn were ravaged by a whooping cough epidemic during the winter of 1863: "All the negroes have been and some are still sick. Two little babies died not long ago." In March 1863 the slaves of William Gordon of Nelson County began to fall ill, starting with the child of the plantation's cook and dairymaid, Jane. Gordon promptly sent for a doctor when another slave, George, was diagnosed with pneumonia. Two days later Archer, Liz, Sylvia, and George were confined to their beds, Jane was desperately ill despite medications, and only five slaves remained well enough to work. Within twenty-four hours most of the slaves were sick with typhoid.

George and Sylvia were better by the third day of April, but Jane was unquestionably sinking fast. Gordon wrote her epilogue on 4 April: "Poor Jane died in the night—She was a good humble creature and we Shall miss her. . . . George no better, indeed I think him worse." This sympathy did not stand in the way of the plantation's needs, however, and the remaining healthy slaves were put to work sowing food crops and tending tobacco. George, who had been on the mend, suffered a relapse on 5 April caused by diphtheria, and Dr. Callaway seemed powerless to relieve any of the other sufferers. As the slaves weakened on the Gordon plantation, the doctor himself became too sick to visit them. The child of the departed Jane, in whom the sickness had first appeared, died on 15 April. Gradually, the rest of Gordon's slaves recovered, but he feared their health might be permanently impaired, not to mention his own financial situation.[5]

Smyth County slave owner James Ward sent his sick slave, Ann, to Dr. Jacob Haller of Wytheville with a note describing her symptoms as a "roaring & numbness" in her head and promised to send payment later. A slave, especially a female of childbearing age, was a commodity.[6]

Slaveholders kept detailed records on slave purchases, births, marriages, sicknesses, and deaths. John C. Cohoon of Cedar Vale plantation in Nansemond County owned slaves ranging from infants to ancients over the age of sixty. Cohoon, himself a septuagenarian, owned real estate and personal property worth $50,000; his account books meticulously logged the birth and death dates, even the times, of his slaves. They reveal that most of his slaves were born in January and November; the fewest, in February and September. One slave couple, Isaac and Lizzy Hodges, had eleven children between 1837 and 1862. Cohoon's records indicate that of his slaves fifty-nine died as infants or juveniles and thirty-seven as adults.[7]

Planters typically registered slave births under the name of their mothers with the child's name, birth and death dates, and occasionally the name of its father. Slave deaths were recorded for tax purposes, and a few owners went so far as to maintain death records of their former chattels during the postbellum period. The slave register of one unidentified Virginia plantation carefully lists the birth dates and ages of its blacks to June 1865. Of the eighteen births recorded, the months of May, March, January, February, August, and September saw the most births, while June, July, and December had the fewest.[8]

Preservation of the health of slaves was imperiled by insects, especially flies attracted by the heavy perspiration of humans and farm animals; flies were so numerous that people ceased to notice them and halfheartedly brushed them away. Also dangerous were bedbugs, gnats, mosquitoes, lice, and ubiquitous rats and mice. Cleanliness was attempted; household rubbish was regularly swept out or discarded at dumps, abandoned wells, rivers, and holes, but it continually accumulated. Fresh water was needed daily for cooking, drinking, washing, and laundry; its retrieval from wells and rivers was a task usually assigned to women and children. Sewage systems did not exist; slaves used discarded chamber pots or hastily constructed privies or sought discreet areas in woods to relieve themselves.

Doctors earned handsome incomes contracting themselves out to plantations and factories to care for slaves. Dr. J. O'Leary was paid $39.75 in November 1862 for cauterizing throats and cupping and blistering sick slaves belong to Samuel Pannill Wilson, a wealthy Pittsylvania County planter with substantial financial and legal interests in Virginia and North Carolina.[9]

Peter T. Coleman, physician for slaves belonging to the estate of John T. Thornton of Farmville, made twelve visits to sick slaves between 11 and 22 July 1863, which cost Thornton's widow $54 ($4.50 per visit). Dr. B. G. Rennolds of Essex County made thirty-five visits between February 1863 and October 1864 to slaves belonging to Sally H. A. Hunter and charged her $81.50 for lancing abscesses, treating mothers who had recently given birth, and prescribing nitric acid, opium, and vitriol. Blacks who succumbed to disease and misguided medical efforts became anatomical cadavers for state medical schools, the bodies usually stolen from black cemeteries shortly before or after burial. In the hope of avoiding these desecrations, Richmond free blacks established the Union Burial Ground Society; $10 enabled a subscriber to purchase a plot where his family would be eternally safe from grave robbers, and certificates were issued as proof of eligibility for internment.[10]

Few doctors were as busy or successful as Charles E. Davidson of Buckingham County, and his account book is predominately a record of visits to and treatments of slaves on approximately 144 occasions between January 1863 and November 1864. He delivered babies, operated on tonsils, extracted teeth, and at times stayed overnight to dispense pills and monitor a patient's progress. For instance, he treated Lucy, a slave owned by Elias Everett, twenty-nine times between 9 June and 28 September 1863 for tonsil problems and other medical exigencies. Nancy, a slave of A. A. Walton, required long-term obstetrical care after the birth of her child on 16 January 1865. Davidson's fourteen subsequent visits to her cost Walton $5 per visit, and when he was compelled to "replace her womb" on 20 January, his fee was $30.[11]

Nor were such doctors hesitant about issuing prescriptions of rest or disability certificates for their black patients, but it is debatable just how often or for how long owners abided by these medical dictates. A slave named Jordan in Pittsylvania County was certified by Dr. John A. Shelton as too ill for "inclement weather or severe physical Exertion" because he had been suffering from dropsy for four months. Physicians also certified certain slaves as having permanent infirmities that interfered with the amount of work they could perform and their resale value (and incidentally kept them out of the clutches of Confederate conscription officers).[12]

Given a choice, slaves tended to balk at medicines offered by their owners. They used folk cures based on memories of African methods and trial-and-error experimentation with indigenous plants and home remedies. One Afro-Virginian belief held that binding of the leaves of a tulip tree around an afflicted area could soothe rheumatism. Authorities on plantation management recommended a daily regimented schedule for slaves that included time set aside for those claiming to be unwell. Medicine, diet, and treatment were to be administered by the slave owner himself or a slave nurse. Black women of intelligence and experience were chosen for this duty and were trusted to administer plantation medicine. White physicians were to be summoned only for the most critical cases.[13]

Of the two classes of Afro-Virginians, free blacks probably received worse medical care and apparently relied heavily on herbal and traditional African-American medicine. The prescription and appointment books of white doctors infrequently mention them unless they were treated for injuries or diseases contracted while serving with labor battalions or in civilian industries. Blacks could not legally practice medicine even for other blacks, but exceptions did occur. (The first African-American woman to earn a medical degree was a native of Richmond, Rebecca Lee. She was graduated from the New England Women's Medical College, Boston, in 1864.)[14]

The potential loss of any slave by accident or otherwise caused some slaveholders to purchase slave life insurance policies. Slaves had to be examined for soundness before the policies were issued; they were valued at two-thirds their market value, with rates for one to five years. A policy for a male slave valued at $700 cost $11.85; covered losses were to be paid sixty to ninety days after proof of death. Policies were null and void if slaves were transported or escaped beyond the borders of the state or died as a result of suicide, dueling, war, "neglect, abuse or mistreatment by his owner" (or the policy's beneficiary), participation in riots, insurrections, or "by the hands of justice." An 1863 policy issued to Joseph Myers insured a Richmond slave named George for a thousand dollars at an annual premium of $17.40 and prohibited his employment on any railroad or steam or sailing vessel, as a miner, or in the manufacture and transportation of gunpowder.

William Guy, agent for the Lynchburg Hose and Fire Company, promoted his company's services (premiums cost $13 per year for a male slave) in this regard not just in Lynchburg but also in Staunton. A. F. Kinney, representing the Albemarle Insurance Company, promised affordable slave insurance "on most reasonable terms." Danville had at least two such companies:

J. M. Johnston's Insurance Agency (it insured slaves for up to four years) and the Danville Insurance Company. The latter's agent, W. W. Flood, was responsible for providing insurance coverage of slaves in Pittsylvania, Henry, and Franklin counties. In the event of death, there were stringent requirements to be met before companies paid claims. A physician's certificate describing the cause and duration of the illness, date of death, and physical description of the deceased slave and an affidavit from the sexton or undertaker who prepared the remains and saw them interred were required. The Petersburg office of the North Carolina Mutual Life Insurance boasted of having paid to one Thomas Smith the sum of $1,000 for the loss of a Virginia slave named Henry.[15]

Northern companies such as the American Life Insurance and Trust Company of Philadelphia offered slave insurance through local agents: "Thousands of Dollars are saved yearly to slave owners, by Life Insurance. This renders them permanent property, equal to real estate!!! Insurance on Slaves for one or five years, the insurer having the privilege of discontinuing the policy at the end of any year; the Company obligating themselves to continue the insurance to the full term of years, if desired by the insurer. Slaves insured between the ages of 8 and 60 years, to remain in Virginia, or to go to and reside in any slaveholding State in the Union." Several companies offering these policies regularly advertised in newspapers; in July 1861 the Virginia Fire & Marine Insurance Company assured its policyholders that neither war nor Yankees could dislodge its liabilities and willingness to assume risks; to customers who renewed their policies it promised business as usual.[16] However, the number of slave insurance ads and companies declined during 1864–65.

Slave infirmaries were established at plantations, and hospitals were opened for hired-out slaves working and residing in urban areas. A year before the war a large hospital for them opened in Richmond. This facility provided a spacious and airy retreat overlooking the James River. Its six physicians (three as full-time residents) were "polite, intelligent, and attentive." The building could accommodate up to forty patients and was wallpapered from basement to attic. The first floor contained a reception room; the second floor, a laboratory. The weekly rate for rooms was $5, each with clean beds and fresh water. Twelve days after its opening it housed sixteen slave patients, indicative of the need for such a facility.

A Richmond correspondent hailed it as "an convenience and of great public utility," for it made available the best personal comfort for sick slaves. But the existence of hospitals and infirmaries for slaves should not be misin-

TABLE 4.1. HOSPITALIZED UNION PRISONERS AND BLACKS AT VARIOUS
VIRGINIA HOSPITALS, 1864–65

Date	Hospital	POW	Blacks
26 March 1864	Richmond, no. 13	5	5
30 June 1864	Richmond (Receiving)	53	4
30 June 1864	Gordonsville (Receiving)	53	4
30 June 1864	Petersburg (Nolea)	0	31
8 Oct 1864	Richmond, no. 13	10	4
8 March 1865	Richmond, no. 13	7	8
Total		128	56

Note: The Petersburg figures are for slaves only.

Source: Folder "Confederate States Army, Office of the Medical Director, Reports. . . , 1862–1865," Papers of the Chase Family, box 5, LC.

terpreted as evidence that they always received good medical care; some were forced to work despite injuries or illnesses. One owner wrote to the slave-trading firm of Dickinson, Hill & Company in Richmond to offer a slave woman for sale even though she had a serious burn: "It does not hurt her in the least as I have had her working at the hoe several days at a time with no complaint." When Charles Gandy accidentally cut his elbow with a sickle while working in the fields, the wound was treated with chimney soot.[17]

Along with Union prisoners, free blacks and slaves were treated at Virginia's Confederate military hospitals. Of 184 Union prisoners of war and blacks treated at hospitals at Gordonsville, Petersburg, and Richmond, 30 percent were Afro-Virginians (table 4.1). As yet another instance of the Confederate paradox of humanity and inhumanity toward blacks, Governor Letcher expressed concern to the General Assembly over the treatment of twelve slave and free black Afro-Virginian convicts recently returned from laboring on public works and fortifications in May 1861.

Letcher reported the black men as having "very grave and dangerous fevers, and some bowel affections." Adam, a slave, had an unhealed left hand from which four fingers had been amputated. "Very feeble, badly used, and much whipped" was Letcher's description of the condition of another slave, Sam, who, in addition to his mistreatment, suffered from phthisis (tuberculosis). Six free blacks fared little better: Emanuel Rick, "very filthy and lousy [i.e., infected with lice]," had undressed wounds consisting of severe contusions and lacerations; one on the inside of his leg was four inches long and constantly exposed to dirt and insects. John Gaines was heavily scarred from severe and too-frequent whippings, and Spencer Pennington suffered from a compound fracture of the left leg near the knee; his injury had not been treated at all. Letcher opposed this sort of treatment and urged reforms.[18]

Some slaves suffering from insanity were admitted to one of the state's two asylums, Western Lunatic (Staunton) or Eastern Lunatic (Williamsburg). They were admitted upon application by their owners "for reasons of humanity as well as other considerations" as long as their admittance did not preclude that of whites. Free blacks were not segregated from white patients, but they were among the last patients scheduled for treatment. White inmates were permitted to treat them as their personal servants. Other insane slaves were cared for on plantations and closely watched "from a respectable distance" lest they harm themselves or others. Virginia law prohibited owners from letting unbalanced slaves roam at large without adequate supervision or provision for their needs.[19]

Afro-Virginians who were handicapped by mental or other diseases were at the mercy of whites and blacks alike. A slave named James stole $25 from a black mute known as "Dummy" during July 1862 but could not be prosecuted because no one could adequately interpret the mute's testimony. Two months later another slave, also named "Dummy," a deaf-mute woman, obtained justice when William, a slave of Powhatan Roberts, was ordered twenty lashes for assaulting her. While on trial in 1864 for stealing a basket of apples, a male slave named Ransom fell into an epileptic fit after being pronounced guilty. Police officers in the courtroom confused his "spasm" for an escape attempt, and three of them tackled him to prevent it. An eyewitness noted of the ensuing struggle that "such rolling and tumbling, kicking and blowing . . . never was, perhaps witnessed in the halls of justice before." The policemen subdued their prisoner but only after receiving extensive bruises and sprains. Ransom was sentenced to a whipping.[20]

Another critical consideration was adequate housing. The quality of the so-called Virginia slave cabins varied greatly; some white observers and blacks themselves described them as meager dwellings that barely had walls or a roof. Ex-slave Louis Hughes described his cabin as a single-room structure of rough logs daubed with mud or clay about fourteen feet square. The floor was dirt, and the only furniture was a bed, a table, and benches. Interior lighting was provided by grease lamps made of iron bowls with rag wicks, and Hughes added that most slave cabins were occupied by two or more families. Austin Steward, another Afro-Virginian slave, agreed: "As was the usual custom, we lived in a small cabin, built of rough boards," with a floor of earth; the entire structure "was put together in the rudest possible manner." Other slaves recalled being housed in barns with farm animals or small huts sheltering as many as sixteen persons and sleeping on mattresses stuffed with straw or chicken feathers. Entire families lived in single rooms behind the houses of their owners or employers.[21]

Booker T. Washington remembered his mother's home as a small log cabin, twelve by sixteen feet, lacking windows. In the center was an opening where sweet potatoes were stored for their owner's family during the winter. Washington's mother cooked meals for the master's family in the cabin as her family slept on pallets made of old rags on the floor. But there were slaveholders who established elaborate specifications for slave quarters. William Massie, a slave owner in Nelson and Rockbridge Counties, ordered a standard set of plans for "framed Negro houses" that were to include three rooms (two were to be thirteen by eleven feet, and one would be twenty-two by eleven feet), each with a door and a fireplace in the center having a hearth three feet wide and a stone chimney. These cabins, comprising twenty-eight by twenty-two feet, could be modified into a two-room frame house for small families or "married men without children." The majority of slave cabins were flimsy, one-room firetraps that were poorly heated and ventilated. A British tourist condemned them as "miserable dwellings" of the worst kind. The shanties of free blacks were hardly better; a white Norfolk schoolteacher described the homes of free black families as little more than hovels with sparse, dilapidated furniture. In their unhygienic and crowded living quarters, the lives of slaves could not have been easy.[22]

When left to their own devices some slaves employed resourcefulness in fabricating comfortable abodes. A runaway slave named Bob built a home for his wife and two sons which escaped detection during the war. Using stolen lumber and a camouflaged cave near a creek, he constructed a ten-foot-square living room with underground piping to carry off smoke and waste, a bed of rails and mattresses made of his wife's old dresses, sawed-off blocks as chairs, and a rock-and-brick fireplace for heating and cooking. This dwelling was so secure that Bob and his family frequently invited other slaves to dine with them.[23]

Slave cabins were whitewashed inside and out for aesthetic and hygienic reasons. Often uncomfortably congested, they were prone to dampness due to leaky roofs and dirt floors. Window openings permitted the necessary modicum of light. Illumination from candles made of animal fat or discarded wax candle stubs became necessary as soon as dusk fell. Virginia was a land of intense heat in summer and cold nights in winter. In the cabins chimneys and fireplaces provided heat and enabled cooking but also meant smoke-laden air breathed by inhabitants and low ceilings covered with deposits of flaking soot. Brushwood, dried animal manure, and vegetable and wood scraps were sources of fuel. Ex-slave Georgia Gibbs remembered fireplaces as the only source of light in her parents' home; fire was produced by striking rocks against pieces of steel to ignite cotton scraps.[24]

Private Henry Martyn Cross of the 48th Massachusetts Volunteers noticed that young unmarried males and old slave men at Fort Monroe were housed in long buildings resembling barracks; unmarried women and families were housed in separate buildings. These structures were whitewashed on the outside and spotlessly clean inside; the single women's quarters were patrolled by soldiers. A Northern missionary described the outskirts of Yorktown as "a city of Negro cabins," each with low doorways, dim lighting, and crowded but neat. Industrious blacks built houses only to have them taken by white Union soldiers too lazy to do such labor. An example of this took place shortly after Confederates burned and abandoned the town of Hampton in 1861. Although only chimneys survived the fire, black families soon built cozy shanties that were so sturdy and attractive that Union soldiers evicted them and commandeered the buildings for themselves. Housing was scarce after the war; ironically, homeless ex-slaves had to seek shelter in the ruins of Confederate fortifications.[25]

Former Confederate general Robert E. Lee journeyed to the national capital in 1866 to be questioned by congressmen about the state of race relations in Virginia. Among the questions put to Lee by Senator Jacob M. Howard of Michigan and Representative Henry T. Blow of Missouri of the Joint Committee on Reconstruction were several pertaining to the education of the freedpeople. Lee stated his belief that their old masters only wished to treat them fairly. Asked about the willingness of whites for blacks to receive an education, he replied that he felt whites would welcome it. But when asked to compare black capacity for knowledge with that of white men, Lee's responses made it clear that whites persisted in believing blacks unqualified for anything other than manual labor:

> Question. General, you are very competent to judge the capacity of black men for acquiring knowledge: I want your opinion on that capacity, as compared with the capacity of white men?
>
> Answer. I do not know that I am particularly qualified on that subject as you seem to intimate; but I do not think that he is as capable of acquiring knowledge as the white man is. There are some more apt than others. I have known some to acquire knowledge and skill in their trade or profession. I have had servants of my own who learned to read and write very well.

In contrast, two weeks before Lee's appearance, the testimony of a black Virginian, Thomas Bain, on the abilities and wants of his race was a direct challenge to notions about the so-called innate ineptitude of blacks:

Question. Are the black people down there [in Virginia] fond of education?

Answer. I think that they are excelled by no people in an eagerness to learn.[26]

Before the Civil War, Afro-Virginians normally did not attend public schools. Most desired to learn, but for a slave to have as much as a written piece of paper (other than a legitimate pass from his master) in his possession was enough to warrant punishment. In the last census before the war, only forty Virginia free blacks were officially attending school. Schools for blacks, even private ones, were subject to extralegal suppression by racial vigilantes. Mrs. Margaret Douglass, a white woman who moved from Charleston, South Carolina, to Norfolk in 1845, was arrested in 1852 and charged with violating the state law that forbade the educational instruction of free black children; a decade passed before another school opened its doors for Norfolk's black children. Nevertheless, the anti–black education laws of 1831 and 1848 were ignored by similar-minded individuals who continued to teach their slaves; because of underground schools in such urban areas as Alexandria, Fredericksburg, Norfolk, Petersburg, and Richmond, many free blacks survived only because they were resourceful and literate.[27]

Slave parents were anxious for their children to learn how to read and write even though such erudition could result in their being sold or put to death. Joseph E. Jones, born a slave in Lynchburg in 1850, was sent to work in a city tobacco factory, but his mother wanted more than a life of slavery and illiteracy for her son. She hired the services of a literate slave to teach him until the slave teacher was caught and sold in 1864. This setback did not deter her, for she then hired a convalescent Confederate soldier as a tutor for Joseph. This arrangement lasted until April 1865 and provided the foundation for his future career. Jones later studied at a private school in Lynchburg, the Richmond Institute, and Madison University in Hamilton, New York. After completing his studies in 1876 and earning an M.A. degree, he was ordained a Baptist minister and appointed professor of Greek at the Richmond Theological Seminary. His life's successes were due to his mother's determination, courage, and resourcefulness in nurturing the abilities of her son.[28]

Blacks learned their letters in secret at Sunday and Bible schools, at isolated farms and in the woods, or wherever sympathetic whites concerned for their welfare could teach them without fear of angry mobs. As slaves took advantage of the war to flee to freedom, the first organized public schools for blacks were begun near Fort Monroe by Mary Peake, a respected and devout free black woman, and at Columbia Street School in Alexandria, operated by Mary Chase. Both schools opened in September 1861, and of the two, Chase's is considered the first wartime school for the state's ex-slaves.

Peake, born in Norfolk in 1823 to a British father and a Virginia free black mother, received her education in Alexandria at a private black school. White vigilance committees tried but failed to thwart Peake's educational mission; within two weeks of her school's opening in Hampton she had forty-five students who learned not only spelling, reading, writing, singing, and arithmetic but also the Lord's Prayer and similar religious texts. Her husband, Thomas, worked as a Union spy. Mary Peake died in 1862 at age thirty-nine from overwork and tuberculosis just four months after founding her school. She was survived by her husband and a five-year-old daughter, Hattie.

The first request of contrabands upon reaching the safety of Union lines was for schools and education for their children. Education was a hazardous subject for Confederate Virginia's blacks. At Camp Porter in January 1862 a slave woman told Oliver Wilcox Norton of the 83d Pennsylvania Volunteer Infantry that her husband had been beaten for refusing to work on rebel fortifications near Leesburg and she had been whipped for trying to learn how to read. Two blacks were arrested in Alexandria in 1863 for "violating the laws of Virginia in keeping a school for Negroes," but nineteen schools were taught by or for the city's Afro-Virginians between May 1861 and September 1864. Albert Jones, a Southampton County slave, recalled, "You better never let mastah catch yer wif a book or paper. . . . If yer done dem things, he sho' would beat yer."[29]

Northerners who came to the Old Dominion as missionaries and teachers for the freedpeople were consternated by the neglected condition of its public education system. These educators, chiefly Yankee schoolmarms with their New England tradition of public schools for all, enthusiastically plunged into their work. The American Missionary Association established schools at Fort Monroe on 3 September 1863 and soon followed with other schools at Arlington Heights, Harpers Ferry, Hampton, Norfolk, Portsmouth, and Ferry Point. By January 1864 the association had sent more than a hundred missionaries to Virginia who founded several schools for blacks. The New England Freedmen's Aid Society (founded in Boston on 7 February 1862) answered the call to teach, clothe, and feed Southern slaves and was "prepared to go anywhere where it [could] be most useful." From Alexandria in December 1864 J. S. Banfield reported that with each passing day his students' interest in their lessons grew. Classes were taught on "the

New-England plan" with three hours of instruction in the morning and in the evening for as long as there was daylight.

S. V. Lawton, who opened his school on 14 November 1864, described his 130 students as progressing far beyond his expectations. Thanks to a recent coat of whitewash and his pupils' passion for learning, his was the best black school in Alexandria. From City Point, Reverend Charles Lowe of the New England Freedmen's Aid Society observed Afro-Virginian employees of the Sanitary Commission at the end of their workday: all six, boys aged sixteen to eighteen, were seated at tables with spelling books and primers in hand learning how to read despite a long, hard day of work. "I know of nothing more gratifying," wrote Lowe approvingly, "in connection with the emerging of a people out of bondage."[30]

Missionaries such as Lowe believed the ex-slaves could, with proper training, become productive, self-sufficient citizens. Areas of tidewater and the peninsula became havens for escaped slaves who learned of contraband camps by word of mouth. Craney Island, located at the mouth of the Elizabeth River near Norfolk, became one of the first such sanctuaries shortly after the capture of that city in 1862. Three teachers were sent by the Educational Committee of Boston; more arrived by the following May. The committee's goals were "to improve the industrial, social, intellectual, moral, and religious" behavior of the freedpeople, and representatives were to teach them the responsibilities of freedom.[31]

Fort Monroe was a significant site of black educational refuge. An $8,000 building capable of accommodating 700 pupils was constructed in December 1864 under the supervision of the office of the superintendent of public education. Federal authorities hoped more of these government schools would be established at places where a large and permanent black population could contribute students and tax dollars to underwrite them. To secure the viability of the government schools and other similar ones, Afro-Virginian children over the age of five and under the age of fourteen were ordered to attend unless gainfully employed; parents who violated this order were to be fined or imprisoned. The government schools, as part of General Butler's Eastern District of Virginia, were headquartered at Fort Monroe's Chesapeake Hospital. Male principals were paid $60 a month, female principals, $30. Soldiers' widows and wives and disabled veterans were preferred as instructors; advertisements for the schools were printed in Boston newspapers.[32]

Approximately nineteen black schools were situated on government farms by February 1864, plantations and estates abandoned by slave owners such as the Taylor Farm near Norfolk and the Whitehead Farm near Portsmouth where a hundred ex-slave families divided the land among themselves, built cabins, grew crops, and sought teachers for their children. A school for black children was founded at Yorktown in June 1864 and consisted of a day school of 300 students and a night school for adults. A nearby contraband village, "Slabtown," possessed its own school and 400 students. Sherwood Forest, the Charles City County estate of John Tyler, near Camp Hamilton, was the site of a school for 2,500 students as old as twenty-five and as young as six years old.

Tyler's mansion opened on 15 September 1861 as a school for blacks and was divided into day and evening classes. The latter were attended by elderly blacks in their sixties, seventies, and eighties, most of whom had but one unpretentious ambition: "I want to be able to read the Bible before I die." Academic exercises included singing, recitations, and spellers, and the teachers reported their students to be quick learners. Sunday school classes for blacks were also held on the grounds. An ex-slave named Carey gave thanks to God, "Though I cannot read thy word I thank thee that thou has written it on the table of my heart, and given me an understanding mind and kept it blazing before my eyes like the sun."[33]

Other than at Fort Monroe offshore Hampton, perhaps the largest concentration of ex-slaves in Virginia was at Norfolk where black schools opened shortly after the arrival of Union occupation forces. School was a new experience for most of the black children, and Northern teachers such as Angelina Ball learned to adjust to their daily patterns: "I have a class of twenty little boys and girls, just learning their letters, coming to school for the first time; and some of them are so full of fun and frolic that it is difficult for them to sit still long at a time, so I take pity on them, and let them go before school is dismissed." The city, divided into three districts with ten teachers each, saw its first black schools being held in churches such as Bute Street Baptist and Fenchurch Street Methodist. One instructor, William L. Coan, conducted a primary day school and evening classes for 1,245 students who studied arithmetic, geography, and history. Plans were made for an industrial school to teach sewing and similar domestic skills. H. R. Smith, another teacher, declared that the black students were progressing as well as, if not better than, white students.

Smith and other ambassadors of learnedness did not confine their endeavors exclusively to the classroom but visited the homes of their students to reinforce and promote the Christian-American traditional family ethic. However, in their letters and reports Northern teachers continued to utilize the standard paternalistic references that has always been applied to blacks: "our little sable friends," "old aunties and uncles," "I have decided that they are capable of being instructed," "wonderfully docile," "they seemed so wild," and "the characteristic [mental] weaknesses of the race."[34]

Mary C. Fletcher, a teacher responsible for fifty students, was among the white Northerners who expressed unconscious racism. She considered black education a success and urged her fellow Northerners to assist the work under way in the Old Dominion. Fletcher had an answer for those who believed it was a foolish waste of time and money to educate blacks for anything other than the kitchen or the plow: "I only wish our Northern friends, who have so strong a prejudice against this oppressed race, could see for themselves how great progress they make, and how they appreciate what we do for them; then, I believe, their prejudice would vanish, and their blindness be removed."[35]

As might be expected, local whites vehemently opposed black education, and students were assaulted. During May 1864 a school at Harpers Ferry was stoned, its windows were broken, and the students and their teachers were verbally harassed. W. W. Wheeler described the town as "a wicked place" and rhetorically asked, "But what more could be expected in the place where John Brown was delivered to the gallows?" Union troops, too, contributed to the harassment of ex-slaves. On 6 August 1862, in Newport News and Hampton, black males were rounded up and taken away by cavalrymen to serve McClellan's army; their homes and shops were plundered, and those who resisted were shot. After pleas by their wives and children to white schoolteachers and General Dix, the men were released when an officer declared the seizures had been a mistake. On the other hand, some Union soldiers volunteered to teach at black schools. But most Afro-Virginians were patient in their sufferings and quietly went about the business of work and education.[36]

Northern education missionaries praised their pupils and the determination of black parents that their children be educated despite the odds. In Norfolk and Portsmouth, of 19,000 ex-slaves, 2,000 were in school by May 1862. None of these students had ever been expelled for unruly behavior, and William Coan, by now superintendent for education, reported that more than three thousand books had been issued with encouraging results. Miss S. L. Daffin, herself an African-American, and other teachers noted their pupils' "strict adherence to the truth, which has been observed in a variety of instances."

Another instructor added, "All is tranquil and peaceful now, and will be while Major-General Butler is at the head of the military department." When a black clergyman from Syracuse, New York, Reverend J. W. Loguen, visited the Old Dominion in 1864, he saw progress among Afro-Virginians and congratulated them on their well-scrubbed schools and classrooms equipped with the latest textbooks, chalkboards, and maps. But he was ever mindful of what remained to be accomplished: "Our white friends seem to be endeavoring by [their] efforts to remove the blot from the country's escutch-eon. But I am convinced that work is ours. We must come forward, make sacrifices, and take our own position for the elevation of our people. . . . If we do not we shall be ashamed hereafter that we have not done so."[37] Lo-guen, Daffin, and their fellow blacks, through dedication, a spirit of charity, and experience, caused their Northern missionary companions to under-stand that Afro-Virginians were capable of reaching for the beckoning light of knowledge.

At the outset of the war there were approximately 417,000 black Christians in the South: 215,000 Methodists, 157,000 Baptists, 38,000 Presbyterians, and 7,000 Protestant Episcopalians. On the subject of religion Afro-Virginians widely believed they were God's chosen people and that he had promised to set them free. This "promise" was derived from the example of the Hebrews who had been held in bondage in Egypt. A slave named Aunt Aggy for twenty years had predicted the freeing of the slaves: "I allers knowed it was a-comin. I allers heerd de rumblin' o' de wheels. I allers 'spected to see white folks heaped up dead. An' de Lor', He's kept His promise, an' 'venged His people, jes' as I knowed He would."[38]

Slaves were willing converts to Christianity, but many Afro-Virginians noted the hypocrisy of religion as practiced by whites. Catherine Broun of Middleburg, Loudoun County, took pride in reading the Bible aloud to her slaves on Sunday evenings and praying with them, and it was her heartfelt belief they all had a good time worshiping together. Slaves thought other-wise, and one Virginia slave woman said: "My mistress was a dreadful pious woman. She would pray, ever so long in the morning, then come out and sit down in her rocking chair, with her cowhide [whip] and cut and slash everybody who passed her. . . . Sometimes I was afraid she was not a Chris-tian, but she was mighty pious." A Fauquier County slave angrily rejected his wife's efforts to convince him to join the church. "How can Jesus be just, if He will allow such oppression and wrong?" he exploded. "Don't the slaveholders justify their conduct by the Bible itself, and say that it tells them to do so? How can God be just, when He not only permits, but sanctions such conduct?"[39]

One proslavery advocate wrote: "The master . . . lays no claim to the soul of the slave. He demands no spiritual service of him, he exacts no divine honors. With his own soul he [the slave] is fully permitted to serve his God." But this statement was in contradiction to a host of laws which denied to blacks freedom of worship or access to Bibles. *De Bow's Review*, a monthly journal devoted to Southern issues, made no effort to excuse white hypoc-risy; not only did it claim an absence of Christianity among free blacks, but it also held that blacks were to be the slaves of either man (whites) or Satan, and furthermore having whites as their natural masters was part of God's worldly order. Yet however religion might be used to control blacks, at the same time it bonded them together as a community, kept alive their hopes of freedom, and made them tougher human beings physically, mentally, morally, and spiritually. One British citizen, irritated by the apparent incapacity of American Northerners and Southerners to settle religious and social problems except through war, exclaimed, "Which of the these two Christian peoples are [we] to pray for?"[40]

Religion as believed and practiced by slaves was paradoxical. Christianity urged resistance to oppression in the Old Testament but taught acceptance of fate and obedience to masters in the New Testament. Faith provided spiritual solace, participation and emotional release through worship, the surreptitious development of a black intelligentsia (preachers, ministers, deacons), and the sense of community in a hostile society. Religion was employed by whites as another method of controlling slaves, and the slaves knew it.

They rejected those parts of Christianity they viewed as inappropriate or hypocritical and created an Afro-Christianity which promised deliverance from earthly slavery, encouraged respect toward one another, and held out the hope of freedom. John Lovell described the spiritual life of a slave "as so full of conflicts of great size that without religion, or something like it he could not have mentally and emotionally survived." Slaves were morally bound to submit patiently to slavery; their owners expected they would serve whites in heaven. The slaves took it for granted that in the afterlife they would be free.[41]

This spiritual nourishment came in many forms, including spirituals, and in them slaves expressed hopes for an end to their bondage; many had double meanings such as those which sang of the Hebrew exodus ("Let My People Go"), "going home," and similar yearnings for freedom. Slaves were known to escape by using the excuse of attending religious services; unsuspecting slave owners, believing churchgoing slaves could be trusted, permitted them to attend services, but some of the good-byes turned into "gone to the Yankees."[42]

Although black churches existed in cities such as Alexandria, Fredericksburg, Lynchburg, Manchester, Norfolk, Petersburg, and Richmond, white ministers usually conducted their services. Dabney Carr Harrison, a Presbyterian, preached to crowds of blacks in Tappahannock, Essex County; they were said to prefer hearing him rather than black preachers. Harrison and ministers like him proudly spoke of their evangelical work among the slaves, which also served as a means to promote slave submissiveness.

Ex-slave Peter Randolph remembered slaves as needing passes to attend services and being freely permitted to dance but not to pray. They were also told, "It is the devil who tells you to be free," but he acknowledged that church services enabled him momentarily to forget his sufferings as a slave and the falseness of the slaveholders' gospel. Nancy Williams of Petersburg complained, "That ol' white preacher used to talk with their tongues without saying nothing, but Jesus told us slaves to talk with our hearts." West Turner agreed and summed up the Bible lessons sanctioned by his master: "Be nice to Masa and Missus, don't be mean; be obedient, and work hard. That was all the Sunday school lesson they taught us." [43]

In the strictest legal sense, only white clergyman could baptize, conduct marriages and burial services, and administer communion to blacks in the churches of Virginia, but there were inherent dangers for black parishioners at white churches. A Prince George County slave named Jem Fulcrum fell asleep one Sunday morning during a sermon by a white minister named Shell who just happened to be his owner. The minister sanctimoniously waited until Monday morning before punishing Fulcrum's transgression. One eyewitness recalled that Fulcrum received "enough cow-hide to last him all the week."

White observers of black churches felt confident that blacks were satisfied with Christianity. A visitor to Richmond's First African Baptist Church during the height of the war praised the all-black congregation as quiet, devotional, and having a good understanding of the Scriptures. The black pastor of Petersburg's African Baptist Church, Reverend Daniel Jackson, after purchasing freedom for himself and his wife Amy in 1819 by paying their respective masters nearly $1,200, ministered to his fellow blacks from 1819 to 1865. Most slaves did not have the luxury of their own formally established church because they were kept busy on isolated farms. Booker T. Washington came to realize that he was a slave because his mother, unable to attend church, would whisper fervent prayers in their cabin every morning that she and her children might be free. [44]

Afro-Virginian churches frequently were visited as tourist attractions by curious Northern soldiers and civilians. In June 1863 Henry E. Simmons visited one such church at the Uniontown contraband camp near Suffolk and described it as made of split logs, with board seats and a dirt floor. Services began at ten in the morning and usually lasted all day with the 300-member congregation on their knees crying aloud, praying, and singing. Their minister preached for fifteen minutes, and Simmons thought it a far better sermon than the one-hour orations customarily delivered by his regimental chaplain. One of the worshipers prayed: "Now Lord didn't you say when one or two ware cum together in your name you come & be wid em?

Now we want you to come jist as you said you would." Another prayed aloud, "De good Lord take dese ere mourners & skake em ober hell but don't luff 'em go." But an employee of the United States Military Railroads at Alexandria, David Probert, who visited a City Point "Neggor Meeting," dismissed it as nothing but a great deal of noise. Another Union soldier, John Albert Monroe, intrigued after regularly hearing voices in the distance, discovered a black prayer meeting in a barn near Falmouth. The building was crammed with kneeling worshipers "shouting and praying." Monroe also saw a living circle comprised of members of both sexes stomping their feet and singing "with the most earnest expressions of countenance." The entire ceremony reminded him of a troupe of jubilee singers.[45]

Tourists at Fort Monroe who witnessed an afternoon worship service in October 1862 came away with more respect for Afro-Christians. In the words of one, "Of a truth I perceive that God is no respecter of persons, but in every nation, he that feareth Him and worketh righteousness is accepted with Him." The black preacher who conducted the service spoke with a "simple eloquence" and led inspiring prayers calling for mercy, forgiveness, and God's protection of President Lincoln and his blessings on the United States. In a similar vein William Davis, an ex-slave from Hampton, addressed an audience of whites in February 1864 on the topic of Christian freedom. Davis claimed that while he was a slave he owned a Bible and prayed daily. He boldly rebuked whites for not accepting blacks as fellow Christians and declared that slaves were superior Christians, for only they knew how to pray properly.

He and dozens of black preachers took advantage of the war to establish churches for their race. Clement Robinson, an ex-slave from Alexandria, became pastor of Beulah Baptist and somehow found time to teach 200 students at a local freedpeople's school. Alexandria possessed at least three black churches in addition to Beulah Baptist (founded in 1863): Alfred Street Baptist (which obtained its first black minister, Reverend Samuel Madden, in 1863), Roberts Chapel, and Zion Baptist (founded in 1864). Hampton blacks founded Zion Baptist and First Baptist. But Afro-Virginians, too, were sectarian in their practice of religion. Afro-Baptists eschewed Methodist hymns, and their ministers shrank from addressing Methodist congregations. Baptist ministers who tried to preach to Presbyterians were shouted down from the pulpit. When asked why most of his race was Baptist, one Afro-Presbyterian minister in Charlotte County tartly replied, "Nothing but ignorance." Afro-Virginian preachers who prayed for and supported the Confederacy were ostracized by their congregations.[46]

William Roscoe Davis, a Norfolk ex-slave, became a lay minister among his people at Fort Monroe in 1861. He never doubted God would free the slaves, and he earned a reputation as an excellent orator. During 1862 Davis undertook a lecture tour sponsored by the American Missionary Association to New York, Massachusetts, and New Hampshire where his intuitive preaching skills raised money on behalf of Afro-Virginians. After the war he was an influential and respected member of Hampton's black community; he founded a school and eventually accepted a federal appointment as a lighthouse keeper.[47]

Preeminent among Afro-Virginian folk preachers was John Jasper who preached his widely acclaimed sermon, "De Sun Do Move," over 250 times. His legend is commemorated among blacks in a folk ballad:

Now all you people kin come,
Tell you whar Jasper took his text from;
God told Joshua to speak to de sun,
Sun stop till right over Gideon.
"De sun do move!"
"De sun do move!"

The "Sun" sermon was not written down until after the war, but there are circumstantial indications that Jasper used portions of it for his wartime sermons.[48]

William Wells Brown, a black abolitionist and contemporary of Jasper, described him as a dark-skinned, tall, slim man with long arms and round shoulders. As one of Virginia's most sought-after speakers, he had a knowledge of the Bible that was matched by few preachers. Born on the Fourth of July in 1812 in Fluvanna County as the twenty-fourth child of his slave parents Philip and Tina, John Jasper answered a vocation that would lead him preach in every city in the state and more than two-thirds of its counties. He began his career shortly after his conversion to Christianity on his twenty-seventh birthday, starting out as a funeral preacher. His master, Samuel Hargrove, supported his conversion and allowed him to preach but charged Jasper a dollar for each workday he missed in order to deliver funeral sermons. A fellow slave taught him how to read, and from then on Jasper's primer was the Bible.

Nineteenth-century Virginia funerals were notable occasions, and eulogies, after brief but respectful references to the deceased, usually focused on weighty spiritual and theological questions and lasted several hours. Slaves traveled great distances to attend, and hasty funerals were considered indecent, even disrespectful. At grave sites blacks were able to vent their grief as well as other powerful emotions arising from their bondage in ways socially acceptable to jittery slaveholders. White persons usually monitored these events.

Such was Jasper's popularity as a funeral speaker that he was able to preach through the end of the war at Confederate hospitals and camps throughout the state and was pastor at Petersburg's Third Baptist Church (although officially it had a white minister). His two most famous sermons, "De Sun Do Move" and "Whar Sin Kum Frum," survive as examples of Afro-Christian oratorical power, majesty, cadence, and soul-stirring timelessness even though they are usually printed in slave dialect.

In his "Sin" sermon Jasper argued that evil came from the doings of man, not God: "Don't you dare ever to say, or think, or to hope, that the temptation to do wrong things comes from God. It does not come from above, but it comes out of your foul and sinful heart." One of his biographers (there were at least four between 1884 and 1954) said of him: "He was a master of assemblies. No politician could handle a crowd with more consummate tact than he. He . . . could sway throngs as the wind shakes the trees. . . . [He] took fire and on eagles' wings he mounted into the heavens and gave such brilliant and captivating addresses that vast crowds went wild with joy and enthusiasm."

The attendance of slave owners at his sermons was proof to some that Christianity could coexist with slavery. "De Sun Do Move," usually preached to whites, was derived largely from the Old Testament books of Joshua (chapters 1–15) and Exodus (15:3). It discusses the continuing fulfillment of Jehovah's promise of the Promised Land (Canaan) to his chosen people, the Israelites. Unbeknownst to his white listeners, Jasper was challenging the foundations of black slavery as a basic tenet of Protestantism. When he exhorted his audiences to "stick with the Bible," he actually meant two different things: for whites to become more humane masters (preferably ex-masters) and for Afro-Virginians to hold on to their faith even though the Bible approved of slavery.[49]

All things considered, Christianity did not eclipse or entirely replace superstitions and folk beliefs among blacks and whites. One Fauquier County slaveholder, upon hearing the distant rumble of thunder and lightning, would hurriedly order at least twenty of his slaves to enter his sitting room and stand in a circle close to him while he sat in their midst. He believed that God would not use lightning to kill poor slaves and hoped that by their presence he, too, might be spared from divine retributive thunderbolts.[50]

Richmond slave Richard Toler recalled how the stinginess of his mistress and her subsequent death was seen by her slaves as a sign of God's displeasure. This woman, Mrs. Henry Toler, was a widow who on Christmas

Eve brusquely refused her slaves' request for additional rations of flour for bread and threatened them with whippings for bothering her. She died mysteriously and suddenly on Christmas Day: "She pulled one boot on, and when she bent over to git the other boot, she just fell over dead." Phenomena such as this surely put the fear of God into some slave owners and became subtle warnings against depriving slaves some enjoyment of the holiday.[51]

Ghosts, spirits, and apparitions known as "the evils" haunted the plantations, if not the minds of their inhabitants. A Gloucester County slave told of how an "evil" followed him one night and "smacked [my] haid cl'ar round on [my] shoulders." Tom Brown, a slave belonging to the Kinloch plantation in King George County, had his throat cut one night during a brawl and staggered home to die at his wife's bedside. Thereafter, Brown's ghost was seen by fellow slaves and members of his master's family as it solemnly walked about, butcher knife in hand, gurgling noises forever emanating from his slit throat.[52]

A few slaves were inadvertently responsible for what can only be described as poltergeistic activities and astral projections. Stories were whispered of furniture and various household objects being flung about by invisible forces only while certain slaves were present and continuing until they were sold or removed. Astral projections of a slave named Millie in 1863 were harbingers of death and illness for the Orrick family of Bath County. So unnerving were these sightings that her mistress forced Millie to sleep alone in a room locked from the outside, but to no avail: a doppelganger of the black maid was seen walking through the walls and rooms of the house! One such nocturnal stroll preceded the death of her master, Captain Johnson Orrick, during a battle near Winchester, and other sightings of an incorporeal Millie were soon followed by the illness of an Orrick daughter and the paralysis of Mrs. Orrick's father. Mrs. Orrick's mother's apoplexy occurred after Millie was seen walking through the bedroom. As for Millie, she obstinately (or balefully) refused to leave the family, even after she was freed.[53]

By 1863–64 there was an increased willingness on the part of whites to permit Afro-Virginians to conduct ceremonies of divine worship openly, particularly if their prayers were for the victory of the Confederacy. Whites assumed blacks were in God's favor and hoped that by easing restrictions against Afro-Christianity, the South might prevail. This attitude was even extended to blacks convicted of heinous crimes. Richard, a King William County slave owned by an absentee New Yorker, was executed on the afternoon of 29 May 1863 at the Henrico County jail for the attempted murder of an overseer. During the weeks before his execution, he was permitted visits by his personal spiritual adviser.[54]

Some slave owners permitted their plantations to house chapels for the spiritual needs of slaves. William Tally, owner of 400 slaves and five plantations, often invited white clergymen to preach to his slaves. A white minister who accepted one of Tally's invitations noted that the blacks who attended were "truly pious"; the planter asked him not to publicize his sermons in advance or else "there will be more negroes [here] than my plantation will hold." In another case, Lucy Skipwith, John Hartwell Cocke's lettered slave, had her absentee owner's permission to conduct a Sunday school for slaves at his Mississipi plantation's chapel, but local whites strongly objected and threatened her with punishment. Skipwith informed Cocke that the slaves would continue their morning prayers and of her bold intent to "commence Teaching again as soon as this talk dies out."[55]

Some God-fearing whites were troubled by slavery. Theological professor Reverend William Sparrow of the Episcopal Seminary in Alexandria publicly opposed slavery. Robert Lewis Dabney, a highly respected Presbyterian minister and formerly General Stonewall Jackson's chief of staff, saw the South's defeats at Gettysburg and Vicksburg as evidence of God's displeasure at slaves being forbidden to read the Bible. Dabney had no love of blacks or concern for the souls of slaves other than as a means to secure the survival of the Confederacy (in one a wartime letter he equated lazy white soldiers with "trifling negroes"). Dabney supported gradual emancipation and believed it would secure a more favorable sentiment by France and Great Britain. Reverend Moses Drury Hoge, chaplain to the Confederate Congress, disagreed; he did not believe slavery was sinful.[56]

A Richmond meeting of Confederate clergymen in April 1863 gravely pronounced Confederate Christianity to be morally compatible with black slavery and the Christianization and civilizing of Africans in a manifesto entitled *An Address to Christians throughout the World by the Clergy of the Confederate States of America*. John Hartwell Cocke, a supporter of the colonization of Liberia by freed Virginia slaves, believed slavery the only true foundation of republican government, hallowed since biblical times: "It is a part . . . of the covenant which God entered into with . . . Man . . . making Abraham the head & Governor of his patriarchate first, of his wife, second of his children & dependents—and thirdly of his slaves."[57]

Increasingly, concern over the spiritual welfare of blacks materialized in ways unheard of before the war. In 1863 one minister baptized 219 blacks in less than a hundred days; with the approval of the town council, black residents founded the Charlottesville African Church, to be led by Reverend John T. Randolph, a white man. After a series of Confederate military rever-

TABLE 4.2. BLACK MEMBERSHIP, DISTRICTS OF THE VIRGINIA CONFERENCE, METHODIST EPISCOPAL CHURCH, 1861–64

District	1861	1862	1863	1864
Norfolk	3,697	3,147	—	—
Petersburg	810	688	682	607
Lynchburg	596	500	541	547
Richmond	459	433	528	151
Farmville	353	233	329	488
Randolph-Macon	240	222	—	—
Charlottesville	207	247	151	204
Henry	159	133	—	—
Washington	61	23	—	—
Fredericksburg	49	67	—	5
Atlantic	—	361	—	—
Danville	—	—	324	367
Miscellaneous	—	—	95	—
Total	6,631	6,054	2,650	2,369

Source: Minutes of the Annual Conferences of the Methodist Episcopal Church, South, for the Years 1861, 1862, 1863, 1864 (Nashville: Southern Methodist Publishing House, 1870), 329, 391, 441, 500. Note: Several districts were unable to file reports after seizure by Union forces.

sals in 1863, God-fearing reformers offered religion as a means to humanize the institution of slavery, influence England to recognize the South, join with it in a military alliance against the North, and put God back on the South's side.

A female correspondent who signed herself "Zarah" wrote to the *Central Presbyterian* in February 1863 to urge that slaves be given regular mandatory spiritual instruction. She judged past neglect as uncivilized and called upon Virginia women to take the lead in this task. Several denominations heeded these exhortations. Methodists were particularly successful in recruiting black members (table 4.2). At a revival in Prince Edward County in October 1863, the white families present decided to permit the full participation of their slaves; 220 were converted, and 170 joined the Methodist church. The Methodist Episcopal Church for Winchester Station licensed approximately eight "coloured preachers" and five exhorters during the war. It routinely renewed certification of its free black members, including Alfred Newman, Robert Armstead, Robert Orrick, and Frank Johnson, as exhorters (assistant pastors) and preachers for African-American Methodists in Frederick County.[58]

Other reformers recommended that blacks and whites worship together and urged repeal of laws prohibiting blacks from learning how to

TABLE 4.3. AFRO-VIRGINIAN PARTICIPATION IN THE PROTESTANT EPISCOPAL
CHURCH, 1861–64

Year	Baptisms	Marriages	Funerals	Sunday schools
1861	250	113	123	695
1862	45	29	27	91
1863	52	55	98	—
1864	15	20	19	200
Total	362	217	267	986

Source: Journals of the Sixty-Sixth, Sixty-Seventh, Sixty-Eighth, and Sixty-Ninth Annual Conventions of the Protestant Episcopal Church in Virginia, Held in St. Paul's Church (Richmond, 1861–64).

read and write. The Protestant Episcopal Church of the Diocese of Virginia shared in the agitation for reform. During annual May conventions held in Richmond between 1861 and 1864, it reported there had been baptisms, marriages, and funerals of blacks, and nearly a thousand black communicants had enrolled in its Sunday schools (table 4.3). The efforts of this denomination to increase black membership and participation thrived. During the four years there were 250 blacks baptized as compared with 840 whites; marriages, 113 blacks, 280 whites; funerals, 123 blacks, 618 whites; and Sunday school enrollment, 695 blacks, 4,393 whites. This did not mean, however, that white Episcopalians favored slavery's abolition.[59]

Any reforms beneficial to blacks were viewed with suspicion by ultraconservatives. One of the leading reformers was Reverend James A. Lyon of the First Presbyterian Church of Columbus, Mississippi, whose article "Slavery, and the Duties Growing Out of the Relationship" appeared in the Southern Presbyterian Review in July 1863. He subscribed to the philosophy that blacks were an inferior species of humanity but proposed certain religious and social reforms. He argued that slaves were religious beings entitled to natural rights, including consecrated marriage, and to deny them these rights was sinful. Religion would make slaves a happier people and better slaves, and Lyon cited the higher prices of religious slaves at auction.[60]

Three months later an anonymous writer published counterarguments in the same journal. This writer accepted some of Lyon's ideas—namely, that the subject of reform made for an interesting discussion—but on the subject of slave marriages questioned why reforms were necessary. He ridiculed the idea as nonsensical because the legalization of slave marriages would interfere with the authority of masters and open the door to qualifying slaves to make legal contracts and exercise other civic obligations.[61]

Ultraconservatives such as Virginia attorney general John Randolph Tucker believed the Confederacy was waging a holy war on behalf of slav-

ery. The African race was debased and "incapable of freedom . . . only fit to
be enslaved," but he was careful to rule out the deportation of their American descendants as impracticable. He boasted of Southern churches as respected institutions where masters and slaves worshiped the same God at
the same communion altar. Tucker brusquely condemned British and
French suggestions that slavery must end before the Confederacy could expect to receive their assistance: "We understand our own business greatly
better than those who are 3,000 miles away." The South needed only the
prayers and moral support of fellow Christians, not guns or ships.[62]

In these religious quarrels outnumbered reformers continued to confront racial conservatives. Reverend Dr. Robert Ryland of Richmond's First
African Baptist Church defended Afro-Christians against printed attacks by
Reverend Dr. J. L. Reynolds, editor of the *Confederate Baptist* of Columbia,
South Carolina, in 1863. The two ecclesiastic protagonists battled for the biracial soul of the Confederacy in the columns of Richmond's *Central Presbyterian*. Ryland, in defense of blacks and his own reputation, portrayed black
congregations as "staid, orderly, and obedient servants of highly respectable
families." His twenty-two years' experience as a pastor and his baptism of
nearly four thousand blacks made him a far better judge of black character
than their critics. Reynolds's caustic rebuttals resorted to race-baiting with
barbs at Ryland and other white ministers of black churches, whom he characterized as degraded white men "ruled by negroes" and lacking in manliness and Christian integrity. He refused even to consider the spiritual
equality of the two races but admitted that "religious meetings of the colored population should be under the control of the whites."[63]

Similar debates persisted in the Old Dominion until the end of the war.
During January 1865 newspapers published more articles on the push to humanize slavery by recognizing the sanctity of slave matrimony. These and
parallel activities in the other Confederate states did not mean Southerners
had completely abandoned slavery or legalized subordination of free
blacks—far from it. Whites, slave owners and non–slave owners, viewed
themselves as legitimate stewards of the South's destiny and God's overseers
of the black race. They insisted slavery was the chosen condition of blacks
even though more than eighty thousand Afro-Virginians were members of
organized churches.[64]

As the war ended, both races hastened to establish separate places of worship. White parishioners at the Roanoke Church in Charlotte County assisted in building a separate church for its black membership because blacks
now made up the majority of the congregation. The whites feared that with-

out their own place of worship, blacks would take control of Roanoke Church and its ministry.[65]

The racially mixed New Hope Baptist Church of Appomattox County reorganized itself in May 1865. Founded during the 1830s, New Hope had black (slaves) and white members throughout the antebellum period. A new constitution and "Rules of Decorum" were drafted, and approximately one hundred members registered in June with blacks comprising 25 percent of the congregation (seven men and seventeen women) and whites 75 percent (twenty-three men and forty-six women). The new spiritual ordinances made no mention of sex or race as qualifications for membership or positions of trust until the white males had second thoughts. The church clerk was authorized to amend the church's constitution to require the approval of two-thirds of the white male members or a majority of the same to conduct worship or business. Blacks were welcome to worship in Christian fellowship at New Hope but under no circumstances allowed any type of authority over whites or any share of church administration.[66]

Before the war slavery had been denounced by some Americans as a violation of Christianity, "that sum of all villainies, the traffic of human flesh" in the words of New York minister A. J. Irving. Fifteen years after Appomattox Episcopalian minister William Nelson Pendleton of Lexington was still defending the South and justifying its use of black involuntary servitude. In a fifteen-page letter he contended that the freedpeople posed more danger to Southerners than the slaves ever had and predicted they would seek bloody revenge and cause "the suffering South" enormous distress. He argued that God had always sanctioned slavery and the right of the superior races to control inferior ones, and anyone who continued to find fault with slavery was sinful and dishonored the Bible. The Virginian asserted that Christ never actually spoke in disapproval of human slavery. Pendleton denied slaves were ever shackled and curtly insisted to the Reverend Mr. Irving that only white Southerners, as the experts on African-Americans and their bondage, were best qualified to handle the "Negro Problem."[67]

A black clergyman, Reverend William Thornton, told a congressional investigative committee in 1866 how white Virginians felt about black churches. Thornton, a former slave who could read and write, obtained a license from the Freedmen's Bureau to conduct marriages for African-Americans and was an ordained minister for two Baptist churches, one in Mathews County and the other in Hampton. He told the congressmen that whites blamed blacks for the South's defeat and were threatening to destroy black churches after Federal troops withdrew from Virginia. After the conclusion of church services, one Afro-Virginian couple were whipped while on their way home because they belonged to a black church. Aghast, the committee asked Thornton:

Question. Why did they not resist being flogged?
Answer. They are that much down.
Question. Did they know that they had a right to resist?
Answer. They dare not do it.

Thornton also recounted how five of his church members took it upon themselves to act as his bodyguard after whites promised to murder any black clergymen who refused to close his church and cease preaching.[68]

Alexander Dunlop of the First Baptist Church of Williamsburg corroborated Thornton's testimony with his own tale of the tribulations faced by black churches. First Baptist's 736 members comprised a thriving community which owned its church free and clear, a singular achievement in a devastated state undergoing hard times. He, too, was marked for death by ex-rebels, and when he asked why, wrathful whites responded: "We want to bring foreign immigration here, and drive every scoundrel of you away from here." Dunlop defended his rights of free speech, worship, and residency. Although his blacksmith's shop was destroyed, Alexander Dunlop and others resolved to stay and assert their rights as citizens: "I tell them that I was born in Virginia, and that I am going to die in Virginia."[69]

After freedom came in the spring of 1865, Patsy, a slave belonging to the Randolph family of New Market, headed for Winchester. A written apologia from her mistress sought to remind her that slavery had been good for Patsy and had provided to her and the rest of the black race the beneficial influences of civilization and Christianity: "I sent you a Bible with the humble hope that you may through the blessings of God meet with some kind friend who will read its blessed pages to you. Keep it & for my sake for your own sake pray that you may understand it & that it may make you wise unto salvation. While you were here I did make an effort to teach you a few things—that you had a soul, which would live forever either in Heaven or Hell. I told you that you were a sinner—I told you of the Blessed Saviour who came down from Heaven to die for us. . . . May God keep you & may you be prepared for Heaven."[70]

But the Randolphs never heard from Patsy again. She was good-bye and gone, her departure an indication that while she and other blacks may have been Christians, they wanted nothing further to do with the distorted piety of white folks.

5 YOURS UNTIL DEATH
Sex, Marriage, and Miscegenation

I could fill pages with my griefs and misfortunes; no tongue could express them as I feel.
—*Elizabeth Keckley*

After enforced debauchery, with the many kindred horrors incident to slavery, it comes with ill grace for the perpetrators of these deeds to hold up the short-comings of some of our race to ridicule and scorn.
—*George H. White*

DINWIDDIE COUNTY ex-slave Elizabeth Keckley bitterly recounted how her fair complexion had caused her humiliation and anguish:

I was regarded as fair-looking for one of my race, and for four years a white man—I spare the world his name—had base designs upon me. I do not care to dwell upon this subject, for it is one that is fraught with pain. Suffice it to say, that he persecuted me for four years, and I—I became a mother. This child of which he was the father was the only child that I ever brought into the world. If my poor boy suffered any humiliating pangs on account of birth, he could not blame his mother, for God knows that she did not wish to give him life; he must blame the edicts of that society which deemed it no crime to undermine the virtue of girls in my position.

This child, light enough to pass for white, abandoned his studies at Wilberforce University in Ohio. He enlisted in the Union army under the name George W. D. Kirkland and died on 10 August 1861 at Wilson's Creek, Missouri. Keckley received a pension for her son's service.[1]

White Virginian women, especially wives of planters, escaped some exploitation of their gender because slave women were available. There was little if any natural alliance between black and white women. As the dominating figures of a patriarchal society, white males could indulge and over-indulge in alcohol, tobacco, gambling, fighting, hunting, fishing, and extramarital liaisons. Sexual escapades before and during matrimony with black or white prostitutes as transient consorts became an acceptable though seldom-discussed part of life.[2]

Sexual intercourse, as vice or virtue, rarely was the subject of public discussion except in criticism of houses of ill repute, harlots, and venereal disease or in coarse jokes exchanged among men. Blacks were stereotyped as sexually promiscuous savages. This image provided many of the rationalizations for slavery and criminal sanctions against interracial marriages. Joseph T. Wilson, an Afro-Virginian who served with distinction in the 54th Massachusetts (Colored) Infantry and later became a founding father of African-American history, rejected white disparagements of blacks: "Slavery offered a premium for licentiousness, but had no punishment for immorality. Those who should have set them a better example, exerted every force of power and law to debauch them and sink them lower in a sea of shame. The glory of wifehood and motherhood was not theirs. No sacred tie ordained of God between man and woman, but was with ruthless hand torn asunder and trampled under foot." In October 1861 a slave woman, whose husband of several years suggested they legally get married by a Union minister, scoffed at the idea. "O! of what use will it be?" she asked. "Master can separate us to morrow."[3]

Slaves spoke guardedly about their sex life during postwar years because they did not want to fuel white stereotypes of blacks as being promiscuous. Still, some white women had long-term sexual relations with black male slaves; such women committed adultery, but there were not so many of them as there were white male adulterers. White husbands accused their wives of committing adultery with blacks and giving birth to mulatto children. Although these outraged husbands sought divorces, such cases were not a matter of rape but of mutual consent between adults.

Rapes of white women by slaves occurred during antebellum times, yet in nearly every case petitions by local whites for pardons on the slaves' behalf attested that these Afro-Virginians had been encouraged by their victims. There were masters who tried to prevent adultery among their slaves. In his "Code of Laws for Island Plantation," Richard Eppes banned slave promiscuity and set up an ascending scale of punishment. For the first offense the man would receive twenty lashes from the husband of the woman and the woman fifteen lashes from her seducer. For the second offense, thirty-nine and thirty lashes, respectively, would be inflicted upon the offending couple.[4]

Afro-Virginian slave women expressed regret about bearing children. "I could not bear the thought of bringing children into slavery—of adding one single recruit to the millions bound to hopeless servitude, fettered and shackled with chains stronger and heavier than manacles of iron," said one to her husband. A twenty-five-year-old mother of three was asked if she could produce a child every year. Glancing down sorrowfully at her children as they stood on the auction block, she boldly retorted, "I will never have anymore and I am sorry I got these."[5]

Interracial sexual liaisons were known as "illicit alliances," "amalgamation," "physical bleachings," "miscegenation," or "race-mixing" and were denounced as barbaric threats to the purity and survival of the white race. Dark-complexioned whites were suspected of having black ancestry, and thousands of blacks were light enough to pass for white. Many did. When a thirteen-year-old slave boy named Ferdinand escaped from the Lynchburg firm of J. H. Hargrove & Company in April 1864, a runaway slave notice advised the public: "He [has a] very bright color, light colored straight hair, and will no doubt attempt to pass himself off as being a white boy. He reads well, is very sprightly and intelligent." Virginia, a breeder state, was a Southern hatchery for slavelings (young slave children): "Those best acquainted with the business of slave-growing, inform us that the actual cost of raising slaves is very trifling. They are grown principally on corn bread, sour milk and the bits and pieces from the master's table . . . the actual cost of keeping young negroes, including the cotton used for their scanty clothing, does not exceed ten dollars per annum."[6]

The fruitfulness of its female slaves was among Virginia's most reliable assets. Shortly after the battle of Williamsburg in the spring of 1862, Union soldiers temporarily occupied a Pamunkey River plantation. The able-bodied males had fled or been taken to the interior by their owner; its remaining slave women, children, and old men were of "all colors." Curious soldiers interrogated the white overseer about the practice and profitability of slave breeding. The man acknowledged the breeding of slaves was his plantation's chief source of income, with an annual production of fifteen to twenty black infants valued at $1,200 each. During the summer of 1864, a member of the 140th Pennsylvania Volunteers visited a King William County estate owned by a seventy-four-year-old farmer named Anderson Scott. The disgusted soldier reported that several of its 150 black slaves were Scott's own children and that he had fathered his grandchildren upon his own black daughters. He denounced Scott as an incestuous heathen: "This old scoundrel . . . I believe I would have been justified in breaking his neck."[7]

According to the 1860 census 40 percent of the Old Dominion's free blacks and 15 percent of its slaves were of mixed ancestry. Contrary to white denials that it occurred at all, miscegenation typically involved a white man and black slave women, and these cases occurred more often was generally admitted. Booker T. Washington never knew the identity of his father but was certain he was a white man. Born a slave in Franklin County in 1856, Washington had light brown skin, reddish hair, and gray eyes; whites attributed his intelligence and organizational abilities to his white blood.[8]

Virginia blacks and mulattoes were listed as "Free Colored" or "Slave" in the census returns of 1860 (Indians were counted as white). Not until the ninth federal census, in 1870, would "black" and "mulatto"—"colored" had been the preferred term—be precisely defined. Virginia law declared any person with at least one black grandparent to be officially black but left it unclear whether blacks having less than one-fourth part of "Negro blood" were legally black or white. By 1860 state law pronounced that a Negro and a mulatto were one and the same.[9]

Mulattoes were known as "white negroes"; their complexions varied from black to white with numerous hues—"cinnamon," "honey," "ginger-bread," "ivory," "dusky"—in between. Mulattoes lived in a sort of purgatory between the races. Perhaps more than a few mulattoes (and blacks) subconsciously preferred to be white. One mulatto girl who resided in a contraband village in Union-held Virginia deemed it beneath her dignity and a betrayal of her racial ancestry to associate with her black half sister (the daughter of her mother's husband) because her own father had been a white man. She and other mulattoes believed it was better to be illegitimate "whites" rather than full-blooded blacks.[10]

The word *miscegenation* is derived from the Latin word *misere*, "to mix" and *genus*, "race." An 1864 book, *Miscegenation: The Theory of the Blending of the Races, Applied to the American White Man and Negro*, argued that whites and blacks were physiologically equal and proclaimed mixed races to be superior breeds. It promoted miscegenation as essential to the American and human condition and predicted the war would end in equality for blacks and marriages between the races. In a passage which infuriated Southerners (who learned of this book through the publicity it received in Northern newspapers), the authors of this explosive book stated that which before had been related only in whispers or barroom conversation: the first sexual experiences of Southern maidens occurred with black lovers. Such accusations directly challenged the idealization of white womanhood that enraptured Southern writers.[11]

Miscegenation was also the title of a play performed at the Richmond Theatre a year before the fall of the city, and it received criticism concerning its star and subject matter from Virginians sensitive about the subject of race mixing. One reviewer blasted actor R. D'Orsay Ogden's impersonation of "the inevitable nigger" and denounced the entire production as an erroneous impersonation of Virginia society and life because everyone knew race mixing only existed in Yankeedom. The repercussions from this satire showed Confederates as willing to be entertained by the farcical aspects of miscegenation while at the same time overly self-conscious about the public unveiling of hidden sins, even those masquerading as fiction.[12]

Throughout the war there were numerous instances when mulattoes caused confusion about their true racial identity. An 1862 Richmond editorial lashed out against the difficulties in determining which persons were of pure blood and which had less than the required fourth of "Negro blood": "Why the framers of our laws ever undertook to draw more than one line of distinction between the white and black population of the country seems a problem equally devoid of philosophy as it is difficult of solutions. The governing race is [and] . . . should be uncontaminated; the white man should be all white, and the negro all negro." In February 1864 Solomon Bones, an employee of the Mount Torry Furnace in Augusta County, was listed on the register page reserved for white men but a dubious clerk noted "supposed to be a white man" beside his name.[13]

Laws passed in 1833 and 1860 permitted free blacks of mixed blood to petition courts to be declared "not a Negro" if he or she offered sufficient proof corroborated by the testimony of a white person. Successful petitioners received a certificate relieving them of black restrictions and legal liabilities. These and similar laws created a society of three classes—whites, "mixed bloods," and blacks. During December 1862 Albert S. Gentry, a free black, was arrested and jailed on charges of not having registration papers. His lawyer obtained a writ of habeas corpus, and a hustings court decided that Gentry was a white man because he had "less than one-fourth of negro blood" and so ordered his release.

In January 1863 another free black named Edward H. Gentry was charged with having beaten a white child with a wagon whip. Gentry's lawyer claimed his client was "a man of mixed blood" because he had less than "one-fourth Negro blood." To muddle matters further, other courts had refused to register Gentry as a free black. Mayor Joseph C. Mayo, acting in his capacity as judge, replied that he would never accept mixed bloods as anything other than black and declared "mixed blooded" men could not, for example, marry white women or testify against whites but could be flogged at whipping posts just like any other black. There were but two classes of people in Virginia, concluded Mayo, whites and blacks, and he did not believe the General Assembly had the power to make "mixed bloods" white men. He sentenced Gentry to be whipped.[14]

A black boy who appeared in August 1864 before a Richmond court claimed to be a runaway from Amherst County. After detailed questioning he confessed to being the son of a white woman, a native of Plymouth, Massachusetts, who had paid free blacks to care for him since his infancy. Sure enough, a black woman materialized in court a few days later with money received from the boy's mother to pay his bail and jail fees, and the surprised judge returned him to her custody. The child's complexion was not even that of a mulatto but of a "regular short-haired negro." The mother of another boy, eight-year-old Charles Taylor, was a mulatto, and her son was described as having a very fair complexion and light, silky hair. His father, Alexander Wethers of Lewis County, sold him to a New Orleans slave trader, but Charles's freedom arrived in the form of Union forces.[15]

Union soldiers, too, were baffled by the degrees of skin color among Afro-Virginians. A soldier stationed at Fort Monroe during 1861 saw more mulattoes than he had expected and described them as "entirely bleached." He noted that one slave employed at the Union breastworks was no darker than his white owner and cousin and afterwards described certain slave women as entirely lacking African features: "They were . . . light-faced and fair-haired. If they were to be brought [north] and their pedigree concealed, they could readily mingle with our population and marry white men, who would never suspect that they were not pure Caucasians." Henry L. Estabrooks, a Union officer who managed to escape from his guards near Richmond, was constantly startled by Afro-Virginians who appeared to be white. One night, while he was hiding in a slave cabin, "a white man came . . . in [a Confederate] uniform. I sprang up and thought I was betrayed; but he advanced and accosted me politely and pleasantly. I did not know what to make of him . . . he was a slave. . . . I could scarcely believe it. He was a large, fine-looking man, with straight, light-colored hair, blue eyes and a florid complexion. Accustomed as I had become to all shades of negro complexion, I was puzzled with him. There was not the least indication of negro blood about him . . . his skin was much lighter than mine." This man's name was Alvin, a runaway slave. Married to a slave named Lucy, Alvin lived secretly in the woods near her owner's plantation; he and other blacks assisted Estabrooks's successful return to Union lines.[16]

Several Afro-Virginians possessed eye colors normally not associated with blacks such as blue, green, gray, even yellow. One Confederate ledger contains an alphabetical record of approximately fifteen hundred free black males enrolled and processed at Richmond's Camp Lee before assignment to duty at various military facilities (ordnance and naval depots, railroads, canals, and armories) from May 1864 to January 1865 (table 5.1). Confederate officers meticulously cataloged complete physical descriptions of these men (age, height, and color of eyes, hair, and skin). The majority of thirteen blue-eyed blacks claimed Washington County (a southwestern county near the North Carolina border) as their place of birth.

For example, James Trent, number 196 to be enrolled, was a Washington County farmer. The county's free black register described him on 25 March 1862 as "a Mulatto man, aged about thirty-six years, five feet nine and one half inches high—right ankle out of place—no other apparent marks or scars—Free born in this County and freedom derived from white female ancestor." Most mulattoes had come by their freedom by a white forebear, usually a woman. Confederate enrollment officers must have been struck

TABLE 5.1. EYE COLORS AND COMPLEXIONS OF SELECTED VIRGINIA FREE
BLACK MEN ENROLLED AT CAMP LEE, 1864–65

Name	Age	County	Description
Dabney Adams	—	—	Blue eyes, light complexion
Washington Bartee	43	Washington	Blue eyes, yellow complexion
Robert Bowers	45	Greensville	Blue eyes
Moore Brockenbrough	31	Essex	Blue eyes
Andrew Cosby	40	Richmond	Blue eyes
Charles Early	25	Washington	Blue eyes
Thomas Foster	30	Richmond (city)	Blue eyes
Charles R. McCrackin	23	Washington	Blue eyes, yellow complexion
Jacob Nash	23	Washington	Blue eyes, yellow complexion
Thompson Quarles	34	Orange	Green eyes, copper complexion
James Ruff	24	Petersburg (city)	Blue eyes
James Smith	20	Washington	Blue eyes
Alexander Spriggs	36	Rockbridge	Yellow eyes
James Trent	39	Washington	Blue eyes, yellow complexion
Davis Watson	25	Washington	Blue eyes, yellow complexion
Atwell Young	22	Spotsylvania	Yellow complexion

Source: Bureau of Conscription, Virginia, Register of Free Negroes Enrolled and Detailed,
May 1864–January 1865, Camp Lee, chap. 1, vol. 241, RG 109, NA.

by the implications of large numbers of blacks who could have passed for
white.[17]

Charles Carleton Coffin, a reporter for the Boston *Journal*, wrote of
meeting a mulatto shortly after Richmond's capture. The young man, more
white than colored, respectfully questioned the journalist about the availability of employment in the North for blacks. When asked about his job
experience, the Afro-Virginian answered: "Well, sir, I have been an assistant
in a drug store. I can put up prescriptions. I paid forty dollars a month for
my time before the Confederate money became worthless, but my master
thought that I was going to run away to the Yankees and sold me awhile
ago; and he was my own father."[18]

"The Negro has domestic relations in as strong degree as a white man, and
however far South his master may drive him he will sooner or later return
to his family," one Union officer admitted. Another Northern observer, Reverend Lewis C. Lockwood, held that Afro-Virginians were a virtuous race:
"To their credit be it spoken that, so far as I have observed, there is no intem-
perance among them." Married slaves sought to remain in the same or
neighboring plantations as their spouses. If this was not possible, weekend

or monthly conjugal visits were customary for these "abroad marriages." Many slaves walked miles to visit their spouses, braving slave patrols, slave stealers, rough roads, and bad weather. The law did not recognize the legality of slave marriages, and the ritual of a couple's "jumping the broom" served more as a hope than an actuality.[19]

Slave owners opposed wartime appeals by reformers for the legal recognition of slave marriages on the grounds that such a modification would foster more problems than it would rectify as far as the relationship between masters and slaves was concerned. Ministers of the gospel believed that by doing so the Confederacy would regain God's grace and thereby attain its independence. Opponents of reform also cited several possible dilemmas with slave divorces. Not all states permitted it for whites. If slaves divorced, this could result in frequent court appearances disruptive of plantation schedules and would create legal expenses to be borne by slave owners. There was the possibility of slaves suing owners for "wrongful" separations from their spouses and families. And if a divorce was granted, which black parent would keep the children and how would these conflicts be resolved to the satisfaction of the slaves and their respective masters?[20]

Although plantation manuals advised against permitting slaves to marry those at other plantations, slave husbands and wives were allowed to visit each other. When a Louisa County slave named Solomon announced plans to marry a slave from a nearby farm, he boldly asked for and received money from his owner to help defray the cost of the nuptials. A Powhatan County slave, Willis Garland, received permission from his owner, W. C. Scott, to wed a Nelson County woman (a distance of approximately forty-five miles) in 1861. Scott praised Garland as "one of the best servants I ever saw" in his letter to the bride's owner, Francis Cabell, approving the arrangement. He promised to allow the groom-to-be to visit his new wife "as often as he can be spared—at least three times annually."[21]

Slaves occasionally held lavish weddings: In the winter of 1861 a British woman at Richmond's Atlantic Hotel witnessed preparations for an all-black ceremony which included chambermaids magically transformed into bridesmaids dressed in finery loaned by their respective mistresses including long white gloves, gold chains and watches, fans, handkerchiefs, and necklaces. The maid of honor, in perfect mimicry of a typical Southern belle, haughtily refused to share a carriage with the bridesmaids and insisted on being transported to the church alone. Church-sanctioned weddings were sought by escaped slaves who customarily requested a renewal of their marriage vows complete with elaborate cakes, lemonade, and the words "Til death do you part" rather than the previous "Til distance [separation by selling] or death do you part." One ex-slave couple's nuptials were announced as: "Married at

Falls Church, Alexandria, Sunday evening, January 24th, 1864, by Rev. J. R. Johnson, missionary of the American Missionary Association, *Mr. Frederick Foote and Miss Margaret Carter.* Frederick has been six times sold as a slave. He has buried one wife, has six children in slavery, and now owns more than thirty acres of land. He thinks, and we think, too, that he can take care of himself and his family also. Heaven bless them!" At Yorktown that same year forty black couples legally reaffirmed their lifelong commitments to each other. The Reverend Mr. Lockwood married couples day and night and asked his Northern colleagues to send more engraved marriage certificates as his supply was nearly exhausted.[22]

Slaves unable or unwilling to escape did manage to keep in contact with their spouses. Granvill Clark, a model of conjugal fidelity, wrote his master on 14 September 1863: "Sir I take the oppounity of Writen you a few Lines to Inform you that I have a favor to ask if you please Sir to Let my Wife Nancy to Remain as she is Until I come up and see you you have done one Peice of Kindness for when I was up there Before and Sorry to troble you again and I am in the hope that you Will Let my Wife Be hire out here in Richmond I will see you next week." Notwithstanding those who declared blacks incapable of expressing to each other the emotions of love, one black woman said: "Selling is worse than flogging. My husband was sold six years ago. My heart has bled ever since, and is not well yet. I have been flogged many times, since he was torn from me, but my back has healed in time."[23]

Afro-Virginian men were attracted to and appreciated black women and praised them as first in everything: love, dancing, and in the sickroom caring for the sick and injured. Black women were also appealing in the eyes of Union and Confederate soldiers who commonly used phrases such as "good-looking," "best-looking," and "quite pretty" to describe them. Union soldier Henry Estabrooks spoke of one such woman as the prettiest in the South.[24]

Union officers were able to engage in practices the common soldier could not. At the battle of Trevilian Station on 11 June 1864, Wade Hampton's cavalry captured the headquarters wagon of General George Armstrong Custer. Among the items confiscated was a carriage containing photographs of Mrs. Custer, assorted equipment, and a very special piece of camp equipage, Custer's mulatto mistress. According to an eyewitness account in the *Richmond Whig,* the rapid approach of Yankee troopers forced the Confederates to cut the horses loose and make their escape, but not before they pushed the carriage, with the lady still inside, over a precipice, her frightened cries delighting the onlookers. Most of Custer's property was eventually returned, but it was observed the general seemed unconcerned about the fate of his unfortunate mistress.[25]

Northern women feared that black women might seduce their men despite white soldiers' protestations that black women were unattractive. The wife of Samuel M. Woods must have wrote her spouse about them. While stationed at Portsmouth he told her of his delight at the abundance and ripeness of Virginia's peaches, plums, pears, apples, and strawberries. Woods frankly confessed that fruit was not the only commodity amply developed and ripe in the Old Dominion: "About the niger women I was out the other knight and see some good big lusty ones but did not derst to tush them for fere I should get my old thing crocked and did not want to come home to soon." George H. Nelson of the 9th Maine Infantry found comfort in the form of "Niger ladies for we have plenty"; a Richmond newspaper avowed that while the black women of the city appeared well fed and good-looking, city white women were "lean and hungry-looking."[26]

Afro-Virginian women had high standards of morality and exhibited a proper and not unexpected decorum when lack of space and poor logistical planning by Federal officers forced them to share sleeping quarters with black men in contraband camps. United States Colored Troops were detailed as armed guards to protect their chastity and privacy from the prying eyes of white soldiers at various freedman's villages and contraband camps.[27]

Some black women unquestionably reciprocated the attentions of Union soldiers. Jim Lee of the 4th Massachusetts Infantry married Candace, a twenty-one-year-old Afro-Virginian woman, one of three slaves who escaped from a slaveholder named Parker West in 1861, and she was sent to the safety of Fort Monroe. "You is a right nice-lookin' man, I declare," another young Afro-Virginian woman straightforwardly told a youthful Union officer upon meeting him for the first time. He reacted as spontaneously as if she had been a member of one of the finest families of society: he blushed.[28]

Mulatto women (sometimes known as mulattresses) were perceived as threats by white women concerned about the attraction of husbands, sons, and brothers toward half-black women. Catherine Hopley grudgingly conceded: "There is a sort of gipsy beauty in the nearly white negro. The large dark eyes retain their brilliancy, while their form is improved; a rich glow in the cheeks, a well-formed nose and full rosy lips, with glossy black ringlets . . . full of feeling, with a smile lingering about the mouth ready to burst forth at a word of encouragement."[29]

According to Elizabeth Fox-Genovese, white male slaveholders were the surrogate husbands and fathers of black females. They provided food, clothing, and shelter, assigned and supervised their labors, and fathered their children. On the other hand, white women perceived black women as titillating Jezebels and seductresses who enticed their husbands and sons. It made little difference that as a class white women were placed atop pedestals as "presiding geniuses over civilization, morality and population," for they feared black women as serious challengers. As one Southern lady explained, "You can understand the fondness of our young men for some of the negro girls when as babies they were suckled by a negro woman."[30]

The application of the label "Jezebel" by white women to attractive black women, especially female slaves who had little choice except surrender to white male lust, was grossly unfair. Historically, Jezebel, the wife of Ahab, one of the biblical kings of Israel, became infamous for her wickedness and idol-worship (1 Kings 16:31, 21:23–25; 2 Kings 9:30–37). Southern women did not publicly discuss the martial transgressions of their husbands, especially if black women were involved. Margaret Douglass, a Norfolk white woman, vented her resentment in 1854: "Southern wives know that their husbands come to them reeking with pollution from the arms of their tawny mistresses. Father and son seek the same source of excitement and alike gratify their inhuman propensities, scarcely blushing when detected and recklessly defying every command of God and every tie of morality and human affection. . . . The whole practice is plainly, unequivocally, shamelessly beastly."[31]

Female slaves were at the physical and sexual mercy of their owners. One Virginia planter, after his wife's frequent complaints, reluctantly promised to whip Fannie, a troublemaker. Suspicious because the slave woman was the mother of three mulatto children whose father had never been identified, this wife secretly followed her husband as he went forth to punish the slave and caught him preparing to make love to a more-than-willing Fannie. As the price for the white couple's return to matrimonial tranquility, Fannie was sold South. Elizabeth Sparks remembered fellow slave Betty Hill as always having decent clothing and special privileges from their owner because "she wuz a favorite of his'n." Although Sparks disapproved of Betty's behavior, she refused to provide more details of the relationship to interviewers after the war.[32]

Common-law liaisons between whites and blacks were not out of the ordinary, and the journal of University of Virginia student William Gibson Field is an indication of this. One of Field's slaves, Flora, married Albert and by him had two children. After his death she married Gabriel, the son of Rosetta by the white overseer of the Field family plantation, Adam Hoffman, in 1862. In another case a white man named William Orville George fell in love with Caroline, his slave, and took her to Pennsylvania where he freed and married her. After his death in 1869, his white relatives sued in Virginia to prevent Caroline and her children by George from inheriting his property. Their attorney argued that despite the fact that certain states permitted marriages between blacks and whites, Virginia law forbade it. George and Caroline's marriage was declared void, and their children illegitimate.[33]

Confederate soldiers sought the company of black women; lifetime habits of gratification flourished with thousands of men away from wives, home, and the disapproving stares of relatives, neighbors, and ministers. Elijah Parker and John L. Sutherlin were arrested in 1862 after being caught in the house of Jordina Mayo, a free black woman. Both men were jailed and forfeited security bonds because they already had been fined for earlier associations with black women. George Norton was arrested for walking down a Richmond street "arm in arm with a Negro wench named Hannah."[34]

Millie Rawls, a fifteen-year-old free black resident of Culpeper County, began a common-law marriage in 1861 with a white man named George W. Jameson and raised a family of five children. Jameson faithfully supported Rawls and the children and transferred all of his property to her name. During Reconstruction she filed a claim for damages to their property caused by Union soldiers. Such interracial couples were threats to the status quo and became part of the South's musical folklore:

> We girls are all for a Union
> Where a marked distinction is laid
> Between the rights of the mistress
> And those of the kinky-haired maid.[35]

Other threats to public decency were brothels and theaters. Editorials demanded their closure as "public nuisances" and "treacherous shoals of the vices." Even the small town of Charlottesville (population 3,000 in 1860) possessed "a pest house of infamy." Private Finch of the 11th New Jersey Infantry, caught in bed with three black women "of notoriously bad character," was ordered to leave the premises by the city's provost marshal. Instead, Finch calmly told the officer to kiss his ass.[36]

When a free black prostitute named Martha Bell arrived in Richmond in 1862, she possessed a genuine certificate of good character from Mayor W. W. Townes of Petersburg. She claimed to be a professional nurse after her arrest in December, but Mayor Mayo, having evidence of her true vocation, ordered her returned to Petersburg. Three black women from Culpeper— Anna Edwards and Ella and Sarah Brown—rented a shanty near the Richmond Exchange and there conducted "one of the most disreputable houses in the city." When arrested in March 1864, they claimed to be white and boasted that certain government officials, who had long provided them with food and other luxuries, would use their influence to obtain their release.

Sure enough, the trio were quickly released and continued to boast of being under the protection of the Confederate government.[37]

Octavia Butler and Sarah Ann Weaver maintained a two-room house of prostitution on Ramcat Alley (a pun?) where they, a fifteen-year-old white girl, and three white men were arrested when a police raid discovered the group "promiscuously sleeping together." Butler and Weaver were whipped, and the white men received jail sentences and fines. The spread of prostitution in the cities and towns of the state led to newspaper and theater advertisements warning women that they would not be admitted to theaters or other public amusements unless accompanied by a gentleman. One reason for this admonition was the custom of prostitutes to rendezvous with their clients near playhouses. Since black men were not viewed as gentlemen under any circumstances, this meant any black woman accosted on the streets could be considered a prostitute.[38]

Long-term interracial romances did exist in Confederate Virginia, but black men who dared cohabit with white women risked being executed under state law. This did not prevent Richard, a Richmond slave, from taking up residence with Delia Mack, a white woman. The couple lived happily together until Delia's sister, Caroline, reported them to the police. Richard was convicted and received 117 lashes over a three-day period in early 1865.[39]

An Albemarle County white woman and her black husband, Jackson, rented a house from the University of Virginia and dwelled there undisturbed until the faculty chairman suddenly demanded their eviction in October 1863. John P. Anderson, another free black man married to a white woman, placed his Fauquier County property in her name, and the couple resided together for the duration of the war and during Reconstruction. Hannah Greenhow, a free woman of color, and Dade Hooe, a white man, both of Stafford County, had eleven children and lived together from 1841 until Hooe's death in 1881.[40]

Rape is the war's least reported crime. One authority on this disturbing subject, Susan Brownmiller, has accused the war's historians of callously portraying the conflict as relatively rape free and thereby contributing to a cover-up of sexual assault, especially of black women.[41]

Black rapists, the scourge of Southern nightmares, caused the General Assembly to raise its voice in self-righteous white wrath against the desecration of Southern womanhood, charging that "refined and virtuous women have been brutally insulted," but few voices were raised in objection to black female concubinage provided by some plantations for white men. Robert Ellet, a King William County slave, recalled: "In those days if you was a slave and had a good looking daughter, she was taken from you. They would put her in the big house where the young masters could have the run of her."[42]

Revenge knows no color, but in the wake of the Union's ill-fated York-town siege of May 1862, slaves sampled forbidden fruit. A slave named Lightfoot convinced a white family that General George McClellan wished to interview them. He then somehow managed to tie them to trees and rape the women.[43]

Two months later two slaves, Stokes Martin and John, received death sentences in Chesterfield County for rape. Details are sketchy, for in the words of one contemporary newspaper, "the particulars of their cases are too revolting for the public print, [and] we refrain from publishing them." A slave named Gilly, valued at $4,000, was hanged on 24 March 1865 at the Petersburg jail for the robbery and rape of a white woman.[44]

White women were allegedly raped by black Union soldiers. After a raid near Richmond and Petersburg in June 1864, members of the 36th United States Colored Infantry were accused by the *Richmond Enquirer* of raping a "Mrs. G.," wife of a Confederate officer, eleven times. In addition, twenty-five or thirty other females (decorum forbade mentioning their names) were also violated by these "demons" who respected "neither age nor color." The *Enquirer* urged no quarter for black Union soldiers. But the newspaper and its readers did not need to protest so much; black soldiers were more likely to be executed by the Union military for raping white women than for any other violation of the articles of war.[45]

One of the war's myths is that black rapists were never lynched before 1865 when the removal of the confines of slavery erased social controls on the black man's lust for white women. In certain areas black men not only had to hastily remove their hats in the presence of white women but came to commit to memory the habit of immediately placing their hats in front of their crotches to prevent any involuntary erections from offending the modesty of white women and thereby avert charges of attempted rape. Any lingering glances at white women that could be interpreted as lustful (later known as "eyeball rape") became a fatal attraction. Moreover, lynchings of blacks did occur during the war. The hanging of a male slave at Saltville on the evening of 7 July 1863 for rape was witnessed by a staff officer assigned there to guard the state's vital saltworks. The "execution," as far as he was concerned, was a lynching plain and simple, and he disapproved of it.[46]

Sexual racism ("racism below the waist"), the sexual exploitation of African-Americans by whites, especially but not limited to the rape or involuntary concubinage of African-American women, is one of the war's silent subjects due to the scarcity of complete documentation. Confederate apologists rationalized white male abuses of black women by claiming such violations enabled the virtue of white womanhood to remain unblemished by carnal appetites. This does not explain why slave woman were punished for refusing to leave their husbands for the beds of overseers and other predatory white males. As one observer explained, "The fear of the lash often causes the female slaves to promise the overseer to visit him of nights, if he will not flog them, which arrangement he is very likely to agree to. . . . Thus slavery being an evil, leads to evil continually."[47] One Union officer accused his comrades of making black women the victims of "unbridled passions." Another soldier, Henry J. H. Thompson, writing from his Suffolk camp during June 1863, told his wife that it was a place not fit for ladies; two unoffending black women were seized, turned upside down upon their heads, and suffered the indignity of "tobacco chips, sticks, lighted cigars & sand [put] into their behinds."[48]

Black women were the victims of the majority of the war's rapes. In April 1862 the family of seventy-seven-year-old B. E. Harrison of Prince William County were eyewitnesses to the rape of one of his slaves. As a squad of Yankee soldiers plundered the Harrison home, a black servant girl was about 150 yards from the building when one of the soldiers saw her. "As she saw him approaching her she ran,—but he caught her and forced [her] to a Brutal act, in full view of my dwelling and Wife and two of her nieces and under the immediate eye of another soldier but a few steps from the spot when the act was committed and in view of same, seven or Eight more soldiers, this Brutal act caused my wife to appeal to me to send her and her nieces . . . to some other place where their persons might be safe from such outrage as had been imposed upon the colored Girl."[49]

Four white Union cavalrymen raped two black women in Newport News during July 1862. A visiting black female acquaintance was in the family yard when one pair of soldiers seized and unmercifully violated her in turn while the other pair stood guard with pistols and swords. The soldiers then entered the home where, as the first pair guarded the door, a young black woman was raped "after a terrible struggle" in the presence of her father and grandfather. However, a few soldiers paid dearly for their lust. A white sailor was shot to death in Yorktown in 1863 by black vigilantes for the attempted rape of a young black girl.[50]

Neither were Confederate soldiers and Richmond police officers models of virtue. Archibald Wilkinson, a Confederate marine, was arrested and transferred to the custody of the provost marshal for raping Margaret Willis, a free black Richmond woman, during November 1862. Dillard McCormick, a member of the city police force, was charged with the rape of Ann Eliza Wells, a crime witnessed by his fellow officers in July 1862. McCormick was committed to trial for "feloniously assaulting and ravishing the person" of

Wells. The case was heard in August in the hustings court after the charges were reduced from assault to beating with attempted rape. He was acquitted but later dismissed from the police force.[51]

Homosexuality is another silent subject of the Civil War. Although the term *homosexual* was not coined until after the conflict, wartime letters and diaries occasionally allude to the practice. A Confederate artilleryman in Augusta County enigmatically wrote his sister about a bizarre episode involving a white Confederate soldier and an officer's black male body servant which aroused the ire of his camp: "The boys . . . rode one of our company on a rail last night for leaving the company and going to sleep with Captain Lowery's black man."[52]

After the war slaves hastened to legalize their marriages though Virginia did not pass an act legitimizing slave matrimony until 1866. Some Afro-Virginian men had good reason for haste in formalizing their vows: black women were eagerly sought out by Union soldiers starved for feminine company (many ex-Confederate women, the most bitter of the defeated rebels, would have nothing to do with Yankees). Danville black men objected when members of the 9th New York Artillery wanted to dance with black women; they claimed that male Yankee odors were offensive to black ladies! A Fredericksburg black woman took action when she found her marriage threatened; she was acquitted of charges of assaulting a white woman who had "stolen the affections" of her husband and induced him to desert his family.[53]

Richard R. Hill, an ex-slave, testified before Congress that most interracial affairs were instigated by whites:

> Question. Do you not think that a Virginia white man would have connexion with a black woman?
>
> Answer. I do, sir; I not only think so, but I know it from past experience. It was nothing but the stringent laws of the south that kept many a white man from marrying a black woman.
>
> Question. It would be looked upon as a very wicked state of things, would it not, for a white man to marry a black woman?
>
> Answer. I will state to you as a white lady stated to a gentleman down in Hampton, that if she felt disposed to fall in love or marry a black man, it was nobody's business but hers; and so I supposed that if the colored race get all their rights, and particularly their equal rights before the law, it would not hurt the nation or trouble the nation.
>
> Question. In such a case do you think the blacks would have a strong inclination to unite with the the whites in marriage?

Answer. No sir; I do not. I do not think that the blacks would have so strong an inclination to unite with the whites as the whites would have to unite with the blacks.

Although the congressmen were incredulous at his statements, Hill's testimony and that of other ex-slaves exposed white demands for racial purity as a hypocritical fabrication.[54]

Afro-Virginian women reciprocated the feelings of love and respect of their husbands and families. Rosette Hill and her slave husband John Henry Hill fled to Canada before the war but subsequently returned to Petersburg where he desperately struggled to find work to support her and six children. Tired and discouraged by white hostility, he talked of giving up. But Rosette stood by him and more importantly reminded John that after surviving slavery they could endure anything: "Dear husband I receve your kine letter and was truly glad to heare from you but sorry you could not get no imployment for I now you are miserable, you must try and bare with things, thare will be a better day not fare distant when thare will be a change and one for the better. . . . My pen is very bad I cant hardly write, I say no more but esespect to see you soon." Rosette's patience and love were vindicated when John was appointed a Petersburg justice of the peace and later was elected to the city council.[55]

6 A COMMONWEALTH OF FEAR
Wartime Racism and Race Relations

Our acts, our angels are, for good or ill,
Our fatal shadows that walk by us still.
—*Virginia ex-slave George Williams, Jr.*

SLAVERY AND racism were powerful forces of oppression whose intolerance enveloped Afro-Virginians and whites. Those who failed to acknowledge and obey their dictates risked swift and fatal consequences. Racism against blacks existed during the Civil War, but some scholars have been content to focus on the testimony of whites to the exclusion of black accounts. Race relations imbued with fear and violence were sanctioned by law and custom. Racism produced and advocated intolerance of blacks; it was motivated by desire for economic, political, and social dominance. It existed simultaneously in the South and the North. It served as an emotional safety valve for whites and yet caused anxieties among both races. Slaves and free blacks had little choice but to outwardly accept the restraints and ideology of white supremacy by wearing masks of passivity. As has been the example of oppressed peoples throughout history, Afro-Virginians resorted to combinations of guile and resistance to survive daily encounters with potentially hostile whites.

Blacks were scapegoats for private, public, and anonymous racist hysteria. Disenfranchised, exploited, ostracized, and suppressed, Afro-Virginians knew their place but did not always stay in it. Some resisted and maintained their self-respect. Others fled or went out of their way to avoid or minimize contact with whites. Some used religion or sought strong familial ties to find solace for being enslaved and discriminated against. Others engaged in prejudicial behaviors against fellow blacks or whites. This chapter surveys racism in wartime Virginia. Its manifestations and evidence in the form of eyewitness accounts, recollections, and testimony of its victims and victimizers indicate a complex and enigmatic society.

A consideration of white attitudes toward blacks can begin by looking at how they were named. Most slaves had but one name. Slave parents, rejecting white people's names, instead named their children after themselves or grandparents, uncles, and aunts or deceased relatives. Sometimes whites bestowed names upon slave children, but black self-consciousness and kinship networks prevailed by calling the children after deceased or sold-away relatives, thus preserving family ties made tenuous by slavery.

Virginia documents indicate the use of African names (Anky, Keziah/Kesiah, Agga), ancient Greek or Roman names (Julius Caesar, Cato, Aphrodite/Venus, Cupid, Cassandra), names that reminded black Virginians of their proud and bitter heritage (Cold Chain, Wright Africa), names of liberty (Lewis Freedman, John Jubilee), or even wordplays (a female slave named Anarchy; a free black male named Major Fortune). Food names might be assigned to slaves such as Lemon (male) or Lettuce (female), or free states such as Indiana (female). Invented names were created out of whim or parts of traditional names: Jubert and Marcharg (males). "Franky/Frankey" was commonly used as a first name by slave and free black Afro-Virginian women.[1]

Many slaves used their owners' family name or took the name of overseers, doctors, prominent local or regional personalities, or famous white Americans (John Quincy Adams, Henry Clay, Benjamin Franklin, Patrick Henry, Andrew Jackson, Thomas Jefferson, and George Washington, for example), perhaps in an attempt to derive some of the status held by these whites. The name of a slave frequently changed from owner to owner; some whites objected to slaves having the same name as they or a member of their family bore, and the slave would be compelled to accept another.

Among slaves African names such as Juba, Dinah/Dina (the belittling female counterpart of Sambo), Mingo, Cuffee, and Sambo (Nigerian for "second son") were common, as were Anglo-American ones: George, Amanda, Liza, Tom, Sam, Will, Mary, Nannie, Jim, Rachel, Chloe, Sadie, Lucinda. Nat fell out of favor after (Nat Turner's 1831 rebellion), but Revolutionary War and ancient Roman ones such as Tarleton, Cassius, Pompey, and Caesar remained popular in Confederate Virginia. No matter how beloved, trusted, or faithful a slave was, he could never expect to receive the titles of social respect and equality that were applied to whites. Elderly blacks were called "uncle" (used since eighteenth-century England as a courteous form of addressing an aged nonrelated male), and aged females were known as "aunt" or "aunty." Free blacks possessed Christian names with surnames; common free Afro-Virginian surnames were Brown, Goins (Goings), Johnson, Jones, Lewis, Robinson, Scott, Smith, White, and Williams.[2]

The names that white Virginians used for Afro-Virginians were diverse and demeaning. The word *negro* appeared in print as a generic term, not a proper noun, and was seldom capitalized. "Nigger" tended to be the preferred designation; depending on the speaker's frame of mind, it could imply criticism, hatred, or fondness. Sometimes it or the word *black* was prefixed to a slave's name and thereby became a permanent part of his or her identity ("Nigger Jim," "Black Susan"). "Old Man" or "John" was employed by whites to address middle-aged or elderly black men.

Other contemporary collective or generic nomenclature included: species of property, sons of Ham, Ethiopians, Africans, slavites, nigros, sable sons of Africa, nigritians, Jeff, Jeb, Dinah, helots, Jezebels (seductive or near-white black women), droves of stock / heads of stock, slavelings, Cuffee, niggerdom, woolly heads, members of the shiney-faced institution, the sable race, species of color, colordom, kinky heads, ebony idols, ebons, Topsies, sooty Africans, black apes, bushy heads, imps of darkness, high yaller / yellow (mulattoes), Anglo-Africans, half-Africans, tatterdemalions, Afro-Saxons, ebonics, Corporal Dick, wooly-headed Congo, and Confederate Ethiopians. "Ham and Eggs" was how one Petersburg slave signed his letters.[3]

When Norfolk County planter George Wallace reported the escape of his hired slaves, he included their surnames, most of which were the same as their owners': Daniel Jones (owned by Demsy Jones); Benjamin Brinkly (owned by Abraham Brinkly); John Wilkins (owned by Jackson Wilkins); and Moses Riddick (owned by Captain James Riddick). In 1862 General Robert E. Lee manumitted approximately two hundred slaves belonging to the estate of his deceased father-in-law, George Washington Parke Custis; of these, only three shared the Custis surname (Chole, her daughter Julia Ann, and a male named Major Custis). None claimed the Lee family name. Among fifty-five slaves belonging to the estate of John and William Thornton of Farmville were those named Henry Clay, Abram Jews, Cupid, and Sheo, along with others who had the less whimsical appellations of Willoughby, Cicely, Mary Ann, and Archer. Most slave parents lacked identity as individuals, and their children had even less. Black slave children were customarily known by the first name of their mothers, i.e., Louisa's Lucy, Beckey's Frances, Sally's Kizzy, Patsy's Robert, and so forth. Gloucester County slave owner William Booth Taliaferro, like many Virginia slaveholders, did not bother to record the names of slave children under the age of two.[4]

Slaves referred to one another as "niggers," "chile / chillums," "darkies / darkeys," or "colored folks." According to Union soldiers stationed at Fort Monroe, blacks preferred to address each other and speak of their race as "darky." Blacks' use of the term *nigger* was a manifestation of internalized oppression, the acceptance and use by members of an oppressed group of negative expressions used by their oppressors to describe them. Some ex-slaves chose new names when freedom came, but just as many appropriated their former masters' names as their own. For example, of thirteen former slaves who signed on as wage laborers on the Pittsylvania County plantation of Samuel Pannill Wilson, only four had surnames different from his. White Virginians did not appreciate this practice.[5]

Slaves addressed their masters by combining their Christian names with the acceptable social titles—"Miss Molly," "Master Harry"—master/ mistress, massa/miss, mars/missy, missus, and sir/sah were permissible. Woe betide any black who failed to address a white person, especially white males, in the proper fashion; linguistic indiscretions could be fatal as Southern males were notoriously sensitive about their reputation, status, and titles, particularly military ones (captain/cap'n, major, colonel, general/ genr'l).[6]

But Afro-Virginians also had derogatory terms for whites: "buckra" (a perfidious, no-account white man), "poor white trash," "poor hickories," and "pattyrollers." (The latter was in reference to paramilitary patrols that monitored the movements of slaves and free blacks by checking their passes or free papers. If a black was caught without a pass or in a place where the patrol felt he did not belong, the offender was whipped, maimed, or killed.) "Poor white trash," "mean whites," and "poor white buckra" (the most awesome epithet in the verbal arsenal of blacks) were used to denote white men who did not own slaves or were otherwise lacking in wealth, power, authority, or prestige. Although poor whites ranked above any black, slaves and free blacks were predisposed to speak of them in scornful terms. (It is no coincidence that it was this class of whites who vehemently supported the Confederacy.) Some writers claimed that slavery brutalized poor whites as much as it dehumanized blacks, but during and after the war it was poor whites who were the frontline troops used to keep African-Americans under control.[7]

White Virginia youngsters imitated their elders by poking fun at blacks and making them the targets of cruel abuse and jokes. Mary Livermore, a native of Boston, Massachusetts, was hired by a planter named Henderson to establish a private school for his six children. She believed herself to be compassionate to blacks yet held the characteristic white attitude toward blacks; her autobiography refers to them as "woolly heads" and states that her reluctance to touch blacks was due to colorphobia. But she gradually became more sympathetic. Henderson prided himself on not allowing his slaves to be whipped by his overseer, but Mrs. Henderson was exempt from this rule. Feared by every slave on the plantation, she kept a rawhide whip on her sewing table for those who did not move fast enough in serving her or who dared question her authority. Mr. Henderson conceded slavery made slaveholders despotic, and his son Dick demonstrated this one day by knocking a slave boy flat with his fist over a minor transgression. When Livermore reprimanded him, the young man replied, "In the South we don't 'low niggers to sass white folks."[8]

At another farm a white boy took a pickle, cut ears and a small nose on it, trimmed the stem, and held it by the end so that it resembled the tail of a mouse. He then approached a black child and ordered him to eat the "mouse." This prankster proudly related the aftermath to his sister: "You ought to have seen his astonishment. He at first very stoutly declined but when I told him if he didn't bite the tail off he shouldn't have any more biscuits he came up & in a most doleful manner bit off the least end! When he tasted the vinegar such a face you never saw! I fixed it and then I went around the quarters & such fun as I had with it." In contrast, black children were generally obedient, well-mannered, and respectful of black and white adults.[9]

Freedwoman Elizabeth Harris of Manchester wrote a scathing letter to the Freedmen's Bureau complaining of white children who constantly insulted black adults and stoned them without provocation. But white Winchester resident John Peyton Clark referred to the "crazy fanaticism" of some Union soldiers and berated them for treating white residents as second-class citizens. He watched a fifteen-year-old white boy being cuffed about the face by a soldier during questioning about the shooting of a black man with a paper ball from a toy blowgun. "They hold the negro as the apple of their eye," Clark impotently fumed in his diary.[10]

Sometimes racism was not monolithic. There were whites and blacks who had feelings of mutual respect for each other, but whites who treated blacks respectfully were held in contempt or pressured to conform with community standards of racial dominance. Whites had a distinctive epithet for those who opposed slavery or exhorted its amelioration: "nigger lover." John Curtiss Underwood experienced the fury of racism and intolerance throughout most of his career. A New Yorker, Underwood married a cousin of Confederate general Thomas J. ("Stonewall") Jackson and settled in Clarke County as a dairy farmer in 1839. As a member of the Free Soil party, he became anathema to his neighbors and after threats and warnings moved from the state following the 1856 elections and joined the Republican party. Appointed by Lincoln as the federal judge for the district court of the United States at Alexandria, Underwood used the federal bench to support civil rights for blacks and the confiscation of property owned by disciples of the Confederacy.[11]

Initial encounters with Afro-Virginians generated commentary in the letters and diaries of Yankee soldiers. To them, blacks were an alien species whose appearances prompted feelings of animosity, amusement, or uneasiness. Even camp dogs displayed such reactions. "Whenever they see a darkey," wrote a Yankee soldier stationed at Fort Tillinghast in 1862, "[they] will run and bark at him, and make such a fuss around him that one not accustomed to the scene would think that darkey was about to be torn in pieces."[12]

Northern soldiers applied their own epithets for blacks including "Jeff" (Jefferson Davis), "Jeb" (Confederate cavalryman Jeb Stuart), "John Henry," and the ubiquitous "Sambo." David Probert, a civilian employee of the United States Military Railroads, had little use for Virginians of either race; in his words the Old Dominion's "Niggers and Whites [are] rather a hard looking Lot." A journalist sketched the biracial panorama of White House, Virginia (site of a Yankee supply depot), in June 1862: "Along the whole way from here to the White House are camps as an ornament for a landscape, but wretched and beggarly-looking camps, filthy and disorderly, and not improved by whole negro families which have established themselves in tents and huts among the soldiers."[13]

Union general George McClellan issued proclamations promising Confederates that he would join in suppressing slave rebellions. Samuel Johnson of the 1st Massachusetts Independent Light Battery angrily expressed the army's stance when McClellan was replaced by General Ambrose Burnside in 1862. He blamed blacks and Lincoln for the dismissal of his hero: "It is just a lucky thing for *you*, *you* poor, miserable, weak minded rail splitter, that the soldiers of this army can't get you into their hands, or I should very much fear for your personal safety." A Union defector in Warrenton remarked that he would rather live in hell than fight to free slaves.[14]

Some Yankee soldiers blamed slaves for the war. A series of illustrated letter envelopes epitomize this racism: "One of the Rebels" depicts a black man picking cotton; a grinning seated black man says: "I'se De Innocent Cause Ob All Dis War Trubble"; and a third proclaims, "Proceedings of U.S. Congress, for '61 and '62: THE NIGGER! THE WHOLE NIGGER! AND NOTHING BUT THE NIGGER!"[15] Robert Cummings of the 8th Pennsylvania Cavalry, hospitalized in Hampton, groused to his nephews: "I did not think when I enlisted that it was the cussed niger that I was going to fight for instead of my country—if I had knowed then half as much as I do now you would not have caught me in this nigger shore." One officer, upon seeing a black nurse tenderly kissing a white child in her care, hurried to inform its mother. The woman laughed and told him that the slave was much devoted to her children and frequently kissed them. "If I saw such a nigger kiss my sister's child, I'd put a bullet through her in a minute," was his indignant response.[16]

Lieutenant J. V. Hadley complained about the presence of blacks as he waited for a friend to get off duty for a Christmas Eve dinner engagement. The friend was "driving Contraband negroes" near a landing at Aquia Creek, and Hadley was miffed at having to "stay with him in the midst of his sable throng." After dinner, the two officers summoned a band of "our would be Equals" to dance for their amusement: "Here Ham was represented in every age . . . and dancing as The Sunbeams. The ring was formed, the birds mated, the collars, unbuttoned and every thing ready for the dance. Sambo called out, 'First four forward' and in one movement more buckets, tin-pans and bones rent the air with their melodies. I never saw such an unbounded universal happiness in 'this low vale of tears' and such music."[17]

Afro-Virginians who joined the Union navy experienced racial harassment. Aboard the USS *Constellation* in January 1863 Henry Martyn Cross, en route to Hampton, noted that of a crew of thirty-six, only three were white but they mistreated the black majority and addressed them as "God Damn nigger," "black dog," "bitches," and kicked, cursed, and shoved them around. As the USS *Delaware* patrolled the James River in June 1864, Acting Master's Mate Benjamin Heath matter-of-factly recorded the death of a black seaman named Richardson who drowned while bathing; "body has not been recovered," Heath noted. But Luther Guiteau Billings praised blacks: "We never were betrayed when we trusted one of them, they were always our friends and were ready, if necessary, to lay down their lives for us."[18]

Public punishments of blacks became diversions from the tedium of camp life. Eleven Afro-Virginians were strung up by their thumbs at Alexandria after a dispute with their white supervisors. As he wrote a letter, Robert Goodyear of a Connecticut regiment described the flogging of a black camp servant for insulting a white man as but a momentary interruption. Another soldier characterized blacks as worse than snakes and bragged how he and his comrades ridiculed them. Army regulations prohibited troops from using insulting, abusing, or ridiculing language or showing contempt for blacks but were routinely disregarded.[19]

Soldiers were known to change black names. At Halltown in 1864 Lieutenant John Sturtevant presumptuously changed the name of his body servant from "Jim" to "Eldridge" in honor of a groceryman back home. Among Afro-Virginians it was customary that once an infant's name was written in a family Bible, it could not be altered. A group of Union soldiers passing near a Orange County plantation asked to have a look at a black newborn, for they had never seen one before. A three-day-old baby girl was presented, and they politely asked permission to name her. Her parents consented and stood beaming as the soldiers wrote a name in the Bible and took their leave. They had christened the infant "Emma Jane Jackson Beauregard Jefferson Davis Abraham Lincoln Christian," and a slave acquainted with the child's family commented that the last time he saw the little girl she was still trying to memorize her elongated name.[20]

A member of a Rhode Island regiment found it hilarious that a group of Falls Church "little nigs" were "as black as night" and owned a black cat. Near Leesburg a Yankee corps on the march passed a group of plantation slaves, and when asked the whereabouts of President Lincoln, the soldiers mischievously answered that he would be along a day or two. The blacks began singing "Lincoln's Coming wid His Chariot" as they settled down to wait for a glimpse of the Great Emancipator. During the occupation of Virginia towns, Union troops took over or established their own newspapers, which included advertisements poking fun at blacks. The *New York Ninth*, published in Warrenton by the 9th New York State Militia in 1862, had an advertisement which read: "I say, Sambo, hab you seen dat YANKEE store on Main Street. I tell you, dat's de place for de SILVER dan all de rest of de fellers in town. I say, Jeb, whar am dat store; Why nigga, don't you know? Why it am de store whar de white flag hangs out." Another publication advertised an "Automation Negro Dancer" which simulated the motions of "a living negro affording infinite amusement to both young and old" for the price of $2.[21]

Afro-Virginians rarely gave Yankee soldiers their complete trust. Following a rainstorm one Union officer received permission to enter a house to change into a dry uniform. Directed to the "nigger loft," he was followed closely by the room's occupant, an elderly black man who constantly muttered that he intended to keep a close eye on "any Yankee" in his room. In a similar instance, a group of soldiers stole the key to the room of an Augusta County slave named Aggy but lacked the nerve to take anything because she followed them everywhere until they sheepishly returned it without molesting her possessions. A free black named Goler, whom other blacks shunned as "a mean cuss," betrayed a group of Yankee soldiers after they took refuge at his home during the fall of 1864. Excusing himself on the pretense of procuring food for his guests, he instead fetched a Confederate patrol who recaptured them.

Afro-Virginians intuitively kept their opinions to themselves, whether whites wore blue or gray uniforms. "I'm on the Lord's side," declared one aged slave when asked which side he favored. Black criticism of either North or the South, at the wrong time to the wrong audience, could be catastrophic. Confederate soldiers often dressed in blue uniforms and approached slaves seeking information on the rebels. If a slave proved loyal or stayed silent, they were unmolested, but if he or she betrayed the South, a noose or a bullet was the reward. In the presence of white strangers, most blacks practiced the wisest sort of paranoia by keeping silent.[22]

There were blacks who were not shy about criticizing Northerners. Several Union soldiers were captured in the waning days of generals James Harrison Wilson and Augustine V. Kautz's Petersburg raid in late June and early July 1864. Among them were Colonel Samuel J. Crooks of the 22d New York Cavalry and his cook, fifteen-year-old Henry Washington. In a *Daily Richmond Enquirer* article, Washington accused Crooks of cowardice and fleeing at the opening shots of the battle. On a Yankee-occupied plantation a slave woman denied permission to prepare her usual dinner for her mistress upbraided the soldiers as "mean, trifling, dirty." Another slave, Burrell Barret of Cold Harbor, slept on the floor outside his owners' bedroom with an ax beginning in 1862. He swore to kill anyone who attempted to attack his master's family or else die in their defense.[23]

Numerous Union soldiers treated blacks with kindness and helped slaves escape, especially Massachusetts, New York, Ohio, and Pennsylvania soldiers. Sympathetic officers pretended ignorance when angry slaveholders appeared and demanded their men's punishment. In 1862 a slave owner recaptured one of his runaway slaves in Alexandria, but the city's provost marshal conducted a quick mock trial and freed the slave. A typical comment was that of a soldier who wrote his wife in June 1862: "I tell you we have some pretty jolly times with them [contrabands], they have got quite well acquainted with [us], and we get some of the smartest of them to . . . tell about their Masters and Mistresses down south. We give them all the spare bread and meat that we have for which they are very grateful, they think there is nobody like *Union soldiers.*" A black preacher received three rousing cheers from the camp's white soldiers after a Union-praising sermon.[24]

Dark-complexioned Northern prisoners of war experienced the added burden of racism in the South. Simon Dawson of the 2d Massachusetts Infantry hotly denied being a black after his capture at the battle of Dranesville in February 1864. "His looks and general appearance, suggestive of *Ethiopian blood* . . . does not bear out his assertion," said the *Daily Richmond Examiner,* which noted that his complexion "is deep olive" and that he had the manners of a black man.[25]

As soldiers learned how insidiously blacks were oppressed, many set aside their racism. One wounded soldier who had previously abhorred blacks was so pleased by the culinary skills of an elderly Afro-Virginian woman that he informed his family that blacks were not so bad after all. While talking with a black laborer, Henry Cross was staggered to learn that the man's mother and brother had been sold to parts unknown years before; Cross wrote his parents that such cruelties increased his hatred of slavery daily.[26]

At Wolf Run Shoals in 1862 George Grenville Benedict of the 12th Vermont Regiment reported that only blacks and white deserters from the rebel armies were welcomed to Union lines; other white refugees were turned back. General Orders no. 46 of the Department of Virginia and North Carolina ordered all officers and soldiers to use every means in their power to aid the escape of blacks to Union territory. Military expeditions were encouraged to transport, aid, protect, and actively encourage slaves to abandon their owners. Any "obstruction of recruiting" by soldiers or civilians was subject to military punishment.[27]

But when Pennsylvania artilleryman Frank Shiras expected slaves to follow the army's march to Winchester and Charles Town during the first month of 1865, he was startled when most instead chose to stay behind with or without their masters and with "little to eat and less to wear." Afro-Virginians preferred to stay home, but thousands of black men did sign up with the army, men like Albert Jones who served for three years and said he was well treated. Charles Gandy (or Grandy) of Norfolk who served with the 19th Wisconsin Infantry and later as a guard at Fort Monroe praised white soldiers for providing good moral training and conducting religious services for blacks. Richard Slaughter proudly enlisted in 1864 with the 19th Maryland Infantry (Union) at the age of seventeen. But then there was Mrs. Candis Goodwin, who accused Yankees of doing nothing except to steal white folks' silver and food by day and sneak around slave cabins at night seeking recruits.[28]

Afro-Virginians helped escaped Union prisoners, who nearly always placed their complete trust in blacks, especially slaves. After the battle of Berryville in September 1864, Lieutenant Henry Estabrooks of the 26th Massachusetts Infantry became a prisoner of war. He and other prisoners were marched to temporary accommodations at Richmond's Libby Prison. As the journey resumed toward Danville, a desperate Estabrooks made a break and plunged into nearby woods. For nearly a month he walked across the state without recapture because slaves and free blacks of both sexes provided him with clothing, food, and safe hiding places until he reached Union headquarters at City Point. He encountered approximately a hundred Afro-Virginians during his escape, but not one betrayed him. A grateful Estabrooks named some of them in his postwar memoirs: Fairborne, Willis, Sam, Justin, Bob Bunyan, George, Mattie, John Randolp, Alex, Jordan, Marie, Alvin, Lucy, and Harriet.[29]

As blacks made the transition from slavery to freedom, they began to assert their independence, especially when Yankee occupation troops arrived. Plantation mistresses complained to Union commanders about depredations committed against property by runaway slaves. One Williamsburg woman enumerated oxen, cows, yokes, wagon wheels, "unoccupied houses, fences, and shade trees" as favorite targets for theft or destruction.[30]

In occupied Fredericksburg newly freed slaves participated in a spontaneous labor strike in 1862 after resentful residents refused to pay them fair wages. Betty Herndon Maury described the tense situation: "Matters are getting worse and worse here every day with regard to the negroes. They are leaving their owners by the hundred and demanding wages. The citizens have refused to hire their own or other peoples slaves so that there are numbers of unemployed negroes in town. Old Dr. Fall agreed to hire his servants but the gentlemen of the town held a meeting and wrote him a letter of remonstrance telling him that he was establishing a most dangerous precedent; that he was breaking the laws of Virginia and was a traitor to his race." Afraid to antagonize his neighbors further and apprehensive over the threat of arrest, the doctor changed his mind. The blacks quit the town in a huff, but residents maintained their racial unanimity in wary fearfulness. Maury dreaded the return of one family slave, Jinny, "a dangerous character" who boasted that it was she who had fetched the Yankees to Fredericksburg in the first place. Maury felt vindicated when two former slaves slipped into town and begged for employment; she refused because "in every case the soldiers have interfered in favor of the negroes."[31]

White racial solidarity was envisioned by state attorney general John Randolph Tucker as the duty of every white Virginian: "If men and women [are] not prepared, at the risk of property and life, to defend home, civilization, and religion, in the fear of God, and without the fear of man, then the South would have proved unworthy of a place among nations and derelict to the mighty trust, which God had confided to their keeping." Blacks, in his words, were "the substratum of Southern society . . . semi-barbarians . . . an inferior race."[32]

A white woman named Elizabeth Lloyd was sent to prison by a Richmond court for "continuing to associate with free blacks" despite her oath to "kiss every book in court" in denial of the charges. Lloyd vainly tried to prove that the only black she associated with was an elderly and sick Afro-Virginian woman named Jane Going to whom she was trying to provide care, but the court would not accept her explanation. Even white foreigners were expected to obey the code of caste and race. A British ship captain was tarred and feathered in 1861 after inviting a black man to have dinner with him.[33]

This solidarity had cracks in its facade. A black child accidentally run over by a Richmond railway car in 1862 was tenderly carried to a local hospital by several white passengers. When free black and slave laborers at city fortifications were cheated of their wages and unjustly whipped, the *Daily Richmond Examiner* complained on their behalf: "In the name of God, is there no justice to be found in the courts of human justice for iniquities like this?" A Winchester newspaper, the *Republican,* issued a stinging dissent after a Frederick County court refused to indict James W. Jones for the willful murder of a black man: "That it was the expectation or intention of Mr. Jones to kill the negro we suppose no one believes, but to say it is no offense for a man to point a deadly weapon directly at another, and deliberately shoot at him twice, in striking distance, is giving license to men to make mark of their fellow-men at their pleasure." [34]

The racial attitude of whites toward blacks was reflected in print. An editorial diatribe by John A. Clark of Alexandria complained of John C. Underwood's "Slanderous Language to the Publick" and accused the judge of trying to make blacks think they were better than whites. Underwood replied in polite admonishment: "Do you not think that a man with black skin and a white heart is quite as respectable as a man with a white skin and a black heart? I know you do; I am quite sure you are not so much prejudiced against the colored people, who, with yourself, have so nobly sustained this flag and union of our country." [35]

"The fact can no longer be disguised; let this war result as it may, African Slavery in Virginia is already virtually swept from her territory," editorialized a Fredericksburg pro-Union newspaper, the *Christian Banner,* in 1862. "The fact is, those who have or may hereafter lose their servants, may just prepare, and nerve themselves for the very worst." A Massachusetts officer wrathfully branded as liars Virginians who professed a desire to eradicate slavery and blamed Northern abolitionist agitation for hampering emancipation. After witnessing a slave auction, one Englishmen wrote in his diary that most Southerners were embarrassed by it, and to him it was a "disagreeable business." [36]

Virginians such as Mary Berkeley Minor Blackford of Fredericksburg boldly defied public opinion. Blackford, who lived across the street from a slave trader, not only opposed slavery but freed her slaves and urged their emigration to Africa; when they decided against leaving, she hired them as servants. She was concerned and interested in the welfare of blacks and taught a Sunday school for them, risking indictment by a local grand jury. Five of her sons served in the Confederate army. When the war ended, she was residing in Lynchburg. There the sight of Afro-Virginians celebrating the first anniversary of the opening of public schools for blacks inspired her to praise God that she had lived long enough to witness their emancipation. [37]

Former slaves looking back at slavery provided historical evidence of the redeeming value of the human spirit. Elizabeth Keckley, a Virginia ex-slave, became an expert seamstress and dressmaker whose reputation and skills provided for seventeen members of her family. In 1860 she obtained a position as the seamstress for Varina Davis (later the first lady of the Confederacy), and eventually she held the same position with Mary Todd Lincoln, in addition to becoming her best friend and confidante. It was Keckley who made the dress that Jefferson Davis allegedly was wearing as a disguise when he was captured on 10 May 1865 near Irwinville, Georgia.[38]

Keckley's autobiography is an insider's account of life in the Lincoln White House and was written on behalf of the widowed Mary. When Keckley was asked how she could so easily forgive slaveholders for the enslavement of her people, she replied: "The past is dear to every one . . . [it] is a mirror that reflects the chief incidents of my life. To surrender it is to surrender the greatest part of my existence—early impressions, friends, and the graves of my father, my mother, my son. These people are associated with everything that memory holds dear."[39]

Isaac D. Williams, whose King George County master owned 760 slaves, summed up slavery's failure: "It is impossible to go through life subject to the will of another and not grow rebellious under it." When he visited President Ulysses S. Grant and mentioned the dangers that blacks faced in the Old Dominion, Grant condescendingly replied that Afro-Virginians would not have any trouble as long as they behaved themselves. Louis Hughes, whose father was a white man, never forgot the humiliation of slave sales, the rough physical examinations he was subjected to by prospective buyers. Arguments that blacks were born to be their slaves held little credibility with him, and he migrated from the state as soon as possible.[40]

While there were slaves such as Richard Hackley who could write to their owners with hopes for national peace, others like Edmund Turner of Petersburg presumed to question white treatment of blacks and warned of a day of Old Testament doom: "Slaveholders, have you seriously thought upon the condition of yourselves, family and slaves. As one that loves your soul repent ye, therefore, and be counted, that your sins may be blotted out." Slavery was the worst of times, another melancholy slave once remarked, and she accused whites of committing every known crime against blacks except eating them.[41]

Slaves sometimes learned there was little difference between Southerners and Northerners. Dave Taylor was owned by Pierre Pickney, a Frenchman who lived in Norfolk. Pickney moved his slaves from Virginia in 1861 and headed for Florida because he feared the South would lose the war. Union forces captured his vessel and imprisoned the white men but permitted the slaves and white women to settle in Key West. Taylor was later shanghaied by a United States naval vessel; three years passed before his family saw him again.[42]

William Davis of Hampton claimed slave children were used as living fences, dikes, and fence posts to prevent livestock from wandering off. One Norfolk slave woman gave a heartrending account to a newspaper reporter: "I had twenty children. My Master and Missus sold them all; one of my girls was sold to buy my Missus' daughter a piano." Then she added with considerable emotion, "I used to stop my ears when I heard her play it; I thought I heard my child crying out that *it was brought with her blood.*"[43]

When Thomas R. Martin, a Confederate stationed at Petersburg, needed a good horse in the summer of 1864, he asked his sister to procure one by trading one of the family slaves. Richard Brooke Garnett told London *Times* correspondent William Howard Russell that America's society was analogous to England's in that some men were born to be slaves, some to be free laborers, others to be mechanics, and at the top a minority of elites were born to rule or own other men. When Russell later visited Fort Monroe and Norfolk in April 1861, he described black waiters at the Atlantic Hotel as "untidy, slip-shod, and careless" and the proximity of blacks during Sunday services as intolerable.[44]

Yet many white Southerners feared African-Americans and considered them quietly terrifying. *Douglass' Monthly* reprinted a conversation between a young white girl and an older woman in 1861. The lady assured the child that the slaves had no interest in the war, but the girl replied: "They are always whispering among themselves, and the other day one told me that in six months she would be as good as I am. They say the war is going to set them free, and they are very anxious for it to come." Lincoln's first inauguration was prematurely interpreted by a group of Petersburg slaves as the start of their freedom, and they courteously bade their owner farewell. As the misinformed slaves traveled down a road, they were rounded up by a posse sent by him and ordered to be sold south.[45]

Among the boldest Afro-Virginian slaves were those who took advantage of Yankee successes to confiscate their masters' farms for their own. In 1862, a Clarke County master placed his slave foreman Morgan Coxen in charge of his property before fleeing to the Confederate interior. Coxen sold horses, brandy, bacon, and lumber to Union forces, pocketed the profits, and filed reimbursement claims when the property was raided by Union soldiers. John R. Howard's master, eighty-one-year-old John B. Cannon, was powerless to prevent this slave from taking over his property and claiming it as his own during 1862–65. Howard told Union authorities that the Prince William County farm was legally his because Cannon had no family and Howard and his niece kept the place profitable by baking and selling pies to soldiers.[46]

Whites blamed the Emancipation Proclamation for giving false ideas to "many noble specimens of the race" and longingly spoke of "cherished institutions and happy reminiscences" of when they owned "splendid negro families" who lived in friendship with whites "from the time they landed on the Southern shores as African heathen" and shared the misfortunes of war and protected their masters' families against Yankees. One Southerner claimed: "No two races ever lived in such harmony as the White and Black races enjoyed . . . before the negro was taught by fanatics that slavery was a yoke. . . . More negroes were emancipated in Virginia than in all the New England States combined."[47]

Afro-Virginians who accepted their ordained social and legal inferiority were praised. J. Willcox Brown wrote in his memoirs about "Aunt Betsy our cook . . . a rather old negro, extremely ugly, and without children." Betsy ruled her kitchen with an iron fist and was so cantankerous that she could not attract a husband. On the other hand, "Mammy" was his favorite because she was "full of fun and would tell us lots of amusing stories." She never abandoned her white folks, even after her emancipation: "She never accepted freedom, for she had never been anything but free so far as she desired to be so." Black women of this class were venerated; a popular colorized postcard contained a maudlin photograph of an aged female survivor of the mammy subcaste in a wheelchair with an angelic halo above her head.[48]

Slavery was the only condition for blacks as far as Confederate president Jefferson Davis was concerned. In response to Lincoln's Emancipation Proclamation, his retaliatory proclamation *An Address to the People of the Free States* ordered that as of 22 February 1863, "All negroes who shall be taken in any of the States in which slavery does not now exist . . . and in all States which shall be vanquished by our arms, all free negroes shall . . . be reduced to the condition of helotism, so that the respective normal conditions of the white and black races may be ultimately placed on a permanent basis" (see Appendix C). Large numbers of free blacks were rounded up by the Army of Northern Virginia during the Gettysburg campaign. Fifty blacks near Greencastle, Pennsylvania, were sent southward not as prisoners of war but slaves.[49]

Another manifestation of racism was minstrel shows. "Dixie," the Confederacy's favorite song, made its debut at an 1859 minstrel show. Minstrel shows mocked blacks in songs with gross exaggerations of black dialect and mannerisms and became wildly popular among whites. They burlesqued the pain of slaves being sold from their families and used black caricatures to mouth proslavery sentiments. Confederates saw these pseudo-blacks as accurate images of African-Americans.

These spectacles stereotyped and demeaned blacks as entertaining clowns while contributing *Jim Crow, coon,* and *blackface* to the language. Jim Crow was a happy-go-lucky, ever-cheerful, nonthreatening plantation slave or dandified free black urbanite known as a high-stepping, snappy-dressing ladies' man who laughed too loud, talked, ate (preferably watermelons and chickens), and drank too much, borrowed without repaying, and exercised his penchant for stealing when he could get away with it. He was a harmless, ear-to-ear-grinning, nappy-haired, eyeball-rolling, shiftless, ne'er-do-well man-child.[50]

Minstrel shows were performed throughout the war, even in Richmond up to the day before the final evacuation of April 1865. Afro-Virginians were prohibited from participating in shows, gambling, exhibitions, or theatrical productions of any kind. They could view them from segregated seating, balconies, or standing room only. The price of admission for blacks at the Richmond Varieties Theatre's "Colored Boxes" was fifty cents; at the New Richmond Theatre, prices for whites were seventy-five cents to a dollar, and its "Colored Gallery" cost fifty cents. Most performances began in the evening and consisted of orchestras playing polkas and other music, dancing, comedies, singing, Shakespearean plays, tragedies, ballet, and joke telling.[51]

One of the plays that appeared on the Richmond stage was William Shakespeare's *The Tragedy of Othello, the Moor of Venice,* a favorite among Southern playgoers even though it was a tale of a black man who married a virginal white bride, Desdemona. Confederates were able to accept and enjoy this tale of miscegenation because Othello was a Moor, not a contemporary black (even though *Moor* was synonymous with *Negro*). Desdemona, attracted to Othello, is eventually killed by him, her fate a kind of poetic justice and subliminal warning to white women about the perils of sexual liaisons with black men. Confederate Virginians understood the playwright's disparaging comments about blacks ("thick lips," "sooty bosom," and "lusty Moor"). Othello, of couse, in the end dies by his own hand.[52]

Groups such as Buckley's Southern Minstrels, "the only organized minstrel band in the Confederate states," were highly popular. Burch's Nightingale Minstrels boasted of being the best "Negro delineatoes," but the Olio Minstrels and Brass Band, which performed regularly at the Richmond Varieties Theatre, claimed to be "the only legitimate minstrel organization." Minstrelsy included original songs, dances, and farces, and some of these shows bordered so closely on the risqué that white ladies were advised to attend them only in the company of gentlemen. The Olio Minstrels, who performed in the city as late as January 1865, were proud that ladies could attend their performances "without fear of having their modesty shocked by obscene gagging and vulgar attempts at wit." Clergymen denounced theaters as "sinks of corruption," public nuisances, and "seats of Satan," but the establishments remained open for the duration of the war. Blacks, too, attended and enjoyed these performances.[53]

Several of the songs of minstrelsy had Virginia settings and customarily told of the black man's longing for the state or his love of black women. In "Old Virginny Break Down" a slave boasts of his Old Dominion heritage:

> My mamma was a wolf—
> My daddy was a tiger—
> I am what you call
> De ole Virginia Nigger,
> Half fire, half smoke,
> A little touch of thunder—
> I am what you call
> De eighth wonder!

Another tune antedated the state song "Carry Me Back to Old Virginia":

> I wish I war at ole Warginny,
> A nursin of my piccaninny,
> And talking very fondly to my Flora,
> Wid beef an soup, an cake before her.
> O rare Warginny am de place sir,
> Where de graceful darkey always shows him ansum face, sir.[54]

One African-American exempted from Virginia's prohibition against black professional entertainers was a Georgia slave, Blind Tom. Born in 1849 near Columbus, Tom made his piano debut in 1858 and was immediately hailed as a musical genius. Although he was born blind and mentally impaired, his remarkable brain could translate sounds into pure music and with total recall play any musical composition with perfection. He performed at benefits across the state to wide acclaim at churches and opera, concert, and vaudeville halls. With a repertoire of 5,000 pieces, Tom played selections from Bach, Beethoven, Chopin, Liszt, Mendelssohn, and Verdi. He undertook a triumphal tour of Virginia in January and February 1862, and advertisements proclaimed him "The Marvel of The World." Tom performed with great success before integrated audiences: "And music, what is it, and where does it dwell? I sink and I rise with its cadence and swell. While it touches my heart with its deep thrilling strain, till pleasure, till pleasure is turned into pain." He possessed an excellent singing voice and earned a fortune for his master but died penniless in 1908 after a lifetime of world-acclaimed performances.[55]

Virginia whites despaired about the preservation of slavery by 1864. Catherine Broun of Loudoun County bewailed increasing examples of black betrayal after her slaves revealed to Yankee raiders the location of her farm's hidden stores of food, weapons, and Confederate uniforms: "I am beginning to lose confidence *in the whole race* I see a growing inclination to the Yanks in our own servants . . . it is hard to see them take a stand against us."[56]

Dr. Benjamin Fleet, owner of fifty slaves in King and Queen County, decided anything was better than black freedom and equality even if it meant rule by a dictator like Caesar, Maximilian, Napoleon, or Queen Victoria. Slavery, Dr. Fleet groused to his son, was dying or already dead. Petersburg army surgeon John H. Claiborne, director of the city's military hospitals, was chagrined by the prospect of defeat but conceded slavery's days were numbered in the Old Dominion. Claiborne professed to be glad to be rid of slaves, for they were exorbitantly troublesome, and he anticipated that blacks would "soon be numbered with the unhappy Indians and *colonized* under the earth."[57]

Were Virginia slaveholders and their nonslaveholding fellow citizens North and South racists? The answer to this question is yes. Slavery was a condition exclusively reserved for blacks. Confederate propaganda, generally addressed to political and racial conservatives, tried to warn Northern whites that slave emancipation and black soldiers imperiled the liberties of all of North America's white inhabitants.[58]

The majority of whites did not have an affinity for slavery, but neither did they abhor it. Although the Civil War evolved into an apocalyptic contest of slavery versus freedom, blacks were generally held in low opinion by Confederates and Yankees. Whites who did not own slaves knew of and benefited by the subordination of African-Americans. Slavery was an American caste system, and racism a psychosexual inferiority complex on the part of whites consisting of attitudes, behaviors, and doctrines involving judicial, political, social, religious, and economic aspects that promoted and maintained a belief in the inherent inferiority of blacks.

One day in the Old Dominion, long after the fighting had ceased, a young white girl paid a visit to John, an ex-slave who before the war had been her favorite and now was a free man working his own plot of ground, rightfully proud of his labor and freedom. She wanted to know if he ever missed the "good old days" of slavery and the plantation past. A long uncomfortable pause ensued before John responded not only for himself but for every former slave: "Miss, there's such a thing as feelings."[59]

7 UNEQUAL JUSTICE
Slaves, Free Blacks, and the Law

Great complaints have been made against the repeated acts of violence perpetuated by gangs of Negro women and men.
—*Richmond Times, 1865*

CONFEDERATE LAWS on slavery and race were codified in the permanent Constitution of the Confederate States of America, modeled after the United States Constitution. There were interesting differences and similarities between the two constitutions on the subject of slavery. Both counted a slave as three-fifths of a free person for apportioning taxes and determining the number of representatives each state could elect to the lower house; both prohibited the importation of "negroes of the African race" from foreign countries (other than slaveholding territories or states of the United States) and provided for the right of property in slaves. Slavery was deemed a permanent part of the Confederacy. Its Congress was forbidden to enact any law impairing slaveholders' right of property in black slaves and protected and recognized the right of transit and sojourn with their slaves without impairing ownership.

Also included in both constitutions was a provision for the apprehension and return of fugitive slaves. The Confederacy guaranteed the perpetuation of slavery by adding a commitment to recognize, protect, and defend "negro slavery, as it now exists" in any territories the Confederacy might acquire in the future. The Confederate document, unlike its Federal counterpart, actually used the words *slave* and *slavery* in its text. Furthermore, states such as Virginia defined treason as inciting slaves to rebel; those who did so were liable to arrest, denial of bail, and the death penalty.[1]

Virginia's state capital, Richmond, makes a good case study for examining the legal system's racial undertones during the war. It became a dual capital in May 1861 with the arrival of the Confederate government. A city on seven hills, was frequently called "the Rome of the South" by its residents and like the Rome of classical times, it was a democracy based on slavery. It was home to 2,576 free blacks and 11,699 slaves: 14,275 Afro-Virginian residents. The population swelled to more than 50 percent black (35 percent slaves) by

1862, a 12 percent increase of the Afro-Virginian population. The entire city population rose from 37,910 in 1860 to a wartime zenith of 150,000. Residential districts such as "Screamersville" and "Penitentiary Bottom" were havens for gambling, brawling, drunkenness, and blowing off steam for both races, and the city fathers tolerated them as long as these activities did not spill over into the better neighborhoods. Just before the war the municipal government adopted an "Ordinance concerning Negroes" itemizing draconian measures designed to hinder Afro-Virginian mobility, stifle protests, and prevent the mingling of slaves and free blacks.

A pass system for slaves was inaugurated, and blacks were forbidden to hire carriages or to assemble near Capitol Square or city hall. Walking canes, a sign of affluence and respectability, were denied to Afro-Virginians unless they were elderly or infirm. Groups of five or more blacks were banned from gathering at public places. Blacks were to yield the right of way to whites on public sidewalks, and loud or insolent language by them was a punishable offense. These and related efforts attempted to maintain acceptable forms of black behavior.[2]

City newspapers editorialized against black criminals and complained of the woeful inadequacy of laws and punishments. The office of the tax recorder, located near the mayor's courtroom, was ransacked on the afternoon of 31 October 1862, an audacious robbery under the very nose of justice when numerous persons were in the building. Four trunks and a large box containing stolen goods being held as evidence were broken into, much to the mortification of police.[3]

Richmond's 1861 police force consisted of a hundred daymen with annual salaries of $800 and seventy-two night watchmen whose main duties were to preserve morals and prevent robberies. Less than a year later, public complaints demanded an increase in the size of the force, for hardly a day passed in which residents were not terrorized by assaults and larcenies; as crimes increased, fewer lawbreakers were arrested. Army conscription shrank the police to a daytime force of eight men and a night watch of thirty-six men by October 1862; the detective department was abolished that same month when Provost Marshal John Henry Winder placed the city under martial law. Convicted troublemakers were put into chain gangs under military guard. This did not suffice: between September 1863 and August 1864 city courts convicted fifty-four slaves on felony charges, and editorials advocated the death penalty, not fines or whippings: "Negroes go a-gadding at night, from one end of the corporation to the other; slave mingle with free and in the counsel of the multitude there is mischief."[4]

Courts were inundated with cases of black criminal activity; from 1861 to early 1862 newspapers simply reported "the usual number of Negroes ordered to be whipped" and "several Negro cases of no great importance were disposed of." Between 1863 and 1865 slaves and free blacks were increasingly identified by name, status, name of owner (if applicable), and crime; the verdict was usually guilty, and that meant whippings or labor at public works and military fortifications. But in a metropolis swarming with slaves and soldiers, white refugees and uprooted free blacks, paroled prisoners of war and sightseers, gamblers and foreign observers, farmers and prostitutes, government administrators and clerks, Northern sympathizers and spies, the population explosion underscored racial, social, and law enforcement tensions that made it difficult to keep crime under control. The resulting backwash materialized in the court system.

Two types of courts dispensed justice. At the hustings court the mayor, the city recorder, an alderman, or an elected judge presided during monthly or quarterly terms. It could summon grand juries, but only the mayor or aldermen could act as justices of the peace. Its jurisdiction extended to a mile outside the city's limits, and slightly less than half of its cases involved blacks. Other hustings courts functioned in Danville, Lynchburg, Norfolk, Petersburg, Portsmouth, Staunton, and Williamsburg.[5]

The other Richmond tribunal was the mayor's court, and there he held the powers of a justice of the peace and civil and criminal authority over misdemeanors and other offenses, especially those committed by blacks. The 1848–49 General Assembly established this court and granted it concurrent jurisdiction with the hustings court "in all cases in which the defendant shall be a resident of said city, or a non-resident of the state." The mayor served as chief law enforcer for Richmond and arbiter of its laws. His court became known as "the place where niggerdom came to time."[6]

City courts were characterized as "a loafer's paradise," places of entertainment for crowds of old white men and young white boys "with nothing better to do." Onlookers were so numerous that small dogs were trampled underfoot, their yelps of pain and rage adding to the carnival atmosphere of the proceedings. "A miserable set of wretches," sneered the *Enquirer*, but it conceded that the courts provided an inexpensive form of diversion.[7]

Richmond's wartime mayor, Joseph Mayo, was first elected in 1853. He boasted he would ride up to his saddle in blood rather than surrender the city to Yankees and promised to "whip every nigger in the city." Any black caught without a pass received thirty-nine lashes and was jailed. Once he encountered a black woman and her child on a city street without passes; he slapped the child's face and had its mother whipped.

At war's end Union officials removed Mayo from office, but he was restored to power by Governor Francis Pierpont and reelected mayor in April 1866. Black Richmonders complained, and by 1868 Mayo was expelled a second time. He moved to New Kent County, and upon his death in 1872 gleeful blacks sang:

> Here lies old Joe Mayo in his grave dead
> Often he whipped us till we bled.
> He will send us no more to the whipping post,
> For he has gone to join the silent host.
> To Judgement seat he must come
> To give account for the deeds he has done.[8]

State laws discriminated against free blacks. They were denied voting rights, public education, civil liberties, and the right to learn and practice most trades despite the fact that they, too, were taxpayers. They were required to pay local and state taxes or else be returned to slavery. A group of one hundred Portsmouth free blacks were sold for failing to pay taxes; this was permissible under the city's charter. Black antismoking ordinances were enacted. The Norfolk select and common councils in March 1861 forbade blacks from smoking in public places; those convicted were to be punished with ten lashes or a $1 fine. "Cuffee," the *Norfolk and Portsmouth Herald* remarked, "will have to puff his villainous weed in private—or take the consequences." Charlottesville authorities enacted a similar regulation of ten lashes and a $10 fine. Smoking was identified with freedom, and it was insulting for any black to do so in the presence of whites. The town also prohibited blacks from going to the railroad terminal unless escorted by a white person.[9]

The testimony of Afro-Virginians was permitted only in the trials of fellow blacks. A Richmond free black, identified as Mrs. Jackson, accused a black boy of having stolen $100 from her, and the young defendant was found guilty. Yet in one instance, the word of a black man resulted in the arrest of a white man. A thief named Bohannon stole $40 from the Richmond Medical Examining Board office, but the board's black employee followed him out and had him arrested by a police officer.[10]

The right of blacks to testify was strongly opposed by whites in Union-held areas such as Alexandria County. There, in September 1864, during a lawsuit between two white men—Israel Graff, plaintiff, and Richard Howard, defendant—an objection was raised when Graff's attorney called on Israel Dorsey, a black man, as a witness. Howard argued that under the laws of Virginia persons of African descent were prohibited from testifying in cases where whites were the only parties involved. Dorsey filed a writ of mandamus in the United States District Court for the Eastern District of

Virginia asking that the Alexandria County court be ordered to accept his testimony.

The Federal Congress had enacted in 1863 a law requiring acceptance of testimony without distinction of color, but the Emancipation Proclamation had not exempted Alexandria from its provisions. As a result Federal judge John C. Underwood sympathized with Dorsey, but he nevertheless reluctantly denied his petition, citing Article IV, section 2, clause 1 of the Constitution ("The citizens of each State shall be entitled to all the privileges and immunities of citizens of the Several States"). Any rights Dorsey possessed as an American citizen evaporated at the borders of the Old Dominion.[11]

A Union newspaper reporter described the scene when Anthony Bright, a recently freed Virginia slave, took the oath for the first time in his life as a witness against a white woman, Mrs. Hudgins, during an 1863 trial near Fort Monroe. When Bright was called forward and asked if he understood the consequences of swearing false oaths, he replied that God would punish him. Satisfied, the judge ordered him to take the stand: "As [Bright] lifted his hand and arm aloft, he seemed to gain several inches in height; his broad chest expanded and his dark eye lighted up with the inspiration of new manhood; and I never saw a nobler specimen of humanity in court or camp, and the African race never produced a worthier model of either physical or intellectual mankind." Hudgins admitted Bright had told the truth.[12]

Booker T. Washington commented that stealing was the one vice most frequently charged against blacks by whites, and he complained that blacks were unfairly blamed for not being honest in accordance with white standards. He recalled how his own mother regularly stole chickens, eggs, and pork to feed her family. Washington acknowledged her actions would have been improper if committed by a free person, but he argued that for slaves certain violations of the law were necessary for survival. Slave owners forewarned their slaves that if their crimes were serious enough, "you will be given up to the laws of your country."[13]

In order of severity there were five felonies for which blacks were regularly punished: murder of or striking a white person, arson, running away, stealing, and impertinent language. Whites were obsessed about and routinely punished black misbehavior; the state code specified fines, whippings, imprisonment, or the death penalty. For conspiring to kill or injure a white person, the penalty for blacks was death or ten years' confinement. Whippings were authorized for impudence, "menacing gestures," possession of firearms, participation in riots, seditious speeches and publications, or selling and administering medicines without the consent of a white person. Blacks accused of felonies were entitled to a jury trial, a lawyer, and the right of appeal.[14]

Black felons were routinely sentenced to be transported beyond the boundaries of Virginia. Between 1861 and 1864 eighty Afro-Virginian slave convicts with a combined value of $97,000 were shipped to other states for sale. Each slave had to be appraised beforehand, and their values ranged from $400 to $6,000. John, a slave of George M. Drewry of Richmond, was sold out of the state for the crime of aiding the escape of slaves. Some slaves were just removed from the locality. Another slave, Ann, was convicted of arson in a Buckingham County court, and her sentence was commuted to "labor on the public works for life." It cost the state $70.25 to transport her from the county to the state penitentiary.[15]

After a slave named Amy was convicted of stealing a letter from the Union Furnace post office, her lawyer unsuccessfully sought to have the verdict overturned on the grounds that she was not a legal person and therefore could not be tried or sentenced. Albemarle County slaves Matt and Reuben, valued at $4,000 each, were found guilty of burglarizing the home of Mrs. Ann Goodwin in September 1864. Their court-appointed lawyer, John Spiece, could offer little by way of a defense as the stolen goods were found on the property of Reuben's master, Robert Wheeler. Reuben, after "questioning," confessed and implicated Matt as his accomplice; they were sentenced to be sold from the state. Thomas Green advised his slave-owning brother to sell a troublesome slave, Pete, "as soon as possible." This slave was so sinister that neighbors feared him as "a terrible fellow" and demanded he be sold.[16]

The wife of one slave owner was a "great scold" who frequently punished blacks by striking them with her heavy household keys until blood flowed. Other extralegal devices used to chastise blacks included manacles, stocks and pillories, and iron neck collars and gags (a circular iron band which passed through the mouth and around the lower part of the head and had a thick piece of metal that covered the tongue and prevented speech) used to punish slaves who gossiped about "white folk's business." "Barrel punishment" was reserved for runaways; the slave was placed in an upright barrel which forced him to crouch and confined his arms, leaving his head exposed. Molasses was smeared on his face to attract flies and intensify his misery.[17]

The form of punishment that has received the most historical attention is the whip. Austin Steward, a Virginia slave, described a typical whip as nine feet in length, made of tough cowhide, and having a butt end weighted with lead. This instrument, capable of slicing the skin of the toughest horse or ox, played bloody tunes on innumerable black backs; several commentators remarked how horribly mutilated slave backs were. Leather straps or paddles were also employed because they did not leave deep scars. Paddles, made of flat, thick pieces of wood with large holes drilled in a pattern, inflicted much pain but seldom drew blood or left permanent marks. Other slaves were whipped with tree branches; afterwards someone had to pick the splinters from their backs.[18]

The standard treatment for lacerated backs consisted of grease (lard) or "Negro plaster," a rubdown concoction of salt, mustard, pepper, and vinegar that healed without scarring (and disguised malcontents during sales); but many of its recipients swore it hurt worse than the whipping itself. Reverend Coleman S. Hodges, a former Virginia slave, observed that planters eschewed corporal punishment of slaves in the presence of their guests. But J. H. Van Evrie belittled criticisms of floggings and described them as no more than the switchings white children received at school and home. Black skin, in his estimation, was just "too susceptible" to pain. Another writer flatly asserted that whippings of slaves were neither painful nor cruel.[19]

A few white men were part-time professional slave whippers. They did not post signs or take out newspaper advertisements to announce their services; word of mouth was sufficient. They performed their duties with discretion, usually in basements or the enclosed yards of their residences. An owner would write a note with the number of lashes he wished his slave to receive and send the luckless servant to deliver the order to the slave whipper. One such note accompanied a female slave named Sookey: "She deserves a whipping I wish you to do it in such a manner as not to injure my property. You must not cut her skin as it can be done equally well without and no injury."[20]

Moncure Daniel Conway, a white Virginian who converted from proslavery to antislavery, disclosed the existence of a slave whipper in his hometown of Falmouth, Stafford County. There a Captain Pickett held this office and Conway recalled how he and other neighborhood boys would peek through the backyard fence to watch the "half-naked cowering slave" and overheard the blows of the lash and the imploring cries of its victims. Pickett was a hard man, a gray-haired loner whose family had left him in disgust because of his profession.

His neighbors apparently ostracized him, but he earned a good living because some urban residents were too squeamish to discipline their slaves themselves. Northerners were not permitted to know of the existence of such men. The tourist "will write in his Diary, that, during several weeks passed at the residence of this or that large slaveholder, he saw no cases of severe punishment. . . . He does not know to this day, perhaps, that in every

Southern community there is a 'Captain Pickett's place,' a dark and unrevealed closet, connected by blind ways with the elegant mansions. His Diary might have had a different entry had he consulted the slaves." One day, after a female slave failed to get an answer upon presenting herself at his doorstep with an order for forty lashes, neighbors broke down Pickett's door and discovered that he had hanged himself beside his whipping post.[21]

Each slave had his or her own bitter recollections of whippings. The first slave young Booker T. Washington ever saw whipped was his own uncle, tied naked to a tree and lashed with cowhide; with each blow he heard his whisper, "Pray, master!"[22]

Charles Grandy recalled how his master beat him crossways with more than a hundred lashes, but Grandy achieved a measure of revenge by later stealing the whip and hiding it in the woods. Lucy Jackson of Fredericksburg said if her mistress promised a whipping, she always gave it; two or three days might pass, but it would always come. Sundays gave no reprieve from whippings. A Portsmouth slave owned by a Mr. Emerson received thirty-nine lashes for praying in his master's garden on the Sabbath. When a Mrs. Pence of Rockingham County, who described herself as the "best hand to whip a wench in the whole county," was chided by a minister for flogging her slaves on Sundays, she waspishly countered, "If I were to whip them any other day I should lose a day's work; but by whipping them on Sunday their backs get well enough by Monday morning."[23]

In 1859 future Confederate general Robert E. Lee ordered whippings for three of his slaves, Wesley Norris and his sister and a cousin, for attempting to flee to Maryland. After their capture and return to Arlington, Lee demanded to know why they had absconded; Norris replied that they considered themselves entitled to freedom. Enraged by this answer, Lee ordered them to be stripped to the waist and given fifty lashes apiece and their backs washed in salt brine. Seven years later Norris stated his reason for telling his story: to dispel myths masquerading as history of Lee as a kindly, humane slave owner. Although the general's biographers have denied that he ever had slaves whipped, Norris knew better: the proof was on his back.[24]

State law forbade more than thirty-nine lashes at one time. However, lashes could be administered in increments of ten, fifteen, twenty, twenty-five, thirty, or fifty blows over a period of several days by court order; dosages up to 500 were not uncommon. William, an Albemarle County slave, earned 117 lashes in 1861 for breaking and entering; a Richmond slave received the same for cohabiting with a white woman in 1864. Charles City County planter Richard Eppes promised 500 lashes to any slave who struck him and 300 stripes for striking his overseer.

One unidentified Richmond free black received 561 lashes in 1862; he collapsed into unconsciousness, his back reduced to a bloody pulp. The *Daily Richmond Examiner,* opposed to this and other barbarities, editorialized that he and similarly mistreated blacks deserved better justice. Afro-Virginians were tied to posts, staked out naked upon the ground, stretched across barrels, or dangled from trees to receive the maximum impact of strokes. Slave whippers spread straw around the whipping site beforehand to prevent blood from saturating their shoes. Despite his protestations of innocence, a black Confederate teamster named Washington was ordered to be severely whipped for "carelessly" driving over a white infant. Another slave, accused of setting a tannery on fire, died at sunset after an all-day whipping in 1865. Other slaves were so violently lashed that their screams could be heard at neighboring plantations.[25]

On rare occasions slaves were able to achieve retribution upon those who had whipped them. William H. Clopton, a slave owner known as the cruelest master in Charles City County, was particularly fond of whipping naked slave women. On 10 May 1864 he was captured by troops under the command of Union brigadier general Edward Augustus Wild, an fanatical abolitionist and recruiter of black soldiers. Wild presented whips to Clopton's slaves and told them to take their revenge. The frightened slaveholder found himself stripped and trussed to a tree in front of the general's headquarters as a black soldier, William Harris of the 1st United States Colored Troops, formerly owned by Clopton, applied a lashing so severe that blood flew at every stroke. After fifteen to twenty blows by Harris, three female slaves "took turns in settling some old scores on their master's back."[26]

Katie Blackwell Johnson achieved a taste of vengeance when the arrival of Union soldiers abruptly interrupted her flogging. Her master was holding her head between his legs with his knees when someone came into his yard to warn of the enemy's approach. As he opened his legs to flee, Johnson suddenly bit him, and for the rest of her days she had the satisfaction of knowing she had had the last word, or rather, bite. Another group of Yankees interrupted the whipping of a slave girl by her mistress. They permitted the slave to strip her owner, whip her, and exchange clothes. Justice served, the slave woman departed with her liberators.[27]

Fredericksburg slave Randall Ward, whipped and jailed for uttering anti-Confederate statements (when asked about the possibility of slave soldiers for the Confederacy, he boldly replied that he would rather kill Southern whites), was later revenged upon his owner, Henry Fitzhugh. Fitzhugh filed a $76,000 claim in 1872 for damages and requisitions of wood, livestock, fodder, and equipment by the Yankee army and testified that he had been a faithful Unionist. But Ward and two ex-slaves swore that Fitzhugh had been a Confederate supporter whose two sons served in the Southern army. Ward recounted how Fitzhugh ordered him to be whipped with a cat-o'-nine-tails, handcuffed, and sent to jail because of his advocacy of the Union. Federal commissioners denied Fitzhugh's claims for restitution.[28]

Capital punishment was inflicted by hanging, and executions of Afro-Virginians were lessons for the entire black community of the consequences of challenging whites. White justice and vigilantism were at times indiscriminate; in 1864–65 blacks in Nottoway and Mecklenburg counties and Richmond earned short ropes and tall trees for aiding Union raids against plantations as well as for petty burglaries.[29]

Two slaves, William and Ben, convicted of stealing $2,500 worth of items, were hanged at Richmond's Poor House Hill in October 1864 before a crowd composed mainly of sympathetic blacks. The doomed men were permitted final prayers before somewhat unsteadily climbing the scaffold. Ben addressed the crowd first and said his sentence was fair. He asked for forgiveness and warned his listeners to "never stray from the paths of virtue." William urged onlookers to abstain from sin. A black employee of the jail named Nelson then spoke: "My brethren, if you all do not turn from your wicked ways you'll sartingly come to some bad end." An unidentified black man, with the permission of the sheriff, mounted the scaffold, shook Ben's hand, and promised to care for his family. The trap was sprung at noon, but both necks failed to break and the condemned suffocated "in the most violent manner." Ben managed to get his feet back on the scaffold three times, and each time the hangman pushed him away. The ensuing month saw a poignant sequel to this execution when the cookshop of a free black, Royall H. Smith, was raided by police for operating without a license. He and two black women were arrested, and one, Elizabeth Valentine, was the widow of the recently hanged Ben. She wore his ambrotype around her neck.[30]

Another method frequently implemented to control black behavior was the threat of sale, usually "sold south." This meant areas of the true cotton kingdom: Alabama, Georgia, Louisiana, Mississippi, and Texas. One afternoon a group of Afro-Virginian slave children made so much noise as to disturb their owner's guests. Cornelius Garner recalled years later how his owner angrily stomped down to the slave quarters and "picked out de family dat got de mos' chillun an' say, 'Fo' God, nigger, I'm going' to sell all dem chillun o' your'n lessen you keep 'em quiet.'" Instant silence descended throughout the quarters. Another method of control utilized cash inducements: payments to slaves for good conduct such as not running away or making serious devilment. It could even be described as conscience money. One

Buckingham County slave, Stirling, regularly received money from his owner "as pay for [his] good behavior."[31]

Slaves were sent to labor on public or military projects, and Confederate engineers had the justly earned reputation of working slaves hard and returning them to owners in worse condition than when received. Afro-Virginians fled or feigned illnesses upon the learning of the arrival of labor conscription and engineering officers. Free blacks, too, were conscripted; Seaton Anderson, caught with stolen potatoes and turnips, found himself sentenced to an indefinite exercise period of "dirt throwing at the batteries."[32]

Accused blacks were not always found guilty. A Richmond slave, Benjamin, though charged with stealing $200 worth of clothing from a trunk, was acquitted in June 1863. The governor pardoned five slaves in 1861 and restored them to their owners: Jack and Ben (Hanover County, property of F. N. Fitzhugh); Tom (convicted by an Amherst County court and property of George W. Clift of Alabama); Bill (Jefferson County, property of Emory Edwards); and John Ricks (New Kent County, property of Charles W. Gilham).[33]

Other Afro-Virginian convicts obtained clemency. Of the forty-eight prisoners pardoned by the governor in 1862, several were black. Free black William Scott was pardoned in May for accepting money under false pretenses, and a slave, John Hicks, obtained amnesty by an act of the General Assembly in May. Jim, a Botetourt County slave, had been convicted with a fellow slave named Oscar for the murder of a white man named Tribbett, and both were sentenced to be executed. But when Oscar exonerated his codefendant of culpability, Jim was pardoned on 22 September 1862. Free black Frederick Fulcher was fifteen years old when convicted in December 1861 in Westmoreland County for helping a slave named George to escape. He was pardoned in January 1862 after a review of the evidence and county residents' vouching for his character.[34]

Five blacks were pardoned in 1863. Thomas Cooper was freed in August on the condition that he sell himself into slavery. He had been convicted in 1860 for grand larceny in Augusta County and sentenced to five years; his exemplary behavior while imprisoned earned him a momentary release, an exchange of one form of bondage for another. Isaac Harris of Chesterfield County was serving eight years for a stabbing, but at the request of his victim and county residents and as a result of his good conduct (and severe rheumatism), a pardon arrived in October. Joseph Farro of Richmond was pardoned within a month of his October 1863 conviction for receiving stolen goods; amnesty was granted in December for William Morton, a convicted burglar. An unusual case concerned a Halifax County slave named Simon who had been convicted of breaking and entering. An examination of the evidence by Governor Letcher led to Simon's unconditional pardon.

The fates of other Afro-Virginian convicts were merely postponed. Sylvanus T. Brown, a free black convicted in October 1863 for grand larceny and sentenced to be sold, obtained a reprieve, not a full pardon. Halifax County slave John was scheduled to hang for burglary until he caught smallpox from a cell mate. A thirty-day reprieve was ordered due to the governor's fear that white spectators at the execution site might be exposed to the disease.[35]

Convicts served their sentences at the state penitentiary in Richmond, described as a "sorry figure for the State prison of the leading State of the South." Construction of this facility began in 1800 on a hill overlooking the James River. Its brick cells were 12 feet by 6½ feet by 9 feet. Convicts were required to spend the first six months and the final month of their sentences in solitary confinement. The outside walls of a dozen or so dungeonlike cells for this purpose were below water level.

The penitentiary lacked indoor plumbing or heating; prisoners shivered in winter and sweltered in summer. The building was so damp that throughout its interior evaporation trickled down its walls. Its location near the James River and Kanawha Canal meant toxic fumes from garbage and wastes in the stagnant water wafted its way, and periodically the place had to be aired out so that the staff and inmates could breathe. The effects of solitary confinement on the mental health of inmates and a bread and water diet contributed to a high mortality rate. Although there was a hospital, the death rate was so appalling that one of its superintendents admitted prisoners suffered more than was necessary.

Penal doctrine held that inmates were to be put to hard work. Virginia subscribed to this ideology, and convict labor was expected earn a profit. They labored in workhouses at the penitentiary where they operated cotton and woolen mills and manufactured boots, nails, and furniture. The facility never became self-supporting, and inmates were kept busy mowing grass and trimming shrubbery. There were no recreational activities, and Sunday services were not permitted until 1835. By the middle of the nineteenth century the state penitentiary was more bastille than reformatory.[36]

Afro-Virginians were seldom incarcerated for "white" crimes such as rape of black women, mail robbery, counterfeiting, or bigamy. They were more likely to be convicted of grand larceny, burglary, second-degree murder, and stabbings. The white population at the state penal institution totaled 292 inmates in 1861, and there were approximately 242 black inmates during 1861–1864. More whites than blacks were confined for slave stealing or aiding runaways or slave conspiracies. Among the ten whites incarcerated

TABLE 7.1. AFRO-VIRGINIAN INMATES, STATE PENITENTIARY, 1861–64

Year	Males	Females	Totals
1861	81	6	87
1862	41	17	58
1863	42	23	65
1864	27	6	33
Total	191	52	242

Source: Message of the Governor of Virginia, and Accompanying Documents: Document No. 13, Annual Report of the Board of Directors of the Penitentiary Institution, Year Ending September 30, 1861 (Richmond, 1861), 20–23, 28, 33; ibid., Document No. 6, . . ., Year Ending September 30, 1862 (Richmond, 1862), 33; ibid., Document No. 9, . . . , Year Ending September 30, 1863 (Richmond, 1863), 18, 19, 30–31; Daily Richmond Enquirer, 19 Jan. 1865. The 1864 figures are for free blacks only.

for aiding runaway slaves was a Captain Bayliss, convicted in 1858 for attempting to smuggle five Petersburg slaves to freedom on his ship. During 1861–64 the black male prison population declined, but the black female population fluctuated (table 7.1). One reason for this fluctuation was the hiring out of several of the black female convicts to the Tredegar Iron Works. Five women were sent to Tredegar furnaces in Botetourt County during 1863–64: Lavina and Ann Taylor to Grace Furnace, where Taylor eventually died, and Ellen, Belinda, and Hetty to Cloverdale Furnace.

Black convicts were an additional source of cheap labor. Thirteen free black convict laborers between the ages of twenty-one and fifty-seven were put to work for Rockbridge County's public works. Convicted felons became slaves; several of these men were sentenced to life terms with this purpose in mind. Afro-Virginian inmates, more frequently than whites, were hired out as county laborers. At one point during the war 408 blacks were sent to the Tredegar Iron Works in Richmond to supplement the company's workforce. The governor reported fifteen black convicts as hired out for the year and ordered the sale of sixteen others.[37]

Incarceration became a death sentence for some. Beverly, a slave convicted and sentenced to be hanged, committed suicide in 1863 before his scheduled execution. His owner, William J. Morgan of Fauquier County, was reimbursed the sum of $1,325 by the state. Ned, a fifty-eight-year-old slave sexton imprisoned for the 1859 rape of a white woman, and Henry Adkins, a thirty-five-year-old butcher sentenced for malicious wounding, died in the state penitentiary while serving time. So, too, did the hapless infant of Mary E. Lewis, a female inmate. Black children born in prison became state property and were sold at auction. Governor Letcher recommended selling these children because they were at the prison "through no fault of or misconduct of their own—they have committed no crime, and humanity requires that some disposition be made of them." At the time of his proposal the oldest of the black children housed in the penitentiary was five years old.[38]

"A negro shall be punished with stripes . . . if he uses provoking language or menacing gestures to a white person," admonished the state legal code. For insulting and threatening a white woman a slave named Solomon earned fifteen lashes in 1862. A free black resident of Charlottesville and waiting maid for the Virginia Central Railroad, Lizzie Burns, directed uncomplimentary remarks at one of the male passengers; a Richmond judge ordered her to receive thirty lashes. John, a slave hack driver, recklessly addressed several of his white female passengers in an insolent manner in November 1864. They were returning from a funeral when John rudely informed them that he had carried them far enough for the amount paid and ordered them out. John's "jawing," which included the comment that "white women could walk," ended with his arrest and thirty-nine lashes.[39]

Allen Tyree, a free black, earned the usual number of stripes for impudence, as did Aylick, a slave who boldly entered the kitchen of Mrs. Margaret H. Vaiden and stole an iron boiler while using "impertinent language." Another free black, James Roberts, was arrested in 1863 for using threatening and abusive language to a white man, Timothy Callahan. Callahan testified that the drunken Roberts appeared before his home "ripping and cutting up" and when ordered to leave cursed him as "a damned white livered son of a bitch" and declared that he was not afraid of any "damned white man." In his defense Roberts identified himself as an employee of Talbott's Foundry and claimed he was not to blame because white coworkers had gotten him drunk.[40]

State law forbade blacks liquor, but they obtained it in illicit ways. A slave named Scott and three other blacks broke into a storehouse and stole twelve bottles of whiskey as refreshments for Scott's impending wedding. The groom-to-be was caught and incarcerated, leaving his bride waiting at the altar. Two black men robbed the Confederate Treasury Department of $12,000 in February 1863 to finance their respective weddings and proceeded to make conspicuous purchases of finery throughout the city. Detectives tracking the pair discovered they had bought wedding goods from free black entrepreneurs Edward Allen and George Mitchell of Franklin Street, Aunty Stewart of Eighth Street, Garrett James of Fifth Street, Biddy Branch of Fourth and Leigh streets, and James Scott of Eighth and Cary streets. "Vigorous applications of the whip" to these storekeepers led to the recovery of stolen money paid to them and information leading to the apprehension of the thieves.[41]

Free black John Randolph regularly purchased apple brandy for $12 a quart without any difficulty, and Afro-Virginian men in Lynchburg could get whiskey for fifty cents a shot. "Gor a mighty, massa," exclaimed one slave when charged a dollar for a small drink. "Why you ask 'mazing price?" The mayor of Petersburg sentenced a free black man, Martin, to toil on the chain gang for three months as punishment for his fondness of "glass and jug." When a drunken free black youth named Arthur Ferguson overimbibed his "Christmas potations" and assaulted a white man, he was easily subdued by the would-be victim and taken to jail. Indecent exposure was a rarer breach of lawlessness. Three "dandy looking" black men were arrested for bathing in the James River and "exposing their naked bodies to public view" in Richmond on a hot August day in 1864.[42]

Virginia laws forbade blacks from owning firearms, and slave patrols were authorized to search slave cabins and free black homes for weapons. But blacks were able to acquire guns if nervy enough. Two slaves, Brown and Joel, were caught with loaded pistols and severely flogged in December 1862.[43]

Additional perils surrounded the pass system. Slaves were not to leave plantations or their owners' businesses or residences without them, and free blacks needed "free papers" (legal documents proving their freedom), especially after sunset. Black employees of the Confederate White House needed passes in order to complete their errands: "Pass Henry to Apothecary's store and back to Presdts House—Jefferson Davis / November 10, 1863." Ordinances banned five or more blacks from congregating at one time. Afro-Virginians ostensibly gathered for weddings, funerals, and religious ceremonies were suspected of plotting rebellion. Laurence, a slave of the South's greatest diarist, Mary Chesnut, learned this hard lesson when he attended a blacks-only party in Richmond. He forgot his pass, and when a brawl erupted the police arrested anyone who lacked one. James Chesnut had to appear personally at the jail to gain Laurence's release.[44]

Twenty-two blacks were arrested in December 1861 by a Richmond city watchman at the home of Alexander Archer for unlawfully congregating and "having a high old time" during a private holiday party. The women were released after their respective employers paid fines, but the men were punished with "a slight flagellation." Owners and employers were advised not to give slaves "liberty to attend these social gatherings, for the Mayor has determined to enforce the law in every instance." This admonition was ignored; another forty-two blacks were seized on 5 August 1864 and charged with unlawful assembly at the home of James Pendleton, a white Richmonder. Two city night watchmen, tipped off in advance, made the arrests; several of the blacks escaped. Those apprehended held passes, but the Pendletons had neglected to obtain permission from a local judge. Evidence presented at the hearing indicated that the blacks were attending a wedding, but the watchmen disputed this and accused the Pendletons of trying to shield slaves from punishment. After a fifty-three-year-old woman and an infant of five months were excused, the other forty blacks got ten lashes apiece.

A similar case in Petersburg in August 1862 involved a late-night meeting of sixty blacks at the home of Thomas Smyth. A warrant for their arrest was issued shortly before midnight while the meeting was still in progress, and three constables arrested thirteen and scattered the others. Half of those arrested were released after showing their passes, but the rest were whipped. A local newspaper warned, "We have no doubt that the law in regard to the assembling of negroes on one's premises, is ignorantly violated in many instances in this city, as probably was the case in the present instance, but this ignorance does not relieve the owner of the premises on which the meeting takes place from the penalty." Five months later forty blacks caught unlawfully assembling for music and dancing were, in the brusque words of the *Daily Richmond Examiner*, "disposed of according to law."[45]

Afro-Virginian women initiated individual acts of resistance that demonstrated their capacity for ferocity. Poisonings, assaults, stabbings, arson, vandalism, escapes, and murders terrified and astounded Confederate Virginians. Family heirlooms were among the casualties of the guerrilla wars that black women waged against white women. "That Nigger Mahala has broke another china plate and saucer," bemoaned the mistress of Glencoe plantation in Norfolk County in 1863. "If she would only confine herself to destroying the stone china I could bear it better, but she always breaks my French china." A young woman, Coley, stoned the house of Adolphus Tyree, destroying thirty-two window panes for which she received two lashes apiece, while another, Susan, tried to burn her employer's home.[46]

During the year 1864 a drug containing nux vomica was prescribed for a member of the Culvin Ford family of Petersburg. This poisonous seed of a tree in the Strychina family has an intensely bitter taste, but nineteenth-century physicians recommended it as a remedy for morning sickness, stomach cramps, rheumatism, impotence, neuralgia, and incontinence. But it could be toxic: fifteen grams could cause death.[47] The Fords' slave Elvira somehow got hold of the bottle and set a glass of buttermilk laced with nux vomica at her mistress's place before a family meal in March 1864. Upon taking a sip Mrs. Ford detected the bitter taste of the drug, and Mr. Ford threatened the servant woman with instant death unless she drank it. Elvira swallowed half a glass and tried to leave the room to disgorge the drug but was prevented. After a few minutes of dizziness, she suffered a series of spasms and collapsed, but a physician saved her life. Found guilty during an August trial, Elvira was sentenced to be sold and transported beyond the boundaries of the state. However, Mr. Ford evidently had second thoughts about suffering a significant monetary loss (owners could receive compensation only for those slaves who received the death sentence), for he petitioned that she be returned to his custody. Despite her murder attempt Elvira, after some sort of scourging, could always be sold to an unsuspecting buyer. The Virginia Supreme Court of Appeals reversed the Petersburg court in February 1865; the court acquitted Elvira and ordered her return to the Fords.[48]

Elvira was not the only would-be slave poisoner. Amanda, a Richmond slave, tried to kill five white schoolgirls at the local school where she was employed as a cook. She baked a cake laced with zinc which made them violently ill. Doctors were called as their condition grew critical, but they all recovered. Amanda and a slave boy accomplice, George, were arrested; bail was set at $700. Later, charges against the pair were dismissed.[49]

Afro-Virginian females did succeed in murdering whites. Margaret, a twenty-year-old slave owned by Mary M. Butt of Oxford, North Carolina, was executed on 9 January 1863 in Richmond for the murder of a white infant. She denied as false the testimony of the chief witness against her, another slave, and accused the latter of having committed the homicide. Margaret smiled to the crowds as she rode from her cell to the gallows.[50]

A free black woman named Robinson killed Mrs. Hester Cooley with a meat cleaver during 1861 at Belle Grove plantation near Winchester. Robinson, hired as a cook by Cooley's husband, Benjamin, exchanged angry words with Mrs. Cooley over the preparation of supper one afternoon while Mr. Cooley was absent. Mrs. Cooley decided to cook the meal herself, but after she and Robinson arrived at a smokehouse, the black woman renewed the quarrel and murdered her. Robinson tried to make the crime look like an accident by tearing her victim's clothing and hanging pieces of it on meat hooks to make it appear that Cooley had fallen from the top of the smokehouse into a fireplace.

Robinson was found guilty of first-degree murder, but before sentence was pronounced, defense attorney Colonel Robert E. Byrd asked the court to set aside the verdict due to a legal technicality: his client was pregnant. The sheriff was ordered to subpoena a panel of eight white women to examine Robinson while the judge and spectators awaited their decision. After an hour's search he was unable to find any women who would obey the court's summons; in fact, several candidates threatened him with bodily harm if he tried to force them to come to the courthouse. When ordered to double his efforts, the sheriff threatened to resign. After several minutes of commotion, the proceedings resumed in absence of proof of Robinson's pregnancy, and the judge remanded her to jail pending execution. This delay proved fortuitous when she vanished shortly after Union troops arrived and freed Winchester's blacks, including those in jail.[51]

Assaults and thefts by Afro-Virginian women were not uncommon. Columbia Anderson, a dishwasher at the Georgia House Hotel in Richmond, was in 1862 a "known man-beater" who when intoxicated sought out and assaulted white men. A slave woman, Louisa, picked up a white boy and hurled him upon a sidewalk with all her might. Dolly, a slave owned by Petersburg resident John Allen, received a court-ordered whipping in 1864 after stealing two ducks and three days later returned to court, this time for threatening Winny, a free black woman who had testified against her. Rose, a slave who lived on Halifax Street in that same city, earned twenty-five lashes for stealing a pair of new sheets from the clothesline of a city housewife; when caught Rose had already converted one into a petticoat, but its owner identified it.[52]

Sarah Putnam, a white Richmond resident, denounced the audaciousness of black women: "We were compelled to keep a rigid practice of barring and bolting and locking; yet all precautions proved ineffectual to prevent the thievish depredations of the negroes, demoralized by the various contending influences which served to develop such propensities in them." One lady returned home after a prayer meeting to discover her two maids had taken several thousand dollars' worth of her possessions. The wife of a Tennessee congressman was in Richmond for a few weeks when her trusted servant woman disappeared with diamonds and clothing valued at $30,000.[53]

Some Afro-Virginians were the victims of white criminals. Edward C. Priest, a member of the Richmond City Battalion, knocked a stack of plates from the head of an unoffending black woman and was ordered to pay a $10 fine. However, Nimrod B. Dickinson, arrested for shooting Sarah, a slave of David McDaniel, was released for lack of evidence in June 1863. Less than a year later an elderly free black woman, Sally White, was victimized by two white men who claimed to be city watchmen. They entered her home, claimed she was under arrest, and ordered her to get dressed. As White complied, they drew pistols and robbed her of $100 in cash, a gold breastpin, and a pair of earrings.

Charges against a white man named Reynolds for assaulting a black girl were dismissed without comment in December 1861, but not for William Langdon, an intoxicated Confederate soldier who tried to shoot Henry Cooper, a hack driver. Cooper, recognizing his passenger's condition, requested payment in advance, but instead Langdon shot him. Cooper's thick overcoat stopped the bullet; Langdon tried to flee but was arrested and indicted for a misdemeanor. Bail was set at $1,000 because the crime had been committed against property, not a person: Cooper was a slave.[54]

Shortly before the capture of Norfolk in 1862, twenty-five of its black residents paid $1,500 in gold to a white man, Joseph Riddle, to smuggle them to Fort Monroe. Riddle kept the money and betrayed them into slavery. On Christmas Day, 1863, a group of black children shooting firecrackers in the middle of a Richmond street were scattered by two constables. One officer struck a boy in the back of the head, knocking him senseless. Thinking he had killed the child, the man fled to Hanover County.

Charles F. Reese brutally whipped a ten-year-old slave girl belonging to a Mrs. Davis and "literally cut her to pieces" for allegedly stealing his wallet. He wrung a confession from her but was overheard by Officer Kelly. When Kelly demanded to know the reason for the horrible beating, Reese replied that the girl had given his wallet to a free black and asked the constable to whip her in order to learn her accomplice's identity. Kelly took both to the mayor's court where a reporter described the black victim as dripping blood, every inch of her body bruised or cut "in the most horrible manner," and bleeding heavily from her scalp. The unrepentant Reese said he would beat her again until she confessed, but instead he was jailed. The girl, battered so badly as to be unable to eat, collapsed during the proceedings, and a physician was summoned to treat her injuries.[55]

A slave named Washington nearly died at the hands of Francis Craven, a Danville depot watchman, on the morning of 30 July 1864 after several blows were inflicted on his head with an iron bar, critically wounding him. An armed passerby who witnessed the assault made a citizens's arrest of Craven. The watchmen first swore that Washington had insulted him, then changed his story to claim the slave had used insolent language against his wife. But white witnesses testified that Washington was walking down a street with two chickens minding his own business when Craven attempted to steal them. Shortly after the fall of Richmond, a city newspaper criticized an assault of two black men by a pair of white men who beat and robbed them. "One of them, happening to be dressed rather genteelly, was stripped to his drawers and shirt. An armed guard is needed to put a stop to outrages of person and property."[56]

Black-on-black crime and overt aggression were disapproved of by whites not for the preservation of order but due to real concerns that they might provoke black insurgence against whites. The courts vigorously dealt with such affairs. Peter Butler, a free black, broke down the door of a black woman's house and threatened her with a knife; a Petersburg newspaper commented that "such conduct [is] very unbecoming even for a Negro." When Jesse and Mary Scott were accused of stealing chickens from another black, it was a white woman, Mrs. McKinney, whose testimony proved their innocence. William, a Petersburg slave, stole an imitation gold chain from his roommate Andrew and sold it to another slave, Toney. He confessed the theft and offered as a defense the best possible reason: his need of money. Andrew's property was returned to him; William got twenty-five lashes and had to reimburse Toney.[57]

These and other Afro-Virginians did not scruple to assault, steal, exploit, or threaten one another. A young boy named William Jackson was accused by a Mrs. Jackson (no relation), "a monstrous big negro woman" weighing 400 pounds, of stealing $100 in cash and other valuables; he confessed to spending the money on ginger cakes. Araminta Murray, a free black woman, assaulted Ellen, a slave, but claimed self-defense because the latter had started the fight. Isham, a prison hospital slave and infamous lawbreaker, stabbed Nat in October 1864; the next month he stabbed another slave, Mack. Isham's propensity for settling his quarrels with a knife cost him thirty-nine lashes. In a similar case a slave named Edmond was ordered in October 1862 to receive twenty-five lashes for threatening to "cut the heart out" of Nathan, another slave. Some blacks were abusive, violent, and dangerous to members of both races. Their misdirected malevolence enabled whites to act as guardians of the Afro-Virginian community.[58]

Afro-Virginian children also violated the law. A boy strolled into a Petersburg establishment in February 1862, snatched a piece of cashmere, and fled at full speed to the Penniston Alley residence of a free black man, Henry Walthall, where he abandoned his prize to cover his escape from a crowd of whites. Walthall promptly turned over the stolen item to the pursuers. "The perpetuation of a theft like this in broad daylight, and almost in the presence of some half a dozen persons, is a very bold deed for a negro boy," declared one city newspaper. A Mrs. Ford of Jones Road complained to the mayor about the theft of thirty chickens and blamed it on two slave families whom she described as dishonest nuisances. Her neighbor John Bishop concealed himself and eventually caught two boys from the families in the act of fowl stealing. A Suffolk slave boy detected stealing from his master, a North Carolina colonel, was so humiliated by his capture that he committed suicide.[59]

By 1864 one of every nine persons arrested in Richmond was black. A slave named George entered a public eating house there and loudly but foolishly offered his services in conveying anyone, white or black, slave or free, to the Union lines at Tappahannock. He quickly found himself under arrest for his bravado. Another slave, Christopher, broke into a city residence and made off with $2,500 worth of clothing and jewelry; William Robertson, a slave, and John Diggs, a free black, openly "visited" the premises of a Mrs. Bragg without permission. The sheriff of Amherst County posted a $2,000 reward for Alick, a slave of Pembroke E. Waugh, who escaped after killing a white woman. The public was urged to assist in Alick's apprehension so that the slave murderer "could receive his just desserts."[60]

City council members and prominent citizens were not immune to black belligerence. Richmond councilman Flemming Griffin was attacked in October 1864 by "a stout negro" near Horse Swamp Hill. The man seized Griffin's horse and stabbed at him with a bayonet, but the councilman escaped by firing a double-barreled shotgun at his assailant, who fled. Laburnum, the home of attorney James Lyons two miles north of Richmond, was set on fire by a slave arsonist named Wilson. The occupants narrowly escaped the flames in their nightclothes. Damage was estimated at $150,000, and Lyons's $30,000 law library, family papers, furniture, shade trees, and Mrs. Lyons's diamonds were destroyed. Wilson held a grudge against the Lyonses because they had had him arrested for aiding in the escape of one of their slaves.[61]

Blacks and whites committed crimes together. David S. Creigh of Greenbrier County (now West Virginia) killed a Union soldier in November 1863. The soldier entered the Creigh home and began ransacking and looting its rooms. Creigh confronted him; both fired pistols simultaneously, but neither was wounded. Creigh grappled with his foe, and the two men tumbled down a flight of stairs. A slave witnessing the fight snatched up an ax, saying, "Master, he will get up," and urged Creigh to kill him. They secretly buried the body, but a neighborhood slave boy notified Union authorities. Creigh was arrested and hanged at Rockbridge County in June 1864.[62]

Jacob N. Hoeflick was a Pennsylvania native who during 1864–65 became involved in several black felonious activities. A Richmond confectioner who resided with his wife, Abigail, a native of New Jersey, and their three children, Hoeflick owned both real and personal property valued at $15,000 each.[63] His troubles began with his March 1864 arrest for selling a barrel of flour to a slave for $275 without the permission of the slave's owner. Dissatisfied with the price quoted, the slave tried to cancel the deal, but Hoeflick refused. Authorities later fined Hoeflick $20 and ordered him to repay four times the flour's value, $1,100. The following October three slaves and a free black were arrested for breaking into Hoeflick's store. They took approximately $3,280 worth of sugar, coffee, pencils, rice, molasses, calico, and coats and then tried to burn the premises to camouflage their crime. Of the three slaves, Jacob (with an appraised value of $4,000) was sold to another Confederate state, and Sam and Curtis were released. Richard Drew, the only free black, was sold into servitude.[64]

Coincidentally, this robbery occurred on the day before the commencement of a legal investigation into the death of one of Hoeflick's slaves, Josephine, a slave child who died in August 1864 under mysterious circumstances. An inquest ruled her death was due to natural causes but included a mild censure which stated that it had been "accelerated by blows or other injuries." Mrs. Hoeflick was suspected but fled north (probably to New Jersey). Hoeflick (described as a member of the city fire brigade) was charged with murder, and bail was granted to allow him time to retrieve his absconded spouse. He posted bail for $500 but did not find his wife. His first trial ended in a hung jury. Hoeflick's next trial required an entire day of testimony on 19 January 1865 following his indictment by a grand jury, along with his still-absent wife. He stood accused of having aided and abetted his wife's "undue" correction of the slave; his luck held out once more as the second jury acquitted him.[65]

The law had not yet finished with Hoeflick. Martha Jackson, a slave who cared for his children during the prolonged absence of his wife, had been a trusted family servant of eleven years' service until she and Tom Fagan, another slave, were convicted of hog stealing. Judge Mayo objected to Jackson or any other black serving as the caretaker of white children and ordered Hoeflick to find someone else to look after for his motherless children. "I don't care, sir," the judge angrily interrupted as Hoeflick attempted to explain his difficulties and faith in Martha's surrogate abilities. "You shall not put your children out to live with negroes."[66]

One of the war's enigmas was voiced by Union naval officer Luther Billings. Baffled over the dearth of black-led wartime slave revolts against Confederates, he rhetorically wondered, "Why they did not band together and rise on their masters to fight for their own freedom?" Carter G. Woodson, the father of African-American history, hypothesized two centuries of slavery and inferior intellectual capacities as the reasons Southern blacks did not rise up in mass revolts against the Confederacy.[67]

Richmond organized a public guard and passed ordinances regulating black movements to forestall gatherings where murder and mayhem might be plotted. Few Virginia whites were killed during slave rebellions until Nat Turner's 1831 uprising. Oftentimes a single slave might resist his oppressors, and on the spur of the moment his friends and family might intervene violently on his behalf; sometimes whites died as a result of such struggles. When these incidents or rumors were reported, they intensified into full-fledged, rampant revolts with each retelling.[68]

Whites held few illusions about internal security threats posed by Afro-Virginians. Black revolts threatened all whites, not just slave owners, and these fears increased their racial and secessionary solidarity. Slavery was based on a triangle of trepidation: slaves were trained to fear their owners and all white persons; whites feared black violence; free blacks distrusted slaves and feared whites.

Black revolts were infrequent during the Civil War because a higher percentage of the white Southern population was more vigilant and armed than before; nearly every household possessed firearms, and slave patrols were tripled. Another school of thought suggests that slaves failed to mount insurrections simply because they did not think of it; many viewed the conflict as a white man's war and remained bystanders. The notion of black revenge caused many whites sleepless nights. One slave offered the harsh promise of such a day of bloody reckoning: "When he lies down at night, he knows not but that ere another morning shall dawn, he may be left mangled and bleeding, and at the mercy of those maddened slaves whom he has so long ruled with a rod of iron."[69]

Southern fears of blacks stoked rumors that were not quenched by the activities of Union generals such as Benjamin Butler, whom Afro-Virginian runaways came to view as a protector, or George B. McClellan. General McClellan despised blacks and promised in his proclamation of May 1861 to loyal Unionist slaveholders to join Virginia whites in putting down any slave insurrections: "Notwithstanding all that has been said by the traitors to induce you to believe that our advent among you will be signalled by interference with your slaves, understand one thing clearly—not only will we abstain from all such intercourse, but we will on the contrary, with an iron hand, crush any attempt at insurrection on their part."[70]

A suspected black revolt in King and Queen County during May 1861 caused mass hysteria and the placing of home guard companies on alert. During October 1862 a slave and free black conspiracy was exposed in Culpeper County; in Surry County one hundred runaway slaves of both sexes thwarted efforts to recapture them, killing three whites. Whenever Union forces visited farms and towns and wherever they remained in force, the practice of slavery became less likely to survive unaffected. Jefferson Davis, echoing the sentiments of Virginia's slavocracy, accused the Lincoln administration of inciting slave rebelliousness. Confederates considered the Emancipation Proclamation a license to drown them in a sea of black rage.[71]

Slaves became increasingly rebellious and threatening. After fleeing a Union raid, two planters returned to their Virginia homes only to be killed by a group of shotgun-wielding slaves. Planters attributed lenient treatment during antebellum times as the cause of rebellious slaves.[72]

Slaves expected liberation as a result of the war. Increasingly they resorted to retaliatory and random acts of rebellion such as work stoppages and slowdowns, breaking tools, faking injuries and illnesses, self-mutilations, sabotage, and similar patterns of resistance. Scattered bands of armed blacks challenged the power of slavery. Farm tools, bricks, poison, ground glass in soups and stews, or clubs could maim and kill slave owners. The war emboldened slaves to inaugurate limited guerrilla warfare. Slave owners in isolated areas and territories in or near Union areas were especially targeted; runaway colonies were organized near cities such as Petersburg, and free blacks risked their lives and freedom by providing them with food and intelligence.

These underground communities survived by raiding and stealing, and wherever they existed whites could venture beyond the limits of urban areas only if heavily armed or in groups. A September 1861 newspaper editorial warned that such black camps would increase to formidable dimensions unless Confederate military authorities destroyed them. Groups of Afro-Virginian "land pirates" even targeted Union troops. As the Army of the Potomac moved through Virginia in 1862, armed bands of these blacks robbed and killed McClellan's soldiers so frequently that travel along the main road from Yorktown was perilous without heavily armed military escorts.[73]

On the afternoon of 21 October 1862, three white men, J. M. Shriver, a British citizen, James A. Graves, formerly commonwealth's attorney for the county, and his young nephew George were rowed from Claremont in Surry County to Jamestown Island by Littleton, Shriver's slave, and Gilbert Wooton, a free black resident of Surry. The white men intended to purchase slaves even though it was common knowledge that the island was inhabited by a colony of fugitive slaves who had established themselves with the aid of Yankee officers stationed at Williamsburg, itself a haven for free blacks and Afro-Virginian runaway slaves from the peninsula and tidewater areas. Approximately a hundred "half-starved" slaves called the island home.[74]

Shortly after making landfall near the old ruins of the first permanent English settlement, where the first African slaves arrived in 1619, Shriver, the Graveses, and Littleton walked toward a bridge. As Wooton guarded the boat, seven armed blacks appeared from the twilight; two of them, George Thomas and Norborne Baker, grabbed and threatened him. Four quick shots were heard from the direction taken by Shriver and the others, and soon the white men, disarmed, emerged in the custody of five of William Allen's slaves, William Parsons, Henry Moore, Jess, Alick, and Mike. The prisoners were taken before their captors' ringleader, a slave named Windsor whom the blacks addressed as "Judge." After a quick mock trial, the whites were ordered to be executed. James Graves, putting on a bold front, demanded they either send him and the other members of his party to Williamsburg (in desperate hope of being placed in the custody of white Union officers) or else release them as it was getting late.

Instead, the prisoners were marched back to the bridge where Shriver made a declaration of bravado similar to Graves's. One of the blacks replied ominously, "I don't think you will go home to-night, or to Williamsburg either." As they loaded their guns, the frightened Graves pleaded for mercy. Wooton detailed what happened next in a deposition four days later: "Six or seven of the negroes then shot together at Mr. Shriver and Mr. Graves. I could not tell their names, we were all so mixed up. Mr. Shriver and Mr. Graves both fell at once. Jim Diggs tried to shoot me, but I held him until George Thomas pulled me back, and he broke my hold; then Jim shot me in the belly. I fell and was shot again, by whom I do not know. During this time little George, who was among the crowd begging for his life, was picked up and thrown from the bridge into the marsh and then shot. I do not know who shot him."[75]

Littleton was commanded to strip the bodies of their coats and search them for money (Wooton's testimony later cleared him of participation in the murders). The bodies of Shriver and the Graveses were thrown from the bridge, but Shriver began swimming; pursued and recaptured, he was bludgeoned to death with an oar. The wounded Wooton took advantage of the distraction to crawl into a nearby marsh. Despite serious injuries he made his way to the residence of a free black named John Cassidy at Green Spring. Cassidy took Wooton to the farm of Mrs. Graves (now the widow of James), and after being treated for his wounds, Wooton returned home. White Virginians denounced the murders as "diabolical" and demanded the extermination of "the nest of runaway negroes . . . whose outrages are doubtless encouraged by the Yankees."[76]

The myth of complacent blacks waned as Southerners became preoccupied with what historian Armstead Robinson has labeled "insurrection anxiety." It was easier for Union soldiers and African-Americans to destroy slavery than for Confederates to defend it. There was a considerable amount of excitement in Norfolk on the night of 1 March 1861 caused by reports that four white men had plotted with blacks to seize control of the city. Six days later forty Northumberland County slaves were arrested for the attempted arsenic poisoning of the Ormsby family and several head of cattle after deciding that Lincoln's inauguration had freed the slaves. They had plotted to kill their owners before leaving the county.[77]

The executive committee of the Fancy Hill (Fancy Hall) Home Guard of Rockbridge County offered a $50 reward in May 1861 for the capture of a gray-haired old man of Irish ancestry dressed in black for "tampering" with slaves and instigating insubordination and insurrection. He may have been a Yankee peddler; they were always suspected of inciting slaves. In April 1861 Peter Hairston apprehended a white man named Williams who had taken it upon himself to inform slaves that the coming war would free them. A Christianburg resident wrote, "We have detected a Scoundrel . . . attempting to incite the Negroes in our County to Robbing and murdering the Whites, but fortunately he was discovered by part of the Home Guards and now have him secure in our jail."[78]

In 1862 Amesville, Culpeper County, blacks engaged in a conspiracy which put whites in a state of "the greatest consternation imaginable." Seventeen blacks, mostly free, were hanged after copies of Northern newspapers containing the text of Lincoln's preliminary Emancipation Proclamation were found in their possession. Bob Richardson, a saloon waiter, was arrested and sent to Castle Thunder in the summer of 1864 on charges that he was the leader of a slave conspiracy; the Richmond *Examiner* exulted that Richardson would soon receive "his desserts right speedily." Other cases probably were instances when blacks were overheard discussing plans of which they possessed little if any firsthand knowledge or were merely indulging in wishful thinking aloud. On the other side of the racial coin, whites marveled at but gratefully accepted the scarcity of slave rebellions and suggested cowardice and subservience as the reasons for their near absence.[79]

Afro-Virginian crime continued after the war. Gangs of black men and women reportedly robbed mourners at city cemeteries, and ex-Confederates shrilly demanded the protection of Union bayonets. At the same time malicious whites were not above taking revenge on ex-slaves and their Yankee allies by subverting the law. When four blacks robbed the store of a disabled Union veteran and killed him, they were caught and sentenced to death by a civilian court. But much to the exasperation of Union military officials, these convicts received reprieves from the state's governor.[80]

A disproportionate number of Afro-Virginians appeared before the courts and whipping posts of Confederate Virginia. Blacks perpetrated crimes, but more often than not they were the victims. Some, as renegades from within, preyed upon their fellow blacks, but the majority were barbarously and unjustly punished by a racially biased judicial system. Disparities in sentencing and punishments for white and black criminals are evidence of this. So perfunctory were Afro-Virginian convictions that the phrase "guilty of the offense wherewith he stands accused" regularly appeared beside the names of those accused.[81]

Black criminals never seriously threatened white hegemony but did pose significant internal security problems, especially in urban areas inhabited by a growing, mobile, and restless black population. Afro-Virginians stretched legal edicts and repressive racial customs to the limit. Crime became one of many collective and individual techniques that blacks exploited in resisting oppression, asserting their freedom, and casting off the physical and psychological shackles of servitude.

Fugitive slaves crossing the Rappahannock River, 1862, below the mill at
Rappahannock Station. *(Library of Congress)*

Family of escaped Virginia slaves, Cumberland Landing, Va., May 1862.
(Library of Congress)

Afro-Virginian contrabands employed by the 13th Massachusetts Infantry, 1862. *(Courtesy of the Massachusetts Commandery Military Order of the Loyal Legion and the U.S. Army Military History Institute)*

Price, Birch & Company, dealers in slaves, Alexandria, Va., 1863. *(Library of Congress)*

Portsmouth slave whipping post, 1863,
approximately seven feet high.
(Courtesy of the Virginia Historical Society)

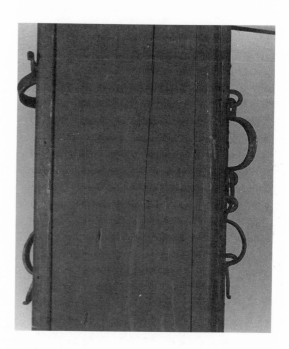

Portsmouth whipping post: close-up of the two sets of
manacles. *(Courtesy of the Virginia Historical Society)*

Marlboro, body servant and Afro-Confederate. *(Courtesy of Thomas R. Towers and Eleanor S. Brockenbrough Library, Museum of the Confederacy, Richmond)*

Afro-Virginian body servant poses with Union soldiers somewhere in Virginia, 1863. Photograph by Mathew Brady. *(Prints File, 10428-E, Manuscripts Division, Special Collections Department, University of Virginia Library)*

Execution of Private William Johnson, 23d United States Colored Troops, Jordan's Farm, Petersburg, June 1864. *(Library of Congress)*

Black Union soldiers, Aiken's Landing, Va., 1864. *(Library of Congress)*

A new generation of free Afro-Virginians. *(Jackson Davis Papers, 3072-A, Manuscripts Division, Special Collections Department, University of Virginia Library)*

PART TWO
GIVE US A FLAG

8 GRAND AND AWFUL TIMES
Body Servants at War

Servants, be obedient to them that are your masters.
—*Ephesians 6:5*

AT CRANEY ISLAND in July 1861, John Thomas Lewis Preston of the 9th Virginia Infantry regarded body servants as indispensable: "We have a great comfort in Jim. . . . He cooks our dinner, waits on us . . . makes our bed, cuts my hair, builds our kitchen . . . can make our cartridges, mend or make our bridles & groom our horses."[1]

When the war was over, Southerners praised African-Americans whom they considered "faithful among the faithless": mammies, house slaves, and body servants. Blacks who comprised these classes, especially body servants, were respected and extolled by nostalgic rebels and welcomed at postbellum Confederate conventions: "It is nothing but simple justice to give each one due credit for services rendered their owners during the war, for the majority of them were good and faithful servants. Those who . . . attend our annual reunions, are treated with the kindest consideration, and mix and mingle with the boys in the most cordial manner, and seem to enjoy the meetings fully as much as their white comrades. Several of them yet attend such meetings, and are honorary members . . . and take seats in our convention hall."[2]

Afro-Virginians camp servants were renowned for their musical and dancing skills and elicited praise from a British journalist: "In our camp we are fortunate enough to possess the most famous banjo-player in the Southern States, and when Sweeny strikes up one of his quaint old Virginian breakdowns, some nigger is sure to 'wade' in and put his legs through a series of marvellous gyrations, to the delight of the sympathetic lookers-on, who beat time for him." Slaves were employed to "wash and cook," with four assigned to each military company. These servants held the official rank of laundress and received the same pay and rations as white Confederate soldiers.[3]

Body servants were attached to the great or would-be great men of the war. They were usually black males between the ages of sixteen to sixty who accompanied Confederate soldiers or officers, typically their masters

185

or masters' sons, to the war. The higher the military rank of an owner, the more status the servant had in relation to other blacks in the camp. Many had been assigned to their masters since childbirth and considered their duties as positions of the highest trust. They were the butt of numerous anecdotes, songs, stories, and jokes but were welcomed at Confederate reunions as living links with a lost past. A few were awarded state pensions.

The fact that a body servant might have served a family for years did not prevent his sale when cash was needed. Culpeper County resident William Gibson Field received as a gift from his father a servant named Martin who quietly accompanied him to school at Gordonsville, Hampden-Sydney, and the University of Virginia, tending to the needs of his young master. Although Martin was "very smart," Field's need for cash became so desperate that he sold his companion for $1,090 and used the money to pay his daily expenses before he joined the army.[4]

The duties of body servants in the military were hard, numerous, and ever present; up before dawn, they had to cook breakfast, brush uniforms, wake their masters, prepare hot water for shaving and bathing, polish swords, and clean pistols. They washed clothes, straightened up living quarters, and were always on the lookout for extra supplies. It was their responsibility to make sure that coffee was always available; at night they were among the last in camp to retire. Other duties were boot cleaning, foraging, and entertainment.

Body servants, in a continuation of the master-slave relationship, tended their wounded owners (or escorted their bodies home) and occasionally fought in battles. Few remained with the Confederate army after 1863 due to supply shortages and the increased need for black industrial and agricultural labor, yet whenever Confederate officers rented civilian lodgings, charges for meals and lodgings costs for them and their body servants were paid by the Confederate government. In 1863 body servants were quartered at the Fredericksburg Hotel at a cost of twenty-five to seventy-five cents per day. A June bill for two servants and their two meals totaled $1.50; in August the supper and breakfast of five cavalry regiment servants cost $2.50, a single night's lodging of three servants was $1.50. These Afro-Virginians had to make do with beds of straw in the stables and a cold breakfast of black molasses, ashcake, and water; if they were lucky, meat might be allocated to them in the form of swine tails or some other offal.[5]

Free blacks voluntarily became body servants for wages and whatever other advantages they might negotiate. Being a body servant also enabled individual Afro-Confederate males to embellish their Confederate allegiance by publicly ingratiating themselves with Virginia whites. Self-preservation was their paramount objective, and when pretense became necessary, body servants were quite capable to taking full advantage of circumstances.

Samuel Page of Appomattox County boasted of his freeborn status when he joined the Confederate army in 1861, serving first as a laborer at the Manassas breastworks and later as a body servant for Company A, 20th Battalion Virginia Heavy Artillery, until the end of the war. The Confederate veteran who endorsed Page's 1924 pension application added a remarkable though typical statement: "I believe he would have taken his place in the ranks with his gun if told to do so."[6] A black teamster named Joe joined the 13th Virginia Cavalry. A black bugler, John H. Bell, enlisted with the Surry Light Artillery for the duration of the war, and surviving payrolls for May 1863 through March 1865 attest to his loyal service. A Tredegar Iron Works battalion comprised of four companies of black and white volunteers was organized for the defense of Richmond.[7]

Six Afro-Virginians voluntarily joined the Goochland Light Artillery during 1863–64 as cooks, blacksmiths, and teamsters and participated in the defense of Richmond at Chaffin's Bluff. Five of these men, Benjamin, Frank, Frederick, Mortimer, and Samuel, apparently were slaves as they lacked surnames; Frederick appeared on the muster roll as an artillerist and earned $12 a month, the same as white soldiers. David ("Davey") Randolph, a twelve-year-old free mulatto boy, enlisted as a cook just five days after the issuance of the Emancipation Proclamation.[8]

Notwithstanding an 1863 ban against their enlistment, Afro-Confederates and Afro-Virginians joined the Confederate navy and served in other necessary capacities. By law ship's crews were not to be more than one-twentieth black, but in February 1865 Secretary of the Navy Stephen R. Mallory admitted that his navy needed an additional 1,150 black seamen. On the other side, the Union navy employed 1,143 blacks by 1862 and 30,000 by 1864.[9]

Some body servants were disloyal. An Afro-Virginian slave named Thadeus escaped from Thomas J. Durrett of the 28th Georgia Infantry in 1861 while wearing "a military cap and pants trimmed in yellow"; a year later he was still at large. Daniel, servant to Franklin Woodall of Hampton's Legion, was apprehended in August 1863 in Lynchburg after his attempt to abscond was foiled when his badly scarred right hand gave him away. Others, not wishing to leave their homes and families, balked at being sent away to their masters' regiments. Levi, owned by a member of the 13th Virginia Infantry, procrastinated for more than a month at the idea of becoming a cook at the Virginia front.[10]

As the Union army advanced into the state, Yankee officers employed Afro-Virginian body servants and treated them with either disdain or compassion. A Quaker officer stationed near Petersburg in 1864, Samuel Rodman Smith of the 4th Delaware Regiment, complained to his father about the high wages demanded by his three body servants and requested a loan to pay the $61 he owed Henry. After he finally gave Henry and the other two servants their wages, they promptly quit: "I have settled my account and paid Henry off . . . [he] has left me now and gone to Gloucester Point, with Philip & the other 'nigs', they had become regular nuisances and I think it good riddance." Henry E. Simmons, a Rhode Island sergeant, noted that one body servant employed in his camp had escaped from the rebel army; to his surprise Simmons found this black man to be "a good fellow" and hard worker. But a soldier encamped at Beverly Ford in September 1863 provided a narrow-minded description of a camp servant: "He is of a very lively disposition, but cannot bear to hear profane language, if any of the men use any in his presence, he absquatulates directly. They worry him considerably about the wenches in this neighborhood; ask him how many pickaninnies he has manufactured since we camped here . . . he puts up with all the abuse the men heap on him with cheerfulness, he attends our regular Sunday worship and prays quite vigorously. He knows he's a negro and that he must not be caught out of place, he thinks he is properly named when called a nigger (at least that is the way the boys brought him up) but he is liked by all the brigade notwithstanding he is black." This letter included an unflattering sketch of a barefooted, smiling, young black man of exaggerated African features in the act of carrying three buckets—one on each arm and the third on top of his head.[11]

Black servants were regarded as sources of stories at the expense of Confederates. One body servant employed at the camp of the 2d Rhode Island Infantry, formerly a laborer at rebel fortifications near Yorktown, caused many a Yankee soldier to guffaw by telling a story about the effect of Union shelling against the Southerners. "The [rebels] were assembled around a fire, where was some meat cooking in a large kettle, and one of our Gunboats threw a shell weighing about a 100 lbs. into the midst of the soldiers aforementioned exploding and knocking men and kettles etc. in all directions," Corporal Henry Blanchard told his brother. "There was some 10 or 12 killed by this shell. He [said] that ever afterwards the rebels used to call these large shells 'Yankee Dinner Pots.'"[12]

Union officers welcomed blacks as storytellers but not as soldiers. When Major Daniel Woodall of a Delaware regiment was ordered to assume command of the 39th New York Volunteers, he soon learned why the regiment was known as the Garibaldi Guard: it had representatives from almost every nation in the world. Woodall mentioned that the regiment's "Negro servants are from Cuba and speak the Spanish language"; to his disgust they were permitted to enlist. He described the entire regiment as nothing more than "thieves, pickpockets, and robbers."[13]

Body servants risked their lives to augment meager rations. A slave named Wesley, entrusted with $500 by his soldier-master Thomas F. Toon and sent to find food in Caroline County, apparently used the entire amount to purchase a turkey and a chicken, prompting Toon to lament, "He would break Jeff Davis in a short time." Bob, employed by a group of midshipmen stationed aboard the CSS *Patrick Henry*, anchored on the James River as the home of the Confederate States Naval Academy and its sole training vessel, was well known for his foraging talents. He attempted to beg some food for the midshipmen from an unsympathetic artillery officer who rebuked him, "You damned black nigger, if you don't get away from here I will blow out your brains!" Bob fearlessly ignored the warning, snatched three hams, and fled, ducking bullets all way back to the ship. In 1861 Lieutenant John L. Cochran joined the 19th Virginia Infantry and accompanying him was a family servant, Tarleton. When Cochran asked him to procure a new suit of clothes for himself, Tarleton bragged that his own shabby clothing would very soon be replaced from the bodies of Yankee soldiers he would slay during his first battle.[14]

Body servants were addressed as "boy" or "uncle" or by their first name (usually they only had one) or skin color ("Black Peter"), never as "Mr." even if they were free blacks. Although one body servant was described as "Mr. Snow," it was in mockery of his race. It is apparent that these black men were highly valued; many were trusted with passes from their owners and traveled hundreds of miles unescorted throughout the state on railroads and other public conveyances, disregarding numerous chances to escape. Stirling, a slave owned by General Philip St. George Cocke, received a pass at Belmead planation in Powhatan County in May 1861. He traveled by packet ship to Fluvanna County and from there by land to Culpeper Court House, where he completed his solitary journey, a distance of more than fifty miles, through five counties.[15]

The Confederate government issued standardized passes for body servants, and these printed forms not only included a description of the slave but instructed military officials to give them free passage:

Negro Passport
Confederate States of America War Department
Richmond, *Feb 16th* 1865.
Pass *Bob svt. of John C. Maynard* to *King & Queen Co.* By *Pike* [turnpike] Subject to the discretion of the Military authorities.

Isaac H. Carrington
Provost Marshal

Description.—Age *25*, Height *5–3*, Color *Dark*

Was Bob a trusted servant allowed home to visit his family? This document bears no clue. Perhaps he was on a special mission to recruit more laborers or even slaves to join the army as soldiers, for by this date Virginia needed all the healthy black men it could find.[16]

Pay rates for free black servants varied, but the General Assembly was concerned about preventing unscrupulous officers from hiring runaway slaves without the permission of their owners. General Orders no. 69 in September 1862 required newspapers to publish the names of these servants and their true owners; General Orders no. 49, issued on 12 May 1863, ordered adjutants to report "all cases of slaves serving with their respective regiments without written authority from their masters." Slaveholders were unwilling for others to employ their slaves without compensation or to entice badly needed black manpower from the fields with promises of wages and the glamour of camp life.[17]

Some body servants volunteered. Tom Hester, a Suffolk slave, accompanied his owner's son to Richmond early in the war and worked as a horse tender. Wounded in the cheek and jaw at First Manassas, Hester was captured by Union forces and taken to an Alexandria hospital; after recovering, he served with a Union ambulance corps. Sixteen Buckingham County Afro-Confederates volunteered as body servants and laborers; a Spotsylvania County slave named Cornelius served with the 47th Virginia Infantry. George T. Antrim, a captain in the 5th Virginia Infantry, furnished his own "colored servant" shortly after his April 1861 enlistment, and Joseph C. Ford was a slave who served with the 30th Virginia Infantry.[18]

As Afro-Confederates, body servants identified with Virginia and the Confederacy. Writing from the 36th Virginia Infantry's "Camp Success" in June 1862, Jack Foster, a slave, told his owner of his delight in serving his young master, a soldier in the regiment. Foster enjoyed living the life of a body servant and apparently even had some free time because he concluded his letter with a request for more fishing hooks. He proudly signed it, "I am, your boy, Jack."[19]

When members of the 9th Virginia Cavalry's Company B contributed $262 for a monument to Confederate general Thomas J. ("Stonewall") Jackson, another $10 was donated by its body servants; after the war Afro-Virginians participated in ceremonies for the dedication of a statue in Jackson's honor. The regiments of the Army of Northern Virginia averaged twenty to thirty body servants each during its Gettysburg campaign. A Confederate officer encountered one of these armed body servants, dressed in a cast-off Yankee uniform, conducting a barefooted white man to the rear as a prisoner of war. When asked to explain himself, the black man replied that the two Confederates assigned to guard the Yankee had gotten drunk so he decided to take charge of the prisoner to prevent his escape.[20]

Body servants fought for the South if given the chance and occasionally replaced fainthearted white rebel soldiers. At the battle of Port Republic in June 1862, Edmund Drew, a black barber assigned to the Charlottesville Light Artillery, joined the fight after an unnerved Irish substitute named Brown abandoned the battery's advance caisson during a Yankee attack. During the Seven Days' battles near Richmond, a Confederate soldier confessed his fright to his superior officer, who disgustedly ordered him to the rear. Westley, "a good-looking darkey," received permission to take the coward's place and arm himself with his weapons. Westley gave a good account of himself during the battle, killing a Yankee with every shot, and was acclaimed as an inspiration to the white soldiers.[21]

Afro-Virginians occasionally encountered black Unionists on the battlefields and treated them with contempt. In the wake of Confederate attacks these blacks would rush upon the body servants of Union officers and seize them as personal prisoners. Such captives, whom Afro-Confederates designated "Lincolnites," were abused and ridiculed as "no count Nordon darkies": "You black rascal you! does you mean to fight agin white folks, you ugly niggers, you?" Also, Afro-Virginians proudly boasted of the fighting prowess of their owners: "Why, massa can whale a dozen of 'em 'fore coffee is hot, fair fight."

Tom and Overton, body servants with the 12th Virginia Cavalry, captured a Union officer's black servant at gunpoint during the gigantic cavalry duel at Brandy Station on 9 June 1863 and thereafter shared him as their personal slave. A more gruesome fate befell a slave boy who escaped but was recaptured after First Manassas by fellow Afro-Virginians. The body servants in the Confederate camp, indignant by this attempt—their personal safety was threatened by any slave who ran away—denounced the boy as a traitor, and he was handed over to them. They promptly executed him as an expression of their loyalty to the Confederacy.[22]

Some slaveholders were proud that their body servants owned servants. A slave with the weighty name of Napoleon Bonaparte, responsible for cleaning the boots of a Virginia major, had a black "under-boy," Solomon, who cleaned his boots. Bonaparte delegated his duties to Solomon whenever possible, and Solomon hated Bonaparte, denouncing him as "a devil." The major declared that "Napoleon's got just as much right to a nigger as I have."[23]

Being a body servant was not without its dangers. A black cook was killed and another had his leg amputated below the knee after the collision of two trains near Orange in June 1861. A servant employed by the 6th Virginia Infantry mistakenly used two live shells as andirons for the camp fireplace until they exploded during the preparations of a meal for the regiment's colonel. An Afro-Virginian cook employed by the 44th North Carolina Infantry was accidentally killed during a manual of arms drill in 1863; a camp favorite, this black's death depressed the soldiers.

On a brighter note Nathan, a body servant belonging to a Lieutenant Williams of the 1st Georgia Regulars, was captured by a Yankee lieutenant who took the slave to a Yankee camp. One morning Nathan was sent by his new owner to a nearby spring for water but instead escaped with two horses to the Confederate lines. As a reward Nathan was allowed to keep both horses; he sold one for $50, kept the other, and returned to his surprised master, who bestowed praises on this faithful servant whom he had given up as a runaway.[24]

Camp life had its lighter moments, and not always at the expense of blacks. Griffin Hawkins, a slave employed by a colonel of the 2d Virginia Cavalry, shared in the serendipitous discovery of a moonshine still in Franklin County. He became thoroughly drunk and proceeded to call and answer the entire roll of his master's regiment in alphabetical order in perfect mimicry of its colonel. As an encore Hawkins sang of his undying love for one Hannah Jane: "Roses is red, Violets is blue, Sugar am sweet, And so is you." Robert Thurston Hubard of the 3d Virginia Cavalry described the nonchalance of a servant named Davy who was only concerned about the fate of his owner's horse during an October 1863 battle: "One day when a heavy cannonade was in progress, someone met Davy riding towards the scene of action and asked, Where are you going? Davy [replied], Gwine arter Marsa's horse, sir. For what? Case he tell me if he got kilt I must take care'n his horse; and all dat firin' must ha' kilt him 'fore now."[25]

But for those servants who steadfastly served until the bitter end freedom was a welcome reward. Sixty-eight-year-old Charles Benger, a black fifer who served in Virginia with Georgia's Macon Volunteers from May 1861 to July 1862, was "honorably discharged" from the Confederate army. During the final evacuation of Petersburg in April 1865, a Confederate surgeon called his servant Romulus to his side and said, "Boy, no Yankee shall ever claim that he gave you your freedom. I will free you right here." He wrote a deed of manumission for Romulus and presented him with a knife and cash.[26]

Among the best-known Afro-Virginians of the war were the body servants of famous Confederates mentioned in memoirs and postwar articles as models of black fidelity or comical interludes among pages of death and battle.

Some looked back at the war with fondness. Aaron Burton, body servant to Colonel John Singleton Mosby, Dixie's celebrated partisan ranger, was a gift to Mosby's mother from her father. Mosby took Burton with him when the war broke out to look after his horses, and Burton spoke with pride of his association with Mosby: "I loved him, and was with him in all his battles. When the war was over Colonel John told me that I was free and could go and do as I pleased. . . . He is a good man, and was a great fighter." Mosby sent Burton checks and told him: "You were always faithful to me, and I shall always remember you for it. I hope you are comfortable in your old age." Burton, eighty-seven at the time of his interview, resided in untroubled retirement with his daughter in Brooklyn, New York.[27]

Edward Porter Alexander claimed that in three and a half years of war he whipped his servant Charley on only two occasions: once for stealing pears from a Richmond garden and the second time for stealing apple brandy at Gettysburg and getting drunk. Jem, a Fredericksburg free black, was the body servant of General Dabney H. Maury for three years. Described as six feet two inches tall and known for habitually doing things his own way, Jem was not a good servant and never bathed, but Maury overlooked this because his servant always seemed to be in good humor. Jem, in Maury's words, was "a black fire-eater," an Afro-Confederate supporter of Virginia's secession. When Maury was sent to Alabama in 1862–63, Jem accompanied him. There the Afro-Virginian bragged to the other body servants of being a "Virginny nigger" and of his soldiery exploits at First Manassas. He claimed Virginia privates were better soldiers than the colonels of other Confederate states. Treated as a comical figure throughout Maury's memoirs, Jem went into the cotton business after the war and during Reconstruction became a politician.[28]

Two of Robert E. Lee's wartime servants were William T. Evans and William Mack Lee. Evans was described in his 1905 obituary as a servant, cook, and bodyguard for the general. Born a slave, Evans was freed at age two; he witnessed the hanging of John Brown, served Lee throughout the war, and was present at the Appomattox surrender. After Lee's death Evans drifted north where he worked as a waiter and at odd jobs until his death at Asbury Park, New Jersey, at the age of eighty-one.[29]

William Mack Lee's 1922 reminiscences were a combination of narrative and excerpts from his newspaper interviews. He proudly included a photograph of himself wearing a chestful of medals from numerous Confederate reunions. Born on 12 June 1835 in Westmoreland County, William, after the death of his mother, was raised at Arlington, the home of his owner, Robert E. Lee. Trained as a cook, William remained with Lee for the entire war and was wounded at Gettysburg. He fathered eight daughters and lived to see twenty-one grandchildren and eight great-grandchildren. William became an ordained Baptist minister, preaching in Washington, Maryland, South Carolina, North Carolina, and elsewhere to raise money for his many churches, and organized black benevolent associations in Washington and Virginia.[30]

In his latter years William developed an effective fund-raising technique. He would enter an office building, usually a newspaper company, and ask, "Kin you white folks gimme a little money fur my church?" When it became apparent that he was being ignored, he would loudly announce that he was "Ole Marse Robert's nigger," and nearly every Southerner in the place would then gladly offer contributions in exchange for the opportunity to ask questions about the immortal Lee. This method helped William to build five churches.[31]

William's narrative contains several incidents regarding General Lee including the time he wept at the death of Stonewall Jackson; he quoted the general as saying, "I'm bleeding at the heart, William." Lee also recalled how the general purchased a black hen from a Petersburg resident and christened the fowl Nellie; she kept him supplied with fresh eggs for the remainder of the war from the safety of an ambulance. A racial accommodationist, William Mack Lee professed support of the cultural dogmas of the Lost Cause: "The best friends we have are the Southern people . . . if we colored people want to get along well with the white people we must show our behavior to, respect and be obedient to them. These are my views to our race." Williams was the type of black that postwar Southern whites could accept: a former slave who adored white folks, still limped from a Yankee bullet, and voted Democratic in every election.[32]

Four Afro-Virginian body servants were associated with Thomas ("Stonewall") Jackson: Joseph Green, a body servant named John, Jeff Shields, and James Lewis. The names of others perhaps have been forgotten. A 1925 obituary for Green simply stated he was "one of the immortal Stonewall's body servants" when it announced his death at Williamsport, Maryland, at age eighty-eight. John is mentioned briefly as a "handyman" in one of Jackson's many biographies; another publication identified Shields as Jackson's personal cook.[33]

James Lewis, "a large and handsome mulatto," is said to have been born in the same year as Jackson, 1824, and as a cook his culinary accomplishments were second to none. Little is known about his antebellum life other than that he was a free black resident of Lexington. He is chiefly remembered for his often-quoted remark about how he knew the secretive Stonewall was about to launch an attack. Whenever the general arose in the middle of the night to pray, Lewis would begin to pack "cos den I knowed

dere wuz a move on hand . . . and hell to pay in the morning." It was this
Afro-Virginian who applied wet towels to Jackson's face as he lay dying after
being accidentally shot by his own troops at Chancellorsville; afterwards
Lewis was an official member of the delegation that accompanied the body
to Richmond. He led Sorrel, Jackson's horse, during the funeral procession.[34]

Lewis then became a servant to Alexander Pendleton until the latter's
death at the battle of Fisher's Hill in 1864. Disconsolate, Lewis died shortly
afterwards and was buried in Lexington's black cemetery. Ten years after
his death former members of Jackson's command solicited funds to erect a
monument over Lewis's grave. Forty years after Jackson's death the Afro-
American congregation of the Roanoke Fifth Avenue Church installed a
stained-glass window in the general's memory as an acknowledgment of
the fact that beginning in 1856, while a Virginia Military Institute professor,
he organized and taught Sunday school classes for Lexington blacks. On the
evening after the battle of First Manassas, despite its momentous significance for the Confederacy, Jackson found the time to send a check for the
school's continued support and urged other whites to underwrite it.[35]

As president of the Confederacy, Jefferson Davis needed the services of
body servants not just for himself but for the Confederate White House.
Five blacks, slave and free, were among his employees. A slave named Jim
Pemberton and a free black woman named Mary Elizabeth Bowser fled to
Union lines after attempting to burn the residence in January 1864. James
Henry Brooks, a black orphan rescued from an abusive owner by Mrs. Davis,
was given his freedom by Davis and became a playmate for the Davis chil-
dren. Robert Brown, a free black, was Varina Davis's personal servant. An-
drew Jackson Davis, a coachman, escaped from his presidential employer in
May 1862 and made his way to England. Brown and James H. Jones, a free
Afro-Confederate, were the most faithful of the Davis family servants.[36]

Jones, a trusted messenger, enjoyed a long and proud association with
Davis and claimed that the Great Seal of the Confederacy was entrusted to
him for safekeeping before the evacuation of Richmond. He accompanied
Davis as he fled from Yankee troopers, and it was Jones who said he threw
a cloak over the Confederate president as he tried to escape when Yankee
cavalrymen finally caught up with him in Georgia in May 1865. Despite alle-
gations in the Northern press, Jones denied to his dying day that Davis had
attempted to disguise himself as woman with the dress made by Elizabeth
Keckley. In June 1865 a servant girl informed Union authorities at Fort Monroe that Jones was on his way to Raleigh, North Carolina, to visit his mother
and retrieve two bags of money worth $10,000 that had been hidden near
one of Davis's camps. He later was employed as a messenger by the United
States Senate, became a member of the board of aldermen in Raleigh, and

was an honored guest at ceremonies for the unveiling of the Davis monument in Richmond in 1907. James H. Jones received tributes at every Confederate reunion he attended until his death in Washington in April 1925.[37]

Several Afro-Virginians servants proudly called themselves Confederate veterans and believed they were entitled to whatever social status this implied. Many whites accepted these men as comrades. Lewis Johnston of Westmoreland County, a well-known "Negro ex-Confederate soldier," was a diligent voter until the 1902 Virginia constitution in effect disenfranchised blacks. Several former body servants claimed to be veterans in census returns in hopes of obtaining pensions. Cornelius S. Lucas, listed in the 1900 census, was born in Fredericksburg and eventually drew a state pension for his wartime services as a cook for the Fredericksburg Artillery. He returned to his native city, married in 1877, and raised a family of twelve children. At his death on 13 May 1927 he owned his Douglas Street home and a profitable grocery store and was a prominent minister highly esteemed by all. Robert Parker and Griffin Dobyns were two former body servants listed in the 1910 census for Lottsburg District in Northumberland County. Both were almost seventy years old, unable to read or write, and had been married for over forty years. Perhaps they were acquainted and entertained each other with tales of their war exploits.[38]

Rockbridge County slave Levi Miller escorted his owner, John J. MacBride of the 5th Texas Infantry Regiment, to the war and nursed him back to health after a near-fatal wounding during the Wilderness campaign. After an unanimous vote by the Texans, Miller was enrolled as a full-fledged soldier and for the remainder of the war saw combat in Virginia, Tennessee, Georgia, Maryland, and Pennsylvania; during the Gettysburg campaign he refused escape overtures from his free relatives. His military service culminated with coolness and bravery in repelling Yankee attacks against his company's position during the battle of Spotsylvania in May 1864. Miller received a full pension from Virginia as an ex-Confederate soldier after his former commander verified Miller's service as a soldier and affectionately spoke of their wartime experiences as comrades at arms. "Levi Miller stood by my side and [no] man never fought and better than he did," wrote Captain J. E. Anderson, "and when the enemy tried to cross our little breastworks and we clubbed and bayonetted them off, no one used his bayonet with more skill and effect than Levi Miller."

During his final years Miller resided in Frederick County and worked as a water dipper for mineral springs tourists at Capon Springs and Rock Enon. He never married and by frugal living was able to purchase land at Opequon where in one year his orchard crop earned him $1,000. He was a member of the Methodist church for fifty years and was held in high regard by members of both races. After his death on 25 February 1921, the *Winchester Evening Star* published a rhapsodic tribute: "Levi Miller, one of the few colored men regularly enlisted in the Confederate army during the civil war . . . was affectionately known among the white as well as colored people of this section as the grand old man of his race. He always had a deep love for everything southern, and although born a slave, it was his loyalty to his state that led him to enter the southern army and fight through the four entire years of war." Miller's coffin was reverently draped with the Stars and Bars and taken to Lexington for a hero's burial in its black cemetery.[39]

When James Mosby of Pulaski died at age seventy in October 1912, his newspaper obituary identified him as a Confederate veteran. A free black, he had joined Floyd's Brigade of Lynchburg in 1861. Henry Clay Lightfoot, a Culpeper slave, served in Longstreet's division as a body servant to Captain William Halcomb. Returning to Culpeper after the war, Lightfoot was elected to the town council, served as juror, purchased his own home, raised a family, and collected a state pension. A large crowd attended his April 1931 funeral at the Antioch Baptist Church; his flower-covered coffin was draped by a silk Confederate flag donated by the Culpeper chapter of the United Daughters of the Confederacy. When "Uncle" Edmund Winslow died in the same city three years later, he was its oldest resident; both races paid tribute to his character and service at Confederate hospitals for which Virginia had awarded him a lifetime pension. Wilson was survived by his wife Lizzie, five children, forty grandchildren, eighty-six great-grandchildren, and seven great-great-grandchildren. Winchester resident George E. Cooke served four years with the 24th Virginia Infantry and was the bodyguard of a Richmond doctor during the war. He was undeniably proud of the fact that his son John, a member of the 513th Engineer Corps of the American Expeditionary Force in France during World War I, was continuing the family's military tradition.[40]

As a group, the body servants appeared to have been long-lived. The last of Virginia's servants each nearly reached the century mark before their deaths during the 1940s: James McKinney of Richmond County (August 1945), Pompey Tucker of McKenny (February 1946), and Lewis Carter of Lanexa (August 1949). State records indicate that other body servant survivors received monthly pensions until the 1950s.[41]

Pensions, the state's way of rewarding citizens for military or civilian service, imply respect and recognition of labors and sacrifices in times of war. Several body servants received them and were welcomed into the Confederate postwar fraternity. Former escaped slaves or those who joined the Republican party were not. Yet the "gray-haired darkies, dressed in Confederate Gray," were treated more like pets, mascots, and good luck charms than social and political equals. However, it was former slave states who provided pensions for them, not the Federal government.[42]

Virginia established pensions for its Confederate veterans as early as 1884 after examples by several localities encouraged the General Assembly to provide a statewide system. The initial act, "Confederate Pension," was passed four years later. From 1911 to 1959 the legislature passed twenty-four appropriations for the care of Confederate graves; between 1912 and 1954 appropriations were also endowed on behalf of Confederate veterans and their widows.[43]

Blacks first became eligible for state pensions with the passage of an act on 14 March 1924; this act amended and reenacted previous acts of 1916 and 1918 regarding Confederate pensions. It referred to the position "body servant" but not to "Negroes" or "slaves": "Under the provisions of this act any person who actually accompanied a soldier in the service and remained faithful and loyal as the body servant of such soldier, or who served as a cook, hostler or teamster or who worked on breastworks under any command of the army and thereby rendered service to the Confederacy, shall be entitled to receive an annual pension of twenty-five dollars, proof of service and right to be enrolled to be prescribed by the auditor of public accounts." This law excluded runaways, Afro-Virginians who served as soldiers and laborers for the Union army, and black women. However, white women who were widows (even those who remarried) of Confederate sailors, soldiers, or marines or who had been hospital matrons were eligible not only for pensions but also to have their funeral expenses paid for by the commonwealth.[44]

To prove his entitlement a petitioner had to file an application with his local hustings or circuit court accompanied by affidavits from two white ex-Confederate soldiers; if none were available, certificates from two local whites of good reputation were acceptable substitutes. The state auditor examined each application for correctness, and county courts appointed a board composed of three pension commissioners, two of whom had to be either Confederate veterans or their sons. These boards reported the merits of the applications to the courts. If one was accepted, the applicant's name was entered on the state pension rolls, and the auditor thereafter issued payment accordingly. Blacks could not serve on these boards, and at any point in the process, vindictiveness and racial prejudice could present formidable obstacles for any would-be black pensioner.[45]

Approximately 270 black male Virginians fulfilled the requirements of the application process annually during the years 1925–1926 (table 8.1). The 1928 General Assembly amended the 1924 act in several respects; one of these

TABLE 8.1. VIRGINIA'S AFRO-CONFEDERATE PENSIONERS, 1924–26

Year	Pensioners	Appropriations	Yearly average
1924–25	254	$5,356.25	$21.08
1925–26	286	$6,730.25	$23.53

Sources: Auditor of Public Accounts, Annual Reports of Officers, Boards and Institutions of the Commonwealth of Virginia for the Twenty-one Months Ending June 30, 1925 (Richmond, 1925), 168, table 42; ibid., Ending June 30, 1926 (Richmond, 1927), 194, table 42; Auditor of Public Accounts, 1925 Roster of Confederate Pensioners of Virginia (Richmond, 1925), 113; Auditor of Public Accounts, 1926 Roster of Confederate Pensioners of Virginia (Richmond, 1926), 106.

was the inclusion of former slaves who had performed guard duty, buried Confederate dead, or "worked in railroad shops, blacksmith shops, or Confederate hospitals." They, too, became eligible for a pension of $25 a year; twenty-six years later this amount was increased when the 1954 assembly gave black Confederates an annuity of $240 per year. White Confederates were to receive $1,200 and their widows $480 annually.[46]

Virginia's pension laws, with the exception of those applying to widows and maiden or widowed daughters of Confederate veterans, were repealed on 10 April 1978; by then the last of its former slaves had long since died. The Old Dominion's pensioning of body servants and black laborers represents one of the few instances when financial compensation was actually paid to American slaves for the deprivation of their freedom and loss of potential income, not to mention the sale and separation of family members. Ironically, white Confederate veterans received pensions from the Federal government beginning in 1958 on the eve of the war's centennial gala. The Eighty-fifth Congress amended the Veterans' Benefits Act of 1957 to permit surviving white ex-rebels to be paid the same monthly pensions as other American military veterans, as if their war service had actually been on behalf of the United States during the Civil War.[47] Several African-American activists in turn issued demands for white churches, synagogues, and the Federal government to pay blacks $500 million to $500 billion as partial restitution for the discrimination and bondage suffered by African-American slaves and their descendants. Periodically, similar demands have been made, but all have been ignored despite numerous historical precedents of granting victims or their survivors compensation and apologies from their oppressors.[48]

"The Confederate negro is the proudest being on earth. . . . I have never seen a Confederate negro that was not full of pride in his record. I believe this sentiment is an evidence of his patriotism as well as a testimony of his love and loyalty to his white folks." Such were the comments resulting from a postwar conversation between a Confederate veteran and an Afro-Virginian residing in Washington, D. C., "eyes beaming with intelligence, and a bearing of modest and courteous dignity." He was a former body servant and proud of it:

> "How long have you been in Washington?" "Since 1870, suh." "Where did you come from?" I could see his chest swelling, and I knew the answer before it was spoken. "From Ferginny, suh." "Were your people in the war?" "Yes, suh," with a smile of enthusiasm and a bow that bespoke reverence for the memories of the olden days. "They tell me you people 'fit' some." I could almost see the lightning dart from his eyes as he straightened himself up. "'Fit?' Why, dey outfit the world, suh; never did whip us, suh. If dey hadn't starved us out, we'd been fightin' yit."[49]

Only in the reminiscences of ex-Confederates are body servants given any sort of appreciation. As intelligent human beings, they were sometimes able to manipulate the slavery system for their own purposes and obtain unprecedented opportunities. Experience had long taught blacks about white perceptions of exceptional black fidelity.

But were Afro-Virginian body servants Confederates or Unionists? If the pension laws of the Commonwealth of Virginia and the reminiscences of Confederate and Union soldiers are taken as a whole, the answer to this question would be that large numbers of enslaved black Virginians were loyal to their owners and the memories of the "gentler" side of slavery. Their support on behalf of a losing effort secured for them the limited gratitude of the Southerners in the form of invitations to attend Confederate reunions and small pensions—but pensions nevertheless. Slaves who ran away, assisted the Union side, or demanded the right to vote during Reconstruction were viewed as traitors as the South shuffled down the road to Jim Crowism.

One of the cruelest ironies of Civil War Virginia is that of the hundreds of thousands of Afro-Virginian slaves, barely three hundred black males sixty years after the conflict received a pittance for their service and sufferings. These body servants were the only slaves ever financially compensated for their enslavement. Some have judged them harshly for their devotion to whites, but they, like other slaves and free blacks, were survivors of a system long opposed to black self-determination.

9 TROUBLESOME ELITES
Free Blacks as Minority Survivalists

No negro, emancipated since [1 May 1806], shall remain in this state more than one year without lawful permission.
—*Code of Virginia*, 1860

ONE MORNING in June 1862, Lucy R. Buck of Front Royal was extremely angry at both the Yankees and her family's slaves. The blacks had met with her father and promised to protect the family after Lincoln's government triumphed. "Insinuating wretches!" Buck angrily wrote in her journal. "To come here and tell Father how kind and good they're going to be to us after our subjugation—how they will soothe the pains of submission. . . . Gracious Heavens! If I thought it were my fate to submit to them I believe it would craze me!"[1] It particularly rankled Lucy that Rob Roy, a free black employed at her father's plantation, by a similar offer of protection and sanctuary had the effrontery to consider himself their equal. These Afro-Virginians were putting whites on notice that times were changing and henceforth they expected to become equitable members of the community.

Indisputably, free blacks were denied complete participation in the social and political mainstream of Confederate culture but at the same time, compelled by their minority status, became more bicultural. They lived and worked within community standards of morality and responsibility while remaining cognizant of their own identity and recognizing the considerable power of whites over their lives.

Free blacks were subjected to vigilantism, racially discriminatory laws, and other forms of prejudice, but their adroitness in preserving their limited liberties was testimony to their ingenuity as minority survivalists within a society of slavery. The white Confederates of Virginia could have learned much from them.

There were approximately 251,000 free blacks in the slaveholding South in 1860; 59,000 lived in Virginia, more than any other slave state except Maryland, which had 84,000. Free blacks were legally freed (either by a white person or through self-purchase) former slaves, slaves who successfully escaped, or those who were born free, inheriting their freedom from parents,

201

usually a white grandparent. They were subjected to stringent laws, arrests as suspected runaway slaves, and reenslavement; by law they were prohibited from engaging in certain occupations. Free blacks comprised 5.5 percent of the state's population and 11.8 percent of all its Afro-Virginians. More than half of all free blacks, 52.2 percent, were female. But many could and did live on the fringes of prosperity, owning property, including slaves, while others managed to obtain a rudimentary education. According to historian Carter G. Woodson, 21 percent of Virginia's free black adults were literate.[2]

Free Afro-Virginians were the black pseudo-aristocracy of the state. They were mindful to show their free status in the way they signed documents: "f.c.p." (free colored person), "f.m.c." or "f.m.o.c." (free man of color), "f.n." (free Negro), "f.n.w." (free Negro woman), "f.p.o.c." (free person of color), "f.w.c." or "f.w.o.c." (free woman of color). It was the proud boast of many a black family after 1865 that it had not been "shot free," i.e., emancipated as a result of the war, the Emancipation Proclamation or the Thirteenth Amendment. Their status was said to be the result of better breeding (but never miscegenation), luck, or conscience-stricken white progenitors who hoped deeds of manumission could be their entrance to heaven.[3]

But this does not answer the question of why free Afro-Virginians lingered in a society of black slavery instead of moving to nonslave states. One answer may be their justifiable fears of permanently sundering family ties or their regarding Virginia as home. Nearly all free blacks had relatives still in bondage and were disinclined to leave them behind. They worked and saved and managed to purchase spouses, siblings, children, parents, and grandparents. Few had well-paying jobs, enough cash to vie against slave traders, or the means to secure loans for the purchase of relatives.

Sometimes disaster struck in the form of white terrorism in response to slave rebellion plots or a reluctance to sell slaves to their free relations. Nat Turner's uprising, increasing difficulties with white mobs caused caused Willis Augustus Hodges of Princess Anne County to abandon Virginia. He took his family North and found prosperity and respect as a leader of New York's black community and even published a newspaper, the *Ram's Horn*. Such talents were impossible for him to exhibit in the antebellum Old Dominion. Another complication was the rural nature of the state itself. Most free blacks dwelled in the same neighborhood for most of their lives and became well known to white locals. They were able to obtain occupations or acquire skills needed in their particular communities.[4]

Free Afro-Virginians had to earn and prove their right to exist in freedom in the nation's state with the most slaves. Although most whites had little use for them, some believed them to be moral and respectable, more so than poor whites. A British visitor during the war characterized Virginia free blacks as contemptuous, sly, impudent, yet pitiful creatures. Slaveholders were antagonistic: "A worthy free negro is known as worthy, and respected accordingly, by his near neighbors only. To all other persons and strangers, he is merely a free negro—a term which always conveys the meaning of a general character of meanness, degradation, and worthlessness. . . . Good habits and morals are rare in that class, still more rarely . . . transmitted to [their] children."[5]

Governor William Smith agreed, branding free blacks as disorderly public nuisances, spies and traitors actively assisting the North. It is true that more than a few boldly and publicly spoke treason by stating what they were going to do to defeated Confederates; by 1864 laws were inadequate to manage them and the General Assembly was urged to enact stringent measures to contain them.[6]

Despite racial enmity, Lynchburg free blacks proved to be so industrious as to pose serious labor competition for whites in the summer of 1861 as mechanics, carpenters, bricklayers, stonemasons, and blacksmiths. There were demands that the Confederate government conscript 150 blacks to avert white unemployment. Yet other whites valued free black labor. The president of the Old Dominion Iron and Nail Works Company appealed to Confederate secretary of war George Wythe Randolph in April 1862 on behalf of free black teamster James Robinson, owner of four wagons. Robinson's wagons were the only ones in Lynchburg that the company could rely upon to deliver its boiler plates, iron, and nails; if he was conscripted, it would be forced to go out of business.[7]

Isle of Wight and Nansemond County residents strongly opposed plans to conscript and remove their free black residents because they were the only persons employed as menial labor. They feared that if those plans became public, Afro-Virginians would desert the counties and seek employment elsewhere. In neighboring Charles City County twelve free black males (with names such as Thomas Jefferson and Oliver Freeman) fled to the Union army in 1862. Rockbridge County residents petitioned in October 1863 for the return of Washington Jackson, a forty-eight-year-old free Afro-Virginian blacksmith impressed for Confederate military labor. Jackson, "a very industrious man," had resided in the county for twenty years, owned more than $1,700 worth of property, and had been their only blacksmith for two years. His absence would pose "a great inconvenience" to the community, not to mention the economic hardship on his wife Letitia and son John. One resident plaintively noted in the petition's postscript: "W. Jackson has done my Smiths work for many years, and I do not know how the farming community can get along if he is Taken from us" (see Appendix D). Two local justices of the peace ordered Confederate military authorities to release Jackson.[8]

Free blacks experienced economic, political, and social discrimination but did create one significant political movement in alliance with sympathetic whites—abolitionism—and established their own schools, churches, and benevolent societies even though they were always threatened by racism and the possibility of enslavement. Some Confederates were sure that all free blacks supported their cause simply because certain Afro-Confederates volunteered to enlist as soldiers in the rebel armies. De Bow's Review declared that free Southern blacks enjoyed "many precious civil rights" and rarely contemplated migration to the North; when they did go north, the journal said, they nearly always regretted it. On rare occasions in Virginia free blacks were treated with courtesy by individual whites. During an 1862 visit to Leesburg, several Confederate soldiers went to the home of an Afro-Virginian, ordered a meal, and insisted on paying for it. So unusual was this behavior that the black owner feared their payment would cause trouble for him if local whites learned of it.[9]

Under no circumstances was any black man, despite pretensions of gentility, considered a gentleman or the equal of whites. William Ferguson, a Richmond free black barber, was arrested in August 1864 and charged with keeping a disorderly house. The "house" was actually a cookshop under the supervision of another black, where, in a scandalous public display, "white men and negroes sit at the same table and devour delicacies." During his trial several blacks testified on behalf of Ferguson's good character and consistently referred to him as "Mr." and a "colored gentleman." These titles of respect were disallowed by the judge who sharply admonished witnesses that the laws of Virginia did not recognize black males as gentlemen; they were only "negroes" no matter how respectable in the Afro-Virginian community.[10]

Free black men tried to conduct themselves as gentlemen, especially in defense of black women. Afro-Virginians employed at Fort Monroe in 1861 refused to associate with an ex-slave named Joe and rejected his application to join their church because of his insistence on the right to beat his wife. One morning in July 1862, Petersburg free black Thomas Hill, while peaceably resting in a second-story room of his Harrison Street home, suddenly overheard a loud domestic altercation at his front door involving a black couple, Henry Adkins and his wife. When Adkins threatened violence against Mrs. Adkins, Hill intervened, ordering Adkins to leave his property and offering Mrs. Adkins sanctuary.[11]

The presence of free blacks technically was a crime under Virginia law because those over the age of twenty-one were required to leave the state within a year of becoming free or else be sold into slavery. The state code did permit blacks who believed themselves unlawfully held in bondage to file lawsuits for their freedom, but if they lost, any person ill fated enough to have aided them in the suit became liable to the slave's owner for reimbursement of damages.[12]

One free black woman sentenced to slavery received gubernatorial absolution: "Whereas Ellen Afto a free negro woman, was condemned by the Circuit Court of the County of Frederick to by sold into absolute slavery for remaining in the State contrary to law, and it appears to me that *she is a fit subject for executive clemency*. Therefore, I, John Letcher, Governor, have thought proper to Pardon the said Ellen Afto for the offense aforesaid, hereby releasing her from all pains or forfeitures that might or would have been inflicted on her had these Letters of Pardon not been made."[13]

A few whites took advantage of free blacks' precarious economic status. James Penn was freed by his owner before the war and migrated to Ohio. But when he reappeared in Rockbridge County in February 1864 to inspect his property, Cornelius Baldwin threatened to have him arrested "as a free negro remaining in the state contrary to law." Baldwin and a Mr. Anderson wanted Penn's property and offered to pay him its full value in cash; "if you want to save trouble, sell out & leave without delay," they told him. Notwithstanding their threats and his inability to read or write, Penn refused to be bullied. Three weeks later Baldwin made good on his threat by swearing out a warrant against Penn.[14]

Other free Afro-Virginians risked residency though denied official permission to stay. Sixty-two-year-old Jacob and forty-year-old Sophy Galloway of Augusta County, manumitted by Nancy Clarke in July 1862, were refused permission to remain in the state or the town of Staunton. Even so, the Galloways dutifully registered with the town's hustings court in 1864 and resided undisturbed.[15]

Black males aged twenty-one and older were required by law to pay taxes; failure to do so could lead to time on a road gang at ten cents a day. Free black men were also subject to conscription as laborers for saltpeter and munitions work but were permitted to hire themselves out rather than being drafted. A thriving practice of blackmailing free blacks to volunteer as laborers existed; victims could choose either to work on fortifications and pay most of their wages to the blackmailers or else be reported to the authorities as shirkers. Those between the ages of eighteen and fifty were required to report to Confederate fortifications for military labor. Promised fair compensation, rations, living quarters, and medical care, these men, by law, were not to be detained for more than 180 days. Failure to report could result in the death penalty under the articles of war on the charges of desertion and disobedience despite the fact that they were civilians.[16]

Municipalities sought to control free blacks tightly. Charlottesville prohibited them from smoking in public on pain of a $10 fine and forbade them from visiting the railroad depot without a white person accompanying them. Richmond ordinances banned blacks from entering the city without a certificate of good character from a justice of the peace; black nonresidents could be arrested and set to labor on public works and military batteries as punishment. Free blacks, slaves, and mulattoes were barred from owning eating establishments or selling newspapers at markets and depots in the Confederate capital. Councilman Richard Frederick Walker opposed these measures as overly harsh because it was blacks who supplied many services needed by city residents. Indeed, free blacks frequently violated city laws by owning illicit, unlicensed cookshops, saloons, grocery stores, adn groggeries whose customers included both races and sexes. City newspapers characterized the registering of free blacks as "unimportant business," but Petersburg free black William Westbrook was arrested for violating city ordinances when he tried to sell a wagonload of potatoes without a permit. His attempt to earn a honest living netted Westbrook fifteen lashes, and his wares were donated to local hospitals.[17]

Perhaps the most odious of the laws directed against free blacks were those which obstructed their freedom of movement. Since colonial times they had been required to register their names, addresses, and physical descriptions once a year if they resided in a city or every three years in counties. Free blacks were prohibited from migrating to the state and could be enslaved if they failed to leave within a certain time period; state funds were appropriated for their removal. Between 1861 and 1864 several conceded defeat and voluntarily became slaves. These cases are tragic when one considers that most had been born free. On the other hand, registration laws were not always strictly enforced; Afro-Virginian requests for extension of residencies were usually granted upon proof of sobriety, good character, and a law-abiding lifestyle. Given the alternatives, most free blacks were not inclined to become public nuisances; laziness could result in reenslavement.[18]

Betty Noel was a free black woman who worked hard to support herself in Smyth County by taking in washing, working in the fields, and spinning thread. She paid rent on her own cabin and avoided trouble. Albert Brooks, a slave tobacco worker in Richmond, purchased his liberty and that of his wife and children in 1862 by subterfuge after his master refused to allow the Brooks family to purchase their freedom. Undeterred, Brooks ingeniously struck a bargain with a third party, the German consul in Richmond, to purchase his family.

There was also the ever-present danger for free blacks of being kidnapped and sold elsewhere counties by conniving slave catchers. Victims found themselves in the position of being adjudged to be slaves having to prove that they had been free, in violation of due process. Free blacks who left Virginia to be educated could not return under threat of severe penalties; they were considered potential revolutionaries with dangerous concepts about freedom for slaves.[19]

Some sympathetic whites respected the personal liberty of individual free blacks and thwarted attempts to kidnap and sell them into slavery. After losing her free papers, forty-two-year-old Nancy Davis and her daughters Virginia and Juliá (ages fourteen and twelve) were taken from Richmond by a white man named David Pounds during February 1862. When Pounds and the three Afro-Virginian women reached the vicinity of Troy, Tennessee, a local official named Adams became suspicious, jailed Pounds, and questioned Davis. She claimed her papers were on file in Lunenburg County, Virginia, and that for several years she had been an employee of Turpin and Yarbrough, a Richmond tobacco manufacturer. Adams, resolving to "do an act of humanity and aid in detecting a scoundrel" after the company confirmed Davis's story, contacted Lunenburg's court clerk for a certified copy of Nancy Davis's free papers in order to procure the family's release. He filed fraudulent enslavement charges against Pounds.[20]

Beginning in 1860, free Afro-Virginians were required to register with county clerks once every five years, and these records noted skin color, name, age, distinguishing marks, and the conditions under which each had been freed. Each person registered received a copy; before it could be renewed, the original had to be produced and then destroyed after the issuing of the new one. Blacks over the age of twelve who lacked such documentation could be jailed. The records indicate that more males than females and more blacks than mulattoes registered. Of the 672 free blacks in Fairfax County, only 251 (37 percent) registered in 1860; in 1861 only 8 bothered to register. Joseph Blantan of Fairfax County, age fifty, was described as having "felon holes" in his ears; Ben Lewis had been emancipated in a will, as were Martha and her four children and Daphney Kelly, a forty-three-year-old mulatto "with straight black hair." Fairfax was lax in enforcing these laws because it needed cheap free black labor to counteract the high wartime cost of slaves.[21]

Fredericksburg's 214 free blacks (84 males, 130 females) were gainfully employed as washers, laborers, seamstresses, draymen, carpenters, cooks, shoemakers, blacksmiths, and bakers. Washington County registered twenty-three free black residents during 1861–63, including John Logan, described as "a mulatto man aged about Thirty three years, five feet nine and a half inches high-scar on the first finger of the left hand, a scar on the left wrist and a scar on the thumb of the same hand—no other apparent marks or scars." Four black families were listed: the Broddys (Fannie, Emely, Charles, Thomas), "born free through a white ancestress"; the Clarks (Polly, Robert, Thomas, Mitchell, Richard); the Trents (James and Clairborne); and the Pools (Simon, Charles, Amanda). They clung to their liberty even as Confederate Virginia fought to preserve slavery.[22]

Christmas was a time when Afro-Virginians attempted to ignore some of the limitations caused by slavery and racism to take advantage of the season of good cheer. But for Richard Adams of Henrico County, Nancy Rex of Petersburg, Nelly Jenkins of Cumberland County, Sarah and Louisa Freeman of Caroline County, and William Cooper of Richmond, the penalty for being caught without their free papers during the 1862 holidays made it a season of the whip instead of mistletoe. While some like freedwoman Lucy Carter possessed one of the better forms of "free papers"—a Yankee military pass which permitted her to pass through the lines at Vienna at her pleasure (she probably was a spy)—for other blacks the loss of their free papers was potentially disastrous. John Pearce was incarcerated at the state penitentiary for this very reason.[23]

William Bowers, Ellen Norman, and George Harvey were caught in Richmond in 1862 without their free papers and received lashes; Harvey made matters worse for himself by having a loaded pistol in his possession. Elizabeth Clarke had better luck; when caught in the city without her free papers, she was allowed leave after a verbal warning. And when two Lynchburg free black women named Margaret Watts and Susan Elizabeth Taylor accidentally destroyed or lost their papers, both hastened to place notices in the newspapers:

> Lost-my freedom papers, which I supposed were burnt. This is to give notice that I shall apply to the Court for others.

> Lost or destroyed by my children, on Thursday last, my free papers issued by the Hustings Court of Lynchburg in 1862. This is to give notice that I shall make application for new papers.

Thirty-year-old Nancy Jenkins, born free in Nelson County, moved to Augusta County and registered in September 1863. Sally Cooper, a free black woman, married a slave named Clarke but was careful to certify her free status legally; daughters Cynthia and Lucy also registered in Augusta County in 1863. Watts, Taylor, Jenkins, and the Coopers understood that not having documentary proof of freedom was not the wisest situation for black women in the heart of the Confederacy.[24]

Free Afro-Virginians were a nascent black middle class under siege, but several acquired property before and during the war. Approximately 169 free blacks owned 145,976 acres in the counties of Amelia, Amherst, Isle of Wight, Nansemond, Prince William, and Surry, averaging 870 acres each. Twenty-nine Petersburg blacks each owned property worth $1,000 and continued to purchase more despite the war.[25]

Gilbert Hunt, a Richmond ex-slave blacksmith, owned two slaves, a house valued at $1,376, and $500 in other properties at his death in 1863. The Union Burial Ground Society of Richmond, a free black organization founded during the 1840s for "the welfare of our race and the importance of advancing in morality, and . . . for the interment of the Dead," obtained additional real estate for its members in October 1864 with the purchase of four lots valued at $4,000 by trustees Benjamin Harris, Braxton Smith, and Nelson P. Vanderval. This society had its own constitution of sixteen articles and annually elected officers in the form of a president, vice president, treasurer, secretary, and nine "Managers" in addition to three trustees. The most stringent requirement for a constitutional officer was that of the treasurer, who had to be "a responsible married man—one who holds real estate."[26]

Suzanne Lebsock's study of Petersburg free women indicates that African-American women not only survived in a white world but in a man's world at that; half of the city's black property owners were female. Lebsock attributes this to their refraining from marriage and thereby retaining control over their own interests. They outnumbered free black men, their best source of eligible husbands, and eagerly assumed the burdens of life on their own terms. It was a hard world for a single black woman, and Lebsock identifies racism as the single barrier in the development of Southern feminism and a natural alliance of black and white women. However, the very nature of Confederate civilization could and did preclude any kind of intuitive bonds between Afro-Virginian free and slave women and almost all white women. White women enjoyed and derived tangible benefits from the enslavement of blacks, and there are many instances in the historical record when they participated in the assertion of white superiority.[27]

The existence of free black women defied racial and gender discrimination. They endured in a society where black women were valued only as slaves and slave breeders. But thirty years before the war Catherine ("Kitty") Foster, an unmarried mulatto seamstress, purchased property in Charlottesville near the University of Virginia. She headed her household until her death in 1863 and bequeathed the property to her daughter and granddaughters. It was held by Foster family women for more than seventy years, and several were buried there.[28]

While the majority of Afro-Virginians lived on the margins of abject poverty, some free black residents of Hampton and Norfolk owned property of considerable value; 17 black Hamptonians possessed property worth a total of $15,000. Thirty-six black men paid taxes as heads of families in Elizabeth City County and were employed as blacksmiths, bricklayers, fishermen, oystermen, and day laborers. In three Norfolk County parishes (Elizabeth City, Portsmouth, and St. Brides), 160 blacks owned a total of $41,158 in real estate and personal property. Black families named Cuffe, Elliot, Civils, Smith, and Wilkins were prominent on the tax rolls. One of the wealthiest, Samuel Smith, Sr., of St. Brides, was a fortune-teller whose net worth was $3,000; Cullen Smith of Portsmouth Parish was worth an astonishing $7,000. Several Petersburg blacks either purchased their freedom or were manumitted outright and became substantial property owners and taxpayers. The Bolling brothers, Thomas and James, together were worth $4,000; blacksmith Armistead Wilson's holdings totaled $1,600, twice the amount he paid for his freedom four years previously. Robert Clark, formerly a hotel slave, owned a carriage and horse-hiring business valued at $9,000.[29]

One of the more curious aspects of the free black existence in Virginia was their ownership of slaves. Black slave masters owned members of their family and freed them in their wills. Free blacks were encouraged to sell themselves into slavery and had the right to choose their owner through a lengthy court procedure. When one-half of the potential slave's value was paid for by his newly chosen master, the status of this black was transformed and it was as if he had been born into slavery.[30]

One free black at Harpers Ferry purchased his wife and children for $1,400 in May 1864, but his former master refused to sell the eldest daughter; she later managed to join her parents. Another Afro-Virginian father in the town worked and saved $1,000 to buy his family only to have Confederate soldiers steal his money. Alexander Dunlop of Williamsburg paid $450 for his wife and $700 for her sister; afterward he was told he could not set them free. Another free black, Aggie Peters, bought her and her husband's freedom and went north. Upon her return to Virginia, she was arrested and "examined" by judges who banished her back to the North with a warning that if she were ever caught in the state again she would be whipped and sold.

William Roscoe Davis saved $1,800 and spent it in litigation to preserve the freedom of his wife and children when the heirs of their former owner tried to set aside the will that manumitted them. The courts ruled in their favor, but not until 1862 could William reclaim and remove them to Union-held Hampton. Betsey Fuller, a self-employed free black woman peddler in Princess Anne County, owned her slave husband. He sided with the Confederacy and after the capture of Norfolk in 1862 unwisely and boisterously continued in his pro-Southern opinions. Yankee occupation authorities put him to work on a city chain gang, and Confederate propagandists praised him as a loyal Afro-Confederate. The mother of five children, Betsey prudently evaded mentioning ownership of her husband to census enumerators.[31]

White Virginians overburdened by the manifold strains of war believed free Afro-Virginians were not doing their fair share of labor for the cause, and there were many calls for black conscription for the army, railroads, and public works. Blacks were criticized as being indifferent to the success of the Southern rebellion. Editorials pointed out that "ten thousand black cooks, nurses, ostlers, draymen and mechanics would mean ten thousand more white men as soldiers." Military commanders, realizing free blacks could be motivated by cash, insisted they be paid promptly so that support of their families would not become an added financial burden to wartime communities. By August 1861 more than a thousand free black males were employed at defensive works on the tidewater peninsula. Billy Wheeler earned $31 in wages for two months' work and was honorably discharged at the end of the year; John Barnes of Nelson County was employed at Augusta County's Mount Torry Furnace at $4 a month.[32]

Repeated calls for slave levies jeopardized agricultural production to such an extent that the General Assembly passed laws regulating the enrollment and employment of free Afro-Virginians. In accordance with a law passed on 1 July 1861, 300 Mecklenburg blacks between the ages of eighteen and fifty were enrolled in August. During February and March 1863, twenty-four counties and towns were issued quotas of 1,029 free black men to labor on the defenses of Richmond and Petersburg. Southampton had to furnish the most (142 men); Charles City County and Petersburg were to supply 100 blacks each, but Madison County needed only 7 blacks for its quota. By the summer of 1863 military engineers were so desperate to complete fortifications that they demanded Richmond police round up 500 free blacks.[33]

So persistent and repugnant were these and subsequent impressments that a few free blacks pretended to be slaves in order to obtain urban employment. Jim Butler successfully passed himself off as a slave and worked at Richmond's Exchange Hotel until his deception was uncovered. Privately, whites desperate to keep farms and businesses functioning were willing to hire Afro-Virginians with no questions asked. Confederate House Speaker Thomas S. Bocock quietly employed Charles Henry, "a free man of color," as a blacksmith on his Appomattox County plantation, paying him $40 a year. Alman William of Gloucester County worked in nearby Mathews County in 1862 for planter Thomas Smith and earned decent wages as a farm laborer. Steady incomes meant free Afro-Virginians could purchase goods on credit just as whites did. A black man named Charles was able to accomplish this during most of 1864 (and somehow avoid being conscripted); he maintained a credit account with a county merchant for which he signed and paid for purchases in his own name. Doubtless, there were many others.[34]

Free Afro-Virginians were in an outlandish situation. Hated and feared, treated like enemy aliens, needed and used to support the survival of a system opposed to their interests, they were vulnerable to prejudice and discrimination. The judicial system contributed to the disparities they encountered. Seemingly, it protected them only when they became the victims of crimes committed against them by other blacks. Ned, a slave, threatened Lewis Sampson, a free black, and was ordered to be punished by a Richmond court. But when Joseph Gray, "f.m.c.," stole a silver watch valued at $40 from a slave named Henry, he was sentenced to be sold into slavery.[35]

The freedom of free blacks was always at risk, but some nevertheless engaged in activities that resulted in their enslavement or imprisonment. Amanda Boyd of Henrico County indiscreetly permitted a slave named Moses to live with her (most likely he was her spouse). The problem was that Moses did not have his owner's permission for this arrangement, and Boyd was whipped for her negligence. Winnie Morton, convicted on 9 June 1862 of stealing $150 worth of clothing, was sold into slavery for $950 and immediately shipped south. Edward Bozeman, a free black, suffered the same fate after being convicted of stealing a $200 watch.[36]

Free Afro-Virginians accused of crimes were sometimes able to hire white lawyers to defend them. Adeline Thacker, charged with allowing her stovepipe to deteriorate to a dangerous condition and keeping a disorderly house, secured an attorney named Crane as her legal counsel. He arranged a plea bargain: Thacker would replace the pipe if the disorderly charges were dropped. Crane's grandiloquent demands that the person who filed the disorderly charge appear in court went unanswered.[37]

A Confederate soldier named Gerard accused John Adams, a prosperous Richmond free black plasterer and property owner, of having stolen his clothes while they were in the care of Gerard's laundress, who had died. It was soon learned that shortly before her death she had bequeathed to Adams all of her worldly goods, including Gerard's clothing, which Adams later sold. His attorney, a Mr. Sands, argued that Adams had sold the items to pay for the deceased's funeral expenses because she was Adams's slave. At this point the presiding judge denied that blacks had the right to own slaves. Sands agreed but pointed out that Adams possessed a bona fide bill of sale. The judge dismissed the charges but hinted that if Adams was prosperous enough to own slaves, he could afford to reimburse Gerard.[38]

The murder of one free black by another or by a white person was not likely to be seriously investigated unless it was of an unusual or particularly atrocious nature. John Roberts, a free black, was stabbed to death in front of his house on a Sunday night in December 1862. A coroner's inquest was held that evening, and the only witness to the crime, Roberts's nephew George Lynch, tearfully testified: "I saw Uncle John run through the gate and heard him holler about 6 or 7 o'clock. Then I heard somebody cuss and say, 'I'll cut your heart out.' I didn't know who it was. He talked like a big colored man. Uncle John then fell dead." A "verdict accordingly" concluded the only official investigation of this unsolved murder.[39]

Some free blacks supported the Southern rebellion. Alexander Dunlop of Williamsburg, a free black, reluctantly acknowledged the presence of "black rebels" in most of the state, and a baffled Union officer told of a free black "rabid secessionist" who lived near Richmond and owned a thousand acres of land. A sexton at the Bruton Parish Church of Williamsburg was described by his contemporaries as a "half-crazed black secessionist." Several Charlottesville free blacks petitioned the town council in 1861 to accept them as military volunteers; the council ducked the issue by pleading lack of authority to accept Afro-Virginian volunteers. The "colored firemen" of Norfolk held a grand parade in December 1861, and observers praised their attractive engines, neat uniforms, and orderly appearance. One eyewitness remarked approvingly: "The sable firemen seemed to enjoy their holiday parade. . . . They had music, too, and marched along in evident consciousness of the importance and usefulness of their position."[40]

George Bundy, caretaker of a Fredericksburg farm belonging to an absentee Confederate soldier, was so faithful to his trust that Union authorities distinguished him as "a rare instance of a colored man who seems to have been for the confederate cause." Alfred Anderson of Jetersville and his brother Francis owned plantations and slaves and were well-known anti-Unionists. James C. Muschett, a resident of Prince William County, owned a store at Quantico Mills and cheerfully furnished food, clothing, and blacksmithing services to the rebel government. He was later imprisoned at Old Capitol Prison as a Confederate spy and loyalist; after the war he filed a $7,000 damage claim against the Federal government.[41]

Spotsylvania County free blacks placed themselves and their property at Virginia's disposal in August 1861, and a black Fairfax County farmer sold

28 acres of his 150-acre farm and donated the money to the defense of Virginia. During the Union occupation of Hampton Roads, Robert Butt of Portsmouth declined nomination as a candidate to represent the district in the United States Congress as long as it remained under Yankee occupation: "No, gentlemen, I will leave this position to some one who is more anxious to act the traitor, and have his name written high upon the page of infamy." James T. Ayer, a black Suffolk farmer, sold so many eggs, slabs of bacon, and chickens to local Confederate quartermasters that Yankees referred to him as an employee of the rebel commissary department.[42]

Free blacks in Richmond, Lynchburg, and Petersburg sought to enlist in the Confederate army in 1861, and an 1862 Baltimore newspaper quoted runaways as saying black men were being armed and organized into regiments for the defense of Richmond. Several were camp auxiliaries. Austin Dix was a free black who served with the 18th Virginia Infantry for two years, and John Hailstock of Stafford County volunteered as a body servant for the 30th Virginia Infantry. William T. Scruggs of Cumberland County and his brother served as cooks for Confederate cavalry. Free black laborers were exchanged or paroled as prisoners of war, and after the Appomattox surrender Robert D. Ruffin of York County and other free black property owners filed claims for reimbursement for damages by Yankee troops. Ruffin's grocery store was plundered by members of the 9th New York Regiment one night in June 1863, resulting in the loss of:

13	kegs cheese	$144.00
18	sliver watches	360.00
2	dozen bottles preserves	4.80
2	dozen pickles	4.80
2	barrels white sugar	74.56
2	barrels brown sugar	59.28
2	dozen pairs of shoes	84.00
100	pounds candies	35.00
1.5	barrels tea-cakes	18.48
3	barrels ginger cakes	24.00
3	boxes raisins	10.50
	TOTAL	$819.42

Such pilfering did not inspire Virginia free black entrepreneurs like Ruffin to support the Union. A decade passed before his petition for compensation was rejected; he and similar Afro-Confederates in Virginia suffered property damage as severe as, if not greater than, the losses of white rebels.[43]

The erratic execution of laws designed to oversee blacks could not thwart their aptitude for endurance. They bided their time, and when the Union armies arrived, some of these Afro-Virginians proved to be eager students of American democracy. Black representatives from the Confederate states of Florida, Louisiana, Mississippi, North Carolina, Tennessee, and Virginia held a National Convention of Colored Men at Syracuse, New York, during October 1864. Five free black Virginians attended: R. D. Beckley and Sampson White of Alexandria, James P. Morrison and E. G. Corprew of Portsmouth, and William Keeling of Norfolk. Keeling was elected one of the convention's vice presidents. This was the first time that Afro-Virginians freely and openly attended a political convention to represent their state and joined with other blacks to address the nation directly about the concerns of their race.

Keeling was especially active in the drafting of a "Declaration of Wrongs and Rights" wherein the delegates pledged their support to Lincoln, the Union, and the defeat of the rebels. In praising the gallantry of black Federal soldiers, the delegates reminded the nation that blacks had served it long and well in peace and war. Now they demanded the rights, privileges, immunities, rewards, and respectful attention to their concerns accorded to other citizens. Declaring their intention to secure an equitable share of the public domain, blacks forewarned both the soon-to-be victorious North and the rapidly disintegrating Confederacy that henceforth they, too, were American citizens.[44]

10 ZEALOTS OF THE WRONG
Afro-Confederate Loyalism

We are willing to aid Virginia's cause to the utmost extent of our ability.
—*Charles Tinsley, spokesman for Petersburg's free blacks, 1861*

Horace Holmes, a black Richmonder, purchased a new Confederate army lieutenant's uniform in the spring of 1863 and proudly wore it as an symbol of his Southern patriotism. City policemen, neither impressed nor pleased at the sight of a black man wearing a uniform, arrested Holmes and hauled him before the provost marshal. He protested that he was unaware that it was illegal for him to make such a purchase or to wear the sacred gray; after a brief consultation, the gold lace and insignia were removed, and a relieved Holmes permitted to go his way, still wearing the uniform.[1]

Afro-Virginians volunteered and supported the Confederacy at the onset of the war even though they had been treated as inferiors and lived in a state of fear. One motivation was the possible improvement in their everyday status and a relaxation of some of the political and legal restraints against them; by identifying and actively supporting the Confederate cause, they anticipated white postwar gratitude in the form of increased privileges and rights. Several free black Virginians were slave and property owners who deemed their way of life threatened by the Northern invasion and yearned to prove to their white neighbors that they, too, were Southern patriots. Those publicly loyal to the Confederacy were pragmatically acknowledging who and where they were. Their determination to stand with the South was akin to free men consciously performing a civic duty. Black Confederate loyalty was more widespread than American history has acknowledged.[2]

In May 1861 Culpeper Court House resident R. L. Patteson observed several black Virginians attached to Confederate military companies passing through the town. One male slave stirred to Southern patriotism fervently vowed: "If old Lincoln does put his foot on old Farginny I can raise a regiment of niggers. . . . the negroes here understand all about it, the people have informed them as to the true state of things, they know that the South are their real friends." By the summer of 1861, Afro-Confederates (Southern blacks who supported and allied themselves with the Confederacy) sought to volunteer, but the Confederate War Department at first declined numerous offers to enlist them.[3]

However, when a Union regiment, the 1st Ohio Volunteers, was attacked on 17 June 1861 near Vienna as it traveled by train to Falls Church, the Confederate attack was led by the 1st South Carolina Infantry accompanied by "a body of 150 armed picked negroes." Six slaves who escaped from Mathews County in July 1861 to the safety of the USS *Mount Vernon* said that when the county's whites attempted to arm blacks, "they deserted in every direction." During that same month Thomas A. Phelps, a slave, wrote to his mother of the pride he felt in being a soldier in the Confederate army: "I will leave . . . today for a scout about the woods for the Yankees. . . . Give my love to mistress and master. . . . P. S. Good by to the white folks until I kill a Yankee."[4]

There were several unaccounted and unheralded Afro-Virginians who could and did pose as white and served in state regiments. George and Stafford Grimes of Caroline County enlisted with the Fredericksburg Artillery in March 1862 though both deserted to Union forces at Yorktown the following April. George was recaptured, and plans were made to court-martial him for desertion until it was decided that as a "Negro" he could not be tried as a soldier. Census records described Stafford as a twenty-three-year-old mulatto laborer with a personal estate valued at $55, and as far as state law was concerned, mulattoes were blacks. Nevertheless, throughout the struggle against slavery and secession, mulattoes passed for white even to the point of serving undetected as Confederate officers.[5]

Early in the war white Virginians found themselves engaging in the same debates and expressing the same fears as their colonial forebears over the problem of arming black men to kill white men, even if those white men happened to be the enemy. The training and promoting of blacks as soldiers posed dire consequences for the future despite the black competency in the art of warfare demonstrated in the Revolutionary and subsequent wars.[6] Confederate civilian and military leaders viewed the mobilization of black men as likely to endanger white superiority. Arming slaves was an issue many Southerners did not care to think about even though slave and free black men represented a viable and accessible military population. Approximately 200,000 white male Virginians (a third of all Southern troops) served in the Confederate military; there were at least 50,000 to 120,000 Afro-Virginian males of military age available for all-black regiments.[7]

Slave soldiers had been suggested by one Southern periodical during the impassioned arguments presaging the impending war: "They contain the best material for a defensive war of the age—a slave population, the most effective laborers for a warm climate under the best discipline and most skillful direction of any other people, in numbers sufficient to raise the means of army subsistence for any probable war, too well fed, clothed and taken care of, to be restless or unruly, and the least dangerous from insurrection."[8]

But various slaveholders were wary of committing their slaves to combat without some sort of government reimbursement, and whenever there was the likelihood of battle, many hoped their slaves would be sent to the rear. A Campbell County planter advised his Confederate soldier son: "I hear you are likely to have a big battle soon, and I write to tell you not to let Sam go into the fight with you. Keep him in the rear, for that nigger is worth a thousand dollars." Nevertheless as early as November 1861, the wife of one Confederate staff officer candidly predicted the South would need black soldiers even though they could not be trusted. Other whites agreed.[9]

Free black and slave loyalty was less likely to be suspected in some areas. In April 1861 the editor of a Tennessee newspaper stated that his state's slaves could be armed and trusted to help repel Yankee invaders; the Louisiana Native Guards, a militia regiment of 1,400 black men and officers who offered their services to Dixie, passed in review at New Orleans. The next year, 3,000 blacks organized as the First Native Guard for the protection of the city were described as "rebel Negroes . . . well drilled . . . [and] . . . uniformed" in the New Orleans *Picayune* of 9 February 1862. Slaves in Mobile, Alabama, were organized as soldiers in the fall of 1861; Mississippi planters and the Alabama legislature petitioned Confederate authorities during 1861–63 to arm slaves.

More than one Virginia slave owner was confident that his slaves would zealously kill other blacks in defense of the South: "Oh, yes! we'll just arm our niggers, and put 'em in the front ranks to make 'em shoot their brothers, Sir!" But not every Southern black man, particularly slaves, wanted to fight for the South. A slave named Tom, when asked about rumors that blacks loved their masters so much that they would not fight white Southerners, replied with much irritability: "I know they says dese tings but dey lies. Our masters may talk now all dey choose; but one ting's sartin,—*dey don't dare to try us.* Jess put de guns into our hans, and you'll soon see dat we not only knows *how* to shoot, but *who* to shoot. *My* master wouldn't be wuff much ef I was a soldier."[10]

Tennessee in June 1861 became the first in the South to legislate the use of free black soldiers. The governor was authorized to enroll those between the ages of fifteen and fifty, to be paid $18 a month and the same rations and clothing as white soldiers; the black men appeared in two black regiments in Memphis by September. But this was early in the war when victory was uncertain, and as yet no one enrolled slaves in the ranks. The free black troops of New Orleans, including the First Native Guards, did not evacuate the city with other Confederates in April 1862 because they did not want to fight the Union army or abandon their families. General Benjamin Butler promptly enlisted these Afro-Confederate veterans into Federal service as three regiments of the Louisiana Native Guard Infantry (later the 73d, 74th, and 75th United States Colored Infantry).[11]

Certain free Afro-Virginian men, like other Southern males, seemed eager to prove their bravery and patriotism against the Yankee hordes. There were reports of local Confederate commanders in Virginia who armed and equipped free blacks and slaves in anticipation of attacks due to manpower shortages and despite well-grounded fears they would turn their weapons against Confederates when Union forces arrived. Another example of the Confederacy's painful drift toward a limited biracial society was in pay equity for African-Americans in its armies. Black musicians employed in Confederate regiments received the same pay as white musicians as of 15 April 1862; one of them, Jacob Jones, enlisted on 14 May 1861 at Salem, Roanoke County, as a drummer for the 9th Virginia Infantry. A Baltimore newspaper announced the arrival of black regiments at Richmond during February 1861 and described the conscription of slaves for service.

Considerable public attention surrounded the arrival of a wreath sent to Richmond by Mrs. Judith C. Judah, a Afro-Virginian woman, as a contribution to the memory of her husband, "A Colored Southern Soldier": "I send . . . my willing contribution of flowers as an offering to the gallant dead of the Richmond Light Infantry Blues, of which my husband was once a musician, and who fell in the service. I hope they all sleep sweetly 'across the river under the shade of the trees' to rise again at another trumpet, as lovely and fresh as these flowers, to flourish forever in the mansions of the blest." Reuben West, another black member of the Richmond Blues, served faithfully during the war and was an honored guest at a postwar ceremony.[12]

African-American historians have deemed the Confederate attempt to enlist blacks a ridiculous, futile, and hypocritical endeavor by one racist society to employ its most oppressed caste against another bigoted society, the North. George Washington Williams, the first black historian to publish a serious and widely received history of African-Americans, wrote, "From the earliest dawn of the war the rebel authorities did not frown upon the action of local authorities in placing arms into the hands of free Negroes." Williams's comment was an exception; six years later Joseph Thomas Wilson, another nineteenth-century black historian, derided such Confederate efforts as "unrealized dreams" and condemned blacks who boasted the loudest of their desire to fight Yankees as doing so only for the approval of whites and in the hopes of obtaining privileges within the confines of slavery.[13]

Wilson's judgments have been echoed by African-American historians including Benjamin Brawley and William E. B. Du Bois, who rejected as absurd the notion of black Confederate soldiers; blacks who volunteered and white Southerners who believed them were both "equally misguided" according to Charles Harris Wesley. These historians acknowledged the value of slaves as agricultural and military laborers for the South and noted that had the Confederacy actually decided to field black troops in 1861–63, large numbers of them would have been obtained. But would they have fought effectively? John Hope Franklin thought not; Benjamin Quarles said, "Perhaps . . . but without their hearts being in it." Yet a Union soldier shot dead by an Afro-Confederate was just as dead as one killed by a white Confederate despite opinions such as that whispered by one slave to a Northerner visitor: "If de Mossas only *do* put guns into our han's, *oh dey'll find out which side we'll turn 'em on!*"[14]

Virginia's legislators pondered a program to conscript Afro-Virginians in 1862. A member of the House of Delegates proposed the enrollment of free black soldiers but admitted their families would lack means of support while they were away. He hastened to add that his proposal was not the result of any personal friendship toward free blacks since if it were in his power he would "convert them all to slaves." Doubtless, other Confederate states would have followed suit had Virginia, with more free blacks than any other Confederate state, initiated such legislation.[15]

During McClellan's 1862 Richmond campaign, numerous planters became so alarmed as to offer their slaves as soldiers and pleaded for the Confederate government to make the necessary arrangements. Allegedly Davis, his cabinet, and state governors privately discussed the idea among themselves. It was agreed that the slaves should enlist with land and freedom as their reward, and that by answering the Southern call for help, Afro-Virginians would instantly "be elevated to a position of trust and confidence unparalleled in the history of the world." Misgivings about a public backlash and Lee's successful Seven Days' defense of the Southern capital nullified the idea.[16]

William C. Oates, an Alabama captain, journeyed to Richmond in 1863 and spent four frustrating days pleading with Confederate congressmen to enlist blacks; he believed they would make good soldiers with proper drilling, discipline, and experienced white commanders. The slave soldiers were to be freed and upon honorable discharge would be entitled to receive eight acres of public land and freedom for their wives and children. The politicians rebuffed his proposals as the overenthusiasm of a young man with patriotic but unfeasible intentions; the disappointed Oates warned that the South would soon encounter thousands of black soldiers armed and led by Yankees. No less a personality than General Richard S. Ewell agreed and glumly predicted the South's need for more military manpower would revive the issue later, perhaps too late: "It is astonishing to me that our people do not pass laws to form regiments of blacks. The Yankees are fighting low foreigners against the best of our people, whereas were we to fight our Negroes they would be a fair offset." [17]

Foreign observers were not so optimistic. Arthur Fremantle, a British colonel who personally observed the Civil War, did not doubt Afro-Confederate troops could fight skillfully under the command of white Southerners. But the high value of slaves and doubt that blacks were capable of civilized warfare led Fremantle to express skepticism that the experiment would ever be attempted except as a last resort: "Any person who has seen negro features convulsed with rage, may form a slight estimate of what the result would be of arming vast numbers of blacks, rousing their passions, and then allowing them free scope." [18]

Southern propaganda in Europe scorned the Union's use of black troops as barbaric but admitted the possibility of using Southern free blacks as warriors for the "vastly better" Confederacy. Sensitive to accusations of hypocrisy, Secretary of War James Seddon bluntly stated that black soldiers were an impossibility, but as white enthusiasm for joining the Confederate army waned, the tide of public opinion also underwent a social metamorphosis. The *Index*, a Confederate propaganda weekly published in London, suggested 500,000 black men could be spared for the front and replaced by black female slaves, who were healthier, hardier, and stronger than European peasant women. Southern blacks and whites possessed "perfect confidence in each other's character," and black soldiers would become steady and effective levies in the manner of the sepoys of India. Blacks possessed obedience, intelligence, and insensibility to danger; the lack of sufficient weapons was to be resolved by a medieval solution: "They would . . . be more effective in the field with the more primitive weapons which the blacksmith's shop on every planation could forge out of the implements of husbandry. A hundred thousand negro pikemen or scythemen could probably be a more formidable body for immediate service than the same number of raw recruits trusted with unwonted weapons. . . . Whether or no the gift of freedom be a boon to the negro, time and experience alone can show." The newspaper conveniently overlooked the fact that in India the sepoys had arisen in a bloody and violent rebellion against their British rulers six years earlier. Nevertheless, excerpts from this article appeared in several Virginian newspapers during the fall of 1863 without editorial objections, an indication of widespread support.[19]

Some Northerners considered it laughable that Southerners, who had long proclaimed the incompetence of blacks in any intellectual activity, would even discuss the subject. "I do not believe that one thinking Southern man . . . has any more idea of arming his negroes," commented one writer in the *Atlantic Monthly*. Nevertheless, eyewitness accounts by Union officers are plausible evidence of African-American participation on the battlefields of Virginia for the Confederacy. New York soldiers on patrol from Newport News were attacked near Newmarket Bridge by Confederate cavalry and a group of 700 armed blacks on 22 December 1861. The Unionists killed six of the blacks before retreating; officers later swore out an affidavit that they were attacked by blacks and complained: "If they [the rebels] fight us with Negroes, why should we not fight them with Negroes, too? . . . Let us fight the devil with fire." This biracial unit and dozens more, paramilitary in nature, were organized by local Confederate and state militia commanders in response to immediate threats in the form of Union raids and were disbanded after the dangers passed. In the same month an armed slave named Davy (Dave) saved a Georgia colonel from capture by single-handedly apprehending several Union soldiers during a Virginia battle. Two "fully armed" Afro-Confederate soldiers were observed on picket duty at the rebel encampment at Fredericksburg in 1862; a sketch of them appeared in *Harper's Weekly*.[20]

The Confederate military had sound, ingenious reasons for employing black men in this manner. After a few hours of training, armed with a few bullets and a rifle and imaginatively camouflaged in simple natural or artificial positions that took advantage of the terrain, a slave or free black could be converted into a cheap but effective killing machine. Any Yankee soldier killed or wounded reduced the number of foes. If an Afro-Confederate sharpshooter was slain, injured, captured, or even deserted, the loss was insignificant, for he could be easily replaced from a constant supply of enthusiastic blacks.

Several extraordinary occurrences of Afro-Confederate soldiering took place near Yorktown on the outskirts of the Federal siege in May 1862. One of the Confederacy's best marksmen apparently was an unidentified Afro-Virginian who outfitted himself with a sniper's roost inside an almost perfect cover—a brick chimney—from which he picked off Yankee soldiers near the perimeter of Camp Scott. Any Union soldier who came into his range was fired upon. Several times the Yankees called upon him to desert, but the black sharpshooter disdained their appeals. Ultimately, a regiment was marched forth to fire a volley at the sniper's hiding place, putting a bullet through his head. A postbellum illustration of this violent finale depicted a coarsely clad young black male, barefoot and hatless, tumbling from a tree after being shot.[21]

Alfred Bellard of the 5th New Jersey Infantry reported the shooting of two black Confederate snipers by members of Berdan's Sharpshooters in April 1862. One of the Afro-Confederates was only wounded, but the other was killed one afternoon after leaving the security of a hollow tree (probably to relieve himself). Two white Confederates tried to retrieve his body but were driven off by Union gunfire.[22] In June 1863 George Hupman, a Union soldier stationed near Newport News with the 89th New York Infantry, matter-of-factly wrote his parents, "I have A ring made from the Tree Californy Joe shot the Rebel sharpshooter Niger out of." The casualness of his reference seems to indicate that Hupman and his comrades frequently encountered black male Virginians employed in this manner. At the headquarters of the 117th New York, a soldier named Hermon Clarke wrote home to describe his visit to the pit from which Joe had ambushed a "nigger" sharpshooter."[23]

Slaves were observed in Southern lines as either Confederate soldiers or conscripted military laborers working under the threat of the lash. Two Afro-Virginians were seen being compelled by a Confederate captain to load and fire cannon at Union lines near Yorktown; a Yankee sharpshooter, taking advantage of the blacks' exposure, shot both. Northerners accused the rebels of putting blacks in the most dangerous posts so that when Union gunners found the range and accurately dropped shells into Confederate fortifications, it was these blacks who suffered the highest casualties.[24]

After the battle of Seven Pines in June 1862, Union soldiers claimed two black Confederate regiments not only had fought but had showed no mercy to the Yankee dead or wounded whom they mutilated, murdered, and robbed. During the Army of Northern Virginia's abortive Antietam campaign in September, eyewitnesses reported the presence of armed blacks in the rebel columns bearing rifles, sabers, and knives and carrying knapsacks and haversacks. They appeared to be an accepted element of Lee's troops. They rode on horses, mules, caissons, and wagons and were led by black buglers, drummers, and fifers as they marched. A Union Sanitary Commission employee who witnessed the occupation of Frederick, Maryland, Dr. Lewis H. Steiner, recorded in his diary: "Most of the negroes . . . were manifestly an integral portion of the Southern Confederacy Army. . . . The fact was patent and rather interesting when considered in connection with the horror rebels express at the suggestion of black soldiers being employed for the National [Federal] defence." And after the battle of Gettysburg in July

1863, the *New York Herald* reported that among the rebel prisoners were seven blacks in Confederate uniforms fully armed as soldiers.[25]

Lieutenant Lewis Thompson of the 2d United States Cavalry encamped at Falmouth, Virginia, beheld an bizarre sight on 7 March 1863 on the Confederate side of the Rappahannock River: he counted more than fifty black soldiers on picket duty. Incredulous, Thompson informed a fellow officer, Henry E. Noyes, and together the two lieutenants returned to the area where, as Noyes later reported to his superiors, "with the aid of a powerful glass, I could distinctly see negroes, with belts and other accoutrements on, the same as white soldiers." Each post was manned with equal numbers of white and black Confederate soldiers. Similar sightings were reported by generals Joseph Hooker and Henry W. Halleck to Secretary of War Edwin M. Stanton.[26]

Who had Dr. Steiner, Noyes, and Thompson seen? Large numbers of blacks were present at the Fredericksburg fortifications as military laborers, and occasionally they may have been assigned picket duty. Obviously, there were a few overexcited body servants and other blacks with Confederate forces, or perhaps Northern witnesses confused begrimed rebel soldiers for blacks. African-Americans were a rare sight for many white Americans, especially those from the North's more rural areas. The first sighting of an African-American was enough to generate comment in white Union soldiers' letters and diaries. To whites, blacks seemed an alien, exotic species of humanity, and their presence at unexpected places and events aroused mixed feelings of shock, amusement, or distrust. The earliest appearance of blacks in the blue uniforms of the Federal government evoked similar commentary by offended white Southerners.[27]

Numerous black Virginians were enthusiastic about fighting Yankees, and conceivably the initial example of this took place before the first major battle of the war at First Manassas. The commander of the 1st Regiment of Virginia Cavalry reported that an Afro-Virginian member of Company H, Captain Richard Carter's Light Horse, single-handedly killed a Union soldier on 2 July 1861 during a skirmish at Falling Waters near Martinsburg. Fifty prisoners, almost an entire company of the 15th Pennsylvania Volunteers, were captured with the exception of three men killed while resisting capture or trying to escape. Philip H. Powers of the Clarke Cavalry informed his wife: "One fellow was creeping away under the cover of a fence when he was shot dead by the only Negro in our party." Another unidentified black, a member of a Captain Patrick's company, was also reported to have slain a Union soldier. Apparently, white Confederates accepted armed Afro-Confederates under specific circumstances during the early stages of the conflict.[28]

Afro-Virginians fought on the Confederate side during the first major battle, Bull Run, on 21 July 1861, which some Confederates derisively christened "Yankees Run." John Parker, a slave from King and Queen County, was employed as a laborer on breastworks and artillery batteries near Richmond, but when the Union army began its advance on Manassas, the Confederate military ordered "all colored people must come and fight." Arriving two days before the battle, Parker and four other slaves were assigned to a battery after a brief stint of training. He and his fellow slaves, as Gun Battery no. 2, opened fire at 10:00 A.M. that fateful morning with grapeshot, and Parker quickly had his hands full handling ammunition, swabbing the cannon, and staying alive.

"Many colored people were killed in the action," he recalled afterwards, and though slaves were promised freedom and cash if they fought well during the battle, they wished in their hearts "that the Yankees would whip [us], and we would have run over to their side but our officers would have shot us." Parker noted that the blacks did not trust the Confederates' promises and fought only because they had no other choice. He also revealed that two regiments of black men, one slave, the other composed of free blacks, participated in the battle. Afterwards, these blacks joined the rebels in stripping Yankee bodies ("the people from the free country") of clothing and valuables. His regiment's colonel claimed the money and watches taken from the Yankee dead; slaves were used to remove weaponry and human debris after the battle. After a visit to his wife, Parker ultimately obtained a pass from Union soldiers at Alexandria on 31 January 1862 and fled in the vicinity of Frederick, Maryland, after serving nine months in the Confederate army. After "travelling for the star," Parker reached Pennsylvania and later New York and subsequently earned a living in the North as a lecturer on the topic "The War and Its Causes, with Slavery Connected" at ten cents per admission, advertising himself as the only black soldier in the Army of Northern Virginia. He later reunited his family and moved to Canada.[29]

A slave attached to the 17th Virginia Infantry was cheered by the regiment as it pursued defeated Yankees after Bull Run: "Our gallant little Colonel, got his meed of hurrahs; and an old negro who rode by with his gun, got no small salute." How many other slaves and free blacks voluntarily or involuntarily assisted in the Southern victory as soldiers or laborers? One hint appears in the comments of the victorious Confederate commander, General Pierre G. T. Beauregard, who noted in his report that most of the army's breastworks were thrown up by slaves of neighboring plantations, thus enabling him to use the respite to concentrate on training his inexperienced forces for the battle. A month after the battle Union soldiers were grousing about the presence of armed blacks at Confederate batteries near

Newport News. The Richmond Howitzers was identified as a Confederate unit manned partly by Afro-Virginians. After the war two of its black members, William Allison and Richard Carter, volunteered to care for the graves of their white comrades at Richmond's Hollywood Cemetery.[30]

The year 1863 was one of considerable foreboding for the Confederacy as its citizens began to wonder aloud about the chances of defeat. Anything less than victory meant black freedom and equality; but a Confederate victory could also generate concessions by augmenting the free black population as reward for the loyal service of slave soldiers on the battlefield. Several Southern whites continued to fear the consequences of arming blacks. In March two Afro-Virginian men on the steamship *West Point* obtained muskets and drilled each other in the manual of arms without interference from white spectators. When one of the weapons accidentally discharged, killing one of the blacks, the Richmond *Sentinel* took advantage of the mishap to denounce of arming of unsupervised blacks as dangerous to themselves as well as whites.[31]

Nine months later officers of the 16th Virginia Infantry posted a young black male named Ben to guard its surplus rations. When a white private approached and ignored commands to desist, the Afro-Virginian sentry fractured the man's skull with his rifle butt, mortally wounding him. Only the intervention of General William Mahone himself (later to achieve fame as the "Hero of the Crater" when his division brutally repulsed a Union attack spearheaded by black troops) prevented Ben from being lynched by the dead soldier's comrades. The service of Ben and other black Virginians influenced the 1928 amendment which awarded state pensions to black males who served on military details or performed guard duty on behalf of the Confederacy.[32]

Some of Virginia's free blacks and slaves contributed funds and labor to the Southern cause as early as April and May 1861. Pompey Scott of Amelia County donated $20 and William, a slave, patriotically invested $150 in Confederate state loan bonds. Blacks so frequently donated large sums of cash to the rebel war effort that one state official remarked that they "contributed thousands of dollars to sustain the Confederacy and many of them stood the test of the battle-field on both sides." Dick Poplar, a black Petersburg chef and caterer who volunteered as a cook for a state regiment, was captured at Gettysburg and held for twenty months in a prison camp; he proudly spurned opportunities to desert to the Union side and proclaimed his loyalty to Jefferson Davis. A black man known as "Uncle Billy," owned by Bedford County customs collector Micajah Davis, buried his owner's official records during a Union raid in May and June 1864 and modestly returned them to a surprised Davis after the war. Lewis, a Mecklenburg County slave who had served with the Boydton Cavalry as its bugler, was denied permission by the Confederate War Department to enlist with the unit when it became the 3d Virginia Cavalry. Undaunted, he donated his $40 bugle and $20 in cash. Confederates viewed such behavior as proof of the righteousness of slavery.[33]

A Petersburg newspaper proposed "three cheers for the patriotic free negroes of Lynchburg" after seventy city blacks proffered their services to Governor Letcher "to act in whatever capacity may be assigned them" in defense of Virginia. Another newspaper article, "Loyalty of the Negro Population," gleefully noted that both free and enslaved Afro-Virginians seemed equally dedicated to the state and the South. Vicksburg, Mississippi, Afro-Confederates held a ball to raise money for "de boys in Varginny" and amassed $1,000; slaves employed at Mobile, Alabama, fortifications promised to fight for "their white folks." Proceeds from a performance by the "Confederate Ethiopian Serenaders" of Charleston, South Carolina, were donated by these black men for the construction of a Confederate gunboat. Back in the Old Dominion, Afro-Confederates in Norfolk voluntarily erected breastworks, while Charles Tinsley, spokesmen for a group of black Petersburg volunteers, vowed that he and his comrades would gladly serve their native state in its hour of trial and stood ready to obey any and all orders. A Confederate recruitment parade in Woodstock illustrated in the October 1861 *Harper's Weekly* was led by a public-spirited black man.

After their capture one group of white Virginia slave owners and Afro-Virginians were asked if they would take the oath of allegiance to the United States in exchange for their freedom. One free negro indignantly replied: "I can't take no such oaf as dat. I'm a secesh nigger." A slave from this same group, upon learning that his master had refused, proudly exclaimed, "I can't take no oath dat Massa won't take." A second slave agreed: "I ain't going out here on no dishonorable terms." On another occasion a captured Virginia planter took the oath, but his slave remained faithful to the Confederacy and refused. This slave returned to Virginia by a flag of truce boat and expressed disgust at his owner's disloyalty: "Massa had no principles." Confederate prisoners of war paid tribute to the loyalty, ingenuity, and diligence of "kind-hearted" blacks who attended to their needs and considered them fellow Southerners.[34]

A January 1862 state newspaper self-righteously reported the outcome after Union raiders carried off eight or nine slaves from Shepherdstown. Upon their arrival in Maryland, the Afro-Virginians were offered a choice of freedom or return to Virginia. They unanimously stated a preference for the Old Dominion because their wives and children were there and they yearned to be with their masters. Flabbergasted, the Union men "set them on the

Virginia shore again and the negroes are now at home contented and happy, fearing nothing but another visit from the [Yankees]." After two weeks of freedom in Pennsylvania, four Clarke County, Virginia, slaves became disgusted with the North and asked to be returned. Two slaves captured in King George County escaped from their "rescuers," complaining that Northerners worked them twice as hard and regularly whipped them. An escaped slave from Gloucester County named Fanny sent $18 in equal amounts of silver, gold, and Union greenbacks for the benefit of her owner's children in August 1863, for which she was hailed as "a bright spot—an 'oasis' in the desert of negro faithfulness."[35]

A small number of pro-Confederate free blacks and slaves spied for the South under the supervision of Confederate spies such as Belle Boyd or military officers like Colonel John Singleton Mosby who appreciated the information they provided on Union troop movements across the Old Dominion. So frequently did Afro-Virginians commit espionage that by 1862 exasperated Union officers were grumbling that military operations in the state suffered more than they gained from ubiquitous black spies and counterspies whom they characterized as sworn allies of the South. Unheralded Afro-Virginian scouts, guides, and safe-house caretakers acted as part-time Southern secret agents; racial prejudice caused many white Confederates to judge them as untrustworthy or lacking in the patriotism, brains, skills, and nerve required for the dangerous task of wartime military intelligence. Furthermore, there were undoubtedly more blacks who preferred to assist Unionists.[36]

Afro-Confederates did not suffer divided loyalties; their attitudes were sincere and were expressed often enough to warrant notice and applause by whites. The pastor of the Brunswick Presbyterian Church, George W. White, described in his memoirs how he always wore pistols, even while conducting Sunday services, as protection against "lawless [white] vagrants," but not blacks. The slaves in Brunswick County outnumbered whites, but White praised their faithfulness: "In time of danger, we always turned over our valuables to our servants to keep and they never failed us. I have often wished that a splendid monument could be erected to the negro commemorating his fidelity." This loyalty was proved when a group of Yankee stragglers passed near White's home. He ordered one slave, Ned, to fetch his horse while another, Judy, brought his gun and pistol belt without being asked. The Reverend Mr. White never even considered how much he was putting his life in their hands; once he and his slave posse captured eight Yankees even though the latter were armed with repeating rifles.[37]

But some Afro-Confederates paid a price for their loyalty to the South.

A free black pastor in Hampton named Bailey, permitted to purchase his family's freedom and two houses, supported the Confederacy in order to protect them. His fellow blacks considered it a sign of divine justice when his houses were destroyed by fire after Confederates burned the town in the summer of 1861. Another black Baptist minister, grateful to whites for allowing him to purchase his beautiful daughter and save her from the sexual advances of lecherous slave owners, was so appreciative that he publicly offered the services of himself and his sons to Virginia. Outraged, other blacks rebuked him for this act. At first he tried to defend his actions with the excuse that he had done what he thought best for Afro-Virginians. Then, as his irate parishioners turned away, he became alarmed, for there are few things a preacher fears more than not having a congregation. He attempted to restore himself in their good graces with more excuses and finally apologies, but they continued to shun him.[38]

The public support and activities of Afro-Confederates, a minority within a minority, received considerable prominence. A Charlottesville newspaper reported an interview with James Ward, a slave who fled "Yankeedom" to warn his fellow slaves of abuse and racism in Union army camps and of blacks being forced to front lines during battles. He preferred being the slave of "the meanest masters in the South" than a free black man in the North: "If this is freedom, give me slavery forever."[39]

When two Union soldiers tried to entice a Shenandoah County slave named George with tales of the good life that awaited him and other blacks in the North, they were met with respectful but firm skepticism. He answered their stories with the curt remark that there were already more people up north than there ought to be. The soldiers then tried a different strategy, asking George if he was free. "No," he replied, "but I am comfortable—got a good house." He had no intention of leaving the Old Dominion. Such examples of black loyalty were praised by whites: "To the honor of the negroes it must be said, that they adhered *in general* with great fidelity to the cause. . . . This was a great surprise to the enemy, who had supposed that at the first signal the whole slave population would be in arms, and rush at every hazard to their standards."[40]

Afro-Confederate patriotism took many forms: slaves personally loyal to individual whites, free blacks who donated money and labor, Afro-Virginians who joined the Confederate army, and blacks who loyally supervised plantations of absentee owners. An unidentified Winchester Afro-Confederate became a local hero after being thrown in jail with nothing but bread and water for three days because of his support of the South and refusal to work for the Union side. On the fourth day, when his captors asked if he had changed his mind, he defiantly replied, "I is secesh yet." The old man was made to chop wood with iron ball and chains attached to his arms and legs, but the curses of his jailers were unavailing: he stubbornly vowed to support the South until death.[41]

Both Confederate and Yankee whites at first loathed the idea of African-American troops, but the events of 1863 and afterwards radically altered this bias. The Union provost marshal of Norfolk anxiously warned Lincoln against enlisting black soldiers for fear that disgruntled white army officers would use them in a coup d'état in favor of General McClellan and the Democratic party. However, Northern blacks, too, were soon given the opportunity to prove their patriotism (but not in exchange for full civil rights) by the elimination of the whites-only draft and the acceptance of black volunteers by the Union's War Department.[42]

Confederates who viewed blacks as pawns for securing Southern independence also feared that black soldier-veterans would be detrimental for race relations in the postwar South. But had the Davis administration exerted decisive leadership at the war's beginning, suspended some of region's caste system, and reanimated an inefficient and lagging Confederate bureaucracy to set up Afro-Confederate regiments speedily, Southern slaves and free blacks would have killed more than their fair share of Yankees.

In August 1863 an anonymous Confederate warned the North not to employ black soldiers, vowing that the South would respond by arming its slaves. This individual, claiming government officials as his source, boasted that 750,000 blacks could be enrolled, drilled, and equipped in three months in segregated regiments with their masters as officers and complete commissary and medical facilities. Southern blacks were "able-bodied fellows, loving and trusting of their masters, and ready to follow them up to the mouths of your [Yankee] cannon." By November the *Richmond Examiner* was critical of slaveholders who were opposed to slaves as soldiers: "The war originated and is carried on in great part for the defence of the slaveholder in his property rights and the perpetuation of the institution, [and] it is reasonable to suppose that he ought to be first and foremost in aiding and assisting by every means in his power, the triumph and success of our arms." Beginning in 1863, slaves were mustered into state militias with promises of freedom and land after the war. Body servants in the army believed they would be freed after the war as a reward for loyal service.[43]

Afro-Confederates were riddles. Whites never formally recognized them as spokesmen for blacks. To Southern racial conservatives they were two-faced; Northerners categorized them as oddities and dupes; most blacks disavowed and feared them as foolhardy traitors and scorned these "skilletheads." Pro-Confederate blacks could not by themselves cure the ills of the African-American community because they were never formally empowered to articulate or negotiate the aspirations of their race (though given time and less pressing circumstances they might have) and lacked political experience. Some were sincerely patriotic; others were alarmed individuals acting on behalf of their own self-preservation and economic interests. Their labors contributed to the rebel war effort, but in the end Confederates failed to appreciate properly and make full use of numerous reliable black allies within their midst.[44]

11 UNCOMMON DEFENDERS
Confederate States Colored Troops as the Great White Hope

Fight for your masters and you shall have your freedom.
—*Confederate secretary of state Judah P. Benjamin, 9 February 1865*

Our wives and daughters and the negroes are the only elements left us to recruit from.
—*Major Thomas P. Turner, Richmond Recruiter, Confederate States Colored Troops, 2 April 1865*

ONE OF the major questions of 1864–65 was: Will the blacks fight? They did. Certain oppressed peoples attempt to cope with their oppressors by professing admiration of them while repudiating their own culture. They actively seek to become members of the oppressor class even as they try to retain some of the "preferable" aspects of their cultural heritage. This is one reason why some Civil War–era blacks referred to each other as "niggers" or preached acceptance of slavery and racial subordination. Their attempts to assimilate were viewed with contempt by both races.[1]

The Confederacy, in dire straits by 1864, began seriously to consider the arming of black men for its armies. Desperate times gave impetus to desperate measures and the need to exploit every possible resource. Southern whites began suggesting the forging of a new biracial military coalition, the war's second, for the North had begun to enroll black soldiers in 1863.

Afro-Virginians had reason to assume that their situation was going to improve, however slightly. It remained to be seen if the Southern revolution's alliance with loyal blacks would lead to legislated policies benefiting blacks and eliminating most slavery. However, Afro-Virginians were likely to comprise the majority of any Confederate States Colored Troops (CSCT). Black political and social equality in the fullest sense was an impossibility, but gaining a few minor rights was not inconceivable. Not all Southern blacks acquiesced in the belief of white supremacy, but most ascertained that their peculiar status might be ameliorated into racial coexistence.[2]

Late in October 1864 the governors of six Confederate states—Alabama, Georgia, Mississippi, North Carolina, South Carolina, and Virginia—

met in Georgia to pass resolutions calling for "changes in policy" and "the increased military use of slaves." Lincoln's reelection in November shattered Southern hopes for a negotiated end to the war. By year's end the states of Arkansas and Louisiana were reorganized under his "ten percent plan." With the disintegration of the Army of the Tennessee after its crushing defeat at the battle of Nashville in December, the third year of the embryonic Confederacy ended on a note of unparalleled gloom.

Added to that, the South faced continued European neutrality, superior and growing Northern manpower (bolstered by the enlistment of blacks), and an increasingly effective naval blockade of its coasts and ports. By December 1864 Virginia was the key; it possessed the number of blacks necessary to produce food, supplies, and, if need be, infantrymen; if it could arm and field its slaves, other surviving slave states might do the same. Inexorably, the South was being strangled between the jaws of the Yankee navy and armies.[3]

Although the Confederate Congress ordered the conscription of all able-bodied white males early in 1864, General Patrick Cleburne did not consider this measure to be enough and offered a plan to use slaves to fill manpower needs. On 2 January 1864 he cited the superior numbers of the North and said the time had come for the South's leaders to discuss the enlistment of slaves. An inexhaustible white Northern population, slaves, and neutral Europeans could overwhelm the Confederacy, said Cleburne, and slavery was becoming a military hindrance.

Cleburne prefaced his recommendation by arguing that if young white boys below the age of eighteen could be trained as soldiers, then so, too, could adult black cooks and teamsters. He urged the emancipation of slaves who "remained true" and cautioned against the foolishness of believing that Great Britain would spend money or send troops to revive slavery after having abolished it throughout its dominions. Ending slavery and arming blacks would gain Britain's support, Cleburne reasoned, hinder the North's recruitment of blacks, and transform the Confederate revolutionary effort into one of independence for all its inhabitants.

Cleburne believed black slaves would fight for their masters as did Sparta's helots or Christian gallery slaves at Lepanto. He also cited the fighting abilities of blacks against the French in Santo Domingo (Haiti) and the Jamaican slave revolt but avoided mention of black American revolutionaries such as Nat Turner, Gabriel Prosser, and Denmark Vesey. Cleburne closed with admonitions: "It is said slavery is all we are fighting for, and if we give it up we give up all. Even if this were true, which we deny, slavery is not all our enemies are fighting for. It is merely the pretense to establish sectional superiority and a more centralized form of government, and to deprive us of our rights and liberties." Cleburne was ahead of his time, and time ran out for him on 30 November 1864 at the battle of Franklin, Tennessee. Davis had ordered the suppression of Cleburne's paper and banned further military petitions on the subject.[4]

In his annual message to the Confederate Congress, Davis rejected the arming of slaves but said that if the rebellion came down to a choice between slave soldiers or defeat, "there seems to be no reason to doubt what should then be our decision." He suggested a corps of 40,000 blacks as fortification laborers to be freed at war's end and recalled his own leadership of slaves against white outlaws before the war. Davis recognized that under certain conditions blacks could become Confederate soldiers. He warned that if the South was defeated, it would be due partially to the adherence to outmoded theories of black inferiority; the tombstone of the Confederacy would be carved with the epitaph "Died of a theory."[5]

Governor William Smith of Virginia suggested that the time had come for masters to volunteer their slaves for the good of the country and "public service" as required. He supported Cleburne's suggestions to arm free blacks and emancipate slaves: "There is not a man that would not cheerfully put the negro in the Army rather than become a slave himself. . . . Standing before God and my country, I do not hesitate to say that I would arm such portion of our able-bodied slave population as may be necessary, and put them in the field, so as to have them ready for the spring campaign." Smith considered Afro-Virginians capable of fighting Afro-Yankees. Public opinion in the state was divided, he conceded, but what if those who were in opposition to black soldiers were mistaken?[6]

A Richmond *Enquirer* editorial demanded that authorities employ 10,000 blacks for military assignments. It assured its readers that Virginia would "fight her blacks to the last man": the *Enquirer* also recommended the government immediately purchase 250,000 slaves to create a biracial army. Vitriolic editorials by John Moncure Daniel of the anti-Davis *Daily Examiner* advocated the conservative position by opposing the enrollment of black soldiers or the freeing of military slave laborers after the war: "While living with the white man in the relation of the slave, he is in a state superior and better for him than that of freedom."[7]

"An Act to Increase the Efficiency of the Army by the Employment of Free Negroes and Slaves in Certain Capacities" was issued on 11 March 1864. It authorized the Confederate Bureau of Conscription to draft up to 20,000 male slaves between the ages of eighteen and fifty for work on fortifications for pay of $11 a month. They were not, however, to be conscripted if sufficient numbers of free blacks were available. Richmond newspapers supported the measure. Owners were encouraged to free their slaves for national defense purposes so that this Southern emancipation policy might not be misinterpreted as abolitionism. Slaves were described as more intelligent than Russian serfs, and with their enlistment Confederate deserters would gladly return to the armies to fight side by side with blacks.[8]

Governor Smith characterized this as "a grave and important question full of difficulty" and praised blacks as representing the means to defeat Grant. He bleakly noted that "the Yankee themselves boast that they have 200,000 of our slaves in arms against us." The *Sentinel* announced approval: "The governor's recommendation about the slaves is prophetic. They will go into the army, if the war goes on through next year. . . . Gov. Smith . . . will be followed by other Governors, and Legislative bodies. We shrewdly suspect the Confederate Government is behind him." But a writer in the *Enquirer* who signed himself "Barbarossa" opposed the idea as an encroachment of property rights; "Virginius" denounced it as an evil but acknowledged that public opinion accepted it.

"Sentinel," writing in the *Daily Richmond Enquirer*, warned that although the South had the right to arm slaves, they would not serve voluntarily. Others recalled a calamitous experiment involving a battalion of Union prisoners, mostly European immigrants, which was hastily disbanded after its members were discovered plotting against the Confederacy. John Goode, representing the state's Sixth District in the Confederate House, protested that the employment of blacks other than as slaves was a confession of weakness: "The right place for Cuffee [is] in the corn field." Some whites accused Davis of using the South's recent military reverses to strengthen his hand in seeking approval for the enlistment of Afro-Confederate soldiers.[9]

Howell Cobb of Georgia predicted national and racial suicide if slave soldiers were employed: "You can't keep white and black troops together, and you can't trust negroes by themselves. . . . Use all the negroes you can get, for all the purposes for which you need them, but don't arm them." Another Georgian told Davis he knew the slaves would fight because they were already doing so for the North. In Great Britain a Liverpool merchant complained to the London *Times* that if the South created a slave army, there would be a cotton famine with perilous consequences for the British economy. Richmond war clerk Robert Kean insisted that the idea had few supporters and was strongly opposed by planters. On Christmas Day, 1864, he wrote in his diary that perhaps it was best for slavery to be abolished if its demise would ensure Confederate independence; by New Year's Day, 1865, he had persuaded himself that Confederates would rather accept black general emancipation than General Grant.[10]

State legislators were still evading the issue in late January 1865 with protestations that the emancipation and enlistment of slaves were affronts to property rights and that slavery had proved beneficial to both races. Formerly vehement antagonists became lukewarm advocates, culminating with the General Assembly's acquiescence in February to governmental employment of Virginia slaves as soldiers.[11]

United States senator John Snyder Carlile of loyal Virginia predicted in 1864, "If it shall become necessary in this struggle for the Confederates to arm their slaves, they will arm and emancipate them." But Lincoln argued that rebel debates on the subject were a sign of impending Union victory: "Slaves cannot fight and stay at home and make bread too. As one is about as important as the other, I do not care which they do." Two years previously, just before his Emancipation Proclamation, Lincoln had claimed that the weapons of any black Union soldier would soon fall into rebel hands.[12]

The Liberator and other Northern newspapers were convinced that Confederates would never chance it: "The negro . . . will sooner tear out his heart-strings than fight [his true friends]. Flattery, or praise or begging, or even the love of freedom cannot conciliate the negro now to join the rebellion. The memory of insults, outrages, broken hearts, scattered families, blasted hopes, rise like a mountain. . . . Let them arm the black man, if they dare—they will be fit out a soldier for our ranks, and place a weapon in the hand surest to smite their cause to the earth." But Ulysses S. Grant, whose City Point headquarters enabled him to gauge Virginia events, ordered his officers in February 1865 to "get all the negro men we can before the enemy can put them in their ranks." The likelihood of hundreds of thousands of blacks in gray could not be taken lightly, and on the eve of victory Grant was for taking no chances.[13]

Relentless hammerblows against the Confederacy's dwindling morale and resources began to take their toll. The capture of Vicksburg, followed by the surrender of Port Hudson, gave the Union control of the Mississippi River and split the Confederacy in half, cutting it off from troops and supplies in the Trans-Mississippi. The elevation of Grant as Lincoln's general-in-chief, the coordination of Northern strategy, Sherman's march through Georgia and the Carolinas, and Phil Sheridan's ravaging of the Valley of Virginia all emphasized the fading Confederacy. The seizure of Mobile Bay by Admiral David Farragut closed one of the South's last two outlets to the Gulf of Mexico; Lee's army was bottled up in Petersburg and lost a third of its soldiers as deserters or casualties; meanwhile, Sherman captured Atlanta, ending its career as a major Confederate supply depot.

Major General Edwin O. C. Ord, commander of the Army of the James, reported the presence of five Afro-Confederate regiments near Petersburg in March 1865. Thomas Morris Chester, the *Philadelphia Press*'s black reporter, claimed 20,000 Afro-Virginians in twenty-two regiments were drilling at Camp Lee west of Richmond. He warned that because runaway slaves feared being returned to their owners or sold to Cuba by Federal officers, Southern blacks were preparing to fight for the Confederacy. An alarmed Frederick Douglass advised Lincoln that unless slaves were guaranteed freedom and land bounties, they would take up arms for the rebels.[14]

The acting superintendent of the Virginia Military Institute, J. L. L. Preston, wrote the Confederate secretary of war in February 1865 that "the call . . . for negro troops will be responded to" and proposed a maximum of 500,000. This goal would "inspire dread" in the enemy and would actually raise 200,000. Preston suggested Richmond's Camp Lee as the perfect training site and claimed that the Institute's officers and cadets were enthusiastic about the prospect of drilling blacks. Three days later Governor Smith advised the General Assembly that "certain volunteer organizations of free negroes" had been formed and that General James Longstreet wanted to employ them at the front without delay. Before Afro-Virginians could fight Afro-Yankees, state laws barring the arming of blacks had to be repealed.[15]

The arming of slaves gained in popularity despite objections from Virginia's neighbor, North Carolina, which passed resolutions denying the Confederacy's right to undertake this precarious war measure. A bill authorizing the use of black soldiers was introduced in the Confederate Congress by Ethelbert Barksdale of Mississippi and approved on 13 March 1865; ten days earlier Virginia's General Assembly had repealed the restrictions on the bearing of arms by black soldiers after General Lee expressed his crucial need of them. The assembly instructed the state's congressional representatives to support a national law to this effect, but Senator Robert M. T. Hunter disagreed. A North Carolina senator protested that the General Assembly's instructing its representatives how to vote was an undemocratic interference of senators' prerogatives.

In fact, Hunter viewed black soldiers as an admission that slavery had been wrong from the beginning: "If we are right in passing this measure we were wrong in denying to the old government the right to interfere with the institution of slavery and to emancipate slaves. Besides, if we offer slaves their freedom . . . we confess that we were insincere, were hypocritical, in asserting that slavery was the best state for the negroes themselves. . . . If we could make them soldiers, the condition of the soldier being socially equal to any other in society, we could make them officers, perhaps, to command white men." He also feared that future dictatorial Confederate presidents might use black troops "to seize the liberties of the country and put white men under his feet." He could not believe "the heroes of Manassas,

Fredericksburg and Cold Harbor were holding out their hands to the negroes to come and save them."[16]

President Davis frequently corresponded with Governor Smith on the value of Afro-Virginians as Confederate defenders and urged Smith to do what was necessary to secure the freedom of slaves who joined the army. Davis promised that upon their honorable discharge they would not only receive their freedom but the right to settle in their old neighborhoods. The amassing of Afro-Virginian recruits at special military camps would serve as a model for other states. Blacks were to be summoned in their home counties, forwarded to the nearest depot for mustering, training, and equipage, then sent to the front in their own regiments under the command of white officers. Davis was even willing to discuss the possibility of noncommissioned black officers and suggested black volunteers should be accepted first.

Davis hoped free Afro-Virginians would volunteer in enough numbers to preclude the drafting of the state's slave population. "It is now becoming daily more evident to all reflecting persons," he declared, "that we are reduced to choosing whether the negroes shall fight for or against us, and that all arguments as to the positive advantages or disadvantages of employing them are beside the question, which is simply one of relative advantage between having their fighting element in our ranks or those of the enemy." His comments were a far cry from earlier pronouncements during 1861–63 during which he damned black soldiers in Northern armies as apocalyptic harbingers of "Servile War" and declared any blacks captured by Southern forces "to be chattels, they and their issue forever, . . . the proper condition of all of African descent."[17]

Smith and Davis took heart at the support voiced by the Richmond press. In its editorial "Colored Soldiers," the Sentinel proclaimed any black who volunteered to be a brother in arms and suggested whites who opposed their enlistment should refrain from public dissent. It prophesied that after the war Confederate States Colored Troops veterans would wear "badges of merit" and hold "certificates of honor" as members of a new black aristocracy. Slave owners should take the lead in this recruitment, and whites were advised not to be "niggard" (a peculiar choice of words) on behalf of this endeavor. "None . . . will deny that our servants are more worthy of respect than the motley hordes which come against us," exclaimed the Sentinel, and Virginians were advised not to become jealous about blacks sharing the honor of killing Yankees. Promises of emancipation, once given, were to be "redeemed with the most scrupulous fidelity and at all hazards. . . . Bad faith [to black Confederate soldiers] must be avoided as an indelible dishonor."[18]

State senator Andrew Hunter wrote to Lee for the general's opinion. Exasperated by delays and complaints, Lee testily replied that notwithstanding his preference for white troops, blacks would do: "We must decide whether slavery shall be extinguished by our enemies and the slaves be used against us, or use them ourselves at the risk of the effects which may produced upon our social institutions. My own opinion is that we should employ them without delay. I believe that with proper regulations they can be made efficient soldiers. They possess the physical qualifications in an eminent degree. Long habits of obedience and subordination, coupled with the moral influence which in our country the white man possesses over the black, furnish an excellent foundation for that discipline which is the best guaranty of military efficiency. Our chief aim should be to secure their fidelity." Lee speculated that the enrollment of black soldiers "would disappoint the hopes which our enemies base upon our exhaustion, deprive them in a great measure of the aid they now derive from black troops, and thus throw the burden of the war upon their own people. In addition to the great political advantages that would result to our cause from the adoption of a system of emancipation, it would exercise a salutary influence upon our whole negro population, by rendering more secure the fidelity of those who become soldiers, and diminishing the inducements to the rest to abscond."

Lee reminded Hunter that the Federal armies' greatest successes in Virginia occurred after Lincoln's proclamation calling for 280,000 black soldiers, many of whom were recruited in the Old Dominion. The Confederacy would have to offer genuine incentives, but if Virginia could accept slave soldiers and was willing to emancipate them, slavery was as dead and buried as if it were a corpse in an unmarked grave.[19]

Confederate diplomats in London found Lee's remarks encouraging and useful; once again they received overtures from the British about possible diplomatic recognition. Davis had appointed Duncan Farrar Kenner in 1864 as his special European envoy to propose a desperate treaty: recognition of the Confederacy in exchange for the gradual emancipation of slaves. The Union blockade prevented Kenner's arrival in Europe until February 1865. There he found that the French were interested but preferred to act in concert with the British. The British bluntly refused to consider formal diplomatic relations because the North was close to victory—and to Canada.

Representative Thomas S. Gholson delivered a jeremiad in the Confederate House denouncing black recruitment as a hazardous experiment, offensive to the army, and a confession of weakness. Slaves were too "credulous and timid" for the pursuits of war; if not, he wondered, why had they not attempted any mass insurrections during the previous four years? Showing particular concern about what would happen after slave soldiers helped the South to achieve independence. Gholson dismissed the entire project as foolhardy.[20]

Two days later, on 3 February, Abraham Lincoln and Secretary of State William Seward met with Confederate representatives at Hampton Roads aboard the *River Queen* to attempt a negotiated settlement. The Confederate commissioners—Assistant Secretary of War John A. Campbell, Vice President Alexander Stephens, and Senator Robert Hunter—wanted to discuss peace between "the two countries" and plans to deal with the French occupation of Mexico. Lincoln began by demanding the surrender of the rebels and their acceptance of slave emancipation. Hunter replied that freedom was cruel to slaves, especially in those areas where all black males had been removed for military labor; emancipation would make black families too helpless to care for themselves. Lincoln answered with a story about a farmer who planted potatoes for his hogs and left them in the ground to be rooted up; the ground froze one winter, but the farmer declared the hogs must root nevertheless ("root, hog, or die"). Seward was asked if he supposed the slavery problem would end with emancipation and if there would be further agitation on the issues of race. Seward agreed to the second proposition, but Lincoln interjected to say that he regarded the North to be as responsible for slavery as the South.[21]

The ill-starred conference broke up on a friendly note. Blacks had been discussed though not permitted to send their own representatives. Afterwards, Seward sent a black servant to the Confederates in a rowboat filled with refreshments and jovially told them to enjoy the food and drinks but to return the black man. Inflexibility gave both sides no choice but to fight to the finish. "All hopes of peace without foreign recognition have died since the return of our Commissioners from Fortress Monroe," lamented a Confederate soldier. "Something must be done and that quickly." Henrico County resident J. H. Stringfellow, in a lengthy missive to Davis, suggested that slave emancipation was the only solution because blacks represented a vast reservoir of untapped strength and their freedom would perpetuate Confederate independence.[22]

On 9 February 1865 resolutions, long speeches, and outpourings of patriotism were presented at Richmond's First African Baptist Church, filled to capacity with whites who turned out to hear their leaders speak on the subject of the war and blacks as soldiers. Senator Robert T. Hunter, previously opposed to the proposal, remarked, "The only hope of the black man is our success . . . the day of his freedom is the day of his doom." Secretary of State Judah P. Benjamin claimed the South had 680,000 black men who could become soldiers and declared: "Let us say to every negro who wants to go into the ranks, go and fight, and you are free. . . . Fight for your masters and you shall have your freedom." Benjamin urged Virginia to be the first to send the black man to the aid of General Lee, and at this remark the audience demonstrated their support with cries and cheers of "Let's try it" and "Now, now, now!" In twenty days, Benjamin asserted, the Army of Northern Virginia could be reinforced with enough black soldiers to resume the offensive.

He apologized for having uttered "some distasteful truths" but excused himself by pointing out that the enemy's black regiments could be repelled only by Confederate blacks: "Let us stop the negro from going over to the enemy by saying, if you go to the Yankee you will get your freedom, but you will perish off the earth, for you cannot live in that cold climate." Richmonders returned to their homes to spread the good news among their slaves: the Confederacy wanted and needed Afro-Virginians for its New Model Biracial Army. They were to be welcomed with open arms into the glorious fold of the New South as symbols of racial cooperation.[23]

Benjamin later described the meeting to Lee and frankly admitted to having spoken of slave volunteers to be freed after the war only to head off further opposition. But Congressman James T. Leach of North Carolina was not fooled. Infuriated by Benjamin's speech, Leach labeled it derogatory and a disgrace by "a high public functionary . . . and an insult to public opinion" and offered a resolution of censure. Deeply concerned about rumors that the army would refuse to accept blacks, Benjamin asked Lee to poll his senior officers discreetly for their views. Should they support the utilization of black soldiers, "there will be no further effective opposition in any of our legislative bodies, State or Confederate." A House minority report rejected slave soldiers: "The doctrine of emancipation as a reward for the services of slaves employed in the army, is antagonistic to the spirit of our institutions, and could effect no permanent good, but would inevitably entail upon the country great present and greater future evil." If and when the supply of white men became exhausted slaves might be permitted to serve; the congressmen offering these resolutions failed to understand that by then it would be too late.[24]

Several bills were proposed to employ black soldiers; most died in committee, victims of stalling tactics by opponents and hesitancy by proponents too timid to defend the question publicly. As his men starved and suffered in the Petersburg trenches, Confederate major general John Brown Gordon, commander of the Army of Northern Virginia's 2d Corps, expressed irritation: "We are having many desertions—caused I think by the despondency in our ranks. It is a terrible blow—the defeat of the negro bill in congress— troops all in favor of it—It would have greatly encouraged the army—they are much disappointed at its defeat. What mean the national Legislators? We shall be compelled to have them or be defeated—with them as volunteers & fighting for their freedom we shall be successful—But I presume we can not hope for any assistance now from this class of our population—If authority

were granted to raise 200,000 of them it would greatly encourage the men &
do so much to stop desertions. I can find excellent officers to take command
of them."[25]

William Porcher Miles, chairman of the Confederate House Military
Affairs Committee, criticized the arming of blacks but conceded it would
take place when the nation reached "the very brink of the precipice of ruin."
Until then, he admitted, the Yankees offered blacks better inducements in
the form of freedom, food, clothing, and whiskey. "The country seems to
have gone wild on the subject of putting negroes in the army," groused Richmond resident J. A. Merritt. "Congress and country seize the abstract question without looking at the question in all its bearings."[26]

But the Confederate Congress could ill afford to ignore what ostensibly
was the will of the people and most army commanders. The Senate and
House military affairs committees passed bills authorizing the raising of
200,000 Negro troops by the president. To placate slave owners their consent
was required before their slaves could enlist; amendments to this measure
specified that manumission of slave soldiers would be granted only with the
consent of the state where they were stationed at the time of they were
discharged. An amendment by Senator Allen T. Caperton of Virginia ordered no more than 25 percent of the male slaves in any state to be enlisted
and with the act was approved on 13 March 1865. The new law established a
quota of 300,000 blacks between the ages of eighteen and forty-five to be
called up from Virginia and the other Confederate states. The slaves and
free blacks were to be organized into companies, regiments, battalions,
and brigades.

Afro-Confederate soldiers were to receive the same allowances, clothing, pay, and rations as their white counterparts. The Confederate Congress,
satisfied with its work, adjourned but not before giving itself a collective pat
on the back in the form of a resolution by Virginia representative Frederick
W. M. Holliday commending its accomplishments. "We shall have a negro
army," wrote a not-too-surprised government clerk. "It is the desperate remedy for the very desperate."[27]

Another resident, recalling the Spanish proverb "A good idea may occur
to a fool which may escape a wise man," proposed that one black man be
allocated to every four white soldiers, each quartet responsible for his drilling and training. A surgeon of the 57th Virginia Infantry proposed the creation of a black corps as a retaliatory mobile force to ravage the North with
the sort of warfare done to Georgia by Sherman's army. He and other Confederate soldiers were willing to have blacks join them in the trenches in the
hope they would fight better for Southerners than Northerners. A poll of
regimental commanders ordered by the Adjutant and Inspector General's

Office in Richmond indicated that most state regiments were ready to receive Afro-Virginians "as co-laborers." And yet, as they issued resolutions in support of the decision, the prejudice of white soldiers resulted in suggestions that blacks serve in segregated regiments.[28]

Robert E. Lee implored Jefferson Davis to hesitate no longer: "The services of these men [blacks] are now necessary to enable us to oppose the enemy." Despite the postwar prospect of increased numbers of free blacks and a decline in slaves, other Confederates agreed. "If [Lee] will but beat back the Yankee invasion, the country will gladly forgive any shock given to its traditional policy of social system," editorialized one newspaper. "Let us be free of our enemy, and let negro labour and the negro race find their lead afterwards as best they may." Blacks, if led by white officers, would fight well, and there would be time enough to sort out their postbellum status later. The shrinking Army of Northern Virginia, already in the crosshairs of Grant's army, desperately awaited Afro-Confederate soldiers.[29]

Editorials addressed Afro-Virginians with appeals to their patriotism and promises of better days: "The Governments, Confederate and state, having settled the policy of employing this element of strength, and [this] class of our population havinggiven repeated evidence of their willingness to take up arms in the defence of their homes, it is believed that it is only necessary to put the matter before them in a proper light to cause them to rally with enthusiasm, for the preservation of the homes in which they have been born and raised, and in which they have found contentment and happiness, and to save themselves and their race from the barbarous cruelty invariably practiced upon them by a perfidious enemy claiming to be friends." The Petersburg *Daily Express* characterized Afro-Virginians as the South's only salvation and declared that they were held in highest esteem by whites in Virginia, North Carolina, South Carolina, Georgia, and other areas east of the Mississippi River. Tennessee congressmen and military officers also championed the arming of slaves.[30]

But dissenters did not remain silent. Texas passed resolutions favoring the perpetuation of slavery. Edward A. Pollard, editor of the *Richmond Examiner*, described the discussion of black recruitment as "an ill-natured debate" and wondered why, if the idea was such a good one, it had not been implemented during the war's earlier phases when blacks might have better served the Confederacy. He also demanded to know how 200,000 black soldiers were to be armed and fed. Another Richmond writer pronounced the concept of black soldiers a colossal blunder and worried that it meant the beginning of racial equality. Diarist Edmund Ruffin, perhaps the most impassioned secessionist in the state, grudgingly acknowledged the necessity of slave soldiers but prophesied that their death within forty years of their enlistment.[31]

In the span of less than four years, Confederate slaves evolved from a hereditary labor force into armed indigenous allies. Dangled promises of future freedom and told there would be racial harmony, they were expected to fight to protect the slaveholders; to be sure, free blacks would fight for something else: acceptance by whites as fledgling social and political partners. White Virginians assured each other that after the war they could easily retain all political rights and the power to control Afro-Virginians. They were not giving up slavery in arming their slaves.[32]

As Virginia geared up for the process of black recruitment, other states considered the Old Dominion a fertile field for slave soldier recruitment. A man might at worse receive an officer's commission or at best a furlough home to raise black troops. An anonymous Georgian implored: "Let negroes fight negroes. . . . Confront them with Yankee negroes and place bayonets behind them." If slave boys and women were kept in bondage, slavery, too, would survive the war. Slave soldiers could be given their freedom and limited civil equality and colonized in Mexico or Central America.[33]

Georgia regiments stationed at Petersburg and Richmond strongly advocated arming blacks and petitioned that the "glorious independence" of the South necessitated their conscription. Azariah Bostwick of the 31st Georgia Infantry demanded that black men be put into military service "the Sooner the better" since the Confederacy was just as much their country as any white man's. Officers of the 49th Georgia forwarded a plan to General Lee detailing the enrollment of blacks and volunteering to send home an officer or enlisted man from each company to recruit them from Georgia's counties. They were willing for the "negro element" to join their ranks, and their suggestions were approved. If this was a ploy for furloughs, it failed; before the 49th could put its scheme into effect, the plans were captured at Fort Gregg a week before the army's surrender.[34]

Captain S. N. Brandon of the 21st Mississippi bragged to Jefferson Davis that he could easily raise a battalion of four black companies; Samuel G. Battle and Robert E. Moffitt of the 3d Alabama promised black infantry and artillery companies. These offers were merely subterfuges for an honorable escape from the Petersburg quagmire; Battle and Moffitt postscripted their intentions as contingent on receiving permission to return to Alabama. Virginia officers had reservations about Afro-Confederate legions. Colonel John De Hart Ross, stationed at the Virginia Military Institute, urged the Confederate Congress to implement their use as "there is no time to lose"; he privately admitted to his wife that he did not want to command black regiments.[35]

Civilians attempted to secure official authorization for black recruitment. A. F. Robertson of Lynchburg proposed to raise either a brigade or a regiment and said that the city's blacks had spoken to him of their interest in joining the army. William S. Southall of Charlotte County described himself as an expert on handling blacks and able to enlist a company of them in a short time; Richmond resident C. E. Thornburn boasted that he could supply 1,200 Afro-Virginians to march at once. James Buchanan of Wythe County wrote: "I am desirous of raising a company of negro troops in this county. . . . I am anxious of [?] the services and to recruit a company of colored troops for the Confederate service. Being full aware of the importance of an early Step in that direction, I respectfully solicit authority for such a purpose."[36]

State officials preferred to leave black mobilization in the hands of military professionals. Adjutant Samuel Wilson, Dr. P. J. Hale, Colonel Kirk Otey of the 11th Virginia, and Lieutenant John L. Cowardin of the 19th Virginia Artillery were commissioned to "recruit, muster, and organize negro troops." Hale recruited blacks in Patrick, Henry, and Franklin counties; Cowardin and Wilson sought recruits in the predominantly black counties of Halifax and Surry. Major Thomas P. Turner, Richmond's recruiter, enthusiastically exhorted fellow recruiters: "Go to work and work, work, work. If the people of Virginia only knew and appreciated General Lee's solicitude on this subject they would no longer hold back their slaves. Their wives and daughters and the negroes are the only elements left us to recruit from."[37]

One Petersburg soldier schemed for command of a black regiment because the army would soon have "two hundred thousand buck Negroes" to defeat Grant. Confederate House Speaker Thomas Bocock received a request from Captain B. J. Hawthorne of the 38th Virginia Infantry for a colonelcy of "a Regiment of Negroes." F. W. Hancock, chief surgeon at Richmond's Jackson Hospital, polled his facility's hired black male slaves on Valentine's Day, 1865, to see "if they would be willing to take up arms to protect their masters' families, homes, and their own from an attacking foe." Of the seventy-two Afro-Virginians, sixty volunteered to fight the Yankees "to the bitter end." Unquestionably, there were Afro-Virginian slaves prepared to die for the Confederacy, who, once enlisted, would have had no alternative except to serve faithfully as long as their families remained at home as hostages.[38]

Lee criticized the slowness in assigning recruiting officers and asked Jefferson Davis to accelerate the process. With potential recruits waiting at Petersburg and in Mecklenburg County, Lee acted on his own authority to send recruiters. Davis distributed a circular to state governors seeking their cooperation and ordering that any officer trusted by slaves and their owners be temporarily appointed as commanders of black companies and battalions. Lee acknowledged lack of progress but blamed the Confederate Congress. His General Order no. 14 established procedures for the induction of black regiments. Only officers with excellent recommendations and creditable proof of their ability to recruit blacks would be appointed to command Afro-Confederate troops, and General Longstreet was ordered to forward the names of such officers to Lee's headquarters immediately.[39]

A report written for Union secretary of war Stanton stated that "the surrender of the rebel armies and the overthrow of the so-called Confederate Government in April, 1865, followed so close . . . that no negro soldiers were recruited under it." This was not correct. Several companies of Afro-Virginians volunteered and served as Confederate soldiers during the months of March and April. A Virginia Military Institute cadet on picket duty at the Richmond front was amazed to be relieved by black soldiers who "politely intimated the character of their orders, and took their positions . . . with all the precision and alacrity of old soldiers."[40]

Sixty blacks at Jackson Hospital saw limited combat on 11 March 1865, two days before the Confederate Congress approved the enlistment of blacks. The Jackson Battalion, comprised of three companies of white convalescent soldiers and two companies of blacks, arrived at the Petersburg front seven days after its organization and saw combat under the command of Colonel Scott Shipp, commandant of the Virginia Military Institute Cadet Corps. Five days later they were withdrawn, and their battalion commander, Major Henry C. Scott, proudly reported: "I ordered my battalion . . . to the front on Saturday night at 12 o'clk and reported by order of Maj. Pegram to Col. Ship. . . . I have great pleasure in stating that my men acted with the utmost promptness and good will. I had the pleasure of turning over to Major Chambliss a portion of my negro company to be attached to his negro command. Allow me to state Sir that they behaved in an extraordinary acceptable manner."[41]

Afro-Virginian volunteers fought due to their own sense of purpose as Confederate Virginians. They suffered hostile fire and attacked Union troops, white men supposedly fighting to free them. While Confederate States Colored Troops never took the field as complete regiments (except for a few isolated squads and companies), the potential existed. In Washington, D. C., the superintendent of the census estimated that 236,990 Afro-Virginian men (12,475 free blacks and 224,515 slaves) were available for service as Confederate soldiers. Approximately 48 percent of the white Virginia male population served in the army; an analogous ratio of Afro-Virginians equaled 113,755 black soldiers. Their mobilization might have tipped the scales of fate in favor of the Confederacy; every man, white or black, was to be armed.[42]

In March 1865 Virginia's state auditor estimated 30,419 black men were available for military service. Governor Smith assured Lee that enlistment depots were being established and were rapidly filling up with black recruits.[43] A black brigade mustered in under the command of majors James W. Pegram and Thomas P. Turner disappointed an integrated crowd on 20 March after announcements that it would march on parade. The blacks failed to appear because their uniforms and equipment had not arrived. A battalion from camps Winder and Jackson commanded by Dr. Jackson Chambliss and a company commanded by Captain Grimes did parade at Capitol Square on the evening of 22 March 1865. Charles McKnight, an ordnance bureau clerk, wrote his brother that there was such a large crowd present that he wondered how the blacks "went through the motions" of the manual of arms; they were hailed as "the first company of negro troops raised in Virginia." One company of thirty-five Afro-Virginians (twelve free blacks and twenty-three slaves) was enrolled five days later.[44]

Black volunteers, each promised a standard gray soldier's uniform, a blanket, and a "serviceable" pair of shoes, rendezvoused in Richmond at Smith's Factory between Main and Cary streets. Military balls were held to raise funds on their behalf. White Virginians were highly pleased with their Afro-Confederate enlistees, and the Winder unit was praised as a superb company which drilled "with pride and alacrity." Petersburg black men became eligible for $100 bounties on 1 April if they would "come forward and show their willingness to save their country." At the Sycamore Street office of recruiting agents W. E. Cameron and S. W. Britton, slaves who enlisted were promised freedom and the right to reside in the Confederacy after the war, but not voting privileges.[45]

Orders from the adjutant general's office established guidelines for Afro-Confederate recruitment. One officer in each state was placed in charge of the process. Depots were to be formed, each with a quartermaster, a commissary, and a surgeon. Enlistments were for the duration of the war, and no slaves were to be accepted unless their owners had given written permission and granted them "the rights of a free man." Volunteers were organized into camps and squads and specially printed forms detailing name, age, description, value, and name of owner were to be submitted on the first Monday of each month. Officers were directed to treat blacks humanely and protect them from "injustice and oppression."[46]

Two black recruits, Ned and Roberts, were arrested in late March while sightseeing in Richmond. They were accused of being runaways though they were dressed in full Confederate uniform complete with knapsacks and bayonets. After proving their military affiliation, they were released to the custody of the provost marshal and returned to their company. Not all blacks were volunteers. Two slaves, Oliver and George, scheduled to hang for burglary, were pardoned by Governor Smith and delivered to Major Pegram as the first of his "volunteers." Understandably, Oliver and Gregory were "delighted with this reversal of their fate." On Poor House Hill near Richmond's Shockoe Cemetery another pair of black convicts in the shadow of the gallows were offered clemency if they joined "the Confederate free negro company." They did but cheated death again when their unit was rejected for conscription.[47]

Among the blacks drilled by Lieutenant Virginius Bossieux at Smith's Factory was a free Afro-Virginian, John Scott. Seeking revenge after Yankees stole his canalboat, robbed him, and destroyed his livelihood during a raid in Goochland County, Scott appeared at the recruiting rendezvous and convinced Bossieux to enroll him. Scott had once believed the Yankees would not harm free blacks but now knew better. He declared army service the duty of Afro-Virginian men, urging them either to "join the Army of the South" or leave Virginia. He told Bossieux: "I wants to jibe right away. I wants to fight dem damn Yankees that hab treated me so bad. For I'se got no nusin in de world but jist what I stands in, and I wants to fight dem dats robbed me. I knows a heap about a gun, jist let me git a bead on 'em and I'll bring 'em every pop." Scott's loyalty did not endure; he deserted on 26 March 1865 with twenty-five pairs of long underwear, shirts, shoes, and socks belonging to his fellow blacks and worth at least $1,000.[48]

Richmond's Camp Lee served as the chief induction center for Afro-Virginian recruits. Many nearby white residents were perturbd because the enlistment of African-Americans offended their views of racial superiority, but the work of enlisting blacks continued with bands, parades, music, and speeches as enticements. "Like flies around a molasses barrel," wrote one soldier in disparagement. Another observer considered this "the last resort of the dying Confederacy; and thus the sublimest tragedy ended in the most absurd and ridiculous comedy—slaves fighting for their own thraldom; freemen unworthy of the name; statesmen, so called, who dared not arm and meet the foe." A Richmond minstrel show lampooned Afro-Confederate soldiers and their white advocates. Recruiting Unbleached Citizens of Virginia for the Confederate States Army played before packed houses to "shouts of applause" a week before the capture of the city.[49]

The planter aristocracy became convinced that blacks could become trustworthy defenders of the racial status quo. Twenty-three of Roanoke

County's largest slave owners pledged to emancipate male slaves of military age if they promised to volunteer for the army. These planters solemnly guaranteed blacks that "they shall be permitted to return to their homes, and that proper provision will be made for them and their families when the war is over."[50]

A "gentlemen refugee" established a special fund for the purchase of slaves who voluntarily enlisted; their manumission papers were to be kept on file pending their honorable discharge or as rewards for meritorious service. Destitute slave owners who could not afford to free their slaves and offer them as "a gift to the army" were encouraged to send them to Richmond or to black recruitment headquarters for compensation from this fund. Every black unit was not enthusiastic. Eyewitnesses spoke of one Afro-Confederate company of sixty dejected blacks in shabby civilian clothes who appeared passive and lethargic as they drilled.[51]

There are few contemporary comments of Afro-Virginians on the subject of their enlistment. It was taken for granted that they were eager to sacrifice themselves upon the state's killing fields. A New Orleans newspaper reported that Afro-Virginians "prayerfully assembled" to discuss the Confederate offer and, after much deliberation, accepted it. The newspaper went on to suggest that once on the field of battle, they intended to turn their guns on Confederates and join Union troops in their annihilation. Yet Joseph A. Mudd, an assistant surgeon at a Richmond hospital, recollected a different Afro-Virginian response. The hospital employed nearly 150 young black men and women as laborers, and when the call came for slave soldiers, Mudd and three other whites learned that the black employees had arranged to hold a meeting outside hospital grounds to deliberate the proposition privately among themselves. Taking care not to be seen, the surgeons were enthralled to overhear a half-hour speech by the leader of the blacks, "a bright young fellow," during which he made "an eloquent and earnest plea for every man to enlist in our glorious cause and help to drive the ruthless invader from the sacred soil of Virginia."[52]

On 2 April 1865 Lee sent a hurried letter to President Davis on the organization and deployment of Afro-Confederate soldiers, reaffirming his willingness to detach whatever officers could be spared from the Petersburg front to lead black troops and promising to send their names to the War Department. The strength of the Union army was growing, thanks to its enlistment of escaped slaves and Northern free blacks. Inundated with requests for transfers to the black regiments that added to the swelling backlog of official correspondence, the general complained that "among the numerous applications which are present, it is difficult for me to decide who are suitable for the duty." As he composed this dispatch, Union troops pounded his thin lines; twenty-four hours later Petersburg fell. Lee's next official communication with Davis announced the surrender of the Army of Northern Virginia.[53]

Nevertheless, a roster of potential officers was submitted for consideration bearing the names of twenty men of nearly every service rank: one brigadier general (Henry Brevard Davidson), five colonels, four majors, four captains, and two each of lieutenants, sergeants, and privates. Exactly what Lee's criteria were in designating these men as the best candidates, as well as their special qualifications, is unknown. Some were unquestionably staff officers seeking their own field commands; they were allowed to state a preference for either recruiting or commanding African-American troops (see Appendix E).

Presumably, few of these twenty volunteers wished to be reminded after the war of their eagerness to command black troops, making them by implication supporters of racial equality. Yet twenty years after the war Jefferson Davis described himself as the only white man in the Confederacy who had ever armed and led black troops against white men. Davis claimed to have always been of the opinion that blacks "would prove efficient in war" and cited his wartime support of the use of organized blacks as military laborers and teamsters as good preliminary training for armed service "if they should be thereupon required." He forgot his and Lee's orders to General Richard S. Ewell, commander of the Confederate Department of Henrico and later of the Richmond defenses, to do whatever was necessary to procure black soldiers and immediately put them in the ranks. Likewise ignored in his memoirs was Lee's list of twenty potential commanders of Afro-Confederate's.[54]

Afro-Virginians saw combat before Lee's surrender. On the first of April 1865, Colonel Shipp's Virginia Military Institute Cadet Corps was ordered to join three battalions of city hospital convalescents and meet General Longstreet's forces along the Darbytown Road for a last-ditch defense of Petersburg. They arrived too late but the next day received orders to burn military warehouses in Richmond to prevent their falling into the hands of the enemy. It is conceivable that remnants of the Jackson Battalion's two black companies participated in these events.

A dawdling white military courier witnessed a bizarre skirmish on 4 April in Amelia County: "I saw a wagon train guarded by Confederate negro soldiers, a novel sight for me." This supply train, protected and manned exclusively by Afro-Confederate infantry, came under attack by Federal cavalry. The blacks formed a battle line and successfully fought off the first charge of their foes. A second charge proved to be too much; the Afro-

Confederates were captured and led away. Who were these "Confederate negro soldiers"? Were they commanded by black noncommissioned officers? How were they armed and trained? What became of them? What happened to their military records? These and similar questions may never be answered. But it is obvious that on this occasion one group of Afro-Virginians in uniforms of gray accepted their duty and fought against the Union army for a cause they believed in.[55]

Two days later a squad of twelve Afro-Confederate soldiers throwing up fortifications along the road to Farmville was seen by white refugees. They were armed with rifles and commanded by white officers who identified them to passersby as "the only company of colored troops in the Confederate service." They were actually the remnants of Major Turner's black command. At Point Lookout, Maryland, in May 1865 "a negro Confederate soldier" was described by a white comrade as "the only dark-skinned reb" in confinement. White soldiers took oaths of allegiance and were released, but this lone Afro-Confederate steadfastly refused to betray Dixie and remained behind bars "unreconstructed and unreconstructible," loyal to the last, last of the loyal.[56]

Accurate and balanced appraisals must take into account the potential contributions of Confederate States Colored Troops: the availability of black manpower, the potential paralysis of segments of the Union war effort due to Northern blacks being viewed as "fifth columns," and carefully fostered divisions among black populations South and North to maintain white superiority. Blacks who wore Confederate gray have been denied or forgotten by history. Under appropriate situations the South could have mobilized them into a potent fighting force for independence, but the successful enlistment of black Confederate soldiers could have transpired only with the active participation of Afro-Virginian males, even though one suspects they were inclined to fight for Virginia rather than the Confederacy. But Virginia disregarded the gallant record of black soldiers and seamen during the Revolutionary War and the War of 1812. Many Afro-Virginians awaited a similar call to arms during the Civil War. It came too late.[57]

12 PLEDGING ALLEGIANCE
The Coming of Citizenship and the Emancipation Proclamation

Negroes, like other people, act upon motives. Why should they do any thing for us, if we will not do nothing for them?
   —*Abraham Lincoln, 1863*

Slavery has stabbed itself to death. It has sinned against the light, committed the unpardonable sin, and must die.
   —*Richmond Whig, 1864*

From 1863 until right now, it seems, colored folks' feet have hurt.
   —*Langston Hughes, African-American poet*

THE YEAR 1938 saw many observances of the seventy-fifth anniversary of the Emancipation Proclamation. At Emery Auditorium in Cincinnati, Ohio, former Virginia slave Richard Toler was the special guest for an evening of pageantry and celebration during ceremonies honoring the progress of African-Americans since the ending of slavery. The 101-year-old recalled being one of 300 slaves on his master's Henrico County plantation and noted that one of his sons (Toler married three times and fathered six sons) was born the year the proclamation was issued. But father and son and the majority of Virginia's slaves were not actually freed until 1865, the year of the Confederate surrender and a constitutional amendment forever outlawing slavery in the United States. Toler recollected the proclamation meant little to him during the war "because the Confederates didn't exactly break any records doing Lincoln's bidding."[1]

In Confederate Virginia in the year 1863, Toler and other slaves could hardly have displayed any awareness of Lincoln's most famous war measure. Other than by running away, or death Virginia slaves could obtain freedom by emancipation (the large-scale freeing of any or all slaves by a government) or through manumission (private acts of freeing a slave or slaves, usually in a slave owner's last will). In 1856 and 1861 state legislators, convinced that free blacks would rather be slaves, enacted appropriate legal procedures. Of the state's 59,000 free blacks, at least 16 took the ghastly option of voluntary enslavement.[2]

When a state constitutional convention met in December 1861, its proposed constitution made it difficult for wavering slave owners to free their slaves or for free blacks to have any hope of remaining in Virginia without the ever-present fear of reenslavement. Future general assemblies were required to reduce to slavery any free black who failed to leave the state more than twelve months after being manumitted. The legislature was given the power to prohibit or impose conditions and restrictions on private manumissions and suggested enslaving free blacks or deporting them. The General Assembly banned itself from emancipating slaves. Within mitigating circumstance, free Afro-Virginians such as the Dean sisters, Julia and Mary Eliza of Richmond, continued to apply for and were "granted papers" to remain in the state after the previously mentioned regulations were mandated.[3]

In 1860 the commonwealth's 490,865 slaves represented approximately one-eighth of America's human chattels (Georgia was second with 462,198 slaves). A smattering of foresighted masters freed their slaves and prudently sent them to free states. "Go on, esteemed daughter of Virginia . . . in the work of patriotism, of freedom and humanity," an editorial letter said in praise of Cornelia Barbour of Orange County after she resolved to free her slaves and send them north; "others will be influenced by your bright and heroic example." Mecklenburg County slave owner Pleasant Burnet sent twenty-two of his manumitted slaves to Hardin County, Ohio, with land and tools with which they could begin new lives as yeoman farmers. Thirty-seven slaves freed by the will of Francis B. Shackelford of Amherst County departed for a free state, but seven others preferred slavery in Virginia. Legally, only 277 (one of every 1,771) Afro-Virginia slaves were manumitted in 1860.[4]

Few Virginia communities welcomed the arrival of large groups of newly freed blacks. When 400 emancipated slaves of John Randolph moved west to Mercer County to set up residence on land purchased through the agency of his last will and testament, local whites were enraged. Subsequently, this county's white citizens passed resolutions in defense of their bigotry: "We will not live among negroes. As we settled here first, we are fully determined that we will resist the settlement of blacks and mulattoes in this county, to the full extent of our means, *the bayonet not excepted.*" They also initiated boycotts against the hiring of Afro-Virginians or the conducting of any business with them "in any manner whatever." The mother-in-law of William Lacy of Stafford County inherited her husband's 95 slaves and Chatham estate (known during the war as Lacy House) after his death. When she planned to free the slaves, her lawyer induced her to offer them their freedom or the right to choose a new master or mistress from among her relatives. After her death Lacy claimed the slaves on behalf of his wife on the grounds that since Virginia law did not recognize a slave as a citizen, the chattels did not have the right to choose. He later sold them south for a huge profit.[5]

Not all white Virginians espoused slavery, including Moncure Daniel Conway, a slaveholder's son whose male relations joined the Confederate army. Conway exiled himself and took up the cause of abolitionism through books and lectures in Great Britain. In July 1862 he helped thirty-one of his father's slaves escape from Virginia and personally resettled them in Ohio. No less a personage than William Lloyd Garrison extolled Conway as "a moral hero."[6]

Northern abolitionists and Radical Republicans pressured Lincoln to fight Southern treason and slavery by liberating Dixie's slaves. Horace Greeley, editor of the *New York Daily Tribune,* published "The Prayer of Twenty Millions," an open letter to the president in August 1862. Greeley reminded the nation that slavery incited and sustained the Confederacy and accused "fossil politicians" and slaveholders in the so-called loyal Union states of Delaware, Maryland, and Kentucky of sympathizing with the rebellion. He declared that no loyal person—meaning Southern slaves—should be held in bondage by traitors; he was particularly angered that Union army officers were allowing runaway slaves who reached the sanctuary of their lines to be returned to their Confederate owners. Unknown to Greeley, Lincoln had prepared and discussed with his cabinet a draft of an emancipation proclamation. He replied by stating his belief that the main goal was the preservation of the Union; whether this could be accomplished without freeing slaves or by emancipating some of them made no difference to him.[7]

Increasingly concerned about the likelihood of the diplomatic recognition of the Confederacy by France or England or both, Lincoln sought a decisive stroke against the rebellious states to forestall this possibility. On 22 September 1862, five days after the battle of Antietam, he issued a preliminary emancipation proclamation warning the Southern states that if they did not end their rebellion and rejoin the Union by 1 January 1863, their slaves would be freed. The initial reaction by Virginia's slaveholders was skepticism that the Yankee president could enforce his order, but there were owners who did not wish to wait around to test Lincoln's sincerity. Some handcuffed and chained their slaves in columns and at bayonet point and under the snaps of whips herded their "species of property" toward the relative safety of Richmond. In Culpeper, Leesburg, and Aldie slaveholders boasted that by the first of the year there would not be a single slave remaining within the reach of the Yankee minions. This custom became known as "running the negroes."[8]

Danville slave Lorenzo Ivy witnessed this practice: "I've seen droves of

Negroes . . . on foot going South. . . . Each one had an old tow sack on his back. . . . Over the hills they came in lines reaching as far as you can see. They walked in double lines chained together in twos. They walked them here to the railroad and shipped them South like cattle." A Union soldier in Alexandria, sickened by slavery's abuses, wrote his wife: "Let the battle come, let slavery and freedom meet in the death struggle and let God give the victory as seem to Him best."[9]

Seated by himself at a table in his office at noon on 1 January 1863, surrounded by members of his cabinet, the president of the United States, in the eighty-seventh year of its independence and the two hundred forty-fourth year of the African Diaspora to its shores, signed the official copy of the Emancipation Proclamation with a gold pen. Afro-Virginians welcomed the announcement even though it bore loopholes and exceptions for the very areas under the control of the Union military: thirteen Louisiana parishes, the forty-eight counties of West Virginia, and "the counties of Berkley, Accomac, Northampton, Elizabeth-City, York, Princess Ann, Norfolk, including the cities of Norfolk and Portsmouth; and which excepted parts are, for the present, left precisely as if this proclamation were not issued." Lincoln admonished slaves freed by his proclamation not to use violence "unless in necessary self-defense" and to work for "reasonable wages." The slaves of the Confederacy, a place where the dictates of the Federal government were not of paramount importance, were "free," and the president pledged the power of his government in preserving their new freedom.[10]

Some Richmond newspapers printed the text, and some ignored it; but Afro-Virginians did not. Confederate president Jefferson Davis, enraged by Lincoln's audacity, retaliated by promising to try Union officers as criminals for inciting slave insurrections (enlisted men would be paroled). He issued a broadside reply, *An Address to the People of the Free States by the President of the Southern Confederacy*, on 5 January 1863 blaming abolitionists for invoking the Union's enlistment of black soldiers. As of 22 February 1863, Davis proclaimed, all Confederate free blacks, their descendants, and free blacks seized in territories hereafter captured by Confederate forces were slaves (see Appendix C).

Governor John Letcher compared Lincoln with John Brown in seeking to "excite servile insurrection and deluge Southern soil in blood." Letcher accused Lincoln of inflaming passions and prejudices that were unquenchable except by violence and complained that state laws prohibiting the removal of slaves without the permission of their owners had been violated every day since the war began. The governor denounced Union soldiers as hirelings and joined Davis in calling for the prosecution of captured United

States officers. He concluded his condemnation on a positive note by assuring Virginians that their slaves, twenty days after the infamous Yankee proclamation, were yet "quietly and contentedly" continuing their labors.[11]

Threats to enslave Virginia free blacks were never put into effect, but at least one Afro-Virginian mother and daughter did not take any chances. Richmond resident Lucy Ann Hughes, born free in Powhatan County, reregistered. Her certificate, no. 2325, described her as a forty-year-old "bright mulatto" five feet three and half inches tall, with a scar on her left elbow and a dark spot on each cheek. Her daughter, Mary Ann, no. 2360, registered in August; she was twenty years old, five feet four and a half inches tall and bore a scar on her forehead. Twenty-one-year-old Thomas Segin of Powhatan County left nothing to chance and registered as no. 894 on 6 July 1863. He was of a "bright yellow complexion" with "a large scar on his left hand where the thumb joins the hand."[12]

Ironically, the only Afro-Virginian slaves who could openly celebrate the proclamation were in areas exempted from its provisions. Norfolk was the scene of one of the largest black public commemorations in the state. Black residents held a parade, led by a band, and marched through the city streets; in one of the displays a group of black women "trampled and tore" up Confederate flags as they rode in a wagon. Four thousand blacks, "of all kinds and colors," participated in or observed the festivities, which concluded at the home of the city's military governor with a burning of Jefferson Davis in effigy. Neighboring Hampton was a different story. There, less exuberant ceremonies were the norm because during the occupation Yankee soldiers constantly mistreated the black population. Fredric Sherman, a Union sailor stationed at Norfolk, remarked that he still liked the navy but not Lincoln or his proclamation. But Henry Simmons of the 11th Rhode Island Volunteers, stationed in Isle of Wight County, pronounced himself pleased with Lincoln's act even though its enforcement meant a delay in his regiment's transfer: "Thank God I belong to the 11th R[hode] I[sland] a regt. that believes in freeing the slaves." Occasionally, it was slaves who first informed Union soldiers about the proclamation. One Union prisoner of war received the news when a slave employed at the prison smuggled in a copy of the *Richmond Enquirer* containing the highlighted text of the proclamation skillfully hidden in the lining of his mended coat.[13]

Elsewhere in the Old Dominion, slaves gathered in secret to rejoice and to spread the good news through the grapevine and in their pervasive spirituals:

> Our bondage here shall end,
>   By and by, by and by;

Our bondage here shall end,
  By and by;
From Egypt's yoke set free,
  Hail the glorious jubilee,
And to Canaan we'll return,
  By and by, by and by,
And to Canaan we'll return
  By and by.

Louise Bowes Rose of Richmond vividly remembered her father's reaction: he jumped into a creek in water up to his neck and joyfully splashed water on his head, shouting, "I'se free! I'se free! I'se free!" After Union soldiers told Williamsburg blacks the news, they promptly packed their few possessions and left town. Charlotte Brown described the first of January as the start of a three-day celebration by the slaves later known as "Stomp down Freedom Day."[14]

Despite the momentous tidings of that Thursday morning, some Virginia slaves did not find out about the proclamation until after the war. Armaci Adams recalled a day when she was being "playfully switched" by her owners' son. The white boy taunted and dared her to fight back, saying that Adams could do so because she was now free. Upon hearing this enlightening news, Adams obliged, beating him senseless. Still, she was not completely convinced until the news was confirmed by neighboring free blacks. For Afro-Virginians the anniversary of the proclamation became a day of celebration with barbecues, dancing, and sermons.

On the first anniversary of the proclamation, four regiments of black troops paraded through Norfolk. Their procession traveled along the city's main streets to the reviewing stand where they were saluted by Union generals. The glorious day concluded with speeches, music, and Masonic ceremonies; the high point came with the presentation of a resplendent flag from the ladies of Washington, North Carolina, to the 3d North Carolina Colored Regiment. The enthusiasm of Norfolk blacks then ebbed into complacency as long as Republican presidents held office; they would not hold celebrations of this magnitude again until the twenty-second anniversary of the proclamation, in response to the defeat of the 1884 Republican presidential candidate. One postwar "Jubellee of Freedom" required elaborate instructions for seating arrangements, sashes, flowers, black dignitaries, lunch for 200 persons, and tricolored rosettes.[15]

While blacks exulted, white Virginians feared that New Year's Day, 1863, marked the start of the long-feared general slave uprising. One Richmond periodical, the *Southern Illustrated News,* inclined to publish damnation of the North rather than news, sarcastically portrayed Lincoln as "a general agent [of the Underground Railroad] for negroes," the Federal Congress as "a body organized for the purpose of appropriating funds to buy Africans," and the Union army as "a provost guard to arrest white men and set negroes free." Confederate Virginians continued to equate black freedom with white destruction.[16]

But just three days before the Emancipation Proclamation went into effect, Confederate general Robert E. Lee, commander of the Army of Northern Virginia, observed the provisions of the antebellum will of his father-in-law George Washington Parke Custis, who died in 1857, and as his legal executor freed approximately 194 slaves belonging to Custis's Arlington, Romancoke, and White House estates. Custis's will directed that his Arlington estate slaves be emancipated within five years of his death; Lee overcame his own private uneasiness at this ironic coincidence to appear before a Spotsylvania County justice of the peace on 29 December 1862. With the stroke of this Confederate general's pen, more than thirty slave groups were transformed into lawful families with the names Grey, Thornton, Norris, Stewart, Johnson, Crump, Burke, Meredith, Crider, Bingham, and even Custis: "Know by all men presents, that I, Robert E. Lee, executor of the last will and testament of George W. P. Custis deceased, acting by and under the authority and direction of the provisions of the said will, do hereby manumit, emancipate and forever set free from slavery the following named slaves. . . . And I do hereby release the aforesaid slaves from all and every claim which I may have upon their services as executor aforesaid" (see Appendix F). Lee sent this deed of manumission to Richmond's hustings court where it was duly recorded by a clerk at noon on 2 January 1863. Lawrence Parks and his nine children: free. Austin and Louisa Bingham and their twelve children: liberated. Three unnamed infants, Old Shaack Check, Leanthe and her two children, Old Davy and Eloy his wife, Patsey Braxton, Charles Syphax, Calvert Dandridge, Chloe Custis and her child Julia Ann, were now emancipated by a man whose every military victory tightened the chains that bound nearly half a million Virginia slaves.[17]

And as his troops fought off Union attacks near Rappahannock Station and Kelly's Ford early in November 1863, Lee consulted with his wife about emancipating more slaves: "As regards the people [slaves]. . . . I directed Mr. Collins as soon as he Could get in the small crops this fall, to obtain from the County Courts their free papers to emancipate them. They can then hire themselves out & support themselves. Their families if they Chose or until they can do better can remain at their present homes. I do not know what to do better for them. The enemy has Carried off all the barns & there is no certainly if they remain of making enough to live on. I wish this done."

Lee's son Custis proposed sending blacks "to heaven (hell?) in a hand basket" but his father's strong sense of duty allowed him to contemplate the slaves' promised freedom despite state laws and secession.[18]

A similar occurrence took place in Carroll County in 1864 when two members of the General Assembly, Delegate James B. Johnson and Senator James C. Taylor, took up the cause of an unspecified number of slaves freed in the will of John Carroll, who had died before the war. The executors of his estate filed suit against the slaves to deny them their freedom, but the courts ruled in favor of the Afro-Virginians. Knowing that they would default their freedom unless they obtained special permission to continue residency as freedpeople or decided to resettle in another state, the former slaves appealed to Johnson and Taylor who in turn contacted Richmond to ask if the freedpeople might receive permission to emigrate to the North. The legislators did not consider Afro-Virginians as constituents but were willing to assist them because newly freed blacks were thought likely to be security threats and bad influences on slaves. The War Department sharply informed Johnson that black Virginians would never receive official Confederate permission "to go to the United States under any circumstances."[19]

Lesser-known Confederates who followed Lee's example included the despairing army surgeon who freed his male slave to prevent Yankee soldiers from boasting of having done so. Despite secessionists and Confederate zealots who labeled those who manumitted their slaves as hypocrites trying to buy their way into heaven, many Virginians admitted in hindsight to having always been in favor of emancipation, "but prejudice stood in the way."[20]

Outwardly, slaveholders and their apologists scoffed at the effrontery of the proclamation. One British visitor to Virginia told her countrymen that the Northern proclamation would not succeed and predicted it would cause the extermination of blacks. An unidentified Norfolk resident told a correspondent that although the city's slaves were "generally gone," the proclamation was Lincoln's last, despairing card and amounted to "abolition by fire and sword, raising the negro above the white man, and in so doing exterminating the whites of the South."[21]

Vigilant Confederate officials uncovered what they considered confirmation of Northern attempts to incite a black rebellion in the South after the capture of two Federal mail steamers in May 1863. Among the mailbags was a letter addressed to Union general John Foster, commander of the Department of North Carolina, concerning a mysterious scheme for insurrection and incendiarism. According to its author, Augustus Montgomery of Washington, D. C., "The plan is to induce the blacks to make a concerted and simultaneous movement or rising on the night of the 1st of August next, over the entire States in rebellion; to arm themselves with any and every kind of weapon that may come to hand. . . . No blood is to be shed except in self-defense. The corn will be in roasting-ears about the 1st of August and with this and hogs running in the woods, and by foraging upon the plantations by night they can subsist. . . . We may make the rising understood by several hundred thousand slaves by the time named." Foster was asked to inform intelligent runaway slaves of the plan and encourage them to disseminate details. General Lee thwarted implementation of the "diabolical project" by warning state governors who concealed the plan to avoid a public panic.[22]

Eight days into the year 1863, the wife of a Middlebrook, Augusta County, minister entered in her diary a smug affirmation that most slaves would continue to be loyal, contented, and satisfied with their lives as chattels. Nancy Emerson attributed her family's abundance of "slaves, sugar, molasses, coffee, clothing, shoes" to the grace of Providence as a sign that all would be well. In an almost audible sigh of relief Emerson noted the peacefulness of her neighborhood and the absence of Afro-Virginian discontent: "The first of the year has come & gone, & Lincoln's proclamation has brought no desolation. What a woeful disappointment will be experienced by our friends the abolitionists. Never was a more quiet & orderly Christmas & New Years. . . . The whole agitation about slavery wh[ich] has prevailed at the N[orth] these years, is the most monstrous humbug ever got up since the flood. I am, if possible, a thousand times better satisfied at the propriety of slavery than I was before the war." Emerson was but one of many Virginians satisfied about the rightness of slavery. But her comments should not be interpreted as yet another indication of Afro-Virginians' reluctance to strike concerted armed blows of their own for freedom. Now more than ever, they understood that they had a better chance of gaining freedom, particularly if they behaved themselves and let events in the form of the Union army advance their day of jubilee. Indeed, it was in July of the next year that many of the Emerson slaves left with Yankee raiders.[23]

Ninety-eight Confederate clergymen representing Baptists, Methodists, Presbyterians, Lutherans, and seven other Protestant denominations met in Richmond during April 1863 and produced a lengthy rebuttal to Lincoln's proclamation, *An Address to Christians throughout the World by the Clergy of the Confederate States of America*. These religious leaders represented every Confederate state except Arkansas, and they confidently espoused proslavery reasoning that emancipation would incite slave insurrections. They assailed abolitionism as interference with God's plan for the improvement and salvation of the African race by its enslavement to Christians, particularly white Southerners. Declaring themselves to be "pious, intelligent, and lib-

eral," the clerics defended slavery: "Most of us have grown up from childhood among the slaves; all of us have preached to and taught them the word
of life; have administered to them ordinances of the Christian church;
sincerely love them as souls for whom Christ died; we go among them
freely.... The South has done more than any other people on earth for
the Christianization of the African race. The condition of slaves here is
not wretched, as northern fictions would have men believe, but prosperous and happy, and would have been yet more so but for the mistaken
zeal of the Abolitionists." As ministers of the gospel and editors of religious periodicals, they claimed to represent 1,550,000 white and 500,000
black communicants.[24]

Incongruously, within two years these and other ministers would call
for modifications of slavery, such as legalizing slave marriages and banning
the selling and separation of slave mothers from their children in order to
find new favor in God's eyes in response to a string of military defeats. Virginians such as J. H. Stringfellow of Henrico County and Charles Ellis of the
Richmond and Petersburg Railroad, while continuing to accept black slavery
as divinely sanctioned, believed the time had come for Jefferson Davis and
the Confederate Congress to "secure & perpetuate" Southern independence
with its own proclamation of limited black emancipation. In early January
1865, after General Lee declared his army's need and willingness to enlist
Afro-Confederate soldiers, Ellis dourly granted that "such a measure means
the emancipation of every slave in the South."[25]

Some Virginian slave owners pragmatically prepared for the inevitable.
Ann Watson carefully listed by name each of the 94 "servants" (including
orphans and families surnamed Braxton, Fox, Hill, Quarles, Ragland, and
Tinsley) she owned at the time of the proclamation in case she needed to
seek restitution from Richmond or Washington upon their liberation. Julia
M. Morris of Hawkwood in Louisa County attested that 104 slaves belonging
to her husband, Richard Morris, were "freed by Abraham Lincoln's proclamation"; during 1862–63 her family owned 94 slaves valued at $65,000. In
December 1892, nearly thirty years after the proclamation, she produced a
list bearing the names of the freed slaves, such as John Carpenter, Uncle
Chapman, Aunt Sally, Kizzy, Sukey, Tildy, and Aramias. Of these, only the
value of John Shoemaker was listed: $4,500. This document was perhaps just
another in the profusion of attempts to obtain financial compensation for
the end of slavery.[26]

Gloucester County planter Colin Clarke tried an unorthodox stratagem by informing his slaves he would not be able to feed them in 1864
but promising to provide each family with a hog of its own in order to
keep them out of his smokehouse. He even offered to free them, but

they preferred to remain with him until the war ended. Time was on their side.[27]

It is usually accepted as a historical fact that not a single slave was directly freed by the proclamation, yet a small number did obtain their freedom under its auspices. Dr. William P. Rucker, forced to flee from Virginia to Marietta, Ohio, due to his Unionist sympathies, freed his slaves, including Charlotte Scott who later spearheaded efforts to raise a monument to Lincoln's memory. William Thornton of Elizabeth City County and Edmund Parsons of Williamsburg claimed after the war to have been emancipated by Lincoln's act. Ex-slave Richard R. Hill told a postwar congressional investigative committee that he had almost immediately escaped from Richmond upon hearing of it. Thomas Bain was another former slave who moved in the opposite direction; although he had fled from Virginia to Massachusetts by way of the Underground Railroad during antebellum times, Bain resolved to return to his native state, trusting in the impending victory of the Union.[28]

Then there was the case of a Virginia slave who reached an agreement with his owner three years before the proclamation to hire himself out for the purpose of purchasing himself. He was permitted to travel to Ohio where wages were better and dutifully sent back payments. He owed $300 on himself when the proclamation was issued; nevertheless, he walked back to Virginia and paid the final installment to his former owner with interest. When asked why he had gone through the trouble and expense of paying for his freedom instead of keeping the money for himself, this ex-slave replied that he had given his word and would not be able to enjoy his freedom unless he paid his debts as promised.[29]

Exactly how many Virginia slaves were emancipated by their owners because of the proclamation cannot be determined, but several hundred is a plausible number. Others, of course, were already on the run or had obtained their freedom by escaping to the Union-occupied areas of Norfolk, Portsmouth, Suffolk, and Hampton, Lincoln's exemptions notwithstanding. Anywhere the Stars and Stripes flew in Virginia now held the promise of sanctuary for runaway slaves. Black Virginians, for the first time in their lives, could genuinely behold the flag of the Union as a beacon of freedom:

> Our glorious banner with its hues of heaven,
> Far, far and wide all lingering doubt dispels.
> No slave beneath its folds now lowly couches,
> But safe beneath its stars securely dwells.

O, God, whose hand or fragile bark did'st save,
Leave us not now, we've dangers yet to brave.[30]

This promise would become the law of the land only after two more years of war and the passage and ratification of the Thirteenth, Fourteenth, and Fifteenth Amendments to the Constitution. Slavery was a paramount cause of the American Civil War. No other cause surpassed it in significance, and slavery was to prove the Confederacy's downfall.

13 FREEDOM FIGHTERS
Black Union Soldiers and Spies

If I was getting up a company of soldiers, I would like in the first place, the Senior Class of Harvard University; next, intelligent farmers and mechanics; next, intelligent Irishmen; next, intelligent Germans; and the negroes in the scale of their intelligence.

—*Union General Benjamin F. Butler, 1862*

General, we come of a fighting race. . . . The only cowardly blood we have got in our veins is the white blood.

—*Reply of a black soldier to General Butler*

TEN DAYS after the fall of Fort Sumter, Jacob Dodson, a $600-a-year free black employee of the United States Senate, wrote a public-spirited letter to the War Department proffering a regiment of African-Americans willing to defend the Union's capital: "I desire to inform you that I know of some 300 reliable colored free citizens of this city who desire to enter the service for the defense of the city. I have been three times across the Rocky Mountains in the service of the country with Fremont and others. I can be found about the Senate Chamber, as I have been employed about the premises for some years." He received a curt response from Secretary of War Simon Cameron: "This Department has no intention at present to call into the service of the Government any colored soldiers."[1]

Two months before the Union's defeat at First Manassas, the *National Anti-Slavery Standard* warned of the nation's peril unless it employed blacks for the army: "While the slaveholders are boasting of their colored soldiers, the commanders of the Northern forces refuse to let the colored men of the North have a chance to fight." Abraham Lincoln nearly risked his political career during the 1850s by claiming that blacks were included under most of the provisions of the Constitution and the Declaration of Independence although like most white Americans of his day he favored white supremacy. By August 1862 President Lincoln expressed a desire to enlist blacks as soldiers yet urged African-Americans to remove themselves, with government sponsorship, to foreign lands in order to prevent postwar problems. In April 1863 his colonization experiment saw 470 ex-slaves sail from Fort Monroe,

Virginia, to Ile à Vache, Haiti. The colony failed when promises of adequate housing and financial assistance did not materialize, combined with the hostility of the Haitian government, smallpox, and starvation. Lincoln admitted failure; 370 sick and discouraged survivors were returned to the United States in 1864, and Congress refused to fund any more overseas colonization attempts.[2]

After compensated emancipation went into effect in the District of Columbia following the abolition of slavery there in 1862–63, the Lincoln administration committed itself to the freeing of Southern slaves as outlined in the Emancipation Proclamation. But abolitionists and black leaders such as Frederick Douglass and their supporters believed Lincoln was moving too slowly to implement the enlistment of blacks. Well aware of the considerable prejudice that existed everywhere against African-Americans, problack advocates pointed to historical antecedents of black military service and fidelity during previous wars. They sought to convince skeptics that at least 700,000 black men, mostly Afro-Southerners, could be trained and armed to crush the rebellion and end slavery.[3]

Although thousands of Northern blacks like Jacob Dodson publicly avowed their enthusiasm to fight, Southern slaves and free blacks, including those in Virginia, showed little desire to participate. Increasing numbers of Afro-Virginians fled to Union-held areas of the state, much to the annoyance of Union officers and white civilians. Residents of Chincoteague Island and Accomack and Northampton counties took oaths of allegiance to the United States in October 1861 in exchange for a promise to deny runaway slaves sanctuary within these areas; the two counties later were among those exempted from the provisions of the Emancipation Proclamation.

General John Dix complained from Fort Monroe about the number of blacks fleeing to his headquarters and suggested they be sent North. His soldiers shared his views. The 2d Delaware Regiment, stationed at Camp Wilkes in Accomack County, published a newspaper, the *Regimental Flag,* which accepted fugitive slave advertisements: "Twenty-five Dollars Reward will be paid for my negro man John, who left my house on Monday, the 13th of this month. The said John is about 5 feet 6 inches high, of a dark Chestnut color. The above reward will be paid if taken in Accomac or Northampton, or fifty dollars if taken out of the State." Delaware was one of the few slave states to remain in the Union, and its soldiers saw no contradiction in preserving slavery while taking up arms against the seceded slave states.[4]

In Williamsburg soldiers of the 5th Pennsylvania Cavalry published a newspaper which bore banners of "Union" and "Freedom" yet whose purpose seemed contradictory: "Let it be distinctly understood that 'white folks' are meant. We do not wish it even insinuated that we have any sympathy with abolitionism." The 5th Connecticut Volunteers' newspaper reassured Winchester residents: "No vindicative feelings toward citizens of the South—with no desire to interfere with their affairs or institutions—but with a fixed and unalterable purpose to enforce obedience to the Government and the Constitution."[5]

The recruitment of black Union soldiers was officially sanctioned by the War Department in August 1862; by 3 March 1863 Northern black males between the ages of twenty and forty-five were subject to conscription. If a Northern slave was drafted, he became a free person and his owner received a $400 bounty. Union soldiers in Virginia were quick to express approval. "I see in the Paper that all able-bodied Negroes are to be drafted (right)," observed George Hupman of the 89th New York, stationed at Newport News. "I say let them fight for their freedom." A member of the 19th Massachusetts Volunteer Infantry at Falmouth, Sergeant Gorham Coffin, echoed Hupman's opinion: "If the darkies will fight, let them fight. We are willing they should." Similar sentiments were expressed in the poem "Sambo's Right to Be Kilt":

> The men who object to Sambo
> > Should take his place an' fight'
> And it's better to have a naygur's hue
> > Than a liver that's wake an' white.
> Though Sambo's black as the ace of spades,
> > His finger a thrigger can pull,
> And his eye runs straight on the barrel-sights
> > From under his thatch of wool!
> > So hear me all, boys, darlings,—
> > Don't think I tippin' you chaff,—
> The right to be kilt I'll divide wid him,
> > And give him the largest half!

But many Northerners disagreed. Two companies of recently recruited blacks were attacked in Georgetown on the evening of 22 May 1863 by "pro-slavery ruffians," but they routed their foes, injuring some badly, and calmly continued on their way. During the New York draft riots of July 1863 a black named Robert (freed some years earlier by his Virginia master's will) was forced to hide in a stable with his two nieces ages five and eight for nearly three days without any water or food except horse oats. "If I could only get down South," he lamented to a news reporter. "I would go there to-night; they never treat coloured folk in such a way down there; they don't hate us."[6]

The Federal superintendent of the census estimated in February 1865 that the number of available Afro-Virginian males between eighteen and forty-five was 101,428 (9,309 free blacks and 92,119 slaves). But by April 1865 only 5,723 Afro-Virginians had enlisted in the Union army as soldiers (despite one postwar black organization's insistence that 25,000 had served). The Confederate states providing the highest number of blacks for the Union were Louisiana (24,052), Tennessee (20,1330), and Mississippi (17,869); those providing the fewest were Florida (1,044) and Texas (47). The number of Old Dominion's enrollees ranked fourth among Southern states.

General Orders no. 46 of the Department of Virginia and North Carolina, issued December 1863, declared it the duty of every soldier and officer to aid the Federal government in recruiting blacks. It promised to issue subsistence support to each black soldier's family for as long as he was in the service (including a $10 bonus for him) and up to six months after his death. Blacks had political rights "for as long as they fulfilled their duties"; clothing, food, medicines, and shelter would be dispensed to their families, but those who refused to work or enlist would be arrested and forced to labor on Federal fortifications. A superintendent of Negro Affairs was appointed to care and protect them.[7]

Recruiting stations were established in Northampton and Accomack counties and the cities of Norfolk, Portsmouth, and Alexandria. John C. Underwood, judge of the district court in Alexandria, raised a company of 150 Afro-Virginian troops. One of these black soldiers later displayed an exceptional lack of vengeance after capturing his former master, telling him, "Wrongs I write in sand." To curry favor with white voters in Accomack and Northampton counties, Virginia Unionist congressman Joseph E. Segar opposed black soldiers: "I gave no vote to arm negroes against white men. I have no sympathy with the rebellion . . . Had I given such a vote, I would not have dared to show my face on the Eastern Shore of Virginia, for I should have expected to be hung on the first tree I could be dragged to." Francis H. Pierpont, governor of the "Loyal Government of Virginia" at Alexandria, also opposed the stationing of black soldiers in the two counties. "I know you would not leave your wife and daughters in a community of armed, undisciplined negroes," he complained to Secretary of War Stanton, "Union men are justly frightened for the safety of their families."[8]

Afro-Virginians participated in the defense of American democracy before the creation of officially sanctioned black regiments. In August 1861 a free black member of a Connecticut regiment named Augustus, captured in a Union army uniform, was identified as a slave who had escaped from Fauquier County several years earlier. A white woman recounted in her diary on 23 August 1861 having seen black Union soldiers in a Richmond hospital. Five days later, at Fort Hatteras, North Carolina, fourteen former Virginia slaves employed as gunners aboard the USS *Minnesota*, flushed with success, "hailed with a victor's pride the Stars and Stripes as they again waved on the soil of the Carolinas."[9]

Nine United States Colored Troops regiments (USCT) were organized in Virginia during 1863–64 from the large pool of available manpower in the form of ex-slaves and free blacks in approximately fifty counties and several towns under Union control. Said one Union general of these recruits, "They instinctively, and without drilling and experience as did white men, kept their camps neat and in better order." Two cavalry regiments, one battery of artillery, and six infantry regiments were enrolled. The 1st Cavalry, organized at Camp Hamilton on 22 December 1863, was comprised of 1,170 blacks from the tidewater region, mostly laborers and farmers. One of its white officers, Lieutenant F. W. Browne, wrote that the regiment "had a better class of men . . . some being from the North and some being the outlaw negroes who in slavery times had been able to maintain their liberty in the swamps of Eastern Virginia and North Carolina." He characterized them as first-rate, well-behaved warriors not afraid to fight Confederates. The regiment saw action at Petersburg, Williamsburg, Bermuda Hundred, and City Point.[10]

The 2d Cavalry Regiment, organized at Fort Monroe in December 1863, fought at Drewry's Bluff, Chaffin's Farm, and Suffolk. An independent company under the command of Captain John Wilder was assigned to this regiment as Company A. Battery B, 2d Regiment, United States Colored Light Artillery, recruited 192 blacks from Virginia, North Carolina, and Maryland and was mustered into Federal service at Fort Monroe during 1864.[11]

Five of the Afro-Virginian infantry regiments, the 10th, 23d, 36th, 37th, and 38th, were organized at Norfolk, Portsmouth, and Camp Casey between October 1863 and March 1865. In addition, there was an Independent Company A organized at Alexandria during September 1864. Four members of the 36th and two from the 38th USCT won the Congressional Medal of Honor. Both regiments participated in battles and campaigns at Petersburg, the Wilderness, Deep Bottom, Fair Oaks, and the occupation of Richmond, suffering 787 casualties in less than two years.[12]

Afro-Virginians also served in Northern regiments, particularly those of Massachusetts. In the 55th Massachusetts Regiment, 106 (11 percent) of its 961 soldiers were from the Old Dominion; its colonel, Norwood P. Hallowell, was impressed by black courage and manliness: "As soldiers, for the first time in his life a black found himself respected and entrusted with duties . . . of which he would be held to strict accountability. . . . He adapts himself more readily to the discipline of a camp, and acquires what is called the drill, in much less time than the average white soldier." Virginia blacks served with the 29th Connecticut Colored Infantry (which had captured 6,000 Confederate soldiers by April 1865), the 5th Massachusetts Colored Cavalry, the 2d and 4th United States Colored Heavy Artillery, and the 15th, 19th, 43d, and 117th USCT. Colonel Robert Gould Shaw of the 54th Massachusetts (Colored) Infantry wrote of a loyal white Virginian mustering officer who originally ridiculed black soldiers but later praised them as a "fine set of men."[13]

At Alexandria a black woman named Maria Lewis served with the 8th New York Cavalry. She "wore uniform & carried a sword & carbine & road & scouted & skirmished & fought like the rest" during her eighteen months of service. Lewis was not a camp follower but a full-fledged soldier who accompanied the New Yorkers to Washington to present seventeen captured rebel flags to the War Department. The flag of the 22d USCT, designed by black Philadelphia artist David Bustill Bower, grimly adopted Virginia's state motto, *Sic Semper Tyrannis,* and depicted a black Union soldier bayoneting a Confederate soldier.[14]

Martin R. Delany became the first black officer in the Union army. Born in Charles Town, Virginia, in 1812 to free black parents, he studied medicine at Harvard and later cofounded the *North Star* with Frederick Douglass; he was also a proponent of African-American emigration to Africa. In February 1865 Delany was commissioned an army surgeon with the rank of major in the 110th USCT and posted to Charleston, South Carolina, as a recruiting officer. After the war he served as a South Carolina judge and ran unsuccessfully for lieutenant governor.[15]

At times it must have seemed to Afro-Virginians that the Union caused them more problems than the Confederacy. Jane Walls of York County complained that her husband was kidnapped and forced to join the Union army in 1863, leaving her and their three children without means of support. John Banks testified in January 1864 that while cutting wood he was seized by black soldiers and threatened with death if he did not enlist. These and other instances of forced impressment made black Virginians wary. When the 19th United States Colored Infantry was sent from Harpers Ferry to recruit blacks in the Shenandoah Valley in 1864, it was assumed that the sight of blacks in uniform would entice volunteers. After two weeks the regiment returned in failure; fearing conscription and mistreatment, Afro-Virginians not only had refused to join but hid themselves.[16]

Black rescue expeditions were more productive. The 1st and 5th USCT, the 1st and 2d North Carolina Colored Volunteers, and the 55th Massachusetts undertook campaigns during December 1863 from bases at Norfolk, Portsmouth, and Pungo Point to Deep Creek, the Great Dismal Swamp, and South Mills, North Carolina. Their mission was to eradicate Confederate guerrillas, break the morale of white civilian rebels, and escort black families to safety. They destroyed distilleries and ammunition, burned homesteads, rounded up hostages, and captured several Confederate soldiers. Newly freed slaves and their horses, carts, and other baggage were escorted back to Union lines. "The men marched wonderfully," reported one of their white commanding officers, "never grumbled, were watchful on picket and always ready for a fight." He concluded that similar ventures could secure numerous recruits and "hosts of negro families would be restored to their rights."[17]

As of July 1864, Federal law allowed Northern states to meet their assigned draft quotas by recruiting blacks from Confederate states. For example, five members of Battery B, 2d Regiment, United States Colored Light Artillery (Charles Green, David Lace, Joseph Lasker, Isham Raney, and Andrew Wilkes) were residents of Norfolk and Sussex counties. They enlisted in the Old Dominion during June 1864 but were credited to New Jersey and New York. In February 1864 Massachusetts governor John Andrew cleverly announced that refugee slaves would be welcomed to his state but privately complained to President Lincoln about military authorities who were unlawfully denying them passes to leave Virginia and the South: "I appeal in behalf of the Commonwealth of Massachusetts . . . to receive immigrants from all parts of the Union." Lincoln saw through the stratagem and replied that the Bay State's plan would interfere with efforts by Governor Pierpont to raise black troops for loyal Virginia's quota: "I should suppose that all the colored people South of Washington were struggling to get to Massachusetts." He opposed the conscription of blacks by fraud or against their will, and his generals tried to stamp out the practice.[18]

Major General Benjamin Butler, commander of the Department of Virginia and North Carolina, cracked down these and similar abuses by banning recently discharged officers from taking their black body servants home with them. Butler reported to the secretary of war that numerous Afro-Virginians were being sold at $50 to $100 each in a cruel parody of slave selling or smuggled North to be auctioned as $500 or $1,000 substitutes for white draftees. He issued orders that blacks above the age of sixteen could not leave the department without official permission. During an August 1864 public meeting held at Williamsburg, New York, blacks accused the American Freedmen's Friend Society and other New York organizations of shipping ex-slaves to the North. Women ages eighteen to thirty and boys and girls ages ten to fifteen, the wives and children of black Union soldiers, were the usual victims. Blacks condemned this as an attempt eradicate their race by breaking up black families. Those gathered at the meeting elected Reverend Willis A. Hodges, a black expatriate from Virginia, to investigate these abuses and to convince Southern blacks to remain in the South, buy land, and become farmers.[19]

Another problem involved black soldiers' pay. Until 1864 both black officers and black privates were paid $7 a month, while white enlisted men received $13 a month. The 54th Massachusetts Volunteers served a year without pay in protest against discriminatory wages. After a public media campaign, petitions, and letters, the situation was partially corrected before the end of the war. Only those who were free as of 19 April 1861 received equal and back pay, and they had to swear an oath and provide corroborative testimony from another source before receiving back pay retroactive from 19 April 1861 to 31 January 1864. Not until March 1865 were all black soldiers assured of the same pay as white soldiers.[20]

Captain George R. Sherman of the 7th USCT hailed black soldiers as quiet, orderly, sober, loyal, and entitled "to be fully equal in all respects, to soldiers of other races and colors." But others perceived blacks as cannon fodder or watermelon-eating clowns. Three USCT regiments in Virginia suffered serious problems of morale because of callous, unprincipled white officers. A lieutenant of the 2d USCT tried to steal his men's money; the body of a soldier in the 23d USCT who died suddenly in camp was horribly mutilated during a botched autopsy, and members of the 38th USCT were brought to the brink of rebellion by abuse from their officers.[21]

Private Abraham Sweat became caught in the middle of a power struggle between two captains of the 27th USCT, Edward Latimer and George Hicks, during July 1864. Latimer requested the return of Sweat to his company (Company C) as soon as possible because he had received orders relieving Sweat of attached duty at the Quartermaster Department in Petersburg. Sweat was ordered and recalled back and forth for most of the month. Members of a black cavalry regiment rioted on the night of 22 March 1865 near Fort Powhatan. The trouble began when the provost marshal, upon hearing a disturbance coming from a tent, curtly ordered its occupants out. They refused, and he had them arrested and dragged to the guardhouse, but as this was taking place twelve black troopers appeared and wrestled one of the guard's rifles away. Quickly, a large crowd of angry blacks, some armed with pistols, gathered at the guardhouse, and during a scuffle a shot was fired at the provost marshal before the crowd dispersed into the night.[22]

In late January 1865 Corporal John Point of the 8th Delaware Regiment witnessed the punishment of a black soldier at City Point: "We drummed a nigar soldier out of the service day before yesterday. We first shaved the wool off of his head and made six men [march with] bayonets on him and six a head of him with [their] guns at a reverse marched clear down the line . . . he had a board on his back with thief on it in big letters."[23]

Petty thievery was not the worst offense a soldier could commit. Twenty-five black soldiers were executed by United States military authorities for various crimes during the war. Black soldiers comprised 8 percent of Union troops but 21 percent of all executed Federal soldiers. At least six Afro-Virginians were executed: William Henderson, 66th USCT, shot by a firing squad in Arkansas on 8 December 1864 for murder; Samuel Mapp, 10th USCT, executed at City Point on 20 April 1865 for mutiny; Alfred Catlett, 1st Heavy Artillery, USCT, executed at Asheville, North Carolina, in May 1865 for rape; John Lewis, hanged in Kentucky in June 1865 for murder; and two sergeants of the 38th USCT, Dandridge Brooks and William Jackson, hanged in Brownsville, Texas, on 30 July 1865 for rape.[24]

Rape was the crime for which mostly black soldiers were executed. Twenty-three-year-old William Johnson of the 23d USCT became a sign of good faith by Union authorities to prove to Confederate officials that black soldiers who committed rape would be punished. Convicted of raping a young white woman at New Kent Court House, he was hanged on 20 June 1864 at nine o'clock in the morning near Jordan's Farm, Petersburg, in the no-man's-land in view of both armies: "He . . . said his punishment was just, and hoped others would take warning by his fate. He appeared quite collected during the whole time, meeting his fate with great resignation, and died apparently very easy, although his neck was not broken by the fall. His pulse ceased to beat at the end of seven minutes." Confederates exploited the propaganda value of Johnson's execution by marching black military laborers past his body and telling them that Yankees always hanged runaways.[25]

Most African-American soldiers were of a more upright character. Twenty-two received the Congressional Medal of Honor. Sergeant William H. Carney of the 54th Massachusetts Volunteers, the first African-American to receive this honor, was a native of Virginia. Born in Norfolk on 29 February 1840, Carney fled to Massachusetts and enlisted with the 54th at New Bedford. During the regiment's doomed attack against Fort Wagner, South Carolina, on 18 July 1863, a color-bearer fell, but before the national flag touched the ground, Carney leaped forward to catch it. Advancing it at the head of the attacking column, he crossed a ditch of waist-deep water and reached the ramparts of the fort, where he fought off Confederates who tried to take the colors. Struck by three bullets, he was ordered to the rear when the retreat was sounded but refused to give up the colors to fellow soldiers. Upon returning to camp, Carney's comrades cheered when he boasted, "The old flag never touched the ground." He did not receive his medal until May 1900, thirty-seven years after the battle.[26]

Robert Blake, a Virginia runaway slave, joined the United States Navy and served aboard the gunboat *Marblehead*. On Christmas Day, 1863, he participated in an engagement off Legareville, Stono River, South Carolina, during a naval assault on John's Island. The *Marblehead*'s commander noted in his report that Blake "excited my admiration by the cool and brave manner in which he served." He was promoted to the rank of seaman and cited for courage in General Orders no. 32, 16 April 1864. James Mifflin, a navy engineer's cook from Richmond, heroically remained at his post aboard the USS *Brooklyn* during the battle of Mobile Bay, 5 August 1864, for which he was mentioned in an report to Rear Admiral David Farragut as "conspicuous for bravely performing [his] duty." General Orders no. 45, issued 31 December 1864, cited his heroism as a significant contribution to the destruction of Fort Morgan and the capture of the Confederate ironclad ram *Tennessee*.[27]

Thirteen blacks, including five Afro-Virginians, earned the Medal of Honor for bravery at the battle of Chaffin's Farm on 29–30 September 1864: Powhatan Beaty, James Gardiner, Miles James, Edward Ratcliff, and Charles Veal. Beaty (or Beatty) was born in Richmond in 1837 and moved to Cincinnati, Ohio, a decade before the war. He joined the army as a member of Company G, 5th USCT, and his moment of supreme military glory came after all of his company's white officers were killed or wounded during the attack. Sergeant Beaty took command and led the regiment until it was ordered to retreat. As the regiment withdrew he noticed that the color-bearer had been killed and the flag was missing. Despite murderous enemy fire he unhesitatingly went back and retrieved the flag.

Private James Gardiner, formerly a Gloucester County slave, surged to the head of his company (Company I, 36th USCT) to bayonet a Confederate officer attempting to rally the defenders. Another ex-slave, Corporal Miles James of Princess Anne County, Company B, 36th USCT, displayed extraordinary determination after his arm was amputated on the field as the battle raged around him. James rejoined the action, loading and firing his rifle with his right arm and advancing to within thirty yards of enemy lines. He was subsequently promoted to sergeant. Edward Ratcliff, a fugitive slave from Charles City County, joined Company C, 38th USCT. He, too, led his company after its commander fell, and he became the first soldier of his unit to enter Confederate lines, for which he was promoted to sergeant major, the highest army rank an African-American soldier could attain.

Portsmouth native Private Charles Veal, Company D, 4th USCT, was a free black; at Chaffin's Farm, after two color-bearers were killed, he held the flags aloft and advanced toward the foe. General Butler witnessed this daring act and promoted him to sergeant on the spot. These eight heroes were awarded their medals officially on 6 April 1865, having proudly fought for the liberation of slaves on the soil of their native state.[28]

Specially trained leadership was needed to avoid abuses by whites and to maintain adequate controls over black soldiers, and there were increased demands for white soldiers to volunteer for duty with black regiments. For some, this was a golden prospect for an officer's commission. "Now there is a number of chances for commissions in colored regiments now raising, infantry or cavalry," wrote a Massachusetts corporal named Austin from his Newport News camp. "And now is my chance to strike. It would make no difference to me what regiment it could be in. I hear Gov. Andrews is raising a colored cavalry and officers must be had for it." Austin urged his brother to contact influential men to secure a commission.

The Free Military School for Applicants for Command of Colored Troops was established in December 1863 in Philadelphia by the Supervisory Committee for Recruiting Colored Regiments to furnish black regiments with humane, educated, and skilled officers to "subdue the Rebellion and exterminate Slavery." Only two students were present when classes began, but a year later there were twelve staff members and 423 candidates learning how to encourage and supervise African-American soldiers. The War Department's General Orders no. 125 (29 March 1864) granted thirty-day furloughs for members of the army to attend the school. Civilians, privates, and commissioned and noncommissioned officers studied the mysteries of leading black men into battle. The only African-American employed by the school was James Buchanan, a messenger.[29]

The school was governed on a military basis, and classes on infantry tactics, army regulations, and mathematics were held three times daily. Students were assigned to companies and practiced drilling at Camp William Penn, an enrollment center for black soldiers; they pledged to accept whatever rank and command were offered them upon completion of the course and acceptance by a board of examiners. Two graduates, First Lieutenant William Baird and Second Lieutenant Henry Whitney, wrote accounts of their experiences at the Free Military School. Baird received his commission on 2 May 1864 and was ordered to report to the 23d USCT at Manassas Junction, Virginia. He remained with the regiment until the end of the war.[30] Whitney enrolled at the school on 14 January 1864. Six weeks later he appeared before the examiners and passed with a rating of "first class" for the rank of second lieutenant. He then proceeded to Clarksburg, West Virginia, purchased a pistol for $200, and from April to May recruited blacks and forwarded them to Camp Casey, Virginia, for mustering in as regiments. He later served with the 45th USCT.[31]

The Free Military School closed on 15 September 1864 due to a decrease in its funding but not before the establishment of an auxiliary school where educated blacks could obtain some training in military science for noncommissioned ranks. Special manuals such as *U.S. Infantry Tactics . . . for the Use of the Colored Troops of the United States Infantry* were devised. This volume contained tactics and drills, bugle calls and drum beats, salutes and marching instructions; it made allowances for the alleged physical disparities between white and black soldiers yet ignored racial differences. The lack of apparent discrimination within its pages—it assumed, for example, that black recruits were able to count and read music and were in the necessary physical condition to carry out drills—betokened confidence in black military competence.[32]

The first combat appearance in Virginia of black Union soldiers occurred on 12 May 1864 when members of Colonel Alonzo G. Draper's expedition from Point Lookout, Maryland, to eastern Virginia, six soldiers of the 36th United States Colored Infantry, demonstrated the fearlessness and energy of seasoned veterans during a melee with nine Confederate marines and cavalrymen in Middlesex County. The blacks were at the center of a three-mile skirmish line, probing and clearing "torpedoes" (land mines) for the expedition after crossing the Potomac and advancing through Mill Creek toward the tip of the peninsula at Stingray Point. Between the Rappahannock and Piankatank rivers were thick woods, underbrush, creeks, and swamps that briefly isolated them from the rest of the line. When the Confederates opened fire, the six blacks unhesitatingly went on the offensive, killing or capturing their foes. The black soldiers battled the enemy entirely on their own initiative because white officers did not arrive on the scene until the fight was over.[33]

The first time entire black Union regiments fought against the Army of Northern Virginia was during the Wilderness campaign of May 1864. The all-black Fourth Division, 9th Army Corps, commanded by General Edward Ferrero, repulsed an attack on wagons they were guarding near Chancellorsville on 15 May. That same day the 23d USCT came to the rescue of the white 2d Ohio and routed the Confederates as the Ohioans were driven back from positions at Piney Branch Creek. At noon an unidentified black regiment beat back an attempt to capture a Union battery; "gallantly repulsed [them]" were the words used by one grateful member of the battery. Black soldiers were beginning to earn a measure of respect if not the admiration of their white Union brothers-in-arms.[34]

Confederates advocated retaliatory measures against blacks and their white officers. An anonymous resident of Orange County grimly vowed that their continued employment "would be sufficient cause to arouse the temper and indignation of every one who was born and reared on Southern soil. . . . Who that is not dead to every sense of honor & humanity, will

Submit to any such thing as negro equality in the sunny South[?] We cannot, we will not."[35]

A white female resident of Northumberland County expressed fears that the stationing of black soldiers in her county would result in "outrages" against her sex but was assured by their commander that the blacks were good men who always obeyed their officers and were respectful of white women and their property. Union general Edward A. Wild threatened to unleash black soldiers against rebellious white civilians as an incentive for their good behavior: "By assisting [freed slaves] . . . with food and transportation, you can save yourselves the necessity of visitations from the colored troops. By thus avoiding the two causes of molestation, you can preserve peace with your borders." The mere presence of black soldiers was enough to frighten rural communities into sullen compliance.[36]

Confederate secretary of war Seddon ordered captured black Union soldiers to be put to death on the spot without trial. Though believing "blood can not restore blood," Lincoln countered with an retaliation order which promised his government would do everything in its power to protect Union soldiers regardless of color: "It is therefore ordered that for every [black soldier] enslaved by the enemy or sold into slavery, a rebel soldier shall be placed at hard labor . . . until the other shall be released and receive the treatment due a prisoner of war." One writer treated the entire subject in a light-hearted Biblical vein:

> Now when it was known in the North that the
>> Rebels sold unto bondage the captives that they had taken from the Ethiopians,
> And has also scourged them, and put them to
>> death shamefully;—the rulers of the North said, Verily, these things must not be so.
> But surely, if these Rebels do this wicked
>> thing to our people, we will visit our vengeance upon them, and do violence to the captives that we have taken from the tribes of the lands of Dixie.[37]

It is ironic that several of the battles in which black soldiers had prominent roles were Union defeats: Fort Wagner, South Carolina; Olustee, Florida; Fort Pillow, Tennessee; Petersburg—the battle of the Crater—and Saltville, Virginia. The Crater assault has been erroneously described as the first time that black Union soldiers engaged in combat in Virginia. In an attempt to break Lee's defensive lines around Petersburg, Union engineers proposed to tunnel beneath them and detonate a large pile of explosives. A controversial part of the plan called for specially trained black soldiers from General Ferrero's divisions to spearhead the attack; but twenty-four hours before the detonation, General George Gordon Meade opposed and General Grant vetoed it. They feared that if the plan failed, the army would be accused of sending blacks to their deaths.

The explosion occurred at 4:45 on the morning of 30 July 1864. Though Ferrero went to off to get drunk and cringe in the safety of the rear, other officers tried to lead black soldiers toward the enemy behind the white Union regiments that paused to gape at the huge crater created by the blast. The blacks pushed through and around them, rushing forward to exploit the gap and hurl themselves at their hereditary foes, who, for several heartbeats, were stunned and demoralized. But as Confederates perceived that many of their attackers were black, they counterattacked in hot fury, shooting, bayoneting, clubbing, and stabbing in hand-to-hand fighting as the men in blue plunged headlong into the still-smoking pit. The compact mass of Yankees struggling to wade through the churned earth was soon trapped in a narrow slaughter pen.

Enraged Confederates butchered the blacks until even veteran Confederate officers sickened at the carnage. One officer later wrote that the "men carved in ebony" were heroes who "commanded the admiration and respect of every beholder that day." John Wise accused fellow Southerners of "a relentless vengeance . . . disregard[ing] the rules of warfare which restrained them in battle with their own race." General Edward Porter praised the blacks as good soldiers and censured his fellow Confederates for killing those who surrendered.

The surrender of white Yankees was accepted, but blacks were shot down in cold blood and with such frequency that General William Mahone personally went among his troops ordering then begging them to cease. Richmond newspapers criticized him. "We regret to learn," said an *Enquirer* editorial, "[that] some negroes were captured instead of being shot . . . go forward . . . until every negro is slaughtered . . . butcher every negro that Grant hurls against [our] brave troops and permit them not to soil their hands with the capture of one negro."[38]

Confederate chaplain Thomas Hume noted in his diary: "We whip[ed] them out of our works with terrible slaughter. Negro troops were bro[ought] up by the Yanks & our men killed them by hundreds." Another soldier, S. S. Watson, bluntly accused Grant of plotting the murder of the blacks: "He made his Negroes charge our line and we killed them all he had on hand and we put them into the hole he blow up which was some thirty feet deep they can't get out of there . . . we put about 1,000 of them in one hole and it was not half full then." Other horrible scenes involved panicky

white Yankees bayoneting their black comrades in the back in order to protect themselves from the vengeance of Confederates, many of whom had
sworn to kill any white soldier serving with black regiments. These pusillani-
mous Northerners boasted of their infamous deeds to their captors or to
each other upon returning to Union lines.[39]

This battle cost the Union side 3,800 casualties including 1,400 blacks
(38 percent of all troops engaged). An investigation by the Joint Committee
on the Conduct of the War faulted Meade and Grant for not allowing the
trained blacks to lead the attack and characterized them as the best chance
for winning the battle. It is difficult to determine the true reasons for Grant's
state of mind and hesitancy during his support of Meade's decision because
his memoirs make only the briefest mention of black soldiers. Perhaps his
reservations were due to the lessons of Fort Wagner and private conversa-
tions with President Lincoln. Samuel Rodman Smith of the 4th Delaware
Regiment wrote his mother of a final indignity against the blacks: "The next
day the 31st several flags of truce were sent from our lines proposing to
recover the wounded and bury the dead, the rebels would not allow us to
take the wounded negroes who laid strewn over the field [and] constituted
the greater part of those who had fallen between the respective Forts of the
opposing parties. The whites they allowed us to take."[40]

Not all surrendering blacks were killed. "We had 8 or 10 colored prisoners in the Crater who I put to work excavating at [the] shaft on our left,"
recalled Lieutenant E. N. Wise of the 1st Confederate States Engineers. A
member of the 46th Virginia Infantry complained that numerous fugitive
slaves from Gloucester, Mathews, and other Virginia counties were captured
and put to work extricating Confederates still trapped in the crater, but he
had no love for the Yankees who had armed and sent them to fight whites:
"Such is the character of the enemy with whom we have to deal—bringing
our own slaves against us." One enterprising Confederate struck a bargain
with a black prisoner of war named Ben who offered to pose as his body
servant rather than being shot as a runaway or sold. The soldier claimed
Ben "belonged" to him, took the slave to Richmond, and sold him for $5,000
in Confederate money to a planter. Events of the following year freed Ben.[41]

During the Petersburg campaign (15 June 1864–3 April 1865), nearly
forty black regiments served with the Union army, and it was difficult for
some Confederate prisoners of war to accept black soldiers. After the battle
of the Crater, Colonel Cleveland J. Campbell of the 23d USCT ordered a
captured Confederate to help carry a wounded black soldier on a stretcher
to the rear. The Southerner cursed loudly and swore he would never assist
a black under any circumstances whereupon Campbell drew his revolver
and shot the man dead. On the other side of the battlefield, Confederates

continued to put black prisoners to work on military projects and sent a few to prison camps. White handkerchiefs raised by black troops in surrender after Chaffin's Farm were respected, but unlike white prisoners they were forced to construct military fortifications while exposed to Union shelling. When General Butler learned of this, he ordered a similar number of Confederate prisoners placed at hard labor on the Dutch Gap Canal near the James River with black soldiers as their guards with instructions to shoot any prisoner attempting to escape. The Confederates withdrew their black prisoners and sent them to prison camps; the Yankees reciprocated.[42]

Southerners categorized battles against black soldiers as "coon fights" and facetiously claimed black skulls were too thick to be crushed by rifle butts. Positions held by black Union soldiers were constantly bombarded, and Confederates gleefully watched for the results of the exploding shells, laughing and cheering whenever, as several quipped in letters home, "nigger meat took a rise."

During a Union assault on Lee's lines at Chaffin's Farm, a black soldier charged forward and called on his comrades to follow him. When he was killed one of his comrades allegedly bewailed, "There! They done killed Corporal Dick! He was the bravest man in the regiment!" One Confederate eyewitness paid him a left-handed compliment: "Yes, Dick was a game kind of nigger, and his boldness was well worthy of a better cause that his efforts to murder Southern people. He led his command and fell at its head, climbing the breastworks at Battery Harrison pierced by the bayonets from our brave boys who nobly defended the fort that day." Thereafter, black Union soldiers were known by Lee's men as "Corporal Dicks."[43]

Aunt Sally, a ninety-five-year-old slave woman who spent nearly a century of bondage on the same Virginia plantation and could remember the Revolutionary War, was asked in 1863 by a journalist which war was worse. Without hesitation she replied, "This be worse war I reckon . . . for everybody is killing everybody."[44] The words of this Afro-Virginia woman were truer that anyone yet suspected.

Henry Chambers admitted that during the battle of Suffolk in March 1864 he and his comrades doubled their pace after officers passed the word that their awaiting foes were black and not to take any prisoners. A group of black soldiers were trapped in a house which was set on fire, but several disappointed Confederates complained they should have been removed from the burning building and shot like dogs. At least eight members of the 2d United States Colored Cavalry died in the house but not before fighting with "desperation and hopelessness."[45]

During the Spotsylvania campaign black prisoners of war were murdered by soldiers from the 9th Virginia Cavalry near Germanna Ford. Byrd C. Willis lamely excused his comrades' behavior: "We captured three negro soldiers the first we had seen they were taken out on the road side and shot & their bodies left there." Black soldiers also were denied the decency of a proper burial. The remains of dead black cavalrymen were left unburied for ten days in a hot summer sun after a cavalry clash on 22 June 1864 between Union general Philip Sheridan and Confederate general Wade Hampton's forces near White House, Virginia.[46]

Some Confederates opposed such brutalities. Andrew Jackson Andrews of the Richmond Howitzers, after witnessing a Texas soldier's cold-blooded shooting of five unarmed black prisoners in revenge for the death of his brother at the battle of Laurel Hill on 8 May 1864, characterized the revenge as a "disgraceful" murder: "I thought this was rather cowardly, as the prisoners were helpless, and most deeply did I condemn such an act. I called this deliberate murder, but as I might be condemned for so freely speaking my open and candid opinion about the killing of an enemy I leave this subject for the reader to say whether or not I am justified in making the above assertions . . . such, dear friends, is the fate of ruthless war." Others were no less opposed but choose their words carefully. "I have seen some few negro soldiers," Rawleigh W. Dunaway, a Virginia Confederate soldier, conceded to his sister; "some few have been taken prisoners. It is needless for me to say what became of them."[47]

During the battle of Chaffin's Farm in September 1864, a member of a Virginia battery claimed to have witnessed General Lee's harsh reprimand of a Confederate soldier herding a pair of captured black soldiers toward nearby woods. According to eyewitness David Gardiner Tyler, when Lee demanded to know what the man intended to do with the prisoners, he replied that he was going to "parole" them. Lee angrily vowed to hang him or any other soldier under his command from the nearest tree who mistreated any prisoner "be he as black as Erebus." Lee commanded the man to return to his unit, placed another guard in charge of the two blacks, and had them forwarded to Richmond with other Union prisoners.[48]

Black cavalrymen of the 5th United States Colored Cavalry were ridiculed and insulted by white Union troops before the blacks' raid into southwestern Virginia. The whites knocked off the blacks' caps, stole their horses, and taunted them by saying they would not fight. The blacks patiently bore the insults. At the battle of Saltville on 2 October 1864, 400 African-American men proved their manhood to friend and foe; during the two-hour battle they led the main Union attack against the Confederate right and center lines; at least 114 were killed or wounded, and upon the regiment's withdrawal most of its members had used their bayonets and fired every bullet in their cartridge boxes. On the return march white soldiers who had derided them were silent and respectful. The blacks brought away most of their wounded, but several were captured by Confederates and murdered after surrendering. Aware of this and earlier Confederate atrocities, black soldiers who were seriously wounded refused to stay behind. One trooper rejoined the column despite the loss of an arm; another had been shot through both lungs and a third through the hips, yet both dragged themselves along with their comrades. In contrast, wounded Confederates who fell into the hands of the black soldiers were humanely treated.[49]

A captured Union surgeon, William H. Gardner of the 13th Kentucky Infantry, reported that on the morning after the battle, several Confederate soldiers came to his field hospital and shot at point-blank range five wounded black enlisted men. Four days later, at the Emory and Henry College Hospital in Washington County, two more hospitalized blacks were shot to death in their beds. A white lieutenant was also shot and other captured Federals were threatened, but after strong protests by the Confederate chief surgeon and his staff, no further killings occurred. Union authorities promised to retaliate unless the Richmond government extradited the murderers for punishment. One hundred wounded Union soldiers were murdered on the field the day after the battle, but Saltville's days as the South's principal salt supplier were numbered; the town was captured and destroyed by the 5th United States Colored Cavalry and other Union troops in December 1864.[50]

Under these conditions one might expect every captured black to be slain, but there were exceptions. Four black prisoners of war arrived at Richmond's Libby Prison on 7 March 1864 after their capture near Williamsburg on 21 February: James W. Corn and P. F. Lewis, 5th United States Volunteers, and R. P. Armistead and John Thomas, 6th United States Volunteers. They were placed in cells with white Union officers as an insult. "The Yankees cannot be degraded lower; the negro probably can be," crowed the *Richmond Daily Examiner.* "This is a taste of negro equality, we fancy, the said Yankee officers do not fancy overmuch," observed the *Richmond Whig* with satisfaction.[51]

By October 1864, 146 black soldiers from the 5th, 7th, and 30th USCT were being held at the city's Confederate States Military Prison; twelve died in hospitals, and another fifty-four remained hospitalized. The remaining eighty-two were given a day's ration and assigned to labor details. Sixty-eight black soldiers at Castle Thunder Prison who had been captured during the battle of the Crater were sent to labor on military fortifications. White prisoners were not expected to perform this type of forced labor. One black soldier who refused to work at a Confederate entrenchment was warned that he would be flogged for noncompliance. He continued to refuse and was whipped to death.[52]

Black soldiers reacted by not taking any chances. Captain Charles Francis Adams, Jr., wrote a description of the type of combat that black regiments practiced against Southerners. "The darkies fought ferociously," he recalled after an attack against Petersburg. "If they murder prisoners, as I heard they did . . . they can hardly be blamed." They were inclined to shoot first and ask questions later when rebel soldiers and guerrillas were involved. During February 1864 a convicted guerrilla named Burroughs under guard at a Portsmouth smallpox hospital while awaiting execution, thinking that a loud distraction in the hallway was a rescue attempt by his friends, tried to escape through a window; but his black guard, "seeing the prisoner in the act of passing out" the window, shot and killed him without first calling on him to halt. Confederates imprisoned in Northern prisons habitually protested that black sentinels were more likely to shoot them for the smallest of infractions and had "the idea that shooting a Rebel meant distinction."[53]

Southern civilians were deeply offended by the sight of black soldiers patrolling their communities. At four o'clock on the afternoon of 11 July 1863 in Norfolk, Second Lieutenant Alanson L. Sanborn of the 1st USCT was leading a squad of black soldiers along a city street when Dr. David Minton Wright, a physician and slave owner, called him a coward. The white lieutenant ordered his men to place the doctor under arrest, but before they could do so, Wright killed the lieutenant with a pistol. Sanborn's men with great difficulty were prevented from avenging their commander with their bayonets.

Wright was tried by a special military commission and in his defense stated he had acted out of fear that the "Southampton menace" (Nat Turner) would be resurrected by arming blacks; he also claimed his honor had been at stake: "Is it to be supposed that a citizen of Norfolk, himself an owner of slaves, not knowing but what even one of my slaves was in that company, would submit to be arrested by Negroes? No sir, I could not submit to that." However, he had been overheard by bystanders boasting as Sanborn's squad approached that he would shoot the first white man whom he encountered with black troops.

Seventeen days after the shooting, Wright was found guilty and sentenced to death. His family and friends made desperate efforts to save his life, going so far as to appeal to Lincoln by attempting to prove that Wright was insane at the time of the crime. Confederate officials did little except praise the condemned Norfolkian for the "prompt vindication of his honor." Major General John G. Foster, commander of the area's Union forces, urged Lincoln to uphold the sentence, pointing out that swift punishment of such acts was essential to the recruitment, morale, and self-respect of blacks and their officers. Lincoln agreed, and on 23 October 1863 Wright died on the gallows at the city's fairgrounds.[54]

Free blacks and slaves formed clandestine alliances with the Union army, infiltrated Confederate camps and fortifications as spies, and passed on valuable military information. Afro-Virginians were auxiliary eyes and ears for Union armies; they knew the roads, rivers, and terrain and excelled as guides. These trusted informants exposed Confederate sympathizers and secret organizations behind Union lines. Afro-Virginians organized secret lodges known as Loyal Leagues to aid the Union and used "Friends of Uncle Abe" and "Light and Liberty" as their watchwords; the leader of one lodge proudly conducted meetings behind a desk draped with an American flag.

Runaway slaves described and sketched enemy batteries, supply depots, troop strengths, and dispositions. At Princess Anne Court House in September 1863, a black guide led a military expedition while another, known as "Specs" Hodges, commanded raids against white civilians. Near Great Bridge an anonymous black man successfully acted as a courier for the Union commander of another raid even though his wagon was stopped and searched. Richmond slaves guided and protected Union prisoners who escaped from Libby Prison in February 1864; of the 109 men who tunneled their way out, 60 reached the safety of Grant's lines thanks to Afro-Virginians who fed and sheltered them.[55]

The names and deeds of fortitude and valor of such blacks appeared in an assortment of military reports. Jim Taylor, a seventeen-year-old slave, escaped on a one-eyed horse from Waterford and crossed over into Union lines at Point of Rocks in Loudoun County in 1862. Previously employed as a teamster on his owner's farm, Taylor had been conscripted as a laborer for a Confederate fort near Edwards Ferry and eagerly identified the camps of several regiments. Twenty-eight-year-old Dick Williams, a Leesburg slave valued at $1,500, kept his eyes and ears open while working at Confederate military projects. He subsequently escaped to report the disposition of 5,000 Confederate soldiers encamped around the town. Henry Strange, a thirty-four-year-old Berryville slave, reported the movements and concentrations of Confederate forces in and around Winchester and Charles Town and hinted that at least thirty slaves were making plans to escape.[56]

A black Falmouth couple provided military intelligence for General Joseph Hooker at Fredericksburg in a novel way. The wife, a laundress for a Confederate general, eavesdropped on meetings and by means of his laundry communicated in code Southern plans for troop movements to her husband, Dabney, a cook and groom in the Union camp. The generals were represented by shirts of different colors; blankets with pins at the bottom indicated phoney Confederate troop movements designed to trick the Yankees. Dabney was also a reliable scout who rooted out Southern agents and supporters in Fredericksburg.

John Scobell, another resourceful Afro-Virginian, spied for the Union by posing as a happy-go-lucky slave who could sing Scottish songs in a Scots accent or plantation melodies in a powerful and sweet voice, much to the delight of Confederate soldiers and civilians starved for entertainment. He posed as a laborer or cook at Centreville, Dumfries, Fredericksburg, Leesburg, Manassas, Occoquan, and Richmond, boldly risking his life. As Scobell sang and worked his way across the state, his keen mind carefully noted Confederate military preparations and related activities. Intelligent and fearless, this former slave and his wife were freed by their owner during the war, and after seeing her safely to Richmond, Scobell offered his services to the North. He participated on several missions with white male and female operatives as an equal, not a subordinate, and was proficient in the use of firearms. Union spymaster Allan Pinkerton praised Scobell as one of the war's best spies: "I employed him in various capacities of importance . . . those in which secrecy and loyalty were essential qualifications and his performance of these duties was all that could be desired."[57]

It was Afro-Virginians who kept the Union apprised of the status of the Confederacy's greatest secret weapon. Fifteen fugitive slaves from Sewell's Point were picked up by a Union tugboat during January 1862 and provided advance information about preparations for the launching of the Confederate ironclad *Virginia* as well as the number and position of Confederate artillery and troops at Sewell's Point, Norfolk and Roanoke Island.[58] In February 1862 Mrs. Mary Louveste, a black woman residing in Norfolk and an employee of the Gosport Navy Yard where the *Virginia* was under construction, crossed Confederate lines and journeyed to Washington, D. C., for a private meeting with Secretary of the Navy Gideon Welles. She produced documents and plans for the Confederate ironclad and described in detail its condition and probable date of completion.

Louveste had regularly rendered important service to the Federal government since the war's beginning, and it was due to her report that Welles remained calm while other members of Lincoln's cabinet became alarmed after the *Virginia* made her spectacular debut at Hampton Roads on 9 March 1862. He knew the Union's own USS *Monitor* was a match for the Confederate vessel. "Mrs. Louveste encountered no small risk in bringing this information . . . and other facts," wrote Welles a decade later in support of her application for a Federal pension. "I am aware of none more meritorious than this poor colored woman whose zeal and fidelity I remember and acknowledge with gratitude." General John E. Wool, military governor of

Norfolk, and Admiral David Porter also attested to her loyalty and dependability.[59]

The victory of the Union's Army of the Shenandoah on 19 September 1864 at the third battle of Winchester (Opequon Creek) shattered the Confederate army in the upper Shenandoah Valley. Partial credit for the success of General Phil Sheridan was due to Thomas Laws, a Berryville, Clarke County, slave owned by prominent Winchester attorney Richard E. Byrd. Sheridan, in need of confirmation about the disposition of Confederate general Jubal Early's 2d Corps, sent two scouts to gather military intelligence. Laws and his wife were sitting outside their cabin one Sunday evening when the pair approached and soon ascertained that the black couple lacked admiration for the Confederacy.

Discovering that Laws possessed a pass from the local Confederate commander permitting him to sell vegetables three times a week in Winchester, the scouts arranged for him to meet Sheridan personally. After the two men discussed the impending mission, Sheridan, completely convinced of Laws's loyalty, composed a message on tissue paper to Rebecca Wright, a Unionist Quaker schoolteacher. The note was compressed into a small pellet and wrapped in tinfoil so that Laws could conceal it in his mouth to be swallowed if he was searched or captured. At worse, Wright risked imprisonment or banishment to Union lines, but for Laws death, the ancient penalty for espionage, loomed as a distinct possibility. Described as "loyal and shrewd" in Sheridan's memoirs (the general did not mention him by name, only as "an old colored man"), Laws delivered the message without detection. Wright's reply confirmed that Early's forces had been substantially reduced by large transfers to Petersburg to reinforce Lee; three days later the Union achieved a major victory, but few knew that the patriotism of one Afro-Virginian had made it all possible. Afterwards Rebecca Wright was rewarded with a position in the Treasury Department in Washington; Thomas Laws died a free and respected citizen in 1898.[60]

Afro-Virginian women spied for the Union. Lucy Carter of Vienna risked her life countless times, and Mary Elizabeth Bowser, an employee at the Confederate White House, secretly eavesdropped as Jefferson Davis and his generals discussed strategy. In January 1864 Bowser came under suspicion and fled with $2,500 and a slave named Jim Pemberton, but not before they tried to burn the mansion to cover their escape. Elizabeth Draper Mitchell, a house servant employed by the head of the Union spy network in Richmond, Elizabeth Van Lew, helped Northern prisoners to escape through a secret tunnel beneath the Van Lew mansion. Described as "medium height, smooth dark skin, snapping black eyes, and passionate lips," Mitchell was Van Lew's right hand, and together they aided the Union undetected.[61]

Neither Confederate nor Union soldiers were squeamish about inflicting death upon spies and collaborators. Ex-slave Virginia Shepherd remembered James Bowser of Nansemond County, a free black who during antebellum times earned the enmity of slaves because he refused to associate with them though some understood that openly helping slaves could cost Bowser and his family their precarious liberty. Bowser yearned to strike a blow for his people's freedom and became a spy for the Union. When his espionage activities were discovered, a mob of angry whites seized and beat him and his son and then beheaded Bowser.[62]

A slave named Henry, regularly sent to labor in New Kent and King William counties, took advantage of these trips to pass information to the Union; after his arrest in June 1863, the Richmond *Sentinel* tartly observed, "His relations with the Yankees were such as did not become a loyal darkey." The same newspaper reported the capture and jailing of "a venerable colored individual named 'Doctor' Harris" at Castle Thunder on charges "affecting his good faith towards the Confederacy"; another Afro-Virginian, Armistead Bently, was jailed for "endeavoring to go the enemy." Meanwhile, Hampton free black Thomas Peake, the husband of teacher Mary Peake, was once arrested by Union forces as a Confederate spy. Peake, who had been freed by his owner in 1846, was indeed a spy—for the Union; perhaps his fair skin and blue eyes were the reason for Yankee suspicions.[63]

Afro-Virginians learned that cooperating with the Union side could be as hazardous as plotting slave rebellions. The body of one such unfortunate, Martin Robinson, became a "gruesome spectacle" and reminder to blacks that the war could bring death from Yankees as well as Confederates. On 28 February 1864 Brigadier General Judson Kilpatrick launched a raid on Richmond to liberate Union prisoners at Belle Isle. While a diversionary raid was under way in Albemarle County under the command of General George Armstrong Custer, Kilpatrick hoped to approach the city from the north as Colonel Ulric Dahlgren and 500 cavalrymen, following the Virginia Central Railroad to Goochland Court House eight miles west of Richmond, forded the James River in order to strike from the south. Since Dahlgren would be traveling deep in the heart of unfamiliar enemy territory, he was sent a reliable and trustworthy guide, Martin Robinson, a free black bricklayer and former slave.

As a resident of Goochland, Robinson supposedly knew the best spots where the Yankees could cross the river and was described to Dahlgren as competent: "Question him five minutes, and you will find him the very man you want." Dahlgren reached Jude's Ferry on the north bank of the river on 1 March 1864, but heavy downpours had left it too swollen to cross. Some writers later accused Robinson of being a double agent who deliberately led the Union column there as part of a Confederate trap, while others claimed that the most likely reasons for Robinson's failure were poor weather, bad memory, bad luck, ignorance, and an impatient Yankee colonel.

Too furious at what he suspected was treachery to consider that Robinson lacked control over the weather, Dahlgren hanged him from a nearby tree. This had an immediate effect on slaves who had spotted the Yankee column and joined it; most slipped back to their plantations. Shortly afterwards Dahlgren and his column rode into an ambush in King and Queen County. He was shot dead, his command decimated, and the remaining slaves with him either fled into the night or were captured. Papers found on Dahlgren's body revealed plans to assassinate Jefferson Davis, execute his cabinet, and burn Richmond.

The North mourned Dahlgren as a hero but almost entirely ignored his arbitrary execution of an innocent black man. Northern newspapers and most of the officers associated with the mission made Robinson the scapegoat. Confederates portrayed Robinson as a martyred Yankee pawn, and for a week local whites pointed his body out to their slaves as it stiffly swayed beneath a gnarled branch. The sight of the decomposing flesh and bulging eyes forever troubled one witness: "I shall never forget when [as] a seven-year-old boy, and passing along the road one evening at twilight, how the cold chills ran over me when this gruesome spectacle met my horrified vision—the neck ... thrice its ordinary length and his [feet] suspended scarcely three feet from the ground."[64]

Despite misadventures such as Robinson's, Afro-Virginians were fundamental components in the Union's efforts against slavery and the Old Dominion. Although some supported or spied for the Confederacy, the majority recognized that their assistance to Yankees would hasten the end of slavery. Union soldiers appreciated blacks as heralds of good news in the war's final days when they confirmed the disintegration of morale among Confederate soldiers and civilians. "We shall have spies constantly," claimed one soldier at Petersburg in April 1865, "including several contrabands [runaway slaves] of more than average ability."[65]

Federal authorities were perplexed about how illiterate slaves always managed to possess accurate military information. One officer, testifying before a congressional committee, spoke of the black aptitude for espionage and noted that time and time again they were the North's most effective spies. When asked to speculate on the reason for this, he replied, "That was a wonder to me, and is to this day. It seemed to pass, as intelligence will, in the strangest manner, from one to another quickly. I do not know how. If there was any preconcert among them I was not aware of it. ... if one met another in the neighborhood he was sure to pass it with unaccountable speed." Like Confederates, this officer overlooked an important detail: as cooks, maids, house servants, body servants, teamsters, and a host of other occupations blacks saw and heard practically the same things as the whites did. There had always been a "grapevine telegraph" used by slaves to keep themselves informed. Although it was said among Union soldiers that "wherever a negro was found he was sure to be a friend," Confederates soldiers could not make such an assumption.[66]

The stability of the alliance between Union soldiers and Afro-Virginian civilians was jeopardized by the former's occasional greed, lechery, and racism. Even General Joseph Hooker, a man infamous for his own alleged lack of moral propriety, felt compelled to criticize the mistreatment of blacks by Federal soldiers. "Regiments have almost filled the camps with negroes, not, I am sorry to say, for any motives of philanthropy but to secure their services without compensation," he observed during the Peninsula campaign. "Nine-tenths . . . would be slave owners today, if they could steal them and in this they are encouraged and applauded by their Officers, for many of them do likewise."[67]

Edmund Parsons, a black Williamsburg resident, told Congress that Union soldiers acting on the orders of the local provost marshal wrongfully evicted him and his wife from their house in January 1865. The Parsons had lived in their home for twenty years unmolested by whites until the soldiers put them out and stole the couple's possessions. "When the Union forces [first] came," recalled Parsons, "a good many officers became attached to me and my wife, and we felt perfectly secure." He felt betrayed and apprehensive, for it seemed Afro-Virginians were caught between former Confederate and Union soldiers.[68]

Two weeks after Lee's surrender Union officers informed the newly freed slaves that they were to remain in the counties where they had been enslaved and sign contracts to work on plantations in exchange for wages. By May 1865 blacks, whether or not they could fully support themselves, were to be herded into government "farms" that were combinations of "poor-houses, penitentiaries, and intelligence offices" under the control of military superintendents who had the power to assign work to adults and minors.[69]

Vindictive and embittered ex-Confederates falsely accused black soldiers of acts "consisting principally in the destruction of buildings and the exciting of the colored people to acts of outrage against the persons and property of white citizens." They reported that "colored soldiers are . . . advising negroes not to work on farms . . . and . . . [suggesting] that if they had not arms to use against their former masters that they (the black soldiers) would furnish them." In Virginia accusations were leveled against members of the all-black 25th Army Corps; it participated in the Appomattox campaign, and its members were among the first Union soldiers to enter and occupy Richmond. Its commander, Major General Godfrey Weitzel, passionately defended the character of his men and denied the charges as racist exaggerations. He blamed the reported incidents on ex-Confederates and escaped inmates from the state penitentiary wearing cast-off Union uniforms. The commander of the Department of Virginia, Major General Ord, added his own endorsement: "I do not consider the behavior of the colored corps . . . to have been bad, considering the novelty of their position. . . . In the city of Richmond their conduct is spoken of as very good."[70]

Overreacting to falsehoods, Secretary of War Stanton ended the enlistment of black troops on 1 June 1865. Their regiments were either mustered out or transferred from Virginia at the moment when black civil rights were imperiled by the resurgence of white reactionaries. Most of the USCT regiments that had been organized in the state and so bravely fought there were sent to faraway Texas. Desperate and alarmed about the safety of their loved ones, members of the 1st Regiment of the United States Colored Cavalry petitioned in December 1865 for discharges so that they could return home, but they and most other regiments were not mustered out until June 1867. Union troop strength in Virginia declined from 46,000 men in June 1865 to less than 400 men by October 1876. Black veterans returned to their families and their own pitiful resources; ahead lay an era of benign neglect.[71]

Some Afro-Virginian Union veterans like Edward Hall received pensions. Born in Jefferson County in 1827, Hall moved to Winchester at age seven and worked as a laborer. He enlisted with the 30th Maryland Regiment (USCT) in March 1864 and served until a bale of hay fell on his back at Morehead City, North Carolina. He was treated at the Roanoke Island Hospital but was left with extreme pain whenever he tried to bend over, lift any kind of weight, or rise from a sitting position; he received an honorable discharge in December 1865. He married twice, survived both wives, raised a family, and collected a Federal pension of $27 a month from 1912 until his death on 24 August 1915 from "the infirmities of old age." He was buried with military honors in Winchester's Orrick Cemetery.[72]

More than 185,000 African-American soldiers (92,000 from the South) and 30,000 sailors risked their lives for the Union. White officers were surprised by their quiet determination and professionalism. One remarked that the blacks were wasted on garrison duty because they possessed a natural aptitude for offensive operations, especially guerrilla warfare. A Union general boasted that his Afro-Virginian cavalrymen, man for man, were as good as other soldiers. Another white commander noted that some of his black troops wrote well enough to prepare daily reports free of errors; he saw no reason why a qualified black should not command the Army of the Potomac or become governor of South Carolina.[73]

Shortly after the war, a lone black soldier on sentry duty in an occupied Virginia town was shoved off a sidewalk by a Southerner. The black soldier ordered the offender to halt but was ignored until the loud clicking of his rifle's cocked hammer forced the Southerner to obey and return to the sentry. As the white man stood anxious and silent, the black soldier quietly announced, "Dis nigger is of no particular account, but you must [respect] dis uniform; white man go on."[74]

14 BABYLON'S FALL
Afro-Virginians at the Gates of Freedom

Go your ways: behold, I send you forth as lambs among wolves.
—*Luke 10:3*

We truly live in a strange age. I cannot realize the freedom of the negroes.
—*Mary Martin, 21 June 1865*

DURING THEIR final months as Confederate citizens, white Virginians issued morale-boosting proclamations pledging undying struggle against the triple serpents of Unionism, abolitionism, and Black Republicanism. A General Assembly resolution circulated among the state's soldiers envisaged an awful future: "A free negro population will be established in your midst who will be your social equals and military governors. Negro guards will, at their pleasure, give you passes and safe conducts, or arrest you to be tried and punished by negro commandants and magistrates: and to these, yourselves, your wives and children will be menial laborers and slaves, except those of you whom the malice of your enemies shall reserve for the dungeons or the gallows." The Texas legislature warned that the virtue of bereaved mothers, widows, sisters, and daughters would be "trampled" unless Confederates as a nation and a people trusted in God and forever spurned "association with the people of the North." Residents of Powhatan County in February 1865 declared unconditional surrender as nothing more than "submission to fanaticism and tyranny."[1]

But to paroled Virginia soldiers the state seemed to be in a surreal state of hopefulness. Shortly after his release from Fort Delaware, Richard C. Taylor expressed dismay at the lackadaisical attitude of fellow Confederates: "It was sad to find that our people in Richmond so little realized that [the] Southern Confederacy was toppling. The officers I met were for the most part buoyant and hopeful. One told me that the Southern people had determined to enlist the negroes as part of our army, and thought that [it] would shortly bring success to our effort."[2]

Afro-Virginians, ignoring the anxiety of whites, increasingly demonstrated newfound assertiveness. Typical of this were three plantation slaves, elected as a committee to represent the wishes of twenty-seven others. This committee of three coolly explained to their master that they were now free but would continue to work for him if they were paid—in Union greenbacks. The piqued but helpless owner could only tell them to go to hell with his hopes that they would get there soon.[3]

Brunswick County blacks initiated raids against whites. An African-American in the uniform of a Union colonel appeared with armed followers claiming to hold a commission to raise a black regiment. This "regiment" grew to such an extent that it was able to attack white-owned homes with impunity. Houses and farms were surrounded at midnight, fired upon, then attacked by a rush of blacks eager for plunder; goods were seized and sent back to the base camp. Even so, these black insurgents imposed self-discipline as far as white women were concerned. On one occasion a member of the party coarsely insulted the lady of the house they were robbing. Their leader stopped his plundering to threaten to kill the man and anyone else who used offensive language toward white women. However, the numbers and successes of these raids put local whites in such a state of terror that they begged Union troops to intervene; the white soldiers successfully hunted down and destroyed marauding blacks.[4]

When the Army of the Potomac finally broke the fighting will of the Army of Northern Virginia at Petersburg on 2 April 1865, that long-besieged city became a Federal prize. The first of the conquering troops to take possession of it were black Union soldiers, including members of the 116th United States Colored Troops. A day later, the first Union soldiers to enter the captured Confederate capital were African-Americans: the 5th Massachusetts Cavalry and the 36th United States Colored Troops, under the command of General Alonzo Draper, along with elements of the 22d, 38th, and 118th USCT, First and Second divisions, 25th Corps. This all-black corps, 14,000 strong, originally consisting of black troops from the 10th and 18th Corps, Army of the James, was the largest single concentration of African-American troops up to that time. These veterans had distinguished themselves on many Virginia battlefields.

They proudly marched into the ruins of Richmond singing their favorite marching song, "John Brown's Body," affirmation of Brown's grim prophecy that the sins of the land could only be purged away with blood. At nine in the morning of 3 April 1865, the black cavalrymen of the 5th Massachusetts Cavalry became the first Union soldiers to arrive, galloping through the burning city to the Exchange Hotel on 14th and Franklin streets where they drew their sabers with a roar of exultation and yelled, "Richmond at last!" Black Richmonders exulted in their new freedom and sang with joy at the fall of the South's Babylon:

Oh, Jesus tell you once before,
   Babylon's fallin' to rise no more;
To go in peace an' sin no more;
   Babylon's fallin' to rise no more.[5]

The world had finally turned right-side up for the newly freed slaves. Those held in the city jails were freed, and for the first time ever black church congregations were able to sing the praises of liberty openly and publicly and give thanks to God for their deliverance.

Ex-slave Moble Hopson chuckled when recalling how he learned from a indignant Confederate that "de nigguhs tuk Richmond." The white soldier's company had taken refuge in a warehouse to make a last stand behind a barricade of cotton and tobacco bales. All night long they heard a distant roaring sound that grew louder with the coming of dawn:

> An den they come. Down de street dey come—a shoutin' an' aprancin' an' a yellin an' asingin' and' aming such uh noise lie as if hell done been turn't loose. Uh mob uh niggahs. Ah ain't nevuh knowed nigguhs—even all uh dem nigguhs—could mek sech uh ruckus. One huge sea uh black faces filt de street fum wall tuh wall, an' dew wan't nothin' but nigguhs in sight. Well, suh, dey warn't no usen us firin' on dem 'cause dey ain't no way we gonna kill all uh dem nigguhs. An' pretty soon dey bus' in de do' uh dat warehouse, an' we stood dere whilst dey pranced 'rounst us a hoopin' an' hollorin', an' not techin' us at all, tell de Yankees soldiers cum up, an' tek away our guns, an' mek us prisoners, an' pretty soon dey march us intuh town an' lock us up in ole Libby Prison.[6]

Black soldiers restrained their enthusiasm and went to work. They reestablished order, rounded up drunken troublemakers, extinguished fires, shared their rations with the jubilant but starving freed slaves, and guarded city streets and surviving buildings. They were detailed to guard white women and children, and there were no complaints of black misbehavior. White Richmonders were surprised that the black soldiers were well behaved, drilled, equipped, and clothed.

One of the war's countless ironies occurred when the wife of General Robert E. Lee was dismayed to find that a black cavalryman had been posted outside her East Franklin Street home by order of the Union provost marshal. Elderly and crippled with arthritis, she had decided to stay in the city while her neighbors successfully extinguished the flames of the Great Richmond Fire as the blaze inched toward her home. She complained that his presence in her front yard was a premeditated insult. Major General Weitzel, commander of the 25th Corps occupying the city, angrily denied accusations that he replaced the black guard with a white soldier at her request and swore he would never do anything so prejudicial as long as he commanded black soldiers.[7]

Some white Union soldiers wanted nothing to do with blacks. Now that the war was over, many wanted the blacks removed from the Confederacy's former capital. "The Niggers ordered away," wrote New Hampshire soldier John Mottram a week after Richmond's capture, "and all things look well." Several blacks headed for Petersburg, twenty miles away, but enough stayed behind for Mottram to complain that the city was filled with tens of thousands of blacks and paroled Confederates, two groups he loathed equally.[8]

Thomas Morris Chester, a black correspondent for the Philadelphia *Press* who accompanied the victorious Union army, entered the State Capitol, seated himself in the chair of the speaker of the House of Delegates, and began writing a story for his newspaper. A paroled Confederate officer, espying him through a doorway, peremptorily ordered him to vacate the chair. Chester ignored him and quietly continued writing, but the Confederate repeated his demand, adding maledictions such as "black cuss" and threatening to knock Chester's brains out. When the black journalist imperturbably disregarded these threats, the white man rushed toward him with clenched fists and more profanities, grabbing the reporter by the collar.

With one smooth motion the tall and muscular Chester rose and "planted a black fist and left a black eye" upon the face of his foe, the force of the blow propelling the dumbfounded rebel backwards over tables and chairs with a loud crash and rendering him hors de combat. Unruffled, Chester resumed his seat, but the Confederate, howling in rage and humiliation, asked a Union officer drawn by the noise for the loan of a sword "to cut the damned nigger's heart out." The officer refused but offered to clear space in the chamber to permit a fair fight, man to man, black fists versus white, and dryly predicted the Confederate would be "thrashed worse than Lee." However, one punch proved enough for the Confederate, who indignantly stomped away. "I thought I would exercise my rights as a belligerent," Chester wryly commented as he picked up his pen and recommenced his work.[9]

Much has been written about the Confederacy's last days and the Appomattox finale, the dignity of the Army of Northern Virginia, and the magnanimity of the Union army on that Palm Sunday when the South surrendered and the peculiar institution died. Among the 29,000 Confederates who surrendered were approximately 30 blacks, including 16 slaves who were part of the ordnance train of Lee's Quartermaster's Department. Four body servants were paroled with the Donaldsonville Artillery of Louisiana. A paroled

South Carolina cavalry brigade included 8 slaves and "free boys," mostly teamsters and sixty-year-old James Barabsha, supervisor of the younger blacks. Many other blacks were present who either escaped or were otherwise not listed or given paroles.[10]

The first casualty of the American Civil War was Heyward Shepherd, an Afro-Virginian killed during John Brown's raid at Harpers Ferry. Ironically, among its final casualties in Virginia was Hannah, a slave owned by Samuel H. Coleman. She was killed by a stray cannonball while standing in the doorway of her cabin one mile west of Appomattox Court House on 9 April 1865. But Appomattox was also the birthplace of African-American freedom.[11]

The man whom blacks regarded as their liberator, President Abraham Lincoln, was idolized by Afro-Virginians in Petersburg and Richmond during his visits on 3–4 April 1865. They kissed his hands, knelt at his feet, and pressed around his carriage so tightly that his traveling companions became concerned for his safety, but his escort of marines and black cavalrymen had little to fear from the joyous multitudes. A member of the presidential entourage, Elizabeth Keckley, a Virginia ex-slave, was keenly interested to see the changes that had occurred since her departure. As she walked through the vanquished city, she idly sifted through a trail of papers and materials abandoned by the Confederate Congress and the General Assembly; among these Keckley discovered an incongruous proclamation prohibiting free blacks from entering the state.[12]

But was "Father Abraham" deserving of being hailed as the Great Emancipator? Shortly before his death Lincoln indicated a willingness to compensate slave owners but not slaves. On 5 February 1865, two days after he failed to come to terms with the Southerners at the Hampton Roads Conference, he submitted to his cabinet a proposed proclamation that he hoped Congress would adopt as a joint resolution. This proclamation, a peace offer to the South, would have empowered the president to reimburse slave owners in the North and the former Confederacy for the freeing of slaves in the Thirteenth Amendment and suggested the sum of $400 million in 6 percent government bonds. The cabinet unanimously rejected this plan, and Lincoln quietly dropped the subject.[13]

Frederick Douglass long had reminded the nation of the injustices of slavery and the right of blacks to be free citizens. Yet it was Lincoln, more than any other single person, who actually freed the slaves. His Emancipation Proclamation was a symbolic document whose words were backed by the reality of Richmond's fall and the achievements of the Union war machine; he knew this, and the slaves understood it. Before the end of April 1865 he was dead, the victim of a bullet fired by a third-rate actor, John

Wilkes Booth, a Southern sympathizer who shouted the state motto of Virginia, *Sic Semper Tyrannis* (Thus always to tyrants) as he murdered the president.

The news stunned Afro-Virginians, who joined in the national outpouring of grief and despondency. They hung mourning cloths from their shacks and cabins, attended memorial services, and rightfully feared that with his death the government's concern and protection of them would end. In Alexandria black hospital chaplain Chauncey Leonard mourned him as the "only earthly Pilot" whom blacks could trust to guide them to "Liberty and Equal Political rights." Elizabeth Keckley, after viewing the body of the president as it lay in state at the Executive Mansion, expressed her sorrow at the death of the person who had been the most powerful man in America but had always addressed her as a fellow citizen: "Never was a man so widely mourned before. The whole world bowed their heads in grief when Abraham Lincoln died."[14]

Sixty-year-old Charlotte Scott, a Virginia ex-slave from Campbell County, became the first person on record to propose that a monument be erected in honor of the Great Emancipator. Scott's owners, refugee Unionists William P. Rucker and his wife, considered her as having been freed by the proclamation. Now a resident of Marietta, Ohio, Scott lamented to her former mistress, "The colored people have lost their best friend on earth; Mr. Lincoln was our best friend, and I will give five dollars of my wages towards erecting a monument to his memory." Ultimately, she and other black Americans, including regiments of United States Colored Troops, raised the remarkable sum of $20,000 for a monument, with Congress providing the pedestal and the land.

And so it was that in the year of the American centennial a Freedmen's Memorial Monument to Abraham Lincoln was dedicated in Washington's Lincoln Park on the eleventh anniversary of his murder. John Mercer Langston, an expatriate Afro-Virginian and dean of Howard University's law school, chaired the national arrangements committee, and Frederick Douglass was the guest speaker. Douglass praised Lincoln's accomplishments and African-Americans, and when President Ulysses S. Grant unveiled the monument, the audience beheld a statue of Lincoln and a slave together breaking chains of bondage. Beneath the two figures a bronze inscription proclaimed that Charlotte Scott, once a slave, was its godmother and had contributed her first earnings as a free woman so that future Americans would remember the deeds of one man and the emancipation of an entire race.[15]

Black Union soldiers detailed to guard Confederate prisoners jeered at their captives with the taunting declaration, "The bottom rail [is now] on the top."

Creed T. Davis, a member of the Richmond Howitzers held as a prisoner of war at Newport News, described in his diary:

> *April 21, 1865.* The negro guards of the prison become more insolent and domineering every day. They abuse us in an infamous manner. Several prisoners have been shot down for the most trivial offences, without even a warning. Two men were shot last night.
>
> *April 29, 1865.* The negro guards are very severe; the slightest breach of discipline means "a dead rebel."
>
> *May 14, 1865.* It is heartily wished by us that the negro guards have been ordered to a very "hot place," [because] they are black devils.[16]

White Virginians were terrorized at the sight of bands of newly freed African-Americans roaming through their neighborhoods in search of sustenance and long-lost family members. Property was attacked or stolen, but whites generally were not molested during isolated ransacking and destruction of farms. These instances of revenge and retribution contributed to the unsettled postwar times. One may draw conclusions from a general order issued by Union military authorities:

> The delusion which many Colored persons, formerly slaves, are laboring under in many instances productive of evil, and giving prospect of much trouble in the future both to themselves and their former masters, it is deemed necessary to correct it, and explain what are the true relations their changed condition places them in towards the Government and their former masters, as well as what their own duties and responsibilities are. Their error consists mainly in the belief that with their liberty they acquire individual rights in the property of their former masters, and that they are entitled to live with and be subsisted by them, without being obliged to labor or give any remuneration for their support. Many even believe that the entire property of . . . former owners belongs now to themselves, and that the owner remains with them only by their sufferance. This mistake has been originated and sustained in many instances by thoughtless, ignorant or mischievous soldiers.
>
> It is therefore stated for the information and guidance of Negroes, formerly slaves . . . that the operation of existing laws is to make them *free*, but not to give them any claim whatever upon, or rights in connection with the property of their former owners. . . . Their former master has the right to refuse them anything that he might deny to a perfect stranger, and is no more bound to feed, clothe, or protect them than if he had never been their master.

Accordingly, this proclamation advised Afro-Virginians not to expect the government to redistribute forty acres and a mule to ex-slave families, but blacks continued to believe themselves entitled to whatever land and goods they could take as compensation for their enslavement. But in Franklin County, nine-year-old Booker T. Washington and his family headed for Malden, West Virginia, where for the first time he could earn wages for his labor and seek an education. When Albert Jones returned home in the uniform of a Union soldier his former master greeted him warmly; his welcome may have been dictated the fact that Jones still had his weapons and plenty of ammunition.[17]

On the day of Lincoln's death, the farm of Mrs. J. L. White was visited by a group of Union soldiers who merely drank some milk and quietly moved on without further incident. "A few hours later, five [male] negroes came into the yard . . . from Nansemond [County]. Our poultry soon announced their presence. They began killing and throwing them together in a heap; grandpa stepped up into the porch, asked them what they were doing with his chickens. He [the black spokesman] replied killing them to eat, that he wanted them & was told to take what he wanted." Their spokesman demanded money, but the grandfather replied that he had none. Glaring up at the house, the leader irritatedly observed that "any one that has such a house as this, must have money"; he cursed the grandfather as "an old whiteheaded copper-faced secesh" and threatened to kill him but was dissuaded by the other blacks. They appropriated dinner plates and utensils and opened nearby beehives, but the insects resisted more successfully than the family, and the blacks soon gave up their painful efforts to obtain honey. They settled in for the night as the Whites anxiously awaited sunrise.

With the arrival of morning, the black spokesman ordered the family's female slaves, Margaret and Maria, to join them; finding Maria to his taste, he made a personal appeal for her to accompany him to Norfolk, promising she would never want to return to her mistress because "Uncle Sam," the Federal government, would provide her with everything she needed. Tearfully and reluctantly Maria agreed; Margaret eagerly accepted a similar proposal. Mrs. White, in a letter to a relative after the incident, expressed shock at the attitude and overall behavior of the blacks, whom she characterized as "very pompous."[18]

Confederate Virginians entered the war convinced that God was on their side. Defeat and black freedom caused former slaveholders such as Robert Kean to characterize slavery as "an inherent weakness when [we] were deeply invaded—from [free black and slave] desertion to the enemy and joining [the Federal] army as recruits." John S. Wise, son of the former state governor and a lieutenant in the Confederate army, belatedly denounced "the curse and misery of human slavery . . . [we] ought to thank God that slavery died at Appomattox."[19]

One slaveholder could not. Union soldiers had killed one of Edmund Ruffin's sons, burned his Charles City County plantation, freed its slaves, sown salt across the fields, and cut down its trees. In June 1865 Ruffin wrote: "With death approaching near, I beg an humble grave for my mortal remains in the soil & among the patriotic & generous people of South Carolina. . . . I commit the care of my reputation & appeal to them for a due appreciation [of my] zealous efforts to promote the best interests of Virginia." He placed the muzzle of a silver gun in his mouth and shot himself.[20]

Other white Virginians, principally those who wanted to keep their slaves in hopes of obtaining monetary compensation, behaved as if they were in a racial maelstrom during the first weeks following the final defeat of the Confederacy. They bombarded Union officials with complaints about the freedpeople and restitution demands for property damaged or stolen by blacks and soldiers. The surrender of Lee did not automatically require Virginia slaveholders to give up their slaves, and there were some who tried to reclaim theirs; for more than a month after Appomattox several slave owners listed fugitive slaves and black employees as runaways in their record books. Anticipating this reaction, military authorities prepared oaths of allegiance forms requiring subscribers to obey Federal laws and proclamations against slavery:

> I will henceforth faithfully support, protect, and defend the Constitution of the United States, and the Union of the States, thereunder and . . . I will, in like manner, abide by and faithfully support all acts of Congress passed during the existing rebellion with reference to slaves, so long and so far as not repealed, modified, or held void by Congress, or by decision of the Supreme Court; and . . . I will, in like manner, abide by and faithfully support all proclamations of the President made during the existing rebellion having reference to slaves, so long and so far as not modified and declared void by decision of the Supreme Court. SO HELP ME GOD.

Not until 9 May 1865 did President Andrew Johnson officially reestablish the authority of the Federal government in the commonwealth by declaring Confederate Virginia's military and civil laws after secession null and void.[21]

Some slaveholders were quite sure they would be compensated for the loss of their slaves. Buckingham County planter Robert Thurston Hubard took comfort in the knowledge that in 1861 a justice of the peace had certified his ownership of 90 slaves ages four to seventy-five with a total market value of $54,000 and registered this information with the county clerk. When a fire destroyed the courthouse in 1869, Hubard took no chances; he prepared a duplicate list for the legal record. A list compiled by Mark Alexander of Mecklenburg County on the day Lee surrendered included 217 slaves (ages two to eighty-four); most of the younger males (ages fifteen to forty) were field hands, and the younger females, ages fourteen to forty, were employed in a variety of tasks such as washers, milkers, seamstresses, and cooks.[22]

A chastened General Assembly accepted the verdict of the war. Early in 1866 it enacted resolutions proclaiming Virginia's unconditional acceptance of Confederate defeat, recognized the secession's unconstitutionality, and endorsed the abolishment of slavery. Furthermore, the assembly pledged, "The Negro race among us should be treated with justice, humanity and good faith; and every means that the wisdom of the legislature can devise, should be used to make them useful and intelligent members of society." But even after military orders to the contrary, impoverished slaveholders still expected the government to ease them through hard times by indemnifying them. Isabella Harrison desperately hoped "a sense of justice may impel the Federal Government to compensate the Southerners for their servants," for she had learned that "some man in Petersburg has offered $10,000 per head for the privilege of the claim." Rumors had it that such compensation was already under way in Alabama.[23]

Ex-slave John Berry of Alexandria sadly learned just how determined some slave owners could be. As a recently discharged black Union soldier, Berry hurried to the home of Benjamin Triplet of Fauquier County to retrieve his waiting family (a wife and six children ages four to fourteen), but Triplet cursed him for having fought for the North and refused to release them. Triplet not only denied that the war was over but also claimed that his slaves still belonged to him and threatened to kill anyone who attempted to rescue them. In April 1865 Armaci Adams was a five-year-old orphan slave girl, but her owners, Reverend and Mrs. Isaac Hunter of Huntersville, Norfolk County, did not tell Adams she was free. They continued to hold her in servitude, accompanied by uninterrupted whippings and mistreatment, on their isolated farm until 1875. Adams later recalled: "I never knowed I was free. . . . Dey didn't tell me. . . . I thought I were still a slave."[24]

Other slave owners were uncertain. "People seem to be at a loss what to do with their servants," wrote Covesville resident Cornelia Boaz. "We have made no change with ours yet none of them have left esceptin 'Big Jim' who has gone to Appomattox to see about his wife & children and Ned who is at the fortifications at the time of Surrender. It appears to be a general plan to let the servants remain as they are till this fall." Judith Page Walker Rives, mistress of Castle Hill in Cobham, grumbled over having to pay wages to scores of freedpeople from her family's plantations to the point of personal bankruptcy.[25]

Union authorities, responding to the bewilderment of embittered whites and the complaints of blacks, issued a military order effective 26 May 1865 terminating forever involuntary hereditary servitude in the Old Dominion. A ledger entry beneath a list of hired slaves employed at one of the state's iron forges tersely noted the change in their status: "May 26 *Declared free by* order of the military authorities." The word of freedom was a long time coming; that such an order became necessary in Virginia denoted the obstinacy of old habits and the entrenchment of racism and malice toward blacks for having backed the winning side of the Civil War.[26]

Sixteen slaves of former Confederate House speaker Thomas S. Bocock of Appomattox County, purchased by him after the surrender of 9 April but before the 26 May order freeing slaves, precipitated an imbroglio shortly after he acquired them in exchange for a hundred bushels of corn and wheat. The majority of these slaves, Lydia and her nine children, Martha and four children, and Sarah, the mother of Lydia and Martha, were sold to Bocock on 17 April by Colonel Thomas A. Flood who, as it later turned out, did not have clear title to them at the time of the sale. When the order ending slavery became public, Bocock told the women they were free and that he would no longer care for them, but they refused to leave his plantation without compensation. To compound the trouble, Bocock's creditors (among them Colonel Flood) hurried to the local federal provost marshal for the District of Lynchburg, a Captain Philips, to disavow any responsibility for their sale or care.

Philips sent word that Bocock was to refund a "liberal compensation" for the slave women's losses in food and clothing. Agitated by the threat of arrest, Bocock reluctantly acquiesced and promised his ex-slaves that he would "make them a suitable *donation* in Corn" and food and clothing if and when his crops came in. But to his annoyance others among his former slaves also demanded to be included in the agreement. "I subsequently agreed to place Ellen on same footing with the men. Sam, Daniel & Tom are to contribute [to] the support of Old Sabra from 25th of June," an infuriated Bocock noted in his memoranda book, and to add insult to injury, his crops for the year were saved only by the agricultural skills of Frank, formerly a slave of one of his neighbors. The chagrined former Confederate House speaker had to pay Frank wages of four and a half bushels of corn.[27]

Virginia's new military overlords made it clear to Bocock and other ex-Confederates whose burden it was to feed and support the freedpeople: "Crops of wheat, rye, oats, corn and other agricultural products have been sown and planted by the present freed people . . . [and these] former slaves . . . will not be permitted to [be turned] loose upon the community without providing for their support. The support of the laborer and his family is a just charge against the product of the land, and the owner cannot escape payment, either as wages paid periodically, or by giving a fair proportion of the crop." Cheating ex-slaves of their wages and entitlements would not be tolerated.[28]

Slavery legally ended in Virginia and the rest of the United States with the proclamation by Secretary of State William Seward on 18 December 1865 of the ratification of the Thirteenth Amendment to the Constitution (though the Five Civilized Tribes, formerly allied with the Confederacy by treaty, did not free their black slaves until 1866). Among the twenty-seven states counted as having ratified the amendment was Virginia. Afro-Virginian slaves were finally and truly emancipated. The Emancipation Proclamation was nearly three years old, and the guns of the Civil War had been silent for nearly eight months.[29]

In the first years of the postbellum era, many Afro-Virginians blacks were willing to let bygones be bygones. Peter Fleming returned to Lexington from Ohio (where he had made a small fortune) fifteen years after being freed by David McKinley to pay his respects at the graves of his former owners. Upon discovering the absence of tombstones, he ordered and paid for two marble markers. "This is an act of generosity that deserves commemoration," commented a local newspaper. "We chronicle it as an exhibition of generous feeling rarely to be met with in our day, and as an evidence of the love and affection existing between this former slave and his master."[30] Other African-Americans, grimly convinced that ex-slaveholders knew the whereabouts of previously sold members of their families and owed it to them to reunite them, were not as forgiving. William Douglass, a former Virginia slave, expressed this attitude to Dr. James Minor of Albemarle County in August 1865.

Douglass, one of hundreds of the Old Dominion's blacks sent to Liberia during the African colonization movement, resided in Careysburg. Restrained but resolute, his letter from Africa took Minor to task for holding his children in bondage and complained that Minor had not kept in touch with him concerning their welfare: "It has been now about four years since I heard from you and I must say I am over anxious to hear from you once more. More so since I heard the war is about over." Douglass boldly appealed as one equal to another and carefully furnished proof of being capable of supporting his family. He had prospered on his eight-acre farm (which produced 8,000 pounds of sugar): "I cannot say that I am sorry that I ever come out here. . . . Here I have realized the meaning of the words Sitting under one's own vine and fig tree and none to molest or make afraid." The only thing missing from his domestic comfort were his children. "Were they with me I should be perfectly satisfied. To be so far separated from them is indeed an affliction hard to bear," he declared.

He had sent Minor $50 in gold toward the purchase of his children before the war, but nothing had come of it. While not accusing the doctor of bad faith, Douglass nevertheless wanted his children returned to him: "You will please let me know whether and when it would be advisable to do so. I would now be able to receive my children as I have built and finished a large house of durable wood consisting of 8 rooms, more than I am able to use." He concluded his letter with a lighthearted comment at the expense of their respective wives: "I tell you that my wife is about as large as your wife and weighs 200 lbs. She enjoys better health than when she was in America." While the letter is polite in tone, there is no mistaking Douglass's consideration of himself as an aggrieved parent and man addressing a thief to demand the immediate restoration of his "property" (in this case, his children). Clearly, all would be forgiven if Minor's indemnity took the form of the Douglass children on board the next ship bound for Liberia.[31]

Another Afro-Virginian father, Frank Marten of Port Gibson, Claiborne County, Mississippi, made similar claims against Joe Perkins of Fluvanna County. Marten had not seen his six sons since his sale to Mississippi in 1855 and promised only his thanks and God's blessings if Perkins aided his quest:

You Will, as I hope, not have quite forgotten old times and old servants and trusting to this, I would like to ask from you a great favor; which might give you some trouble; but trusting your kindness I hope you will help me.
You will remember Frank Marten who used to belong to Mr. James Fisher, the husband of Luci and Marten (Brooks), who was sold in 1855 and taken to Clairborne County Miss.
I had to leave my children, 6 boys behind and as much as I know with you; I have failed since the surrender hoping to make enough to back to the old home and see it and my children once more; but have not been able to accomplish it and so seeing no other way I direct these lines and in them my wish to you.
Do you know anythink about my children Please let me know where they are when you only could let me know something of of one of them; you would do me the greatest favor any mankind could do for me, and my thanks, which I can not give for you when I am so far from you, I will send in prayer to heaven.
I have enjoyed since you have seen me last, 19 years ago, good health, (which I hope to hear from you the same) and have been married in this state, having with my wife 3 children, 2 girls and 1 boy but I am getting old and have not been able to make anythink, I am as poor [as] I was when a slave; might be lit-

tle poorer but I would verget age and poverty in the joy to hear something from my boys.

Marten did not feel self-conscious or awkward about his supplication, for in his mind the previous owner and seller of his sons, Perkins, bore responsibility for knowing where they were, war or no war, and for restoring them to their natural father.[32]

Milly Richard (formerly Milly Armstrong, a slave) sent a heartrending request to Williamsburg resident Thomas Russell seeking genealogical information about her family and the health and addresses of those still living in Virginia. To refresh his memory she stated her sisters' names as Dolly Blackburn and Lucindy Barber and their grandmother's name as Franky. Milly, who signed herself with the respectable title of "Mrs.," also mentioned that her father, Caesar, had not been seen or heard from by the family for thirty-five years. As for herself, she resided in Vicksburg, Mississippi, with the family that had purchased her before the war, but her heart ached to hear from her own kinfolk. She hoped to restore familial bonds violated by slavery and poignantly expressed her sense of loss and lonesomeness: "I do not know whether any of my people white or black are living but thinking that probably this letter may fall into the hands of one who knows the old family I have concluded at last to write."[33]

Union soldiers basked in the vindication of Northern military prowess and the preservation of the nation's honor. For the defeated rebels who capitulated at Appomattox Court House and in North Carolina, Alabama, and the Trans-Mississippi, their former foes offered respect and sympathy as fellow Americans and soldiers. On Christmas Day, 1868, this mutual admiration was capped by a proclamation from the president of the United States declaring "unconditionally and without reservation, to all and to every person who directly or indirectly, participated in the late insurrection or rebellion a full pardon and amnesty for the offense of treason."[34]

But little honor was extended to African-Americans, for in the minds of most white Americans they were the cause of the conflict. Everywhere they were treated with punitive animosity. White Richmond children assaulted and intimidated black schoolchildren. Unoffending black adults were kicked and beaten in the streets of Northern cities, and when rioting white soldiers attacked and drove off blacks from their homes near Washington, D. C., the African-Americans rallied out fought back; guns were used by both sides, and military force became necessary to quell the dispute.[35] Few whites wanted to sing the praises of the slaves who risked their lives to aid Union prisoners of war in escaping from rebel prisons, the runaway slaves who fled with or returned for their families despite rewards offered by their owners, or the free blacks who aided runaway slaves and spied for the Union army or paradoxically volunteered to man Virginia's farms and industries in its most desperate hour of need. Nor did they find praiseworthy the 38,000 blacks (5,000 of them Afro-Virginians) who died for the liberation of their race, for their country, and—in the words of Lincoln's 1863 Gettysburg Address (which curiously omitted any mention of slavery)—for the promise of "a new birth of freedom" and a people's government which would never perish from the earth.

Black Americans wanted the country to remember and reward their struggles and sacrifices during the war and to acknowledge difficult unfinished tasks ahead. It would be their erstwhile allies, the abolitionists, the Union army, and the Republican party, who would lose sight of these goals and, as a consequence, delay for a century the complete implementation and integration of constitutional protections and civil rights of black people. The war was over, and everyone wanted to put it behind them. National reunification came first; black civil rights were at the bottom of the nation's social and political agenda.

What did these hopeful, God-fearing people deserve other than their personal freedom? Land, protection, social justice, and a recognition of their rights as citizens at the ballot box, in the courthouse, in schools, and in dealings with fellow citizens who just happened to have white skins. One possible solution to the race problems surrounding black suffrage and civil rights after the war might have been the reconstruction of South Carolina or a tract of western territory as an all-black state, an enlarged version of the Port Royal and Sea Islands experiments. This idea smacks of separatism but is not so far-fetched as it sounds. As a flawed historical precedent West Virginia seceded from Virginia, and more for military than political purposes the Lincoln administration consistently refused to consider its return to the Old Dominion after the war regardless of the outcome. Contemporary schemes to give all or parts of defeated Confederate states to blacks were not implausible. White Americans saw the former slaves as having a collective usefulness—elsewhere.

Northern gubernatorial and senatorial candidates urged that Florida and the coastal areas of Georgia and South Carolina be carved into an all-black state. One member of Congress, Kansas Republican senator James H. Lane, proposed giving half of Texas to African-Americans and introduced legislation in January 1864 during the first session of the Thirty-eighth Congress. He insisted that "justice" required the United States to establish a home for "Anglo-Africans" within its territories and suggested the "Territory of Rio Grande," an area stretching 600 to 700 miles from the Gulf of Mexico north to New Mexico and 250 to 300 miles from the Colorado River west to the Rio Grande, as the perfect site, which by coincidence was suitable for growing cotton.

Afro-Virginians would have been among the first of the former slaves sent to the new state under this plan for three reasons. First, there were more of them than any other group of blacks in North America. Second, the Union military was large and strong enough in Virginia to force their removal. Third, if the experiment worked, blacks in other ex-Confederate states would have little choice but to expect deportation to Texas, with the free blacks of the North scheduled next. But Lane's measure failed, and the war and Reconstruction ended without the establishment of an African-American state.[36]

A better possibility was South Carolina, where blacks already comprised the majority in twenty of thirty-one counties. The nation's entire population of African-Americans could have been resettled there had their leaders publicly supported this as one of several permanent solutions to their long-standing problems: the lack of both land and political and economic empowerment. With the USCT keeping the peace during the transition, Federal compensation could have been provided for white South Carolinians who voluntarily emigrated from the state (those who wished to stay could have done so at their own risk, retaining citizenship rights). Reimbursement of blacks for their relocation costs plus a generous thirty-year financial package to assist them in establishing themselves would have smoothed this process.

Another benefit beckoned in the political honing and seasoning of leaders such as Frederick Douglass, Martin Delany, P. B. S. Pinchback, James Mercer Langston, Thomas Morris Chester, Robert Brown Elliott, and Robert Smalls for public office as governors, auditors, state treasurers, education superintendents, constables, legislators, judges, and mayors to create an experienced black body politic.

Such a plan, more feasible and less costly than antebellum and wartime colonization schemes proposed by slaveholders and Lincoln, would have ensured the election of black senators and representatives and provided African-Americans with a well-established political base. The lives of generations of blacks would have been changed for the better, possibly preventing the rise of the Klan, lynchings, or the sort of civil rights protests and racial turmoil still infesting America.

In the late spring of 1865 slaves celebrated their passage from the valley of humiliation to a dawn of freedom:

Slavery chain done broke at las',
Broke at las', broke at las',
Slavery chain done broke at las',
Goina serve God 'twil I die![37]

As the animosity of Southern whites toward the newly freed slaves intensified, most blacks—landless, homeless, powerless, voteless—faced ambiguous futures. Nevertheless, Afro-Virginians were determined to exercise their hard-won rights. Within a month after war's end, Norfolk blacks held a meeting at Bute Street Baptist Church and resolved: "The rights and interests of the colored citizens of Virginia are more directly, immediately and deeply affected in the restoration of the State to the Federal Union than any other class of citizens . . . we have peculiar claims to be heard in regard to the question of reconstruction, and . . . we cannot keep silent without dereliction of duty to ourselves, to our country, and to our God."[38] A cataclysmic page of history had been turned; another was about to begin. And the freedpeople soon discovered that freedom had a heavy price.

Epilogue

THE CONFEDERACY was a biracial phenomenon; the presence of blacks can never have been far from the minds of whites, any more than that of whites can have been far from the consciousness of blacks. The history of African-Americans and of the Confederacy are forever intertwined. The phenomenal number of Civil War studies have led us to believe that we know a great deal about our most calamitous national experience. Nothing could be further from the truth.

"While the neglected past of the Negro must long remain a fertile and fitting field, the Negroes thus concerned must treat history in its broad aspects in order to show how it has been colored by racial antipathy," wrote Carter G. Woodson in 1938.[1] The history of the United States of America is lessened if the story of the South and the Confederacy is overlooked; any history of the South is incomplete without Virginia; the nation, the South, or the Old Dominion cannot be appreciated unless the African-American struggle becomes an equitable component in the flow of human history.

The fortitude and courage of nineteenth-century Afro-Virginians in confronting and overcoming physical and psychological oppression are impressive. The slighting or absence of African-American experiences from the record distorts reality and contradicts their historical legitimacy.

In spite of laws threatening freed slaves with reenslavement, laws barring educated blacks from returning on pain of punishment, despite everything that happened to them, Afro-Virginians viewed Virginia as their home. On the eve of his departure to the free climate of New York, Willis Augustus Hodges could not resist a lingering look back: "Virginia! With all thy faults, I love thee still."[2]

Elizabeth Keckley left as a slave but years later returned a free woman, a citizen, and a member of the president of the United States' official touring party in April 1865. Without vindictiveness but with her freedom vindicated, Keckley compared her return with that of a long-lost child: "Dear old Virginia! A birthplace is always dear, no matter under what circumstances you were born, since it revives in memory the golden hours of childhood . . . and the warm kiss of a mother."[3]

These and similar testimonials symbolized Virginia's potential as a true abode of liberty. Blacks held high expectations for themselves and their country, and in the face of an absence of full opportunities in society, freed slaves vanquished passivity and rejected the culture of demoralization to work, raise families, obey the laws, and seek new lives for themselves. African-Americans are and will continue to be vital participants in the ageless panoramic drama known as the human adventure. Their unique and praiseworthy contributions are reminders of freedom's promises unfulfilled yet within our grasp.

As dwellers in the crucible of race, Afro-Virginians of the Civil War era are shining examples for present and future generations. They were heroic in every sense of the word as warriors, musicians, farmers, craftsmen, revolutionaries, and survivors. They were and have always been Africans and Southerners, Virginians and Americans.

APPENDIXES
NOTES
BIBLIOGRAPHY OF PRIMARY SOURCES
INDEX

Appendix A

STATE OF RACE

Racial Population of Virginia's 148 Counties, 1860

County	Population	Black	White
Accomack	18,586	7,925 (43%)	10,661 (57%)
Albemarle	26,625	14,522 (54%)	12,103 (46%)
Alexandria[1]	12,656	2,801 (28%)	9,851 (72%)
Alleghany	6,765	1,122 (19%)	5,643 (81%)
Amelia	10,741	7,844 (73%)	2,897 (37%)
Amherst	13,742	6,575 (48%)	7,167 (52%)
Appomattox	8,889	4,771 (53%)	4,118 (47%)
Augusta	27,749	6,202 (22%)	21,547 (77%)
Barbour	8,958	203 (2.5%)	8,728 (97.5%)
Bath	3,676	1,024 (27%)	2,652 (73%)
Bedford	25,068	10,680 (42%)	14,388 (58%)
Berkeley[2]	12,525	1,936 (15%)	10,589 (85%)
Boone	4,840	159 (3%)	4,681 (97%)
Botetourt	11,516	3,075 (26%)	8,441 (74%)
Braxton	4,992	107 (2%)	4,885 (98%)
Brooke	5,494	69 (1%)	5,425 (99%)
Brunswick	14,809	9,817 (66%)	4,992 (34%)
Buchanan	2,793	31 (1%)	2,762 (99%)
Buckingham	15,212	9,171 (60%)	6,041 (40%)
Cabell	8,020	329 (4%)	7,691 (96%)
Calhoun	2,502	10 (0.3%)	2,492 (99.7%)
Campbell	26,197	12,609 (48%)	13,588 (52%)
Caroline	18,464	11,516 (63%)	6,948 (37%)
Carroll	8,012	293 (3.5%)	7,719 (96.5%)
Charles City	5,609	3,803 (67%)	1,806 (33%)
Charlotte	14,471	9,490 (65%)	4,981 (35%)
Chesterfield	19,016	8,997 (47%)	10,019 (53%)
Clarke	7,146	3,439 (48%)	3,707 (52%)
Clay	1,787	26 (1.4%)	1,761 (98.6%)
Craig	3,553	450 (12%)	3,103 (88%)
Culpeper	12,063	7,104 (58%)	4,959 (42%)
Cumberland	9,961	7,015 (70%)	2,946 (30%)
Dinwiddie	30,198	16,520 (54%)	13,678 (46%)
Doddridge	5,203	35 (0.6%)	5,168 (99.4%)
Elizabeth City	5,798	2,618 (45%)	3,180 (55%)
Essex	10,469	7,173 (68.5%)	3,296 (31.5%)
Fairfax	11,834	3,788 (32%)	8,046 (68%)
Fauquier	21,706	11,276 (51%)	10,430 (49%)

Racial Population of Virginia's 148 Counties, 1860 (*continued*)

County	Population	Black	White
Fayette	5,997	281 (4.6%)	5,716 (95.4%)
Floyd	8,236	491 (6%)	7,745 (94%)
Fluvanna	10,353	5,260 (51%)	5,095 (49%)
Franklin	20,098	6,454 (32%)	13,642 (67%)
Frederick	16,546	3,467 (20%)	13,079 (80%)
Giles	6,883	845 (12%)	6,038 (88%)
Gilmer	3,759	74 (2%)	3,685 (98%)
Gloucester	10,956	6,439 (58%)	4,517 (42%)
Goochland	10,656	6,842 (64%)	3,184 (36%)
Grayson	8,252	599 (7%)	7,653 (93%)
Greenbrier	12,211	1,711 (14%)	10,500 (86%)
Greene	5,022	2,007 (39%)	3,015 (61%)
Greensville	6,347	4,400 (69%)	1,974 (31%)
Halifax	26,520	15,460 (58%)	11,060 (42%)
Hampshire	13,913	1,435 (10%)	12,478 (90%)
Hancock	4,445	3 (1%)	4,442 (99%)
Hanover	17,222	9,740 (56%)	7,482 (44%)
Hardy	9,864	1,343 (13%)	8,521 (87%)
Harrison	13,790	614 (4%)	13,176 (96%)
Henrico	61,616	23,631 (38%)	37,985 (62%)
Henry	12,105	5,332 (44%)	6,773 (56%)
Highland	4,319	429 (9%)	3,890 (91%)
Isle of Wight	9,977	4,940 (49%)	5,037 (51%)
Jackson	8,306	66 (1%)	8,240 (99%)
James City	5,798	3,631 (62%)	2,167 (38%)
Jefferson[2]	14,535	4,471 (30%)	10,064 (70%)
Kanawha	16,150	2,365 (14%)	13,785 (86%)
King George	6,571	4,061 (61%)	2,510 (39%)
King and Queen	10,328	6,527 (63%)	3,801 (37%)
King William	8,530	5,941 (69%)	2,589 (31%)
Lancaster	5,151	3,170 (61%)	1,981 (39%)
Lee	11,032	837 (7%)	10,195 (92%)
Lewis	7,999	263 (3%)	7,736 (97%)
Logan	4,938	149 (3%)	4,789 (97%)
Loudoun	21,774	6,753 (31%)	15,021 (69%)
Louisa	16,701	10,518 (63%)	6,183 (37%)
Lunenburg	11,983	7,562 (63%)	4,421 (37%)
McDowell	1,535	0	1,535 (100%)
Madison	8,854	4,494 (50%)	4,360 (49%)
Marion	12,722	66 (1%)	12,655 (99%)
Marshall	12,997	86 (1%)	12,911 (99%)

Racial Population of Virginia's 148 Counties, 1860 (*continued*)

County	Population	Black	White
Mason	9,173	423 (5%)	8,750 (95%)
Mathews	7,091	3,226 (45%)	3,865 (55%)
Mecklenburg	20,096	13,318 (66%)	6,778 (34%)
Mercer	6,819	391 (6%)	6,428 (94%)
Middlesex	4,364	2,501 (57%)	1,863 (43%)
Monongalia	13,048	47 (1%)	12,901 (99%)
Monroe	10,757	1,221 (11%)	9,536 (89%)
Montgomery	10,617	2,366 (22%)	8,251 (78%)
Morgan	3,732	118 (3%)	3,614 (97%)
Nansemond	13,693	7,961 (58%)	5,732 (42%)
Nelson	13,015	6,366 (48%)	6,649 (52%)
New Kent	5,884	3,738 (63%)	2,146 (37%)
Nicholas	4,627	156 (3%)	4,471 (97%)
Norfolk	36,227	11,807 (32%)	24,420 (68%)
Northampton	7,832	4,834 (61%)	2,998 (39%)
Northumberland	7,531	3,661 (48%)	3,870 (52%)
Nottoway	8,836	6,566 (74%)	2,270 (26%)
Ohio	22,422	226 (1%)	22,196 (99%)
Orange	10,851	6,298 (58%)	4,553 (42%)
Page	8,109	1,234 (15%)	6,875 (85%)
Patrick	9,359	2,201 (23%)	7,158 (77%)
Pendleton	6,164	294 (5%)	5,870 (95%)
Pittsylvania	32,104	14,999 (46%)	17,105 (54%)
Pleasants	2,945	20 (1%)	2,925 (99%)
Pocahontas	3,958	272 (6%)	3,686 (94%)
Powhatan	8,392	5,812 (69%)	2,580 (31%)
Preston	13,312	112 (1%)	13,200 (99%)
Prince Edward	11,844	7,807 (65%)	4,037 (35%)
Prince George	8,411	5,512 (65%)	2,899 (35%)
Prince William	8,565	2,875 (33%)	5,690 (67%)
Princess Anne	7,714	3,381 (43%)	4,333 (57%)
Pulaski	5,416	1,602 (29%)	3,814 (71%)
Putnam	6,301	593 (9%)	5,708 (91%)
Raleigh	3,367	76 (2%)	3,291 (98%)
Randolph	4,990	197 (4%)	4,793 (96%)
Rappahannock	8,850	3,832 (43%)	5,018 (57%)
Richmond	6,856	3,286 (47%)	3,570 (52%)
Ritchie	6,847	38 (1%)	6,809 (99%)
Roane	5,381	74 (1%)	5,307 (99%)
Roanoke	8,048	2,798 (34%)	5,250 (66%)
Rockbridge	17,248	4,407 (25%)	12,841 (75%)

Racial Population of Virginia's 148 Counties, 1860 (*continued*)

County	Population	Black	White
Rockingham	23,408	2,919 (12%)	20,489 (88%)
Russell	10,280	1,150 (11%)	9,130 (89%)
Scott	12,072	542 (4%)	11,530 (96%)
Shenandoah	13,896	1,069 (7%)	12,827 (93%)
Smyth	8,952	1,220 (13%)	7,732 (87%)
Southampton	12,915	7,202 (55%)	5,713 (45%)
Spotsylvania	16,076	8,360 (52%)	7,716 (48%)
Stafford	8,555	3,633 (42%)	4,922 (58%)
Surry	6,133	3,799 (61%)	2,334 (38%)
Sussex	10,175	7,057 (69%)	3,118 (30%)
Taylor	7,463	163 (2%)	7,300 (98%)
Tazewell	9,920	1,295 (13%)	8,625 (87%)
Tucker	1,428	36 (3%)	1,392 (97%)
Tyler	6,517	29 (1%)	6,488 (99%)
Upshur	7,292	228 (3%)	7,064 (97%)
Warren	6,442	1,859 (28%)	4,583 (72%)
Warwick	1,740	1,078 (61%)	662 (39%)
Washington	16,891	2,796 (16%)	14,095 (84%)
Wayne	6,747	143 (2%)	6,604 (98%)
Webster	1,555	3 (0.1%)	1,553 (99%)
Westmoreland	8,282	4,895 (59%)	3,387 (41%)
Wetzel	6,703	12 (1%)	6,691 (99%)
Wirt	3,751	23 (1%)	3,728 (99%)
Wise	4,508	92 (2%)	4,416 (98%)
Wood	11,046	255 (2%)	10,791 (98%)
Wyoming	2,861	66 (2%)	2,795 (98%)
Wythe	12,305	2,319 (18%)	9,986 (82%)
York	4,949	2,607 (52%)	2,342 (48%)
Total	1,596,146	548,847	1,047,299

Note: The counties listed include those which became West Virginia. Free blacks and slaves are collectively listed as "blacks"; the state's 112 Indians were counted as "white" by the census enumerators. Omitted is Bland County (formed from parts of Giles, Wythe, and Tazewell counties), organized on 30 March 1861, the last county crated before the war.

[1]Alexandria County, consisting of thirty square miles ceded to the District of Columbia in 1801, was returned by Congress to Virginia in 1846 and renamed Arlington County in 1920.

[2]Berkeley and Jefferson counties remained a part of Virginia until 1866 when they were transferred by the Federal government to West Virginia.

Source: Joseph C. G. Kennedy, Superintendent of the Census, *Population of the United States in 1860; Compiled from the Original Returns of the Eighth Census, under the Direction of the Secretary of the Interior* (Washington, D.C.: PO, 1864), 501–13, 516–18.

Appendix B

PLANTATION MANAGEMENT
"Standing Rules for the Government of Slaves on a Virginia
Plantation, with Notes & Observations"

Rule 1st No negro should be permitted to go off the Plantation on his or her
own business without a written Pass
2nd No negro should be presented to sell any thing without a written Permit
3d Fighting should be strictly forbidden
4th It should [be] made the duty of every negro to take up or give information
to the Overseer of every negro who may come among them & cannot give a
strick account of himself, they should be especially prohibited from entertaining
watermen.
5th Quarrelling, or vexations & insulting language, from one to another &
especially from a younger to an older negro, should be strictly forbidden.
6th Every working hand under the authority of the Overseer upon the
plantation should appear with a clean shirt & decent clothes every [Sunday?]
morning.

DIRECTIONS FOR UNEXPERIENCED OVERSEERS

Permit no negro to Pass through your Plantation who has not a written Pass, &
who cannot give a satisfactory account of himself. [K]ill every stray dog that appears
lurking about the plantation without a master & give this in charge also to the negroes.

Never permit any orders you give to be disobeyed or disregarded without a
strict inquiry into it & punish the offender if necessary.

Set the first example of strict attention to your duties & you may with the
more Justice & propriety inflict Punishment upon others for the neglect of these.
Therefore never make an order without Punctually attending to it, for if you make
a rule & forget it yourself with what face could you Punish others for neglecting it
also. If you punish only according to justice & reason with uniformity you can never
be too Severe, & will be the more respected for it, even by those who suffer. Arrangement & regularity form the great secret of doing things well; you must therefore, as far as possible have every thing done according to a [firm?] rule.

Your People should all turn out in the morning together by some established
signal & let no one be permitted to be a moment behind the rest.

Have your stock of every kind, attended to at stated times, & by particular
persons who should be bound to finish by a certain time.

317

The [Stable] Boys should carry their Horses to water at stated hours & your [gear?] should be placed in some particular part of the Stable, & kept well oiled & repaired.

You are expected to have learned by your own experience, calculation & trials, & enquire of other Persons what is a days work for a hand in every variety of plantation business & daily compare what your People do with what they ought to do & thus Perfect your Judgement in such matters, enabling you to calculate beforehand what can be Performed.

The cook should be required to serve the Peoples food in a clean & decent manner, & at stated regular hours; every article be made well done. You should constantly examine into the manner in which your hands are Performing their work & if there be any defect in the Tool or implement they are using, or in the manner of applying it, let it be corrected or give such instructions as may be necessary.

You should never Scold or talk more to your people upon any occasion than may be absolutely necessary to make them understand you.

You should arrange in your mind the work that is to imploy you, at least 3 or 4 days beforehand & under every variety of circumstances as to rainy weather, fair, frozen, or moderate weather.

You should always keep under shelter for seasoning, an ample supply of every description of Timber likely to be required on the farm. And finally you Should bear in mind that it is the duty of a faithful, active, & industrious agent, to be the first on the ground in the morning & the last to leave it at night, to see to the giving out of all grain, & to the feeding, comfortable sheltering, & counting of every description of stock under your charge, night and morning; & that you are bound not only to give orders, but Personbly [*sic*] see that they are well & faithfully executed—

Source: Cocke Family Papers, 640, box 184, UVA.

Appendix C

CONFEDERATE RESPONSE TO THE EMANCIPATION
PROCLAMATION
An Address to the People of the Free States by the President of the
Southern Confederacy

Richmond, January 5, 1863.

Citizens of the non-slaveholding States of America, swayed by peaceable motives, I have used all my influence, often thereby endangering my position as the President of the Southern Confederacy, to have the unhappy conflict now existing between my people and yourselves, governed by those well established international rules, which heretofore have softened the asperities which necessarily are the concomitants of a state of belligerency, but all my efforts in the premises have heretofore been unavailing. Now, therefore, I am compelled *e necessitati rei* to employ a measure, which most willingly I would have omitted to do, regarding, as I always must, State Rights, as the very organism of politically associated society.

For nearly two years my people have been defending their inherent rights—their political, social and religious rights against the speculators of New England and their allies in the States heretofore regarded as conservative. The people of the Southern Confederacy have—making sacrifices such as the modern world has never witnessed—patiently, but determinedly, stood between their home interests and the well paid, well fed and well clad mercenaries of the Abolitionists, and I need not say that they have nobly vindicated the good name of American citizens. Heretofore, the warfare has been conducted by white men—peers, scions of the same stock; but the programme has been changed, and your rulers despairing of a triumph by the employment of white men, have degraded you and themselves, by inviting the co-operation of the black race. Thus, while they deprecate the intervention of white men—the French and the English—in behalf of the Southern Confederacy, they, these Abolitionists, do not hesitate to invoke the intervention of the African race in favor of the North.

The time has, therefore, come when a becoming respect for the good opinion of the civilized world impels me to set forth the following facts:—

First. Abraham Lincoln, the President of the Non-Slaveholding States, has issued his proclamation, declaring the slaves within the limits of the Southern Confederacy to be free.

Second. Abraham Lincoln has declared that the slaves so emancipated may be used in the Army and Navy, now under his control, by which he means to employ, against the Free People of the South, insurrectionary measures, the inevitable tendency of which will be to inaugurate a Servile War, and thereby prove destructive, in a great measure, to slave property.

Now, therefore, as a compensatory measure, I do hereby issue the following Address to the People of the Non-Slaveholding States:—

On and after February 22, 1863, all free negroes within the limits of the Southern Confederacy shall be placed on the slave status, and be deemed to be chattels, they and their issue forever.

All negroes who shall be taken in any of the States in which slavery does not now exist, in the progress of our arms, shall be adjudged, immediately after such capture, to occupy the slave status, and in all States which shall be vanquished by our arms, all free negroes shall, *ipso facto,* be reduced to the condition of helotism, so that the respective normal conditions of the white and black races may be ultimately placed on a permanent basis, so as to prevent the public peace from being thereafter endangered.

Therefore, while I would not ignore the conservative policy of the Slave States, namely, that a Federal Government cannot, without violating the fundamental principles of a Constitution, interfere with the internal policy of several States; since, however, Abraham Lincoln has seen fit to ignore the Constitution he has solemnly sworn to support, it ought not be considered polemically or politically improper in me to vindicate the position which has been at an early day of this Southern republic, assumed by the Confederacy, namely, that slavery is the corner-stone of a Western Republic. It is not necessary for me to elaborate this proposition. I may merely refer, in passing, to the prominent fact, that the South is emphatically a producing section of North America; this is equally true of the West and Northwest, the people of which have been mainly dependent on the South for the consumption of their products. The other States, in which slavery does not exist, have occupied a middle position, as to the South, West and Northwest. The States of New England, from which all complicated difficulties have arisen, owe their greatness and power to the free suffrages of all other sections of North America; and yet, as is now evident, they have, from the adoption of the Federal Constitution, waged a persistent warfare against the interests of all the other States of the old Union. The great centre of their opposition has been Slavery, while the annual statistics of their respective State Governments abundantly prove that they entertain within all their boundaries fewer negroes than any single State which does not tolerate slavery.

In view of these facts, and conscientiously believing that the proper condition of the negro is slavery, or a complete subjection to the white man,—and entertaining the belief that the day is not distant when the old Union will be restored with slavery nationally declared to be the proper condition of all of African descent,—and in view of the future harmony and progress of all the States of America, I have been induced to issue this address, so that there may be no misunderstanding in the future.

JEFFERSON DAVIS

Source: Broadside, Jefferson Davis Papers, University Library, Washington and Lee University, Lexington, VA.

Appendix D

Petition on Behalf of Washington Jackson, a Free Afro-Virginian
Blacksmith Drafted by the Confederate Army, October 1863

To the worshipful Court of the County of Rockbridge:

Your petitioners respectfully represent, that they have learned that Washington
Jackson (a free man of color) has been impressed into the Confederate service in
said County, and they further represents that the said Washington Jackson is a Blacksmith by trade, and a very industrious man, and the only reliable Smith now in this
Town of Brownsburg or vicinity. Therefore we pray that he may be exempted as
the county and the Town, will be subject to great inconvenience Should they be
deprived of his labour at this time, the said Jackson has been doing the work of this
community for the last two years—almost entirely—

[33 signatures]

N. B. I fully concur in
the above & would farther
State that W. Jackson has
done my Smiths work for
many years, and I do not
know how the farming community
can get along if he is
Taken from us
   Henry B. Jones
I concur in Capt Jones Statement
     P. [?]

[Endorsement]
Capt. T. H. Tutwiler, Assistant Quartermaster, C. S. S.
      Having considered this written pe-
      tition, You will please release
      Washington Jackson herein named.
October 5th 1863   W. C. Davis, Justice of the Peace
      William Doel(?), Justice of the Peace

Source: Washington Jackson Petition, Rockbridge County Historical Society, University
Library, Washington and Lee University, Lexington, Va.

Appendix E

General Robert E. Lee's "List of Officers Who Ask Authority to Raise or Be Assigned to the Command of Negro Troops," [2 April 1865]

Name and rank	Service branch	Command goal
Brig. Gen. Henry Brevard Davidson		Desires to command Division
Colonel William T. Robins	24th Virginia Calvary	Desires to command Brigade
Lt. Col. D. S. Troy	60th Alabama	Desires to raise Brigade
Lt. Col. Bolivar H. Gee	59th Georgia	" " "
Lt. Col. A. S. Cunningham	Artillery, P.A.C.S.	Desires to raise Regiment
Lt. Col. Clinton M. Winkler	4th Texas	" " "
Capt. John W. Kerr	Assistant Adjutant General, Texas Brigade	" " "
Major Hatch Book	60th Alabama	" " "
Major William J. Mims	43rd Alabama	" " "
Major John M. Jeffries	41st Alabama	" " "
Major James W. Pegram	Assistant Adjutant General	" " "
Capt. J. B. Moorehead	41st Alabama	" " "
Capt. M. L. Randolph	Signal Corps	Desires to command Regiment
Capt. E. Willoughby Anderson	Ordnance	" " "
Lt. M. M. Lindsay	Aide-de-Camp [formerly 19th Mississippi]	" " "
Lt. J. Warren Jackson	8th Louisiana	Desires to raise Regiment
Sergt. Eugene [McLea?]	43rd Alabama	" " "

Name and rank	Service branch	Command goal
Private Alfred T. Glover	43rd Alabama	″ ″ ″
Private Harry Wooding	5th Virginia Calvary	Desires to command Regiment
Sergt. F. R. Smith	1st Engineer Troops	Desires to command Company

Source: "List of Officers who ask authority to raise or be assigned to the command of Negro Troops," Robert Edward Lee Headquarters Papers, 1855–78, VH Society. I am indebted to the late Waverly Winfree, Librarian of the society, for locating this document and granting permission to reproduce it. I have made a few minor editorial modifications for clarity. Officers were identified by consulting Joseph H. Crute, Jr., *Units of the Confederate States Army* (Midlothian, Va., 1987), and U.S. Department of War, *List of Staff Officers of the Confederate States Army, 1861–1865,* comp. Gen. Marcus J. Wright, (Washington, D.C.: GPO, 1891).

Appendix F

DEED OF MANUMISSION
Confederate General Robert E. Lee Emancipates
ca. 194 Afro-Virginian Slaves,
December 1862

Know all men by these presents, that I, Robert E. Lee, executor of the last will and testament of George W. P. Custis deceased, acting by and under the authority and direction of the provisions of the said will, do hereby manumit, emancipate and forever set free from slavery the following named slaves belonging to the Arlington estate, viz: Eleanor Harris, Ephraina Dimicks[?], George Clarke, Charles Syphax; Selina and Thornton Grey and their six children Emma, Sarah, Harry, Anise, Ada, Thornton; Margaret Taylor and her four children Dandridge, [John], Billy, Quincy; Lawrence Parks and his nine children—Perry, George, Amanda, Martha, Lawrence, James, Magdalena, Leno, William; Julia Ann Check and her three children Catharine, Louis, Henry and an infant of the said Catharine; Sally Norris [and?] Len Norris and their three children Mary, Sally, and Wesley; Old Shaack Check; Austin Bingham and Louisa Bingham and their twelve children Harrison, Parks, Reuben, Henry, Edward, Austin, Lucius, Leanthe, Louisa, Caroline, Jem, and an infant; Obadiah Grey; Austin Banham, Michael Merriday, Catharine Burk and her child; Marianne Burke and Agnes Burke: Also the following slaves belonging to the White House estate, viz: Robert Crider and Desiah his wife, Locky, Zack Young and two other children[,] Fleming Randolph and child; Maria Meredith and Henry her husband and their three children Nelson, Henry, and Austin; Lorenzo Webb, Old Daniel, Clavert Dandridge, Claiborne Johnson, Mary and John Stewart, Harrison, Jeff, Pat and Gadsby, Dick, Joe, Robert, Anthony, Davy, Bill Crump, Peyton, Dandridge, Old Davy and Eloy his wife, Milly and her two children[,] Leanthe and her five children; Jasper, Elisha and Rachael his wife, Lavinia and her two children, Major, Phill, Miles, Mike and Scilla his wife and their five children Lavinia, Israel, Isaiah, Loksey[?] and Delphy; Old Fanny and her husband, Patsy, [L]ittle Daniel, and Cloe, James Henry, Milly, Ailsey and her two children, Susan Pollard[,] Armistead and Molly his wife, Airy, Jane Piler[?], Bob, Polly, Betsy and her child, Molly, Charity, John Reuben, George Crump, Minny, Grace, Martha and Matilda: Also the following belonging to the Romancoke estate, viz: Louis, Jem, Edward, Kitty and her children[,] Mary Dandridge and an infant; Nancy; Dolly, Esther, Serica[?], Macon and Louisa his wife, Walker, Peggy, Ebbee, Fanny, Chloe Custis and her child Julia Ann, Elvey Young and her child Charles, Airy Johnson, Anne Johnson, William and Sarah Johnson and their children Ailey, Crump, Molly, and George, James Henry and Anderson Crump,

Major Custis and Lucy Custis, Nelson Meredith and Phoebe his wife, and their children Robert, Elisha, Nat, Rose and Sally, Ebbee Macon, Martha Jones & her children Davy & Austin; Patsey Braxton, Susan Smith and Mildred her child, Anne Brown, Jack Johnson, Marwell Bingham and Henry Baker.

And I do hereby release the aforesaid slaves from all andevery claim which I may have upon their services as executor aforesaid.

Witness my hand and seal this 29th day of December in the year in the year of Our Lord eighteen hundred sixty-two

[signed]   R. E. Lee [seal]

Ex. of G. W. P. Custis

State of Virginia, County of Spotsylvania to wit:

I, Benj[amin] S. Cason, Justice of the Peace in and for said County, do hereby certify that Robert E. Lee, executor of the last will and testament of George W. P. Custis, a party to the foregoing deed of manumission, this day appeared before me, and acknowledged the same to be his act and deed.

Given under my hand this 29 day of Dec 1862

[signed]   Benj[amin] S. Cason J. P.

City of Richmond, to wit:

In the Office of the Court of Hustings for the said City, the 2d day of January 1863

This deed was presented and with the Certificate annexed, admitted to record at twelve o'clock N.

Teste   Ro[bert] Howard, Clerk

Source: Robert E. Lee: Custis Executor Document, Museum of the Confederacy.

Notes

ABBREVIATIONS AND SHORT TITLES

Berlin,
  Black
  Military
  Experience
Ira Berlin, Joseph Reidy, and Leslie S. Rowland, eds. *Freedom: A Documentary History of Emancipation, 1861–1867, Selected from the Holdings of the National Archives of the United States*. Ser. 2, *The Black Military Experience*. New York, 1982.

Berlin,
  Destruction
  of Slavery
Ira Berlin et al., eds. *Freedom: A Documentary History of Emancipation, 1861–1867, Selected from the Holdings of the National Archives of the United States*. Ser. 1, vol. 1, *The Destruction of Slavery*. New York, 1985.

Brewer
James H. Brewer. *The Confederate Negro: Virginia's Craftsmen and Military Laborers, 1861–1865*. Durham, N.C., 1969.

*Code of
  Virginia*
The Code of Virginia. 2d ed. Including Legislation to the Year 1860. Richmond: Ritchie, Dunnavant & Co., 1860.

*Collected
  Works of
  Lincoln*
Lincoln, Abraham. *The Collected Works of Abraham Lincoln*. Ed. Roy P. Basler. 9 vols. New Brunswick, N.J., 1953–55.

CSA
Confederate States of America

CV
Confederate Veteran

Duke
Special Collections Department, William R. Perkins Library, Duke University, Durham, N.C.

Flournoy
H. W. Flournoy. *Calendar of Virginia State Papers and Other Manuscripts from January 1, 1836, to April 15, 1869; Preserved in the Capitol at Richmond*. Vol. 11. Richmond, 1893.

Guild
June Purcell Guild. *Black Laws of Virginia: A Summary of the Legislative Acts of Virginia concerning Negroes from Earliest Times to the Present*. 1936. Reprint, New York, 1969.

Index
The Index: A Weekly Journal of Politics, Literature, and News: Devoted to the Exposition of the Mutual Interests, Political and Commercial, of Great Britain and the Confederate States of America. London, 1861–65.

JNH
Journal of Negro History

Joint
  Committee
U.S. Congress. Joint Committee on Reconstruction. *Report of the Joint Committee on Reconstruction, at the First Session Thirty-ninth Congress*. Pt. 2, Virginia, North Carolina, South Carolina. Washington, D.C.: GPO, 1866.

Keckley
Elizabeth Keckley. *Behind the Scenes. Or, Thirty Years a Slave and Four Years in the White House*. New York: G. W. Carleton, 1868.

LC
Manuscripts Division, Library of Congress, Washington, D.C.

Museum
of the
  Confederacy
Eleanor S. Brockenbrough Library, Museum of the Confederacy, Richmond.

NA
National Archives, Washington, D.C.

Negro in Virginia	Virginia Writers' Project. *The Negro in Virginia.* New York, 1940.
Negro Military Service	The Negro in the Military Service of the United States, 1636–1886. National Archives Microfilms Publication. Washington, D.C., 1963. M-858 (formerly Microcopy T-823). 5 rolls.
OR	U.S. War Department. *The War of the Rebellion: A Compilation of the Official Records of the Union and Confederate Armies.* Ser. 1–4. 128 vols. Washington, D.C.: GPO, 1880–1901.
ORN	U.S. Navy War Records Office. *Official Records of the Union and Confederate Navies in the War of the Rebellion.* Ser. 1–2. 30 vols. Washington, D.C.: GPO, 1894–1922.
RG	Record Group
SHC	Southern Historical Collection, Wilson Library, University of North Carolina at Chapel Hill.
SHSP	*Southern Historical Society Papers.* 52 vols. 1876–1959.
USCT	United States Colored Troops
UVA	Manuscripts Division, Special Collections Department, University of Virginia Library, Charlottesville.
Va. Tech	University Libraries, Special Collections Department, Virginia Polytechnic Institute and State University, Blacksburg.
VHS	Virginia Historical Society, Richmond.
VMHB	*Virginia Magazine of History and Biography*
VSLA	Virginia State Library and Archives, Richmond.
VSU	Johnston Memorial Library, Special Collections and University Archives, Virginia State University, Petersburg.
W&M	Manuscripts and Rare Books Department, Swem Library, College of William and Mary, Williamsburg, Va.
WFCHS	Winchester–Frederick County Historical Society, Winchester, Va.

PREFACE

1. See Vincent Harding, *There is a River: The Black Struggle for Freedom in America* (New York: Vintage Books, 1983), 6 May 1988.

2. W. E. B. Du Bois, "Robert E. Lee," *Crisis* 35 (March 1928): 97.

3. Letters by black Union soldiers and their families are reproduced to good effect in Berlin, *Black Military Experience.*

4. For an insightful discussion, see "Shift to 'African-American' May Prove There is Much in a Name," *Washington Post,* 16 Oct. 1990.

PROLOGUE: SPHINXES WEARING MASKS

1. Oswald Garrison Villard, *John Brown, 1800–1859: A Biography Fifty Years After* (Boston, 1911), 678. Harpers Ferry had been the site of a federal arsenal since 1796. The 1860 Census enumerated 14,535 persons in Jefferson County: 511 free blacks and 3,960 slaves (Joseph C. G. Kennedy, Superintendent of the Census, *Population of the United States in 1860; Compiled From the Original Returns of the Eighth Census* . . . [Washington, D.C.: GPO, 1864], 501, 507, 511; U.S. Congress, Senate, Select Committee on the Harper's Ferry Invasion, *Report of the Select Committee Appointed to Inquire into the Late Invasion and Seizure of*

the Public Property at Harper's Ferry, 36th Cong., 1st ses., Rep. Com. no. 278 (Washington, D.C., 1860), testimony of Dr. John D. Starry, 24. [Hereafter cited as *Select Committee on Harper's Ferry*]). The spelling of Heyward Shepherd's name has caused much historical confusion; I have selected this version for the sake of consistency. He is not listed in the index for the 1850 Virginia census. As a free black, Shepherd filed for and received the permission of the Jefferson County court to reside in the county.

2. Villard, *John Brown*, 684–87; Flournoy, 310–11. Harriet's letters were brought to the attention of state authorities by her Prince William County owner.

3. Villard, *John Brown*, 433, 437, 441; Robert E. Lee's report to Adj. Gen. Samuel Cooper in *Select Committee on Harper's Ferry*, 40–44; *Anglo-African Magazine*, Nov. 1859, 347–60, Dec. 1859, 398–99; Dorothy Sterling, ed., *We Are Your Sisters: Black Women in the Nineteenth Century* (New York, 1984), 455; Benjamin Quarles, *Allies for Freedom: Blacks and John Brown* (New York, 1974), 93–94, 103–5, 182–84.

4. Ralph W. Widener, *Confederate Monuments: Enduring Symbols of the South and the War Between the States* (Washington, D.C., 1982), 303; *Scottsville Register* as quoted in *Liberator*, 30 Dec. 1859, "Mock Hanging of John Brown by Negroes," 206, and 21 Nov. 1863, 187.

5. *Select Committee on Harper's Ferry*, 38; Osborne Perry Anderson, *A Voice from Harper's Ferry: A Narrative of Events at Harper's Ferry; with Incidents Prior and Subsequent to Its Capture by Captain Brown and His Men* (Boston, 1861), 34–62.

6. Willis Augustus Hodges, *Free Man of Color: The Autobiography of Willis Augustus Hodges*, ed. Willard B. Gatewood, Jr. (Knoxville, Tenn., 1982), l–li.

7. Anderson, *A Voice from Harper's Ferry*, 72.

8. *Old John Brown: A Song for Every Southern Man* (1859), Rare Books Division, UVA.

9. Anderson, *A Voice from Harper's Ferry*, 68.

10. Abraham Spengler to his brother, [28 Nov. 1859], Abraham S. Spengler Papers, SHC.

11. *Plan for the Abolition of Slavery / To the Non-Slaveholders of the South* [1860?], UVA.

12. Daniel R. Hundley, *Social Relations in our Southern States* (New York: Henry B. Price, 1860), 19–273; Shields McIlwaine, *The Southern Poor-White from Lubberland to Tobacco Road* (Norman, Okla., 1939), xviii, 4; Kenneth Stampp, *The Peculiar Institution: Slavery in the Ante-bellum South* (New York, 1956), 153; Moncure Daniel Conway, *Testimonies concerning Slavery* (London: Chapman and Hall, 1864), 120–22.

13. Frederic Bancroft, *Slave Trading in the Old South* (New York, 1959), 90, 91, 237, 252, 270, 274, 287, 295, 305, 309, 316, 320–21; Michael Tadman, *Speculators and Slaves: Masters, Traders, and Slaves in the Old South* (Madison, Wis., 1989), 7; Ethan Allen Andrews, *Slavery and the Domestic Slave-Trade in the United States* (Boston: Light and Stearns, 1836), 135–43; William Chambers, *Things As They Are in America* (London and Edinburgh: William and Robert Chambers, 1854), 273–86; *De Bow's Review*, June 1859, 647–57, March 1860, 354; Hector Davis letters to an unidentified person, 13, 20, 31, Jan. 1860, in folder "1840–1862 Slavery," Southside Virginia Family Papers, 550, box 5, UVA.

14. Louis Hughes, *Thirty Years a Slave* (Milwaukee: South Side Printing, 1897; reprint, New York, 1969), 12; Louis R. Harlan, ed., *The Booker T. Washington Papers* (Urbana, Ill., 1972—), 1:3, 5, 11–12; "Negroes of M. M. Bolling Sold at Buckingham Court House, February 1861," Hubard Family Papers, box 16, folder 180, SHC; Chambers, *Things As They Are in America*, 280–81; Keckley, 28–29; "Dear Sir" form letter, 5 Jan. 1861, Dickinson, Hill & Co., Richmond, in Negro Collection: Slavery Division, Duke.

15. G. B. Wallace to Andrew Grinnan, 15 April 1855, Grinnan Family Papers, 49, box 4, UVA; James Jackson to Alfred Dearing, 20 Jan. 1850, Dearing Family Papers, 10565,

UVA; George P. Rawick, ed., *The American Slave: A Composite Autobiography*, vol. 1, ser. 1, *From Sundown to Sunup: The Making of the Black Community* (Westport, Conn., 1972), 88.

16. Hughes, *Thirty Years a Slave*, 11–12; Peter Randolph, *From Slave Cabin to Pulpit* (Boston: J. H. Earle, 1893), 184–86.

17. John S. Wise, *The End of an Era* (Boston: Houghton, Mifflin and Company, 1899), 80–87.

18. Eyre Crowe, *With Thackeray in America* (New York: Charles Scribner's Sons, 1893), 130–36; Chambers, *Things As They Are in America*, 279, 284–85; "Dear Sir" form letter, 28 Dec. 1860, Dickinson, Hill & Co., Richmond, in Negro Collection: Slavery Division, Duke.

19. Richard Swainson Fisher, *A New and Complete Statistical Gazetteer of the United States of America, Founded on and Compiled from Official Federal and State Returns, and the Seventh National Census* (New York: J. H. Colton, 1859), 883–87; Richard Edwards, ed., *Statistical Gazetteer of the States of Virginia and North Carolina* (Richmond, 1856), 67–71; Clement A. Evans, *Confederate Military History* 3 (Atlanta: Confederate Publishing Company, 1899): 7–8.

20. Geographical and topographical discussion drawn from Evans, *Confederate Military History* 3:4–5, 11–12; *De Bow's Review*, March 1860, 354; Sam Bowers Hilliard, *Atlas of Antebellum Southern Agriculture* (Baton Rouge, La., 1984), 6–33; Otis P. Starkey et al., *The Anglo-American Realm*, 2d ed. (New York, 1975), chap. 6; Alison Goodyear Freehling, *Drift toward Dissolution: The Virginia Slavery Debate of 1831–1832* (Baton Rouge, La., 1982), 13–16; Edwards, *Statistical Gazetteer*, 355–61; "Topography of Hampton Roads," *Warrenton Flag of '98*, 6 June 1861; *De Bow's Review*, March 1860, 354; Wilbur Zelinsky, *The Cultural Geography of the United States* (Englewood Cliff, N.J., 1973).

21. U.S. Department of Interior, *Statistics of the United States, (Including Mortality, Property, &c.,) in 1860: Compiled from the Original Returns and Being the Final Exhibit of the Eighth Census, under the Direction of the Secretary of the Interior* (Washington, D.C.: GPO, 1866), 339. Virginia was not the only biracial southern state; South Carolina was 59 percent black and Mississippi, 55 percent black. There were more free blacks in Maryland (84,000) than Virginia. Blacks comprised 37 percent of all Southerners.

22. "History of Slavery in the United States," London *Times*, 4 Jan. 1861; *Code of Virginia*, 508–10; Donald B. Dodd and Wynelle S. Dodd, *Historical Statistics of the South, 1790–1970* (University, Ala., 1973), 58; *American Jubilee*, Feb. 1855, 76–77; Tipton Ray Snavely, *The Taxation of Negroes in Virginia*, Phelps-Stokes Fellowship Papers, no. 3 (Charlottesville, Va., 1916), 10–11; George Washington Carleton, *The Suppressed Book about Slavery!* (New York: Carleton, 1864), 22; *A Southern Document. To the People of Virginia. The Great Issue! Our Relations to It* (Wytheville, Va.: D. A. St. Clair, 1861), 2, 19, 28–29.

23. Kennedy, *Population of the United States in 1860*, 507–8, 518; Luther Porter Jackson, *Free Negro Labor and Property Holding in Virginia, 1830–1860* (New York, 1942), 70.

24. U.S. Department of Interior, *Statistics of the United States in 1860*, 350; Wise, *End of an Era*, 148; Virginius Dabney, *Virginia: The New Dominion* (New York, 1971), 254; "Estate of Philip St. George Cocke, Summary of Property," folder, Feb. 1860, Cocke Family Papers, 640, box 159, UVA; Marshal Hairston, 6th U.S. Census, 1840, Virginia, Henry County, Eastern District of Virginia, 280; Joseph C. Kennedy, Superintendent of the Census, *Agriculture of the United States in 1860; Compiled from the Original Returns of the Eighth Census . . .* (Washington, D.C.: GPO, 1864), 243–45; Stampp, *Peculiar Institution*, 30; *De Bow's Review*, March 1860, 354.

25. *Message of the Governor of Virginia, and Accompanying Documents, 1861: Document 1,*

Biennial Report of the Auditor of Public Records, 1860 and 1861 (Richmond: William F. Ritchie, 1861), 633, 647.

26. New York (State), Court of Appeals, *Report of the Lemmon Slave Case: Containing Points and Arguments of Counsel on Both Sides, and Opinions of All the Judges* (New York: Horace Greeley, 1860), 3–4; *New York Times*, Nov. 8, 18, 1852. Louis Napoleon signed the petition with his mark.

27. *Report of the Lemmon Slave Case*, 4; *New York Times*, 9 Nov. 1852.

28. *Report of the Lemmon Slave Case*, 4–6; *New York Times*, 2 Oct., 10, 15, 19, 20, 22, 27 Nov., 24 Dec. 1852.

29. *Report of the Lemmon Slave Case*, 12–15, 51, 127–28; *New York Times*, 3, 6 Oct., 11 Dec. 1852, 8 Dec. 1857, 25, 26, 30 Jan., 26, 30 April 1860; Alfred H. Kelley and Winfred A. Harbinson, *American Constitution: Its Origins and Development*, 4th ed. (New York, 1970), 385, 389.

30. Harrison Berry, *Slavery and Abolitionism, as Viewed by a Georgia Slave* (Atlanta: M. Lynch, 1861), 7, 10, 24–25, 28, 32–35, 37–46.

31. *New Star* (Christianburg), 16 Feb. 1861.

32. *Alexandria Gazette and Virginia Advertiser*, 14 Jan. 1860.

33. Henry Shanks, *The Secession Movement in Virginia, 1847–1861* (Richmond, 1934), 116–17; Keckley, 66–73.

34. Richmond *Examiner* quoted in *Spirit of the South towards Northern Freedmen and Soldiers Defending the American Flag against Traitors of the Deepest Dye* (Boston: R. F. Wallcut, 1861), 12; *A Southern Document*, 2, 19, 28–29.

35. G. D. Gray, Culpepper Court House, to Angus R. Blakey, 31 Dec. 1860, Angus R. Blakey Papers, Duke; Pittsylvania County Resolutions [1861], 6458, UVA; Frank Moore, comp. and ed., *Rebel Rhymes and Rhapsodies* (New York: George P. Putnam, 1864), 13–17.

36. Charlottesville *Review* of 15 March 1861 as quoted in the Winchester *Republican*, 22 March 1861; *Warrenton Flag of '98*, 9 May 1861; *OR*, ser. 4, 3:803–16; Pegram to Charles Ellis, 18 April 1861, Munford-Ellis Family Papers, Duke; John Thomas Lewis Preston Diary, 20 Aug. 1861, LC.

37. Arthur James Lyon Fremantle, *Three Months in the Southern States, April–June, 1863* (New York: J. Bradbury, 1864), 210; Moore, *Rebel Rhymes*, 38–40; Milton White to his brother, 20 Oct. 1861, "1860–1910 Correspondence of the White Family," White Family Papers, 9372-B, box 2, UVA; N. Harnson to William B. Randolph, 28 Sept. 1862, William B. Randolph Papers, LC.

38. The text of the proposed 1861 constitution appeared in several of the state's leading newspapers, including the Petersburg *Daily Express* of 3 Jan. 1862, and copies were sent to county clerks and courts before a voter referendum in March 1862. It was rejected by a margin of less than 680 votes (Clement Eaton, *A History of the Southern Confederacy* [New York, 1954], 45–46).

39. Ollinger Crenshaw, *The Slave States in the Presidential Election of 1860* (Baltimore, 1945), 147; Charles H. Ambler, *Francis H. Pierpont: Union Governor of Virginia and Father of West Virginia* (Chapel Hill, N.C., 1937), 35, 38, 40–41, 68–69; David H. Strother to Francis Pierpont, 25 June 1862; Flournoy, 381.

40. Ambler, *Francis H. Pierpont*, 41–42, 169–72, 202–5, 213–18; J. G. Randall and David Herbert Donald, *The Civil War and Reconstruction*, 2d ed., rev. (Lexington, Mass., 1969), 237–42; letter of B. F. Caldwell, 6 Sept. 1862, and of 2d Lt. John E. Parkinson, 20 Oct. 1862, Flournoy, 390–92, 397.

41. C. M. Hubbard to John Letcher, Governor of Virginia, 26 April 1861, *OR*, ser. 1,

5:47; Virginia State Convention of 1861, *Ordinances Adopted by the Convention of Virginia, at the Adjourned Session, in June and July, 1861* (Richmond: W. M. Elliot, 1861), 47–48.

42. E. N. Elliot, *Cotton is King, and Proslavery Arguments* (Augusta, Ga.: Pritchard, Abbot & Loomis, 1860), 639–40; John Hawkins Simpson, *Horrors of the Virginia Slave Trade and of the Slave-Rearing Plantations. The True Story of Dinah, an Escaped Virginia Slave, on Whose Body Are Eleven Scars Left by Her Master, Her Own Father . . .* (London: A. W. Bennett, 1863), 50; Henry L. Swint, ed., *Dear Ones at Home: Letters from Contraband Camps* (Nashville, 1966), 107; *Connecticut Fifth*, the newspaper of the 5th Connecticut Volunteers in occupied Winchester, Va., 23 March 1862; "The Contrabands at Fortress Monroe," *Atlantic Monthly*, Nov. 1861, 637; *American Missionary*, Nov. 1861, 258; Catherine Cooper Hopley, *Life in the South; From the Commencement of the War*, (London: Chapman and Hall, 1863): 1:344–45; Fredric Sherman to father, 22 Sept. 1862, and to mother, 12 Oct. 1862, Fredric Sherman Letters, SHC.

43. N. Wilson, Troy, N.Y., to Eliza Wilson, Rockbridge County, 6 May 1861, Wilson, Whitehead, and Houston Family Papers, 38–490, UVA.

44. Snead to Aunt Peggy, 21 July 1861, Robert Winn Snead Papers, VHS. Blacks habitually and secretly reversed their public behavior and word meanings. If they promised to pray for someone (i.e., "I will pray for you" or "I wish you were in heaven"), especially persons who had wronged them (fellow blacks or white slave owners, overseers, and other authority figures), such prayers instead sought retribution by God against that person in the form of injury, sickness, bad luck, or death (Earl E. Thorpe, *The Mind of the Negro: An Intellectual History of Afro-Americans* [Baton Rouge, La., 1961], 79–82).

45. Ewell to wife, 13, 25 Jan., 5 Feb., 24 March 1861, John S. Ewell Letters, Duke.

46. *Harper's Weekly*, 18 May 1861, 311. This black Jeff Davis was born in July 1861 and is listed in "Register of My Negroes in Nelson," 1858–62, Robert Thurston Hubard Papers, 8708, box 10, UVA.

47. Confederate president Jefferson Davis's inaugural addresses (February 1861 and 1862) contain such phrases as "enjoyment of . . . independence," "government rests on the consent of the governed," "to obtain respect for the rights to which we were entitled," "sense of justice," "time-honored bulwarks of civil and religious liberty," "our traditions of peace and love of justice," "the value of our liberties," "resistance," "just cause," and "consecrated right to constitutional representative government [vindicated] by an appeal to arms" (James D. Richardson, *A Compilation of the Messages and Papers of the Confederacy* 1 [Nashville, 1906]: 32–34, 184–88).

I. HERITAGE OF SERVITUDE

1. Folder, "Omohundro Business Records, Oak Nole Farm Account Book," Silas Omohundro Papers, VSLA.

2. *Negro in Virginia*, 71; Chambers, *Things As They Are in America*, 276, 278; Barbara M. Starke, "A Mini View of the Microenvironment of Slaves and Freed Blacks Living in the Virginia and Maryland Areas from the 17th through the 19th Centuries," *Negro History Bulletin* 41 (Sept.–Oct. 1976): 878–79; Frederick Law Olmsted, *The Cotton Kingdom*, ed. Arthur M. Schlesinger, Sr. (New York, 1984), 37; Thomas and Charles Ellis & Company and Christian & Lathrop advertisements of "Negro Clothing," *Richmond Enquirer*, 28 Oct. 1851; "Prices of Goods & Groceries" section, 1846–63, "Notebook of Farming Advice, Knowledge, Observations, etc., Kept by R. T. Hubard for the Education of His Sons," 1846–1863, Robert Thurston Hubard Papers, 8708, box 10, UVA.

3. Randolph, *Slave Cabin to Pulpit*, 178–79; Richard Toler interview, "Former Slave Reflects," Cincinnati *Enquirer*, 31 Dec. 1938.

4. Keckley, 20; Booker T. Washington, *The Story of My Life and Work* (Toronto, 1900), 34–35.

5. Theodore Weld, *American Slavery As It Is* (New York: American Anti-Slavery Society, 1839), 101; Isaetta R. Hubard to her mother, 23 May 1862, Hubard-Randolph Family Papers, 4717, box 2, UVA.

6. Francis T. Glasgow, Fincastle, to Joseph Reid Anderson, 11 March 1863, bound volume "Negroes and Rations at Catawba," Tredegar Iron Company Records, box 31, VSLA; ledger (1780–84, 1864–65) of an unidentified King and Queen County woman, Joseph Westmore Papers, Duke; ——, Gloucester County, to his nephew, Col. Christopher Lumpkins, 10 June 1863, William Patterson Smith Papers, box 10, Duke; Colin Clarke to Maxwell Clarke, 20 Sept. 1863, folder 20, Maxwell Troax Clarke Papers, SHC.

7. Thomas Hughes, *A Boy's Experiences in the Civil War, 1860–1865* (Baltimore, 1904), 46–55; Holland Nimmons McTyeire, *Duties of Masters to Servants* (1851; reprint, Freeport, N.Y., 1971), 9–28, 35–39; *Code of Virginia*, 510.

8. *Richmond Enquirer*, 14 Nov. 1862; *Harper's Weekly*, 31 Jan. 1863; *Richmond Times*, 25 April 1865.

9. Stuart Berg Flexner, *I Hear America Talking* (New York, 1976), 32–33.

10. Keckley, 167–69.

11. Reay Tannahill, *Food in History* (New York, 1973), 300; "Rules & Regulations for Island Plantation," Eppes Family Papers, VHS; Randolph, *Slave Cabin to Pulpit*, 178–79.

12. Randolph, *Slave Cabin to Pulpit*, 157; [Richard Eppes, Charles City County], "Code for Laws for Island Plantation," Eppes Family Papers, VHS; William Wells Brown, *My Southern Home: or, The South and Its People*, 3d ed. (Boston: A. G. Brown, 1882), 210.

13. Sam Bowers Hilliard, "Hog Meat and Cornpone: Foodways in the Antebellum South," in *Material Life in America, 1600–1860*, ed. Robert Blair St. George (Boston, 1988), 325–28.

14. William H. Wiggins, Jr., *O Freedom!: Afro-American Emancipation Celebrations* (Knoxville, Tenn., 1987), 46; Eileen Southern, *The Music of Black Americans: A History*, 2d ed. (New York, 1983), 177; Arthur R. Ashe, Jr., *A Hard Road to Glory: A History of the African-American Athlete, 1619–1918* (New York, 1988), 10.

15. Ashe, *Hard Road to Glory*, 10; Charles L. Perdue, Jr., Thomas E. Barden, and Robert K. Phillips, *Weevils in the Wheat: Interviews with Virginia Ex-Slaves* (Charlottesville, Va., 1976), 155.

16. C. Vann Woodward, *Mary Chesnut's Civil War* (New Haven, 1981), 458; Lt. J. V. Hadley to Miss Pett Barbour, 2 Jan. 1863, Lucian Barbour Papers, LC; Southern, *Music of Black Americans*, 188.

17. Arnold Shaw, *Black Popular Music in America* (New York, 1986), 9–13; William Francis Allen, Charles Pickford, and Lucy Garrison McKim, comps. and eds., *Slave Songs of the United States* (New York: A. Simpson, 1867), 458–70.

18. Allen, *Slave Songs*, 70, 72.

19. Folder 9, "Slave Life," W.P.A. Folklore, 1547, box 1, UVA.

20. George L. Severs Account Book, 289, WFCHS.

21. Leslie J. Pollard, "Aging and Slavery: A Gerontological Perspective," *JNH* 66 (Fall 1981): 232–33; Department of Interior, *Statistics of the United States in 1860*, 514–15; Account Book, 1858–59, Watson Family Papers, 530, box 5, UVA.

22. Weld, *American Slavery*, 133; Simpson, *Horrors of the Virginia Slave Trade*, 50–51;

Carleton, *Suppressed Book about Slavery;* Guild, 82, 166; Lynchburg *Daily Republican,* 17 Dec. 1862.

23. Ulrich Bonnell Phillips, *Life and Labor in the Old South* (Boston, 1929), 196–205; Weld, *American Slavery,* 105; "Rules & Regulations for Island Plantation," Eppes Family Papers, VHS.

24. Austin Steward, *Twenty-two Years a Slave, and Forty Years a Freeman; Embracing a Correspondence of Several Years, While Resident of Wilberforce Colony, London, Canada West* (Rochester, N.Y.: William Alling, 1857), 15–16; A Southern Planter, *Plantation and Farm Instruction, Regulation, Record, Inventory and Account Book* (Richmond: J. W. Randolph, 1852), 10.

25. John Lovell, Jr., *Black Song: The Forge and the Flame* (New York, 1972), 185–86; Maria Gordon Pryor Rice Reminiscences, 1, VHS; A Southern Planter, *Plantation and Farm Instruction,* 10.

26. [Richard Eppes, Charles City County], "Code of Laws for Island Plantation," Eppes Family Papers, VHS.

27. Frederick's Hall Plantation Books, vol. 19, SHC.

28. Account Book, 1858–59, Watson Family Papers, 530, box 5, UVA; Olmsted, *Cotton Kingdom,* 186, 191, 494; Keckley, 18–21.

29. Perdue, *Weevils in the Wheat,* 281, 322.

30. Francis Colburn Adams, *A Troopers Adventures in the War for the Union* (New York: Hurst, n.d.), 425–26.

31. Contract, 15 Nov. 1862, Saunders Family Papers, VSLA.

32. "1846–1863, Notebook of Farming Advice, Knowledge, Observations, etc., Kept by R. T. Hubard for the Education of His Sons" (overseers section), 5–8, Robert Thurston Hubard Papers, 8708, box 10, UVA.

33. [Richard Eppes, Charles City County], "Code of Laws for Island Plantation: Laws for the Foreman or Driver and Privileges of the Foreman and the Headplougher," Eppes Family Papers, VHS.

34. CSA [Congress], *An Act to Diminish the Number of Exemptions and Details (An Amendment to the Conscription Act Approved Feb. 17, 1864)* (Richmond, 1864).

35. Charles C. Wellford to Gen. D. Ruggles, 24 May 1861, 1663-A, UVA; Berlin, *Destruction of Slavery,* 732.

36. Petition of John Hartwell Cocke to Jefferson Davis, 1863, box 170, and Cocke to Mr. [Albert] Wood, 27 Jan. 1864, box 171, 640, Cocke Family Papers, UVA.

37. Robert Ritchie, Brandon, to George Harrison, 21 Oct. 1861, Ritchie-Harrison Family Papers, W&M; Edmund Ruffin, *The Diary of Edmund Ruffin,* vol. 3, *A Dream Shattered, June 1863–June 1865,* ed. William Kauffman Scarborough (Baton Rouge, La., 1989), entries for 14 Dec. 1863, 12 April, 4 June 1864, 141–42, 394, 449.

38. Swint, *Dear Ones at Home,* 78–79; Richmond *Sentinel,* 30 May 1863; Mrs. Nancy Williams interview, 18 May 1937, p. 2, Ex-Slave Interviews, 3462, UVA.

39. William Gordon, Diary 4, 3 March 1863, Papers of the Gordon Family, 9553, UVA.

40. Beverly B. Munford, *Virginia's Attitude toward Slavery and Secession* (New York, 1909), 142–43; Weld, *American Slavery,* 182–83; Olmsted, *Cotton Kingdom,* 45–47; W. E. B. Du Bois, *Black Reconstruction: An Essay of the Part Which Black Folk Played in the Attempt to Reconstruct Democracy in America, 1638–1870* (New York, 1935), 42–44; Pulliam & Company notice, 15 Jan. 1860, Negro Collection: Slavery Division, Duke; *Index,* 20 Nov. 1863, 58. For a discussion of slave-breeding records, see Charles L. Blockson, *Black Genealogy* (Englewood Cliffs, N.J., 1977), 72–74.

41. *Charlottesville Advocate*, 16 March 1860.

42. Bancroft, *Slave Trading in the Old South*, 91–93; Conway, *Testimonies concerning Slavery*, 19–26; James Barber, *Alexandria in the Civil War* (Lynchburg, Va., 1988), 26, 63; Josiah to Phebe, 6 Oct. 1862, Clifton Waller Barrett Papers, 6526-E, UVA.

43. Simpson, *Horrors of the Virginia Slave Trade*, 4, 59; Carleton, *Suppressed Book about Slavery*, 154; *Acts of the General Assembly . . . , passed in 1861–62, in the Eighty-seventh Year of the Commonwealth* (Richmond: William F. Ritchie, 1862), 15, 17–19; *Acts of the General Assembly . . . , Passed at Adjourned Session, 1863, in the Eighty-seventh year of the Commonwealth* (Richmond: William F. Ritchie, 1863), 18, 21.

44. Lt. George Garrett to Dickinson & Hill, 8 Oct. 1861, an unidentified Henrico County owner to same, 3 Feb. 1862, Dr. J. H. Burnett to E. H. Stokes, 23 July 1862, Papers of the Chase Family, boxes 5, 6, LC; Hector Davis to Angus R. Blakey, 20 March 1862, Angus R. Blakey Papers, Duke. Davis's firm was succeeded by Lee & James in 1862–63 ("City Intelligence" column, "The Negro Market," *Richmond Examiner*, 28 Feb. 1863).

45. George S. Morris and Susan L. Foutz, *Lynchburg in the Civil War* (Lynchburg, Va., 1984), 26; Lynchburg *Daily Republican*, 17 Dec. 1862; *Liberator*, 1 April 1864, 55. "We learn from the Richmond papers that the prices of negroes in that city have had an upward tendency ever since the inauguration of Lincoln"(*Alexandria Gazette*, 14 March 1861).

46. Phillips, *Life and Labor*, 175–77, 181, 186–87; Bell Irwin Wiley, *Southern Negroes, 1861–1865* (New Haven, 1938), 86–89; Randolph B. Campbell, *An Empire for Slavery: The Peculiar Institution in Texas, 1821–1865* (Baton Rouge, La., 1989), 242–43; Lynchburg *Daily Republican*, 17 Dec. 1862.

47. Silas & R. H. Omohundro Business Ledger, 4122, UVA; folder, Omohundro Business Records, "Money Paid Out and Received, No. 1, 1851–1877," Omohundro Papers, VSLA.

48. Receipt dated 20 Jan. 1863, Graham Family Papers, 38–106, box 3, UVA; bill of sale, 16 Jan. 1863, "Letters to Mrs. Thornton," John T. Thornton Papers, 4021, UVA; Mrs. B. L. Blankenship to E. H. Stokes, 29 March 1863, Correspondence of R. H. Dickinson & Brother, Slavery in the United States Collection, box 2, folder 1, American Antiquarian Society, Worcester, Mass.

49. "Inventory of Negroes upon Pea Hill Plantation Taken from 1st Jan. 1863," Cocke Family Papers, 640, UVA.

50. Valuation of Confederate Slaves, 15 Feb. 1864, 10938, UVA.

51. Bettie to Nellie, 10 Jan. 1864, Edgehill School letter, 38–421, UVA; Wiley, *Southern Negroes*, 94; John B. Jones, *A Rebel War Clerk's Diary*, ed. Earl Schenck Miers (New York, 1961), 522 (entry of 22 March 1865); *Richmond Daily Dispatch*, 24 July 1862.

52. Valuation of Confederate Slaves, 15 Feb. 1864, 10938, UVA.

53. "Last Will and Testament of J. H. Cocke," box 166, Skipwith to Cocke, 30 May 1861, box 164, 5 Aug. 1861, box 165, Cocke Family Papers, 640, UVA.

54. Skipwith to Cocke, 30 May 1862, box 167, 28 March 1864, box 171, ibid.

55. Order of Capt. Charles B. Atchinson, 13 May 1865, box 172, Skipwith to Cocke, 7 Dec. 1865, box 173, ibid.

56. *Rockingham Register and Advertiser*, 6 Sept. 1861; *Fredericksburg News*, 2 Aug. 1861; Petersburg *Daily Express*, 9 Nov. 1861; *Staunton Spectator*, 31 Dec. 1861; *Lexington Gazette*, 15 July, 1864; Petersburg *Daily Express*, 23 July 1864; Richardson ad, *Richmond Whig*, 21 Dec. 1864. Petersburg and Richmond slave brokers actively solicited of this type of business; slave owners offered slaves for hire in consignments of thirty or more, and sometimes several combined their slaves and commissioned hiring agents or slave brokers.

See advertisements of B. A. Cooke (Richmond) and William Gee, Thomas Temple, Alexander and James Donnan, and John Dodson (Petersburg) in *Richmond Enquirer,* 24 Dec. 1861, and Petersburg *Daily Express,* 28 Dec. 1861.

57. Slave hire bond signed "Varina Davis for Jefferson Davis," 1 Jan. 1865, Jefferson Davis Collection, Museum of the Confederacy; Joseph R. Anderson, Richmond, to Angus R. Blakey, 9 April 1864, Angus R. Blakey Papers, Duke.

58. "Slave hiring contracts," Financial Records folder, Black History Collection, box 1, LC; Petersburg *Daily Express,* 28 Dec. 1861; bonds for slave hires, 1 Jan. 1861 and 1 Jan. 1863, Boatwright Family Papers, VHS; letter, 31 Jan. 1865, Grinnan Family Papers, 49, box 4, UVA.

59. Richmond *Sentinel,* 31 Dec. 1863; *Staunton Spectator,* 8 April 1862; letter, 1 Jan. 1863, Grinnan Family Papers, 49, box 4, UVA; "List of Negroes at Mt. Torry Furnace, Feby. 1st 1864" in bound volume "Negroes and Rations at Catawba," Tredegar Iron Company Records, box 31, VSLA.

60. Charles Tibbs to Andrew Grinnan, 10 April 1861, Grinnan Family Papers, 49, box 4, UVA.

61. John J. Fry to William D. Cabell, 5 Dec. 1863, William D. Cabell Papers, 276, box 2, UVA; "List of Hands at Glenwood Furnace, 1863," Tredegar Iron Company Records, bound volume "Negroes and Rations at Catawba," box 31, VSLA.

62. William T. Mitchell folder, Southside Virginia Family Papers, 550, box 3, UVA; folder "1855–1863, Business and Legal Papers," bound volume listing slaves, 1861–64, and slave births, 1853–65, Morris Family Papers, 38–79, box 9, UVA.

63. OR, ser. 4, 3:798; Magruder to Cooper, 28 Dec. 1861, OR, ser. 1, 4:716. The commonwealth of Virginia's ownership of slaves is recorded in the 8th U.S. Census, 1860, Slave Schedules, Richmond, Henrico County, 16 June 1860, 61.

64. James M. Taylor file, vouchers for hire of slave Isaac, June 1863–June 1864, Confederate Papers Relating to Citizens or Business Firms, M346, roll 1011 (microfilm), RG 109, War Department Collection of Confederate Records, NA. I am grateful to Michael Musick of the National Archives for information about this collection, and to my wife, Lorraine Frye Jordan, for bringing Isaac's case to my attention during my research visit.

65. E. W. Massey file, miscellaneous vouchers for boarding for blacks (hired and conscripted), 3 July 1863–16 Jan. 1864, Confederate Papers Relating to Citizens or Business Firms, M346, roll 1011 (microfilm), RG 109, NA.

66. Folder, "1840–1862 Slavery," Southside Virginia Family Papers, 550, box 5, UVA.

67. *Daily Lynchburg Virginia,* 1 Jan. 1863.

68. E. C. Waddell to Dear Sir, 29 Dec. 1864, A. J. Rike to Mrs. Majette, 2 Feb. 1865, Waddell to Majette, 4 March 1865, Majette Family Papers, VHS.

2. THE COLOR OF SWEAT

1. Robert S. Starobin, *Industrial Slavery in the Old South* (New York, 1970), 191–214; Richard C. Wade, *Slavery in the Cities: The South, 1820–1860* (New York, 1964), 243–81; Stampp, *Peculiar Institution,* 426–27.

2. Barbara J. Fields, *Slavery and Freedom on the Middle Ground: Maryland during the Nineteenth Century* (New Haven, 1985), 54–55; Starobin, *Industrial Slavery,* 153–63; Bruce Laurie, *Artisans into Workers: Labor in Nineteenth-Century America* (New York, 1989), 43; Thomas Putnam Fenner, *Cabin and Plantation Songs: As Sung by the Hampton Students* (New York: G. P. Putnam's, 1877), 218, 200–201; James E. Newton and Ronald L. Lewis,

eds., *The Other Slaves: Mechanics, Artisans, and Craftsmen* (Boston, 1978), 243–45; Wade, *Slavery in the Cities*, 30–37.

3. *Acts of the General Assembly, 1861–2*, 103; *Acts of the General Assembly . . . Passed at Called Session, 1863, in the Eighty-eighth Year of the Commonwealth* (Richmond: William F. Ritchie, 1863), 25; *Acts of the General Assembly Passed at Session of 1863–4, in the Eighty-eighth Year of the Commonwealth* (Richmond: William F. Ritchie, 1864), 54; Ronald L. Lewis, *Coal, Iron, and Slaves: Industrial Slavery in Maryland and Virginia, 1715–1865* (Westport, Conn., 1979), 234; F. N. Boney, *John Letcher of Virginia: The Story of Virginia's Civil War Governor* (University, Ala., 1966), 197.

4. Lynchburg *Daily Republican*, 5 Aug. 1861; *Daily Lynchburg Virginian*, 15 May 1862; Lewis, *Coal, Iron, and Slaves*, 71–73, 116, 118; Richmond *Daily Examiner*, 27 Oct. 1864.

5. *Richmond Examiner*, 8 Aug. 1864. A Confederate sabotage explosion three days later at General Grant's City Point supply depot killed an undetermined number of Afro-Virginian workmen.

6. *Richmond Examiner*, 5 Aug. 1864; Richmond *Daily Dispatch*, 5 Aug. 1864.

7. Charles Dew, *Ironmaker to the Confederacy: Joseph R. Anderson and the Tredegar Iron Works* (New Haven, 1966), 26–27, 92, 250, 262–63; Brewer, 57, 62, 64; Lewis, *Coal, Iron, and Slaves*, 34, 195–96; Joseph Reid Anderson ownership of slaves recorded by the 8th U.S. Census, 1860, Slave Schedules, Richmond, Henrico County, Virginia, 15 Aug. 1860, 74–75; Wade, *Slavery in the Cities*, 71, 139; Francis T. Glasgow to Joseph Reid Anderson, 22 Jan. 1863, bound volume "Negroes and Rations at Catawba," box 31, VSLA; Eli N. Evans, *Judah P. Benjamin: The Jewish Confederate* (New York, 1988), 246.

8. Francis T. Glasgow to Joseph Reid Anderson, 29 May 1863, and "List of Negroes at Catawba Furnace, 1863," bound volume "Negroes and Rations at Catawba," Tredegar Iron Company Records, box 31, VSLA; Brewer, 66–67; "List of Rations, etc., at Catawba Furnace, T. K. Menefee, Manager, Feb. 23, 1864," 2, Tredegar Iron Company Records, box 31, VSLA; Newton and Lewis, *Other Slaves*, 92–93; Wiley, *Southern Negroes*, 60; *Message of the Governor of Virginia, and Accompanying Documents, 1863: Document 9, Annual Report of the Board of Directors of the Penitentiary Institution, Year Ending September 30, 1863* (Richmond: William F. Ritchie, 1863), 19; *Journal of the House of Delegates of the State of Virginia, for the Session of 1863–64: Document No. 1, Messages* [of the governor] (Richmond: William F. Ritchie, 1863), xviii.

9. Contract signed by John W. Robinson, 3 April 1862, account of David Graham with William ——, 1863, promissory note between Robinson and John Cork, 2 April 1862, Graham Family Papers, 38–106, box 3, UVA.

10. Weaver-Brady Iron Works & Grist Mill Papers, ledger no. 10, "Journal, W. W., Buffalo Forge, 1859 June 1–1866 Sept. 29," 172, 223, 186, 304, Weaver-Brady Papers, 38–98, UVA; "Descriptive List of Negroes at Buffalo Forge," William Weaver Papers, Duke; Wiley, *Southern Negroes*, 117. Virginia authorities were careful not to offer free blacks more than $11 a month, the same wage paid to soldiers. Eventually, hired slaves were paid $16–20 monthly by the government due to competition from civilian firms. Free blacks earned higher wages than white soldiers after 1862 (Brewer, 8, 146, 159).

11. Gov. John Letcher, 7 Dec. 1863, *Journal of the House of Delegates, 1863–64: Document No. 1, Message* [of the governor], xiii; Brewer, 79–94; B. G. Brown to his brother, 14 Dec. 1861, Correspondence of A. D. and B. G. Brown, 371, Albemarle County Historical Society (acc. no. 3513 at UVA); Richmond *Sentinel*, 8 July 1863.

12. Starobin, *Industrial Slavery*, 25; Ella Lonn, *Salt as a Factor in the Confederacy* (New York, 1933), 123, 131, 135, 138–40; *Harper's Weekly*, 14 Jan. 1865, 22; Brewer, 45–48; Col.

I. M. St. John to CSA Secretary of War James A. Seddon, 22 Nov. 1864, Letters Received by the Confederate Secretary of War, 1861–65, roll 151, frame 68, NA (microfilm).

13. Brewer, 75–78; Minutes, 9 Dec. 1861, 27 Oct. 1862, 23 Oct. 1865, James River and Kanawha Canal Company, Minute Book of the Annual Stockholders Meetings, 10421–A, UVA.

14. "Weekly Statements of Receipts & Expenditures of Richmond *Examiner*" folder, 1862–65, Daniel-Moncure MSS, 4802, UVA.

15. Wyndham B. Blanton, *Medicine in Virginia in the Nineteenth Century* (Richmond, 1933), 309; Ervin L. Jordan, Jr., *Charlottesville and the University of Virginia in the Civil War* (Lynchburg, Va., 1988), 46, 55, 117–18; Brewer, 98, 102, 125, 127.

16. *Staunton Vindicator,* 6 Jan. 1865; *Richmond Dispatch,* 9 Dec. 1864; Lynchburg *Daily Republican,* 3 May 1862; Norman Dain, *Disordered Minds: The First Century of Eastern State Hospital in Williamsburg, Virginia, 1766–1866* (Williamsburg, Va., 1971), 175–77, 184–86.

17. *Message of the Governor of Virginia, 1863: Document 11, Report of the Dean of the Faculty of the Medical College of Virginia,* 10; Berlin, *Destruction of Slavery,* 726–28.

18. Berlin, *Destruction of Slavery,* 703; Brewer, 106; *OR,* ser. 4, 3:1193; Maj. Henry C. Scott to Col. Shipp, 16 March 1865, Confederate Information Index, Slaves, entry 453, RG 109, NA; *American Missionary,* July 1864, 173.

19. List of black vaccinations on inside back endpaper, 1859–63, Weaver-Brady Iron Works & Grist Mill Papers, ledger no. 10, "Journal, W. W., Buffalo Forge, 1859 June 1–1866 Sept. 29," Weaver-Brady Papers, 38–98, UVA; D. Graham & Son Account with [Dr.] R. W. Sanders, 1858–62 folder, Graham Family Papers, 38–106, box 3, UVA.

20. W. W. Rex to "Dear Mr. Brady," 22 March 1862, Weaver-Brady Iron Works & Grist Mill Papers, box 1, and David Brady to James Stewart, 7 July 1864, item 19, Buffalo Forge Letter Book, 1860 Nov. 3–1865 March 22, Weaver-Brady Papers, 38–98, UVA; *Staunton Spectator,* 26 May 1863; Lexington *Gazette,* 5 March 1863; Francis T. Glasgow to Joseph Reid Anderson, 25 Jan. 1863, bound volume "Negroes and Rations at Catawba," Tredegar Iron Company Records, box 31, VSLA.

21. David Brady to James Stewart, 7 July 1864, Weaver-Brady Iron Works & Grist Mill Papers, item 19, Buffalo Forge Letter Book, 1860 Nov. 3–1865 March 22, Weaver-Brady Papers, 38–98; UVA; Lynchburg *Daily Republican,* 21 Sept. 1864; *Richmond Dispatch,* 9 Dec. 1864; William M. E. Rachal, "The Occupation of Richmond, April 1865: The Memorandum of Events of Colonel Christopher Q. Tompkins," *VMHB* 73 (1965): 189–93.

22. *New York Daily Tribune,* 27 June 1861.

23. Brewer, 18–30; Bernard Nelson, "Confederate Slave Impressment Legislation," *JNH* 31 (Oct. 1946): 393, 395, 408. At Camp Winder a hired slave named Marshal, employed as a bread carrier, earned $25 a month for his owner ("Report of Persons Hired and Employed at Camp Winder during the Month of Jan. 1863 by Capt. John Knox, Jr.," MS 5120, entry 183, RG 109, NA).

24. Wilson to sister, 8 May 1861, James Peter Wilson Papers, 490, box 4, UVA; Yorktown Defences, New Kent County, for Oct. & Dec. 1861, Slave Roll no. 1553, entry 57, RG 109, NA; Berlin, *Destruction of Slavery,* 684–85; *National Anti-Slavery Standard,* 4, 25, May 1861.

25. Louis H. Manarin, ed., *Richmond at War: The Minutes of the City Council, 1861–1865,* Richmond Civil War Centennial Committee, Official Publication no. 17 (Chapel Hill, N.C., 1966), 63; Mayor Joseph Mayo's proclamation, 31 Dec. 1863, Richmond *Whig,* 1 Jan. 1864; Perdue, *Weevils in the Wheat,* 325.

26. Berlin, *Destruction of Slavery*, 686, 688, 745–46; John Tyler and Hill Carter to the Secretary of War, 26 Aug. 1861, J. Bankhead Magruder to Gen. S. Cooper, 20 Sept. 1861, and Magruder proclamation, 7 Sept. 1861, D. Leadbetter to Magruder, 9 Nov. 1861, *OR*, ser. 1, 4:636, 654, 697; William M. Robinson, Jr., "The Confederate Engineers," *Military Engineer* 22 (1930): 416.

27. Statement on behalf of Jason B. Douglass of Albermarle County signed by his General Assembly representatives Benjamin H. Magruder (House of Delegates) and William D. Hart (Virginia Senate), 20 Feb. 1863, in "1860–1869 Legal Documents" folder, Jason Douglass Papers, 702, box 2, UVA; Thomas Garland affidavit, 22 Dec. 1862, Thomas Walker to Capt. K. Johns, 23 Dec. 1862, Ira Garrett, Albemarle County court clerk, court order to Garland, 6 Jan. 1863, Garland to Magruder, 7 Jan. 1863, Magruder and Hart to the Secretary of War, 10 Jan. 1863, Letters Received, Confederate Secretary of War (M437), file M46 (WD), 1863, NA; *Acts of the General Assembly, 1863–4*, 87.

28. Maj. Gen. John Bankhead Magruder, General Orders no. 154, Yorktown, 1 March 1862, Negro Military Service, roll 1, frame 746; Charles Harris Wesley, *The Collapse of the Confederacy* (Washington, D.C., 1937), 147; *Douglass' Monthly*, Feb. 1862, 605; *Acts of the General Assembly of the State of Virginia, Passed at Called Session, 1862, in the Eighty-seventh Year of the Commonwealth* (Richmond: William F. Ritchie, 1862), 6–8.

29. *Acts of the General Assembly, Called Session, 1862*; Flournoy, 224–25; *OR*, ser. 4, 2:426–30.

30. Valuation documents from UVA MS collections: 29 Oct. 1864 (slaves Andrew, Spencer, and Tarleton), box 168, 28 July 1864 (slaves Ben, Carter, Willis), box 171, Cocke Family Papers, 640; "1860–1869 Business Papers" folder and receipts signed by F. Lamb, 23 Sept. 1863 (in folder "1863 Letters re Confederacy), William D. Cabell Papers, 276, box 2; 24 Oct. (slaves Charles, Peter, Harrison) and 9 Nov. 1864 (slave Gil Bass), Papers of Samuel Pannill Wilson, 10721, box 2; 24 Oct. (slave Henry), 9 and 11 Nov. 1864 (slaves Reuben and Wiley), "1863–1865 Confederate Papers of Dr. George Clements," Pocket Plantation Papers, 2027, box 9; discharge & pass to John, slave of J. W. Robinson, 38-436-B, UVA.

31. Rembert W. Patrick, ed., *Opinions of the Confederate Attorneys General* (Buffalo, 1950), 51–53; Brewer, 143–44, 151; J. F. Gilmer, Colonel of Engineers and Chief of Bureau, to James A. Seddon, Secretary of War, 4 March 1863, *OR*, ser. 1, 51: pt. 2, 684.

32. *Acts of the General Assembly, Adjourned Session, 1863*, 42–46; *Acts of the General Assembly, Called Session, 1863*, 4–6; Robert Thurston Hubard, Journal of Annual Receipts and Disbursement, 3 Nov. 1862, 27 Jan. 1863, Hubard Family Papers, 8039, box 24, UVA.

33. List of slaves of Rockbridge drafted for the defenses of Richmond, 22 Sept. 1863, and [12 Sept.] 1863 "List of Slaves in Rockbridge County," Cocke Family Papers, 640, box 170, UVA; "The Rockbridge Negroes on the Fortifications," Lexington *Gazette*, 10 Feb. 1863.

34. Wesley, *Collapse of the Confederacy*, 155; *Message of the Governor of Virginia, 1863, and Accompanying Documents: Documents 4 and 6, 6, 7, 8, 16–17.*

35. CSA War Department, *General Orders from the Adjutant and Inspector General's Office, Confederate States Army, from January, 1862, to December, 1863, (Both Inclusive) in Two Series. Prepared from Files of Head-Quarters, Department of S.C., Ga., and Fla. with Full Indexes* (Columbia, S.C.: Presses of Evans & Cogswell, 1864), 184–86; (CSA War Department, *General Orders from the Adjutant and Inspector General's Office, Confederate States Army, for the Year 1863, with a Full Index. Compiled and Corrected under Authority of Gen'l S. Cooper,*

by R. H. P. Robinson (Richmond: A. Morris, 1864), 190–92; Robinson, "The Confederate Engineers," 413; Berlin, *Destruction of Slavery*, 727–28, 748–54; *Message of the Governor, 1863 . . . Document 1*, xviii.

36. CSA Congress, House of Representatives, *A Bill to Be Entitled, "An Act to Provide Payment for Slaves Impressed under State Laws, and Lost in the Public Service"* (Richmond, 1864); Patrick, *Opinions of the Confederate Attorneys General*, 300, 345–51, 501–2.

37. *Richmond Daily Examiner*, 6 Oct. 1864.

38. CSA Engineer Department, *Estimate of Five Hundred Thousand Dollars Reqired to Meet the Just Claims Presented, or to Be Presented Hereafter, for the Loss of Slaves Who Have Been Impressed in the State of Virginia* (Richmond, 1864); James M. Matthews, ed., *The Statutes at Large of the Provisional Government of the Confederate States of America* (Richmond: R. M. Smith, 1864), 202; Gilmer to James A. Seddon, 27 Oct., *OR*, ser. 4, 3:778. The attorney general ruled in April 1864 that owners could not file claims for slaves who died from "neglect or improper exposure" while employed by the government as laborers (Patrick, *Opinions of the Confederate Attorneys General*, 437–38).

39. CSA Congress, House of Representatives, *A Bill to Increase the Efficiency of the Army by the Employment of Free Negroes and Slaves in Certain Capacities* (Richmond, 1864); Matthews, *Statutes at Large*, 235–36; *OR*, ser. 4, 3:208. Shortly after the passage of this 17 Feb. act, the adjutant and inspector general's office in Richmond issued General Orders no. 32 to put these provisions into effect; no more than a fifth of an owner's male slaves could be conscripted under this order (Robinson, "The Confederate Engineers," 413).

40. *Journal of the House of Delegates, 1863–64*, 196–97, 205; Brewer, 13; CSA Congress, Senate, *An Act to Amend an Act Entitled "An Act to Increasd the Efficiency of the Army by Employing Free Negroes and Slaves in Certain Capacities," Approved February 17th, 1864*, Senate Bill no. 19, 22 Nov. 1864 (Richmond, 1864), and *A Bill to Provide for the Employment of Free Negroes and Slaves to Work upon Fortifications and Perform Other Labor Connected with the Defence of the Country*, Senate bill no. 129, 6 Dec. 1864 (Richmond, 1864).

41. *OR*, ser. 4, 3:162; Grant to Maj. Gen. H. W. Halleck, 19 July 1864, *OR*, ser. 1, 41: pt. 3, 334.

42. Seddon to Gen. Robert E. Lee, 22 Sept. 1864, Jeremy F. Gilmer, Engineer Bureau, to Gen. Lee, 19 Nov. 1864, Lee to Gilmer, 21 Nov. 1864, Negro Military Service, roll 3, frames 703–4, 712–17; Robinson, "The Confederate Engineers," 416.

43. CSA War Department, *Communication from [the] Secretary of War [relative to the Impressment of Slaves], January 10, 1865* (Richmond, 1865), 3–5.

44. *OR*, ser. 4, 3:798; Walter Lynwood Fleming, *Jefferson Davis, the Negroes, and the Negro Problem* (Baton Rouge, La., 1908), 4–5; CSA War Department, *Communication from [the] Secretary of War [relative to the recent impressment of slaves, by his order, in the state of Virginia]* (Richmond, 1864), 1–4.

45. Robinson, "The Confederate Engineers," 413; Flournoy, 254–56; Virginia, Governor's Requisition, [16 Dec.] 1864 (broadside), Rare Book Division, UVA; Henry County clerk certificate, 4 Jan. 1865, Luther Porter Jackson Papers, box 55, folder "Henry County," VSU; Brewer, 150–51; Jordan, *Charlottesville*, 40.

46. Petition to the Confederate States Department of Engineers from James H. Evans, 1865, James H. Evans Papers, VHS.

47. John A. McKinney and Thomas S. Bocock to Lt. W. T. Fentress, 21 Dec. 1864, and Fentress Report to Commandant, 21 Dec. 1864, Papers of the Thornhill Family and Thomas S. Bocock, 10612, box 7, UVA.

48. Flournoy, 259–61.

49. Ibid., 259–62; Wesley, *Collapse of the Confederacy*, 143; CSA Congress, Senate, *Amendments Proposed by the House of Representatives to the Bill of The Senate (S. 129) to Provide for the Employment of Free Negroes and Slaves to Work upon Labor Fortifications, and Perform Other Labor Connected with the Defence of the Country* (Richmond, 1865); Gov. William Smith to the Honorable Courts of the Counties, Cities, &c., Named in the Annexed Schedule, *OR*, ser. 4, 3:1138–43; William F. Fry, "Report of Negro Slaves Received and Dispersed Of under Circular No. 69, Conscript Office, 1864, Camp Lee, 28th Feb. 1865" and "Report of Negro Slaves Impressed in the State of Virginia under Circular 69, Conscript Office, 1861 to 1st March 1865," Generals, Staff Officers, Compiled Military Records, M-331, RG 109: NA.

50. "Register of Free Negroes Enrolled and Detailed, May 1864–Jan. 1865, Camp Lee," chap. 1, vol. 241, Bureau of Conscription, Virginia, RG 109, NA.

3. MANY THOUSANDS GONE

1. *Central Presbyterian* (Richmond), 3 April 1862; *Charlottesville Advocate*, 16 March 1860.

2. Rawick, *American Slave*, vol. 16, ser. 2, *Kansas, Kentucky, Maryland, Ohio, Virginia, and Tennessee Narratives*, 49; Eric Foner, *Freedom's Lawmakers: A Directory of Black Office-holders during Reconstruction* (New York, 1993), 162–63; William Still, *Underground Rail Road Records*, rev. ed. (Philadelphia, 1886), 81–86.

3. Charles L. Blockson, *The Underground Railroad* (New York, 1987), 96, 127–28; J. H. Eckenrode, "Negroes in Richmond in 1864," *VMHB* 46 (1938): 200.

4. *Harper's Weekly*, 7 June 1862; American Anti-Slavery Society, *The Anti-Slavery History of the John Brown Year: Being the Twenty-Seventh Annual Report of the American Anti-Slavery Society* (New York, 1861), 49; John McCray letter, 28 March 1861, Colson-Hill Family Papers, box 1, and 14 Dec. 1857 application of John Hill, in a temporary box labeled "Colson Documents," VSU; Still, *Underground Rail Road Records*, 189–197; R. J. M. Blackett, *Thomas Morris Chester, Black Civil War Correspondent* (Baton Rouge, La., 1989). The McCray family name is spelled "McCrea" in various documents.

5. George Holbert Tucker, *Norfolk Highlights, 1584–1881* (Norfolk, Va., 1972), 122.

6. John Quincy Adams, *Narrative of the Life of John Quincy Adams When in Slavery and Now as a Freeman* (Harrisburg, Pa.: Seig, 1872), 5–14, 28, 35, 39, 47, 58.

7. Mary A. Livermore, *My Story of the War* (Hartford: A. D. Worthington, 1889), 270–71.

8. George T. Wallace to J. R. Saunders, 1 July 1862, George T. Wallace Papers, Duke.

9. T. Green to Col. William Bailey, n.d. [ca. Aug. 1861], William Bailey Papers, 10586, box 1, UVA; Boaz to her brother [Henry St. George Harris], 9 July 1863, Henry St. George Harris Papers, Duke; Petersburg *Daily Express*, 18 April 1864; Harvey Wish, "Slave Disloyalty under the Confederacy," *JNH* 23 (1938): 447; C. G. Woodson, "My Recollections of Veterans of the Civil War," *Negro History Bulletin* 7 (Feb. 1944): 103–4, 115.

10. White, Lake Farm, Hanover County, to wife Nannie, 5 June 1862, H. B. White Papers, SHC.

11. *Harper's Weekly*, 7 June 1862; Benjamin Quarles, *Black Mosaic* (Amherst, 1988), 89–90; Quarles, *The Negro in the Civil War* (Boston, 1969), 81–82; Wise, *End of an Era*, 210; Craig M. Simpson, *A Good Southerner: The Life of Henry A. Wise of Virginia* (Chapel Hill, N.C., 1985), 223, 314.

12. Joseph Cephas Carroll, *Slave Insurrections in the United States, 1800–1865* (1938: re-

print, Westport, Conn., 1968), 208; Frank Moore, *The Civil War in Song and Story, 1860–1865* (New York: P. F. Collier, 1889), 76; Lynchburg *Daily Republican*, 18 Jan. 1864; Berlin, *Destruction of Slavery*, 77, 181–82; Petersburg *Daily Express*, 9 Nov. 1861; Fields, *Slavery and Freedom*, 115–16.

13. U.S. Department of Interior, *Statistics of the United States in 1860*, 337–38; *Message of the Governor of Virginia, and Accompanying Documents, Document 19, Communication from the Auditor of Public Accounts, Transmitting Statistical Tables, 1864* (Richmond: William F. Ritchie, 1863), 11.

14. *Code of Virginia*, 513–18.

15. *Message of the Governor of Virginia, and Accompanying Documents, Document 2, Biennial Report of the Auditor of Public Accounts, 1862 & 1863* (Richmond, 1863), 7; George H. Reese, ed., *Journals and Papers of the Virginia State Convention of 1861* 3 (Richmond, 1966): 20–21; Virginia State Convention of 1861, *Ordinances Adopted by the Convention of Virginia, in Secret and Adjourned Sessions in April, May, June and July, 1861* (Richmond: W. M. Elliot, 1861), 23; *Journal of the House of Delegates of the State of Virginia, for the Called Session of 1863* (Richmond, 1863), 28.

16. Matthews, *Statutes at Large*, 207; CSA, Department of State, *Notice to Judicial Officials Taking Testimony in Cases of Slaves Abducted or Harbored by the Enemy, and of Other Property Seized, Wasted, or Destroyed by Them*, William M. Browne, Acting Secretary of State, 25 Oct. 1861 (Richmond, 1861).

17. *Acts of the General Assembly, Called Session, 1862*, 12–13; *Acts . . . , Adjourned Session, 1863*, 34; *Acts of the General Assembly, 1863–4*, 55; *Message of the Governor of Virginia . . . Document 13, Report of the President and Directors of the Central Lunatic Asylum, for the Fiscal Year Ending September 30, 1863* (Richmond, 1863), 41; John H. Lifsey, commissioner of revenue, Greensville County, "Reports of Escaped Slaves, 1863," Auditor of Public Accounts: Runaway and Escaped Slaves, Receipts and Reports, 1863, entry 759, box 1977, RG 48.759, VSLA. *Message of the Governor of Virginia . . . Document 19, Communication from the Auditor of Public Accounts, Transmitting Statistical Tables, 1864* reports that in 1863 approximately 37,706 slaves (10 percent) absconded or were seized by the enemy out of a population of 346,848 taxable slaves (the 1860 tax rolls listed 378,399 slaves), 11. See Kennedy, *Population of the United States in 1860*, 509–13.

18. Patrick, *Opinions of the Confederate Attorneys General*, 34; Matthews, *Statutes at Large*, 278.

19. Richmond *Enquirer*, 21 Oct., 8 Dec. 1864; Lynchburg *Daily Republican*, 12 Aug., 10 July 1863; Moore, *Civil War in Song*, 134.

20. Richmond *Examiner*, 10 Oct., 21 June 1864; *Staunton Spectator*, 31 May 1864.

21. *Danville Register*, 10 April 1863; Petersburg *Daily Express*, 23 July 1864; *Richmond Dispatch*, 9 Dec. 1864; *Richmond Daily Dispatch*, 1 April 1865.

22. Petersburg *Daily Express*, 18 April 1864; Lynchburg *Virginian*, 13 April 1864; *Winchester Republican*, 10 Jan. 1862.

23. *Rockingham Register and Advertiser*, 6 March, 16 Jan. 1863, 6 Sept. 1861.

24. Lexington *Valley Star*, 7 March 1861.

25. *Daily Richmond Examiner*, 5 March 1864; Mrs. Preston to Sabina Lewis Creigh Woods, 17 Dec. [1863], folder "1861–1864, ca. 1864 Correspondence of the Woods Family," Micajah Woods Papers, 10279, box 1, UVA. Sabina's brother, David Creigh, was executed in June 1864 for the murder of a Union soldier. See *A Brief Sketch of the Life and Character of the Late David S. Creigh . . .* (Lewisburg, W.V.: "Weekly Times" Print, 1865), 8–10.

26. Blackett, *Thomas Morris Chester*, 220; *Freedman's Journal* (Boston, Mass.), Jan.

1865, 7, 4–5; M. Stickler to Dr. Nelson Waller, 30 July, 13 Sept. 1864, Civil War Collection, W&M.

27. Berlin, *Destruction of Slavery*, 75–76, 82; *OR*, ser. 1, 4:630–31.

28. *Acts of the General Assembly, 1861–2*, 104; *Acts of the General Assembly, 1863–4*, 40.

29. Wallace to James R. Saunders, 25 June 1862, George T. Wallace Papers, Duke; Colin Clarke, Hickory Fork, Gloucester County, to his son Maxwell, folder 2, Maxwell Troax Clarke Papers, SHC; Wise to Col. T. J. Page, 27 Oct. 1862, Papers of Samuel Barron, 10134, box 2, UVA.

30. Shirley Plantation Journals, 14 and 16 July 1863, 10 June 1864, vol. 4, 1851–72, LC.

31. Ruffin plantation diary entries for 26 May to 24 June 1862, 1865 entry "Redmoor in Amelia County," Edmund Ruffin, Jr., Diary [1851–73], SHC. Ruffin's wartime entries conclude on 25 June 1862 and do not resume until April 1865.

32. *OR*, ser. 1, 33:26–28; Mary T. Hunley Diary (typescript), 12 May, 6 June 1861, 5 June 1863, 19 March, 13 May 1864, SHC.

33. Sigismunda Stribling Kimball Journal, 11, 13 March 1862, 2534, UVA.

34. Ibid., 24, 25 Feb. 1863.

35. Ibid., 27 Feb., 7 March 1863.

36. Richmond *Enquirer*, 16 April 1861; Lynchburg *Virginian*, 13 April 1864; *Daily Richmond Enquirer*, 7 Nov. 1864.

37. Richmond *Enquirer*, 19 Nov. 1864; Richmond *Examiner*, 1 July 1864; Richmond *Daily Dispatch*, 1 July 1864; John Woods to Micajah Woods, 2, 12 July 1863, Micajah Woods Papers, 10279, box 1, UVA.

38. Richmond *Daily Dispatch*, 2 Oct. 1862; CSA, *Communication from the Secretary of War* [relative to steps taken to carry out the provisions of the acts of Congress "in relation to the arrest and disposition of slaves who have been recaptured from the enemy"] (Richmond, 1864).

39. Richmond *Sentinel*, 21 Aug. 1863.

40. *Daily Richmond Examiner*, 10 Oct. 1864.

41. Diary of Nancy Emerson, 7 June, 8, 15 July 1864, Emerson Family Papers, 9381, UVA.

42. Richmond *Daily Dispatch*, 30 June 1864; *Daily Richmond Enquirer*, 1–5 July 1864; Wickham Family Papers, 4 July 1863, VSLA. Seventeen slaves had escaped from this family a year earlier. See also William Stokes Diary, 28–29 June 1864, 7896, UVA.

43. James A. Seddon, Secretary of War, War Department, to Gen. Pierre G. T. Beauregard, 30 Nov. 1862, Negro Military Service, roll 5, frame 333.

44. Report of Trial of Negro Soldiers Captured as Prisoners of War: *The State of South Carolina* vs. *George Council, Henry Worthington, Henry Kirk, William Harrison*, 10 Sept. 1863, ibid., roll 5, frames 450–51; Thomas Wentworth Higginson, *Massachusetts in the Army and Navy during the War of 1861–65* 1 (Boston: Wright & Potter Printing, 1896): 522, 561.

45. "Lo! The Poor Negro!" *Daily Richmond Examiner*, 28 May 1864.

46. Thomas A. Smith to My Dear Sister, 4 Aug. 1864, Thomas A. Smith Letters, 6846-CT, UVA; Joseph T. Wilson, *The Black Phalanx* (Hartford: American Publishing, 1888), 417–18; Alfred Lewis Scott Reminiscences, 26–27, VHS; Gilbert Adams case, "T. Rowland Book," 6–7, Kate Mason Rowland Collection, Museum of the Confederacy.

47. Maj. M. P. Turner, Confederate States Military Prison, Richmond, to Capt. W. H. Hatch, 14 Oct. 1864, T. O. Chester, Assistant Adjutant General, Headquarters Dept. of Richmond, to Maj. J. H. Carrington, 5 Oct. 1864, Negro Military Service, roll

5, frames 518–19; *Richmond Daily Dispatch*, 1 April 1865; Charlottesville *Daily Chronicle*, 1 Jan. 1865.

48. "The Contrabands at Fortress Monroe," *Atlantic Monthly*, Nov. 1861, 627, 637; item nos. 240 and 241 of Civil War Pictorial Envelopes collection, SHC; *Liberator*, 14 Feb. 1862, "Colored Refugees," 26. "Superintendent of Contrabands," *American Missionary*, April 1862, 83, used the word *vagrants*.

49. *OR*, ser. 1, vol. 4:64.

50. Benjamin F. Butler, *Butler's Book* (Boston: A. M. Thayer, 1892), 256–65; "The Contrabands at Fortress Monroe," *Atlantic Monthly*, Nov. 1861, 627–28, 630; Robert Francis Engs, *Freedom's First Generation: Black Hampton, Virginia, 1861–1890* (Philadelphia, 1979), 18–20; Moore, *Civil War in Song*, 31.

51. *Freedman*, Jan. 1864; *Principia*, 16 July 1863; Henry E. Simmons Letters, folder 3, SHC.

52. *National Anti-Slavery Standard*, 16, 30 Nov. 1861; *ORN*, ser. 1, 6:535; Berlin, *Destruction of Slavery*, 88–91; John Hope Franklin, *From Slavery to Freedom*, 5th ed. (New York, 1980), 208; Swint, *Dear Ones at Home*, 99.

53. *Index*, 26 Feb. 1863, 287; Betty Herndon Maury Diary, 22 June 1862, LC.

54. William Martin to sister, 11 Dec. 1862, Atcheson L. Hench Collection, 8474-U, UVA; Robert to wife, 1 June 1862, Letters from Federal Soldiers, 1242, UVA.

55. Maj. Gen. John A. Dix, Fort Monroe, to Secretary of War Edwin M. Stanton, 12 Sept. 1862, P. H. Watson, Assistant Secretary of War to Gen. Dix, 19 Sept. 1862, Dix to Stanton, 22 Nov. 1862, Dix to Brig. Gen. M[ichael] Corcoran, Newport News, 26 Nov. 1862, Negro Military Service, roll 1, frames 614, 648–50; General Orders no. 21, Headquarters, Department of Virginia, Fort Monroe, 15 March 1862, in "Superintendent of Contrabands," *American Missionary*, April 1862, 82–83.

56. James Morrison MacKaye to the American Freedmen's Inquiry Commission, 8 May 1863, Papers of James Morrison MacKaye, LC.

57. O. Brown to G. T. Chapman, Secretary, American Freedmen's Inquiry Commission, New York, 25 May 1863, ibid., *New York Daily Tribune*, 9 Jan. 1863; Barber, *Alexandria in the Civil War*, 93–95; *Freedman*, March 1864.

58. "Freedman's Village at Arlington," *American Missionary*, Feb. 1864, 31; *Principia*, 21 Dec. 1863; *Harper's Weekly*, 7 May 1864; Virginia Trist to Martha Burke, 7 Feb. 1864, Trist-Burke Papers, 6696, box 1, UVA; Joseph P. Reidy, "Coming from the Shadow of the Past: The Transition from Slavery to Freedom at Freedman's Village, 1863–1900," *VMHB* 95 (1987): 403–28.

59. *Principia*, 29 May 1862; *New York Daily Tribune*, 9 Jan. 1863.

60. John Peyton Clark Journal, 28 July 1862, WFCHS.

61. U.S. War Department, Adjutant General's Office, General Orders no. 296, *Transportation of Stores and Books for Freedom*, 2 Dec. 1864 (Washington, D.C., 1864); Keckley, 105, 111–12, 113–16.

62. Rev. I. W. Brinckerhoff, *Advice to Freedmen* (New York: American Tract Society, 1863); Rev. J. B. Waterbury, *Friendly Counsels for Freedom* (New York: American Tract Society, 1864); Robert Dale Owen, *The Wrong of Slavery, the Right of Emancipation, and the Future of the African Slave Race in the United States* (Philadelphia: J. B. Lippincott, 1864), 226–28.

63. Mortimer to Helen Briggs, 12 Jan. 1865, folder "Richmond Papers," Black History Collection, box 1, LC.

64. "To Whom It May Concern," document signed by James I. Ferre(?), "Comman-

dant, Contraband Camp," 11 April 1863, Papers of James Morrison MacKaye, LC; *American Missionary*, July 1864, 163, 175.

65. *Harper's Weekly*, 17 Jan. 1863; *Richmond Times*, 25 April 1865; *Rockingham Register and Advertiser*, 20 Jan. 1865; see also Harding, *There Is a River*, 254.

4. BODY AND SOUL

1. Judith B. Smith to Dr. Iverson B. Twyman, 3 May 1863, Austin-Twyman Papers, W&M.

2. "Notebook of Farming Advice, Knowledge, Observations, etc., Kept by R. T. Hubard for the Education of His Sons" (entry "Medicine"), Robert Thurston Hubard Papers, 8708, box 10, UVA.

3. Taxation Records (southwestern district), 1862, and "Slaves Exempt from Draft" folder, 28 Dec. 1862, Rockbridge County Historical Society, University Library, Washington and Lee University, Lexington, Va.; Account Book and Diary of Lancelot Minor, 30 Dec. 1863, Minor Family Papers, 6055 and 6055-A, UVA.

4. Printed petition of Mary Clark in folder "Claims for Recompense on Death of Slaves," Black History Collection, box 1, LC.

5. W. H. Glenn to Henry St. George Harris, 18 Dec. 1863, Henry St. George Harris Papers, Duke; William Gordon, diary 5, 28 March–16 April 1864, Papers of the Gordon Family, 9553, UVA.

6. James Ward to Dr. Jacob Haller, 19 Feb. 1863, Haller Medical Accounts, 981, UVA.

7. Eighth U.S. Census, 1860, Slave Schedules, Nansemond County, Virginia, 25 June 1860, 124; John C. Cohoon Account Book, 8868, UVA.

8. Plantation and farm record book, 1853–64, pp. 20–21, 86, acc. MsV Af27, W&M.

9. Accounts, 4 Nov. 1862, Papers of Samuel Pannill Wilson, 10721, box 1, UVA.

10. Receipt, 30 Aug. 1863, John T. Thornton Papers, 4021, UVA; miscellaneous doctor's fees, 10 Feb. 1863–15 Oct. 1864, in Dr. B. G. Rennolds Papers, Duke; Todd Savitt, *Medicine and Slavery: The Diseases and Health Care of Blacks in Antebellum Virginia* (Urbana, Ill., 1978), 194–96, 198–200, 291–92, 299; Union Burial Ground Society, City of Richmond Papers, VSLA.

11. Charles E. Davidson Account Book, vol. 1863–65, 4146, UVA.

12. Southside Virginia Family Papers, "1840–1862 Slavery" folder, 550, box 5, UVA.

13. Frances Anne Kemble, *Journal of a Residence on a Georgia Plantation in 1838–1839* (London: Longman, Green, Longman, Roberts, & Green, 1863), 76; A Southern Planter, *Plantation and Farm Instruction*, 5, 6.

14. Suzanne Lebsock, *Virginia Women, 1600–1945: "A Share of Honour"* (Richmond, 1987), 99.

15. Archibald Alexander Little to Andrew Glassel Grinnan, 21 March 1850, Grinnan Family Papers, VHS; slave policy no. 3670, George, slave of Joseph Myers, 1858–63, Joseph Myers Papers, Museum of the Confederacy; *Staunton Spectator*, 7 May 1861 (Lynchburg Hose and Fire Company), 7 Jan. 1862 (Albemarle Insurance); *Danville Register*, 15 March 1860 (J. M. Johnston's), 8 Aug. 1861 (Danville Insurance); Petersburg *Daily Express*, 6 Aug., 28 Sept. 1861 (North Carolina Mutual); receipt for Charles Davis, 17 Dec. 1860, Kersey and Davis Company, VSLA.

16. American Life Insurance and Trust Company, Philadelphia, *INSURE YOUR SLAVES!!!*, policy for 1858–63, Joseph Myers Papers, Museum of the Confederacy; W. L.

Cowardin, Richmond, Virginia Fire & Marine Insurance Company, to W. P. Smith, 27 July 1861, William Patterson Smith Papers, box 10, Duke.

17. Savitt, *Medicine and Slavery*, 192–93; Richmond *Enquirer*, 20 March 1860; letter to Dickerson, Hill & Company, 10 April 1861, folder " Slave Traders," box 6, Papers of the Chase Family, LC; Rawick, *American Slave* 16:21–33.

18. *Message of the Governor: Document 13, Annual Report of the Board of Directors of the Penitentiary Institution, Year Ending Sept. 30, 1860, Memorandum, May 25, 1861* (Richmond, 1861), 41.

19. Dain, *Disordered Minds*, 105, 109–13, 186; Guild, 82, 87–89, 116, 118, 166; Joseph Martin, *A New and Comprehensive Gazetteer of Virginia and the District of Columbia* (Charlottesville, Va., 1835), 85; comments regarding "Uncle Sam" (an insane slave cobbler), Maria Gordon Pryor Rice Reminiscences, 1, VHS. Erasmus, a seventeen-year-old "idiotic" slave, is listed in "Negroes Belonging to Mark Alexander Senior of the County of Mecklenburg State of Virginia on the Day of the Surrender of the Army of Northern Virginia by Gen. Robert E. Lee April 9th, 1865," Mark Alexander Papers, W&M.

20. Richmond *Enquirer*, 18 July, 23 Sept. 1862; *Richmond Whig*, 1 Nov. 1864.

21. Olmstead, *Cotton Kingdom*, 42–43, 81, 161, 290, 346; Louis Hughes, *Thirty Years a Slave*, 26–27; Steward, *Twenty-two Years a Slave*, 13; Perdue, *Weevils in the Wheat*, 82, 103, 149, 153, 155, 227, 237.

22. Washington, *Story of My Life*, 32, 34; "Memorandum Book of Work to Be Done, Timbers to Be Gotten, and Architecture of Tobacco Houses and Slave Cabins, etc.," William Massie Papers, Eugene C. Barker Texas History Center, University of Texas at Austin; Chambers, *Things As They Are in America*, 271–72; "The Contrabands at Fortress Monroe," *Atlantic Monthly*, Nov. 1861, 632; Hopley, *Life in the South*, 1:45; Margaret Douglass, *Educational Laws of Virginia: The Personal Narrative of Mrs. Margaret Douglass, a Southern Woman, Who Was Imprisoned for One Month in the Common Jail of Norfolk, under the Laws of Virginia, for the Crime of Teaching Free Colored Children to Read* (Boston: John P. Jewett, 1854), 12.

23. Interview of Reverend Massey [Ishrael Massie], 5–6, Ex-Slave Interviews, 3462, UVA.

24. Perdue, *Weevils in the Wheat*, 105.

25. William Cullen Bryant II, ed., "A Yankee Soldier Looks at the Negro," *Civil War History* 7 (June 1961): 137; Swint, *Dear Ones at Home*, 107–8; Engs, *Freedom's First Generation*, 34; Henry Latham, *Black and White: A Journal of a Three Months' Tour in the United States* (London: Macmillan, 1867), 105–6.

26. Testimony of Gen. Robert E. Lee, 17 Feb. 1866, testimony of Thomas Bain, 3 Feb. 1866, Joint Committee, 130, 59.

27. Douglass, *Educational Laws of Virginia*, 1, 5–6, 7–21, 25, 37, 44; Guild, 155–76, 178–79; James D. Anderson, *The Education of Blacks in the South, 1860–1935* (Chapel Hill, N.C., 1988), 281; George Washington Williams, *History of the Negro Race in America from 1619 to 1880* (New York: G. P. Putnam's Sons, 1882), 181; Tommy L. Bogger, "The Slave and Free Black Community in Norfolk, 1775–1865" (Ph.D. diss., University of Virginia, 1976), 217–21. I am indebted to Professor Bogger for permission to consult his dissertation.

28. Walter R. Vaughan, *Vaughan's "Freedmen's Pension Bill"* (1891; reprint, Freeport, N.Y., 1971), 77–79; Wendell Phillips Dabney, *Cincinnati's Colored Citizens: Historical, Sociological, and Biographical* (Cincinnati, 1926), 296.

29. "The Virginia Freedmen; Their Moral and Intellectual Improvement," *American*

Missionary, Nov. 1861, 256, 258–59; "Death of Mrs. Peake," ibid., April 1862, 83; report of William H. Ruffner, Superintendent of Public Instruction, Department of Education, *Virginia School Report, 1871, First Annual Report of the Superintendent of Public Instruction, for the Year Ending August 31, 1871* (Richmond: C. A. Schaffter, Superintendent Public Printing, 1871), 116; Lewis C. Lockwood and Charlotte L. Forten, *Two Black Teachers during the Civil War: Mary S. Peake; the Colored Teacher at Fortress Monroe [by] Rev. Lewis C. Lockwood, and, Life on the Sea Islands [by] Charlotte Forten* (1863 and 1864; reprint, New York, 1969), 5–6, 15, 30–36, 44–51; Samuel L. Horst, *Education for Manhood: The Education of Blacks in Virginia during the Civil War* (Lanham, Md. 1987), 8–9, 15, 25, 61–74; Engs, *Freedom's First Generation*, 12–13; Anderson, *Education of Blacks*, 7; *National Anti-Slavery Standard*, 16 May 1863; Annette Tapert, ed., *The Brother's War* (New York, 1988), 36; *Alexandria Gazette*, 22 May 1863; Rawick, *American Slave* 16:42.

30. "Freedmen," *American Missionary*, July 1864, 162–63; *Freedmen* (Boston, Mass.), Jan. 1864; *Freedmen's Journal* (Boston), Jan. 1865, 2, 4, 7, 10.

31. *First Annual Report of the Educational Commission for Freedmen, May 1863* (Boston: Prentiss & Deland, 1863), 4, 9, 11, 14–15.

32. *Freedmen's Journal*, Jan. 1865, 8–10; Swint, *Dear Ones at Home*, 147.

33. "Old Dominion," *American Missionary*, Feb. 1864, 30; "Freedmen—Virginia," ibid., July 1864, 173–74; opening of the "Tyler" school, ibid., Oct. 1861, 247–48; Swint, *Dear Ones at Home*, 110–11, 120, 147; *Principia*, 28 May 1863; William Martin, 11th Pennsylvania Cavalry, to his sister, 11 Dec. 1862, Atcheson L. Hench Collection, 8474-U, UVA; Quarles, *Negro in the Civil War*, 122; "Prayer of a Contraband," *Liberator*, 21 Feb. 1862, 32.

34. *Freedmen's Journal*, Jan. 1865, 5–7, 10; Sing-Nan Fen, "Notes on the Education of Negroes at Norfolk and Portsmouth, Virginia, during the Civil War," *Phylon* 28 (Summer 1967): 199, 204.

35. Extract of a letter from Mary C. Fletcher, Norfolk, 6 Dec. 1864, as quoted in *Freedmen's Journal*, Jan. 1865, 5.

36. *American Missionary*, Sept. 1862, 208–9, and July 1864, 174; Henry E. Simmons [11th Rhode Island Volunteers], to his wife, 28 April 1862, Henry E. Simmons letters, folder 2, SHC.

37. "Old Dominion," *American Missionary*, Feb. 1864, 30; "Freedmen—Virginia" and "Mr. Loguen's Visit to Virginia," ibid., July 1864, 172–73, 175–76.

38. *Christian Observer*, 7 Feb. 1861 (a Presbyterian weekly); Livermore, *My Story of the War*, 259–62.

39. Catherine Barbara Broun Diary, 27 Dec. 1863, 2:31, SHC; *Principia*, 16 July 1863; Francis Fedric, *Slave Life in Virginia and Kentucky* (London: Wertheim, Macintosh, and Hunt, 1863), 11.

40. Albert Taylor Bledsoe, *An Essay on Liberty and Slavery* (Philadelphia: J. B. Lippincott, 1857), 90; *De Bow's Review*, May and June 1861, 651, 658; Rawick, *From Sundown to Sunup* 1:33–34; London *Times*, 16 Jan. 1863.

41. Lovell, *Black Song*, 185.

42. James S. Olson, *Slave Life in America* (Lanham, Md. 1983), 16; *Memorial Edition of the National Jubilee Melody Song Book* (Nashville, n.d.), 71; Sarah A. Brock Putnam, *Richmond during the War* (New York: G. W. Carleton, 1867), 265.

43. William James Hoge, *Sketch of Dabney Carr Harrison: Minister of the Gospel and Captain in the Army of the Confederate States of America* (Petersburg, Va.: Evangelical Tract Society, 1863), 14–15; Randolph, *Slave Cabin to Pulpit*, 196–204; Albert J. Raboteau, *Slave Religion: The "Invisible Institution" in the Antebellum South* (New York, 1978), 294; *Negro in*

Virginia, 44, 49–50, 108; Luther P. Jackson, "Negro Religious Development in Virginia," *JNH* 16 (April 1931): 194–228; Hundley, *Social Relations*, 350–51.

44. Jackson, "Negro Religions Development," 222, 228; Randolph, *Slave Cabin to Pulpit*, 199; Hopley, *Life in the South* 1:188–190; Washington, *Story of My Life*, 30; Luther P. Jackson, "Manumission in Certain Virginia Cities," *JNH* 15 (July 1930): 292.

45. Simmons to wife, 7 June 1863, folder 3, Henry E. Simmons Letters, SHC; Civil War Diary of David Probert, 3 July 1864, 10776, UVA; John Albert Monroe, *Reminiscences of the War of the Rebellion of 1861–65* (Providence: N. Bangs Williams, 1881), 73–74.

46. *New York Daily Tribune*, 9 Jan. 1863; *Religious Herald* (Richmond), 4 Feb., 1 Dec. 1864; Elsa S. Rosenthal, "1790 Names—1970 Faces: A Short History of Alexandria's Slave and Free Black Community," in *Alexandria: A Composite History*, ed. Elizabeth Hambleton and Marian Van Landingham (Alexandria, Va., 1975), 89–90; Engs, *Freedom's First Generation*, 76; Livermore, *My Story of the War*, 267; Mary A. Livermore, *The Story of My Life* (Hartford: A. D. Worthington, 1897), 347–48; Maria Gordon Pryor Rice Reminiscences, 10–12, VHS; *American Missionary*, Oct. 1861, 245; "The Contrabands at Fortress Monroe," *Atlantic Monthly*, Nov. 1861, 638.

47. *American Missionary*, Oct. 1861, 244, 246–49, April 1862, "William Davis the Ex-Slave," 83; Charles T. Davis, *Black Is the Color of the Cosmos*, ed. Henry Louis Gates, Jr. (New York, 1982), 335–48.

48. William Eldridge Hatcher, *John Jasper: The Unmatched Negro Philosopher and Preacher* (New York, 1908), 20; "Ballad—DE SUN DO MOVE by John Jasper," folder "Virginia Negro Lore," box A6888, Records of the U.S. Works Projects Administration, LC.

49. Brown, *My Southern Home*, 204; Isaac James, *"The Sun Do Move": The Story of the Life of John Jasper* (Richmond, 1954), 8–44; Phillip T. Drotning, *A Guide to Negro History in America* (Garden City, N.Y., 1968), 215; Hatcher, *John Jasper*, 36–42, 47–57; John Jasper letter, 26 March 1884, Valentine Museum, Richmond. After the war Jasper founded and became pastor of Richmond's Sixth Mount Zion Baptist Church. During his thirty-five-year pastorate, its congregation grew from a handful to 2,000 members. Virginians of both races attended his funeral after his death on 31 March 1901.

50. Fedric, *Slave Life in Virginia*, 3–4.

51. "Former Slave Reflects," Cincinnati *Enquirer*, 31 Dec. 1938. Toler did not speculate as to the cause of his mistress's death, but poison administered by a disgruntled slave cannot be ruled out.

52. "Ghost Stories," folder "Virginia Negro Love," box A6888, Records of the U.S. Works Projects Administration, LC; Marguerite Du Pont Lee, *Virginia Ghosts*, rev. ed. (Berryville, Va., 1966), 156–57.

53. Lee, *Virginia Ghosts*, 237–38.

54. Raboteau, *Slave Religion*, 308–9; Thomas Lewis Johnson, *Twenty-eight Years a Slave* (Bournemouth, Eng., 1909), 29–30; Richmond *Sentinel*, 30 May 1863. If any slaves prayed for the Confederacy, it was in the best interests of African-Americans and their desire for freedom and divine vengeance against the heartless oppression of whites. See Thorpe, *The Mind of the Negro*, 81–82, 107, 116–17, 198–99.

55. Memoirs of Rev. George W. White, 10837, UVA, 43; Lucy Skipwith to John H. Cocke, 15 Aug. 1863, Cocke Family Papers, 640, box 170, UVA.

56. Cornelius Walker, *The Life and Correspondence of Rev. William Sparrow, D.D., Late Professor of Systematic Divinity and Evidence, in the Episcopal Seminary of Virginia* (Philadelphia: James Hammond, 1876), 246, 255, 257; Thomas Cary Johnson, *The Life and Letters of Robert Lewis Dabney* (Richmond, 1903), 67–68, 128–29, 242, 282–83; Robert Lewis Dabney,

A Defence of Virginia, and through Her, of the South, in Recent and Pending Contests against the Sectional Party (New York: E. J. Hale & Son, 1867), 215; Peyton Harrison Hoge, *Moses Drury Hoge: Life and Letters* (Richmond: Presbyterian Committee of Publication, 1899), 136, 149–50, 239.

57. *Central Presbyterian* (Richmond), 23 April 1863, contains a complete text of the *Address,* but for a slightly different version, see Edward McPherson, *The Political History of the United States of America . . . ,* 2d ed. (Washington, D.C.: Philip & Solomons, 1865), 519; Journal [of John Hartwell Cocke], "Earliest Recollections of Slavery," Aug. 1863, Cocke Family Papers, 640, box 170, UVA; H. Shelton Smith, *In His Image, but . . . Racism in Southern Religion, 1780–1910* (Durham, N.C., 1972), 190–91, 196–97.

58. *Religious Herald* (Richmond), 20 June 1861; *Central Presbyterian* (Richmond), 10 Feb., 8 Oct. 1863; Minute Book, Market Street United Methodist Church Records, box 2, WFCHS. Other meetings were held at Norfolk (1861), Petersburg (1862), Richmond (1863), and Lynchburg (1864).

59. *Journal of the Sixty-Sixth Annual Convention of the Protestant Episcopal Church in Virginia, Held in St. Paul's Church, Richmond, on the 16th and 17th of May, 1861* (Richmond: Charles H. Wynne, 1861), 58–59; *Journal of the Sixty-Seventh Annual Convention . . . on the 21st and 22nd May, 1861* (Richmond: MacFarlane & Ferguson, 1862), 24; *Journal of the Sixty-Eighth Annual Council . . . on the 20th, 21st and 22nd May, 1863* (Richmond, 1863), 26; *Journal of the Sixty-Ninth Annual Council . . . on the 18th and 19th May, 1864* (Richmond, 1864), 27; *Christian Observer,* 7 Feb. 1861.

60. James A. Lyon, "Slavery, and the Duties Growing Out of the Relationship," *Southern Presbyterian Review* 16 (July 1863): 33–35; Smith, *In His Image,* 202.

61. "A Slave Marriage Law," *Southern Presbyterian Review* 16 (Oct. 1863): 145–61.

62. John Randolph Tucker, *The Southern Church Justified in Its Support of the South in the Present War: A Lecture Delivered before the Young Men's Christian Association, of Richmond, on the 21st May, 1863; by Hon. John Randolph Tucker* (Richmond: Wm. H. Clemmitt, 1863), 6–35; *Richmond Daily Dispatch,* 25 May 1863.

63. *Central Presbyterian* (Richmond), 28 May 1863.

64. "Religious Duties of Masters to Slaves," *Richmond Daily Dispatch,* 30 Jan. 1865.

65. Rice reminiscences, pp. 10–12, VHS.

66. Minute Book of the New Hope Baptist Church, 1830–68, 6:96–98, Papers of the Thornhill Family and Thomas S. Bocock, 10612, box 5, UVA.

67. Rev. George Bourne, *A Condensed Anti-Slavery Bible Argument: by a Citizen of Virginia* (New York: S. W. Benedict, 1845), 89; Pendleton to Irving, 27 Jan. 1880, 1–6, 9, 15, and 12 Feb. 1880, folder 63, William Nelson Pendleton Papers, SHC.

68. Testimony of Reverend William Thornton (colored) of Hampton, Va., 3 Feb. 1866, Joint Committee, 52–53.

69. Testimony of Alexander Dunlop (colored) of Williamsburg, Va., 3 Feb. 1866, ibid., 57.

70. Lucy Randolph letter, n.d., Va. Tech.

5. YOURS UNTIL DEATH

1. Keckley, 38–39, 42, 105; John E. Washington, *They Knew Lincoln* (New York, 1942), 209–12; U.S. Congress, House, Representative George H. White, 56th Cong., 2d sess., 29 Jan. 1901, *Congressional Record* 34:1636. White was the only black member of Congress in 1897–1901 and the last until 1929.

Preliminary drafts of this chapter were presented as papers at various historians' conferences including the Virginia Center for the Humanities (Charlottesville, Va., 1990), the National Association of African-American Studies (Petersburg, Va., 1993), and the 78th annual meeting of the Association for the Study of Afro-American Life and History (Baltimore, 1993). I am indebted to these scholars for their thoughtful comments and critiques: Dina Copelman, George Mason University; Sarah Shaver Hughes, Shippensburg University; Lucious Edwards, Virginia State University; Matthew Holden, University of Virginia; Deborah White (author of *Ar'n't I a Woman?*), Rutgers University; Delores P. Aldridge, Emory University.

2. Eugene D. Genovese, *Roll, Jordan, Roll: The World the Slaves Made* (New York, 1974), 93-97, 297-98; George C. Rable, *Civil Wars: Women and the Crisis of Southern Nationalism* (Urbana, Ill., 1989), chap. 3.

3. Lerone Bennett, Jr., *Before the Mayflower: A History of Black America*, 6th ed. (Chicago, 1988), 296-321; Du Bois, *Black Reconstruction*, 34-35, 43-44; Joseph T. Wilson, *Emancipation: Its Course and Progress from 1481 B.C. to A.D. 1875* (Hampton, Va., 1882), 145; *American Missionary*, Oct. 1861, 249.

4. James Hugo Johnston, *Race Relations in Virginia and Miscegenation in the South, 1776–1860* (Amherst, Mass., 1970), 250–63; Sterling, *We Are Your Sisters*, 19; "Code of Laws for Island Plantation," Eppes Family Papers, VHS.

5. Keckley, 46; Carleton, *Suppressed Book about Slavery*, 145–47.

6. *Lynchburg Virginian*, 13 April 1864; unidentified newspaper clipping, 28 July [1862], John Curtiss Underwood Scrapbook, p. 19, LC.

7. Adams, *A Troopers Adventures*, 425, 430–31; "The 'Patriarchal' System: 'Miscegenation' in Perfection," *Natural Anti-Slavery Standard*, 23 July 1864. According to the article, Scott, described as an "old man," resided at a plantation approximately "four miles north of the Pamunkey River" near White House Landing. This suggests an area in or near King William County. A seventy-four-year-old unmarried King William County farmer named Anderson Scott is enumerated in 1860 census returns as the owner of $200,000 in real estate and personal property, including 108 slaves (8th U.S. Census, 23 June 1860, King William County, Virginia, Aylett township, dwelling no. 384, p. 575; 8th U.S. Census, 1860, Slave Schedules, King William County, 4 July 1860, no. 13, Anderson Scott, pp. 275–76). Another Union solider, after encountering evidence of rampant miscegenation and breeding of slave children for export, characterized Virginia as "a slave-breeding country" ("The Contrabands at Fortress Monroe," *Atlantic Monthly*, Nov. 1861, 637). For an example of a South Carolina slave woman used as a "breeder," see Foner, *Freedom's Lawmakers*, 101.

8. Ira Berlin, *Slaves without Masters: The Free Negro in the Antebellum South* (New York, 1974), 178; Washington, *Story of My Life*, 29, 32; Harlan, *Booker T. Washington Papers* 1:6; Calder Loth, ed., *The Virginia Landmarks Register*, 3d ed. (Charlottesville, Va., 1986), 155. For another contemporary example of "physical bleaching," see Hopley, *Life in the South* 2:123.

9. Kennedy, *Population of the United States in 1860*, 516–18; U.S. Department of Commerce, Bureau of the Census, *Negro Population in the United States, 1790–1915* (1918; reprint, New York, 1968), 53, 207–9; John Codman Hurd, *The Law of Freedom and Bondage in the United States* 2 (Boston: Little, Brown & Co., 1862; reprint, New York, 1968): 4; J. Tivis Wicker, "Virginia's Legitimization Act of 1866," *VMHB* 86 (1978): 343; *Code of Virginia*, 510.

10. Joel Williamson, *New People: Miscegeneation and Mulattoes in the United States* (New York, 1980), 4; *OR*, ser. 3, 3:431.

11. David G. Croly and George Wakeman, *Miscegenation: The Theory of the Blending*

of the Races, Applied to the American White Man and Negro (London: Trubner, 1864), vii, 14–15, 18, 24, 27–28, 56; W. J. Cash, *The Mind of the South* (New York, 1941), 86. For additional opposing Civil War views on this subject, see *Liberator*, 8 April 1864, and J. H. Van Evrie, *Negroes and Negro "Slavery": The First an Inferior Race: The Latter Its Normal Condition* (New York: Van Evrie, Horton & Co., 1861), 146–47. An overview of *Miscegenation* as a Democratic escapade to undermine abolitionists and Republicans is discussed in George M. Frederickson, *The Black Image in the White Mind: The Debate on Afro-Ameican Character and Destiny, 1817–1917* (New York, 1971), and as a hoax in Sidney Kaplan, *American Studies in Black and White: Selected Essays, 1949–1989*, ed. Allan D. Austin (Amherst, Mass., 1991), 47–100.

12. *Southern Illustrated News*, 16 April 1864. Ogden was an actor and the stage manager of the Richmond Theatre; see E. Merton Coulter, *The Confederate States of America, 1861–1865* (Baton Rouge, La., 1950), 487–89.

13. Richmond *Enquirer*, 5 Dec. 1862; "List of White Men at Mt. Torry Furnace, Feby. 1st 1864," entry no. 9, in bound volume "Negroes and Rations at Catawba," Tredegar Iron Company Records, box 31, VSLA. Another example of the confusion that "white negroes" caused is in Hopley, *Life in the South*, 1:188, 2:122, 124.

14. Richmond *Daily Examiner*, 5 Dec. 1862, 26 Jan. 1863; Guild, 32; *Code of Virginia*, chap. 107, sec. 17, 522.

15. *Richmond Whig*, 20 Aug. 1864; *Harper's Weekly*, 30 Jan. 1864, 69, 71; Rebecca Aleene Ebert, "A Window on the Valley: A Study of the Free Black Community of Winchester and Frederick County, Virginia, 1785–1860" (M.A. thesis, University of Maryland, 1986), 9. I am indebted to her for providing a copy of her master's thesis.

16. "The Contrabands at Fortress Monroe," *Atlantic Monthly*, Nov. 1861, 636; Henry L. Estabrooks, *Adrift in Dixie* (New York: Carleton, 1866), 122–23, 174–76.

17. "Register of Free Negroes Enrolled and Detailed, May 1864–January 1865, Camp Lee," chap. 1, 241:1–126, Bureau of Conscription, Virginia, RG 109, NA. Each enrolled free black was numbered at the time of his enlistment; several were later exempted by medical boards or deserted. A modest theory is necessary for the apparent preponderance of blue-eyed blacks born in Washington County among these enrollees. One of this county's surviving free black registers (144 names) did not reveal any unusual numbers of blue-eyed Afro-Virginians. Washington County was 16 percent black according to the 1860 census (2,800 out of 16,900 persons). There were 249 free blacks (126 males), comprising 8 percent of the Afro-Virginian population; of these, 191 (6 percent of the black population and 76 percent of the free black population) were listed as mulattoes (95 males). See Register of Free Blacks, Washington County, 1838–63, 41-A, UVA, and Kennedy, *Population of the United States in 1860*, 518.

18. Charles Carleton Coffin, *The Boys of '61: or, Four Years of Fighting* (Boston: Estes and Lauriat, 1881), 518.

19. *OR*, ser. 3, 3:1142; *American Missionary*, Oct. 1861, 245; Lovell, *Black Song*, 185–86; Deborah Gray White, *Ar'n't I a Woman?: Female Slaves in the Plantation South* (New York, 1985), 76, 104, 112, 153–55; Jeanne Noble, *Beautiful, Also, Are the Souls of My Sisters: A History of the Black Woman in America* (Englewood Cliffs, N.J.: 1978), 40–41, 46; Herbert G. Gutman, *The Black Family in Slavery and Freedom, 1750–1925* (New York, 1976), 275–77, 281–83.

20. "A Slave Marriage Law," *Southern Presbyterian Review* 16 (Oct. 1863): 145–58.

21. A Southern Planter, *Plantation and Farm Instruction*, 10; Account Book, 1858–95, 5 Aug. 1859, Watson Family Papers, 530, box 5, and W. C. Scott to Mrs. Francis Cabell, 9 Jan. 1861, Cabell Papers, 5084, box 5, UVA.

22. Hopley, *Life in the South* 2:53–56; Gutman, *Black Family*, 412; "Marriages among

Ex-Slaves," *American Missionary*, April 1864, 92–93; "Marrying the Freedmen" and "Sabbath-Day Exercises," ibid., Nov. 1861, 256, 258; Swint, *Dear Ones at Home*, 121. Whites frequently commented on how well-dressed some blacks were during antebellum times: "Dashing satin bonnets now cover woolly false curls. . . . These gentry leave their visiting cards at each other's kitchens" (Samuel Mordecai, *Virginia, Especially Richmond, in By-Gone Days*, 2d ed. [Richmond, 1860; reprint, 1946], 360).

23. Clark to William D. Cabell, 18 Sept. 1863, William D. Cabell Papers, 276, box 2, UVA; Fedric, *Slave Life in Virginia*, 10.

24. *Southern Illustrated News*, 1 Nov. 1862; Estabrooks, *Adrift in Dixie*, 119, 145, 170, 172, 178, 202–3.

25. *Richmond Whig*, 29 June 1864; Charles K. Mills, *Harvest of Barren Regrets: The Army Career of Frederick William Benteen, 1834–1898* (Glendale, Calif., 1985), 209–10; Bell Irvin Wiley, *The Life of Billy Yank* (Garden City, N.Y.: 1971), 117 n. 36.

26. Woods to wife, 24 May 1863, Samuel M. Woods Letters, 10698, UVA; Nelson to Elbridge Libby, 13 April 1863, Letters of Union and Confederate Soldiers, 10694, UVA; *Richmond Times*, 25 April 1865.

27. Fedric, *Slave Life in Virginia*, 8; *OR*, ser. 3, 3:431; Feb. 12, 21, 1864, Papers of Christian Abraham Fleetwood, reel 1, LC.

28. "Report of Negroes Forwarded to Col. Alanson Crane at Fortress Monroe on the Steamer *Cataline*," 6 June 1861, Roswell Farnham Letters, Vermont Historical Society; Estabrooks, *Adrift in Dixie*, 203.

29. Hopley, *Life in the South*, 2:122–23.

30. Elizabeth Fox-Genovese, *Within the Plantation Household: Black and White Women of the Old South* (Chapel Hill, N.C., 1988), 229, 292; Elliot, *Cotton Is King*, 728; Mrs. Nicholas Ware Eppes, *The Negro of the Old South* (Chicago, 1925), 73.

31. Douglass, *Educational Laws of Virginia*, 63–64.

32. Perdue, *Weevils in the Wheat*, 227, 332.

33. William Gibson Field Journal, 10538, UVA; Conway Robinson, *Case of the Heirs of William O. George, a White Person, between Whom and a Negro It Is Alleged, There Was a Marriage in Pennsylvania* (n.p., 1869), 3–6; Conway Robinson, *Supreme Court of Appeals of Virginia: (March Session 1877): Observations of Conway Robinson upon the Application for a Rehearing in George and others against Pilcher and others* (n.p., 1877), 26–27.

34. *Richmond Enquirer*, 28 Nov. 1862; *Daily Richmond Enquirer*, 18 Jan. 1865.

35. House Committee on War Claims, *Summary Reports of the Commissioners of Claims in all Cases Reported to Congress as Disallowed under the Act of March 3, 1871 . . .* (Washington, D.C.: GPO, 1871–80), 2(1875–76):253, Moore, *Rebel Rhymes*, 7.

36. Eckenrode, "Negroes in Richmond in 1864," 198; Lynchburg *Daily Republican*, 5 Jan. 1863; "The Richmond Theatre," *Central Presbyterian* (Richmond), 15 Oct. 1862; Jordan, *Charlottesville*, 36, 94.

37. *Richmond Enquirer*, 16 Dec. 1862; *Richmond Daily Dispatch*, 18, 19 March 1864.

38. *Richmond Daily Examiner*, 6 May 1864.

39. *Code of Virginia*, 815–16; *Richmond Daily Examiner*, 15 March 1865.

40. Jordan, *Charlottesville*, 40; House Committee on War Claims, *Summary Reports* 3 (1877–78):143; *Greenhow & Als v. James' Ex'or*, George W. Hansbrough, *Reports of Cases Decided in the Supreme Court of Appeals of Virginia*, vol. 80, *from January 1st, 1885, to November 1st, 1885* (Richmond, 1886), 636–50. Dade Hooe is enumerated in the 8th U.S. Census, 1860, Virginia, Stafford County, p. 889; Hooe and Greenhow are enumerated in the 9th U.S. Census, 1870, Virginia, Stafford County, Aquia Township, p. 11. The couple married

in 1875 in the District of Columbia in an unsuccessful attempt to legitimatize their children.

41. Susan Brownmiller, *Against Our Will: Men, Women, and Rape* (New York, 1975), 88; Gutman, *Black Family,* 386–87, 613. A review of the standard books on the war failed to locate substantial comments on rape or sex with the exception of Burke Davis, *Our Incredible Civil War* (New York, 1960), 158–66.

42. *Address of the General Assembly to the Soldiers of Virginia* (Richmond, 1864), 2; see also W.P.A. Folklore, 1547, box 1, folder 8, "Ex-Slaves," UVA.

43. Reid Mitchell, *Civil War Soldiers* (New York, 1988), 118.

44. Petersburg *Daily Express,* 16 July 1862, 25 March 1865.

45. *Daily Richmond Enquirer,* 7 July 1864; *OR,* ser. 1, 36: pt. 3, 278, 472, 37: pt. 1, 163–67; Joseph T. Glatthaar, *Forged in Battle* (New York, 1990), 118; Robert I. Alotta, *Civil War Justice: Union Army Executions under Lincoln* (Shippensburg, Pa., 1989), 30, 187.

46. Genovese, *Roll, Jordan, Roll,* 428; Gutman, *Black Family,* 536; Bennett, *Before the Mayflower,* chap. 10, "Red, White, and Black: Race and Sex"; Giles Buckner Cooke Diary, 7 July 1863, VHS. Eyeball rape and incidental contact with white women posed dangers for black male Southerners well into the twentieth century; see John Dollard, *Caste and Class in a Southern Town* (New Haven, 1937), 165, and Stetson Kennedy, *Jim Crow Guide to the U.S.A.* (London, 1959), 171, 211.

47. John Roles, *Inside Views of Slavery on Southern Plantations* (New York: John A. Gray & Green, 1864), 21; George H. Hepworth, *The Whip, Hoe, and Sword; or, the Gulf Department in '63* (Boston: Walker, Wise, and Company, 1864), 193; John W. Blassingame, *The Slave Community* (1972; reprint, New York, 1982), 82.

48. Randall C. Jimerson, *The Private Civil War* (Baton Rouge, La., 1988), 73; Sterling, *We Are Your Sisters,* 239–40; Henry J. H. Thompson to wife, 20 June 1863, Henry J. H. Thompson Papers, Duke.

49. Harrison to A. Lincoln, 28 July 1862, Records of the Office of the Secretary of War, RG 107, microfilm 494, roll 1, NA.

50. *American Missionary,* Sept. 1862, 208; Engs, *Freedom's First Generation,* 78.

51. Richmond *Enquirer,* 4 Nov., 25 July 1862; *Daily Richmond Examiner,* 25 July, 15 Aug. 1862; Richmond *Daily Dispatch,* 25 July, 15 Aug. 1862. A few newspaper accounts list Wells's last name as "Wills."

52. Stuart Berg Flexner, *Listening to America: An Illustrated History of Words and Phrases from Our Lively and Splendid Past* (New York, 1982), 283; George McClaugherty to sister, 2 Jan. 1865, Albert B. McClaugherty Letters, Manassas National Military Park; see also Perdue, *Weevils in the Wheat,* 89, 105. Another taboo topic, incest, is also shrouded in silence.

53. Gutman, *Black Family,* 11–14, 389, 414; *OR,* ser. 1, 46: pt. 3, 1221; Wicker, "Virginia's Legitimization Act of 1866," 340–42; Wiley, *Life of Billy Yank,* 117; Leon F. Litwack, *Been in the Storm So Long: The Aftermath of Slavery* (New York, 1979), 266.

54. Joint Committee, 56. Virginia's antimiscegenation law was declared unconstitutional by the U.S. Supreme Court in the 1967 case *Loving v. the Commonwealth of Virginia* (Kelley and Harbinson, *American Constitution,* 941; "Woman Who Changed Laws That Prevented Mixed Marriage Tells What It Was Like Then," *Jet,* 9 Nov. 1992, 12–15). For a succinct account of the relationship between Southern women and black men, see Cash, *Mind of the South,* 116.

55. Rosette Hill to Dear Husband, 5 Aug. 1867, Colson-Hill Family Papers, box 2, VSU; 9th U.S. Census, 11 Aug. 1870, Dinwiddie County, Virginia, 6th Ward, Petersburg,

John H. Hill, dwelling no. 199 and family no. 208, 409; Luther P. Jackson, *Negro Office-Holders in Virginia, 1865–1895* (Norfolk, Va., 1945), 56, 58, 86; *Negro in Virginia*, 138. I am grateful to my mentor and colleague, Professor and University Archivist Lucious Edwards of Virginia State University, for bringing the Hill papers to my attention.

6. A COMMONWEALTH OF FEAR

1. Newbell N. Puckett, "American Negro Names," *JNH* 23 (Jan. 1938): 38; Carter G. Woodson, *Free Negro Owners of Slaves in the United States in 1830* (Washington, D.C., 1924), 163–92; Murray Heller, ed., *Black Names in America: Origins and Usage* (Boston, 1975), chap. 5; "One Negro woman, Anarchy" advertised for sale in "Trust Sale," *Virginia Advocate* (Charlottesville), 22 March 1833. Lemon, Jubert, Marchary, Indiana, and Lettuce are listed in "Negroes Belonging to Mark Alexander Senior of the County of Mecklenburg State of Virginia on the Day of the Surrender of the Army of Northern Virginia by Gen. Robert E. Lee, April 9th 1865," Mark Alexander Papers, W&M. A variety of documents indicated several Afro-Virginian women were named "Franky/Frankey."

2. Ogonna Chuks-orgi, *Names from Africa* (Chicago, 1972), 75–80, and Ihechukwu Madubuike, *A Handbook of African Names* (Washington, D.C., 1976), 7–22.

3. Olmsted, *Cotton Kingdom*, 106; the generic "John" appears in Charles A. Page, *Letters of a War Correspondent* (Boston: L. C. Page, 1899), 310; Carter G. Woodson, *The Mind of the Negro as Reflected in Letters Written during the Crisis, 1800–1860* (New York, 1969), 559.

"Species of color" appeared with surprising frequency in numerous wartime periodicals published in Virginia and Confederate documents as well as such Northern periodicals as *Harper's Weekly*, 8 Nov. 1862; "helotism" was used by Jefferson Davis in his 5 Jan. 1863 address reprinted below as App. C; "Topsies" is, of course, from Harriet Beecher Stowe, *Uncle Tom's Cabin* (Boston: John P. Jut, 1853); "members of the shiney-faced institution," *Southern Illustrated News*, 23 March 1863, 5; "tatterdemalion negroes," Livermore, *Story of My Life*, 284; "wooly-headed Congo," *Alexandria Gazette and Virginia Advertiser*, 14 Jan. 1860; "droves of stock / heads of stock," Vincent Colyer, *Report of the Services Rendered by the Freed People to the United States Army in North Carolina, in the Spring of 1862, after the Battle of Newbern* (New York: Vincent Colyer, 1864), 19.

4. George T. Wallace to J. R. Saunders, 1 July 1862, George T. Wallace Papers, Duke; Lee, Custis Executor Document, printed as App. F below; "Negroes Belonging to the Estate of John T. Thornton Nov. 26th 1863" in folder "1863–65 & 1870 Letters to Mrs. Thornton, etc.," John T. Thornton Papers, 4021, UVA; bound volume of Afro-Virginian slave births and names, 1861–64 and 1953–65, respectively, Morris Family Papers, 38–79, box 9, UVA. Of approximately fifty-three slaves in a "List of Slaves Belonging to W. B. Taliaferro of Gloucester—1862 June 1st (over One Years Old)" (Taliaferro Family Papers, 4536, UVA), four girls under the age of two and three boys a year old or less lacked names.

5. "The Contrabands at Fortress Monroe," *Atlantic Monthly*, Nov. 1861, 637; Litwack, *Been in the Storm*, 250–51; folder "1861–1883 Wages Paid (Chiefly to Negroes)," Papers of Samuel Pannill Wilson, 10721, box 2, UVA.

6. Hopley, *Life in the South*, 1:55.

7. John Hope Franklin, *The Militant South* (Cambridge, Mass., 1970), 69–70, 72–73, 191–92; *Index*, 26 Feb. 1863, 287; "Tales of Slavery Told by Mrs. Fannie Berry—Anecdotes," 3, Ex-Slave Interviews, 3462, UVA ("poor hickories"); Cash, *Mind of the South*, 82–83; Bell

Irvin Wiley, *The Plain People of the Confederacy* (Baton Rouge, La., 1943), 64; McIlwaine, *Southern Poor-White*, 83. The concept of black superiority is discussed in Thomas L. Webber, *Deep like the Rivers: Education in the Slave Quarter Community* (New York, 1978), 91–101.

8. Livermore, *Story of My Life*, 154–65, 183, 202, 364–65. Livermore returned to New England, having had her fill "to the lips in horrors of the Virginia plantation." During the Civil War she organized the Chicago branch of the Sanitary Commission and subsequently lectured, published, and agitated on behalf of temperance and women's rights movements. She described her wartime experiences in *My Story of the War*.

9. J. Randolph Bryan to his sister, 31 Dec. 1865, Grinnan Family Papers, 49, box 4, UVA; Webber, *Deep like the Rivers*, 93.

10. Elizabeth Harris to Col. Brown, 20 Nov. 1865, "Unregistered Letters and Telegrams Received: Individuals, A—W," Records of the Assistant Commissioner for Virginia, Freedmen's Bureau, roll 40 (microfilm), NA; John Peyton Clark Journal, 17 July 1862, WFCHS. His "apple" reference is taken from Deuteronomy 32:10: "He found him in a desert land, and in the waste howling wilderness; he led him about, he instructed him, he kept him as the apple of his eye."

11. Jordan, *Charlottesville*, 97; Dabney, *Virginia: The New Dominion*, 367–73.

12. "Robert" to wife, 28 March 1863, Fort Tillinghast, Va., Letters from Federal Soldier, 1242, UVA.

13. Michael Shaara, *The Killer Angels* (New York, 1974), 176 ("John Henry"); Bruce Catton, *Mr. Lincoln's Army* (Garden City, N.Y., 1951), 180; Civil War Diary of David Probert, 9 July 1864; 10766, UVA; "The Civil War in America," London *Times*, 19 July 1863.

14. Samuel S. Johnson Diary, 9 Nov. 1862, 8493, UVA; Catherine Barbara Broun Diary, 2:9, 1 Feb. 1863, SHC.

15. Item nos. 24, 156, 190, Civil War Pictorial Envelopes Collection, SHC.

16. Cummings to nephew, 23 Dec. 1862, Robert Cummings Papers, Special Collections and Archives, Rutgers University Libraries; Memoirs of Rev. George W. White, p. 39, 10837, UVA.

17. Lt. J. V. Hadley to Miss Pett Barbour, 2 Jan. 1863, Lucian Barbour Papers, LC.

18. Bryant, "A Yankee Soldier Looks at the Negro," 137; Benjamin Heath, Jr., Civil War Journal, 6 June 1864, Special Collections and Archives, Rutgers University Libraries; Luther Guiteau Billings Memoirs, "Only Yesterday," 81, LC.

19. Probert Diary, 16 May 1864, 10776, UVA; Tapert, *Brother's War*, 117, 130; *OR*, ser. 3, 3:1142.

20. Tapert, *Brother's War*, 211–12; *Negro in Virginia*, 202.

21. Henry Simmons to his wife Anna, 12 Nov. 1862, Henry E. Simmons Letters, folder 1, SHC; Bruce Catton, *Glory Road* (Garden City, N.Y., 1952), 249–50; *New York Ninth* (Warrenton), 31 July 1862; *Harper's Weekly*, 17 Dec. 1864.

22. Monroe, *Reminiscences of the War*, 18–19; Kimball Journal, 7 April 1863, 2534, UVA; Estabrooks, *Adrift in Dixie*, 105; "On the Safe Side," London *Times*, 20 Oct. 1863.

23. *Daily Richmond Enquirer*, 4 July 1864; Felix Gregory De Fontaine, *Marginalia Gleanings from an Army Note-Book* (Columbia, S.C.: Steam Power Press of F. G. De Fontaine, 1864), 23; I. G. Bradwell, "The Irresponsible Race," *CV* 31 (April 1923): 134. Samuel Crook's first name is incorrectly given in this article as Daniel. He apparently was released or exchanged as he is listed in one source as having been discharged from the army in March 1865 (U.S. Adjutant General's Office, *Official Army Register of the Volunteer Force of the United States Army for the Years 1861, '62, '63, '64, '65* [Washington, D.C.: Adjutant General's Office, 1867; reprint, Gaithersburg, Md., 1987], pt. 2, 352).

24. Fields, *Slavery and Freedom*, 103–6, 108; Charles Lewis Wagandt, *The Mighty Revolution: Negro Emancipation in Maryland, 1862–1864* (Baltimore, 1964), 120; Robert to wife, 1 June 1862, Letters from Federal Soldier, 1242, UVA.

25. *Daily Richmond Examiner*, 1 March 1864.

26. Robert Cummings to his sister, 20 Sept. 1862, Robert Cummings Papers, Special Collections and Archives, Rutgers Universities Libraries; Bryant, "A Yankee Soldier Looks at the Negro," 136.

27. George Grenville Benedict, *Army Life in Virginia* (Burlington, Vt.: Free Press Association, 1895), 137; *OR*, ser. 3, 3:1142.

28. Wallace F. Workmaster, ed., "The Frank H. Shiras Letters, 1862–1865," *Western Pennsylvania Historical Magazine* 40 (Fall 1957): 189; Rawick, *American Slave*, 16:19, 21–23, 43, 47–49; "Slave Narratives: A Folk History of Slavery in the United States from Interviews with Former Slaves" (typescript, Washington, D.C., 1941), 17–20, 21–23, U.S. Works Project Administration, box A932, LC.

29. Estabrooks, *Adrift in Dixie*, 69, 80, 82, 88, 89, 95, 100–101, 111, 216–19.

30. Mrs. M. N. Munford, Williamsburg, to Gen. Naglee, 19 Nov. 1862, Virginia Cities Collection: Williamsburg Papers, W&M.

31. Betty Herndon Maury Diary, 16 May 1862, LC.

32. Tucker, *The Southern Church Justified*, 10, 15, 17, 34.

33. Richmond *Enquirer*, 4 Oct. 1864; London *Times*, 26 Feb. 1861.

34. Richmond *Daily Dispatch*, 2 Oct. 1862; "City Fortifications—Abuses," *Daily Richmond Examiner*, 9 Jan. 1862; "Acquittal of Mr. James W. Jones," *Winchester Republican*, 22 March 1861. See also Carl N. Degler, *The Other South: Southern Dissenters in the Nineteenth Century* (New York, 1974).

35. Clark to Underwood, 18 July 1865, Underwood to Clark, 21 July 1865, John Curtiss Underwood Scrapbook, LC, 95; John C. Underwood, U.S. District Court, Clerk's Office, Alexandria, to Edwin M. Stanton, Secretary of War, 2 Feb. 1864, Negro Military Service, roll 3, frame 54.

36. *Christian Banner* (Fredericksburg), 24 June 1862; George H. Gordon, *A War Diary of Events in the War of the Great Rebellion, 1863–1865* (Boston: James R. Osgood, 1882), 99–100; Fremantle, *Three Months in the Southern States*, 191.

37. L. Minor Blackford, *Mine Eyes Have Seen the Glory* (Cambridge, Mass., 1954), 1, 24, 41, 47, 49, 249–50.

38. Keckley, 17, 45, 65–75.

39. Ishbel Ross, *The President's Wife* (New York, 1973), 266–67; Ruth Painter Randall, *Lincoln's Sons* (Boston, 1955), 252–55; Justin G. Turner and Linda Lovitt Turner, *Mary Todd Lincoln* (New York, 1972), 471–72; Keckley, 241–42. For Keckley's later years, see Washington, *They Knew Lincoln*, 214–15, 223–24. The only reference to Keckley in the standard biography of Robert Lincoln, John S. Goff, *Robert Todd Lincoln* (Norman, Okla., 1969), makes no mention of his efforts to suppress her book when it appeared in 1868. Several skeptics doubted that Keckley wrote *Behind the Scenes;* for a discussion of this controversy, see Washington, *They Knew Lincoln*, 226–41.

40. Isaac D. Williams, *Sunshine and Shadow of Slave Life* (East Saginaw, Mich.: Evening News Printing and Binding House, 1885; reprint, New York, 1975), 5, 9–10, 60, 81; Hughes, *Thirty Years a Slave*, 5–9.

41. Woodson, *Mind of the Negro*, 536–37, 572; *Slave Voices: Things Past Telling* (Washington, D.C., 1987), sound cassette.

42. Rawick, *American Slave*, vol. 17, ser. 2, *Florida Narratives*, 311–26.

43. *National Anti-Slavery Standard*, 10 May 1862, 24 Jan. 1863.

44. Martin to Susan P. Martin, 17 July 1864, Perry-Martin-McCue Papers, 6806-B, UVA; Sir William Howard Russell, *My Diary North and South*, ed. Fletcher Pratt (New York, 1954), 48–50.

45. *Douglass' Monthly*, June 1861, 477; *National Anti-Slavery Standard*, 10 May 1862, 24 Jan. 1863.

46. House Committee on War Claims, *Summary Reports* 1 (1871–74): 561, 563, 573.

47. T. K. Cartmell, *Shenandoah Valley Pioneers and Their Descendants* (Winchester, Va., 1909), 521–22.

48. "Negro Slaves As I Have Known Them," 3, 17–18, J. Willcox Brown Collection of Reminiscences, VSLA; John Charles McNeill, *Lyrics from Cotton Land* (Charlotte, N.C., 1907), photograph facing p. 100.

49. Moore, *Civil War in Song*, 523.

50. Shaw, *Black Popular Music*, 19, 22; Southern, *Music of Black Americans*, 89.

51. Guild, 109, 121–22, 169; *Southern Illustrated News*, 25 Oct. 1862, 14 Feb. 1863. Performances by Bud and Buckley's Minstrels and Band occurred as late as 1 April 1865 ("Highest price paid for old and new CORK at the Hall," *Richmond Daily Examiner*, 31 March and 1 April 1865).

52. Hardin Craig and David Bevington, eds., *The Complete Works of Shakespeare*, rev. ed. (Glenview, Ill., 1973), 947–49, 956.

53. *Richmond Enquirer*, 18 Nov. 1862; Richmond *Examiner*, 7–13 Sept. 1864; *Central Presbyterian* (Richmond), 15 Oct. 1862.

54. *Duncombe's Ethiopian Songster, and Mississippi Screamer, Containing All the Newest and Most Popular Nigger Songs*, collected, edited, and arranged by J. H. Cave (London: T. J. Allman, 1861), 14, 76.

55. *Richmond Enquirer*, 23, 31 Jan., 4, 7, 11, 18, 29 Feb. 1862; *The Marvelous Musical Prodigy, Blind Tom: The Negro Boy Pianist, Whose Performances at the Great St. James and Egyptian Halls, London, and Salle Hertz, Paris, Have Created Such a Profound Sensation. Anecdotes, Songs, Sketches of the Life, Testimonials of Musicians, and Savans, and Opinions of the American and English Press, of "Blind Tom"* (Baltimore: Sun "Book" and Job Printing Establishment, 1876). The 1867 edition of this pamphlet (New York: French & Wheat) contains a phrase omitted from the 1876 edition: ". . . and everywhere to good houses except in Boston" (p. 9), perhaps an example of lingering Southern antipathy toward New Englanders.

56. Catherine Barbara Broun Diary, 1 May 1864, 2:34, SHC.

57. Betsy Fleet and John D. Fuller, eds., *Green Mount: A Virginia Plantation Family during the Civil War* (Lexington, Ky., 1962), 356; Claiborne to wife, 21 Dec. 1864, Letters of Dr. Claiborne, 3633, UVA.

58. See Appendix C below. See also Raymond Starr and Robert Detweiler, *Race, Prejudice, and the Origins of Slavery in America* (Cambridge, Mass., 1975).

59. Maria Gordon Pryor Rice Reminiscences, 8, VHS.

7. UNEQUAL JUSTICE

1. Barrett Hollander, *Slavery in America* (New York, 1963), 186–210; text of the Confederate Constitution, Matthews, *Statutes at Large*, 11–23. The Confederacy had two constitutions, one provisional (February-March 1861) and the other permanent (March 1861-April 1865). Treason in Virginia was defined as "levying war against the State, adher-

ing to its enemies or giving them aid and comfort" (broadside, *Treason in Virginia*, 15 May 1861, Rare Book Division, UVA; Lexington *Valley Star*, 6 June 1861).

2. Kennedy, *Population of the United States in 1860*, xiii, 519; Evans, *Judah P. Benjamin*, 161–62; Wade, *Slavery in the Cities*, 106–9; Richard H. Clark, Thomas Read Rootes Cobb, and David Irwin, eds., *The Code of the State of Georgia* (Atlanta: John H. Seals, 1861), 266, 320–21, 875–82.

3. *Daily Richmond Examiner*, 5 March 1864; Richmond *Daily Whig*, 1 Nov. 1862.

4. Richmond *Enquirer*, 24 Dec. 1861, 24, 31 Oct., 4 Nov. 1862; Eckenrode, "Negroes in Richmond in 1864," 197; Philip J. Schwarz, *Twice Condemned: Slaves and the Criminal Laws of Virginia, 1705–1865* (Baton Rouge, La., 1988), 302; "Crime among Our Servile Population," *Daily Richmond Examiner*, 5 March 1864.

5. *Code of Virginia*, 277, 661–62, 675–77; Eckenrode, "Negroes in Richmond in 1864," 199.

6. *Acts of the General Assembly of the State of Virginia, Passed at the Session Commencing Dec. 4, 1848, and Ending March 19, 1849, in the Seventy-third Year of the Commonwealth* (Richmond: William F. Ritchie, 1849), 51; *Richmond Examiner*, 14 Oct. 1864.

7. *Richmond Examiner*, 23 June 1864; Richmond *Enquirer*, 18 Nov. 1862.

8. Randolph, *Slave Cabin to Pulpit*, 81–82.

9. *Code of Virginia*, 508–13; Snavely, *Taxation of Negroes*, 10–15; *Liberator* (Boston, Mass.), 29 July 1989; *Richmond Times*, 22 April 1865; *Message of the Governor of Virginia, Document 2, Biennial Report of the Auditor of Public Accounts, 1862 & 1863*, 7; *Norfolk and Portsmouth Herald*, 27 Feb. 1861; Jordan, *Charlottesville*, 82. The Norfolk law was repealed in August 1863 by Union occupation authorities.

10. Richmond *Examiner*, 29 June 1864; *Richmond Whig*, 2 March, 24 Oct. 1864. Bohannon, previously certified as a lunatic, was returned to an asylum. Several months later he shot a white child to death at Seabrook Hospital.

11. *New York Daily Tribune*, 4 Oct. 1864; *Equal Suffrage: Address from the Colored Citizens of Norfolk, Va., to the People of the United States, Also an Account of the Agitation among the Colored People of Virginia for Equal Rights* (Bedford, Mass., 1865); reprint, in Afro-American History Series, Collection 3, *The Black Intellectual* (Wilmington, Del., n.d.), 23–26.

12. *National Anti-Slavery Standard*, 30 Jan. 1864.

13. Washington, *Story of My Life*, 30, 32; [Richard Eppes, Charles City County], "Code for Laws for Island Plantation," Eppes Family Papers, VHS.

14. *Code of Virginia*, 815–17, 847–49.

15. "Condemned Slaves, Transported" folders, 1861, 1862, 1865, Auditor of Public Accounts: Condemned Blacks Executed or Transported, 1783–1865, entry 756, box 1792, RG 48.756, VSLA.

16. Helen Tunnicliff Catterall, *Judicial Cases concerning American Slavery and the Negro*, vol. 1, *Cases from the Courts of England, Virginia, West Virginia, and Kentucky* (Washington, D.C., 1926), 247–48; Executive Papers of Gov. William Smith, 6 Feb. 1865, box 467, VSLA; Thomas Green, Petersburg, to mother, 19 Feb. 1865, Green W. Penn Papers, Duke.

17. Steward, *Twenty-two Years a Slave*, 24; Roles, *Inside Views of Slavery*, 16–20.

18. Steward, *Twenty-two Years a Slave*, 15; George Ryley Scott, *The History of Torture throughout the Ages* (London, 1954), 196; "Tales of Slavery Told by Mrs. Fannie Berry—Anecdotes," 1, Ex-Slave Interviews, 3462, UVA.

19. "Tales of Slavery Told by Mrs. Fannie Berry—Anecdotes," 1, Ex-Slave Interviews, 3462, UVA; Weld, *American Slavery*, 178, 127, 88; *Negro in Virginia*, 155; J. H. Van

Evrie, *White Supremacy and Negro Subordination* (New York: Van Evrie & Horton, 1868), 121–22; Eckenrode, "Negroes in Richmond in 1864," 198.

20. Undated draft of a note ordering the whipping of a female slave, Austin-Twyman Papers, folder 165, W&M.

21. Conway, *Testimonies concerning Slavery,* 28–31, 38–41, 44–47; 7th U.S. Census, 1850, Virginia, Stafford County, Falmouth, Eastern District, frame 027. Neither a George Pickett nor any other white male fitting Captain Pickett's description was enumerated in the 1860 census of Falmouth. For Conway's antislavery views, see Conway, *The Rejected Stone; or, Insurrection vs. Resurrection in America,* 2d ed. (Boston: Walker and Wise, 1862), 93–112, 124–31, and John D'Entremont, *Southern Emancipator: Moncure Conway, the American Years, 1832–1865* (New York, 1987), 158.

22. Washington, *Story of My Life,* 36–37; interview of Reverend Massie [Ishrael Massie], 2–3, Ex-Slave Interviews, 3462, UVA.

23. *Negro in Virginia,* 154–55; W.P.A. Folklore, 1547, box 1, "Recollections," UVA; Weld, *American Slavery,* 88, 178. Confederate soldiers were occasionally punished by flogging. Prt. Owen Maguire, Company H, 1st Virginia Infantry, received one hundred lashes for desertion in 1862 (Richmond *Daily Dispatch,* 6 Oct. 1862).

24. *National Anti-Slavery Standard,* 14 April 1866; Douglas Southall Freeman, *R. E. Lee: A Biography* (New York, 1934–35), 1:390–93; Wyatt-Brown, *Southern Honor,* 371–72.

25. *Code of Virginia,* 817; Richmond *Examiner,* 15 March 1865; Jordan, *Charlottesville,* 28; "Code for Laws for Island Plantation," Eppes Family Papers, VHS; Randolph, *Slave Cabin to Pulpit,* 162–64; Hopley, *Life in the South* 1:148; "City Fortifications—Abuses," *Daily Richmond Examiner,* 9 Jan. 1862; *Daily Richmond Examiner,* 10 Feb. 1863; "Tales of Slavery Told by Mrs. Fannie Berry—Anecdotes," 1, and interview of Reverend Massie [Ishrael Massie], 2–3, Ex-Slave Interviews, 3462, UVA.

Confederate Virginia newspapers employed a variety of euphemisms for whippings: "teasings," "to pass under the lash," "a dressing," "hug the post," "to hug the widow," "kiss the cowhide," "strap-hopping," "dance the cowhide tune," "paddling," "jump and twitch," "corrections," "floppings," "nigger desserts," "leather-lessons," "dressings," "disciplinings," "ordered to be thrashed," "ordered to stripes," "hand-sawings," "flagellations," "switchings," and "ticklings." Apparently there was an unspoken arrangement to use code words to minimize giving offense to the sensibilities of the British and French (in order that their governments would grant the Confederacy diplomatic recognition) and to discredit reports of Southern slave brutality that frequently appeared in Northern newspapers. Afro-Virginians were extrajudicially and disproportionately punished by whippings after the war. See Joint Committee, 1866 testimony of Madison Newby and Thomas Bain, 55, 59.

26. Berlin, *Destruction of Slavery,* 95–98; Ezra J. Warner, *Generals in Blue* (Baton Rouge, La., 1964), 557–58; Richmond *Examiner,* 30 June 1864; *Daily Richmond Enquirer,* 1 July 1864 (both newspapers erroneously identify Clopton as "Clayton"). Clopton is enumerated in 1860 census returns as owning real estate and personal property valued at $22,873, including 25 slaves (ages 2 to 70) (8th U.S. Census, 3 July 1860, Charles City County, Virginia, dwelling no. 198 and family no. 198, 140; 8th U.S. Census, 1860, Slave Schedules, Charles City County, 25 June 1860, 151).

27. Perdue, *Weevils in the Wheat,* 162.

28. House Committee on War Claims, *Summary Reports,* 1:194–95.

29. Schwarz, *Twice Condemned,* 311; Richmond *Examiner,* 15 March 1865.

30. *Daily Richmond Enquirer*, 21, 22 Oct. 1864; *Daily Richmond Enquirer*, 4, 5 Nov. 1864. An assessment of Ben before his execution established his value at $5,000. (Folder "Executed Slaves 1861," Auditor of Public Accounts: Condemned Blacks Executed and Transported, 1783–1865, entry 756, box 1792, RG 48.756, VSLA). Royall Smith paid a $50 fine.

31. *Negro in Virginia*, 74; "Journal of Annual Receipts and Disbursements, Robert Thurston Hubard, 1835–1871," 12 April 1863, Hubard Family Papers, 8039, box 24, UVA.

32. Richmond *Daily Examiner*, 11 Oct. 1864.

33. Richmond *Sentinel*, 15 June 1863; *Acts of the General Assembly of the State of Virginia, Passed in 1861, in the Eighty-Fifth Year of the Commonwealth* (Richmond: William F. Ritchie, 1861), 255–57, and *Journal of the House of Delegates of the State of Virginia, for the Extra Session, 1861* (Richmond: William F. Ritchie, 1861), 265.

34. *Message of the Governor of Virginia, and Accompanying Documents (Appendix to the Governor's Messages, 1863), Document 7, Communication Relative to Reprieves, Pardons, etc.* (Richmond, 1863), 4, 5, 10; Richmond *Examiner*, 29 Jan. 1863.

35. *Message of the Governor of Virginia, and Accompanying Documents: Document No. 16, Communication Relative to Pardons, Reprieves, etc., December 1863* (Richmond, 1863), 11, 16, 17–18, 21.

36. Alfred Hoyt Bill, *The Beleaguered City: Richmond, 1861–1865* (New York, 1946), 14; Orlando Faulkland Lewis, *The Development of American Prisons and Prison Conditions, 1776–1845* (Albany, 1922), 210–16.

37. *Message of the Governor of Virginia, and Accompanying Documents: Document No. 13, Annual Report of the Board of Directors of the Penitentiary Institution. Year Ending September 30, 1861* (Richmond, 1861), 20–23, 28, 33; *Message of the Governor of Virginia, and Accompanying Documents: Document No. 6, Annual Report of the Board of Directors of the Penitentiary Institution, Year Ending September 30, 1862* (Richmond, 1862), 33; *Message of the Governor of Virginia, Document 9, Annual Report of the Board of Dirctors of the Penitentiary Institution, Year Ending September 30, 1863*, 18, 19, 30–31; *Daily Richmond Enquirer*, 19. Jan. 1865; "List of Negroes at Grace Furnace, 1863" and "List of Negroes at Cloverdale Furnace, 1863," Tredegar Iron Company Records, bound volume "Negroes and Rations at Catawba," box 31, VSLA. Bayliss remained in the penitentiary until his release by Union forces in April 1865 (John Herbert Claiborne, *Seventy-five Years in Old Virginia* [New York, 1904], 137; *Negro in Virginia*, 138).

38. Guild, 92; *Message of the Governor, Document 9, 1863*, 30–31; *Journal of the House of Delegates, 1863–64, Document No. 1, Messages* [of the governor], xviii.

39. *Code of Virginia*, 816; Richmond *Enquirer*, 21 Jan. 1862, 12 Nov. 1864; Charlottesville *Daily Chronicle*, 11 March 1864.

40. Richmond *Examiner*, 27 Feb., 20 Jan. 1865, 10 Feb. 1863.

41. Guild, 107, 120–21, 166; Richmond *Sentinel*, 30 Dec. 1863; "The Nigger Treasury Robbery," Richmond *Examiner*, 7 Feb. 1863.

42. Estabrooks, *Adrift in Dixie*, 169; Lynchburg *Daily Republican*, 16 Jan. 1863; Petersburg *Daily Express*, 16 Aug. 1861; Richmond *Daily Dispatch*, 28 Dec. 1861; Richmond *Enquirer*, 9 Aug. 1864.

43. Guild, 45–46, 51, 62, 64, 96, 107, 112, 168; Richmond *Enquirer*, 5 Dec. 1862.

44. Pass for Henry, 1863, Jefferson Davis Collection, Museum of the Confederacy; Wade, *Slavery in the Cities*, 108, 89; Woodward, *Mary Chesnut's Civil War*, 458.

45. Richmond *Daily Dispatch*, 30 Dec. 1861; Richmond *Whig*, 6 Aug. 1864; Petersburg *Daily Express*, 25 Aug. 1862; *Daily Richmond Examiner*, 26 Jan. 1863.

46. Eleanor P. Cross and Charles B. Cross, Jr., eds., *Glencoe Diary* (Chesapeake, Va.,

1968), 24; Richmond *Enquirer*, 11 Feb. 1862, 25 Dec. 1861. For a discussion of slave resistance and the white response to it, see James L. Roark, *Slaves without Masters: Southern Planters in the Civil War and Reconstruction* (New York, 1977), 80–85, 99–110, 122–24.

47. Robert Christison, *A Dispensatory, or Commentary on the Pharmacopoeias of Great Britain (and the United States); Comprising the Natural History, Description, Chemistry, Pharmacy, Actions, Uses, and Doses of the Articles of the Materia Medica*, 2d ed. (Philadelphia: Lee and Blanchard, 1848), 687–89; George B. Wood, M.D., and Franklin Bache, *The Dispensatory of the United States of America*, 10th ed. (Philadelphia: Lippincott and Grambo, 1854), 490–93; Robley Dunglison, *New Remedies: With Formulae for Their Preparation and Administration*, 7th ed. (Philadelphia: Blanchard & Lea, 1856), 540–47; *Code of Virginia*, 512.

48. *Lynchburg Daily Virginian*, 28 March 1864; Catterall, *Judicial Cases* 1:254–55; Peachy R. Grattan, *Reports of Cases Decided in the Supreme Court of Appeals and in the General Court of Virginia*, vol. 16, *From July 1, 1860, to April 1, 1865*, 2d ed. (Richmond, J. H. O'Bannon, Superintendent Public Printing, 1895), 561–71 (hereafter cited as Grattan).

49. *Daily Richmond Enquirer*, 29 Oct., 19 Nov. 1864.

50. *Richmond Whig*, 10 Jan. 1863.

51. Cartmell, *Shenandoah Valley Pioneers*, 111; "The Tragedy near Middletown," *Alexandria Gazette*, 14 March 1861, and "Belle Grove Tragedy," *Strasburg News*, 3 April 1913, Belle Grove Collection, box 12, Handley Library, Winchester, Va. According to the 1913 article, the day before her scheduled execution Robinson was carried to Richmond (and she later died there in prison as part of the Confederate evacuation of the Valley. Another version of this incident represents Robinson as a nameless female cook at Belle Grove who predicted that any white woman who entered the house as its mistress would not live long; the prophecy came true when she slew the victim (identified as Mrs. Benjamin Collie in this source) with an ax and hid the body in the smokehouse (Lee, *Virginia Ghosts*, rev. ed., 191–92).

52. Richmond *Enquirer*, 29 Oct. 1862; Richmond *Examiner*, 28 June 1864; Petersburg *Daily Express*, 18 April 1864.

53. Putnam, *Richmond during the War*, 264–66; Eckenrode, "Negroes in Richmond in 1864," 200.

54. Richmond *Enquirer*, 4 Nov. 1862, 13 Dec. 1861; Richmond *Sentinel*, 8 June 1863; *Richmond Whig*, 23 Feb. 1864; Richmond *Daily Dispatch*, 28 Dec. 1861.

55. *Principia*, 23 July 1863; Richmond *Sentinel*, 28 Dec. 1863; *Richmond Whig*, 7 March 1864; *Liberator*, 1 April 1864, 55.

56. *Richmond Times*, 22 April 1865.

57. Petersburg *Daily Express*, 13 April 1864 (Butler's punishment was twenty-five lashes); Richmond *Examiner*, 21 June 1864.

58. *Richmond Daily Examiner*, 29 June 1864; Richmond *Enquirer*, 18, 21 Oct., 15 Nov. 1864; Richmond *Daily Dispatch*, 2 Oct. 1862.

59. Petersburg *Daily Express*, 20 Feb. 1862, 13 April 1864, 25 Nov. 1861.

60. *Daily Richmond Examiner*, 5 March 1864; Schwarz, *Twice Condemned*, 311; *Richmond Whig*, 7 March 1864; Petersburg *Daily Express*, 18 April 1864; Lynchburg *Daily Republican*, 14 July 1864.

61. *Richmond Daily Examiner*, 10 Oct. 1864; *Richmond Whig*, 17 March 1864; *Richmond Daily Dispatch*, 17 March 1864; Woodward, *Mary Chesnut's Civil War*, 134, 587.

62. *Brief Sketch of the Life of David Creigh*, 8–10; folder "1863–1865 Correspondence and Papers re Execution of David S. Creigh (1864 June)," Micajah Woods Papers, 10279, box 1, UVA.

63. Seventh U.S. Census, 1850, Virginia, Henrico County, Richmond, frame 349; M. Ellyson, *The Richardson Directory and Business Advertiser, for 1856* (Richmond: H. K. Ellyson, 1856), 149; 8th U.S. Census, 1860, Henrico County, Richmond, Second Ward, frame 240. Several variations of Hoeflick's name appear in print: "Hoeflick" (*Richmond Whig,* 1864, and Ellyson); "Hoeflish" (1850 census); "Hoelich" (1860 census), and "Hoefflick" (Richmond *Examiner,* 1864). "Hoeflick" is the most consistently used version of his surname.

64. *Richmond Daily Examiner,* 18 Oct. 1864; *Daily Richmond Enquirer,* 18 Oct., 18 Nov. 1864.

65. *Richmond Whig,* 20 Aug. 1864; *Daily Richmond Enquirer,* 20 Oct. 1864; *Richmond Daily Examiner,* 14 Oct. 1864.

66. *Daily Richmond Enquirer,* 19 Jan. 1865; 20 Oct. 1864; *Richmond Daily Examiner,* 19, 20 Jan. 1865.

67. Luther Guiteau Billings Memoirs, "Only Yesterday," 82, LC; Lorenzo J. Greene, *Working with Carter G. Woodson, the Father of Black History: A Diary, 1928–1930,* ed. Avarah E. Strickland (Baton Rouge, La., 1989), 226.

68. Franklin, *Militant South,* 74, 77.

69. Bertram Wilbur Doyle, *The Etiquette of Race Relations in the South: A Study in Social Control* (Chicago, 1937), 107; Steward, *Twenty-two Years a Slave,* 32.

70. Proclamation, *To the Union Men of Western Virginia,* 26 May 1861, Negro Military Service, roll 1, frame 0401.

71. Carroll, *Slave Insurrections,* 204; Herbert Aptheker, *The Negro in the Civil War* (New York, 1938), 21, 24; Fleet and Fuller, *Green Mount,* 55; Richardson, *Compilation of the Messages and Papers* 1:233, 290–91, 495.

72. Wiley, *Plain People of the Confederacy,* 82.

73. Petersburg *Daily Express,* 24 Sept. 1861; Providence, R.I., *Post,* 6 June 1862, as quoted in the *Southern Federal Union* (Milledgeville, Ga.), 22 July 1862.

74. Flournoy, 233–34; *Daily Richmond Examiner,* 24 Oct. 1862; Lynchburg *Daily Virginian,* 27 Oct. 1862; Richmond *Daily Whig,* 24 Oct. 1862.

75. Flournoy, 235–36.

76. Ibid., *Daily Lynchburg Virginian,* 27 Oct. 1862; *Daily Richmond Examiner,* 24 Oct. 1862.

77. Carroll, *Slave Insurrections,* 208, 213–16; Wish, "Slave Disloyalty under the Confederacy," 450; Armstead L. Robinson, "In the Shadow of Old John Brown: Insurrection Anxiety and Confederate Mobilization, 1861–1863," *JNH* 65 (Fall 1980): 280–81, 294–95; Van Evrie, *Negroes and Negro "Slavery,"* 150; *Alexandria Gazette,* 14 March 1861.

78. Lexington *Valley Star,* 6 June, 7 March, 30 May 1861; Bertram Wyatt-Brown, *Southern Honor: Ethics and Behavior in the Old South* (New York, 1982), 451; Peter W. Hairston, Oak Hill, Va., to Fanny C. Hairston, Salisbury, N.C., 4 April 1861, Peter Wilson Hairston Papers, SHC; Davidson L. W. Charlton to Friend Oliver, 23 May 1861, Charlton Family Papers, Va. Tech.

79. *Liberator,* 24 Oct. 1862; *Richmond Daily Examiner,* 13 June 1864; Eckenrode, "Negroes in Richmond in 1864," 194; Ruffin, *Diary of Edmund Ruffin,* 3:630–31.

80. *Richmond Times,* 22 April 1865; Eckenrode, "Negroes in Richmond in 1864," 199–200; James E. Sefton, *The United States Army and Reconstruction, 1865–1877* (Baton Rouge, La., 1967), 194–95.

81. As an example, before John Buck was hanged at Lunenburg County on 20 June 1862, the following phrase appeared on the execution warrant: "Condemned Slave 1862,

Executed" (Auditor of Public Accounts: Condemned Blacks Executed or Transported, 1783–1865, entry 756, box 1792, RG 48.756, VSLA). A Petersburg newspaper wasted little space on black lawbreakers: "Two petty cases of theft were tried before the Mayor yesterday morning—both of the parties being negroes. . . . Both were whipped" (Petersburg *Daily Express,* 25 March 1865).

8. GRAND AND AWFUL TIMES

1. John Thomas Lewis Preston Diary, 24 July 1861, LC.

2. Henry W. Thomas, *History of the Doles-Cook Brigade Army of Northern Virginia, C.S.A.* (Atlanta, 1903), 615. See also the letters of James Graham Tate, 4th Virginia Infantry, [1861] and 21 Dec. 1862, Graham-Tate Family Papers, 9232-N, box 1, UVA. Tate asked his father to send Burkhart or Charles to cook and take care of his camp needs and mentions another camp cook, Bill.

3. *Illustrated London News,* 10 Jan. 1863, 41, 44; *OR,* ser. 1, 32: pt. 2, 683.

4. William Gibson Field Journal (typescript), 110, 10538, UVA.

5. Bradwell, "The Irresponsible Race," 133–34; Bell Irvin Wiley, *The Life of Johnny Reb: The Common Soldier of the Confederacy* (Indianapolis, 1943), 117, 327–28; Fredericksburg Hotel (?) Ledger, June–Aug. 1863, pp. 59–60, Dr. John Eugene Coles Papers, 9982, UVA.

6. Samuel Page pension application, 8 April 1924, Confederate Pension Applications for Body Servants, boxes 151–52, VSLA.

7. Daniel T. Balfour, *13th Virginia Cavalry* (Lynchburg, 1986), 84; Benjamin Washington Jones, *Under the Stars and Bars: A Private History of the Surry Light Artillery* (Richmond, 1909), 210; Surry Light Artillery roster, John H. Bell, Virginia Confederate Rosters, 18:380, and Bells' service record, Compiled Service Records of Confederate Soldiers Who Served in Organizations from Virginia (NA microfilm), roll 8, VSLA; roster of the Tredegar Battalion (6th Battalion, Local Defense Troops), Virginia Confederate Rosters, 17:20–52, ibid.; Lee A. Wallace, *A Guide to Virginia Military Organizations, 1861–1865,* 2d ed. (Lynchburg, 1986), 183–84.

8. Goochland Light Artillery, Compiled Service Records of Confederate Soldiers Who Served in Organizations from Virginia (NA microfilm), rolls 299–300, VSLA; Wallace, *Guide to Virginia Military Organizations, 1861–1865,* 22. I am grateful to Jeff Weaver (currently writing a history of the Goochland Artillery) of Arlington, Va., for bringing these Afro-Virginians to my attention. David Randolph is enumerated in the 1860 census for Goochland where he resided with his grandmother Judy (head of the household, age eighty, unable to read or write) and his mother Polly (age fifty-five, apparently unmarried). He is listed as a mulatto, but his mother and grandmother are described as black (8th U.S. Census, June 1860, Goochland County, Virginia, dwelling and family no. 23, p. 849). David's motives for enlistment were probably practical (to provide a regular source of income for his family) instead of patriotic.

9. *OR,* ser. 4, 2:941; Tom Henderson Wells, *The Confederate Navy: A Study in Organization* (University, Ala., 1971), 25, 27, 38, 65, 70; Brewer, 34–35; Wesley, *Collapse of the Confederacy,* 149.

10. Lynchburg *Daily Republican,* 5 Aug. 1862, 21 Oct. 1863; Balfour, *13th Virginia Cavalry,* 3.

11. Samuel Rodman Smith, Petersburg, to his father, 19 Oct. 1864 (p. 345 in a bound volume of his typescript letters), Samuel Rodman Smith Letters, Historical Society of Delaware, Wilmington; U.S. Adjutant General's Office, *Official Army Register,* pt. 3, 1052;

Simmons to wife, 7 June 1863, folder 3, Henry E. Simmons Letters, SHC; Carl to Uncle George, Sept. 1863, Civil War Collection, W&M.

12. Henry T. Blanchard to brother, 26 Aug. 1862, Civil War letter, 10756, UVA.

13. Woodall to his sister, 31 July 1863, Daniel Woodall Papers, Historical Society of Delaware, Wilmington. Notwithstanding Woodall's opinion, the Garibaldi Guard fought valiantly at Gettysburg where it successfully defended the Union center, captured three battle flags, and received a unit commendation for valor (U.S. Adjutant General's Office, *Official Army Register*, pt. 2, 476–78). Woodall received the rank of brevet brigadier general on 15 June 1865 for services rendered during the war (ibid., pt. 3, 1048; Warner, *Generals in Blue*, 595).

14. Toon to his brother, 2 Dec. 1862, Thomas Fentress Toon letter, Duke; W. F. Clayton, *A Narrative of the Confederate States Navy* (Weldon, N.C., 1910), 104–5; Ervin L. Jordan, Jr., and Herbert A. Thomas, Jr., *19th Virginia Infantry* (Lynchburg, Va., 1987), 3.

15. Henry Kyd Douglas, *I Rode with Stonewall* (Chapel Hill, N.C., 1940), 336; slave pass signed by C. B. Cocke, 1 May 1861, Cocke Family Papers, 640, box 163, UVA.

16. CSA document, VHS.

17. CSA War Department, *General Orders, Confederate States Army, January, 1862, to December, 1863*, 80; CSA War Department, *General Orders, Confederate States Army*, 59.

18. See W.P.A. Folklore, 1547, box 1, folder 8, "Ex-Slaves," UVA; Charles W. White, *The Hidden and the Forgotten: Contributions of Buckingham Blacks to American History* (Marceline, Mo., 1985), 54; Ruth Coder Fitzgerald, *A Different Story: A Black History of Fredericksburg, Stafford, and Spotsylvania, Virginia* (n.p., 1979), 90; Lee A. Wallace, *5th Virginia Infantry* (Lynchburg, Va., 1988), 90; Fredericksburg *Free Lance-Star*, 6 June 1932.

19. Jack Foster to his master, 24 June 1862, Tompkins Family Papers, VHS.

20. "A Noble Contribution," Richmond *Sentinel*, 31 July 1863; Fremantle, *Three Months in the Southern States*, 234, 281. James Lawson Kemper, governor of Virginia 1874–77, defended black participation in postwar commemorations of Jackson: "It would be an appropriate and striking tribute to the great Confederate (Jackson) for the negroes to unite [with us] in honor to his name" (Kemper to Fitzhugh Lee, 4 Nov. 1875, Fitzhugh Lee Papers, W&M).

21. "Memoirs of Leroy Wesley Cox," acc. no. 940, Albemarle County Historical Society (acc. no. 5049 at UVA); An English Combatant, *Battle-Fields of the South, from Bull Run to Fredericksburgh; with Sketches of Confederate Commanders, and Gossip of the Camps* (New York: John Bradburn, 1864), 284.

22. Ibid., 110–11, 252–53; Wayne P. Austerman, "Virginia's Black Confederates," *Civil War Quarterly* 8 (March 1987): 47; George Baylor, "The Army Negro," *SHSP* 31 (1903): 365–66; An English Combatant, *Battle-Fields of the South*, 279.

23. Myrta Lockett Avary, ed., *A Virginia Girl in the Civil War, 1861–1865* (New York, 1903), 293–96.

24. Lexington *Valley Star*, 6 June 1861; Thomas Joseph Macon, *Reminiscences of the First Company of Richmond Howitzers* (Richmond, 1909), 81–82; 7 Sept. 1863, Montpelier Letters, 10631-A, UVA; *Southern Federal Union* (Milledgeville, Ga.), 22 July 1862.

25. Rufus H. Peck, *Reminiscence of a Confederate Soldier of Co. C, 2nd Virginia Cavalry* (Fincastle, Va., 1913), 63–64; Civil War Reminiscence of Robert Thurston Hubard, Jr., chap. 11, p. 194 in the original volume, p. 85 of the typescript, Hubard Family, 10522, UVA.

26. Macon *Georgia Weekly Telegraph*, 28 July 1862; Claiborne, *Seventy-Five Years in Old Virginia*, 267.

27. John Singleton Mosby Scrapbooks, 3:34, 7872-A, UVA.

28. Edward Porter Alexander, *Fighting for the Confederacy*, ed. Gary W. Gallagher (Chapel Hill, N.C., 1989), 76–77, 229; Dabney Herndon Maury, *Recollections of a Virginian in the Mexican, Indian, and Civil Wars*, 3d ed. (New York: Charles Scribner's Sons, 1894), 160–63, 165.

29. Fredericksburg *Free Lance*, 7 Nov. 1905.

30. William Mack Lee, *History of the Life of Rev. William Mack Lee, Body Servant of General Robert E. Lee, through the Civil War, Cook from 1861 to 1865; Still Living under the Protection of the Southern States* (Norfolk, Va., 1922), 3, 12–13.

31. Ibid., 3–6, 10–11, 14.

32. Ibid., 4, 7, 9, 11, 13.

33. "Comrades of Hagerstown, Maryland," *CV* 33 (1925): 468; Frank Vandiver, *Mighty Stonewall* (New York, 1957), 448; Bell Irvin Wiley, *Embattled Confederates: An Illustrated History of Southerners at War* (New York, 1964), 235.

34. Burke Davis, *They Called Him Stonewall* (New York, 1954), 25; Mary Anna Jackson, *Life and Letters of General Thomas J. Jackson* (New York: Harper, 1892), 288, 372; John Overton Casler, *Four Years in the Stonewall Brigade* (Girard, Kans., 1906), 92; Douglas, *I Rode with Stonewall*, 154–55; Vandiver, *Mighty Stonewall*, 492; Robert Lewis Dabney, *Life and Campaigns of Lieu.-Gen. Thomas J. Jackson* (New York: Blelock, 1866), 716; William Gleason Bean, *Stonewall's Man: Sadie Pendleton* (Wilmington, N.C., 1987), 69, 81, 121, 124.

35. *Lexington Gazette and Citizen*, 17 Dec. 1875; Francis Springer, "Beyond the Call of Duty," *Southern Partisan*, Spring 1985, 29; Joseph B. Earnest, Jr., *The Religious Development of the Negro in Virginia* (Charlottesville, Va., 1914), 83–84.

36. Lebsock, *Virginia Women*, 81; Woodward, *Mary Chesnut's Civil War*, 535, 545; *Harper's Weekly*, 7 June 1862; Quarles, *Negro in the Civil War*, 81–82; Fleming, *Jefferson Davis*, 12–14.

37. Fleming, *Jefferson Davis*, 14; Quarles, *Negro in the Civil War*, 25; *OR*, ser. 1, 46: pt. 3, 1249; Edward Augustus Johnson, *A School History of the Negro Race in America from 1619 to 1890* (Philadelphia: Sherman, 1893), 136–37; Monroe Work, comp., *Negro Year Book: An Annual Encyclopedia of the Negro, 1921–1922* (Tuskegee Institute, Ala., 1922), 375.

38. James Joseph McDonald, *Life in Old Virginia*, ed. J. A. C. Chandler (Norfolk, Va., 1907), photograph adjacent to p. 220; 12th U.S. Census, 1900, Virginia, City of Fredericksburg, p. 221, sheet 20B; Robert K. Krick, *The Fredericksburg Artillery* (Lynchburg, Va., 1986), 105; Fredericksburg *Free Lance*, 14 May 1927; 13th U.S. Census, 1910, Virginia, Northumberland County, Lottsburg District, 11 May 1910, p. 8B.

39. "Levi Miller, Confederate Veteran," *CV* 29 (1921): 358; "Confederate Pension for a Colored Man," "Levi Miller Has a Good War Record," and "Levi Miller, Colored War Veteran, Dead," Winchester *Evening Star*, 17 June 1908, Feb. 25, 26, 1921. My thanks to Ben Ritter of Winchester, Va., for copies of the *Evening Star* articles. Black Hawk, an ex–body servant residing in Woodstock, had his picture displayed in an pro-Confederate postbellum periodical and proudly told of his service with Chew's Battery and his capture on two occasions by Yankees ("Gratitude of a Faithful Servant," *CV* 20 [1912]: 410).

40. Fredericksburg *Daily Star*, 23 Oct. 1912; *Culpeper Virginia Star*, 9 April 1931, 8 March 1934; "Colored Vet's Son in France," *Winchester Evening Star*, 9 June 1918.

41. Jay S. Hoar, *The South's Last Boys in Gray* (Bowling Green, Ohio, 1986), 55, 212–14, 28, 392–93; *Acts and Joint Resolutions of the General Assembly of the Commonwealth of Virginia, Session 1954 Which Commenced at the State Capitol, Richmond, on Wednesday, January 13, 1954* (Richmond, 1954), 942.

42. Wiley, *Southern Negroes*, 145.

43. Alice Clark Peirce, comp., *Index of Acts of the General Assembly of the Commonwealth of Virginia, 1912–1959* (Richmond, 1959), 84–86.

44. *Acts and Joint Resolutions (Amending the Constitution) of the General Assembly of the State of Virginia, Session Which Commenced at the State Capitol on Wednesday, January 9, 1924* (Richmond, 1924), 295–97.

45. Ibid., 298–302.

46. Auditor of Public Accounts, *Annual Report of Officers, Boards, and Institutions of the Commonwealth of Virginia for the Twenty-one Months Ending June 30, 1925* (Richmond, 1925), 168; *Annual Report . . . Ending June 30, 1926* (Richmond, 1927), 194; *1925 Roster of Confederate Pensioners of Virginia* (Richmond, 1925), 113; *1926 Roster . . .* (Richmond, 1926), 106; General Assembly, *Acts and Joint Resolutions (Amending the Constitution) of the General Assembly of the State of Virginia, Session Which Commenced at the State Capitol on Wednesday, January 11, 1928* (Richmond, 1928), 555–56; *Acts and Joint Resolutions, 1954,* 941–42.

47. General Assembly, *Acts and Joint Resolutions . . . , Session 1978 Which Commenced at the State Capitol, Richmond, on Wednesday, January 11, 1978 and Ended on Saturday, March 11, 1978* (Richmond, 1978), 1506; U.S. Congress, *Veterans' Benefits Act of 1957,* in *U.S. Statutes at Large* 72 (1958): 133–34; U.S. Congress, Committee on the Judiciary, *Veterans' Benefits Act,* in *U.S. Code,* title 38, 7: sec. 510 (1958), 6240.

48. Boris I. Bittker, *The Case for Black Reparations* (New York, 1973), 4–5, 19, 159–75. The former East German government officially apologized to Israel and Jews for the Holocaust. West Germany paid reparations to the state of Israel for the crimes of Nazi Germany against Jews during World War II even though neither country existed at the time. In 1988 the United States Congress approved payments of $20,000 apiece and a presidential letter of apology to 60,000 Japanese-Americans who were forcibly interned or evacuated to concentration camps during the Second World War.

49. Joseph A. Mudd, "The Confederate Negro," *CV* 23 (1915): 411.

9. TROUBLESOME ELITES

1. Diary of Lucy Rebecca Buck, 18 June 1862, Buck Family Papers, 4932, box 3, UVA; *Code of Virginia,* 520.

2. Kennedy, *Population of the United States in 1860,* vii, 214, 509, 515; *Journal of the House of Delegates of the State of Virginia, for the Session of 1861–62* (Richmond: William F. Ritchie, Public Printer, 1861), 338; *Journal of the House of Delegates, 1863–64,* 101; Carter G. Woodson, *The Education of the Negro Prior to 1861* (New York, 1915), 240.

3. John Hammond Moore, *Albemarle: Jefferson's County, 1727–1976* (Charlottesville, Va., 1976), 428; Gutman, *Black Family,* 91; Perdue, *Weevils in the Wheat,* 67, 259.

4. Hodges, *Free Man of Color,* xxx–xlii.

5. Andrews, *Slavery and the Domestic Slave-Trade,* 162; Hopley, *Life in the South* 2:123; *De Bow's Review,* Jan. 1861, 121–22.

6. *OR,* ser. 4, 3:914.

7. Berlin, *Destruction of Slavery,* 760–62.

8. Ibid., 764–65; "Free Negroes / Charles City County (1863), Fredricksburg (1862)," Auditor of Public Accounts: Free Blacks, entry 757, box 1974, RG 48.756, VSLA; Jackson, "Manumission in Certain Virginia Cities," 295–300; Washington Jackson MS, 5 Oct. 1865, Rockbridge County Historical Society, University Library, Washington and Lee University, Lexington, Va.; Washington Jackson, 6th U.S. Census, 1840, Virginia, Rockbridge County, 199; and 8th U.S. Census, 1860, Virginia, Rockbridge County, 6th District, 275.

Jackson is not listed in the 1850 census for Rockbridge County, but in the 1860 enumeration he is described as a forty-five-year-old mulatto blacksmith with a forty-year-old wife and eight-year-old son.

9. *De Bow's Review*, May–June 1868, 475; Robert Wallace Shand files of Robert K. Krick, chief historian, Fredericksburg and Spotsylvania National Military Park.

10. Richmond *Enquirer*, 4 Aug. 1864. One free black who abruptly returned to Virginia after seeking his fortune in the North was asked why. He haughtily replied, "The North is no place for a Virginia gentleman" (Bishop William Meade, *Sketches of Old Virginia Family Servants* [Philadelphia: Isaac Ashmead, 1847], 83).

11. "The Contrabands at Fortress Monroe," *Atlantic Monthly*, Nov. 1861: 635, Petersburg *Daily Express*, 2 July 1862.

12. Jackson, *Free Negro Labor*, 6; Guild, 72; *Code of Virginia*, 518–20.

13. Ellen Afto Collection, 10 Jan. 1861, WFCHS.

14. C. C. Baldwin to James Penn, 1 Feb. 1864, and arrest warrant of 27 Feb. 1864, Cocke Family Papers, 640, box 171, UVA. Penn (a fifty-six-year-old mulatto), his wife Jane, and a ten-year-old boy named William Washington are enumerated in the 1870 census of Rockbridge County. He owned $500 in personal property and real estate (9th U.S. Census, 1870, Virginia, Rockbridge County, Natural Bridge Township, 8 Sept. 1870, 517).

15. Katherine G. Bushmen, ed., *The Registers of Free Blacks, 1810–1864, Augusta County, Virginia, and Staunton, Virginia* (Verona, Va., 1989), 144.

16. *Acts of the General Assembly, 1861–2*, 4, 146, 61–63; *Code of Virginia*, 522; *Acts of the General Assembly, Adjourned Session, 1863*; *Public Hiring of Free Negroes*, broadside, [Fredericksburg], 5 Feb. 1855, Rare Book Division, UVA; "City Fortifications—Abuses," *Richmond Daily Examiner*, 9 Jan. 1862.

17. Jordan, *Charlottesville*, 82; Manarin, *Richmond at War*, 344, 346, 349, 518–19; Eckenrode, "Negroes in Richmond in 1864," 197; Berlin, *Slaves without Masters*, 242–43; *Daily Richmond Examiner*, 10 Feb. 1863; Petersburg *Daily Express*, 5 Nov. 1862.

18. Donald Sweig, ed., *"Registration of Free Negroes Commencing September Court 1822, Book No. 2" and "Registers of Free Blacks 1835, Book 3": Being the Full Text of the Two Extant Volumes, 1822–1861, of Registration of Free Blacks Now in the County Courthouse, Fairfax, Virginia* (Fairfax, Va., 1977), 1–5; Guild, 95–122; Jackson, *Free Negro Labor*, 194–95; Hurd, *The Law of Freedom and Bondage* 2:10; Jordan, *Charlottesville*, 78.

19. Entry for Betty Noel, Smyth and Wythe Counties, Va., Ledger, 13, Va. Tech; Charlotte K. Brooks, Joseph K. Brooks, and Walter H. Brooks 3rd, *A Brooks Chronicle: The Lives and Times of an African-American Family* (Washington, D.C., 1989), 3, 5, 8, 11, 29, 35, 38; Jackson, "Manumission in Certain Virginia Cities," 305.

20. L. Adams to clerk of Lunenburg County, Va., 5 March 1862, Luther Porter Jackson Family Papers, box 55, folder "Lunenburg County," VSU; 8th U.S. Census, 1860, Virginia, Henrico County, Richmond, Eastern District, p. 775, entry 849, Nancy Davis. The census lists another daughter, Anne; she and Nancy were literate.

21. *Code of Virginia*, 521; Sweig, *Registration of Free Negroes*, 4, 7, 255–57; Jackson, *Free Negro Labor*, 58; Ebert, "A Window on the Valley," 14–15.

22. "Free Negroes / Charles City County (1863), Fredericksburg (1862)," a list compiled by Robert W. Hart, Commissioner of the Revenue, 1 Feb. 1862, in Auditor of Public Accounts: Free Blacks, entry 757, box 1974, RG 48.756, VSLA; Register of Free Blacks, Washington County, 1838–63, entry no. 127, 41-A, UVA; Ebert, "A Window on the Valley," 16.

23. Richmond *Examiner*, 1 Jan. 1863; pass for Lucy Carter, 21 Feb. 1864, signed by Lt.

Col. Geo. P. Hollister, 16th New York Cavalry, Carter G. Woodson Collection, reel 9, frame 492, LC; *Code of Virginia*, 521–22; *Richmond Daily Examiner*, 22 June 1864.

24. *Richmond Enquirer*, 24 Jan., 21 Oct., 2 Dec. 1862; *Richmond Daily Examiner*, 22 June 1864; Lynchburg *Virginian*, 28 March, 13 April 1864. Harvey's pistol was confiscated. Jenkins and the Coopers are listed in Bushmen, *Registers of Free Blacks, 1810–1864, Augusta County*, 32, 91–93.

25. Jackson, *Free Negro Labor*, 3–33, 247–51; Ebert, "A Window on the Valley," 29–30.

26. Marie Tyler-McGraw and Gregg D. Kimball, *In Bondage and Freedom: Antebellum Black Life in Richmond, Virginia* (Richmond, 1988), 54–58; Jackson, *Free Negro Labor*, 157, 197, 218; Henrico County Deed Book no. 51 (microfilm reel 34), 23 March 1847, pp. 146–47, and no. 81 (microfilm reel 49), 28 Sept., 10 Oct. 1864, pp. 47–48, 55–56, VSLA; see also the society's constitution, Union Burial Ground Society, City of Richmond Papers, VSLA.

27. Suzanne Lebsock, *The Free Women of Petersburg: Status and Culture in a Southern Town, 1784–1860* (New York, 1984), 89–100, 240–41.

28. Ervin L. Jordan, Jr., "The Catherine Foster Family: Free Blacks in the Slavery Era," *Charlottesville-Albemarle Tribune*, 10 June 1993; Amy E. Grey, M. Drake Patten, and Mark S. Warner, "A Preliminary Assessment of the Venable Lane Site" (Charlottesville: Department of Anthropology, University of Virginia, 1993).

29. Engs, *Freedom's First Generation*, 11–13; "Property Owners, Norfolk County, 1860," *Lower Norfolk County Antiquary* 2 (1899): 1–11, 3 (1899): 12–18, 3 (1900): 62–69; Jackson, "Manumission in Certain Virginia Cities," 301–2, 307–9.

30. John H. Russell, "Colored Freemen as Slave Owners in Virginia," *JNH* 1 (June 1916): 234–40; Woodson, *Free Negro Owners of Slaves*, 33–42; *Code of Virginia*, 509–10.

31. *American Missionary*, July 1864, 174; Joint Committee, 57; Swint, *Dear Ones at Home*, 161; "The Contrabands at Fortress Monroe," *Atlantic Monthly*, Nov. 1861, 637; Davis, *Black Is the Color of the Cosmos*, 337; 8th U.S. Census, 1860, Virginia, Princess Anne County, p. 682. Fuller's age is listed as forty, and she described herself as a Virginia native. Her children were: Sarah, age 16; William, age 12; John, age 2; James, age 1; and Isaiah, age 10. See also "Slave Owners, Princess Anne County, 1840," *Lower Norfolk Antiquary* 4 (1903): 174–78, and Jackson, "Manumission in Certain Virginia Cities," 296–97, 301–5.

32. *Richmond Whig*, 20 Jan. 1864; *OR*, ser. 1, 4:573; Billy Wheeler document, 6 Dec. 1861, Museum of the Confederacy; "List of Negroes at Mt. Torry Furnace, Feb. 1st 1864," bound volume "Negroes and Rations at Catawba," Tredegar Iron Company Records, box 31, VSLA.

33. List of Free Black Males, 19 Aug. 1861, Luther Porter Jackson Family Papers, box 55, folder "Mecklenburg County," VSU; *OR*, ser. 1, 51: pt. 2, 682–83, 734; see also pp. 472–73.

34. *Richmond Enquirer*, 22 April 1862; Memoranda Book of Thomas S. Bocock, Papers of the Thornhill Family and Thomas S. Bocock, 10612, box 8, UVA; Thomas A. Smith Letters, 6846-T, UVA; D. Graham & Sons, Hands Book, 1864–69, Graham-Robinson Papers, 38–107, vol. 13, UVA.

35. *Daily Richmond Enquirer*, 25 Oct. 1864; *Daily Richmond Whig*, 10 Dec. 1861.

36. *Richmond Examiner*, 27 June 1864; *Richmond Enquirer*, 10 June 1862; *Richmond Sentinel*, 15 June 1863.

37. *Daily Richmond Enquirer*, 18 Oct. 1864.

38. Ibid., 7 Nov. 1864; Guild, 120. John Adams (ca. 1825–1873), is enumerated in the 7th U.S. Census, 1850, Virginia, Henrico County, city of Richmond, frame 277, and 8th U.S. Census, 1860, Virginia, 3d Ward, city of Richmond, Henrico County, frame 573; see

also Jackson, *Free Negro Labor*, 151, 157–58, 161–62; "Death of a Wealthy Colored Citizen," *Richmond Daily Whig*, 16 Jan. 1873, and John Adams Papers, 11078, UVA.

39. Richmond *Enquirer*, 9 Dec. 1862.

40. Joint Committee, 57–58; Gordon, *A War Diary*, 76; Swint, *Dear Ones at Home*, 109; Berlin, *Slaves without Masters*, 386–87; Jordan, *Charlottesville*, 28; Richmond *Daily Dispatch*, 28 Dec. 1861.

41. House Committee on War Claims, *Summary Reports* 2 (1875–76):240, 3 (1877–78):143, 4 (1879–80):231; Tinsley Lee Spraggins, "Mobilization of Negro Labor for the Department of Virginia and North Carolina, 1861–1865," *North Carolina Historical Review* 24 (April 1947): 168.

42. De Fontaine, *Marginalia*, 16, 72; Spraggins, "Mobilization of Negro Labor," 166. This department was also known as the Subsistence Department, Office of the Chief Commissary of Virginia.

43. Wilson, *The Black Phalanx*, 491; Williams, *History of the Negro Race in America from 1619 to 1880*, 278; Wesley, *Collapse of the Confederacy*, 142; James I. Robertson, Jr., *18th Virginia Infantry* (Lynchburg, Va., 1984), 50; Fitzgerald, *A Different Story*, 89; William T. Scruggs pension application, 29 Aug. 1924, Confederate Pension Applications for Body Servants, boxes 151–52, VSLA; Flournoy, 11:238; House Committee on War Claims, *Summary Reports* 1 (1871–74):401.

44. Howard Holman Bell, ed., *Minutes of the Proceedings of the National Negro Conventions, 1830–1864* (New York, 1969), 5, 8, 42.

10. ZEALOTS OF THE WRONG

1. Richmond *Daily Dispatch*, 25 May 1863; Tinsley quote, Petersburg *Daily Express*, 26 April 1861.

2. Charles Harris Wesley, "The Employment of Negroes as Soldiers in the Confederate Army," *JNH* 4 (1919): 241, and *Collapse of the Confederacy*, 142; Hopley, *Life in the South* 1:264–65, 318–19; J. K. Obatala, "The Unlikely Story of Blacks Who Were Loyal to Dixie," *Smithsonian Magazine* 9 (March 1979): 94–101; Berlin, *Slaves without Masters*, 386–87.

3. R. L. Patteson to Dear Uncle [Maj. James M. Patteson, Glenmore, Buckingham County], 14 May 1861, folder 15 May 1861–21 Dec. 1861, item 89–89b, box 4, Patteson Family Papers, VSLA. I am grateful to Ricky Patteson of Scottsville, Va., for bringing this letter to my attention.

4. *OR*, ser. 1, 2:124–30; Berlin, *Destruction of Slavery*, 75; Phelps's letter quoted in *Southern Hatred of the American Government, the People of the North, and Free Institutions* (Boston: R. F. Wallcut, 1862), 20.

5. Robinson, "Confederate Engineers," 412; Krick, *The Fredericksburg Artillery*, 71, 103; 8th U.S. Census, 1860, Virginia, Caroline County, p. 723 (George Grimes was not found in these records); *Code of Virginia*, 510; Wilson, *The Black Phalanx*, 123, 179–80.

6. Henry C. Baird, *General Washington and General Jackson on Negro Soldiers* (Philadelphia: H. C. Baird, 1863). See also Daniel Pipes, *Slave Soldiers and Islam: The Genesis of a Military System* (New Haven, 1981), 25, 29–30, 35–45.

7. Quarles, *Black Mosaic*, 25–47; Robert K. Krick, chief historian, Fredericksburg and Spotsylvania National Military Park, letter to the author, 8 June 1989. A typical Confederate regiment consisted of 900 men, and using this figure Krick estimates that more than 120,000 white Virginians served in the Confederate army; an aggregate of 196,587 men between the ages of eighteen and forty-five was suggested by Evans, *Confederate Military*

History 3:14. The estimate of 50,000 black soldiers is based on the *Message of the Governor: Document 1, Biennial Report of the Auditor of Public Records, 1860 and 1861,* 633, 647, which includes enumerations of slaves over the age of twelve and free blacks aged twenty-one and older in 1860–61. The 8th U.S. Census (1860) lists 249,805 white Virginia males between the ages of fifteen and fifty, and 12,475 free blacks and 224,515 slaves—a total of 236,990 blacks—of prime military age. If but half of these Afro-Virginians were successfully enlisted, this would have meant 120,000 black men in approximately 133 regiments; a third of this estimate would result in nearly 79,000 blacks for 87 regiments (Kennedy, *Population of the United States in 1860,* 514).

8. *De Bow's Review,* May 1853, 443–45.

9. Hepworth, *The Whip, Hoe, and Sword,* 110; *Negro in Virginia,* 193; Woodward, *Mary Chesnut's Civil War,* 241, 255–56, 340, 678, 794.

10. John Cimprich, *Slavery's End in Tennessee, 1861–1865* (University, Ala., 1985) 13–14; Wilson, *The Black Phalanx,* 481–82; George Washington Williams, *A History of the Negro Troops in the War of the Rebellion, 1861–1865* (New York: Harper, 1888), 84–85; Wiley, *Southern Negroes,* 147–48; Mary F. Berry, "Negro Troops in Blue and Gray: The Louisiana Native Guards, 1861–1865," *Louisiana History* 8 (Spring 1967): 167–69; Fitz-Hugh Ludlow, "If Massa Puts Guns into Our Han's," *Atlantic Monthly* 15 (April 1865): 512; Hepworth, *The Whip, Hoe, and Sword,* 186–87.

11. Wiley, *Southern Negroes,* 147; Wilson, *The Black Phalanx,* 483; Work, *Negro Year Book, 1921–1922,* 186; Berry, "Negro Troops in Blue and Gray," 169, 172–77; Arthur W. Bergeron, Jr., "Free Men of Color in Grey," *Civil War History* 32 (1986): 247–55.

12. An English Combatant, *Battle-Fields of the South,* 282; *National Anti-Slavery Standard,* 1 June 1861; *OR,* ser. 4, 3:1059; Bernard C. Nalty and Morris J. MacGregor, eds., *Blacks in the United States Armed Forces: Basic Documents,* vol. 2, *Civil War And Emancipation* (Wilmington, Del., 1977), 192; Benjamin H. Trask, *9th Virginia Infantry* (Lynchburg, Va., 1984), 76; *Baltimore Traveller,* 4 Feb. 1862, as quoted in Williams, *History of the Negro Troops,* 84; Mrs. Judah's letter in "A Colored Southern Soldier," in Lexington *Gazette and Banner,* 23 May 1866. Reuben West was among the guests identified in Henry A. Wise, *R[ichmond] L[ight] I[nfantry] Blues. Speech of Gen. H. A. Wise, War Roll of Honorary Members and the Present Roll of the Company, 1874* (Richmond: Clemmitt & Jones, 1874), 16. The Blues were Company A of the 46th Virginia Infantry.

13. John Hope Franklin, *George Washington Williams: A Biography* (Chicago: 1985), 235; Williams, *History of the Negro Race in America from 1619 to 1880,* 278; Wilson, *The Black Phalanx,* 483, 495, 499.

14. Benjamin Brawley, *A Short History of the American Negro,* rev. ed. (New York, 1924), 113; Du Bois, *Black Reconstruction,* 119–120; Wesley, *Collapse of the Confederacy,* 42; Franklin, *From Slavery to Freedom,* 221; Bennett, *Before the Mayflower,* 464; Quarles, *Negro in the Civil War* 281; Ludlow, "If Massa Puts Guns into Our Han's," 512. See also Carter G. Woodson, "Charles H. Wesley Unmasks the Confederacy" (book review), in *New York Age,* 5 Feb. 1938, p. 6.

15. McPherson, *The Political History of the United States of America, during the Great Rebellion,* 281–83. The free black population in 1860 consisted of: Virginia, 58,042; North Carolina, 30,463; Louisiana, 18,547; South Carolina, 9,914; Tennessee, 7,300; Georgia, 3,500; Alabama 2,690; Florida, 932; Mississippi, 773; Texas, 355; and Arkansas, 144 (Kennedy, *Population of the United States in 1860,* 7, 17, 53, 71, 193, 269, 357, 451, 465, 479, 515).

16. London *Times,* 14 Sept. 1863.

17. William C. Oates, *The War between the Union and the Confederacy* (New York,

1905), 496–99; Percy Hamlin, ed., *The Making of a Soldier: Letters of General R. S. Ewell* (Richmond: 1935), 113.

18. Fremantle, *Three Months in the Southern States*, 282. Confederates had already proved their capability for committing atrocities. James B. Painter of the 28th Virginia Infantry bragged after the battle of First Manassas of his participation in the mutilation of dead Union soldiers: "[Some of] us roasted the grease out of their heads. . . . I seen near [passing] a yankee out of his grave . . . took his teeth out and buried him again. . . . I could walk over them like they was brutes—they smelled like brutes." Less than a year after the battle, 21 March 1862, an Afro-Virginia woman at Sudley Church guided a Union grave-hunting expedition to the remains of Major Sullivan Ballou of the 2d Rhode Island Infantry. Georgia soldiers had dug up, beheaded, and burned the corpse (James B. Painter Letters, 21 July 1861, 10661, UVA; Virgil Carrington Jones, *Gray Ghosts and Rebel Raiders* [New York, 1956], chap. 8, "The Dead Behead Easily," 66–73, 379–81).

19. *OR*, ser. 4, 2:941, 1:1095; *Index*, 20 Aug. 1863, 3, 10 Nov. 1864, "Arming the Negroes," 10 Sept. 1863; Lynchburg *Daily Virginian*, 9 Oct. 1863.

20. Ludlow, "If Massa Puts Guns into Our Han's," 508; *Douglass' Monthly*, Feb. 1862, 598; Savannah *Daily Morning News*, 7 Dec. 1861, quoted in Clarence L. Mohr, *On the Threshold of Freedom: Masters and Slaves in Civil War Georgia* (Athens, 1986), 287; *Harper's Weekly*, 10 Jan. 1863. After a failed Union naval expedition up the Blackwater River near Franklin, Va., on 3 Oct. 1862, its commander reported his gunboats were attacked by rebel soldiers including "men without uniforms, and also some negroes" (*ORN*, ser. 1, 8:113).

21. Wilson, *The Black Phalanx*, 498; *National Anti-Slavery Standard*, 10 May 1862. Black Confederate sharpshooters also served in South Carolina; see James Henry Gooding, *On the Altar of Freedom*, ed. Virginia Matzke Adams (Amherst, Mass., 1991), 54.

22. Alfred Bellard, *Gone for a Soldier: The Civil War Memoirs of Private Alfred Bellard*, ed. David Herbert Donald (Boston, 1975), 56–57. Berdan's Sharpshooters, organized under Col. Hiram G. Berdan as the 1st U.S. Sharpshooters, were equipped with Sharps breech-loading rifles, an extremely deadly and accurate rifle that in the hands of an experienced marksman was capable of being fired ten times per minute. Some were fitted with telescopic sights.

23. George Hupman to his parents, 25 June 1863, George Hupman Papers, Special Collections and Archives, Rutgers University Libraries; Harry F. Jackson and Thomas F. O'Donnell, *Back Home in Oneida: Hermon Clarke and His Letters* (Syracuse, N.Y., 1965), 87.

24. *Harper's Weekly*, 10 May 1862, 17 Jan. 1863. The incident of the two blacks and the rebel captain was witnessed through a telescope and sketched by *Harper's* most famous war artist, Alfred R. Waud (1828–1891).

25. Mitchell, *Civil War Soldiers*, 25; Lewis H. Steiner, *Report of Lewis H. Steiner, M.D., Inspector of the Sanitary Commission . . . during the Campaign in Maryland, September, 1862* (New York: Anson D. F. Randolph, 1862), 20–21; *New York Herald*, 11 July 1863. I am indebted to Ronald L. Waddell of Lebanon, Pa., and Greg Coco of Bendersville, Pa., for bringing these sources to my attention.

26. 1st Lt. Lewis Thompson, Camp of the 2d U.S. Cavalry, Falmouth, Va., to 1st Lt. Henry E. Noyes, 11 March 1863, Noyes to Capt. T. C. Bacon, 11 March 1863, Negro Military Service, roll 2, frames 67–68.

27. Mitchell, *Civil War Soldiers*, 117–18. Gen. Robert E. Lee reported the presence of 1,000 blacks at work on the Confederate trenches at Fredericksburg to Gen. Arnold Elzey on 22 May 1863 (Negro Military Service, roll 2, frame 970).

28. *OR*, ser. 1, 2:185–86, 484; Robert J. Trout, Myerstown, Pa., letter to the author, 21 Jan 1990; Joseph H. Shepherd, "Company D, Clarke County," *SHSP* 24 (1896): 146. Falling Waters was a Union victory.

29. Brewer, 38; *Douglass' Monthly*, March 1862, 617; John Parker lecture notice, Jan. 1863, owned by Michael P. Musick of Washington, D.C.

30. George Wise, *History of the Seventeenth Virginia Infantry, C.S.A.* (Baltimore: Kelly & Piet, 1870), 31; report of Gen. G. T. Beauregard on the battle of Manassas, 26 Aug. 1861 (submitted 14 Oct. 1861), *OR*, ser. 1, 2:501; Austerman, "Virginia's Black Confederates," 50; *OR*, ser. 1, 4:569; "Hollywood: Graves of the Confederate Dead" (column heading "Two Faithful Negroes"), *Daily Richmond Examiner*, 29 May 1866.

31. Richmond *Sentinel*, 30 March 1863.

32. Benjamin Trask, *16th Virginia Infantry* (Lynchburg, Va., 1986), 28; *Acts and Joint Resolutions, Session Which Commenced January 11, 1928*, 556.

33. Warrenton *Flag of '98*, 21 May 1861; report of Ruffner, *Virginia School Report, 1871*, 118; Springer, "Beyond the Call of Duty," 26, 28; Thomas P. Nanzig, *3rd Virginia Cavalry* (Lynchburg, Va., 1990), 3–4; Edward Spencer, "Confederate Negro Enlistments," in *The Annals of the War Written by Leading Participants North and South* (Philadelphia: Times Publishing, 1879), 536–42.

34. April issue of the Lynchburg *Republican* as quoted in the Petersburg *Daily Express*, 23 April 1861; Lynchburg *Tri-Weekly Republican*, 17 April 1861; English Combatant, *Battle-Fields of the South*, 282; Coulter, *The Confederate States of America*, 256; Harry A. Ploski and James Williams, comps. and eds., *The Negro Almanac*, 4th ed. (New York, 1983), 836; Richard Taylor, *Destruction and Reconstruction* (New York: D. Appleton, 1879), 210; Quarles, *Negro in the Civil War*, 36; *Harper's Weekly*, 5 Oct. 1861, 632; "T. Rowland Book," 21, Kate Mason Rowland Collection, Museum of the Confederacy; Jones, *A Rebel War Clerk's Diary*, 500 (16 Feb. 1865 entry); *Central Presbyterian* (Richmond), 15 Oct. 1862.

35. "Negro Subordination," Winchester *Republican*, 3 Jan. 1862; Colin Clarke to Maxwell Clarke, 3 Aug. 1863, Maxwell Troax Clarke Papers, SHC.

36. John Bakeless, *Spies of the Confederacy* (Philadelphia and New York, 1970), 116, 139, 143, 149–50, 317–18; *Norfolk Union*, 8 June 1862.

37. Memoirs of Rev. George W. White, 10837, UVA.

38. *American Missionary*, Oct. 1861, 245; "The Contrabands at Fort Monroe," *Atlantic Monthly*, Nov. 1861, 638.

39. Charlottesville *Daily Chronicle*, 30 March 1864.

40. Sigismunda Stribling Kimball Journal, 29 March 1863, 2534, UVA; *De Bow's Review*, March 1867, 226–27.

41. Diary of Nancy Emerson, 26 June 1863, Emerson Family Papers, 9381, UVA. Afro-Confederate loyalism was not confined to the South. A black New York City resident, John Jones, delivered a speech announcing his suport of the Confederacy before a large audience in October 1861. He was arrested and treated as a lunatic ("A Negro Preaching Secession Doctrine," *New York Herald*, 5 Oct. 1861).

42. Maj. Alvin E. Bovay, 19th Wisconsin Volunteers, provost marshal of Norfolk, to Abraham Lincoln, 19 Feb. 1863, Negro Military Service, roll 2, frames 48–49; Ervin L. Jordan, Jr., "A Painful Case: The Wright-Sanborn Incident in Norfolk, Virginia, July–October, 1863" (M.A. thesis, Old Dominion Univ., 1979), 12.

43. London *Times*, 13 Aug. 1863; *Richmond Examiner* as quoted by the *Liberator*, 21 Nov. 1863, 187; Robert F. Durden, *The Gray and the Black: The Confederate Debate on Emancipation* (Baton Rouge, La., 1972), 33–34, 44, 47–48.

44. As exemplified in Nottoway County in 1993, efforts by whites and Confederate memorial groups to erect monuments honoring "loyal" Confederate blacks have met stiff opposition from African-Americans and the National Association for the Advancement of Colored People (NAACP). See "Memorial to Honor Black Confederates Meets Opposition," Charlottesville *Daily Progress*, 10 Oct. 1993.

II. UNCOMMON DEFENDERS

1. Albert Memmi, *The Colonizer and the Colonized* (1957; reprint, Boston, 1965), 96–97, 108–12, 120–24.

2. Mohr, *On the Threshold of Freedom*, 291. The label "Confederate States Colored Troops" appears in *OR*, ser. 4, 3:1206.

3. Durden, *The Gray and the Black*, 99–100; James M. McPherson, *Battle Cry of Freedom: The Civil War Era* (New York, 1988), 833; Ezra J. Warner and W. Buck Yearns, *Biographical Register of the Confederate Congress* (Baton Rouge, La., 1975), 305; Jefferson Davis, *The Rise and Fall of the Confederate Government* 1 (New York: D. Appleton, 1881): 514.

4. *OR*, ser. 1, 52: pt. 2, 586–92.

5. *OR*, ser. 4, 3:799; Davis, *Rise and Fall* 1:518–19; Fleming, *Jefferson Davis*, 12.

6. Governor [William Smith], *From the Governor of Virginia Communicating a Series of Resolutions Passed at a Meeting of the Governors . . . November 7, 1864* (Richmond, 1864), 1–3; John W. Bell, *Memoirs of Governor William Smith* (New York: Moss Engraving, 1891), 21; Ezra J. Warner, *Generals in Gray* (Baton Rouge, La., 1959), 285; Alvin A. Fahrner, "William 'Extra Billy' Smith, Governor of Virginia, 1864–1865, a Pillar of the Confederacy," *VHMB* 74 (1966): 78–86; Richmond *Daily Dispatch*, 9 Dec. 1864; Report of Governor Smith to the General Assembly, 7 Dec. 1864, *OR*, ser. 4, 3:915; see also W. Buck Yearns, ed., *The Confederate Governors* (Athens, Ga., 1985).

7. *Daily Richmond Enquirer*, 6 Oct. 1864; *Richmond Daily Examiner*, 8 Nov. 1864.

8. Woodward, *Mary Chesnut's Civil War*, 586; CSA War Department, *General Orders from the Adjutant and Inspector General's Office, Confederate States Army, from January 1, 1864, to July 1, 1864* (Columbia, S.C.: Presses of Evans & Cogswell, 1864), 59–61; Richmond *Enquirer*, 18 Oct. 1864.

9. Smith to General Assembly, 7 Dec. 1864, *OR*, ser. 4, 3:915–16; *Charlottesville Daily Chronicle* as quoted in the Richmond *Sentinel*, 21 Dec. 1864; *Daily Richmond Enquirer*, 15 Nov. 1864; *Daily Richmond Enquirer*, 2 Nov. 1864; Robinson, "The Confederate Engineers," 412; minutes of the 2d (Confederate) Cong., 2d sess., *SHSP*, n.s., 13, whole no. 51 (1959), 296; Charles Ellis to My Dear Pa, 8 March 1865, Munford-Ellis Family Papers, Duke. Goode later voted to arm slaves but not to free them (Warner and Yearns, *Biographical Register of the Confederate Congress*, 102). Union prisoners of war and deserters who joined the Confederacy were known as "galvanized Yankees."

10. Howell Cobb to James A. Seddon, Richmond, 8 Jan. 1865, *OR*, ser. 4, 3:1009–10; letter to Jefferson Davis, 10 Jan. 1865, ibid., 1010; London *Times*, 9 Nov. 1864; Journals of Robert G. H. Kean, vol. 2 (1864–66), 20 Nov. and 25 Dec. 1864, 1 Jan. 1865, 3070, UVA.

11. Thomas M. Preisser, "The Virginia Decision to Use Negro Soldiers in the Civil War, 1864–1865," *VMHB* 83 (1975): 104, 110; Durden, *The Gray and the Black*, 165–66.

12. Negro Military Service, roll 3, frame 81; *Collected Works of Lincoln* 8:360–62, 5:423; "President Lincoln's Views on Arming Slaves," *Liberator*, 24 March 1865, 47. Under the authority of the "Restored Government of Virginia," John Snyder Carlile (1817–1878) was elected in July 1861 to fill the Senate vacancy caused by the resignation and formal expul-

sion of Virginia senator Robert M. T. Hunter, who became the Confederacy's second secretary of state.

13. "Rebel Adulation of the Black Man," *Liberator*, 7 April 1865, 53–54; Grant to Maj. Gen. E. R. S. Canby, 27 Feb. 1865, *OR*, ser. 1, 49: pt. 1, 780–81.

14. Hepworth, *The Whip, Hoe, and Sword*, 176–77; *OR*, Ord to Rawlins, 15 March 1865, ser. 1, 46: pt. 2, 991; Mitchell, *Civil War Soldiers*, 191; Blackett, *Thomas Morris Chester*, 248–50, 282–83; Durden, *The Gray and the Black*, 161.

15. J. L. L. Preston to James C. Breckinridge, 17 Feb. 1865, *OR*, ser. 4, 3:1093; Flournoy, 11:261–62.

16. North Carolina General Assembly, *Resolutions against the Policy of Arming Slaves* [ratified 3 Feb. 1865] (Richmond, 1865); Durden, *The Gray and the Black*, 202–3, 249–50; *OR*, ser. 1, 46: pt. 3, 1315; minutes of the 2d (Confederate) Cong., 2d sess., *SHSP*, n.s., 14, whole no. 52 (1959): 452–57; Preisser, "Virginia Decision," 110–12; McPherson, *Battle Cry*, 837.

17. Davis to Smith, 25, 30 March 1865, *OR*, ser. 1, 46: pt. 3, 1348–49, 1366–67; Davis to John Forsyth, 21 Feb. 1865, *OR*, ser. 4, 4:1110; Appendix C below.

18. Richmond *Sentinel*, 24 March 1865.

19. Andrew Hunter to Robert E. Lee, 7 Jan. 1865; Lee to Hunter, 11 Jan. 1865, *OR*, ser. 4, 3:1007–9, 1012–13.

20. *ORN*, ser. 3, 3:1258–59; Thomas Saunders Gholson, *Speech to Hon. Thos. S. Gholson, of Virginia, on the Policy of Employing Negro Troops, and the Duty of All Classes to Aid in the Prosecution of the War, Delivered in the House of Representatives of the Congress of the Confederate States, on the 1st of February, 1865* (Richmond: Geo. P. Evans, 1865).

21. "Memorandum of Lincoln-Stephens Conference at Hampton Roads," 13 March 1865, Papers of R. M. T. Hunter, Hunter-Garnett Collection, 38–45, box 33, UVA; Mark Mayo Boatner III, *The Civil War Dictionary* (New York, 1959), 116, 371. See Lincoln's report to Congress of the meeting, *Collected Works of Lincoln* 8:284–85.

22. Douglas J. Cater to Cousin Fannie, 11 Feb. 1865, Douglas J. and Rufus W. Cater Papers, LC; J. H. Stringfellow to Jefferson Davis, 8 Feb. 1865, Negro Military Service, roll 4, frames 398–405.

23. *Richmond Daily Examiner*, 10 Feb. 1865.

24. "Resolution Introduced by Mr. James T. Leach of North Carolina in the House of Representatives, Feb. 15, 1865," Negro Military Service, roll 4, frame 423; Benjamin to Lee, 11 Feb. 1865, *OR*, ser. 1, 46: pt. 2, 1229; Nigel Rogers, CSA Congress, House of Representatives, *Minority Report* [on recruitment of black troops] (Richmond, 1865). Dr. James T. Leach (1805–1883), elected in 1863, was a leading opponent of Jefferson Davis (Warner and Yearns, *Biographical Register of the Confederate Congress*, 148–49).

25. *Richmond Daily Examiner*, 16 Feb. 1865; Gordon to W. H. Taylor, 18 Feb. 1865, *OR*, ser. 1, 61: pt. 2, 1063; J. B. Gordon to Dear Major, 26 Feb. 1865, John Brown Gordon Collection, University of Georgia.

26. Miles to Gen. Pierre G. T. Beauregard, 14 Jan. 1865, William Porcher Miles Papers, SHC; J. A. Merritt (on stationery of the Mississippi Relief Agency), Richmond, to William H. E. Merritt, 9 Nov. 1864 and 21 Feb. 1865, William H. E. Merritt Papers, Duke.

27. CSA Congress, House of Representatives, *A Bill to Be Entitled An Act to Increase the Military Force of the Confederate States* (Richmond, 10 Feb. 1865); CSA Congress, Senate, *A Bill to Provide for Raising Two Hundred Thousand Negro Troops* (Richmond, 10 Feb. 1865); *Amendment Proposed by the Committee on Military Affairs to the Bill (S. 190) to Provide for Raising Two Hundred Thousand Negro Troops* (Richmond, 13 Feb. 1865); minutes of the 2d

(Confederate) Cong., 2d sess., *SHSP*, n.s., 14, whole no. 52 (1959): 465, 470, 499; Oates, *The War between the Union and the Confederacy*, 501–2; Jones, *A Rebel War Clerk's Diary*, 518–19.

28. Louis Cruger to Jefferson Davis, 10 Feb. 1865, Edward Pollard, Assistant Surgeon, 57th Virginia Infantry, to Davis, 13 Jan. 1865, Negro Military Service, roll 4, frames 0413, 0350–51; Oates, *The War between the Union and the Confederacy*, 500; Langston James Goree V, ed., *The Thomas Jewett Goree Letters* (Bryan, Tex., 1981), 233. The 6th, 12th, and 61st Virginia regiments voted for black soldiers; the 41st Virginia Infantry opposed them (Brig. Gen. D[avid] A[ddison] Weisiger to Lt. Col. W. H. Taylor, 17 Feb. 1865, Negro Military Service, roll 4, frames 0429–32; Michael A. Cavanaugh, *6th Virginia Infantry* [Lynchburg, Va., 1988], 58). In his letter Pollard volunteered to command a black regiment: "I think the aspect of our condition now requires the introduction of the blacks, not only as laborers; but as the chief basis of the rank & file. . . . Raised and educated in New Orleans, I am familiar with all the diseases of the negro race, and a practice of six years in Claiborne County Mississippi, has informed me of the discipline & management of this class."

29. Lee to Jefferson Davis, 24 March 1865, *OR*, ser. 1, 46: pt. 3, 1339; *Index*, 30 March, 6 April 1865; Simpson, *A Good Southerner*, 223.

30. Richmond *Sentinel*, 20 March 1865; Petersburg *Daily Express*, 27 March 1865; Woodward, *Mary Chesnut's Civil War*, 794; Cimprich, *Slavery's End in Tennessee*, 17–18.

31. Texas Legislature, *Resolutions of the Legislature of the State of Texas, concerning Peace, Reconstruction, and Independence* (Austin, Tex., 1865); Ella Lonn, *Desertion during the Civil War* (Gloucester, Mass., 1966), 36; Edward A. Pollard, *The Last Year of the War* (New York: Charles B. Richardson, 1866), 177; Edward A. Pollard, *The Lost Cause: A New Southern History of the War of the Confederates* (New York: E. B. Treat, 1866), 659–60; Journals of Robert G. H. Kean, vol. 2 (1864–66), 24 Jan., 23 March 1865, 3070, UVA; Ruffin, *Diary of Edmund Ruffin* 3:748–49.

32. J. H. Stringfellow to Jefferson Davis, 8 Feb. 1865, Negro Military Service, roll 4, frame 400.

33. "A Native Georgian" to CSA Secretary of War James Seddon, 29 Sept. 1864, *OR*, ser. 4, 3:693–94.

34. Mohr, *On the Threshold of Freedom*, 278–79; Azariah Bostwick to parents, 23 Feb. 1865, enclosure with letter from Robert K. Krick, chief historian, Fredericksburg and Spotsylvania National Military Park, to the author, 20 April 1990; M. Newman, "The Old Forty-ninth Georgia," *CV* 21 (1923): 181. See Compiled Service Records of Confederate General and Staff Officers and Nonregimental Enlisted Men, M-331, reel 11, NA, for other examples of Georgians volunteering as black recruitment officers, especially Rutherford to Gen. Samuel Cooper, 27 March 1865, and R. K. Atkinson to Cooper, 26 March 1865. My thanks to Robert Krick ("Miscellaneous Files on Negroes") and Lee A. Wallace of Falls Church, Va. ("Notes on Black Virginia Troops"), for their suggestions.

35. Capt. S. N. Brandon, Samuel G. Battle, Jr., and Robert E. Moffitt (two letters), to Secretary of War James C. Breckinridge, 29 March 1865, Letters Received by the Confederate Secretary of War, 1861–65, roll 146, frames 718, 745–48, NA (microfilm); Richard W. Oram, "Harpers Ferry to the Fall of Richmond: Letters of Colonel John De Hart Ross, C.S.A., 1861–1865," *West Virginia History* 45 (1984): 173.

36. A. F. Robertson, William S. Southall, and C. E. Thornburn (three letters), 21, 20, 26 March 1865, James Buchanan, ca. 29 March 1865, all to Secretary of War James C. Breckinridge, Letters Received by the Confederate Secretary of War, 1861–65, roll 151, frames 0368, 0597, 0786–88, and roll 146, frame 691, NA (microfilm).

37. "Commissioned to Raise a Negro Regiment," *Richmond Daily Examiner*, 24 March 1865; *Daily Lynchburg Republican*, 28–29 March, 2 April 1865; Turner to Shin, 2 April 1865, *OR*, ser. 4, 3:1193–94. Halifax County was 58 percent black (15,460) in 1860; Surry, 61 percent black (3,799) (Kennedy, *Population of the United States in 1860*, 501–13).

38. Samuel to Lewis, 2 Feb. 1865, Harriet C. Lewis Papers, Duke; Hawthorne to Bocock, 17 March 1865, Papers of the Thornhill Family and Thomas S. Bocock, 10612, box 8, UVA; *OR*, ser. 4, 3:1193; *Richmond Daily Examiner*, 18 March 1865; Richmond *Sentinel*, 15 March 1865.

39. Lee to Secretary of War, 27 March 1865, and Davis to Lee, 1 April 1865, *OR*, ser. 1, 46: pt. 3, 1356–57, 1370–71; Pugh comments, 16 March 1865, minutes of the 2d (Confederate) Cong., 2d sess., *SHSP*, n.s., 14, whole no. 52 (July 1959), 495; Lee to General Longstreet, 28 March 1865, Walter Fairfax Papers, VHS.

40. Report to James B. Fry, Provost Marshal General, to E. M. Stanton, 17 March 1866, *OR*, ser. 3, 5:599, 712; *Lynchburg Virginian*, 23 March 1865.

41. H. C. Scott to Col. Scott Shipp, 16 March 1865, Confederate Information Index, Slaves, entry 453, RG 109, NA. Scott, employed at the Jackson Hospital since 1863, was captured in Richmond on 3 April 1865 and later released upon taking the oath of allegiance. For a description of Colonel Shipp's Cadet Corps, see Wallace, *Guide to Virginia Military Organizations, 1861–1865*, 229–31.

42. Kennedy, *Population of the United States in 1860*, 514. The 1860 census enumerated the state's male population as: age 15 and under 20, 56,601; age 20 and under 30, 88,405; age 30 and under 40, 61,164; age 40 and under 50, 43,635, for a total of 249,805 men. It has been estimated by various scholars that 48 percent (+120,000) to 79 percent (+196,587) of all white Virginia males served in the Confederate military. See also chap. 10, n. 7 above.

43. "Statement of Auditor of the Numbers of slaves for Service, March 25, 1865," Executive Papers of Gov. William Smith, box 467, VSLA. Black historian James Brewer has suggested that 27,771 free Afro-Virginian males of military age were available by 1864 (Brewer, 11). An optimistic estimate of black manpower per regiment using the auditor's figures suggests that Afro-Virginian male slaves could have made up approximately 38 regiments of 800 men each.

44. Richmond *Sentinel*, 20–24 March 1865; Charles McKnight to Dear Willie, 22 March 1865, McKnight Family Civil War Letters, Alexandria Library, Lloyd House; "The Company of Negroes," *Richmond Daily Examiner*, 27 March 1865. Pegram, formerly a member of Gen. Richard Ewell's staff, was captured at Sayler's Creek on 6 April and fifteen days later sent to Johnston's Island, a prisoner of war camp at Lake Erie; he was paroled in June. Chambliss, a native of Louisiana, was assigned to the Winder Hospital in 1864; he was captured on 3 April 1865 and paroled seventeen days later.

45. Richmond *Sentinel*, 20 March 1865; *Lynchburg Daily Republican*, 29 March 1865; Pollard, *Last Year of the War*, 177; *Richmond Daily Examiner*, 18 March 1865; Petersburg *Daily Express*, 1 April 1865.

46. *Richmond Dispatch*, 25 March 1865, and General Orders no. 14, Adjutant and Inspector General's Office, as quoted in "Instructions for the Enlistment of Negroes," *Daily Lynchburg Republican*, 29 March 1865.

47. Richmond *Daily Dispatch*, 25, 31 March 1865; Richmond *Sentinel*, 30 March 1865; *Richmond Daily Examiner*, 15 March 1865; Ernest Taylor Walthall, *Hidden Things Brought to Light* (Richmond, 1933), 34.

48. Richmond *Daily Dispatch*, 25 March 1865; *Richmond Daily Examiner*, 29 March 1865; Richmond *Sentinel*, 30 March 1865.

49. William Miller Owen, *In Camp and Battle with the Washington Artillery of New Orleans* (Boston: Ticknor, 1885), 366; Wise, *End of an Era*, 395; John Newton Opie, *A Rebel Cavalryman with Lee, Stuart, and Jackson* (Chicago: W. B. Conkey, 1899), 325; Bud and Buckley advertisements, *Richmond Daily Dispatch*, 31 March, 1 April 1865.

50. Letter from Salem (Roanoke County) in *Lynchburg Virginian*, 24 March 1865; "Liberal Gift of Colored Troops," *Richmond Daily Examiner*, 27 March 1865.

51. Hughes, *A Boy's Experiences in the Civil War*, 7, 12–13; *Richmond Dispatch*, 25 March 1865.

52. Du Bois, *Black Reconstruction*, 119–20; Mudd, "The Confederate Negro," 411. See also Spencer, "Confederate Negro Enlistments," 536–42, 545, 549, 552.

53. Lee to Davis, 2 April 1865, Letter Book of Gen. R. E. Lee, April 2, 1865–Nov. 27, 1866, reel A2, Lee Family Papers, VHS.

54. Jefferson Davis to Maj. Campbell Brown, 14 Jan. 1886, letter no. 208–9, box 3, Papers of George Washington Campbell, LC.

55. Report of Gen. Richard S. Ewell, 20 Dec. 1865, p. 2, Papers of Richard Stoddert Ewell (microfilm), LC (also printed in *OR*, ser. I, 46: pt. 1, 1292–95); R. M. Doswell, "Union Attack on Confederate Negroes," *CV* 23 (1915): 404.

56. *Watchman* (New York), ca. April 1866 (?), Robert K. Krick, chief historian, Fredericksburg and Spotsylvania National Military Park, letter to the author, 15 June 1989; Royall W. Figg, *"Where Men Only Dare to Go!"* (Richmond: Whittet & Shepperson, 1885), 236.

57. Guild, 191–92; see also Durden, *The Gray and the Black*. American Civil War novels are devoid of black Confederate soldiers.

12. PLEDGING ALLEGIANCE

1. "Former Slave Reflects," Cincinnati *Enquirer*, 31 Dec. 1938; Henry C. Toler, 6th U.S. Census, 1840, Madison Ward (ward no. 2), Henrico County, Richmond (city), 17 Oct. 1840, p. 178.

2. Guild, 119–22; *Acts of the General Assembly*, 1861, 52, 53, 251–54; *Code of Virginia*, 509–10.

3. *New Constitution of the Commonweath of Virginia, Adopted by the State Convention, Sitting in the City of Richmond, on the 5th Day of December, 1861*, in Reese, *Journals and Papers of the Virginia State Convention*, (Richmond, 1966); Richmond *Enquirer*, 17 Oct. 1862. State law (1860) permitted the emancipation of slaves by last will, and apparently a few scattered instances of this occurred before 1863 (*Code of Virginia*, 511).

4. U.S. Department of Commerce, *Negro Population in the United States*, 56–57; John Curtiss Underwood to Barbour, unidentified 1860 newspaper clipping, John Curtiss Underwood Scrapbook, 70, LC; American Anti-Slavery Society, *Anti-Slavery History of the John Brown Year*, 44; U.S. Department of Interior, *Statistics of the United States in 1860*, 337. For a study of black manumissions from 1784 to 1860, see Jackson, "Manumission in Certain Virginia Cities," 278–314.

5. *Central Presbyterian* (Richmond), 3 April 1862; London *Times*, 4 June 1862.

6. John Bright, *Speeches of John Bright, M.P., on the American Question* (Boston: Little & Brown, 1865), 194–96; D'Entremont, *Southern Emancipator*, 166–71.

7. *New York Daily Tribune*, 20 Aug. 1862; *Collected Works of Lincoln* 5:388–89.

8. *Harper's Weekly*, 8 Nov. 1862.

9. Perdue, *Weevils in the Wheat*, 153; Josiah to Phebe, Alexandria, Va., 6 Oct. 1862, Clifton Waller Barrett Papers, 6526-E, UVA.

10. *Collected Works of Lincoln* 6:28–30.

11. Flournoy, 238–43.

12. Carter G. Woodson Collection, reel 9, frame 540, LC; Thomas Segin certificate no. 894, 6 July 1863, Negro Collection: Slavery Division, Duke.

13. New York *Times*, 4 Jan. 1863; Thomas J. Wertenbaker, *Norfolk: Historic Southern Port*, 2d ed., ed. Marvin W. Schlegel (Durham, N.C., 1962), 220–21; Engs, *Freedom's First Generation*, 36; John Hope Franklin, *The Emancipation Proclamation* (Garden City, N.Y., 1963), 114–15, 124–26; Sherman to mother, 7 March 1863, Fredric Sherman Letters, SHC; Simmons, Isle of Wight plantation, 25 May 1863, Henry E. Simmons Letters, folder 3, SHC; John James Geer, *Beyond the Lines: or a Yankee Prisoner Loose in Dixie* (Philadelphia: J. W. Daughaday, 1864), 238–39.

14. *Memorial Edition of the National Jubilee Melody Song Book*, 63; *Negro in Virginia*, 208, 211–12; Perdue, *Weevils in the Wheat*, 58–59, 242.

15. *Negro in Virginia*, 209; Wiggins, *O Freedom*, xix, 47; J. C. Rowe to Craig and Fulton, 1 Jan. 1864, Negro Military Service, roll 3, frame 4; Thomas F. Paige, *Twenty-two Years of Freedom* (Norfolk, Va., 1885), 7–27; "Jubellee of Freedom" (1883?), in folder "Rules, Jubellee of Freedom," Colson-Hill Family Papers, box "Colson Documents," VSU. Rowe refers to the regiment as the "2nd North Carolina" but it was actually the 3d Regiment, organized in Norfolk during January 1864. Its designation was changed to the 37th Regiment, United States Colored Troops, in February 1864 (U.S. Adjutant General's Office, *Official Army Register*, pt. 8, 141).

16. *Southern Illustrated News*, 23 May 1863.

17. *Negro in Virginia*, 207; Mrs. William Cabell Flournoy, "Arlington," *CV* 31 (April 1923): 135; Freeman, *R. E. Lee* 1:380–81, 2:474, 3:228, 4:385.

18. Lee to Mrs. R. E. Lee, 11 Nov. 1863, Lee Family Papers, VHS; Woodward, *Mary Chesnut's Civil War*, 464.

19. J. B. Johnson and J. C. Taylor to Sir, 24 Feb. 1864, and, James A. Seddon, CSA War Department, Richmond, to J. B. Johnson, 27 Feb. 1864, Negro Military Service, roll 3, frames 675–76. Senator Taylor represented Carroll, Floyd, Grayson, Montgomery, and Pulaski counties in the General Assembly.

20. Claiborne, *Seventy-five Years in Old Virginia*, 267; Woodward, *Mary Chesnut's Civil War*, 757; John Henderson Russell, *The Free Negro in Virginia, 1619–1865* (Baltimore, 1913), 85–86.

21. Hopley, *Life in the South* 2:384–87; "Between Two Stools," Norfolk letter of 13 Oct. 1862, London *Times*, 11 Nov. 1862.

22. Zebulon B. Vance to Jefferson Davis, 21 May 1863, Augustus S. Montgomery to Maj. Gen. Foster, 12 May 1863, Robert E. Lee to Secretary of War, 26 May 1863, and Lee to Vance, 26 May 1863, all in *OR*, ser. 1, 18:1067–69, 1072–73.

23. Diary of Nancy Emerson, 8 Jan. 1863, Emerson Family Papers, 9381, UVA.

24. McPherson, *Political History of the United States of America, during the Great Rebellion*, 517–21.

25. Berlin, *Black Military Experience*, 291–96; J. H. Stringfellow to Jefferson Davis, 8 Feb. 1865, Negro Military Service, roll 4, frames 398–405; Charles Ellis (on stationery of the Office of Richmond and Petersburg Railroad Company) to Capt. Powhatan Ellis, Jackson, Miss., 8 Jan. 1865, Munford-Ellis Family Papers, Duke.

26. Morris Family Papers, 38–79, box 9, UVA: "List of Servants Owned by Mrs. Ann Watson at the Time That the Slaves of the Southern States Were Proclaimed Free," in an undated "Business and Legal Papers" folder (insert folder labeled "Slavery Material");

"List of Slaves formerly Belonging to Richard O. Morris Freed by Abram Lincoln's Proclamation of January 1st 1863 and the Surrender of Gen. Robert E. Lee April 9th 1865" (insert folder "List of Freed Slaves / 10 Dec. 1892"), "1864–1898 Business and Legal Papers" folder; "1855–1863 Business and Legal Papers" folder (insert folder "1862 Taxables").

27. Colin Clarke to Maxwell Troax Clarke, 7 Dec. 1863, folder 5, Maxwell Troax Clarke Papers, SHC.

28. Wilson, *Emancipation*, 163–65, 174, 176; Joint Committee, 52–53, 55, 58–59.

29. Booker T. Washington, *Up from Slavery* (New York, 1901), 14–15.

30. Wilson, *Emancipation*, 34.

13. FREEDOM FIGHTERS

1. Jacob Dodson to Simon Cameron, 23 April 1861, and Cameron to Dodson, 29 April 1861, *OR*, ser. 3, 1:107, 133; U.S. Department of Interior, *Register of Officers and Agents, Civil, Military, and Naval, in the Service of the United States, on Thirtieth September, 1861 . . .* (Washington, D.C.: GPO, 1862), 208; U.S. Department of Interior, *Register of Officers and Agents . . . Thirtieth September, 1863 . . .* (Washington, D.C.: GPO, 1864), 274.

2. *National Anti-Slavery Standard*, 4 May 1861; *Collected Works of Lincoln* 5:419–25, 6:41–42, 178–79, 7:164–65; George Sinkler, *The Racial Attitudes of American Presidents, from Abraham Lincoln to Theodore Roosevelt* (New York, 1971), 35; Romero B. Garrett, *The Presidents and the Negro* (Peoria, Ill., 1982), 116–28.

3. Baird, *General Washington and General Jackson on Negro Soldiers*, 3, 8; George Livermore, *An Historical Research respecting the Opinions of the Founders of the Republic on Negroes as Slaves, as Citizens, and as Soldiers* (Boston: John Wilson and Son, 1862), 118–200.

4. Spraggins, "Mobilization of Negro Labor for the Department of Virginia and North Carolina," 190; *Regimental Flag*, 16 Jan. 1862.

5. *Cavalier*, 25 June 1862; *Connecticut Fifth* (published by the 5th Connecticut while it was in stationed in Winchester), 18 March 1862.

6. Jack Franklin Leach, *Conscription in the United States: Historical Background* (Rutland, Vt., 1952), 398; Hupman to his parents, 15 Feb. 1863, George Hupman Papers, Special Collections and Archives, Rutgers University Libraries; Herbert A. Wisbey, Jr., ed., "Civil War Letters of Graham Coffin," *Essex Institute Historical Collections* 93 (Jan. 1957): 89; Moore, *Civil War in Song*, 269; *Principia*, 28 May 1863, 1123; *Index*, 27 Aug. 1863, 277–78. The poem was written by Lt. Col. Charles Halpine under the pen name "Private Miles O'Reilly."

7. Kennedy, Superintendent of the Census, to John P. Usher, Secretary of the Interior, 11 Feb. 1865, Negro Military Service, roll 2, frames 35–38; *OR*, ser. 3, 3:1102, 1139–44, 1270; *Equal Suffrage: Address from the Colored Citizens of Norfolk*, 2.

8. *OR*, ser. 3, 3:860, 938; John Curtis Underwood Scrapbook, 83, 85, LC: Joseph Eggleston Segar, *To the Voters of Accomac and Northampton, April 10, 1863*, UVA; Pierpont to Stanton, 27 Jan. 1864, Flournoy, 11:424–25.

9. *Fredericksburg News*, 2 Aug. 1861; Woodward, *Mary Chesnut's Civil War*, 159; "The Contrabands at Fortress Monroe," *Atlantic Monthly*, Nov. 1861, 640.

10. Frederick Henry Dyer, *A Compendium of the War of the Rebellion* (New York, 1959), 3:1720; U.S. Adjutant General's Office, *Official Army Register*, pt. 8, 141; Butler, *Butler's Book*, 494; Lt. F. W. Browne, "My Service in the First U.S. Colored Calvary," 2–3, Black History Collection, box 3, LC.

11. Dyer, *Compendium* 3:1720, 1722; U.S. Adjutant General's Office, *Official Army Regis-*

ter, pt. 8, 142, 165; E. D. Townshend, Special Orders no. 288, Adjutant General's Office, Washington, 30 June 1863, Negro Military Service, roll 2, frame 0318; "Field & Staff of 2nd USCT," folder "Military Papers" in Black History Collection, box 3, LC.

12. Dyer, *Compendium* 3:1725, 1727, 1730; U.S. Adjutant General's Office, *Official Army Register*, pt. 8, 165, 180, 194, 207–11, 319; Wilson, *The Black Phalanx*, 377–462, 478; Bogger, "The Slave and Free Black Community in Norfolk," 301–4; William Paquette, *United States Colored Troops from Lower Tidewater in the Civil War* (Portsmouth, Va., 1982), 5–80; Paquette, "Lower Tidewater's Black Volunteers," in *Readings in Black & White: Lower Tidewater Virginia*, ed. Jane H. Kobelski (Portsmouth, 1982), 17–22.

13. Norwood Penrose Hallowell, *The Negro as a Soldier in the War of the Rebellion, Read before the Military Historical Society of Massachusetts, January 5, 1892* (Boston: Little, Brown and Company, 1897), 7–8, 10–11; U.S. Adjutant General's Office, *Official Army Register*, pt. 8, 315; White, *The Hidden and the Forgotten*, 77–81; Robert Gould Shaw, *Memorial: RGS* (Cambridge, Mass.: University Press, 1864), 8.

14. Julia William Diary, 4 April 1865, Quaker Collection, Haverford College Library, Haverford, Pa.; Henry Norton, *Deeds of Daring, or History of the Eighth N.Y. Volunteer Cavalry* (Norwich, N.Y.: Chenango Telegraph Printing House, 1889), 108–9, 182. I am indebted to T. Michael Miller, Research Historian, Alexandria Library, for calling the Wilbur diary to my attention (a microfilm copy is available at the library). Julia Wilbur (1815–ca. 1890) was a New York Quaker and abolitionist who moved to Alexandria during the war to assist the freed slaves (Diana Franzusoff Peterson, Manuscripts Cataloger, Haverford College Library, letter to author, 6 Dec. 1990).

The 22d USCT, organized in Philadelphia in January 1864, later participated in the Petersburg campaign (U.S. Adjutant General's Office, *Official Army Register*, pt. 8, 193; Kaplan, *American Studies in Black and White*, 107 and fig. 44; Williams, *History of the Negro Troops*, 298).

15. Leon F. Litwack and August Meier, eds., *Black Leaders of the Nineteenth Century* (Urbana, Ill., 1988), 162–63; Quarles, *Negro in the Civil War*, 328–29; Glatthaar, *Forged in Battle*, 9, 179.

16. Berlin, *Black Military Experience*, 138–40; Laura Virginia Hale, *Four Valiant Years in the Lower Shenandoah Valley, 1861–1865* (Strasburg, Va., 1975), 336–37.

17. *OR*, ser. 1, 29: pt. 1, 911–14, 28 Dec. 1863.

18. *Public Laws of the United States of America, Passed at the First Session of the Thirty-Eighth Congress, 1863–1864*, ed. George P. Sanger, 13 (Boston: Little, Brown and Co., 1864): 379; Paquette, *United States Colored Troops*, 7; *Collected Works of Lincoln* 7:190–91, 204, 8:266.

19. Maj. Gen. Benjamin F. Butler to Edward M. Stanton, 10 Aug. 1864, Negro Military Service, roll 3, frame 0462; "The Freedmen," *New York Daily Tribune*, 11 Aug. 1864.

20. Petition to Congress, 8 Dec. 1864, Thomas Wentworth Higginson Collection, 6968-B, Clifton Waller Barrett Library of American Literature, UVA; Glatthaar, *Forged in Battle*, 169–75; "Who Are Freemen," *New York Daily Tribune*, 11 Aug. 1864.

21. George R. Sherman, *The Negro as a Soldier* (Providence, 1913), 15–18; Monroe, *Reminiscences of the War*, 66–67; Glatthaar, *Forged in Battle*, 89, 112, 192.

22. Folder "1864 March–Nov.," Irvine-Saunders Papers, 38–33, box 16, UVA; Capt. Henry Spaulding to Lt. E. G. Smith, Adjutant, 38th New York Volunteers, 25 March 1865, Henry Spaulding Papers, 38–156, UVA. The reasons for the disturbance are unknown.

23. John Point, City Point, to his brother George, New Castle, Del., 20 Jan. 1865, John Point Papers, Historical Society of Delaware, Wilmington.

24. Dyer, *Compendium* 1:18; Glatthaar, *Forged in Battle*, 118; Alotta, *Civil War Justice*, 138, 165, 168, 172.

25. Alotta, *Civil War Justice*, 117; "Execution of William Johnson," *Cavalier*, 27 June 1864; Davis, *Our Incredible Civil War*, 159–60; William A. Frassanito, *Grant and Lee: The Virginia Campaigns, 1864–1865* (New York, 1983), 216–22.

26. Joseph Brady Mitchell, *Badge of Gallantry: Recollections of Civil War Congressional Medal of Honor Winners* (New York, 1968), 132–34; Walter Frederick Beyer and O. F. Keydel, *Deeds of Valor* (Detroit, 1907), 258–59; Sharp & Dunnigan, *The Congressional Medal of Honor: The Names, the Deeds* (Forest Ranch, Calif., 1984), 739.

27. *ORN*, ser. 1, 15:191, 197, 21:448, 452.

28. Sharp & Dunnigan, *Congressional Medal of Honor*, 715, 721, 781, 817, 854, 885, 934–35; Brent Tarter, "'Gallantry in Action': Medal of Honor Winners from Virginia, 1862–1865," *Virginia Cavalcade* 37 (Summer 1987): 33–37; Dabney, *Cincinnati's Colored Citizens*, 344–45.

29. Austin to Benjamin Austin, 1 Jan. 1864, Newport News, Va., letter, 1864, Va. Tech; Mitchell, *Badge of Gallantry*, 139; Supervisory Committee for Recruiting Colored Regiments, *Free Military School for Applicants for Commands of Colored Troops, No. 1210 Chestnut Street, Philadelphia: Established by the Supervisory Committee for Recruiting Colored Regiments, Chief Preceptor, John H. Taggart, Late Colonel 12th Regiment Pennsylvania Reserves*, 2d ed. (Philadelphia: King & Baird, 1864). The second printing of 28 Dec. 1864 required 8,000 copies.

30. Supervisory Committee, *Free Military School*; William Baird Memoirs, 7–14, Michigan Historical Collections, Bentley Historical Library, University of Michigan, Ann Arbor; U.S. Adjutant General's Office, *Official Army Register*, pt. 8, 194.

31. Henry Whitney Diary, 23 April 1864, Special Collections and Archives, Rutgers University Libraries.

32. Hondon B. Hargrove, *Black Union Soldiers in the Civil War* (Jefferson, N.C., 1988), 110; U.S. War Department, *U.S. Infantry Tactics, for the Instruction, Exercise, and Manoeuvers of the Soldier, a Company, Line of Skirmishers, and Battalion, for the Use of the Colored Troops of the United States Infantry, Prepared under the Direction of the War Department* (Washington, D.C.: GPO, 1863), copy, previously owned by the 26th United States Colored Troops, Company D, at UVA; Glatthaar, *Forged in Battle*, 103–4.

33. *OR*, ser. 1, 37: pt. 1, 71–73. During the 36th's participation in Draper's raid to Pope's Creek in June 1864, several of its members were accused by the Richmond press of the rape of a Confederate officer's wife (*Daily Richmond Enquirer*, 7 July 1864).

34. *Negro in Virginia*, 195; *OR*, ser. 1, 36: pt. 1, 986–87, 990–91; Charles A. Cuffel, *History of Durell's Battery in the Civil War (Independent Battery D, Pennsylvania Volunteer Artillery)* (Philadelphia, 1903), 183. A week before this action, the 23d USCT guarded wagon trains at Germanna Ford and were deployed in a line of battle from four in the afternoon until four o'clock in the morning. They were ordered to fall back without engaging the enemy, but when a small body of Confederates attempted to stampede them, the 23d USCT drove them off: "Our boys got behind the wagons and done good work for green boys. They fired three or four rounds and captured quite a number of saddles when the confederates left" (Baird Memoirs, 15–17, Michigan Historical Collections, University of Michigan, Ann Arbor).

35. Unidentified CSA soldier to Shelly, 1 May 1864, Papers of the Wall Family, 10482, UVA.

36. Maj. Gen. Benjamin F. Butler, Fort Monroe, to Elizabeth T. Upshur, Franktown, Va., 10 Jan. 1864, Negro Military Service, roll 3, frames 0020–21; *OR*, ser. 1, 29: pt. 1, "A Timely Warning," 917.

37. Seddon to Gen. Pierre G. T. Beauregard, 30 Nov. 1862, Negro Military Service, roll 5, frame 0333; *Collected Works of Lincoln* 7:345–46, 357, 8:1–2; Rev. Allen M. Scott, *Chronicles of the Great Rebellion from the Beginning of the Same until the Fall of Vicksburg*, 13th ed. (Cincinnati: C. F. Vent, 1864), 324–26.

38. Michael A. Cavanaugh and William Marvel, *The Petersburg Campaign: The Battle of the Crater* (Lynchburg, Va., 1989), 16–19, 21, 52–53, 56, 89, 98, 111; Henry Goddard Thomas, "The Colored Troops at Petersburg," *Century Magazine* 34 (Sept. 1887): 778–82; Wise, *End of an Era*, 366; Alexander, *Fighting for the Confederacy*, 462; *Daily Richmond Enquirer*, 1 Aug. 1864.

39. Hume pocket diary, July 1864, Thomas Hume Papers, SHC; S. S. Watson, Petersburg, to Mrs. Harriet C. Lewis, 20 Aug. 1864, Harriet C. Lewis Papers, Duke; George L. Kilmer, "The Dash into the Crater," *Century Magazine* 34 (Sept. 1887): 776; Dudley Taylor Cornish, *The Sable Arm* (New York, 1966), 276.

40. Samuel Rodman Smith, Petersburg, to his mother, 1 Aug. 1864, p. 313 of a bound typescript volume, Samuel Rodman Smith Letters, Historical Society of Delaware, Wilmington.

41. Cuffel, *History of Durell's Battery*, 197–99; *Negro in Virginia*, 197; E. N. Wise to John Warwick Daniel, 1905 folder "Civil War Material: Petersburg, 1864–1865," John Warwick Daniel Papers, 158 & 5385–A–E, box 23, UVA; Thomas A. Smith to My dear Sister, 4 Aug. 1864, Thomas A. Smith Letters, 6846-CT, UVA; Wise, *End of an Era*, 368–71.

42. Cornish, *The Sable Arm*, 266; Baird Memoirs, 17, 20, Michigan Historical Collections, University of Michigan, Ann Arbor; Berlin, *Black Military Experience*, 590–91; Richard J. Sommers, "The Dutch Gap Affair: Military Atrocities and Rights of Negro Soldiers," *Civil War History* 21 (1975): 51–64; *Negro in Virginia*, 198; J. H. Martin, "Another Account of the Battle of Fort Harrison," *Watson's Magazine* 15 (June 1912): 145–49.

43. J. M. Hudson, "A Stirring Incident of the Days of '61," *Watson's Magazine* 14 (April 1912): 980; Martin, "Another Account of the Battle of Fort Harrison," 149; Alexander, *Fighting for the Confederacy*, 478; Andrew J. Andrews, *A Sketch of the Boyhood Days of Andrew J. Andrews, of Gloucester County, Virginia* (Richmond, 1905), 49.

44. "Aunt Sally on the War," London *Times*, 21 May 1863.

45. Diary entry of 9 March 1864, Henry A. Chambers Papers, North Carolina State Archives; Bruce Suderow, "The Suffolk Slaughter: 'We Did Not Take Any Prisoners,'" *Civil War Times Illustrated* 23 (May 1984): 38–39. The 2d U.S. Colored Cavalry, commanded by Col. George W. Cole, suffered casualties of eight killed and one wounded during the battle (U.S. Adjutant General's Office, *Official Army Register*, pt. 8, 142, 341).

46. Robert K. Krick, *9th Virginia Calvary*, 2d ed. (Lynchburg, Va., 1982), 34; Byrd C. Willis Diary, 8 May 1864, VSLA; Jones, *Under the Stars and Bars*, 205–6.

47. Andrews, *A Sketch of Boyhood Days*, 47–48; Rawleigh W. Dunaway to Mary Fannie Dunaway, 12 May 1864, Civil War Correspondence of Rawleigh W. Dunaway, microfilm roll 517, VSLA.

48. D. Gardiner Tyler, "Address of Judge D. Gardiner Tyler on the Occasion of the Anniversary of the Birth of Robert E. Lee Delivered at the College of William & Mary, January 19, 1911," *Bulletin of the College of William and Mary* 4, no. 3 (Jan. 1911): 5–6.

49. *OR*, ser. 1, 39: pt. 1, 556–57; G. K. Miller, "History of the Eighth Regiment, Confederate Cavalry," 48–49, acc. no. 1, UVA.

50. *OR*, ser. 1, 39: pt. 1, 554–55; Brainerd Dyer, "The Treatment of Colored Union Troops by the Confederates," *JNH* 20 (1935): 273–86.

51. *Richmond Daily Examiner*, 8 March 1864; *Richmond Whig*, 8 March 1864; McPherson, *Battle Cry of Freedom*, 795–96.

52. Maj. M. P. Turner, Office, Confederate States Military Prison, Richmond, to Capt. W. H. Hatch, Assistant Agent of Exchange, 14 Oct. 1864, and T. O. Chester, Assistant Adjutant General, Headquarters Dept. of Richmond, to Maj. J. H. Carrington, Provost Marshal, 5 Oct. 1864, Negro Military Service, roll 5, frames 0518–19; Estabrooks, *Adrift in Dixie*, 92. Turner and Carrington became recruiters of Confederate States Colored Troops in 1865.

53. McPherson, *Battle Cry*, 795; *Harper's Weekly*, 20 Feb. 1864, 117; "Recollections by Isaac Coles" (typescript), 9, Pocket Plantation Papers, 2027, box 9, UVA.

54. Jordan, "A Painful Case," 10–13, 24, 30, 34, 37–38, 44–45, 49–51; Wilson, *The Black Phalanx*, 466; Flournoy, 11:412.

55. Woodward, *Mary Chesnut's Civil War*, 153; Ass. Adj. Gen. E. P. Halstead to Col. John D. Shaul, 76th New York Volunteers, 6 April 1862, Negro Military Service, roll 1, frames 0492–93; *OR*, ser. 1, 4:630–31, 29: pt. 1, 137, 483; Allan Pinkerton, *The Spy of the Rebellion* (Toronto: Rose Publishing, 1884), 204–5; Hodges, *Free Man of Color*, lii; Jordan, *Charlottesville*, 65, 173; Estabrooks, *Adrift in Dixie*, 179.

56. Description of Refugees, Deserters, and Contrabands, 1862 (for Headquarters, Gen. N. P. Banks's Division, Army of the Potomac), ca. 17 Dec. 1861–14 May 1862, RG 393, Records of the U.S. Army Continental Commands, vol. 18, pt. 2, entries 2223 and 5493, NA.

57. Moore, *Civil War in Song*, 263–64, 268–69; *Negro in Virginia*, 199–200; Pinkerton, *Spy of the Rebellion*, 199–227.

58. *ORN*, ser. 1, 6:535.

59. Gideon Welles, "The First Iron-Clad Monitor," in *Annals of the War Written by Leading Participants North and South*, 20; Gideon Welles letter, Hartford, 17 Aug. 1872, Portsmouth Public Library, Portsmouth, Va. I am indebted to Professor Tommy Bogger, Norfolk State University's archivist, for bringing the Welles letter to my attention and to Dean Burgess, director of the Portsmouth Library, for graciously allowing it to be quoted.

60. Philip H. Sheridan, *Personal Memoirs of P. H. Sheridan* 2 (New York: Charles L. Webster, 1888): 1–9; James E. Taylor, *With Sheridan up the Shenandoah Valley in 1864* (Dayton, Ohio, 1989), 348–55; 8th U.S. Census, 1860, Virginia, Winchester, Frederick County, 376; 1860 Slave Schedules, Virginia, Winchester, Frederick County, 160.

61. Jack D. Foner, *Blacks and the Military in American History: A New Perspective* (New York, 1974), 46; Lebsock, *Virginia Women*, 81; Evans, *Judah P. Benjamin*, 256; Woodward, *Mary Chesnut's Civil War*, 535, 545; Bakeless, *Spies of the Confederacy*, 81, 134, 162; Muriel Branch and Dorothy Rice, *Miss Maggie: A Biography of Maggie Lena Walker* (Richmond: Marlborough House, 1984), 15–19, 36. Elizabeth Mitchell's daughter, Maggie Lena Walker, became the first African-American female bank president (Wendell Phillips Dabney, *Maggie L. Walker and the I. O. of Saint Luke: The Woman and Her Work* [Cincinnati, 1927], 24–25).

62. Perdue, *Weevils in the Wheat*, 259–60.

63. Richmond *Sentinel*, June 26, 30, 1863; Engs, *Freedom's First Generation*, 12–13, 131, 177. Castle Thunder was far from being the most pleasant place to spend the war regardless of one's crimes. One Union spy recalled: "I was imprisoned in Castle Thunder from

the 20th day of January 1865 until 2d April 1865. . . . but forebear to enumerate the sufferings endured, which can be better imagined than described" (S[amuel] Ruth to Edwin M. Stanton, 21 Dec. 1865, folder "S. Ruth—claims for services to the Army as a spy," William S. Hillyer Papers, 10645, box 2, UVA).

64. Jordan, *Charlottesville*, 65–66; Virgil Carrington Jones, *Eight Hours before Richmond* (New York, 1957), 46–47, 74–75, 101, 105; Richard G. Crouch, "The Dahlgren Raid," *SHSP* 34 (1906): 183–84; "Woman Saved Richmond City," Richmond *News-Leader*, 16 May 1906; *Daily Richmond Examiner*, 5 March 1864; *OR*, ser. 1, 33:170–71, 183–84, 187–91, 194–95, 216–17, 221. Dahlgren's father, Adm. John Adolph Bernard Dahlgren, omitted Martin Robinson and his fate in *Memoir of Ulric Dahlgren* (Philadelphia: J. B. Lippincott, 1872), 214; Byron Sunderland, *A Sermon in Memory of Colonel Ulric Dahlgren* (Washington, D.C.: McGill and Witherow, 1864), 35, refers to possible treachery on the part of Robinson but makes no mention of his name, race, or execution. Ulric Dahlgren's ring was returned to the provost marshal of the Department of Virginia on 21 Oct. 1865: "Received of Mr. F. W. E. Lohman a gold ring marked with the initials 'L. D.' which ring was worn by the late Col. Ulric Dahlgren at the time of his death and taken from his person by Cornelius Martin, 9th Va. Cav. Recovered by Mr. Lohman after a long search on the 19th of October 1865," (receipt, 21 Oct. 1865, Albert Ordway to Lohman, folder "Miscellaneous Military Papers," William S. Hillyer Papers, 10545, box 1, UVA).

65. *Grant's Petersburg Progress*, 5 April 1865.

66. Joint Committee, testimony of Lt. George O. Sanderson, 177.

67. Hooker to Sen. Henry Wilson, 4 April 1862, Papers of Henry Wilson, LC.

68. Joint Committee, 3 Feb. 1866, testimony of Edmund Parsons, 59–60.

69. *Index*, 25 May 1865, 327; *Lynchburg Daily Republican*, 25 May 1865; *OR*, ser. 1, 46: pt. 3, 1216.

70. *OR*, ser. 1, 46: pt. 3, 11, 48, 1160–61.

71. *OR*, ser. 3, 4:48; Berlin, *Black Military Experience*, 725–27; Wilson, *The Black Phalanx*, 464, 478; Dyer, *Compendium*, 3:1720, 1723, 1725, 1727, 1730; U.S. Adjutant General's Office, *Official Army Register*, pt. 8, 319; Sefton, *The United States Army and Reconstruction*, 261–62.

72. Edward Hall Collection, Handley Library, Winchester, Va.

73. Dyer, *Compendium*, 1:12, 18, 38; Glatthaar, *Forged in Battle*, 270–74; Butler, *Butler's Book*, 494; "An Officer on the Colored Soldiers," *Liberator*, 24 Feb. 1865, 32.

74. Norman Barton Wood, *The White Side of a Black Subject* (Chicago: American Publishing House, 1897), 258.

14. BABYLON'S FALL

1. *Address of the General Assembly to the Soldiers of Virginia*, 2–3; Texas Legislature, *Resolutions concerning Peace, Reconstruction, and Independence*; *Magnolia Weekly* (Richmond), 13 Feb. 1864; CSA Congress, House of Representatives, *Resolutions Adopted by a Meeting of the People of Powhatan, Held in the Courthouse on February Court Days, 1865* [Richmond, 1865].

2. "Hospital Life and Prison Experiences," 13, Taylor Family Papers, 9965-B, box 11, UVA.

3. *Richmond Times*, 25 April 1865.

4. Memoirs of Rev. White, pp. 41–42, 10837, UVA.

5. Blackett, *Thomas Morris Chester*, 313, 289, 303, 624–25; Harding, *There Is a River*,

274; Burke Davis, *To Appomattox: Nine April Days, 1865* (New York, 1959), 159–60; Richard Wheeler, *Witness to Appomattox* (New York, 1989), 107; Putnam, *Richmond during the War*, 367; Mrs. Fannie Walker Miller, "The Fall of Richmond," *CV* 13 (1905): 305; "Testimony of Major-General Godfrey Weitzel, Commanding 25th Army Corps, before the Congressional Committee on the Conduct of the War, May 18, 1865," Negro Military Service, roll 4, frame 0145; Fenner, *Cabin and Plantation Songs*, 248–49.

6. "The Story of Uncle Moble Hopson," 4–5, folder "Virginia Slave Narratives," box A916, Records of the U.S. Works Projects Administration, LC.

7. James I. Robertson, Jr., ed., "English Views of the Civil War: A Unique Excursion to Virginia, April 2–8, 1865," *VMHB* 77 (1969): 210; Blackett, *Thomas Morris Chester*, 293, 299; Henry Chapin to his father, Richmond, 21 April 1865, 10310-G, UVA; "Testimony of Major-General Godfrey Weitzel," Negro Military Service, roll 4, frames 0143–45.

8. Diary of John Mottram, 13th New Hampshire Volunteers, 12–13, 18–19 April 1865, 10988, UVA.

9. Coffin, *The Boys of '61*, 519; Page, *Letters of a War Correspondent*, 326–27; J. Cutler Andrews, *The North Reports the Civil War* (Pittsburgh, 1955), 635; Davis, *To Appomattox*, 139; Blackett, *Thomas Morris Chester*, 42. Chester became involved in a similar affair in 1866; see William Ira Smith, *A Card to the Public*, (broadside), 14 July 1866, Rare Books Division, UVA, and *Richmond Enquirer*, 2 March 1866.

10. R. A. Brock, ed., "Paroles of the Army of Northern Virginia," *SHSP* 15 (1887): 45, 63, 487.

11. Chris M. Calkins, *The Battles of Appomattox Station and Appomattox Court House, April 8–9, 1865* (Lynchburg, Va., 1987), 138.

12. Donald C. Pfanz, *The Petersburg Campaign: Abraham Lincoln at City Point, March 20–April 9, 1865* (Lynchburg, Va., 1989), 61–63, 66; Putnam, *Richmond during the War*, 372; C. Percy Powell, *Lincoln Day by Day: A Chronology, 1809–1865*, vol. 3, *1861–1865* (Washington, D.C., 1960), 325–26; *OR*, ser. 1, 46: pt. 3, 96; Keckley, 166.

13. *Collected Works of Lincoln*, 8:260–61.

14. Berlin, *Black Military Experience*, 652; Keckley, 191; *Negro in Virginia*, 214. Two Afro-Virginians informed pursuing Union cavalry of Booth's movements as he fled toward Port Royal, Va.; their assistance lead to his eventual entrapment and death (ibid., 213–14).

15. Wilson, *Emancipation*, 157–92; George Cantor, *Historic Landmarks of Black America* (Detroit: Gale Research, 1991), 274. Thomas Ball was its sculptor and received $17,000 for his work. This bronze monument, *Freedom's Memorial*, sometimes known as the Emancipation Statue, still stands on a granite pedestal in Lincoln Park, Washington, D.C.

16. Opie, *A Rebel Cavalryman*, 324; *Contribution to a History of the Richmond Howitzer Battalion*, pamphlet no. 4, *Prison Diary of Creed T. Davis, of Second Company* (Richmond: J. W. Randolph & English, 1886), 6, 8, 12. Confederates who surrendered or were captured before the 9 April 1865 surrender of Lee were not included in the Appomattox parole agreement and became prisoners of war. Some were not released until August 1865 upon taking the oath of allegiance to the United States.

17. *Lynchburg Daily Republican*, 25 May 1865; Rawick, *American Slave* 16:43.

18. White to Irene, 13 May 1865, Ada P. Bankhead Papers, 38–463, UVA.

19. Journals of Robert G. H. Kean, 2 (1864–66):121–22, 3070, UVA; Wise, *End of an Era*, 88.

20. "Note by Edmund Ruffin re His Burial and Reputation," 1865, Bland-Ruffin Papers, 3026, UVA.

21. Oath signed by Dr. F. Y. Clark, 2 March 1865, in folder "Miscellaneous Military Papers," Williams S. Hillyer Papers, 10645, Box 1, UVA; *OR*, ser. 3, 5:13–15. My thanks to the owner of the Hillyer Papers, John H. Walker of Scottsville, Va., for graciously allowing the form signed by Dr. Clark to be quoted.

22. "List of Slaves of Robert Thurston Hubard, Sr., and Their Value at Emancipation," 25 Oct. 1869, Hubard Family Papers, 8039, box 21, UVA; "Negroes Belonging to Mark Alexander Senior of the County of Mecklenburg, State of Virginia, on the day of the Surrender of the Army of Virginia by Gen. Robert E. Lee, April 9th 1865," Mark Alexander Papers, W&M.

23. Resolutions of 16 Feb. 1866, *Acts of the General Assembly of the State of Virginia, Passed in 1865–66, in the Eighty-Ninth Year of the Commonwealth* (Richmond: Allegre & Goode, 1886), 57: Isabella Harrison to My Dearest Brother, 20 Oct. 1865, Ritchie-Harrison Family Papers, W&M.

24. Berlin, *Black Military Experience*, 799; *Negro in Virginia*, 209; Perdue, *Weevils in the Wheat*, 1–5. Adams contradicted herself during her interviews: she claimed to be fifteen when she finally escaped the Hunters but in another account gave her age as thirteen. Her owner, a Norfolk County farmer, owned $13,000 worth of real estate and personal property in 1860, including six female slaves (8th U.S. Census, 1860, Virginia, Elizabeth River Parish, Norfolk County, p. 038, entry 22, Isaac R. Hunter; 8th U.S. Census, 1860, Slave Schedules, Elizabeth River Parish, Norfolk County, Virginia, 25 Aug. 1860, frame 223 [schedule p. 69], entry 34, Isaac R. Hunter).

25. Boaz to My Dear Brother [Henry St. George Harris], 21 June 1865, Henry St. George Harris Papers, Duke; Judith Page Walker Rives to William Cabell Rives, Jr., 15 Jan. 1866, Additional Papers of the Rives Family, 10596-C, UVA. Tennessee whites openly discussed continuing slavery and and kept many isolated freed people in near bondage until the end of 1865; see Cimprich, *Slavery's End in Tennessee*, 119–20.

26. Lynchburg *Daily Virginian*, 23 May 1865; Buffalo Forge Journal, 1859 June 1–1866 Sept. 29, p. 304, item 10, Weaver-Brady Papers, 38–98, UVA. For an analysis of African-American emancipation observances, see Wiggins, *O Freedom*.

27. General Orders no. 9, *Lynchburg Daily Republican*, 28 May 1865; Memoranda Book of Thomas S. Bocock, undated entry, probably post–17 April to Aug. 1865, Papers of the Thornhill Family and Thomas S. Bocock, 10612, box 8, UVA.

28. General Orders no. 13, *Lynchburg Daily Republican*, 28 May 1865.

29. Randall and Donald, *Civil War and Reconstruction*, 396–97; Wilson, *Emancipation*, 194–201, 210–13. The Seminole, Choctaw, Chickasaw, Creek, and Cherokee Indian nations did not formally free their 12,606 black slaves until the signing of treaties between May and July 1866. See Annie Heloise Abel, *The American Indian under Reconstruction* (Cleveland, 1925; reprint, New York, 1970).

30. "Gratitude," 6 May 1866, Peter Fleming newspaper clipping, 38–412, UVA.

31. William Douglass to Dr. James Minor, 15 Aug. 1865, Letters from Ex-Slaves in Liberia, 10460, UVA.

32. Frank Marten to Col. Joe Perkins, ca. 1874, "Letter from a Freed Slave Enquiring about His Family," nos. 75–707 and 75–711, Fluvanna County Historical Society, Old Stone Jail, Palmyra, Va. I am grateful to Minnie Lee McGehee for permission to quote this document (a copy is available as 8386, microfilm 1725, UVA).

33. Mrs. Milly Richard to Capt. Thomas Russell, 8 July 1868, Virginia Cities Collection: Williamsburg Papers, W&M.

34. Jonathan Truman Dorris, *Pardon and Amnesty under Lincoln and Johnson: The Res-*

toration of the Confederates to Their Rights and Privileges, 1861–1898 (Chapel Hill, N.C., 1953), 357.

35. London *Times,* June 22, 24, 1865.

36. Fredrickson, *The Black Image in the White Mind,* 175–77; *Senate Journal,* 38th Cong., 1st sess., 7 Dec. 1863, 66, 89, 129, 146; *Congressional Globe,* 38th Cong., 1st sess., 1864, N.S. 10, 145, 238, 480, 586, 672–75; Senate Committee on Territories, *Report* [to accompany bill S. no. 45], *"to Set Apart a Portion of the State of Texas for the Use of Persons of African descent,"* 38th Cong., 1st sess., 1864, Reporting Committee no. 8, 1–3; Campbell, *Empire for Slavery,* 21, 29, 34, 44, 63; Dudley G. Wooten, ed., *A Comprehensive History of Texas, 1685 to 1897* 2 (1898; reprint, Austin, 1986), 8; John Gauss, "Give the Blacks Texas," *Civil War Times Illustrated* 29 (May/June 1990): 55.

37. Folder "Virginia Negro Lore," box A6888, Records of the U.S. Works Project Administration, LC.

38. *Equal Suffrage: Address from the Colored Citizens of Norfolk,* 10.

EPILOGUE

1. Woodson, "Charles H. Wesley Unmasks the Confederacy," 6.
2. Hodges, *Free Man of Color,* 73.
3. Ibid.; Keckley, 165.

Bibliography of Primary Sources

MANUSCRIPT COLLECTIONS

Albemarle County Historical Society, Charlottesville, Va.
  Correspondence of A. D. Brown, ACHS 371 (housed at the University of Virginia's Special Collections Department as accession number 3513)
  Memoirs of Leroy Wesley Cox, ACHS 940. (housed at the University of Virginia's Special Collections Department as acc. no. 5049)
Alexandria Library, Lloyd House, Alexandria, Va.
  McKnight Family Civil War Letters
American Antiquarian Society, Worcester, Mass.
  Slavery in the United States Collection: Correspondence of R. H. Dickinson & Brother
College of William and Mary, Manuscripts and Rare Books Department, Swem Library, Williamsburg, Va.
  Mark Alexander Papers
  Austin-Twyman Papers
  Civil War Collection
  Fitzhugh Lee Papers
  Plantation and farm record book, 1853–64
  Ritchie-Harrison Family Papers
  Virginia Cities Collections: Williamsburg Papers
Duke University, Special Collections Department, William R. Perkins Library, Durham, N.C.
  Angus R. Blakey Papers
  John S. Ewell Letters
  Henry St. George Harris Papers
  Harriet C. Lewis Papers
  William H. E. Merritt Papers
  Munford-Ellis Family Papers
  Negro Collection: Slavery Division
  Green W. Penn Papers
  B. G. Rennolds Papers
  William Patterson Smith Papers
  Henry J. H. Thompson Papers
  Thomas Fentress Toon letter
  George T. Wallace Papers
  William Weaver Papers
  Joseph Westmore Papers

Fluvanna County Historical Society, Old Stone Jail, Palmyra, Va.
  Letter from freed slave [Frank Marten], ca. 1874
The Handley Library, Winchester, Va.
  Belle Grove Collection
  Edward Hall Collection
Haverford College Library, the Quaker Collection, Haverford, Pa.
  Julia Wilbur Diaries
Historical Society of Delaware, Wilmington.
  John Point Papers
  Samuel Rodman Smith Letters
  Daniel Woodall Letters
Robert K. Krick, Chief Historian, Fredericksburg & Spotsylvania National Military
    Park, Fredericksburg, Va.
  Miscellaneous files and information on "Negroes"
Library of Congress, Washington, D.C.
  Lucian Barbour Papers
  Luther Guiteau Billings Memoirs
  Black History Collection
  Papers of George Washington Campbell
  Douglas J. and Rufus W. Cater Papers
  Papers of the Chase Family
  Papers of Richard Stoddert Ewell (microfilm)
  Christian Abraham Fleetwood Papers (microfilm)
  Papers of James Morrison MacKaye
  Betty Herndon Maury Diary
  John Thomas Lewis Preston Diary
  William B. Randolph Papers
  Shirley Plantation Journals
  John Curtiss Underwood Scrapbook
  Records of the U.S. Works Projects Administration
  Papers of Henry Wilson
  Carter G. Woodson Collection (microfilm)
Manassas National Battlefield Park, Manassas, Va.
  Albert B. McClaugherty Letters
Michigan Historical Collections, Bentley Historical Library, University of Michigan,
    Ann Arbor
  William Baird Memoirs
Museum of the Confederacy, Eleanor S. Brockenbrough Library, Richmond
  Jefferson Davis Collection
  Robert E. Lee: Custis Executor Document
  Joseph Myers Papers
  Kate Mason Rowland Collection
  Billy Wheeler document
Michael P. Musick, Washington, D.C.
  John Parker lecture notice, 1863

National Archives and Records Administration, Washington, D.C.

Compiled Service Records of Confederate General and Staff Officers and Nonregimental Enlisted Men, M-331

Letters Received by the Confederate Secretary of War, 1861–65. Washington, D.C.: National Archives, 1963. National Archives Microfilm Publications: Microcopy no. 437.

The Negro in the Military Service of the United States, 1639–1886. Washington, D.C.: National Archives Microfilms Publications, 1963. M-858 (formerly Microcopy T-823).

Population Schedules of the Fourth (1820), Fifth (1830), Sixth (1840), Seventh (1850), Eighth (1860), Twelfth (1900) and Thirteenth (1910) Censuses of the United States: Virginia

Records of the Assistant Commissioner for the State of Virginia, Bureau of Refugees, Freedmen, and Abandoned Lands, 1865–69. Washington: National Archives and Records Service, General Services Administration, 1977. National Archives Microfilm: Microfilm Publication M1048.

Records of the Office of the Secretary of War, M-494

Records of U.S. Army Continental Commands, RG 393, Descriptions of Refugees, Deserters, and Contrabands, vol. 18, pt. 2, entries 2223 & 5493

Slave Schedules, 8th Census (1860): Virginia

War Department Collection of Confederate Records, RG 109

Compiled Military Service Records, Generals, Staff Officers, etc.: William H. Fry, Report of Negro Slaves Received and Dispersed Of under Circular No. 69, Conscript Office, 1864, Camp Lee, 28 February 1865, and Report of Negro Slaves Impressed in the State of Virginia under Circular No. 69, Conscript Office, 1861 to 1st March 1865, M-331

Confederate Information Index: Slaves, entry 453

Confederate Papers Relating to Citizens or Business Firms, Washington, D.C.: National Archives, 1961. National Archives Microfilm Publications: M346. 1982.

Register of Free Negroes Enrolled and Detailed, May 1864–January 1865, Camp Lee, chap. 1, vol. 241, Bureau of Conscription, Virginia

Report of Persons Hired and Employed at Camp Winder during the Month of January 1863 by Capt. John Knox, Jr., MS 5120, entry 183

Yorktown Defences, New Kent County, for October & December 1861, Slave Roll no. 1553, entry 57

North Carolina State Archives, Raleigh

Henry A. Chambers Papers

C. J. Cowles Papers

Portsmouth Public Library, Portsmouth, Va.

Gideon Welles letter, 1872, on behalf of Mary Louveste

Rockbridge County Historical Society, Lexington, Va. (housed at the University Library, Washington and Lee University)

Washington Jackson petition

Rockbridge County, Virginia, Papers

Rutgers University Libraries, Special Collections and Archives, New Brunswick, N.J.
  Robert Cummings Papers
  Benjamin Heath, Jr., Civil War Journal
  George Hupman Papers
  Henry Whitney Diary
University of Georgia, Hargrett Rare Book and Manuscript Library, Athens
  John Brown Gordon Collection
University of North Carolina at Chapel Hill, Southern Historical Collection, Wilson Library
  Catherine Barbara Broun Diary
  Civil War Pictorial Envelopes
  Maxwell Troax Clarke Papers
  Frederick's Hall Plantation Books
  Peter Wilson Hairston Papers
  Hubard Family Papers
  Thomas Hume Papers
  Mary T. Hunley Diary
  William Porcher Miles Papers
  William Nelson Pendleton Papers
  Edmund Ruffin, Jr., Diary
  Fredric Sherman Letters
  Henry E. Simmons Letters
  Abraham S. Spengler Papers
  H. B. White Papers
University of Texas at Austin, Eugene C. Barker Texas History Center
  William Massie Papers
University of Virginia, Manuscripts Division, Special Collections Department, Charlottesville
  Irvine-Saunders Papers, 38–33
  Papers of R. M. T. Hunter, Hunter-Garnett Collection, 38–45
  Morris Family Papers, 38–79
  Weaver-Brady Papers, 38–98
  Graham Family Papers, 38–106
  Graham-Robinson Papers, 38–107
  Henry Spaulding Papers, 38–156
  Peter Fleming newspaper clipping, 38–412
  Edgehill School letter, 38–421
  Discharge and pass to John, slave of J. W. Robinson, 38–436–B
  Ada P. Bankhead Papers, 38–463
  Wilson, Whitehead, and Houston Family Papers, 38–490
  G. K. Miller, "History of the Eighth Regiment, Confederate Cavalry," no. 1
  Register of Free Blacks, Washington County, 41–A
  Grinnan Family Papers, 49, etc.
  John Warwick Daniel Papers, 158 & 5383 A—E

William D. Campbell Papers, 276
James Peter Williams Papers, 490
Watson Family Papers, 530
Southside Virginia Family Papers, 550
Cocke Family Papers, 640, etc.
Jason Douglass Papers, 702
Haller Medical Accounts, 981
Letters from Federal Soldiers, 1242
W. P. A. Folklore, 1547
Charles C. Wellford letter, 1663–A
Pocket Plantation Papers, 2027
Sigismunda Stribling Kimball Journal, 2534
Bland-Ruffin Papers, 3026
Journals of Robert G. H. Kean, 3070
Ex-Slave Interviews, 3462
Letters of Dr. John H. Claiborne, 3633
John T. Thornton Papers, 4021
Silas and R. H. Omohundro Business Ledger, 4122
Charles E. Davidson Account Books, 4156
Taliaferro Family Papers, 4536
Hubard-Randolph Family Papers, 4717
Daniel-Moncure Manuscripts, 4802
Buck Family Papers, 4932
Cabell Papers, 5084
Minor Family Papers, 6055 & 6055–A
Pittsylvania County Resolutions, 6458
Clifton Waller Barrett Papers, 6526–E
Trist-Burke Papers, 6696
Perry-Martin-McCue Papers, 6806–B
Thomas A. Smith Letters, 6846–CT
Thomas Wentworth Higginson Collection, 6968–B
John Singleton Mosby Scrapbooks, 7862–A
William Stokes Diary, 7896
Hubard Family Papers, 8039
Booker T. Washington Collection, 8337
Atcheson L. Hench Collection, 8474–U
Samuel S. Johnson Diary, 8493
Robert Thurston Hubard Papers, 8708
John C. Cohoon Account Book, 8868
Clifton Waller Barrett: Langston Hughes Collection, 8870–B
Graham-Tate Family Papers, 9232–N
White Family Papers, 9372
Emerson Family Papers, 9381
Papers of the Gordon Family, 9553

Taylor Family Papers, 9965–B
Dr. John Eugene Coles Papers, 9982
Papers of Samuel Barron, 10134
Micajah Woods Papers, 10279
Henry Chapin letter, 10310–G
James River and Kanawha Canal Company Minute Book of the Annual Stock-
    holders Meetings, 10421–A
Letters from Ex-Slaves in Liberia, 10460, 10460–A, & 10595
Papers of the Wall Family, 10482
Hubard Family, 10522
William Gibson Field Journal and Papers, 10538
Dearing Family Papers, 10565
William Bailey Papers, 10586
Additional Papers of the Rives Family, 10596–C
Papers of the Thornhill Family and Thomas S. Bocock, 10612
"Montpelier Letters," 10631–A
William S. Hillyer Papers, 10645
James B. Painter Letters, 10661
Letters of Union and Confederate Soldiers, 10694
Samuel M. Woods letter, 10698
Papers of Samuel Pannill Wilson, 10721
Civil War letter [of Henry T. Blanchard], 10756
Civil War Diary of David Probert, 10776
Memoirs of Rev. George W. White, 10837
Valuation of Confederate Slaves, 10938
Diary of John Mottram, 13th New Hampshire Volunteers, 10988
Rare Book Division: Broadsides
    Public Hiring of Free Negroes. 1855.
    Old John Brown: A Song for Every Southern Man. 1859.
    Plan for the Abolition of Slavery / To The Non-Slaveholders of the South. [1860?].
    Segar, Joseph Eggleston. *To the Voters of Accomac and Northampton.* 10 April
        1863.
    Smith, William Ira. *A Card to the Public.* 1866.
    Treason in Virginia. 1861.
    Virginia. Governor's Requisition. 1864.
Valentine Museum, Richmond
    John Jasper letter
Vermont Historical Society, Montpelier
    Roswell Farnham Letters
Virginia Historical Society, Richmond
    Boatwright Family Papers
    Confederate States of America document
    Giles Buckner Cooke Diary
    Eppes Family Papers

James H. Evans Papers
Walter Fairfax Papers
Grinnan Family Papers
Robert Edward Lee Headquarters Papers, 1858–78
Lee Family Papers
Majette Family Papers
Maria Gordon Pryor Rice Reminiscences
Robert Winn Snead Papers
Tompkins Family Papers
Virginia Polytechnic Institute and State University, University Libraries, Special Collections Department, Blacksburg
    Charlton Family Papers
    Newport News, Va., letter, 1864
    Lucy Randolph letter
    Smyth and Wythe counties, Va., Ledger
Virginia State Library and Archives, Richmond
    Auditor of Public Accounts
        Condemned Blacks Executed or Transported, 1783–1865
        Free Blacks, box 1794
        Runaway and Escaped Slaves, Receipts and Reports, 1863
    J. Willcox Brown Collection of Reminiscences
    Compiled Service Records of Confederte Soldiers Who Served in Organizations from the State of Virginia (National Archives microfilm)
    Confederate Pension Applications for Body Servants, boxes 151–52
    Rawleigh W. Dunaway, Civil War Correspondence (microfilm)
    Henrico County Deed Books, nos. 51 & 81 (microfilm)
    Kersey and Davis Company Papers
    Silas Omohundro Papers
    Patteson Family Papers
    Saunders Family Papers
    Executive Papers of Gov. William Smith
    Tredegar Iron Company Records
    Union Burial Ground Society, City of Richmond, Papers
    Virginia Confederate Rosters, 20 vols.
    Wickham Family Papers
    Byrd C. Willis Diary
Virginia State University, Johnston Memorial Library, Special Collections and University Archives, Petersburg
    Colson-Hill Family Papers
    Luther Porter Jackson Family Papers
Lee A. Wallace, Jr., Falls Church, Va.
    Notes on Black Virginia Troops
Washington and Lee University, University Library, Lexington, Va.
    Jefferson Davis Papers

Winchester-Frederick County Historical Society, Winchester, Va. (housed at the
    Handley Library)
    Ellen Afto Collection
    John Peyton Clark Journal
    Market Street United Methodist Church Records
    George L. Severs Account Book

GOVERNMENT PUBLICATIONS

Richard H. Clark, Thomas Read Rootes Cobb, and David Irwin, eds. *The Code of the
    State of Georgia.* Atlanta: John H. Seals, Crusader Book and Job Office, 1861.
The Code of Virginia. 2d Ed. Including Legislation to the Year 1860. Richmond: Rit-
    chie, Dunnavant & Co., 1860.
Confederate States of America. Congress. House of Representatives. *Amendment to
    the Negro Soldier Bill.* Richmond, 1865.
————.————.————. *A Bill to Increase the Efficiency of the Army by the Employment of Free
    Negroes and Slaves in Certain Capacities.* Richmond, 1864.
————.————.————. *A Bill to Be Entitled An Act to Increase the Military Force of the Confeder-
    ate States.* Richmond, 1865.
————.————.————. *A Bill to Be Entitled "An Act to Provide Payment for Slaves Impressed under
    State Laws, and Lost in the Public Service."* Richmond: C.S.A., 1864.
————.————.————. *Minority Report* [on recruitment of black troops]. [Richmond, 1865?].
————.————.————. *Resolutions Adopted by a Meeting of the People of Powhatan, Held in the
    Courthouse on February Court Days, 1865.* [Richmond, 1865].
————.————. Senate. *Amendments Proposed by the House of Representatives to the Bill of the
    Senate, (S. 129) to Provide for the Employment of Free Negroes and Slaves to Work upon
    Fortifications, and Perform Other Labor Connected with the Defence of the Country.*
    Richmond, 1865.
————.————.————. *A Bill to Provide for the Employment of Free Negroes and Slaves to Work
    upon Fortifications and Perform Other Labor Connected with the Defences of the Coun-
    try.* Richmond, 1864.
————.————.————. *A Bill to Provide for Raising Two Hundred Thousand Negro Troops.* Rich-
    mond, 1865.
————.————.————. Committee on Military Affairs. *Amendment Proposed by the Committee
    on Military Affairs to the Bill (S. 190) to Provide for Raising Two Hundred Thousand
    Negro Troops.* Richmond, 1865.
————.————. [Senate]. *An Act to Amend an Act Entitled "An Act to Increase the Efficiency of
    the Army by Employing Free Negroes and Slaves in Certain Capacities," Approved Feb-
    ruary 17th, 1864.* Richmond, 1864.
————. [Congress.] *An Act to Diminish the Number of Exemptions and Details.* [An amend-
    ment to the Conscription Act approved 17 Feb. 1864.] Richmond, [1864?].
————. Department of State. *Notice to Judicial Officers Taking Testimony in Cases of Slaves
    Abducted or Harbored by the Enemy, and of Other Property Seized, Wasted, or De-*

stroyed by Them. William M. Browne, Acting Secretary of State, 25 Oct. 1861. [Richmond, 1861].

——. Engineer Department. *Estimate of Five Hundred Thousand Dollars Required to Meet the Just Claims Presented, or to Be Presented Hereafter, for the Loss of Slaves Who Have Been Impressed in the State of Virginia*. Richmond: C.S.A., 1864.

——. *Communication from [the] Secretary of War* [relative to the recent impressment of slaves, by his order, in the state of Virginia]. Richmond, 1864.

——. *Communication from the Secretary of War* [relative to steps taken to carry out the provisions of the acts of Congress "in relation to the arrest and disposition of slaves who have been recaptured from the enemy"]. Richmond, 1864.

——. War Department. *Communication from [the] Secretary of War* [relative to the impressment of slaves], 10 Jan. 1865. [Richmond, 1865].

——.——. *General Orders from the Adjutant and Inspector General's Office, for the Year 1863, with a Full Index. Compiled and Corrected under Authority of Gen'l S. Cooper, by R. H. P. Robinson*. Richmond: A. Morris, 1864.

——.——. *General Orders from the Adjutant and Inspector General's Office, Confederate States Army, from January, 1862, to December, 1863, (Both Inclusive) in Two Series. Prepared from Files of Head-quarters, Department of S.C., Ga., and Fla. with Full Indexes*. Columbia: Presses of Evans & Cogswell, 1864.

——.——. *General Orders from the Adjutant and Inspector General's Office, Confederate States Army, from January 1, 1864, to July 1, 1864, Inclusive. Prepared from Files of Head-quarters, Department of South Carolina, Georgia, and Florida. by R. C. Gilchrist. With Full Index, Explanatory Notes and Such Decisions of the War Department as Could Be Collected Touching Matters of General Concern to the Service*. Columbia: Presses of Evans & Cogswell, 1864.

Congressional Globe. 46 vols. Washington, D.C., 1834–73.

Flournoy, H. W., Secretary of the Commonwealth and State Librarian. *Calendar of Virginia State Papers and Other Manuscripts from January 1, 1836, to April 15, 1869; Preserved in the Capitol at Richmond*. Vol. 11. Richmond, 1893.

Grattan, Peachy R. *Reports of Cases Decided in the Supreme Court of Appeals of Virginia*, vol. 16, *From July 1, 1860, to April 1, 1865*. 2d ed. Richmond: J. H. O'Bannon, Superintendent of Public Printing, 1895.

Hansbrough, George W. *Reports of Cases Decided in the Supreme Court of Appeals of Virginia*, vol. 80, *From January 1st, 1885, to November 1st, 1885*. Richmond, 1886.

Kennedy, Joseph C. Superintendent of the Census. *Agriculture of the United States in 1860; Compiled from the Original Returns of the Eighth Census, under the Direction of the Secretary of the Interior*. Washington, D.C.: GPO, 1864.

Kennedy, Joseph C. G. Superintendent of the Census. *Population of the United States in 1860; Compiled from the Original Returns of the Eighth Census, under the Direction of the Secretary of the Interior*. Washington, D.C.: GPO, 1864.

Matthews, James M., ed. *The Statutes at Large of the Provisional Government of the Confederate States of America*. Richmond: R. M. Smith, printer to Congress, 1864.

New York (State). Court of Appeals. *Report of the Lemmon Slave Case: Containing Points and Arguments of Counsel on Both Sides, and Opinions of All the Judges.* New York: Horace Greeley & Co., 1860.

North Carolina. General Assembly. *Resolutions against the Policy of Arming Slaves* [ratified 3 Feb., 1865]. Richmond, 1865.

Office of Historic Alexandria. *The Confederate Statue.* Alexandria, Va.: Office of Historic Alexandria, n.d. Brochure.

[Peirce, Alice Clark, comp.]. *Index of Acts of the General Assembly of the Commonwealth of Virginia, 1912–1959.* Richmond, 1959.

Reese, George H., ed. *Journals and Papers of the Virginia State Convention of 1861 in Three Volumes.* Richmond, 1966.

Robinson, Conway. *Case of the Heirs of William O. George, a White Person, between Whom and a Negro It Is Alleged, There Was a Marriage in Pennsylvania.* N.p., 1869.

——. *Supreme Court of Appeals of Virginia: (March Session 1877): Observations of Conway Robinson upon the Application for a Rehearing in George and Others Against Pilcher and Others.* N.p., 1877.

Texas. Legislature. *Resolutions of the Legislature of the State of Texas, concerning Peace, Reconstruction, and Independence.* [Austin, 1865].

U.S. Adjutant General's Office. *Official Army Register of the Volunteer Force of the United States Army for the Years 1861, '62, '63, '64, '65.* 9 pts. 1867. Reprint. Gaithersburg, Md., 1987.

U.S. Congress. House of Representatives. Committee on the Judiciary. *Veterans' Benefits Act. U.S. Code,* title 38, vol. 7, sec. 510 (1958).

——.——. Committee on War Claims. *Summary Reports of the Commissioners of Claims in All Cases Reported to Congress as Disallowed under the Act of March 3, 1871 . . .* Washington, D.C.: GPO, 1871–80.

——. Joint Committee on Reconstruction. *Report of the Joint Committee on Reconstruction, at the First Session Thirty-ninth Congress.* (Pt. 2. Virginia, North Carolina, South Carolina.) Washington, D.C.: GPO, 1866.

——. Laws and Resolutions. *Veterans' Benefits Act of 1957.* In *U.S. Statutes at Large,* vol. 72 (1958).

——. Senate. *Journal.* 38th Cong., 1st sess., 7 Dec. 1863.

——.——. Select Committee on the Harper's Ferry Invasion. *Report of the Select Committee Appointed to Inquire into the Late Invasion and Seizure of the Public Property at Harper's Ferry.* 36th Cong., 1st sess., Rep. Com. no. 278. Washington, D.C., 1860.

U.S. Department of Commerce. Bureau of the Census. *Negro Population in the United States, 1790–1915.* 1918. Reprint. New York, 1968.

U.S. Department of Interior. *Register of Officers and Agents, Civil, Military, and Naval, in the Service of the United States, on Thirtieth September, 1861; Showing the State Or Territory from Which Each Person Was Appointed to Office, the State of Country in Which He Was Born, and the Compensation, Pay, and Emoluments Allowed to Each; the Names, Force, and Condition of All Ships and Vessels Belonging to the United States, and When and Where Built; Together with the Names and Compensation of All Printers in Any Way Employed by Congress, or Any Department of Officer of the Government.* Washington, D.C.: GPO, 1862.

——. *Register of Officers and Agents, Civil, Military, and Naval, in the Service of the United States, on Thirtieth September, 1863; Showing the State or Territory from Which Each Person Was Appointed to Office, the State or Country in Which He Was Born, and the Compensation, Pay, and Emoluments Allowed to Each; Together with the Names and Compensation of All Printers in Any Way Employed by Congress, or Any Department of Officer of the Government.* Washington, D.C.: GPO, 1864.

——. *Statistics of the United States, (Including Mortality, Property, &c.,) in 1860: Compiled from the Original Returns and Being the Final Exhibit of the Eighth Census, under the Direction of the Secretary of the Interior.* Washington, D.C.: GPO, 1866.

U.S. Naval War Records Office. *Official Records of the Union and Confederate Navies in the War of the Rebellion.* Ser. 1–2. 30 vols. Washington, D.C.: GPO, 1894–1922.

U.S. War Department. Adjutant General's Office. *General Orders, no. 296. Transportation of Stores and Books for Freedmen.* 2 Dec. 1864. Washington, D.C.: 1864.

——.——. *List of Staff Officers of the Confederate States Army, 1861–1865.* Washington, D.C.: 1891.

——.——. *U.S. Infantry Tactics, for the Instruction, Exercise, and Manoeuveres of the Soldier, a Company, Line of Skirmishers, for the Use of the Colored Troops of the United States Infantry, Prepared under Direction of the War Department.* Washington, D.C.: GPO, 1863.

——.——. *The War of the Rebellion: A Compilation of the Official Records of the Union and Confederate Armies.* Ser. 1–4. 128 vols. Washington, D.C.: GPO, 1880–1901.

Virginia. Auditor of Public Accounts. *Annual Reports of Officers, Boards and Institutions of the Commonwealth of Virginia for the Twenty-One Months Ending June 30, 1925.* Richmond, 1925.

——.——. *Annual Reports of Officers, Boards and Institutions of the Commonwealth of Virginia for the Twenty-One Months Ending June 30, 1926.* Richmond, 1927.

——.——. *1925 Roster of Confederate Pensioners of Virginia.* Richmond, 1925.

——.——. *1926 Roster of Confederate Pensioners of Virginia.* Richmond, 1926.

——. Department of Education. *Virginia School Report, 1871. First Annual Report of the Superintendent of Public Instruction, for the Year Ending August 31, 1871.* Richmond: C. A. Schaffter, Superintendent Public Printing, 1871.

——. General Assembly. *Acts and Joints Resolutions (Amending the Constitution) of the General Assembly of the State of Virginia. Session Which Commenced at the State Capitol on Wednesday, 9 Jan. 1924.* Richmond, 1924.

——.——. *Acts and Joint Resolutions (Amending the Constitution) of the General Assembly of the State of Virginia. Session Which Commenced . . . on Wednesday, 11 Jan. 1928.* Richmond, 1928.

——.——. *Acts and Joint Resolutions of the General Assembly of the State of Virginia. Session 1954. . . .* Richmond, 1954.

——.——. *Acts and Joint Resolutions of the General Assembly of the Commonwealth of Virginia. Session 1978. . . .* Richmond, 1978.

——.——. *Acts of the General Assembly of Virginia, Passed at the Session Commencing December 4, 1848, and Ending March 19, 1849, in the Seventy-third Year of the Commonwealth.* Richmond: William F. Ritchie, Printer to Commonwealth, 1849.

——.——. *Acts of the General Assembly of the State of Virginia, Passed in 1861, in the Eighty-fifth Year of the Commonwealth*. Richmond: William F. Ritchie, Public Printer, 1861.

——.——. *Acts of the General Assembly of the State of Virginia, Passed in 1861–2, in the Eighty-sixth Year of the Commonwealth*. Richmond: William F. Ritchie, Public Printer, 1862.

——.——. *Acts of the General Assembly of the State of Virginia, Passed at Called Session, 1862, in the Eighty-seventh Year of the Commonwealth*. Richmond: William F. Ritchie, Public Printer, 1862.

——.——. *Acts of the General Assembly of the State of Virginia, Passed at Adjourned Session, 1863, in the Eighty-seventh Year of the Commonwealth*. Richmond: William F. Ritchie, Public Printer, 1863.

——.——. *Acts of the General Assembly of the State of Virginia, Passed at Called Session, 1863, in the Eighty-eighth Year of the Commonwealth*. Richmond: William F. Ritchie, Public Printer, 1863.

——.——. *Acts of the General Assembly of the State of Virginia, Passed at Session of 1863–4, in the Eighty-eighth Year of the Commonwealth*. Richmond: William F. Ritchie, Public Printer, 1864.

——.——. *Acts of the General Assembly of the State of Virginia, Passed in 1865–66, in the Eighty-ninth Year of the Commonwealth*. Richmond: Allegre & Goode, 1866.

——.——. House of Delegates. *Journal of the House of Delegates of the State of Virginia, for the Extra Session of 1861*. Richmond: William F. Ritchie, 1861.

——.——.——. *Journal of the House of Delegates of the State of Virginia, for the Session of 1861–62*. Richmond: William F. Ritchie, 1861.

——.——.——. *Journal of the House of Delegates of the State of Virginia, for the Called Session of 1863*. Richmond: William F. Ritchie, 1863.

——.——.——. *Journal of the House of Delegates of the State of Virginia, for the Session of 1863–64*. Richmond: William F. Ritchie, 1863.

——.——. [Senate and House Committees.] *Address of the General Assembly to the Soldiers of Virginia*. [Richmond, 1864].

——. Governor. *Message of the Governor of Virginia, and Accompanying Documents*. Richmond: William F. Ritchie, Public Printer, 1861.

——. ——. *Message of the Governor of Virginia, and Accompanying Documents*. Richmond: William F. Ritchie, Public Printer, 1862.

——. ——. *Message of the Governor of Virginia, and Accompanying Documents*. Richmond: William F. Ritchie, Public Printer, 1863.

——.——. [William Smith]. *Letter from the Governor of Virginia Communication a Series of Resolutions Passed at a Meeting of the Governors . . .* 7 Nov. 1864. Richmond, 1864.

——. State Convention of 1861 (Richmond). *Ordinances Adopted by the Convention of Virginia, at the Adjourned Session, in June and July, 1861*. Richmond: W. M. Elliot, 1861.

——.——. *Ordinances Adopted by the Convention of Virginia, in Secret and Adjourned Sessions in April, May, June and July, 1861*. Richmond: W. M. Elliot, 1861.

NEWSPAPERS AND PERIODICALS

Alexandria Gazette
American Jubilee
American Missionary
Anglo-African Magazine
Atlantic Monthly
Bulletin of the College of William and Mary
Cavalier (Yorktown)
Central Presbyterian (Richmond)
Century Magazine
Charlottesville Advocate
Charlottesville-Albemarle Tribune
Charlottesville *Daily Chronicle*
Charlottesville *Daily Progress*
Christian Banner (Fredericksburg)
Christian Observer
Cincinnati *Enquirer*
Civil War History
Civil War Quarterly
Civil War Times Illustrated
Confederate Veteran
Connecticut Fifth (Winchester)
Culpeper Virginia Star
Danville Register
De Bow's Review
Douglass' Monthly
Essex Institute Historical Collections
Fredericksburg *Daily Star*
Fredericksburg *Free Lance*
Fredericksburg *Free Lance-Star*
Fredericksburg News
Freedman (Boston)
Freedmen's Journal (Boston)
Georgia Weekly Telegraph (Macon)
Grant's Petersburg Progress
Harper's Weekly: A Journal of Civilization
The Index: A Weekly Journal of Politics, Literature, and News: Devoted to the Exposition of the Mutual Interests, Political and Commercial, of Great Britain and the Confederate States of America (London)
Jet
Journal of Negro History
Journal of Southern History
Lexington *Gazette*

Lexington *Gazette and Banner*
Lexington *Gazette and Citizen*
Lexington *Valley Star*
Liberator (Boston)
London Illustrated News
Louisiana History
Lower Norfolk County Antiquary
Lynchburg *Daily Republican* and *Lynchburg Daily Republican*
Daily Lynchburg Virginian and *Lynchburg Virginian*
Lynchburg *Tri-Weekly Republican*
Magnolia Weekly (Richmond)
Military Engineer
National Anti-Slavery Standard
Negro History Bulletin
New Star (Christianburg)
New York Age
New York Daily Tribune and *New York Tribune*
New York Herald
New York Ninth (Warrenton)
New York Times
Norfolk and Portsmouth Herald
Norfolk Union
North Carolina Historical Review
Petersburg Daily Express
Petersburg *Daily Register*
Philadelphia Daily Evening Bulletin
Phylon
Principia
Regimental Flag (Accomack County)
Religious Herald (Richmond)
Richmond Daily Examiner and *Daily Richmond Examiner*
Richmond Dispatch and Richmond *Daily Dispatch*
Richmond Enquirer, Richmond *Enquirer,* and *Daily Richmond Enquirer*
Richmond *Examiner, Richmond Daily Examiner,* and *Daily Richmond Examiner*
Richmond *News-Leader*
Richmond *Sentinel*
Richmond Times
Richmond Whig, Richmond Daily Whig, and *Daily Richmond Whig*
Rockingham Register and Advertiser
Scottsville Register
Smithsonian Magazine
Southern Exposure
Southern Federal Union (Milledgeville, Ga.)
Southern Historical Society Papers

Southern Illustrated News
Southern Partisan
Southern Presbyterian Review
Staunton Spectator
Staunton Vindicator
Times (London)
Virginia Cavalcade
Virginia Law Review
Virginia Magazine of History and Biography
Warrenton Flag of '98
Washingtonian (Leesburg)
Washington Post
Waterford News (Loudoun County)
Watson's Magazine
West Virginia History
Western Pennsylvania Historical Magazine
William and Mary Quarterly
Winchester *Evening Star*
Winchester *Republican*

Index

Willis, Byrd C. (Confederate soldiers), 280

Willis, Margaret (free black), 133

Wilson, Armstead (free black), 210

Wilson, Eliza (slaveholder), 21–22

Wilson, Gen. James Harrison, 80, 144

Wilson, Joseph T. (black soldier and historian), 120, 219–20

Wilson, Samuel (recruiter of Confederate States Colored Troops), 245

Wilson, Samuel Pannill (slaveholder), 59, 94, 139

Winchester, 9, 87, 171, 229–30, 289

Winchester (Opequon Creek), battle of, 285

Winchester Evening Star, 197

Winchester *Republican,* opposes murder of blacks, 147

Winder, John Henry (Confederate provost marshal), 156

Windsor (slave), 178

Winny (free black woman), 172

Winslow, Edmund (black Confederate pensioner), 197

Wisconsin: 19th Infantry, 145

Wise, Lt. E. N. (Confederate soldier), 278

Wise, Henry A. (former governor), 72, 77

Wise, John S. (Confederate officer), 6, 277, 298

Wolf Run Shoals, 144

Women, Afro-Virginian: abuse by husbands, 204; assault each other, 87; assault white men, 172; assault white women, 134; attractiveness, 127–28; black men attracted to, 127, 192; chastity defended, 128; complain of husbands forced into Union army, 269; Confederate soldiers as lovers of, 130; convicted criminals, 160; dresses of, 29; elderly slaves, 11, 22, 43; female Union cavalryman, 269; final casu-

alties of the war, 295; first to earn a medical degree, 95; "Frankey/ Franky" as typical first name, 137, 304, 354n1; free black, 202; initiators of violence, 170–72, 174; kidnapping of, 207; number incarcerated in state penitentiary, 166; ownership of relatives, 210–11; quoted, 6; percentage of population, 12; Petersburg, 209; preferred as slaves, 39; prices, 41; prosperity of, 87; punishments of, 34–35; rape victims, 131–33; self-supporting, 206, 209–10; spies, 283–85; weight, disparaging descriptions of, 174, 303; sexual racism, 132–33; Underground Railroad agents, 70; white child care providers, 176; white men as husbands, 128, 131; white women's jealousy and fear of, 128–29. *See also* Afro-Virginians; Hill, Rosette; Johnson, Katie Blackwell; Keckley, Elizabeth; Lane, Annetta; Lee, Rebecca; Lewis, Maria; Louveste, Mary; Men, Afro-Virginian; Millie; Newby, Harriet; Richard, Milly; Skipwith, Lucy; Slaves, female; United Order of Tents

Wood, Albert (overseer), 37

Woodall, Daniel (Union officer), 188

Woods, Albert (slave), 30

Woods, Jim (slaveholder), 79

Woods, Samuel M. (Union soldier), 128

Woodson, Carter G. (historian), 71, 176, 202, 308

Woodson, James Henry (runaway slave and father of Carter G.), 71

Wool, Gen. John E., 83, 284–85

Wooton, Gilbert (free black), 178–79

Worthington, Henry (black Union soldier), 81–82

Wright, Dr. David Minton (slaveholder), 282–83